CISSP:
Certified Information Systems Security Professional
Study Guide
3rd Edition

CISSP®:
Certified Information Systems Security Professional

Study Guide

3rd Edition

James Michael Stewart

Ed Tittel

Mike Chapple

San Francisco • London

Publisher: Neil Edde
Acquisitions and Developmental Editor: Heather O'Connor
Production Editor: Lori Newman
Technical Editor: Ed Tittel
Copyeditor: Judy Flynn
Compositor: Jeffrey Wilson, Happenstance Type-O-Rama
CD Coordinators and Technicians: Dan Mummert, Keith McNeil, Kevin Ly
Proofreaders: Nancy Riddiough, Jim Brook, Candace English
Indexer: Ted Laux
Book Designer: Bill Gibson, Judy Fung
Cover Designer: Archer Design
Cover Illustrator/Photographer: Victor Arre and Photodisc

Library of Congress Card Number: 2005929270

ISBN: 0-7821-4443-8

SYBEX and the SYBEX logo are either registered trademarks or trademarks of SYBEX Inc. in the United States and/or other countries.

Screen reproductions produced with FullShot 99. FullShot 99 © 1991-1999 Inbit Incorporated. All rights reserved. FullShot is a trademark of Inbit Incorporated.

The CD interface was created using Macromedia Director, COPYRIGHT 1994, 1997-1999 Macromedia Inc. For more information on Macromedia and Macromedia Director, visit http://www.macromedia.com.

This study guide and/or material is not sponsored by, endorsed by, or affiliated with International Information Systems Security Certification Consortium, Inc. (ISC)²® and CISSP® are registered service and/or trademarks of the International Information Systems Security Certification Consortium, Inc. All other trademarks are the property of their respective owners.

TRADEMARKS: SYBEX has attempted throughout this book to distinguish proprietary trademarks from descriptive terms by following the capitalization style used by the manufacturer.

Manufactured in the United States of America

10 9 8 7 6 5 4 3 2 1

Wiley Publishing Inc End-User License Agreement

To Cathy, *whenever there is trouble, just remember "Some beach, somewhere..."*

Acknowledgments

Wow, I can't believe it has already been a year since the last revision and lots of things have changed in the world of CISSP. I hope our efforts to improve this study guide will lend themselves handily to your understanding and comprehension of the wide berth of CISSP concepts. I'd like to express my thanks to Sybex for continuing to support this project. Thanks to Ed Tittel co-author (1st and 2nd editions) and technical editor (3rd edition) for a great job making sure as few errors as possible made it into print. Also thanks to all my CISSP course students who have provided their insight and input to improve my training courseware and ultimately this tome.

To my fiancé, Cathy, I'm looking forward to a wonderful life shared with you. To my parents, Dave and Sue, thanks for your love and consistent support. To my sister Sharon and nephew Wesley, it's great having family like you to spend time with. To Mark, we'd all get along better if you and everyone else would just learn to worship me. To HERbert and Quin, brace yourself, the zoo is about to invade! And finally, as always, to Elvis—I just discovered you've been re-incarnated in the Cow Parade as Cowlvis!

—James Michael Stewart

Contents At A Glance

Contents

Chapter   8   Malicious Code and Application Attacks   257

Introduction

The *CISSP: Certified Information Systems Security Professional Study Guide, 3rd Edition* offers you a solid foundation for the Certified Information Systems Security Professional (CISSP) exam. By purchasing this book, you've shown a willingness to learn and a desire to develop the skills you need to achieve this certification. This introduction provides you with a basic overview of this book and the CISSP exam.

This book is designed for readers and students who want to study for the CISSP certification exam. If your goal is to become a certified security professional, then the CISSP certification and this study guide are for you. The purpose of this book is to adequately prepare you to take the CISSP exam.

Before you dive into this book, you need to have accomplished a few tasks on your own. You need to have a general understanding of IT and of security. You should have the necessary 4 years of experience (or 3 years if you have a college degree) in one of the 10 domains covered by the CISSP exam. If you are qualified to take the CISSP exam according to (ISC)², then you are sufficiently prepared to use this book to study for the CISSP exam. For more information on (ISC)², see the next section.

(ISC)²

The CISSP exam is governed by the International Information Systems Security Certification Consortium, Inc. (ISC)² organization. (ISC)² is a global not-for-profit organization. It has four primary mission goals:

- Maintain the Common Body of Knowledge for the field of information systems security

- Provide certification for information systems security professionals and practitioners

- Conduct certification training and administer the certification exams

- Oversee the ongoing accreditation of qualified certification candidates through continued education

The (ISC)² is operated by a board of directors elected from the ranks of its certified practitioners. More information about (ISC)² can be obtained from its website at www.isc2.org.

CISSP and SSCP

(ISC)² supports and provides two primary certifications: CISSP and SSCP. These certifications are designed to emphasize the knowledge and skills of an IT security professional across all industries. CISSP is a certification for security professionals who have the task of designing a security infrastructure for an organization. System Security Certified Practitioner (SSCP) is a certification for security professionals who have the responsibility of implementing a security infrastructure in an organization. The CISSP certification covers material from the 10 CBK domains:

1. Access Control Systems and Methodology
2. Telecommunications and Network Security

3. Security Management Practices

4. Applications and Systems Development Security

5. Cryptography

6. Security Architecture and Models

7. Operations Security

8. Business Continuity Planning and Disaster Recovery Planning

9. Law, Investigations, and Ethics

10. Physical Security

The SSCP certification covers material from 7 CBK domains:

- Access Controls

- Administration

- Audit and Monitoring

- Cryptography

- Data Communications

- Malicious Code/Malware

- Risk, Response, and Recovery

The content for the CISSP and SSCP domains overlap significantly, but the focus is different for each set of domains. CISSP focuses on theory and design, whereas SSCP focuses more on implementation. This book focuses only on the domains for the CISSP exam.

Prequalifications

(ISC)[2] has defined several qualification requirements you must meet to become a CISSP. First, you must be a practicing security professional with at least 4 years' experience or with 3 years' experience and a recent IT or IS degree. Professional experience is defined as security work performed for salary or commission within one or more of the 10 CBK domains.

Second, you must agree to adhere to the code of ethics. The CISSP Code of Ethics is a set of guidelines the (ISC)[2] wants all CISSP candidates to follow in order to maintain professionalism in the field of information systems security. You can find it in the Information section on the (ISC)[2] website at www.isc2.org.

(ISC)[2] has created a new program known as an Associate of (ISC)[2]. This program allows someone without any or enough experience to take the CISSP exam and then obtain experience afterward. They are given 5 years to obtain 4 years of security experience. Only after providing proof of experience, usually by means of endorsement and a resume, does (ISC)[2] award the individual the CISSP certification label.

To sign up for the exam, visit the (ISC)[2] website and follow the instructions listed there on registering to take the CISSP exam. You'll provide your contact information, payment details, and security-related professional experience. You'll also select one of the available time and location settings for the exam. Once (ISC)[2] approves your application to take the exam, you'll receive a confirmation e-mail with all the details you'll need to find the testing center and take the exam.

Overview of the CISSP Exam

The CISSP exam consists of 250 questions, and you are given 6 hours to complete it. The exam is still administered in a booklet and answer sheet format. This means you'll be using a pencil to fill in answer bubbles.

The CISSP exam focuses on security from a 30,000-foot view; it deals more with theory and concept than implementation and procedure. It is very broad but not very deep. To successfully complete the exam, you'll need to be familiar with every domain but not necessarily be a master of each domain.

You'll need to register for the exam through the (ISC)² website at www.isc2.org.

(ISC)² administers the exam itself. In most cases, the exams are held in large conference rooms at hotels. Existing CISSP holders are recruited to serve as proctors or administrators over the exams. Be sure to arrive at the testing center around 8:00 a.m., and keep in mind that absolutely no one will be admitted into the exam after 8:30 a.m.

CISSP Exam Question Types

Every single question on the CISSP exam is a four-option multiple choice question with a single correct answer. Some are straightforward, such as asking you to select a definition. Some are a bit more involved, such as asking you to select the appropriate concept or best practice. And some questions present you with a scenario or situation and ask you to select the best response. Here's an example:

1. What is the most important goal and top priority of a security solution?

    A. Prevention of disclosure

    B. Maintaining integrity

    C. Human safety

    D. Sustaining availability

You must select the one correct or best answer and mark it on your answer sheet. In some cases, the correct answer will be very obvious to you. In other cases, there will be several answers that seem correct. In these instances, you must choose the best answer for the question asked. Watch for general, specific, universal, superset, and subset answer selections. In other cases, none of the answers will seem correct. In these instances, you'll need to select the least incorrect answer.

By the way, the correct answer for this question is C. Protecting human safety is always your first priority.

Advice on Taking the Exam

There are two key elements to the CISSP exam. First, you need to know the material from the 10 CBK domains. Second, you must have good test-taking skills. With 6 hours to complete a

250-question exam, you have just under 90 seconds for each question. Thus, it is important to work quickly, without rushing but without wasting time.

A key factor to keep in mind is that guessing is better than not answering a question. If you skip a question, you will not get credit. But if you guess, you have at least a 25-percent chance of improving your score. Wrong answers are not counted against you. So, near the end of the sixth hour, be sure an answer is selected for every line on the answer sheet.

You can write on the test booklet, but nothing written on it will count for or against your score. Use the booklet to make notes and keep track of your progress. We recommend circling each answer you select before you mark it on your answer sheet.

To maximize your test-taking activities, here are some general guidelines:

1. Answer easy questions first.

2. Skip harder questions and return to them later. Consider creating a column on the front cover of your testing booklet to keep track of skipped questions.

3. Eliminate wrong answers before selecting the correct one.

4. Watch for double negatives.

5. Be sure you understand what the question is asking.

Manage your time. You should try to keep up with about 50 questions per hour. This will leave you with about an hour to focus on skipped questions and double-check your work.

Be very careful to mark your answers on the correct question number on the answer sheet. The most common cause of failure is making a transference mistake from the test booklet to the answer sheet.

Study and Exam Preparation Tips

We recommend planning out a month or so for nightly intensive study for the CISSP exam. Here are some suggestions to maximize your learning time; you can modify them as necessary based on your own learning habits:

- Take one or two evenings to read each chapter in this book and work through its review material.

- Take all the practice exams provided in the book and on the CD.

- Review the (ISC)[2]'s study guide from www.isc2.org.

- Use the flashcards found on the CD to reinforce your understanding of concepts.

I recommend spending about half of your study time reading and reviewing concepts and the other half taking practice exams. My students have found that the more time they spend taking practice exams, the better the topics were retained in their memory.

You might also consider visiting resources such as www.cccure.org, www.cissp.com, and other CISSP-focused websites.

Completing the Certification Process

Once you have been informed that you successfully passed the CISSP certification, there is one final step before you are actually awarded the CISSP certification label. That final step is known as endorsement. Basically, this involves getting someone familiar with your work history to sign and submit an endorsement form on your behalf. The endorsement form is sent to you as an attachment on the e-mail notifying you of your achievement in passing the exam. Simply send the form to a manager, supervisor, or even another CISSP along with your resume. The endorser must review your resume, ensure that you have sufficient experience in the 10 CISSP domains, and then submit the signed form to (ISC)² via fax or snail mail. You must have completed endorsement files with (ISC)² within 90 days after receiving the confirmation of passing e-mail. Once (ISC)² receives your endorsement form, the certification process will be completed and you will be sent a welcome packet via snail mail.

Post CISSP Concentrations

(ISC)² has added three concentrations to its certification lineup. These concentrations are offered only to CISSP certificate holders. The (ISC)² has taken the concepts introduced on the CISSP exam and focused on specific areas; namely, architecture, management, and engineering. The three concentrations are as follows:

- ISSAP (Information Systems Security Architecture Professional)
- ISSMP (Information Systems Security Management Professional)
- ISSEP (Information Systems Security Engineering Professional)

For more details about these concentration exams and certifications, please see the (ISC)² website at www.isc2.org.

Notes on This Book's Organization

This book is designed to cover each of the 10 CISSP Common Body of Knowledge (CBK) domains in sufficient depth to provide you with a clear understanding of the material. The main body of this book comprises 19 chapters. The first 9 domains are each covered by 2 chapters, and the final domain (Physical Security) is covered in Chapter 19. The domain/chapter breakdown is as follows:

Chapters 1 and 2   Access Control Systems and Methodology

Chapters 3 and 4   Telecommunications and Network Security

Chapters 5 and 6   Security Management Practices

Chapters 7 and 8   Applications and Systems Development Security

Chapters 9 and 10   Cryptography

Chapters 11 and 12   Security Architecture and Models

Chapters 13 and 14   Operations Security

Chapters 15 and 16   Business Continuity Planning (BCP) and Disaster Recovery Planning (DRP)

Chapters 17 and 18   Law, Investigation, and Ethics

Chapter 19   Physical Security

Each chapter includes elements to help you focus your studies and test your knowledge. These include Exam Essentials, key terms, and review questions. The Exam Essentials point out key topics to know for the exam. Unique terminology is presented in the chapter, and then each key term is also later defined in the glossary at the end of the book for your convenience. Review questions test your knowledge retention for the material covered in the chapter.

There is a CD included that offers many other study tools, including lengthy practice exams (all of the questions from each chapter plus over 300 additional unique questions) and a complete set of study flashcards.

The Elements of this Study Guide

You'll see many recurring elements as you read through the study guide. Here's a description of some of those elements.

Key Terms and Glossary   In every chapter, we've identified *key terms,* which are important for you to know. You'll also find these key terms and their definitions in the glossary.

Summaries   The summary is a brief review of the chapter to sum up what was covered.

Exam Essentials   The Exam Essentials highlight topics that could appear on one or both of the exams in some form. While we obviously do not know exactly what will be included in a particular exam, this section reinforces significant concepts that are key to understanding the body of knowledge area and the test specs for the CISSP exam.

Chapter Review Questions   Each chapter includes 20 practice questions that have been designed to measure your knowledge of key ideas that were discussed in the chapter. After you finish each chapter, answer the questions; if some of your answers are incorrect, it's an indication that you need to spend some more time studying that topic. The answers to the practice questions can be found at the end of the chapter.

What's on the CD?

We worked really hard to provide some essential tools to help you with your certification process. All of the following gear should be loaded on your workstation when studying for the test.

The Sybex Test Preparation Software

The test preparation software, made by experts at Sybex, prepares you for the CISSP exam. In this test engine, you will find all the review and assessment questions from the book, plus five additional bonus exams that appear exclusively on the CD. You can take the assessment test, test yourself by chapter, take the practice exams, or take a randomly generated exam comprising all the questions.

Electronic Flashcards for PCs and Palm Devices

Sybex's electronic flashcards include hundreds of questions designed to challenge you further for the CISSP exam. Between the review questions, practice exams, and flashcards, you'll have more than enough practice for the exam!

CISSP Study Guide in PDF

Sybex offers the *CISSP Study Guide* in PDF format on the CD so you can read the book on your PC or laptop. So if you travel and don't want to carry a book, or if you just like to read from the computer screen, Acrobat Reader 5 is also included on the CD.

How to Use This Book and CD

This book has a number of features designed to guide your study efforts for the CISSP certification exam. It assists you by listing the CISSP body of knowledge at the beginning of each chapter and by ensuring that each of them is fully discussed within the chapter. The practice questions at the end of each chapter and the practice exams on the CD are designed to assist you in testing your retention of the material you've read to make you are aware of areas in which you should spend additional study time. Here are some suggestions for using this book and CD:

1. Take the assessment test before you start reading the material. This will give you an idea of the areas in which you need to spend additional study time, as well as those areas in which you may just need a brief refresher.

2. Answer the review questions after you've read each chapter; if you answer any incorrectly, go back to the chapter and review the topic, or utilize one of the additional resources if you need more information.

3. Download the flashcards to your hand-held device and review them when you have a few minutes during the day.

4. Take every opportunity to test yourself. In addition to the assessment test and review questions, there are five bonus exams on the CD. Take these exams without referring to the chapters and see how well you've done—go back and review any topics you've missed until you fully understand and can apply the concepts.

Finally, find a study partner if possible. Studying for, and taking, the exam with someone else will make the process more enjoyable, and you'll have someone to help you understand topics that are difficult for you. You'll also be able to reinforce your own knowledge by helping your study partner in areas where they are weak.

About the Authors

James Michael Stewart, CISSP, has been writing and training for over 11 years, with a current focus on security. He has taught dozens of CISSP training courses, not to mention numerous sessions on Windows security and the Certified Ethical Hacker certification. He is the author of several books and courseware sets on security certification, Microsoft topics, and network administration. He is also a regular speaker at Interop and COMDEX. More information about Michael can be found at his website: www.impactonline.com.

Ed Tittel is a full-time freelance writer, trainer, and consultant specializing in matters related to information security, markup languages, and networking technologies. He's a regular contributor to numerous TechTarget websites, is technology editor for *Certification Magazine,* and writes an e-mail newsletter for CramSession called "Must Know News."

Mike Chapple, CISSP, is an IT security professional with the University of Notre Dame. In the past, he was chief information officer of Brand Institute and an information security researcher with the National Security Agency and the U.S. Air Force. His primary areas of expertise include network intrusion detection and access controls. Mike is a frequent contributor to TechTarget's SearchSecurity site, a technical editor for *Information Security Magazine,* and the author of several information security titles including Wiley's *GSEC Prep Guide* and *Information Security Illuminated* from Jones and Bartlett Publishers.

Assessment Test

1. In what phase of the Capability Maturity Model for Software (SW-CMM) are quantitative measures utilized to gain a detailed understanding of the software development process?

    A. Repeatable

    B. Defined

    C. Managed

    D. Optimizing

2. You are the security administrator of a large law firm. You have been asked to select a security model that supports your organization's desire to ensure data confidentiality and integrity. You must select one or more models that will protect data from internal and external attacks. What security model(s) will you choose? (Choose all that apply.)

    A. Bell-LaPadula

    B. Take Grant Model

    C. Clark-Wilson

    D. TCSEC

3. Why are military and intelligence attacks among the most serious computer crimes?

    A. The use of information obtained can have far-reaching detrimental strategic effect on national interests in an enemy's hands.

    B. Military information is stored on secure machines, so a successful attack can be embarrassing.

    C. The long-term political use of classified information can impact a country's leadership.

    D. The military and intelligence agencies have ensured that the laws protecting their information are the most severe.

4. What is the length of a message digest produced by the MD5 algorithm?

    A. 64 bits

    B. 128 bits

    C. 256 bits

    D. 384 bits

5. Which of the following is most likely to detect DoS attacks?

    A. Host-based IDS

    B. Network-based IDS

    C. Vulnerability scanner

    D. Penetration testing

6. How is annualized loss expectancy (ALE) calculated?

    A. SLE*AS (single loss expectancy * asset value)

    B. AS*EF (asset value * exposure factor)

    C. ARO*V (annualized rate of occurrence * vulnerability)

    D. SLE*ARO (single loss expectancy * annualized rate of occurrence

7. At what height and form will a fence deter determined intruders?

    A. 3- to 4-feet high chain link

    B. 6- to 7-feet high wood

    C. 8-feet high with 3 strands of barbed wire

    D. 4- to 5-feet high concrete

8. A VPN can be established over which of the following?

    A. Wireless LAN connection

    B. Remote access dial-up connection

    C. WAN link

    D. All of the above

9. What is the Biba access control model primarily based upon?

    A. Identity

    B. Analog

    C. Military

    D. Lattice

10. Which one of the following database backup techniques requires the greatest expenditure of funds?

    A. Transaction logging

    B. Remote journaling

    C. Electronic vaulting

    D. Remote mirroring

11. What is the value of the logical operation shown here?

    ```
    X:          0 1 1 0 1 0
    Y:          0 0 1 1 0 1
    _____

    X ∨ Y:      ?
    ```

    A. 0 1 1 1 1 1

    B. 0 1 1 0 1 0

    C. 0 0 1 0 0 0

    D. 0 0 1 1 0 1

12. Which one of the following security modes does not require that a user have a valid security clearance for all information processed by the system?

   A. Dedicated mode

   B. System high mode

   C. Compartmented mode

   D. Multilevel mode

13. You are the security administrator for an international shipping company. You have been asked to evaluate the security of a new shipment tracking system for your London office. It is important to evaluate the security features and assurance of the system separately to compare it to other systems that management is considering. What evaluation criteria should you use (assume the year is 1998)?

   A. TCSEC

   B. ITSEC

   C. The Blue Book

   D. IPSec

14. What is the last phase of the TCP/IP three-way handshake sequence?

   A. SYN packet

   B. ACK packet

   C. NAK packet

   D. SYN/ACK packet

15. Which of the following is a requirement of change management?

   A. Changes must comply with Internet standards.

   B. All changes must be capable of being rolled back.

   C. Upgrade strategies must be revealed over the Internet.

   D. The audit reports of change management should be accessible to all users.

16. Which of the following is a procedure designed to test and perhaps bypass a system's security controls?

   A. Logging usage data

   B. War dialing

   C. Penetration testing

   D. Deploying secured desktop workstations

17. At which layer of the OSI model does a router operate?

   A. Network layer

   B. Layer 1

   C. Transport layer

   D. Layer 5

18. Which of the following is considered a denial of service attack?

    A. Pretending to be a technical manager over the phone and asking a receptionist to change their password

    B. While surfing the Web, sending to a web server a malformed URL that causes the system to use 100 percent of the CPU to process an endless loop

    C. Intercepting network traffic by copying the packets as they pass through a specific subnet

    D. Sending message packets to a recipient who did not request them simply to be annoying

19. Audit trails, logs, CCTV, intrusion detection systems, antivirus software, penetration testing, password crackers, performance monitoring, and cyclic redundancy checks (CRCs) are examples of what?

    A. Directive controls

    B. Preventive controls

    C. Detective controls

    D. Corrective controls

20. Which one of the following vulnerabilities would best be countered by adequate parameter checking?

    A. Time-of-check-to-time-of-use

    B. Buffer overflow

    C. SYN flood

    D. Distributed denial of service

21. What technology allows a computer to harness the power of more than one CPU?

    A. Multitasking

    B. Multiprocessing

    C. Multiprogramming

    D. Multithreading

22. What type of backup stores all files modified since the time of the most recent full or incremental backup?

    A. Full backup

    B. Incremental backup

    C. Partial backup

    D. Differential backup

23. What law allows ISPs to voluntarily provide government investigators with a large range of user information without a warrant?

    A. Electronic Communications Privacy Act

    B. Gramm-Leach-Bliley Act

    C. USA Patriot Act

    D. Privacy Act of 1974

24. What type of detected incident allows the most time for an investigation?

   A. Compromise

   B. Denial of service

   C. Malicious code

   D. Scanning

25. Auditing is a required factor to sustain and enforce what?

   A. Accountability

   B. Confidentiality

   C. Accessibility

   D. Redundancy

26. Which type of firewall automatically adjusts its filtering rules based on the content of the traffic of existing sessions?

   A. Static packet-filtering

   B. Application-level gateway

   C. Stateful inspection

   D. Dynamic packet-filtering

27. Which one of the following is a layer of the ring protection scheme that is not normally implemented in practice?

   A. Layer 0

   B. Layer 1

   C. Layer 3

   D. Layer 4

28. In what type of cipher are the letters of the plaintext message rearranged to form the ciphertext?

   A. Substitution cipher

   B. Block cipher

   C. Transposition cipher

   D. One-time pad

29. What is the formula used to compute the ALE?

   A. ALE = AV*EF

   B. ALE = ARO*EF

   C. ALE = AV*ARO

   D. ALE = EF*ARO

30. Which of the following is the principle that objects retain their veracity and are only intentionally modified by authorized subjects?

   A. Privacy

   B. Authentication

   C. Integrity

   D. Data hiding

31. E-mail is the most common delivery vehicle for which of the following?

   A. Viruses

   B. Worms

   C. Malicious code

   D. All of the above

32. What type of physical security controls are access controls, intrusion detection, alarms, CCTV, monitoring, HVAC, power supplies, and fire detection and suppression?

   A. Technical

   B. Administrative

   C. Physical

   D. Preventative

33. In the United States, how are the administrative determinations of federal agencies promulgated?

   A. Code of Federal Regulations

   B. United States Code

   C. Supreme Court decisions

   D. Administrative declarations

34. What is the first step of the Business Impact Assessment process?

   A. Identification of priorities

   B. Likelihood assessment

   C. Risk identification

   D. Resource prioritization

35. If Renee receives a digitally signed message from Mike, what key does she use to verify that the message truly came from Mike?

   A. Renee's public key

   B. Renee's private key

   C. Mike's public key

   D. Mike's private key

36. The "something you are" authentication factor is also known as what?

   A. Type 1

   B. Type 2

   C. Type 3

   D. Type 4

37. What is the primary goal of risk management?

   A. To produce a 100-percent risk-free environment

   B. To guide budgetary decisions

   C. To reduce risk to an acceptable level

   D. To provide an asset valuation for insurance

Answers to Assessment Test

1. C. The Managed phase of the SW-CMM involves the use of quantitative development metrics. The Software Engineering Institute (SEI) defines the key process areas for this level as Quantitative Process Management and Software Quality Management. For more information, please see Chapter 7.

2. A, C. Because your organization needs to ensure confidentiality, you should choose the Bell-LaPadula model. To ensure the integrity of your data, you should also use the Clark-Wilson model, which addresses separation of duties. This feature offers better protection from internal and external attacks. For more information, please see Chapter 12.

3. A. The purpose of a military and intelligence attack is to acquire classified information. The detrimental effect of using such information could be nearly unlimited in the hands of an enemy. Attacks of this type are launched by very sophisticated attackers. It is often very difficult to ascertain what documents were successfully obtained. So when a breach of this type occurs, you sometimes cannot know the full extent of the damage. For more information, please see Chapter 18.

4. B. The MD5 algorithm produces a 128-bit message digest for any input. For more information, please see Chapter 10.

5. B. Network-based IDSs are usually able to detect the initiation of an attack or the ongoing attempts to perpetrate an attack (including DoS). They are, however, unable to provide information about whether an attack was successful or which specific systems, user accounts, files, or applications were affected. Host-based IDSs have some difficulty with detecting and tracking down DoS attacks. Vulnerability scanners don't detect DoS attacks; they test for possible vulnerabilities. Penetration testing may cause a DoS or test for DoS vulnerabilities, but it is not a detection tool. For more information, please see Chapter 2.

6. D. Annualized loss expectancy (ALE) is the possible yearly cost of all instances of a specific realized threat against a specific asset. The ALE is calculated using the formula SLE*ARO. For more information, please see Chapter 6.

7. C. A fence that is 8 feet high with 3 strands of barbed wire deters determined intruders. For more information, please see Chapter 19.

8. D. A VPN link can be established over any other network communication connection. This could be a typical LAN cable connection, a wireless LAN connection, a remote access dial-up connection, a WAN link, or even an Internet connection used by a client for access to the office LAN. For more information, please see Chapter 4.

9. D. Biba is also a state machine model based on a classification lattice with mandatory access controls. For more information, please see Chapter 1.

10. D. Remote mirroring maintains a live database server at the remote site and comes at the highest cost. For more information, please see Chapter 16.

11. A. The ∨ symbol represents the OR function, which is true when one or both of the input bits are true. For more information, please see Chapter 9.

12. D. In multilevel security mode, some users do not have a valid security clearance for all information processed by the system. For more information, please see Chapter 11.

13. B. ITSEC was developed in Europe for evaluating systems. Although TCSEC (also called the Orange Book) would satisfy the evaluation criteria, only ITSEC evaluates functionality and assurance separately. For more information, please see Chapter 12.

14. B. The SYN packet is first sent from the initiating host to the destination host. The destination host then responds with a SYN/ACK packet. The initiating host sends an ACK packet and the connection is then established. For more information, please see Chapter 8.

15. B. One of the requirements of change management is that all changes must be capable of being rolled back. For more information, please see Chapter 5.

16. C. Penetration testing is the attempt to bypass security controls to test overall system security. For more information, please see Chapter 14.

17. A. Network hardware devices, including routers, function at layer 3, the Network layer. For more information, please see Chapter 3.

18. B. Not all instances of DoS are the result of a malicious attack. Errors in coding OSs, services, and applications have resulted in DoS conditions. Some examples of this include a process failing to release control of the CPU or a service consuming system resources out of proportion to the service requests it is handling. Social engineering and sniffing are typically not considered DoS attacks. For more information, please see Chapter 2.

19. C. Examples of detective controls are audit trails, logs, CCTV, intrusion detection systems, antivirus software, penetration testing, password crackers, performance monitoring, and CRCs. For more information, please see Chapter 13.

20. B. Parameter checking is used to prevent the possibility of buffer overflow attacks. For more information, please see Chapter 8.

21. B. Multiprocessing computers use more than one processor, in either a symmetric multiprocessing (SMP) or massively parallel processing (MPP) scheme. For more information, please see Chapter 11.

22. D. Differential backups store all files that have been modified since the time of the most recent full or incremental backup. For more information, please see Chapter 16.

23. C. The USA Patriot Act granted broad new powers to law enforcement, including the solicitation of voluntary ISP cooperation. For more information, please see Chapter 17.

24. D. Scanning incidents are generally reconnaissance attacks. The real damage to a system comes in the subsequent attacks, so you may have some time to react if you detect the scanning attack early. For more information, please see Chapter 18.

25. A. Auditing is a required factor to sustain and enforce accountability. For more information, please see Chapter 14.

26. D. Dynamic packet-filtering firewalls enable real-time modification of the filtering rules based on traffic content. For more information, please see Chapter 3.

27. B.   Layers 1 and 2 contain device drivers but are not normally implemented in practice. Layer 0 always contains the security kernel. Layer 3 contains user applications. Layer 4 does not exist. For more information, please see Chapter 7.

28. C.   Transposition ciphers use an encryption algorithm to rearrange the letters of the plaintext message to form a ciphertext message. For more information, please see Chapter 9.

29. C.   The annualized loss expectancy (ALE) is computed as the product of the asset value (AV) times the annualized rate of occurrence (ARO). The other formulas displayed here do not accurately reflect this calculation. For more information, please see Chapter 15.

30. C.   The principle of integrity states that objects retain their veracity and are only intentionally modified by authorized subjects. For more information, please see Chapter 5.

31. D.   E-mail is the most common delivery mechanism for viruses, worms, Trojan horses, documents with destructive macros, and other malicious code. For more information, please see Chapter 4.

32. A.   Technical security controls include access controls, intrusion detection, alarms, CCTV, monitoring, HVAC, power supplies, and fire detection and suppression. For more information, please see Chapter 19.

33. A.   Administrative determinations of federal agencies are published as the Code of Federal Regulations. For more information, please see Chapter 17.

34. A.   Identification of priorities is the first step of the Business Impact Assessment process. For more information, please see Chapter 15.

35. C.   Any recipient can use Mike's public key to verify the authenticity of the digital signature. For more information, please see Chapter 10.

36. C.   A Type 3 authentication factor is something you are, such as fingerprints, voice print, retina pattern, iris pattern, face shape, palm topology, hand geometry, and so on. For more information, please see Chapter 1.

37. C.   The primary goal of risk management is to reduce risk to an acceptable level. For more information, please see Chapter 6.

Chapter

1

Accountability and Access Control

THE CISSP EXAM TOPICS COVERED IN THIS CHAPTER INCLUDE:

- ✓ Accountability
- ✓ Access Control Techniques
- ✓ Access Control Administration
- ✓ Identification and Authentication Techniques
- ✓ Access Control Methodologies and Implementation

The Access Control Systems and Methodology domain of the *Common Body of Knowledge (CBK)* for the CISSP certification exam deals with topics and issues related to the *monitoring,* identification, and authorization of granting or restricting *user* access to resources. Generally, an *access control* is any hardware, software, or organizational administrative policy or procedure that grants or restricts access, monitors and records attempts to access, identifies users attempting to access, and determines whether access is authorized.

In this chapter and in Chapter 2, "Attacks and Monitoring," the Access Control Systems and Methodology domain is discussed. Be sure to read and study the materials from both chapters to ensure complete coverage of the essential material for this domain of the CISSP certification exam.

Access Control Overview

Controlling access to resources is one of the central themes of security. Access control addresses more than just controlling which users can access which files or services. Access control is about the relationships between subjects and objects. The transfer of information from an object to a subject is called *access. However, access is not just a logical or technical concept; don't forget about the physical realm where access can be disclosure, use, or proximity.* A foundational principle of access control is to deny access by default if access is not granted specifically to a subject.

Subjects are active entities that, through the exercise of access, seek information about or data from passive entities, or *objects.* A subject can be a user, program, process, file, computer, database, and so on. An object can be a file, database, computer, program, process, file, printer, storage media, and so on. The subject is always the *entity* that receives information about or data from the object. The subject is also the entity that alters information about or data stored within the object. The object is always the entity that provides or hosts the information or data. The roles of subject and object can switch as two entities, such as a program and a database or a process and a file, communicate to accomplish a task.

Types of Access Control

Access controls are necessary to protect the *confidentiality, integrity,* and *availability* of objects (and by extension, their information and data). The term *access control* is used to describe a broad range of controls, from forcing a user to provide a valid username and *password* to log on to preventing users from gaining access to a resource outside of their sphere of access.

CIA Triad

The essential security principles of confidentiality, integrity, and availability are often referred to as the *CIA Triad*. All security controls must address these principles. These three security principles serve as common threads throughout the CISSP CBK. Each domain addresses these principles in unique ways, so it is important to understand them both in general terms and within each specific domain:

- Confidentiality is the principle that objects are not disclosed to unauthorized subjects.

- Integrity is the principle that objects retain their veracity and are intentionally modified by authorized subjects only.

- Availability is the principle that authorized subjects are granted timely access to objects with sufficient bandwidth to perform the desired interaction.

Different security mechanisms address these three principles in different ways and offer varying degrees of support or application of these principles. Objects must be properly classified and prioritized so proper security access controls can be deployed. These and many other issues related to the CIA Triad are discussed throughout this book.

Access controls can be divided into the following seven categories of function or purpose. You should notice that some security mechanisms can be labeled with multiple function or purpose categories.

Preventative access control   A *preventative access control* (or *preventive access control*) is deployed to stop unwanted or unauthorized activity from occurring. Examples of preventative access controls include fences, locks, biometrics, mantraps, lighting, alarm systems, separation of duties, job rotation, data classification, penetration testing, access control methods, encryption, auditing, presence of security cameras or closed circuit television (CCTV), smart cards, callback, security policies, security awareness training, and antivirus software.

Deterrent access control   A *deterrent access control* is deployed to discourage the violation of security policies. A deterrent control picks up where prevention leaves off. The deterrent doesn't stop with trying to prevent an action; instead, it goes further to exact consequences in the event of an attempted or successful violation. Examples of deterrent access controls include locks, fences, security badges, security guards, mantraps, security cameras, trespass or intrusion alarms, separation of duties, work task procedures, awareness training, encryption, auditing, and firewalls.

Detective access control   A *detective access control* is deployed to discover unwanted or unauthorized activity. Often detective controls are after-the-fact controls rather than real-time controls. Examples of detective access controls include security guards, guard dogs, motion detectors, recording and reviewing of events seen by security cameras or CCTV, job rotation, mandatory vacations, audit trails, intrusion detection systems, violation reports, honey pots, supervision and reviews of users, incident investigations, and intrusion detection systems.

Corrective access control   A *corrective access control* is deployed to restore systems to normal after an unwanted or unauthorized activity has occurred. Usually corrective controls are simple in nature, such as terminating access or rebooting a system. Corrective controls have only a minimal capability to respond to access violations. Examples of corrective access controls include intrusion detection systems, antivirus solutions, alarms, mantraps, business continuity planning, and security policies.

Recovery access control   A *recovery access control* is deployed to repair or restore resources, functions, and capabilities after a violation of security policies. Recovery controls have a more advanced or complex capability to respond to access violations than a corrective access control. For example, a recovery access control can repair damage as well as stop further damage. Examples of recovery access controls include backups and restores, fault tolerant drive systems, server clustering, antivirus software, and database shadowing.

Compensation access control   A *compensation access control* is deployed to provide various options to other existing controls to aid in the enforcement and support of a security policy. Examples of compensation access controls include security policy, personnel supervision, monitoring, and work task procedures.

Compensation controls can also be considered to be controls used in place of or instead of more desirable or damaging controls. For example, if a guard dog cannot be used because of the proximity of a residential area, a motion detector with a spotlight and a barking sound playback device can be used.

Directive access control   A *directive access control* is deployed to direct, confine, or control the actions of subjects to force or encourage compliance with security policies. Examples of directive access controls include security guards, guard dogs, security policy, posted notifications, escape route exit signs, monitoring, supervising, work task procedures, and awareness training.

Access controls can be further categorized by how they are implemented. In this case, the categories are administrative, logical/technical, or physical:

Administrative access controls   *Administrative access controls* are the policies and procedures defined by an organization's *security policy* to implement and enforce overall access control. Administrative access controls focus on two areas: personnel and business practices (e.g., people and policies). Examples of administrative access controls include policies, procedures, hiring practices, background checks, data classification, security training, vacation history, reviews, work supervision, personnel controls, and testing.

Logical/technical access controls   *Logical access controls* and *technical access controls* are the hardware or software mechanisms used to manage access to resources and systems and provide protection for those resources and systems. Examples of logical or technical access controls include encryption, smart cards, passwords, *biometrics,* constrained interfaces, *access control lists (ACLs),* protocols, firewalls, routers, intrusion detection systems, and clipping levels.

 The words *logical* and *technical* may be used interchangeably within this concept.

Physical access controls   *Physical access controls* are the physical barriers deployed to prevent direct contact with systems or portions of a facility. Examples of physical access controls include guards, fences, motion detectors, locked doors, sealed windows, lights, cable protection, laptop locks, swipe cards, guard dogs, video cameras, mantraps, and alarms.

Access Control in a Layered Environment

No single access control mechanism is ever deployed on its own. In fact, combining various types of access controls is the only means by which a reasonably secure environment can be developed. Often multiple layers or levels of access controls are deployed to provide layered security or defense in depth. This idea is described by the notion of concentric circles of protection, which puts forth the concept of surrounding your assets and resources with logical circles of security protection. Thus, intruders or attackers would need to overcome multiple layers of defenses to reach the protected assets. Layered security or defense in depth is considered a more logical approach to security than a traditional fortress mentality. In a fortress mentality security approach, a single giant master wall is built around the assets like the massive rock walls of a castle fortress. The major flaw in such an approach is that large massive structures often have minor weakness and flaws; are difficult if not impossible to reconfigure, adjust, or move; and are easily seen and avoided by would be attackers (i.e., they find easier ways into the protected area).

In a layered security or concentric circles of protection deployment, your assets are surrounded by a layer of protection provided for by administrative access controls, which in turn is surrounded by a layer of protection consisting of logical or technical access controls, which is finally surrounded by a layer of protection that includes physical access controls. This concept of defense in depth highlights two important points. First, the security policy of an organization ultimately provides the first or innermost layer of defense for your assets. Without a security policy, there is no real security that can be trusted. Security policies are one element of administrative access controls. Second, people are your last line of defense. People or personnel are the other focus of administrative access control. Only with proper training and education will your personnel be able to implement, comply with, and support the security elements defined in your security policy.

The Process of Accountability

One important purpose of security is to be able to hold people accountable for the activities that their online personas (i.e., their user accounts) perform within the digital world of the computer network. The first step in this process is identifying the subject. In fact, there are several steps leading up to being able to hold a person accountable for online actions: identification, authentication, authorization, auditing, and accountability.

Identification

Identification is the process by which a subject professes an identity and *accountability* is initiated. A user providing a username, a logon ID, a *personal identification number (PIN)*, or a smart card represents the identification process. Providing a process ID number also represents the identification process. Once a subject has identified itself, the identity is accountable for any further actions by that subject. Information technology (IT) systems track activity by identities, not by the subjects themselves. A computer doesn't know one human from another, but it does know that your user account is different from all other user accounts.

Authentication

Authentication is the process of verifying or testing that the claimed identity is valid. Authentication requires that the subject provide additional information that must exactly correspond to the identity indicated. The most common form of authentication is a password, which falls under the first of three types of information that can be used for authentication:

Type 1   A Type 1 authentication factor is something you know. It is any string of characters that you have memorized and can reproduce on a keyboard when prompted. Examples of this factor include a password, personal identification number (PIN), lock combination, *pass phrase,* mother's maiden name, favorite color, and so on.

Type 2   A Type 2 authentication factor is something you have. It is a physical device that you are in possession of and must have on your person at the time of authentication. Examples of this factor include a smart card, *token device,* memory card, USB drive, and so on. This can also include your physical location, referred to as the "somewhere you are" factor.

The main difference between a memory card and a smart card is that a memory card is only used to store information while a smart card has the ability to process data. We'll discuss these security methods in more detail in Chapter 19, "Physical Security Requirements."

Type 3   A Type 3 authentication factor is something you are. It is a body part or a physical characteristic of your person. Examples of this factor include *fingerprints,* voice print, retina pattern, iris pattern, face shape, palm topology, hand geometry, and so on. (We'll discuss these in more detail in just a moment).

Each type of authentication factor is roughly the same in terms of the level of security provided; only a single attack must be successful to overcome a single authentication factor. However, each type is more secure than the one before it. For instance, a Type 3 factor is the most difficult security to breach of the three factors. It can be overcome by creating a fake duplicate (like a gummy fingerprint). A Type 2 factor, the next most difficult security to breach, can be overcome by physical theft, and a Type 1 factor can be overcome by a password cracker. As you can see, the Type 3 factor is slightly more secure than a Type 2 factor, which is in turn more secure than a Type 1 factor.

"Something" and "Somewhere"

In addition to these three commonly recognized factors, there are at least two others. One is called "something you do," such as writing a signature, typing out a pass phrase (keyboard dynamics), or saying a phrase. Something you do is often included in the "something you are," or Type 3, category.

Another factor, mentioned earlier, is called "somewhere you are," such as the computer terminal from which you logged in or the phone number (identified by caller ID) or country (identified by your IP address) from which you dialed up. Controlling access by physical location forces the subject to be present rather than connecting remotely. Somewhere you are often included in the "something you have," or Type 2, category.

Logical Location

Logical location can combine the ideas of "somewhere you are," "something you have," and "something you know." A logical location access control restricts access based upon some form of logical identification, such as IP address, MAC address, client type, or protocol used. However, it should be noted that logical location control should not be the only factor used because any type of address information can be spoofed with hacking tools.

Access can further be restricted to date and time of day or by transaction type. The former prevents access accept within defined time periods. The latter is a type of content- or context-dependant control where access is dynamic based on the transactions being attempted by the subject.

Multiple-Factor Authentication

Two-factor authentication occurs when two different factors are required to provide authentication. For example, when cashing a check at the grocery store, you often have to provide your driver's license (something you have) and your phone number (something you know). Strong authentication is simply any authentication that requires two or more factors but not necessarily different factors. However, as a general rule, when different factors are employed, the resultant authentication is more secure.

The concept behind two-factor authentication is that when two of the same factors are used together, the strength of the system is no greater than just one of the factors used alone. More specifically, the same attack that could steal or obtain one instance of the factor could obtain all instances of the factor. For example, using two passwords together is no more secure than using a single password because a password cracking attack could discover both with a single successful attack. However, when two or more different factors are employed, two or more different types or methods of attack must be successful to collect all relevant authentication elements. For example, if a password, a token, and a biometric factor are all used for a single authentication, then a password crack, a physical theft, and a biometric duplication attack must all be successful simultaneously to gain entry to the system.

Once the *logon credentials* of the offered identity and the authentication factor(s) are provided to the system, they are checked against the database of identities on the system. If the identity is located and the correct authentication factor(s) have been provided, then the subject has been authenticated.

Authorization

Once a subject is authenticated, its access must be authorized. The process of *authorization* ensures that the requested activity or object access is possible given the rights and privileges assigned to the authenticated identity (which we will refer to as the subject from this point forward). Authorization indicates who is trusted to perform specific operations. In most cases, the system evaluates an *access control matrix* that compares the subject, the object, and the intended activity (we discuss the access control matrix in greater detail in Chapter 11 "Principles of Computer Design"). If the specific action is allowed, the subject is authorized. If the specific action is not allowed, the subject is not authorized.

Keep in mind that just because a subject has been identified and authenticated, it does not automatically mean they have been authorized. It is possible for a subject to be logged onto a network (i.e., identified and authenticated) but blocked from accessing a file or printing to a printer (i.e., by not being authorized to perform that activity). Most network users are authorized to perform only a limited number of activities on a specific collection of resources. Identification and authentication are "all or nothing" aspects of access control. Authorization has a wide range of variations between all and nothing for each individual subject or object within the environment. A user may be able to read a file but not delete it. A user may be able to print a document but not alter the print queue. A user may be able to log onto a system but not access any resources.

It is important to understand the differences between identification, authentication, and authorization. Although they are similar and are essential to all security mechanisms, they are distinct and must not be confused.

Auditing and Accountability

Auditing is the process by which the online activities of user accounts and processes are tracked and recorded. Auditing produces audit trails. Audit trails can be used to reconstruct events and to verify whether or not security policy or authorization was violated. By comparing the contents of audit trails with authorization against authenticated user accounts, the people associated with user accounts can be held accountable for the significant online actions of those user accounts.

According to the National Institute of Standards and Technology Minimum Security Requirements (MSR) for Multi-User Operating Systems (NISTIR 5153) document, audit data recording must comply with the following requirements:

- The system shall provide a mechanism for generating a security audit trail that contains information to support after-the-fact investigation of loss or impropriety and appropriate management response.

- The system shall provide end-to-end user accountability for all security relevant events.

- The system shall protect the security audit trail from unauthorized access.

- The system shall provide a mechanism to dynamically control, during normal system operation, the types of events recorded.

- The system shall protect the audit control mechanisms from unauthorized access.

- The system shall, by default, cause a record to be written to the security audit trail for [numerous specific security-related] events.

- The system shall provide a privileged mechanism to enable or disable the recording of other events into the security audit trail.

- For each recorded event, the audit record shall identify [several specific datapoints] at a minimum.

- The character strings input as a response to a password challenge shall not be recorded in the security audit trail.

- The audit control mechanism shall provide an option to enable or disable the recording of invalid user IDs during failed user authentication attempts.

- Audit control data (e.g., audit event masks) shall survive system restarts.

- The system shall provide a mechanism for automatic copying of security audit trail files to an alternative storage area after a customer-specifiable period of time.

- The system shall provide a mechanism for automatic deletion of security audit trail files after a customer-specifiable period of time.

- The system shall allow site control of the procedure to be invoked when audit records are unable to be recorded.

- The system shall provide tools to monitor the activities (i.e., capture the keystrokes) of specific terminals or network connections in real time.

> This list was taken directly from the NISTIR 5153 document. It has been edited for length. We have provided only a small excerpt of the entire material. To view all of the details of this MSR, see the NISTIR 5153 document at http://csrc.nist.gov.

An organization's security policy can be properly enforced only if accountability is maintained. In other words, security can be maintained only if subjects are held accountable for their actions. Effective accountability relies upon the capability to prove a subject's identity and track their activities. Thus, accountability builds on the concepts of identification, authentication, authorization, access control, and auditing.

Identification and Authentication Techniques

Identification is a fairly straightforward concept. A subject must provide an identity to a system to start the authentication, authorization, and accountability processes. Providing an identity can be typing in a username, swiping a smart card, waving a token device, speaking a phrase, or positioning your face, hand, or finger for a camera or scanning device. Without an identity, a system has no way to correlate an authentication factor with the subject. A subject's identity is typically considered to be public information.

Authentication verifies the identity of the subject by comparing one or more factors against the database of valid identities (i.e., user accounts). The authentication factor used to verify identity is typically considered to be private information. The ability of the subject and system to maintain the secrecy of the authentication factors for identities directly reflects the level of security of that system.

Identification and authentication are always together as a single two-step process. Providing an identity is step one and providing the authentication factor(s) is step two. Without both, a subject cannot gain access to a system—neither element alone is useful.

There are several types of authentication information a subject can provide (e.g., something you know, something you have, etc.). Each authentication technique or factor has its unique benefits and drawbacks. Thus it is important to evaluate each mechanism in light of the environment in which it will be deployed to determine viability.

Passwords

The most common authentication technique is the use of passwords, but they are also considered to be the weakest form of protection. Passwords are poor security mechanisms for several reasons, including the following:

- Users typically choose passwords that are easy to remember and therefore easy to guess or crack.

- Randomly generated passwords are hard to remember, thus many users write them down.

- Passwords are easily shared, written down, and forgotten.

- Passwords can be stolen through many means, including observation, recording and playback, and security database theft.

- Passwords are often transmitted in cleartext or with easily broken encryption protocols.

- Password databases are often stored in publicly accessible online locations.

- Short passwords can be discovered quickly in brute force attacks.

Password Selection

Passwords can be effective if selected intelligently and managed properly. There are two types of passwords: static and dynamic. *Static passwords* always remain the same. *Dynamic passwords* change after a specified interval of time or use. *One-time passwords* or *single-use passwords* are a variant of dynamic passwords that are changed every time they are used. One-time passwords are considered the strongest type of password, at least in concept. Humans don't have the ability to remember an infinite series of lengthy random character strings, which have only a single-attempt use before expiring. Thus, one-time passwords are often implemented as Type 2 factors using a processing device known as a token (see later this chapter for more details).

As the importance of maintaining security increases, so does the need to change passwords more frequently. The longer a password remains static and the more often the same password is used, the more likely it will be compromised or discovered.

In some environments, the initial passwords for user accounts are automatically generated. Often the generated password is a form of composition password. A composition password is a password constructed from two or more unrelated words joined together with a number or symbol in between. Composition passwords are easy for computers to generate, but they should not be used for extended periods of time because they are vulnerable to password guessing attacks. If the algorithm for computer-generated passwords is discovered, all passwords created by the system are in jeopardy of being compromised.

A password mechanism that is slightly more effective than a basic password is a pass phrase. A *pass phrase* is a string of characters usually much longer than a password. Once the pass phrase is entered, the system converts it into a virtual password for use by the authentication process. Pass phrases are often modified natural language sentences to allow for simplified memorization. Here's an example: "She ell C shells ByE the c-shor." Using a pass phrase has several benefits. It is difficult to crack a pass phrase using a brute force tool and the pass phrase encourages the use of a password with numerous characters yet is still easy to remember.

Another interesting password mechanism is the *cognitive password*. A cognitive password is usually a series of questions about facts or predefined responses that only the subject should know. For example, three to five questions might be asked of the subject, such as the following:

- What is your birth date?
- What is your mother's maiden name?
- What is the name of your division manager?
- What was your score on your last evaluation exam?
- Who was your favorite baseball player in the 1984 World Series?

If all the questions are answered correctly, the subject is authenticated. The most effective cognitive password systems ask a different set of questions each time. The primary limitation of cognitive password systems is that each question must be answered at the time of user *enrollment* (i.e., user account creation) and answered again during the logon process, which increases the time to log on. Cognitive passwords are often employed for phone-based authentication by financial organizations, such as your bank. However, this type of password is considered to be inappropriate and insecure for protecting IT.

Many systems include password policies that restrict or dictate the characteristics of passwords. Common restrictions are minimum length, minimum age, maximum age, requiring three or four character types (i.e., uppercase, lowercase, numbers, symbols), and preventing password reuse. As the need for security increases, these restrictions should be tightened.

However, even with strong software-enforced *password restrictions,* easily guessed or cracked passwords can still be created. An organization's security policy must clearly define both the need for *strong passwords* and what a strong password is. Users need to be trained about security so they will respect the organization's security policy and adhere to its requirements. If passwords are created by end users, offer suggestions such as the following for creating strong passwords:

- Don't reuse part of your name, logon name, e-mail address, employee number, Social Security number, phone number, extension, or other identifying name or code.
- Don't use dictionary words, slang, or industry acronyms.
- Do use nonstandard capitalization and spelling.
- Do switch letters and replace letters with numbers.

Password Security

When a malicious user or attacker seeks to obtain passwords, there are several methods they can employ, including network traffic analysis, password file access, brute force attacks, dictionary attacks, and social engineering. Network traffic analysis (also known as sniffing) is the process of capturing network traffic when a user is entering a password for authentication. Once the password is discovered, the attacker attempts to replay the packet containing the password against the network to gain access. If an attacker can gain access to the password database file, it can be copied and a password cracking tool can be used against it to extract usernames and passwords. Brute force and dictionary attacks are types of password attacks that can be waged against a stolen password database file or a system's logon prompt. In a *dictionary attack,* the attacker uses a script of common passwords and dictionary words to attempt to discover an account's password. In a *brute force attack*, a systematic trial of all possible character combinations is used to discover an account's password. Finally, a *hybrid attack* attempts a dictionary attack and then performs a type of brute force attack. The follow-up brute force attack is used to add prefix or suffix characters to passwords from the dictionary to discover one-upped constructed passwords, two-upped constructed passwords, and so on. A *one-upped constructed password* is a password with a single character difference from its present form in the dictionary. For example, "password1" is one-upped from "password," and so are "Password," "1password," and "passXword."

No matter what type of password attack is used, only read access is required to the password database. Write access is not required. Therefore, a wider number of user accounts can be employed to launch password cracking attacks. From an intruder's perspective, this makes finding a weak user account more attractive than having to attack the administrator or root account directly and initially to gain system access.

A *social engineering* attack is an attempt by an attacker to obtain logon capabilities through deceiving a user, usually over the telephone, into performing specific actions on the system, such as changing the password of an executive who's on the road or creating a user account for a new fictitious employee.

There are several ways to improve the security of passwords. *Account lockout* is a mechanism used to disable a user account after a specified number of failed logons occur. Account lockouts stop brute force and dictionary attacks against a system's logon prompt. Once the logon attempt limit is reached, a message displaying the time, date, and location (i.e., computer name or IP address) of the last successful or failed logon attempt is displayed. Users who suspect that their account is under attack or has been compromised can report this to the system administrator. *Auditing* can be configured to track logon success and failure. An intrusion detection system can easily identify logon prompt attacks and notify administrators.

There are other options to improve the security offered by password authentication:

- Use the strongest form of *one-way encryption* available for password storage.

- Never allow passwords to be transmitted over the network in cleartext or with weak encryption.

- Use password verification tools and password cracking tools against your own password database file. Require that weak or discovered passwords be changed.

- Disable user accounts for short periods of inactivity, such as a week or a month. Delete user accounts that are no longer used.

- Properly train users about the necessity of maintaining security and the use of strong passwords. Warn about writing down or sharing passwords. Offer tips to prevent shoulder surfing or keyboard logging to capture passwords. Offer tips and recommendations on how to create strong passwords, such as the following:

  - Require that users change passwords consistently. The more secure or sensitive the environment, the more frequently passwords should be changed.

  - Never display passwords in clear form on any screen or within any form. Instead, mask the display of the password at all times. This is a commonly recognized feature of software, such as the display of asterisks instead of letters when typing in your password in a logon dialog box.

  - Longer passwords, such as those with 16 characters or more, are harder for a brute force password cracking tool to discover. However, it's harder for people to remember longer passwords, which often lead to users writing the password down. Your organization should have a standard security awareness rule that no passwords should ever be written down. The only possible exception to that rule is that very long very complex passwords for the most sensitive accounts, such as administrator or root, can be written down and stored in a vault or safety deposit box.

  - Create lists of passwords users should avoid. Easy-to-memorize passwords are often easily discovered by password cracking tools.

  - If the root or administrator password is ever compromised, every password on every account should be changed. (In a high-security environment, a compromised system can never be fully trusted again. Thus it may require formatting the drives and rebuilding the entire system from scratch.)

  - Passwords should be handed out in person after the user has proved their identity. Never transmit passwords via e-mail.

Biometrics

Another common authentication and identification technique is the use of biometric factors. Biometric factors fall into the Type 3 "something you are" authentication category. A biometric factor is a behavioral or physiological characteristic that is unique to a subject. There are many types of biometric factors, including *fingerprints, face scans, iris scans, retina scans, palm scans* (also known as *palm topography* or *palm geography*), *hand geometry, heart/pulse patterns, voice patterns, signature dynamics,* and *keystroke patterns (keystroke dynamics).*

Let's discuss these biometric factors in more detail, taking into account the human body part they utilize and the information that each quantifies in order to make the most accurate identification possible.

Fingerprints   The macroscopic (i.e., visible to the naked eye) patterns on the last digit of fingers and thumbs are what make fingerprinting so effective for security. A type of fingerprinting known as minutia matching examines the microscopic view of the fingertips. Unfortunately, minutia matching is affected by small changes to the finger, including temperature, pressure, and minor surface damage (such as sliding your fingers across a rough surface).

Face scans   Face scans utilize the geometric patterns of faces for detection and recognition. They employ the recognition technology known as eigenfeatures (facial metrics) or eigenfaces. (The German word *eigen* refers to recursive mathematics used to analyze intrinsic or unique numerical characteristics.)

Iris scans   Focusing on the colored area around the pupil. Iris scans are the second most accurate form of biometric authentication. However, iris scans cannot differentiate between identical twins. Iris scans are often recognized as having a longer useful authentication life span than any other biometric factor. This is because the iris remains relatively unchanged throughout a person's life (barring eye damage or illness). Every other type of biometric factor is more vulnerable and more likely to change over time. Iris scans are considered acceptable by general users because they don't involve direct contact with the reader and don't reveal personal medical information.

Retina scans   Retina scans focus on the pattern of blood vessels at the back of the eye. They are the most accurate form of biometric authentication (they are able to differentiate between identical twins) but also the least acceptable because retina scans can reveal medical conditions, such as high blood pressure and pregnancy. In addition, these types of scans often require the subject to place their eye onto a cup reader that blows air into the eye.

Palm scans (also known as palm topography or palm geography)   Palm scans utilize the whole area of the hand, including the palm and fingers. Palm scans function as a hand-sized fingerprint by analyzing the grooves, ridges, and creases as well as the fingerprints themselves.

Hand geometry   Hand geometry recognizes the physical dimensions of the hand. This includes width and length of the palm and fingers. This can be a mechanical or image-edge (i.e., visual silhouette) graphical solution.

Skin scans are not used as a form of biometric authentication because they cannot be used to differentiate between all individuals.

Heart/pulse patterns   This involves measuring the pulse or heartbeat of the user to ensure that a real live person is providing the biometric factor. This is often employed as a secondary biometric to support one of the other types.

Voice pattern recognition   This type of biometric authentication relies on the sound of a subject's speaking voice. This is different than speech recognition, which extracts communications from sound (i.e., automatic dictation software). In other words, voice pattern recognition differentiates between one person's voice and another, while speech recognition differentiates between words within any person's voice.

Voice pattern recognition is often thought to have numerous benefits, such as its reliability and its function as a "natural" biometric factor. However, the idea of speech recognition is commonly confused with voice pattern recognition. Remember, voice pattern recognition differentiates between one person's voice and another, while speech recognition differentiates between words within any person's voice. The benefits of speech recognition include flexibility, hands-free and eyes-free operation, reduction of data entry time, elimination of spelling errors, and improved data accuracy.

Signature dynamics   This recognizes how a subject writes a string of characters. Signature dynamics examine how the subject performs the act of writing as well as the features of the resultant written sample. The success of signature dynamics relies upon pen pressure, stroke pattern, stroke length, and the points in time when the pen is lifted from the paper. However, the speed at which the written sample is created is usually not an important factor.

Keystroke patterns (keystroke dynamics)   Keystroke patterns measure how a subject uses a keyboard by analyzing flight time and dwell time. Flight time is how long it takes between key presses and dwell time is how long a key is pressed. Using keystroke patterns is inexpensive, nonintrusive, and often transparent to the user (both use and enrollment). Unfortunately, use of keystroke patterns for security is subject to wild variances. Simple changes in user behavior greatly affect this biometric authentication, such as only using one hand, being cold, standing rather than sitting, changing keyboards, and having an injured hand/finger.

Biometric factors can be used as an identifying or authentication technique. Using a biometric factor instead of a username or account ID as an identification factor requires a one-to-many search of the offered biometric pattern against the stored database of enrolled and authorized patterns. As an identification technique, biometric factors are used in physical access controls. Using a biometric factor as an authentication technique requires a one-to-one match of the offered biometric pattern against the stored pattern for the offered subject identity. As an authentication technique, biometric factors are used in logical access controls.

The use of biometrics promises universally unique identification for every person on the planet. Unfortunately, biometric technology has yet to live up to this promise. For biometric factors to be useful, they must be extremely sensitive. The most important aspect of a biometric device is its accuracy. To use biometrics as an identifying mechanism, a biometric device must be able to read information that is very minute, such as the variations in the blood vessels in a person's retina or the tones and timbres in their voice. Because most people are basically similar, the level of detail required to authenticate a subject often results in false negative and false positive authentications.

Biometric Factor Ratings

Biometric devices are rated for their performance against false negative and false positive authentication conditions. Most biometric devices have a *sensitivity* adjustment so they can be tuned to be more or less sensitive. When a biometric device is too sensitive, a *Type 1 error* occurs. A Type 1 error occurs when a valid subject is not authenticated. The ratio of Type 1 errors to valid authentications is known as the *False Rejection Rate (FRR)*. When a biometric device is not sensitive enough, a *Type 2 error* occurs. A Type 2 error occurs when an invalid subject is authenticated. The ratio of Type 2 errors to valid authentications is known as the *False Acceptance Rate (FAR)*. The FRR and FAR are usually plotted on a graph that shows the level of sensitivity adjustment against the percentage of FRR and FAR errors (see Figure 1.1). The point at which the FRR and FAR are equal is known as the *Crossover Error Rate (CER)*. The CER level is used as a standard assessment point from which to measure the performance of a biometric device. The CER is used for a single purpose: to compare the accuracy of similar biometric devices (i.e., those focusing on the same biometric factor) from different vendors or different models from the same vendor. On the CER graph, the device with the lowest CER is overall the most accurate. In some situations, having a device more sensitive than the CER rate is preferred, such as with a metal detector at an airport.

FIGURE 1.1   Graph of FRR and FAR errors indicating the CER point

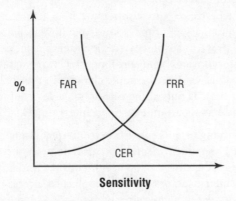

Biometric Registration

In addition to the sensitivity issues of biometric devices, there are several other factors that may cause them to be less than effective—namely, enrollment time, throughput rate, and acceptance. For a biometric device to function as an identification or authentication mechanism, the subject must be enrolled or registered. This means the subject's biometric factor must be sampled and stored in the device's database. The stored sample of a biometric factor is called a reference profile or a reference template. The time required to scan and store a biometric factor varies greatly by what physical or performance characteristic is used. The longer it takes to enroll with a biometric mechanism, the less a user community accepts the inconvenience. In general, enrollment times longer than two minutes are unacceptable. If you use a biometric characteristic that changes with time, such as a person's voice tones, facial hair, or signature pattern, enrollment must be repeated at regular intervals.

Once subjects are enrolled, the amount of time the system requires to scan and process them is the *throughput rate.* The more complex or detailed the biometric characteristic, the longer the processing will take. Subjects typically accept a throughput rate of about six seconds or faster.

A subject's acceptance of a security mechanism is dependent upon many subjective perceptions, including privacy, invasiveness, and psychological and physical discomfort. Subjects may be concerned about transfer of body fluids or revelations of health issues via the biometric scanning devices.

Appropriate Biometric Usage

When selecting a biometric solution for a specific environment, numerous aspects must be considered. These aspects include which type of biometric factor is most suitable for your environment as well as the effectiveness and acceptability of the biometric factor. When comparing different types of biometric factors, often a Zephyr chart is used. A Zephyr chart rates various aspects, functions, or features of different biometrics together on a single easy-to-read diagram (see Figure 1.2).

FIGURE 1.2   An example Zephyr chart

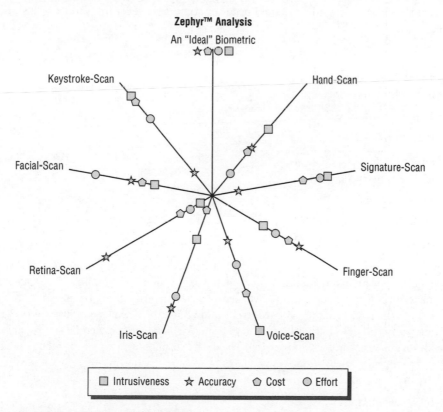

The effectiveness of biometrics is dependent on how accurate one type of biometric factor is in comparison to others. Here is a commonly accepted order of effectiveness from most to least:

- Palm scan
- Hand geometry
- Iris scan
- Retina pattern
- Fingerprint
- Voice verification
- Facial recognition
- Signature dynamics
- Keystroke dynamics

The acceptance of biometrics is a rating of how well people accept the use of specific biometric factors in their environment. The rating of acceptance incorporates a person's view of how invasive and easy to use a specific type of biometric factor is and the level of health risk it presents. Here is a commonly accepted order of acceptance level from most to least:

- Iris scan
- Keystroke dynamics
- Signature dynamics
- Voice verification
- Facial recognition
- Fingerprint
- Palm scan
- Hand geometry
- Retina pattern

Tokens

Tokens (or smart tokens) are password-generating devices that subjects must carry with them. A token device is an example of a Type 2 factor, or "something you have." A token can be a static password device, such as an ATM card or other memory card. To use an ATM card, you must supply the token (the ATM card itself) and your PIN. Tokens can also be one-time or dynamic password devices that look a bit like small calculators or even be smart cards (to read more about smart cards, see Chapter 19). The device displays a string of characters (a password) for you to enter into the system.

There are four types of token devices:

- Static tokens
- Synchronous dynamic password tokens

- Asynchronous dynamic password tokens

- Challenge-response tokens

A *static token* can be a swipe card, a smart card, a floppy disk, a USB RAM dongle, or even something as simple as a key to operate a physical lock. Static tokens offer a physical means to provide identity. Static tokens still require an additional factor to provide authentication, such as a password or biometric factor. Most device static tokens host a *cryptographic key*, such as a private key, digital signature, or encrypted logon credentials. The cryptographic key can be used as an identifier or as an authentication mechanism. The cryptographic key is much stronger than a password because it is pre-encrypted using a strong encryption protocol, it is significantly longer, and it resides only in the token. Static tokens are most often used as identification devices rather than as authentication factors.

A *synchronous dynamic password token* generates passwords at fixed time intervals. Time interval tokens require that the clock on the authentication server and the clock on the token device be synchronized. The generated password is entered into the system by the subject along with a PIN, pass phrase, or password. The generated password provides the identification, and the PIN/password provides the authentication.

An *asynchronous dynamic password token* generates passwords based on the occurrence of an event. An event token requires that the subject press a key on the token and on the authentication server. This action advances to the next password value. The generated password and the subject's PIN, pass phrase, or password are entered into the system for authentication.

One-Time Password Generators

As we discussed earlier, one-time passwords are dynamic passwords that change every time they are used. They can be very effective for security purposes, except that humans rarely have the capacity to remember passwords that change so frequently. One-time password generators create the passwords for your users and make one-time passwords reasonable to deploy. Users only need to possess the token device (i.e., password generator), have knowledge of the logon procedure, and possibly have memorized a short PIN, depending on which generator you use. With device-based authentication systems, an environment can benefit from the strength of one-time passwords without placing a huge burden of memorization on the users.

The five widely recognized one-time password generator systems are synchronous, PIN synchronous, asynchronous, PIN asynchronous, and transaction synchronous. The systems with a PIN in their name simply require an additional memorized key sequence to be entered to complete the authentication process.

Challenge-response tokens generate passwords or responses based on instructions from the authentication system. The authentication system displays a challenge, usually in the form of a code or pass phrase. This challenge is entered into the token device. The token generates a response based on the challenge, and then the response is entered into the system for authentication.

Using token authentication systems is a much stronger security measure than using password authentication alone. Token systems use two or more factors to establish identity and provide authentication. In addition to knowing the username, password, PIN, code, and so on, the subject must be in physical possession of the token device.

However, token systems do have failings. If the battery dies or the device is broken, the subject is unable to gain access. Token devices can be lost or stolen. Tokens should be stored and managed intelligently because once a token system is compromised, it can be difficult and expensive to replace. Furthermore, human factors can render tokens less secure than they are designed to be. First and foremost, if the user writes their access code or PIN on the token device, the security of the token system is compromised. Users should understand that loaning out a token and PIN, even to a coworker, is a violation of security.

Tickets

Ticket authentication is a mechanism that employs a third-party entity to prove identification and provide authentication. The most common and well-known ticket system is *Kerberos*. Kerberos was developed under Project Athena at MIT. Its name is borrowed from Greek mythology. A three-headed dog named Kerberos guards the gates to the underworld, but in the myth, the three-headed dog faced inward, thus preventing escape rather than preventing entrance. Kerberos and its tickets are discussed later in this chapter.

Single Sign On

Single Sign On (SSO) is a mechanism that allows a subject to be authenticated only once on a system and be able to access resource after resource unhindered by repeated authentication prompts. With SSO, once a subject is authenticated, they can roam the network freely and access resources and services without being rechallenged for authentication. This is considered the primary disadvantage to SSO: Once an account is compromised, the malicious subject has unrestricted access. Or in other words, the maximum level of unauthorized access is gained simply through password disclosure. SSO typically allows for stronger passwords because the subject must memorize only a single password. Furthermore, SSO offers easier administration by reducing the number of locations on which an account must be defined for the subject. SSO can be enabled through authentication systems or through scripts that provide logon credentials automatically when prompted.

Kerberos, SESAME, KryptoKnight, NetSP, thin clients, directory services, and scripted access are examples of SSO mechanisms. Two or more SSO mechanisms can be combined into a single security solution. It is most common for Kerberos to be combined with another SSO mechanism. For example, under Windows 2003 (as well as Windows 2000), it is possible to employ the native directory service (Active Directory), which is integrated with Kerberos with other SSO options, including thin clients (i.e., Terminal Services) and scripted access (i.e., logon scripts).

Kerberos

Kerberos is a trusted third-party authentication protocol that can be used to provide a single sign-on solution and to provide protection for logon credentials. Kerberos relies upon symmetric key cryptography (a.k.a. private key cryptography), specifically Data Encryption Standard (DES), and provides end-to-end security for authentication traffic between the client and the *Key Distribution Center (KDC)*. Kerberos provides the security services of confidentiality and integrity protection for authentication traffic.

The Kerberos authentication mechanism centers on a trusted server (or servers) that hosts the functions of the KDC, *Ticket Granting Service (TGS)*, and *Authentication Service (AS)*. Generally, the Kerberos central server that hosts all of these services is simply referred to as the KDC. Kerberos uses symmetric key cryptography to authenticate clients to servers. All clients and servers are registered with the KDC, so it maintains the secret keys of all network members.

A complicated exchange of tickets (i.e., cryptographic messages) between clients, network servers, and the KDC is used to prove identity and provide authentication. This allows the client to request resources from the server with full assurance that both the client and the server are who they claim to be. The exchange of encrypted tickets also ensures that no logon credentials, session keys, or authentication messages are ever transmitted in cleartext.

Kerberos tickets have specific lifetimes and use parameters. Once a ticket expires, the client must request a renewal or a new ticket to continue communications with a server.

The Kerberos logon process is as follows:

1. User types username and password into client.

2. Client encrypts credentials with DES for transmission to KDC.

3. KDC verifies user credentials.

4. KDC generates a TGT by hashing the user's password.

5. The TGT is encrypted with DES for transmission to the client.

6. The client installs the TGT for use until it expires.

The Kerberos server or service access process is as follows:

1. The client sends its TGT back to the KDC with a request for access to a server or service.

2. The KDC verifies the ongoing validity of the TGT and checks its access control matrix to verify that the user has sufficient privilege to access the requested resource.

3. A Service Ticket (ST) is generated and sent to the client.

4. The client sends the ST to the server or service host.

5. The server or service host verifies the validity of the ST with the KDC.

6. Once identity and authorization is verified, Kerberos activity is complete. The server or service host then opens a session with the client and begins communications or data transmission.

Limitations of Kerberos

Kerberos is a versatile authentication mechanism that can be used over local LANs, local logons, remote access, and client-server resource requests. However, Kerberos has a single point of failure—the KDC. If the KDC is ever compromised, then the secret key of every system on the network is also compromised. Also, if the KDC goes offline, no subject authentication is possible.

There are other limitations or problems with Kerberos:

- Dictionary and brute force attacks on the initial KDC response to a client may reveal the subject's password. In fact, direct password guessing attacks can be waged against the KDC unimpeded. A countermeasure to such attacks is to deploy a preauthentication service to check logon credentials and watch for access attacks before granting a subject access to the KDC.

- Issued tickets are stored in memory on the client and server.

- Malicious subjects can replay captured tickets if they are reused within their lifetime window.

- Issued tickets, specifically the Ticket Granting Ticket (TGT), are based on a hash of the user's password with an added time stamp for expiration.

- Kerberos only encrypts authentication traffic (i.e., mechanisms for proving identity), it does not provide any security for subsequent communication sessions or data transmissions.

Other Examples of Single Sign On

While Kerberos seems to be the most widely recognized (and deployed) form of single sign on, it is not the sole example of this moniker. Here is a quick review of other SSO mechanisms that you may encounter.

Secure European System for Applications in a Multivendor Environment (SESAME) was a system developed to address the weaknesses in Kerberos. However, it was incomplete in its attempt to compensate for all of problems with Kerberos. Eventually Kerberos's later versions and various vendor implementation techniques resolved the initial problems. In the professional security world, SESAME is no longer considered a viable product.

KryptoKnight is a peer-to-peer-based authentication solution developed by IBM. It was incorporated into the *NetSP* product. Like SESAME, KryptoKnight and NetSP never gained a foothold and is no longer a widely used product.

Thin clients are low-end client systems that connect over a network to a server system. Thin clients originated in the mainframe world where host-terminal connections allowed for dumb terminals to interact with and control centralized mainframes. The terminals had no processing or storage capabilities. The idea of thin clients has been replicated on modern client-server environments using interface software applications that act as clients to server-hosted environments. All processing and storage takes place on the server, while the client provides an interface for the subject through the local keyboard, mouse, and monitor. Sometimes thin clients can be called remote control tools.

A *directory service* is a centralized database of resources available to the network. It can be thought of as a telephone directory for network services and assets. Users, clients, and processes consult the directory service to learn where a desired system or resource resides. Then once this address or location is known, access can be directed toward it. A directory service must be authenticated to before queries and lookup activities can be performed. Even after authentication, the directory service will only reveal information to a subject based on that subject's assigned privileges. Directory services are often based upon the Lightweight Directory Access Protocol (LDAP). Some well-known commercial directory services include Microsoft's Active Directory and Novell's NetWare Directory Services (NDS), recently renamed eDirectory.

Scripted access or *logon scripts* are used to establish communication links by providing an automated process by which logon credentials are transmitted to resource hosts at the start of a logon session. Scripted access can often simulate SSO even though the environment still requires a unique authentication process to connect to each server or resource. Scripts can be used to implement SSO in those environments where true SSO technologies are not available. However, scripts and batch files should be stored in a protected area as they usually contain access credentials.

Access Control Techniques

Once a subject has been identified and authenticated and accountability has been established, it must be authorized to access resources or perform actions. Authorization can occur only after the subject's identity has been verified through authentication. Systems provide authorization through the use of access controls. Access controls manage the type and extent of access subjects have to objects. There are two primary categories of access control techniques: discretionary and nondiscretionary. Nondiscretionary can be further subdivided into specific techniques, such as mandatory, *role-based,* and *task-based access controls.*

Discretionary Access Controls (DAC)

A system that employs *discretionary access controls (DAC)* allows the *owner* or creator of an object to control and define subject access to that object. In other words, access control is based on the discretion (i.e., a decision) of the owner. Access is granted or denied in a discretionary environment based on the identity of the subject (which is typically the user account name). For example, if a user creates a new spreadsheet file, they are the owner of that file. As the owner of the file, they can modify the permissions on that file to grant or deny access to other subjects. DACs are often implemented using access control lists (ACLs) on objects. Each ACL defines the types of access granted or restricted to individual or grouped subjects. Discretionary access control does not offer a centrally controlled management system because owners can alter the ACLs on their objects. Thus, access is more dynamic than it is with mandatory access controls.

DAC environments can be extended beyond just controlling type of access between subjects and objects via ACLs by including or applying time controls, transaction controls, and other forms of ID-focused controls (i.e., device, host, protocol, address, etc.). Within a DAC environment, a user's privileges can be suspended while they are on vacation, resumed when they return, or terminated when they have left the organization.

The United States government labels access controls that do not rely upon policy to define access as discretionary; however, corporate environments and nongovernment organizations will often label such environments as need-to-know.

Nondiscretionary Access Controls

Nondiscretionary access controls are used in a rule-based system in which a set of rules, restrictions, or filters determines what can and cannot occur on the system, such as granting subject access, performing an action on an object, or accessing a resource. Access is not based on administrator or owner discretion and is not focused on user identity. (Thus, nondiscretionary access control is the opposite of discretionary in much the same way as Non-A is the opposite of A.) Rather, access is managed by a static set of rules that governs the whole environment (i.e., centrally controlled management system). In general, rule-based access control systems are more appropriate for environments that experience frequent changes to data permissions (i.e., changing the security domain or label of objects). This is so because rule-based systems can implement sweeping changes just by changing the central rules without having to manipulate or "touch" every subject and/or object in the environment. However, in most cases, once the rules are established, they remain fairly static and unchanged throughout the life of the environment.

In rule-based access control systems, control is based on a specific profile created for each user. A common example of such a system is that of a firewall. A firewall is governed by a set of rules or filters defined by the administrator. Users are able to communicate across the firewall because they have initiated transactions that are allowed by the defined rules. Users are able to accomplish this because they have client environments configured to do so; these are the specific profiles. The formalized definition of a rule-based access control (or specifically, a rule-based security policy) is found in RFC 2828, entitled "Internet Security Glossary." This document includes the following definition for the term *rule-based security policy*: "A security policy based on global rules imposed for all users. These rules usually rely on comparison of the sensitivity of the resource being accessed and the possession of corresponding attributes of users, a group of users, or entities acting on behalf of users."

Mandatory Access Controls

Mandatory access controls rely upon the use of classification labels. Each classification label represents a security domain or a realm of security. A security domain is a realm of common trust that is governed by a specific security policy for that domain. Subjects are labeled by their level of clearance (which is a form of privilege). Objects are labeled by their level of classification or sensitivity. For example, the military uses the labels of top secret, secret, confidential, sensitive but unclassified (SBU), and unclassified (see Chapter 5 "Security Management Concepts and Principles"). In a mandatory access control system, subjects are able to access objects that have the same or a lower level of classification. An expansion of this access control method is known as need-to-know. Subjects with higher clearance levels are granted access to highly sensitive resources only if their work tasks require such access. If they don't have a need to know, even if they have sufficient clearance, they are denied access. Mandatory access control (MAC) is prohibitive rather than permissive. If an access is not specifically granted, it is forbidden. MAC is generally recognized as being more secure than DAC but not as flexible or scalable. This relative scale of security is evident via the TCSEC evaluation criteria, which lists mandatory protection as a higher level of security than discretionary protection (for more information about TCSEC, see Chapter 12 "Principles of Security Models").

The use of *security labels* in mandatory access controls presents some interesting problems. First, for a mandatory access control system to function, every subject and object must have a security label. Depending on the environment, security labels can refer to sensitivity, value to the organization, need for confidentiality, classification, department, project, and so on. The military security labels mentioned earlier range from highest sensitivity to lowest: top secret, secret, confidential, sensitive but unclassified (SBU), and unclassified. Common corporate or commercial security labels are confidential, proprietary, private, sensitive, and public. Security classifications indicate a hierarchy of sensitivity, but each level is distinct.

Classifications within a mandatory access control environment are of three types: hierarchical, compartmentalized, or hybrid. Let's discuss these in more detail.

Hierarchical environments   *Hierarchical environments* relate the various classification labels in an ordered structure from low security to medium security to high security. Each level or classification label in the structure is related. Clearance in a level grants the subject access to objects in that level as well as to all objects in all lower levels but prohibits access to all objects in higher levels.

Compartmentalized environments   In *compartmentalized environments,* there is no relationship between one security domain and another. In order to gain access to an object, the subject must have the exact specific clearance for that object's security domain.

Hybrid environments   A *hybrid environment* combines the hierarchical and compartmentalized concepts so that each hierarchical level may contain numerous subcompartments that are isolated from the rest of the security domain. A subject must not only have the correct clearance but also the need-to-know for the specific compartment in order to have access to the compartmentalized object. Having the need to know for one compartment within a security domain does not grant the subject access to any other compartment. Each compartment has its own unique and specific need-to-know. If you have the need to know (which is based on your assigned work tasks), then you are granted access. If you don't have the need to know, then your access is blocked. A hybrid MAC environment provides for more granular control over access but becomes increasingly difficult to manage as the size of the environment (i.e., number of classifications, objects, and subjects) increases.

Role-Based Access Control (RBAC)

Systems that employ role-based or task-based access controls define the ability of a subject to access an object through the use of subject roles (i.e., job descriptions) or tasks (i.e., work functions). If a subject is in a management position, they will have greater access to resources than someone who is in a temporary position. Role-based access controls are useful in environments with frequent personnel changes because access is based on a job description (i.e., a role or task) rather than on a subject's identity.

Role-based access control (RBAC) and *groups within a DAC environment* may serve a similar purpose, but they are different in their deployment and use. They are similar in that they both serve as containers to collect users into manageable units. However, a user can be a member of more than one group. In addition to collecting the rights and permissions from each group, an individual user account may also have rights and permissions assigned directly to it. In a DAC system, even with groups, access is still based on discretion of an owner and focuses control on the identity of the user. When an RBAC system is employed, a user may have only a single role, but there are new trends emerging where a user is assigned multiple roles. Users have only the rights and permissions assigned to such roles and there are no additional individually assigned rights or permissions. Furthermore, access is not determined by owner discretion; it is determined by the inherent responsibilities of the assigned role (i.e., job description). Also, access focuses on the assigned role, not on the identity of the user. Two different users with the same assigned role will have the exact same access and privileges. Role-based access control is becoming increasingly attractive to corporate entities that have a high rate of employee turnover. RBAC also allows company-specific security policies to be directly mapped and enforced in such a way as to map directly with the organization's hierarchy and management structure. This implies that the roles or job descriptions within an RBAC system are often hierarchical, meaning that the roles are related in a low-to-high fashion so that the higher roles are created by adding access and privileges to lower roles. Often, MAC and DAC environments can be replaced by RBAC solutions.

A related method to RBAC is task-based access control (TBAC). TBAC is the same basic idea as RBAC, but instead of being assigned a single role, each user is assigned dozens of tasks. However, the assigned tasks all relate to the assigned work tasks of the person associated with the user account. Under TBAC, access is still based on rules (i.e., the work tasks) and still focuses on controlling access based upon tasks assigned rather than user identity.

Lattice-Based Access Controls

Some, if not most, nondiscretionary access controls can be labeled as *lattice-based access controls*. Lattice-based access controls define upper and lower bounds of access for every relationship between a subject and object. These boundaries can be arbitrary, but they usually follow the military or corporate security label levels. A subject with the lattice permissions shown in Figure 1.3 has access to resources up to private and down to sensitive but does not have access to confidential, proprietary, or public resources. Subjects under lattice-based access controls are said to have the least upper bound and the greatest lower bound of access to labeled objects based on their assigned lattice position. Lattice-based access controls were originally developed to address information flow, which is primarily concerned with confidentiality. One common example of a lattice-based access control is a mandatory access control.

FIGURE 1.3   A representation of the boundaries provided by lattice-based access controls

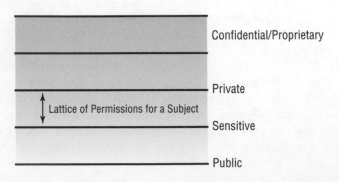

Access Control Methodologies and Implementation

There are two primary access control methodologies: centralized and decentralized (or distributed). *Centralized access control* implies that all authorization verification is performed by a single entity within a system. *Decentralized access control,* or *distributed access control,* implies that authorization verification is performed by various entities located throughout a system.

Centralized and Decentralized Access Control

Centralized and decentralized access control methodologies offer the benefits and drawbacks that any centralized or decentralized system offers. Centralized access control can be managed by a small team or an individual. Administrative overhead is lower because all changes are made in a single location. A single change affects the entire system. However, centralized access control also has a single point of failure. If system elements are unable to access the centralized access control system, then subject and objects cannot interact. Two examples of centralized access control are Remote Authentication Dial-In User Service (RADIUS) and Terminal Access Controller Access Control System (TACACS).

Decentralized access control often requires several teams or multiple individuals. Administrative overhead is higher because the changes must be implemented in numerous locations. Maintaining homogeneity across the system becomes more difficult as the number of access control points increases. Changes made to an individual access control point affect only aspects of the systems that rely upon that specific access control point. Decentralized access control does not have a single point of failure. If an access control point fails, other access control points may be able to balance the load until the control point is repaired, plus objects and subjects that don't rely upon the failed access control point can continue to interact normally. Domains and trusts are commonly used in decentralized access control systems.

A *domain* is a realm of trust or a collection of subjects and objects that share a common security policy. Each domain's access control is maintained independently of that for other domains. This results in decentralized access control when multiple domains are involved. To share resources from one domain to another, a trust is established. A *trust* is simply a security bridge that is established between two domains and allows users from one domain to access resources in another. Trusts can be one-way only or they can be two-way.

RADIUS and TACACS

Remote Authentication Dial-In User Service (RADIUS) is used to centralize the authentication of remote dial-up connections. A network that employs a RADIUS server is configured so the remote access server passes dial-up user logon credentials to the RADIUS server for authentication. This process is similar to the process used by domain clients sending logon credentials to a domain controller for authentication. Use of an authentication server, such as RADIUS or

TACACS, that is separate from the primary remote access server system provides the benefit of keeping auditing and access settings on a system other than the remote access server, thus providing greater security. RADIUS and other remote authentication protocols and services are designed to transport authentication, authorization, and session configuration information between a remote access server (a.k.a. a network access server) and a centralized authentication server (often known as a domain controller).

RADIUS is defined in RFC 2138. It is primarily used to provide an additional layer of protection against intrusions over dial-up connections. RADIUS supports dynamic passwords and callback security. It acts as a proxy for the remote client because it acts on behalf of the client to obtain authentication on the network. RADIUS acts as a client for the network by requesting authentication in much the same manner as a typical client would. Likewise, within the RADIUS architecture, the remote access server is configured as a client of RADIUS.

Due to the success of RADIUS, an enhanced version of RADIUS named DIAMETER was developed; it is designed for use on all forms of remote connectivity, not just dial-up. However, RADIUS and DIAMETER are not interoperable. Eventually, the features of DIAMETER were added back into RADIUS. Now, only a version of RADIUS that supports all types of remote access connectivity is available.

Terminal Access Controller Access Control System (TACACS) is an alternative to RADIUS. TACACS is available in three versions: original TACACS, XTACACS (Extended TACACS), and TACACS+. TACACS integrates the authentication and authorization processes. XTACACS keeps the authentication, authorization, and accounting processes separate. TACACS+ improves XTACACS by adding two-factor authentication. TACACS and RADIUS operate similarly, and TACACS provides the same functionality as RADIUS. However, RADIUS is based on an Internet standard, whereas TACACS is more of a proprietary (although widely used) solution. TACACS is defined in RFC 1492.

These forms of centralized access control, specific to remote access, provide an additional layer of security for your private network. They prevent LAN authentication systems and domain controllers from being attacked directly by remote attackers. By deploying a separate system for remote access users, even if that system is compromised, only the remote access users are affected; the rest of the LAN still functions unhindered.

Access Control Administration

Access control administration is the collection of tasks and duties assigned to an administrator to manage user accounts, access, and accountability. A system's security is based on effective administration of access controls. Remember that access controls rely upon four principles: identification, authentication, authorization, and accountability. In relation to access control administration, these principles transform into three main responsibilities:

- User account management
- Activity tracking
- Access rights and permissions management

Account Administration

User account management involves the creation, maintenance, and closing of user accounts. Although these activities may seem mundane, they are essential to the system's access control capabilities. Without properly defined and maintained user accounts, a system is unable to establish identity, perform authentication, prove authorization, or track accountability.

Creating New Accounts

The creation of new user accounts is a simple process systematically, but it must be protected or secured through organizational security policy procedures. User accounts should not be created at the whim of an administrator or at the request of anyone. Rather, a stringent procedure should be followed that flows from the HR department's hiring or promotion procedures.

The HR department should make a formal request for a user account for a new employee. That request should include the classification or security level that should be assigned to the new employee's user account. The new employee's department manager and the organization's security administrator should verify the security assignment. Once the request has been verified, only then should a new user account be created. Creating user accounts outside of established security policies and procedures simply creates holes and oversights that can be exploited by malicious subjects. A similar process for increasing or decreasing an existing user account's security level should be followed.

As part of the hiring process, new employees should be trained on the security policies and procedures of the organization. Before hiring is complete, employees must sign an agreement committing to uphold the security standards of the organization. Many organizations have opted to craft a document that states that violating the security policy is grounds for dismissal as well as grounds for prosecution under federal, state, and local laws. When passing on the user account ID and temporary password to a new employee, a review of the *password policy* and acceptable use restrictions should be performed.

The initial creation of a new user account is often called an enrollment. The enrollment process creates the new identity and establishes the factors the system needs to perform authentication. It is critical that the enrollment process be completed fully and accurately. It is also critical that the identity of the individual being enrolled be proved through whatever means your organization deems necessary and sufficient. Photo ID, birth certificate, background check, credit check, security clearance verification, FBI database search, and even calling references are all valid forms of verifying a person's identity before enrolling them into your secured system.

Account Maintenance

Throughout the life of a user account, ongoing maintenance is required. Organizations with fairly static organizational hierarchies and low employee turnover or promotion will have significantly less account administration than an organization with a flexible or dynamic organizational hierarchy and high employee turnover and promotion. Most account maintenance deals with altering rights and privileges. Procedures similar to the procedures used when new accounts are created should be established to govern how access is changed throughout the life of a user account. Unauthorized increases or decreases in an account's access capabilities can result in serious security repercussions.

When an employee is no longer present at an organization, their user account should be disabled, deleted, or revoked. Whenever possible, this task should be automated and tied into the HR department. In most cases, when someone's paychecks are stopped, that person should no longer have logon capabilities. Temporary or short-term employees should have a specific expiration date programmed into their user account. This maintains a degree of control established at the time of account creation without requiring ongoing administrative oversight.

Account, Log, and Journal Monitoring

Activity auditing, account tracking, and system monitoring are also important aspects of access control management. Without these capabilities, it would not be possible to hold subjects accountable. Through the establishment of identity, authentication, and authorization, tracking the activities of subjects (including how many times they access objects) offers direct and specific accountability. Auditing and monitoring as an aspect of operations security and as an essential element of a secure environment are discussed in Chapter 14, "Auditing and Monitoring."

Access Rights and Permissions

Assigning access to objects is an important part of implementing an organizational security policy. Not all subjects should be granted access to all objects. Not all subjects should have the same functional capabilities on objects. A few specific subjects should access only some objects; likewise, certain functions should be accessible only by a few specific subjects.

The Principle of Least Privilege

The *principle of least privilege* arises out of the complex structure that results when subjects are granted access to objects. This principle states that subjects should be granted only the amount of access to objects that is required to accomplish their assigned work tasks. This principle has a converse that should be followed as well: subjects should be blocked from accessing objects that are not required by their work tasks. The principle of least privilege is most often linked with DAC, but this concept applies to all types of access control environments, including Non-DAC, MAC, RBAC, and TBAC.

Keep in mind that the idea of privilege usually means the ability to write, create, alter, or delete data. Thus, by limiting and controlling privilege based upon this concept, it serves as a protection mechanism for data integrity. If users can change only those data files that their work tasks require them to change, then the integrity of all other files in the environment is protected.

This principle relies upon the fact that all users have a distinctly defined job description. Without a specific job description, it is not possible to know what privileges a user does or does not need.

Need-to-Know Access

A related principle in the realm of mandatory access control environments is known as need-to-know. Within a specific classification level or security domain, some assets or resources may be sectioned off or compartmentalized. Such resources are restricted from general access even to those subjects with otherwise sufficient clearance. These compartmentalized resources require an additional level of formalized access approval before they can be used by subjects. Subjects are granted access when they can justify their work-task-related reason for access or their need to know. Often, the need to know is determined by a domain supervisor and is granted only for a limited period of time.

Determining which subjects have access to which objects is a function of the organizational security policy, the organizational hierarchy of personnel, and the implementation of an access control model. Thus, the criteria for establishing or defining access can be based on identity, roles, rules, classifications, location, time, interfaces, need-to-know, and so on. Access control models are formal descriptions of a security policy. A security policy is a document that encapsulates the security requirements of an organization and prescribes the steps necessary to achieve the desired security. Access control models (or security models) are used in security evaluations and assessments as well as in tools used to prove the existence of security.

Excessive Privilege and Creeping Privileges

It's important to guard against two problems related to access control: excessive privilege and creeping privileges. Excessive privilege is when a user has more access, privilege, or permission than their assigned work tasks dictate. If a user account is discovered to have excessive privilege, the additional and unnecessary privileges should be immediately revoked. Creeping privileges involve a user account accumulating privileges over time as their job roles and assigned tasks change. This can occur because new tasks are added to a user's job and the related or necessary privileges are added as well but no privileges or access is ever removed, even if the related work task is not longer associated with or assigned to the user. Creeping privileges result in excessive privilege. Both of these issues can be prevented with the proper application of the principle of least privilege.

Users, Owners, and Custodians

When discussing access to objects, three subject labels are used: user, owner, and custodian. A user is any subject who accesses objects on a system to perform some action or accomplish a work task. An owner, or information owner, is the person who has final corporate responsibility for classifying and labeling objects and protecting and storing data. The owner may be liable for negligence if they fail to perform *due diligence* in establishing and enforcing security policies to protect and sustain sensitive data. A *custodian* is a subject who has been assigned or delegated the day-to-day responsibility of proper storage and protection of objects.

A user is any end user on the system. The owner is typically the CEO, president, or department head. The custodian is typically the IT staff or the system security administrator.

Separation of Duties and Responsibilities

Separation of duties and responsibilities is a common practice that prevents any single subject from being able to circumvent or disable security mechanisms. When core administration or high-authority responsibilities are divided among several subjects, no one subject has sufficient access to perform significant malicious activities or bypass imposed security controls. Separation of duties creates a checks-and-balances system in which multiple subjects verify the actions of each other and must work in concert to accomplish necessary work tasks. Separation of duties makes the accomplishment of malicious, fraudulent, or otherwise unauthorized activities much more difficult and broadens the scope of detection and reporting. It is easy for an individual to perform an unauthorized act if they think they can get away with it. Once two or more people are involved, the committal of an unauthorized activity requires that each person agree to keep a secret. This typically serves as a significant deterrent rather than as a means to corrupt a group *en masse*. Separation of duties can be static or dynamic. Static separation of duties is accomplished by assigning privileges based on written policies that don't change often. Dynamic separation of duties is used when security requirements cannot be determined until the system is active and functioning.

An example of a properly enforced separation of duties is to prevent the security administrator from being able to access system administration utilities or to perform changes to system configuration not related to security. For example, a security administrator needs no more than read access to system logs. In this manner, separation of duties helps to prevent conflicts of interest in the types of privileges assigned to administrators as well as users in general. Figure 1.4 illustrates common privileges that should not be combined with others in order to properly enforce separation of duties.

The Segregation of Duties Control Matrix is not an industry standard, but a guideline indicating which positions should be separated and which require compensating controls when combined. The matrix is illustrative of potential segregation of duties and should not be viewed or used as an absolute, but rather it should be used to help identify potential conflicts so proper questions may be asked to identify compensating controls.

Summary

The first domain of the CISSP CBK is Access Control Systems and Methodology. Access controls are central to the establishment of a secure system. They rely upon identification, authentication, authorization, and accountability. Access control is the management, administration, and implementation of granting or restricting subject access to objects.

The first step in access control is verifying the identities of subjects on the system, commonly known as authentication. There are a number of methods available to authenticate subjects, including passwords and phrases, biometric scans, tokens, and tickets.

Once a subject is authenticated, their access must be managed (authorization) and their activities logged, so ultimately the person can be held accountable for the user account's online actions.

There are various models for access control or authorization. These include discretionary and nondiscretionary access controls. There are at least three important subdivisions of nondiscretionary access control: mandatory, role-based, and task-based access control.

Access can be managed for an entire network at once. Such systems are known as Single Sign On solutions. Remote access clients pose unique challenges to LAN security and often require specialized tools such as RADIUS or TACACS.

Finally, once all these systems are in place, they must be maintained. It does very little good to set up system security only to let it go stale over time. Proper role assignment and object maintenance are key aspects to keeping a system secure over time.

FIGURE 1.4   A Segregation of Duties Control Matrix

	Control Group	Systems Analyst	Application Programmer	Help Desk and Support Mgr.	End User	Data Entry	Computer Operator	DB Administrator	Network Administrator	System Administrator	Security Administrator	Tape Librarian	Systems Programmer	Quality Assurance
Control Group		X	X	X		X	X	X	X	X			X	
Systems Analyst	X			X	X		X				X	X		
Application Programmer	X			X	X	X	X	X	X	X	X	X	X	
Help Desk and Support Mgr.	X	X	X		X	X		X	X	X		X	X	
End User		X	X	X			X	X	X			X	X	X
Data Entry	X		X	X			X	X	X	X	X		X	
Computer Operator	X	X	X		X	X		X	X	X	X		X	
DB Administrator	X		X	X	X	X	X		X	X			X	
Network Administrator	X		X	X	X	X	X	X				X		
System Administrator	X		X	X		X	X	X				X		
Security Administrator		X	X			X	X					X	X	
Tape Librarian		X	X	X	X				X	X	X		X	
Systems Programmer	X		X	X	X	X	X	X			X	X		X
Quality Assurance					X							X	X	

X—Combination of these functions may create a potential control weakness.

Exam Essentials

Understand the CIA Triad.   The CIA Triad comprises confidentiality, integrity, and availability. Confidentiality involves making sure that each aspect of a system is properly secured and accessible only by subjects who need it. Integrity assures that system objects are accurate and reliable. Availability ensures that the system is performing optimally and that authenticated subjects can access system objects when they are needed.

Know the common access control techniques.   Common access control techniques include discretionary, mandatory, nondiscretionary, rule-based, role-based, and lattice-based. Access controls are used to manage the type and extent of access subjects have to objects, which is an important part of system security because such controls define who has access to what.

Understand access control administration.   The secure creation of new user accounts, the ongoing management and maintenance of user accounts, auditing/logging/monitoring subject activity, and assigning and managing subject access are important aspects of keeping a system secure. Security is an ongoing task, and administration is how you keep a system secure over time.

Know details about each of the access control models.   There are two primary categories of access control techniques: discretionary and nondiscretionary. Nondiscretionary can be further subdivided into specific techniques, such as mandatory, role-based, and task-based access control.

Understand the processes of identification and common identification factors.   The processes of identification include subject identity claims by using a username, user ID, PIN, smart card, biometric factors, and so on. They are important because identification is the first step in authenticating a subject's identity and proper access rights to objects.

Understand the processes of authentication and the various authentication factors.   Authentication involves verifying the authentication factor provided by a subject against the authentication factor stored for the claimed identity, which could include passwords, biometrics, tokens, tickets, SSO, and so on. In other words, the authentication process ensures that a subject is who they claim to be and grants object rights accordingly.

Understand the processes of authorization.   Authorization ensures that the requested activity or object access is possible given the rights and privileges assigned to the authenticated identity. This is important because it maintains security by providing proper access rights for subjects.

Understand the strengths and weaknesses of passwords.   Users typically choosing passwords that are easy to remember and therefore easy to guess or crack is one weakness associated with passwords. Another is that randomly generated passwords are hard to remember, thus many users write them down. Passwords are easily shared and can be stolen through many means. Additionally, passwords are often transmitted in cleartext or with easily broken encryption protocols, and password databases are often stored in publicly accessible online locations. Finally, short passwords can be discovered quickly in brute force attacks. On the other hand, passwords can be effective if selected intelligently and managed properly. It is important to change passwords frequently; the more often the same password is used, the more likely it will be compromised or discovered.

Know the two access control methodologies and implementation examples.   Access control methodologies include centralized access control, in which authorization verification is performed by a single entity within a system, and decentralized access control, in which authorization verification is performed by various entities located throughout a system. Remote authentication mechanisms such as RADIUS and TACACS are implementation examples; they are used to centralize the authentication of remote dial-up connections.

Understand the use of biometrics.   Biometric factors are used for identification or authentication. FRR, FAR, and CER are important aspects of biometric devices. Fingerprints, face scans, iris scans, retina scans, palm topography, palm geography, heart/pulse pattern, voice pattern, signature dynamics, and keystroke patterns are commonly used in addition to other authentication factors, such as a password, to provide an additional method to control authentication of subjects.

Understand Single Sign On.   Single Sign On (SSO) is a mechanism that allows a subject to be authenticated only once on a system and be able to access resource after resource unhindered by repeated authentication prompts. Kerberos, *SESAME, KryptoKnight, NetSP,* thin clients, directory services, and *scripted access* are examples of SSO mechanisms.

Review Questions

1. What is access?
   A. Functions of an object
   B. Information flow from objects to subjects
   C. Unrestricted admittance of subjects on a system
   D. Administration of ACLs

2. Which of the following is true?
   A. A subject is always a user account.
   B. The subject is always the entity that provides or hosts the information or data.
   C. The subject is always the entity that receives information about or data from the object.
   D. A single entity can never change roles between subject and object.

3. What are the elements of the CIA Triad?
   A. Confidentiality, integrity, and availability
   B. Confidentiality, interest, and accessibility
   C. Control, integrity, and authentication
   D. Calculations, interpretation, and accountability

4. Which of the following types of access control uses fences, security policies, security awareness training, and antivirus software to stop an unwanted or unauthorized activity from occurring?
   A. Preventative
   B. Detective
   C. Corrective
   D. Authoritative

5. _____ access controls are the hardware or software mechanisms used to manage access to resources and systems and to provide protection for those resources and systems.
   A. Administrative
   B. Logical/technical
   C. Physical
   D. Preventative

6. What is the first step of access control?
   A. Accountability logging
   B. ACL verification
   C. Subject authorization
   D. Subject identification

7. _____ is the process of verifying or testing the validity of a claimed identity.

   A. Identification

   B. Authentication

   C. Authorization

   D. Accountability

8. Which of the following is an example of a Type 2 authentication factor?

   A. Something you have, such as a smart card, ATM card, token device, and memory card

   B. Something you are, such as fingerprints, voice print, retina pattern, iris pattern, face shape, palm topology, and hand geometry

   C. Something you do, such as type a pass phrase, sign your name, and speak a sentence

   D. Something you know, such as a password, personal identification number (PIN), lock combination, pass phrase, mother's maiden name, and favorite color

9. Which of the following is not a reason why using passwords alone is a poor security mechanism?

   A. When possible, users choose easy-to-remember passwords, which are therefore easy to guess or crack.

   B. Randomly generated passwords are hard to remember, thus many users write them down.

   C. Short passwords can be discovered quickly in brute force attacks only when used against a stolen password database file.

   D. Passwords can be stolen through many means, including observation, recording and playback, and security database theft.

10. Which of the following is not a valid means to improve the security offered by password authentication?

   A. Enabling account lockout controls

   B. Enforcing a reasonable password policy

   C. Using password verification tools and password cracking tools against your own password database file

   D. Allowing users to reuse the same password

11. What can be used as an authentication factor that is a behavioral or physiological characteristic unique to a subject?

   A. Account ID

   B. Biometric factor

   C. Token

   D. IQ

12. What does the Crossover Error Rate (CER) for a biometric device indicate?

   A. The sensitivity is tuned too high.

   B. The sensitivity is tuned too low.

   C. The False Rejection Rate and False Acceptance Rate are equal.

   D. The biometric device is not properly configured.

13. Which if the following is not an example of an SSO mechanism?

   A. Kerberos

   B. KryptoKnight

   C. TACACS

   D. SESAME

14. _____ access controls rely upon the use of labels.

   A. Discretionary

   B. Role-based

   C. Mandatory

   D. Nondiscretionary

15. A network environment that uses discretionary access controls is vulnerable to which of the following?

   A. SYN flood

   B. Impersonation

   C. Denial of service

   D. Birthday attack

16. What is the most important aspect of a biometric device?

   A. Accuracy

   B. Acceptability

   C. Enrollment time

   D. Invasiveness

17. Which of the following is not an example of a deterrent access control?

   A. Encryption

   B. Auditing

   C. Awareness training

   D. Antivirus software

18. Kerberos provides the security services of _____ protection for authentication traffic.

  A. Availability and nonrepudiation

  B. Confidentiality and authentication

  C. Confidentiality and integrity

  D. Availability and authorization

19. Which of the following forms of authentication provides the strongest security?

  A. Password and a PIN

  B. One-time password

  C. Pass phrase and a smart card

  D. Fingerprint

20. Which of the following is the least acceptable form of biometric device?

  A. Iris scan

  B. Retina scan

  C. Fingerprint

  D. Facial geometry

Answers to Review Questions

1. B. The transfer of information from an object to a subject is called access.

2. C. The subject is always the entity that receives information about or data from the object. The subject is also the entity that alters information about or data stored within the object. The object is always the entity that provides or hosts the information or data. A subject can be a user, a program, a process, a file, a computer, a database, and so on. The roles of subject and object can switch as two entities, such as a program and a database or a process and a file, communicate to accomplish a task.

3. A. The essential security principles of confidentiality, integrity, and availability are often referred to as the CIA Triad.

4. A. A preventative access control is deployed to stop an unwanted or unauthorized activity from occurring. Examples of preventative access controls include fences, security policies, security awareness training, and antivirus software.

5. B. Logical/technical access controls are the hardware or software mechanisms used to manage access to resources and systems and to provide protection for those resources and systems. Examples of logical or technical access controls include encryption, smart cards, passwords, biometrics, constrained interfaces, access control lists, protocols, firewalls, routers, intrusion detection systems, and clipping levels.

6. D. Access controls govern subjects' access to objects. The first step in this process is identifying who the subject is. In fact, there are several steps preceding actual object access: identification, authentication, authorization, and accountability.

7. B. The process of verifying or testing the validity of a claimed identity is called authentication.

8. A. A Type 2 authentication factor is something you have. This could include a smart card, ATM card, token device, and memory card.

9. C. Brute force attacks can be used against password database files and system logon prompts.

10. D. Preventing password reuse increases security by preventing the theft of older password database files, which can be used against the current user passwords.

11. B. A biometric factor is a behavioral or physiological characteristic that is unique to a subject, such as fingerprints and face scans.

12. C. The point at which the FRR and FAR are equal is known as the Crossover Error Rate (CER). The CER level is used as a standard assessment point from which to measure the performance of a biometric device.

13. C. Kerberos, SESAME, and KryptoKnight are examples of SSO mechanisms. TACACS is a centralized authentication service used for remote access clients.

14. C. Mandatory access controls rely upon the use of labels. A system that employs discretionary access controls allows the owner or creator of an object to control and define subject access to that object. Nondiscretionary access controls are also called role-based access controls. Systems that employ nondiscretionary access controls define a subject's ability to access an object through the use of subject roles or tasks.

15. B. A discretionary access control environment controls access based on user identity. If a user account is compromised and another person uses that account, they are impersonating the real owner of the account.

16. A. The most important aspect of a biometric factor is its accuracy. If a biometric factor is not accurate, it may allow unauthorized users into a system.

17. D. Antivirus software is an example of a recovery or corrective access control.

18. C. Kerberos provides the security services of confidentiality and integrity protection for authentication traffic.

19. C. A pass phrase and a smart card provide the strongest authentication security because it is the only selection offering two-factor authentication.

20. B. Of the options listed, retina scan is the least accepted form of biometric device because it requires touching a shared eye cup and can reveal personal health issues.

Chapter

2

Attacks and Monitoring

THE CISSP EXAM TOPICS COVERED IN THIS CHAPTER INCLUDE:

- ✓ Monitoring
- ✓ Intrusion Detection
- ✓ Penetration Testing
- ✓ Access Control Attacks

The Access Control Systems and Methodology domain of the Common Body of Knowledge (CBK) for the CISSP certification exam deals with topics and issues related to the monitoring, identification, and authorization of granting or restricting user access to resources. Generally, access control is any hardware, software, or organizational administrative policy or procedure that grants or restricts access, monitors and records attempts to access, identifies users attempting to access, and determines whether access is authorized.

This domain is discussed in this chapter and in the previous chapter (Chapter 1, "Accountability and Access Control"). Be sure to read and study the materials from both chapters to ensure complete coverage of the essential material for the CISSP certification exam.

Monitoring

Monitoring is the programmatic means by which subjects are held accountable for their actions while authenticated on a system. It is also the process by which unauthorized or abnormal activities are detected on a system. Monitoring is necessary to detect malicious actions by subjects, as well as to detect attempted intrusions and system failures. It can help reconstruct events, provide evidence for prosecution, and produce problem reports and analysis. *Auditing* and logging are usually native features of an operating system and most applications and services. Thus, configuring the system to record information about specific types of events is fairly straightforward.

Using log files to detect problems is another matter. In most cases, when sufficient logging and auditing is enabled to monitor a system, so much data is collected that the important details get lost in the bulk. There are numerous tools to search through log files for specific events or ID codes. The art of data reduction is crucial when working with large volumes of monitoring data obtained from log files. The tools used to extract the relevant, significant, or important details from large collections of data are known as *data mining tools*. For true automation and even real-time analysis of events, a specific type of data mining tool is required—namely, an intrusion detection system (IDS). See the next section for information on IDSs.

Accountability is maintained by recording the activities of subjects and objects as well as core system functions that maintain the operating environment and the security mechanisms. The audit trails created by recording system events to logs can be used to evaluate a system's health and performance. System crashes may indicate faulty programs, corrupt drivers, or intrusion attempts. The event logs leading up to a crash can often be used to discover the reason a system failed. Log files provide an audit trail for re-creating a step-by-step history of an event, intrusion, or system failure.

For more information on configuring and administering auditing and logging, see Chapter 14, "Auditing and Monitoring."

Intrusion Detection

An *intrusion detection system (IDS)* is a product that automates the inspection of audit logs and real-time system events. IDSs are primarily used to detect intrusion attempts, but they can also be employed to detect system failures or rate overall performance. IDSs watch for violations of confidentiality, integrity, and availability. The goal of an IDS is to provide perpetrator accountability for intrusion activities and provide a means for a timely and accurate response to intrusions. Attacks recognized by an IDS can come from external connections (such as the Internet or partner networks), viruses, malicious code, trusted internal subjects attempting to perform unauthorized activities, and unauthorized access attempts from trusted locations. An IDS is considered a form of a technical detective security control.

An IDS can actively watch for suspicious activity, peruse audit logs, send alerts to administrators when specific events are discovered, lock down important system files or capabilities, track slow and fast intrusion attempts, highlight vulnerabilities, identify the intrusion's origination point, track down the logical or physical location of the perpetrator, terminate or interrupt attacks or intrusion attempts, and reconfigure routers and firewalls to prevent repeats of discovered attacks. IDS alerts can be sent or communicated with an on-screen notification (the most common), by playing a sound, via e-mail, via pager, or by recording information in a log file.

A response by an IDS can be active, passive, or hybrid. An active response is one that directly affects the malicious activity of network traffic or the host application. A passive response is one that does not affect the malicious activity but records information about the issue and notifies the administrator. A hybrid response is one that stops unwanted activity, records information about the event, and possibly even notifies the administrator.

Generally, an IDS is used to detect unauthorized or malicious activity originating from inside or outside of your trusted network. The capability of an IDS to stop current attacks or prevent future attacks is limited. Typically, the responses an IDS can take against an attack include port blocking, source address blocking, and disabling all communications over a specific cable segment. Whenever an IDS discovers abnormal traffic (e.g., spoofed) or violations of its security policy, filters, and rules, it records a log detail of the issue and then drops, discards, or deletes the relevant packets.

An IDS should be considered one of the many components a well-formed security endeavor comprises to protect a network. An IDS is a complementary security tool to a firewall. Other security controls, such as physical restrictions and logical access controls, are necessary components (refer to Chapter 1 for a discussion of these controls).

Intrusion prevention requires adequate maintenance of overall system security, such as applying patches and setting security controls. It also involves responding to intrusions discovered via an IDS by erecting barriers to prevent future occurrences of the same attack. This could be as simple as updating software or reconfiguring access controls, or it could be as drastic as reconfiguring a firewall, removing or replacing an application or service, or redesigning an entire network.

When an intrusion is detected, your first response should be to contain the intrusion. Intrusion containment prevents additional damage to other systems but may allow the continued infestation of already compromised systems. Later, once compromised systems are rebuilt from scratch, be sure to double-check compliance with your security policy—including checking ACLs, service configurations, and user account settings—before connecting the reestablished system to your network. You should realize that if you wipe and re-create a system, none of the previous system, nor any intrusion footprints, will remain.

WARNING It is considered unethical and risky to actively launch counterstrikes against an intruder or to actively attempt to reverse-hack the intruder's computer system. Instead, rely upon your logging capabilities and sniffing collections to provide sufficient data to prosecute criminals or to simply improve the security of your environment accordingly.

Host-Based and Network-Based IDSs

IDS types are most commonly classified by their information source. There are two primary types of IDSs: host based and network based. A *host-based IDS* watches for questionable activity on a single computer system. A *network-based IDS* watches for questionable activity being performed over the network medium.

Host-Based IDS

Because the attention of a host-based IDS is focused on a single computer (whereas a network-based IDS must monitor the activity on an entire network), it can examine events in much greater detail than a network-based IDS can. A host-based IDS is able to pinpoint the files and processes compromised or employed by a malicious user to perform unauthorized activity.

Host-based IDSs can detect anomalies undetected by network-based IDSs; however, a host-based IDS cannot detect network-only attacks or attacks on other systems. Because a host-based IDS is installed on the computer being monitored, crackers can discover the IDS software and disable it or manipulate it to hide their tracks. A host-based IDS has some difficulty with detecting and tracking down denial of service (DoS) attacks, especially those of a bandwidth consumption nature. A host-based IDS also consumes resources from the computer being monitored, thereby reducing the performance of that system. A host-based IDS is limited by the auditing capabilities of the host operating system and applications.

Host-based IDSs are considered more costly to manage than network-based IDSs. Host-based IDSs require that an installation on each server be monitored and require administrative attention at each point of installation, while network-based IDSs usually only require a single installation point. Host-based IDSs have other disadvantages as well; for example, they cause a significant host system performance degradation and they are easier for an intruder to discover and disable.

Network-Based IDS

Network-based IDSs detect attacks or event anomalies through the capture and evaluation of network packets. A single network-based IDS is capable of monitoring a large network if installed on a backbone of that network, where a majority of the network traffic occurs. Some versions of network-based IDSs use remote agents to collect data from various subnets and report to a central management console. Network-based IDSs are installed onto single-purpose computers. This allows them to be hardened against attack, reduces the number of vulnerabilities to the IDS, and allows the IDS to operate in stealth mode. In stealth mode, the IDS is invisible to the network and intruders would have to know of its exact location and system identification to discover it. A network-based IDS has little negative affect on overall network performance, and because it is deployed on a single-purpose system, it doesn't adversely affect the performance of any other computer.

On networks with extremely large volumes of traffic, a network-based IDS may be unable to keep up with the flow of data. This could cause the IDS to miss an attack that occurred during high traffic levels. Network-based IDSs do not usually work well on switched networks, especially if the routers do not have a monitoring port. Network-based IDSs are used to monitor the content of traffic if it is encrypted during transmission over the network medium. They are usually able to detect the initiation of an attack or the ongoing attempts to perpetrate an attack (including DoS), but they are unable to provide information about whether an attack was successful or which specific systems, user accounts, files, or applications were affected.

Often, a network-based IDS can provide some limited functionality for discovering the source of an attack by performing Reverse Address Resolution Protocol (RARP) or Domain Name System (DNS) lookups. However, because most attacks are launched by malicious individuals whose identity is masked through spoofing, this is not usually a fully reliable system capability.

An IDS should not be viewed as a single universal security solution. It is only part of a multi-faceted security solution for an environment. Although an IDS can offer numerous benefits, there are several drawbacks to consider. A host-based IDS may not be able to examine every detail if the host system is overworked and insufficient execution time is granted to the IDS processes. A network-based IDS can suffer the same problem if the network traffic load is high and it is unable to process packets efficiently and swiftly. A network-based IDS is also unable to examine the contents of encrypted traffic. A network-based IDS is not an effective network-wide solution on switched networks because it is unable to view all network traffic if it is not placed on a mirror port (i.e., a port specifically configured to send all data to the IDS). An IDS may initially produce numerous false alarms and requires significant management on an ongoing basis.

A switched network is often a preventative measure against rogue sniffers. Just like an IDS off of a switch, if the switch is not configured to mirror all traffic, then only a small portion of network traffic will be accessible. However, numerous attacks, such as MAC or ARP flooding, can cause a switch to default into hub mode, thus granting the attacker access to all data (as well as greatly reducing the efficiency and throughput of your network).

Knowledge-Based and Behavior-Based Detection

There are two common means by which an IDS can detect malicious events. One way is to use *knowledge-based detection*. This is also called *signature-based detection* or *pattern-matching detection.* Basically, the IDS uses a signature database and attempts to match all monitored events to it. If events match, then the IDS assumes that an attack is taking place (or has taken place). The IDS vendor develops the suspect chart by examining and inspecting numerous intrusions on various systems. What results is a description, or signature, of common attack methods. An IDS using knowledge-based detection functions in much the same way as many antivirus applications.

The primary drawback to a knowledge-based IDS is that it is effective only against known attack methods. New attacks or slightly modified versions of known attacks often go unrecognized by the IDS. This means that the knowledge-based IDS lacks a learning model; that is, it is unable to recognize new attack patterns as they occur. Thus, this type of IDS is only as useful as its signature file is correct and up-to-date. Keeping the signature file current is an important aspect in maintaining the best performance from a knowledge-based IDS.

The second detection type is *behavior-based detection.* A behavior-based IDS is also called *statistical intrusion detection, anomaly detection,* and *heuristics-based detection.* Basically, behavior-based detection finds out about the normal activities and events on your system through watching and learning. Once it has accumulated enough data about normal activity, it can detect abnormal and possible malicious activities and events.

A behavior-based IDS can be labeled an expert system or a pseudo artificial intelligence system because it can learn and make assumptions about events. In other words, the IDS can act like a human expert by evaluating current events against known events. The more information provided to a behavior-based IDS about normal activities and events, the more accurate its anomaly detection becomes.

The primary drawback of a behavior-based IDS is that it produces many false alarms. The normal pattern of user and system activity can vary widely, and thus establishing a definition of normal or acceptable activity can be difficult. The more a security detection system creates false alarms, the less likely security administrators will heed its warnings, just as in the fable of the boy who cried wolf. Over time, the IDS can become more efficient and accurate, but the learning process takes considerable time. Using known behaviors, activity statistics, and heuristic evaluation of current versus previous events, a behavior-based IDS can detect unforeseen, new, and unknown vulnerabilities, attacks, and intrusion methods.

Although knowledge-based and behavior-based detection methods do have their differences, both employ an alarm-signal system. When an intrusion is recognized or detected, an alarm is triggered. The alarm system can notify administrators via e-mail or pop-up messages or by executing scripts to send pager messages. In addition to administrator notification, the alarm system can record alert messages in log and audit files as well as generate violation reports detailing the detected intrusions and discoveries of vulnerabilities.

IDS-Related Tools

Intrusion detection systems are often deployed in concert with several other components. These IDS-related tools expand the usefulness and capabilities of IDSs and make them more efficient and less prone to false positives. These tools include honey pots, padded cells, and vulnerability scanners.

Honey pots are individual computers or entire networks created to serve as a snare for intruders. They look and act like legitimate networks, but they are 100 percent fake. Honey pots tempt intruders by containing unpatched and unprotected security vulnerabilities as well as by hosting attractive and tantalizing but faux data. They are designed to grab an intruder's attention and direct them into the restricted playground while keeping them away from the legitimate network and confidential resources. Legitimate users never enter the honey pot; there is no real data or useful resources in the honey pot system. Thus, when honey pot access is detected, it is most likely an unauthorized intruder. Honey pots are deployed to keep an intruder logged on and performing their malicious activities long enough for the automated IDS to detect the intrusion and gather as much information about the intruder as possible. The longer the honey pot retains the attention of the intruder, the more time an administrator has to investigate the attack and potentially identify the person perpetrating the intrusion.

The use of honey pots raises the issue of enticement versus entrapment. A honey pot can be legally used as an enticement device if the intruder discovers it through no outward efforts of the honey pot owner. Placing a system on the Internet with open security vulnerabilities and active services with known exploits is enticement. Entrapment occurs when the honey pot owner actively solicits visitors to access the site and then charges them with unauthorized intrusion. It is considered to be entrapment when you trick or encourage a perpetrator into performing an illegal or unauthorized action. Enticement occurs when the opportunity for illegal or unauthorized actions is provided but the perpetrator makes their own decision to perform the action.

A *padded cell* system is similar to a honey pot, but it performs intrusion isolation using a different approach. When an intruder is detected by an IDS, the intruder is automatically transferred to a padded cell. The padded cell has the look and layout of the actual network, but within the padded cell the intruder can neither perform malicious activities nor access any confidential data. A padded cell is a simulated environment that offers fake data to retain an intruder's interest. The transfer of the intruder into a padded cell is performed without informing the intruder that the change has occurred. Like a honey pot, the padded cell system is heavily monitored and used by administrators to gather evidence for tracing and possible prosecution.

Another type of IDS-related tool is a *vulnerability scanner*. Vulnerability scanners are used to test a system for known security vulnerabilities and weaknesses. They are used to generate reports that indicate the areas or aspects of the system that need to be managed to improve security. The reports may recommend applying patches or making specific configuration or security setting changes to improve or impose security. A vulnerability scanner is only as useful as its database of security issues. Thus, the database must be updated from the vendor often to provide a useful audit of your system. The use of vulnerability scanners in cooperation with IDSs may help reduce false positives by the IDS and keep the total number of overall intrusions or security violations to a minimum. When discovered vulnerabilities are patched quickly and often, the system provides a more secure environment.

Penetration Testing

In security terms, a penetration occurs when an attack is successful and an intruder is able to breach the perimeter of your environment. The breach can be as small as reading a few bits of data from your network or as big as logging in as a user with unrestricted privileges. One of the primary goals of security is to prevent penetrations.

One common method to test the strength of your security measures is to perform *penetration testing*. Penetration testing is a vigorous attempt to break into your protected network using any means necessary. It is common for organizations to hire external consultants to perform the penetration testing so the testers are not privy to confidential elements of the security's configuration, network design, and other internal secrets.

Penetration testing seeks to find any and all weaknesses in your existing security perimeter. Once a weakness is discovered, countermeasures can be selected and deployed to improve the security of the environment. One significant difference between penetration testing and actual attacking is that once a vulnerability is discovered, the intrusion attempt ceases before the vulnerability is actually exploited and causes system damage.

Penetration testing can be performed using automated attack tools or suites or performed manually with common network utilities and scripting. Automated attack tools range from professional vulnerability scanners to wild, underground cracker/hacker tools discovered on the Internet. Tools are also often used for penetration testing performed manually, but much more onus is placed on knowing how to perpetrate an attack.

Penetration testing should be performed only with the consent and knowledge of the management staff. Performing unapproved security testing could result in productivity loss, trigger emergency response teams, or even cost you your job.

Regularly staged penetration attempts are a good way to accurately judge the security mechanisms deployed by an organization. Penetration testing can also reveal areas where patches or security settings are insufficient and where new vulnerabilities have developed. To evaluate your system, benchmarking and testing tools are available for download at `www.cisecurity.org`.

Penetration testing is discussed further in Chapter 14.

Methods of Attacks

As discussed in Chapter 1, one of the goals of access control is to prevent unauthorized access to objects. This includes access into a system (a network, a service, a communications link, a computer, etc.) or access to data. In addition to controlling access, security is also concerned with preventing unauthorized alteration and disclosure and providing consistent availability (remember the *CIA Triad* from Chapter 1).

However, malicious entities are focused on violating the security perimeter of a system to obtain access to data, alter or destroy data, and inhibit valid access to data and resources. The actual means by which attacks are perpetrated vary greatly. Some are extremely complex and require detailed knowledge of the victimized systems and programming techniques, whereas others are extremely simple to execute and require little more than an IP address and the ability to manipulate a few tools or scripts. But even though there are many different kinds of attacks, they can be generally grouped into a handful of classifications or categories.

These are the common or well-known classes of attacks or attack methodologies:

- Brute force and dictionary
- Denial of service

- Spoofing
- Man-in-the-middle attacks
- Spamming
- Sniffers
- Crackers

Brute Force and Dictionary Attacks

Brute force and dictionary attacks are often discussed together because they are waged against the same entity: passwords. Either type of attack can be waged against a password database file or against an active logon prompt.

A brute force attack is an attempt to discover passwords for user accounts by systematically attempting every possible combination of letters, numbers, and symbols. With the speed of modern computers and the ability to employ distributed computing, brute force attacks are becoming successful even against strong passwords. With enough time, all passwords can be discovered using a brute force attack method. Most passwords of 14 characters or less can be discovered within 7 days on a fast system using a brute force attack program against a stolen password database file (the actual time it takes to discover passwords is dependent upon the encryption algorithm used to encrypt them).

The longer the password (or the greater the number of keys in an algorithm's key space), the more costly and time consuming a brute force attack becomes. When the number of possibilities is increased, the cost of performing an exhaustive attack increases as well. In other words, the longer the password, the more secure against brute force attacks it becomes.

A *dictionary attack* is an attempt to discover passwords by attempting to use every possible password from a predefined list of common or expected passwords. This type of attack is named such because the possible password list is so long it is as if you are using the entire dictionary one word at a time to discover passwords.

Password attacks employ a specify cryptographic attack method known as the birthday attack (see Chapter 10, "PKI and Cryptographic Applications"). This attack can also be called reverse hash matching or the exploitation of collision. Basically, the attack exploits the fact that if two messages are hashed and the hash values are the same, then the two messages are probably the same. A way of expressing this in mathematical or cryptographic notation is $H(M)=H(M')$. Passwords are stored in an accounts database file on secured systems. However, instead of being stored as plain text, passwords are hashed and only their hash values are actually stored. This provides a reasonable level of protection. However, using reverse hash matching, a password cracker tool looks for possible passwords (through either brute force or dictionary methods) that have the same hash value as a value stored on the accounts database file. When a hash value match is discovered, then the tool is said to have cracked the password.

Combinations of these two password attack methodologies can be used as well. For example, a brute force attack could use a dictionary list as the source of its guesswork.

Dictionary attacks are often successful due to the predictability of human nature to select passwords based on personal experiences. Unfortunately, those personal experiences are often broadcast to the world around you simply by the way you live and act on a daily basis. If you are a sports fan, your password might be based on a player's name or a hit record. If you have children, your password might be based on their names or birth dates. If you work in a technical industry, your password might be based on industry acronyms or product names. The more data about a victim learned through intelligence gathering, dumpster diving, and social engineering, the more successful a custom dictionary list will be.

Protecting passwords from brute force and dictionary attacks requires numerous security precautions and rigid adherence to a strong security policy. First, physical access to systems must be controlled. If a malicious entity can gain physical access to an authentication server, they can often steal the password file within seconds. Once a password file is stolen, all passwords should be considered compromised.

Second, tightly control and monitor electronic access to password files. End users and non–account administrators have no need to access the password database file for normal daily work tasks. If you discover an unauthorized access to the database file, investigate immediately. If you cannot determine that a valid access occurred, then consider all passwords compromised.

Third, craft a password policy that programmatically enforces strong passwords and prescribe means by which end users can create stronger passwords. The stronger and longer the password, the longer it will take for it to be discovered in a brute force attack. However, with enough time, *all* passwords can be discovered via brute force methods. Thus, changing passwords regularly is required to maintain security. Static passwords older than 30 days should be considered compromised even if no other aspect of a security breach has been discovered.

Fourth, deploy two-factor authentication, such as using biometrics or token devices. If passwords are not the only means used to protect the security of a network, their compromise will not automatically result in a system breach.

Fifth, use account lockout controls to prevent brute force and dictionary attacks against logon prompts. For those systems and services that don't support account lockout controls, such as most FTP servers, employ extensive logging and an IDS to look for attempted fast and slow password attacks.

Sixth, encrypt password files with the strongest encryption available for your OS. Maintain rigid control over all media that have a copy of the password database file, such as backup tapes and some types of boot or repair disks.

Passwords are a poor security mechanism when used as the sole deterrent against unauthorized access. Brute force and dictionary attacks show that passwords alone offer little more than a temporary blockade.

Denial of Service

Denial of service (DoS) attacks are attacks that prevent the system from processing or responding to legitimate traffic or requests for resources and objects. The most common form of denial of service attacks is transmitting so many data packets to a server that it cannot processes them all. Other forms of denial of service attacks focus on the exploitation of a known fault or vulnerability in an operating system, service, or application. Exploiting the fault often results in system crash or 100 percent CPU utilization. No matter what the actual attack consists of, any attack that renders the victim unable to perform normal activities can be considered a denial of service attack. Denial of service attacks can result in system crashes, system reboots, data corruption, blockage of services, and more.

Unfortunately, denial of service attacks based on *flooding* (i.e., sending sufficient traffic to a victim to cause a DoS) a server with data are a way of life on the Internet. In fact, there are no known means by which denial of service flood attacks in general can be prevented. Furthermore, due to the ability to spoof packets or exploit legitimate Internet services, it is often impossible to trace the actual origin of an attack and apprehend the culprit.

There are several types of DoS flood attacks. The first, or original, type of attack employed a single attacking system flooding a single victim with a steady stream of packets. Those packets could be valid requests that were never completed or malformed or fragmented packets that consume the attention of the victimized system. This simple form of DoS is easy to terminate just by blocking packets from the source IP address.

Another form of attack is called the *distributed denial of service (DDoS)*. A distributed denial of service occurs when the attacker compromises several systems and uses them as launching platforms against one or more victims. The compromised systems used in the attack are often called slaves or zombies. A DDoS attack results in the victims being flooded with data from numerous sources. DDoS attacks can be stopped by blocking packets from the compromised systems. But this can also result in blocking legitimate traffic because the sources of the flood packets are victims themselves and not the original perpetrator of the attack. These types of attacks are labeled as distributed because numerous systems are involved in the propagation of the attack against the victim.

A more recent form of DoS, called a *distributed reflective denial of service (DRDoS),* has been discovered. DRDoS attacks take advantage of the normal operation mechanisms of key Internet services, such as DNS and router update protocols. DRDoS attacks function by sending numerous update, session, or control packets to various Internet service servers or routers with a spoofed source address of the intended victim. Usually these servers or routers are part of the high-speed, high-volume Internet backbone trunks. What results is a flood of update packets, session acknowledgment responses, or error messages sent to the victim. A DRDoS attack can result in so much traffic that upstream systems are adversely affected by the sheer volume of data focused on the victim. This type of attack is called a reflective attack because the high-speed backbone systems reflect the attack to the victim. Unfortunately, these types of attacks cannot be prevented because they exploit normal functions of the systems. Blocking packets from these key Internet systems will effectively cut the victim off from a significant section of the Internet.

Not all instances of DoS are the result of a malicious attack. Errors in coding operating systems, services, and applications have resulted in DoS conditions. For example, a process failing to release control of the CPU or a service consuming system resources out of proportion to the service requests it is handling can cause DoS conditions. Most vendors quickly release patches to correct these self-inflicted DoS conditions, so it is important to stay informed.

There have been many forms of DoS attacks committed over the Internet. Some of the more popular ones ("popular" meaning widespread due to affecting many systems or well known due to media hype) are discussed in the remainder of this section.

A *SYN flood attack* is waged by breaking the standard three-way handshake used by TCP/IP to initiate communication sessions. Normally, a client sends a SYN packet to a server, the server responds with a SYN/ACK packet to the client, and the client then responds with an ACK packet back to the server. This three-way handshake establishes a communication session that is used for data transfer until the session is terminated (using a three-way handshake with FIN and ACK packets). A SYN flood occurs when numerous SYN packets are sent to a server but the sender never replies to the server's SYN/ACK packets with the final ACK.

    A TCP session can also be terminated with a RES (reset) packet.

In addition, the transmitted SYN packets usually have a spoofed source address so the SYN/ACK response is sent somewhere other than to the actual originator of the packets. The server waits for the client's ACK packet, often for several seconds, holding open a session and consuming system resources. If a significant number of sessions are held open (e.g., through the receipt of a flood of SYN packets), this results in a DoS. The server can be easily overtaxed by keeping sessions that are never finalized open, thus causing a failure. That failure can be as simple as being unable to respond to legitimate requests for communications or as serious as a frozen or crashed system.

One *countermeasure* to SYN flood attacks is increasing the number of connections a server can support. However, this usually requires additional hardware resources (memory, CPU speed, etc.) and may not be possible for all operating systems or network services. A more useful countermeasure is to reduce the timeout period for waiting for the final ACK packet. However, this can also result in failed sessions from clients connected over slower links or can be hindered by intermittent Internet traffic. Network-based IDSs may offer some protection against sustained SYN flood attacks by noticing that numerous SYN packets originate from one or only a few locations, resulting in incomplete sessions. An IDS could warn of the attack or dynamically block flooding attempts.

A *Smurf attack* occurs when an amplifying server or network is used to flood a victim with useless data. An amplifying server or network is any system that generates multiple response packets, such as ICMP ECHO packets or special UDP packets, from a single submitted packet. One common attack is to send a message to the broadcast of a subnet or network so that every node on the network produces one or more response packets. The attacker sends information request packets with the victim's spoofed source address to the amplification system. Thus, all of the response packets are sent to the victim. If the amplification network is capable of producing sufficient response packet traffic, the victim's system will experience a DoS. Figure 2.1 shows the basic elements of a Smurf attack. The attacker sends multiple IMCP PING packets with a source address spoofed as the victim (V) and a destination address that is the same as the broadcast address of the amplification network (AN:B). The amplification network responds with multiplied volumes of echo packets to the victim, thus fully consuming the victim's connection bandwidth. Another DoS attack similar to Smurf is called Fraggle. Fraggle attacks employ spoofed UDP packets rather than ICMP packets.

Countermeasures for Smurf attacks include disabling directed broadcasts on all network border routers and configuring all systems to drop ICMP ECHO packets. An IDS may be able to detect this type of attack, but there are no means to prevent the attack other than blocking the addresses of the amplification network. This tactic is problematic because the amplification network is usually also a victim.

FIGURE 2.1   A Smurf attack

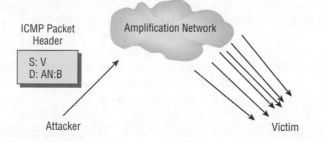

A *ping of death attack* employs an oversized ping packet. Using special tools, an attacker can send numerous oversized ping packets to a victim. In many cases, when the victimized system attempts to process the packets, an error occurs, causing the system to freeze, crash, or reboot. The ping of death is more of a buffer overflow attack, but because it often results in a downed server, it is considered a DoS attack. Countermeasures to the ping of death attack include keeping up-to-date with OS and software patches, properly coding in-house applications to prevent buffer overflows, avoiding running code with system- or root-level privileges, and blocking ping packets at border routers/firewalls.

A *WinNuke* attack is a specialized assault against Windows 95 systems. Out-of-band TCP data is sent to a victim's system, which causes the OS to freeze. Countermeasures for this attack consist of updating Windows 95 with the appropriate patch or changing to a different OS.

A *stream attack* occurs when a large number of packets are sent to numerous ports on the victim system using random source and sequence numbers. The processing performed by the victim system attempting to make sense of the data will result in a DoS. Countermeasures include patching the system and using an IDS for dynamic blocking.

A *teardrop attack* occurs when an attacker exploits a bug in operating systems. The bug exists in the routines used to reassemble (i.e., resequence) fragmented packets. An attacker sends numerous specially formatted fragmented packets to the victim, which causes the system to freeze or crash. Countermeasures for this attack include patching the OS and deploying an IDS for detection and dynamic blocking.

A *land attack* occurs when the attacker sends numerous SYN packets to a victim and the SYN packets have been spoofed to use the same source and destination IP address and port number as the victim. This causes the system to think it sent a TCP/IP session opening packet to itself, which causes a system failure and usually results in a system freeze, crash, or reboot. Countermeasures for this attack include patching the OS and deploying an IDS for detection and dynamic blocking.

Spoofing Attacks

Spoofing is the art of pretending to be something other than what you are. *Spoofing attacks* consist of replacing the valid source and/or destination IP address and node numbers with false ones. Spoofing is involved in most attacks because it grants attackers the ability to hide their identity through misdirection. Spoofing is employed when an intruder uses a stolen username and password to gain entry, when an attacker changes the source address of a malicious packet, or when an attacker assumes the identity of a client to fool a server into transmitting controlled data.

Two specific types of spoofing attacks are impersonation and masquerading. Ultimately, these attacks are the same: someone is able to gain access to a secured system by pretending to be someone else. These attacks often result in an unauthorized person gaining access to a system through a valid user account that has been compromised. Impersonation is considered a more active attack because it requires the capture of authentication traffic and the replay of that traffic in such a way as to gain access to the system. Masquerading is considered a more passive attack because the attacker uses previously stolen account credentials to log on to a secured system.

Countermeasures to spoofing attacks include patching the OS and software, enabling source/destination verification on routers, and employing an IDS to detect and block attacks. As a general rule of thumb, whenever your system detects spoofed information, it should record relevant data elements into a log file; then the system should drop or delete the spoof itself.

Man-in-the-Middle Attacks

A *man-in-the-middle attack* occurs when a malicious user is able to gain a position between the two endpoints of a communication's link. There are two types of man-in-the-middle attacks. One involves copying or sniffing the traffic between two parties; this is basically a sniffer attack (see the next section). The other involves attackers positioning themselves in the line of communication where they act as a store-and-forward or proxy mechanism (see Figure 2.2). The attacker functions as the receiver for data transmitted by the client and the transmitter for data sent to the server. The attacker is invisible to both ends of the communication link and is able to alter the content or flow of traffic. Through this type of attack, the attacker can collect logon credentials or sensitive data as well as change the content of the messages exchanged between the two endpoints.

To perform this type of attack, the attacker must often alter routing information and DNS values, steal IP addresses, or defraud ARP lookups to impersonate the server from the perspective of the client and to impersonate the client from the perspective of the server.

An offshoot of a man-in-the-middle attack is known as a *hijack attack*. In this type of attack, a malicious user is positioned between a client and server and then interrupts the session and takes it over. Often, the malicious user impersonates the client to extract data from the server. The server is unaware that any change in the communication partner has occurred. The client is aware that communications with the server have ceased, but no indication as to why the communications were terminated is available.

FIGURE 2.2   A man-in-the-middle attack

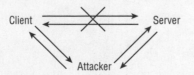

Another type of attack, a *replay attack* (also known as a *playback attack*), is similar to hijacking. A malicious user records the traffic between a client and server; then the packets sent from the client to the server are played back or retransmitted to the server with slight variations of the time stamp and source IP address (i.e., spoofing). In some cases, this allows the malicious user to restart an old communication link with a server. Once the communication session is reopened, the malicious user can attempt to obtain data or additional access. The captured traffic is often authentication traffic (i.e., that which includes logon credentials, such as username and password), but it could also be service access traffic or message control traffic. Replay attacks can be prevented by employing complex sequencing rules and time stamps to prevent retransmitted packets from being accepted as valid.

Countermeasures to these types of attacks require improvement in the session establishment, identification, and authentication processes. Some man-in-the-middle attacks are thwarted through patching the OS and software. An IDS cannot usually detect a man-in-the-middle or hijack attack, but it can often detect the abnormal activities occurring via "secured" communication links. Operating systems and many IDSs can often detect and block replay attacks.

Sniffer Attacks

A *sniffer attack* (also known as a *snooping attack*) is any activity that results in a malicious user obtaining information about a network or the traffic over that network. A sniffer is often a packet-capturing program that duplicates the contents of packets traveling over the network medium into a file. Sniffer attacks often focus on the initial connections between clients and servers to obtain logon credentials (e.g., usernames and passwords), secret keys, and so on. When performed properly, sniffing attacks are invisible to all other entities on the network and often precede spoofing or hijack attacks. A replay attack (discussed in the preceding section) is a type of sniffer attack.

Countermeasures to prevent or stop sniffing attacks require improvement in physical access control, active monitoring for sniffing signatures (such as looking for packet delay, additional routing hops, or lost packets, which can be performed by some IDSs), and using encrypted traffic over internal and external network connections.

Spamming Attacks

Spam is the term describing unwanted e-mail, newsgroup, or discussion forum messages. Spam can be as innocuous as an advertisement from a well-meaning vendor or as malignant as floods of unrequested messages with viruses or Trojan horses attached. Spam is usually not a security threat but rather a type of denial of service attack. As the level of spam increases, locating or accessing legitimate messages can be difficult. In addition to the nuisance value, spam consumes a significant portion of Internet resources (in the form of bandwidth and CPU processing), resulting in overall slower Internet performance and lower bandwidth availability for everyone.

Spamming attacks are directed floods of unwanted messages to a victim's e-mail inbox or other messaging system. Such attacks cause DoS issues by filling up storage space and preventing legitimate messages from being delivered. In extreme cases, spamming attacks can cause system freezes or crashes and interrupt the activity of other users on the same subnet or ISP.

Spam attack countermeasures include using e-mail filters, e-mail proxies, and IDSs to detect, track, and terminate spam flood attempts.

Crackers

Crackers are malicious users intent on waging an attack against a person or system. Crackers may be motivated by greed, power, or recognition. Their actions can result in stolen property (data, ideas, etc.), disabled systems, compromised security, negative public opinion, loss of market share, reduced profitability, and lost productivity.

A term commonly confused with *crackers* is *hackers,* who are technology enthusiasts with no malicious intent. Many authors and the media often use the term *hacker* when they are actually discussing issues relating to crackers.

Thwarting a cracker's attempts to breach your security or perpetrate DoS attacks requires vigilant effort to keep systems patched and properly configured. IDSs and honey pot systems often offer means to detect and gather evidence to prosecute crackers once they have breached your controlled perimeter.

Access Control Compensations

Access control is used to regulate or specify which objects a subject can access and what type of access is allowed or denied. There are numerous attacks designed to bypass or subvert access control. These are discussed in the previous sections. In addition to the specific countermeasures for each of these attacks, there are some measures that can be used to help compensate for access control violations. A compensation measure is not a direct prevention of a problem but rather a means by which you can design resiliency into your environment to provide support for a quick recovery or response.

Backups are the best means to compensate against access control violations. With reliable backups and a mechanism to restore data, any corruption or file-based asset loss can be repaired, corrected, or restored promptly. RAID technology can provide fault tolerance to allow for quick recovery in the event of a device failure or severe access violation.

In general, avoiding single points of failure and deploying fault tolerant systems can help to ensure that the loss of use or control over a single system, device, or asset does not directly lead to the compromise or failure of your entire network environment. Fault tolerance countermeasures are designed to combat threats to design reliability. Having backup communication routes, mirrored servers, clustered systems, failover systems, and so on can provide instant automatic or quick manual recovery in the event of an access control violation.

Your business continuity plan should include procedures for dealing with access control violations that threaten the stability of your mission-critical processes. Likewise, you should include in your insurance coverage categories of assets for which you may require compensation in the event of severe access control violations.

Summary

Managing a system's access control involves a thorough understanding of system monitoring and common forms of malicious attacks. Monitoring a system provides the basis for accountability of authenticated users. Audit trails and logging files provide details about valid and unauthorized activities as well as system stability and performance. The use of an IDS can simplify the process of examining the copious amount of data gathered through monitoring.

There are two types of IDSs: host based and network based. A host-based IDS is useful for detecting specific intrusions on single systems. A network-based IDS is useful for detecting overall aberrant network activity. There are two types of detection methods employed by IDSs: knowledge based and behavior based. A knowledge-based IDS uses a database of attack signatures to detect intrusion attempts. However, it fails to recognize new attack methods. A behavior-based IDS uses learned patterns of activity to detect abnormal events, but it produces numerous false positives until it has gained sufficient knowledge about the system it is monitoring.

Honey pots and padded cells are useful tools for preventing malicious activity from occurring on the actual network while enticing the intruder to remain long enough to gather evidence for prosecution.

Vulnerability scanners are signature-based detection tools that scan a system for a list of known vulnerabilities. These tools produce reports indicating the discovered vulnerabilities and provide recommendations on improving system security.

Penetration testing is a useful mechanism for testing the strength and effectiveness of deployed security measures and an organization's security policy. Be sure to obtain management approval before performing a penetration test.

There are numerous methods of attacks that intruders perpetrate against systems. Some of the more common attacks include brute force, dictionary, denial of service, spoofing, man-in-the-middle, spamming, and sniffing attacks. Each type of attack employs different means to infiltrate, damage, or interrupt systems and each has unique countermeasures to prevent them.

Exam Essentials

Understand the use of monitoring in relation to access controls.   Monitoring is used to hold subjects accountable for their actions and to detect abnormal or malicious activities.

Understand the need for intrusion detection systems (IDSs) and that they are only one component in a security policy.   An IDS is needed to automate the process of discovering anomalies in subject activity and system event logs. IDSs are primarily used to detect intrusions or attempted intrusions. An IDS alone will not secure a system. It must be used in cooperation with access controls, physical security, and maintaining secure systems on the network.

Know the limits of using host-based IDSs.   Host-based IDSs can monitor activity on a single system only. In addition, they can be discovered by attackers and disabled.

List the pros and cons of network-based IDSs. Network-based IDSs can monitor activity on the network medium, and they can be made invisible to attackers. They do not, however, work well on switched networks.

Be able to explain the differences between knowledge-based and behavior-based IDS detection methods. Knowledge-based detection employs a database of attack signatures. Behavior-based detection learns what is normal about a system and assumes that all unknown activities are abnormal or possible signs of intrusion.

Understand the purpose of a honey pot and a padded cell. A honey pot is a fake system or network that is designed to lure intruders with fake data to keep them on the system long enough to gather tracking information. A padded cell is a simulated environment that intruders are seamlessly moved into once they are detected on the system. The simulated environment varies from the real environment only in that the data is fake and therefore malicious activities cause no harm.

Be able to explain the purpose of vulnerability scanners and penetration testing. Vulnerability scanners are used to detect known security vulnerabilities and weaknesses. They are used to generate reports that indicate the areas or aspects of the system that need to be managed to improve security. Penetration testing is used to test the strength and effectiveness of deployed security measures with an authorized attempted intrusion attack.

Know how brute force and dictionary attacks work. Brute force and dictionary attacks are carried out against a password database file or the logon prompt of a system. They are designed to discover passwords. In brute force attacks, all possible combinations of keyboard characters are used, whereas a predefined list of possible passwords is used in a dictionary attack.

Understand the need for strong passwords. Strong passwords make password cracking utilities less successful. Strong passwords are dynamic passwords and should be strengthened by using two-factor authentication, enabling account lockouts, and using strong encryption on the password database file.

Know what denial of service (DoS) attacks are. DoS attacks prevent the system from responding to legitimate requests for service. There are two types: traffic flooding and fault exploitation.

Be able to explain how the SYN flood DoS attack works. The SYN flood DoS attack takes advantage of the TCP/IP three-way handshake to inhibit a system by requesting numerous connection sessions but failing to provide the final acknowledgment packet.

Know how the Smurf DoS attack works. Smurf attacks employ an amplification network to send numerous response packets to a victim.

Know how ping of death DoS attacks work. Ping of death attacks send numerous oversized ping packets to the victim, causing the victim to freeze, crash, or reboot.

Know how the WinNuke DoS attack works. Only Windows 95 systems are vulnerable to WinNuke. WinNuke sends out-of-band TCP/IP data to the victim, causing the OS to freeze.

Understand stream DoS attacks. Stream attacks send a large number of packets to numerous ports on the victim system by using random source and sequence numbers. The processing performed by the victim system attempting to make sense of the data will result in a DoS.

Be able to explain teardrop DoS attacks.   A teardrop attack occurs when an attacker exploits a bug in operating systems. The bug exists in the routines used to reassemble fragmented packets. An attacker sends numerous specially formatted fragmented packets to the victim, which causes the system to freeze or crash.

Understand land DoS attacks.   A land attack occurs when an attacker sends numerous SYN packets to a victim and the SYN packets have been spoofed to use the same source and destination IP address and port number as the victim's. This causes the victim to think it sent a TCP/IP session opening packet to itself, which in turn causes a system failure, usually resulting in a freeze, crash, or reboot.

Be able to list the countermeasures to all types of DoS attacks and to spoofing, man-in-the-middle, sniffer, and spamming attacks.   Countermeasures include patching the OS for vulnerabilities, using firewalls and routers to filter and/or verify traffic, altering system/protocol configuration, and using IDSs.

Understand spoofing attacks.   Spoofing attacks are any form of attack that uses modified packets in which the valid source and/or destination IP address and node numbers are replaced with false ones. Spoofing grants the attacker the ability to hide their identity through misdirection.

Understand man-in-the-middle attacks.   A man-in-the-middle attack occurs when a malicious user is able to gain position between the two endpoints of a communications link. There are two types of man-in-the-middle attacks. One involves copying or sniffing the traffic between two parties; this is basically a sniffer attack. The other involves the attacker being positioned in the line of communication where they act as a store-and-forward or proxy mechanism.

Be able to explain hijack attacks.   The hijack attack is offshoot of a man-in-the-middle attack. In this type of attack, a malicious user positions himself between a client and server and then interrupts the session and takes it over. Often, the malicious user impersonates the client so they can extract data from the server. The server is unaware that any change in the communication partner has occurred.

Understand replay or playback attacks.   In a replay attack, a malicious user records the traffic between a client and server. Then the packets sent from the client to the server are played back or retransmitted to the server with slight variations of the time stamp and source IP address (i.e., spoofing). In some cases, this allows the malicious user to restart an old communication link with a server.

Know what sniffer attacks are.   A sniffer attack (or snooping attack) is any activity that results in a malicious user obtaining information about a network or the traffic over that network. A sniffer is often a packet-capturing program that duplicates the contents of packets traveling over the network medium into a file.

Understanding spamming attacks.   *Spam* is the term describing unwanted e-mail, newsgroup, or discussion forum messages. Spam can be as innocuous as an advertisement from a well-meaning vendor or as malignant as floods of unrequested messages with viruses or Trojan horses attached. Spam is usually not a security threat but rather a type of denial of service attack. As the level of spam increases, locating or accessing legitimate messages can be difficult.

Review Questions

1. What is used to keep subjects accountable for their actions while they are authenticated to a system?

   A. Access controls

   B. Monitoring

   C. Account lockout

   D. Performance reviews

2. Which of the following tools is the most useful in sorting through large log files when searching for intrusion-related events?

   A. Text editor

   B. Vulnerability scanner

   C. Password cracker

   D. IDS

3. An intrusion detection system (IDS) is primarily designed to perform what function?

   A. Detect abnormal activity

   B. Detect system failures

   C. Rate system performance

   D. Test a system for vulnerabilities

4. IDSs are capable of detecting which type of abnormal or unauthorized activities? (Choose all that apply.)

   A. External connection attempts

   B. Execution of malicious code

   C. Unauthorized access attempts to controlled objects

   D. None of the above

5. Which of the following is true for a host-based IDS?

   A. It monitors an entire network.

   B. It monitors a single system.

   C. It's invisible to attackers and authorized users.

   D. It's ineffective on switched networks.

6. Which of the following types of IDS is effective only against known attack methods?

   A. Host-based

   B. Network-based

   C. Knowledge-based

   D. Behavior-based

7. Which type of IDS can be considered an expert system?

   A. Host-based

   B. Network-based

   C. Knowledge-based

   D. Behavior-based

8. Which of the following is a fake network designed to tempt intruders with unpatched and unprotected security vulnerabilities and false data?

   A. IDS

   B. Honey pot

   C. Padded cell

   D. Vulnerability scanner

9. When a padded cell is used by a network for protection from intruders, which of the following is true?

   A. The data offered by the padded cell is what originally attracts the attacker.

   B. Padded cells are a form of entrapment.

   C. The intruder is seamlessly transitioned into the padded cell once they are detected.

   D. Padded cells are used to test a system for known vulnerabilities.

10. Which of the following is true regarding vulnerability scanners?

   A. They actively scan for intrusion attempts.

   B. They serve as a form of enticement.

   C. They locate known security holes.

   D. They automatically reconfigure a system to a more secured state.

11. When using penetration testing to verify the strength of your security policy, which of the following is not recommended?

   A. Mimicking attacks previously perpetrated against your system

   B. Performing the attacks without managements consent

   C. Using manual and automated attack tools

   D. Reconfiguring the system to resolve any discovered vulnerabilities

12. Which of the following attacks is an attempt to test every possible combination against a security feature in order to bypass it?

   A. Brute force attack

   B. Spoofing attack

   C. Man-in-the-middle attack

   D. Denial of service attack

13. Which of the following is not a valid measure to take to improve protection against brute force and dictionary attacks?

    A. Enforce strong passwords through a security policy.

    B. Maintain strict control over physical access.

    C. Require all users to log in remotely.

    D. Use two-factor authentication.

14. Which of the following is not considered a denial of service attack?

    A. Teardrop

    B. Smurf

    C. Ping of death

    D. Spoofing

15. A SYN flood attack works by what mechanism?

    A. Exploiting a packet processing glitch in Windows 95

    B. Using an amplification network to flood a victim with packets

    C. Exploiting the three-way handshake used by TCP/IP

    D. Sending oversized ping packets to a victim

16. Which of the following attacks sends packets with the victim's IP address as both the source and destination?

    A. Land

    B. Spamming

    C. Teardrop

    D. Stream

17. In what type of attack are packets sent to a victim using invalid resequencing numbers?

    A. Stream

    B. Spamming

    C. Distributed denial of service

    D. Teardrop

18. Spoofing is primarily used to perform what activity?

    A. Send large amounts of data to a victim.

    B. Cause a buffer overflow.

    C. Hide the identity of an attacker through misdirection.

    D. Steal user accounts and passwords.

19. Spamming attacks occur when numerous unsolicited messages are sent to a victim. Because enough data is sent to the victim to prevent legitimate activity, it is also known as what?

   A. Sniffing

   B. Denial of service

   C. Brute force attack

   D. Buffer overflow attack

20. What type of attack occurs when malicious users position themselves between a client and server and then interrupt the session and takes it over?

   A. Man-in-the-middle

   B. Spoofing

   C. Hijack

   D. Cracking

Answers to Review Questions

1. B. Accountability is maintained by monitoring the activities of subject and objects as well as of core system functions that maintain the operating environment and the security mechanisms.

2. D. In most cases, when sufficient logging and auditing is enabled to monitor a system, so much data is collected that the important details get lost in the bulk. For automation and real-time analysis of events, an intrusion detection system (IDS) is required.

3. A. An IDS automates the inspection of audit logs and real-time system events to detect abnormal activity. IDSs are generally used to detect intrusion attempts, but they can also be employed to detect system failures or rate overall performance.

4. A, B, C. IDSs watch for violations of confidentiality, integrity, and availability. Attacks recognized by IDSs can come from external connections (such as the Internet or partner networks), viruses, malicious code, trusted internal subjects attempting to perform unauthorized activities, and unauthorized access attempts from trusted locations.

5. B. A host-based IDS watches for questionable activity on a single computer system. A network-based IDS watches for questionable activity being performed over the network medium, can be made invisible to users, and is ineffective on switched networks.

6. C. A knowledge-based IDS is effective only against known attack methods, which is its primary drawback.

7. D. A behavior-based IDS can be labeled an expert system or a pseudo artificial intelligence system because it can learn and make assumptions about events. In other words, the IDS can act like a human expert by evaluating current events against known events.

8. B. Honey pots are individual computers or entire networks created to serve as a snare for intruders. They look and act like legitimate networks, but they are 100 percent fake. Honey pots tempt intruders with unpatched and unprotected security vulnerabilities as well as attractive and tantalizing but faux data.

9. C. When an intruder is detected by an IDS, they are transferred to a padded cell. The transfer of the intruder into a padded cell is performed automatically, without informing the intruder that the change has occurred. The padded cell is unknown to the intruder before the attack, so it cannot serve as an enticement or entrapment. Padded cells are used to detain intruders, not to detect vulnerabilities.

10. C. Vulnerability scanners are used to test a system for known security vulnerabilities and weaknesses. They are not active detection tools for intrusion, they offer no form of enticement, and they do not configure system security. In addition to testing a system for security weaknesses, they produce evaluation reports and make recommendations.

11. B. Penetration testing should be performed only with the knowledge and consent of the management staff. Unapproved security testing could result in productivity loss or trigger emergency response teams. It could even cost you your job.

12. A. A brute force attack is an attempt to discover passwords for user accounts by systematically attempting every possible combination of letters, numbers, and symbols.

13. C. Strong password policies, physical access control, and two-factor authentication all improve the protection against brute force and dictionary password attacks. Requiring remote logons has no direct affect on password attack protection; in fact, it may offer sniffers more opportunities to grab password packets from the data stream.

14. D. Spoofing is the replacement of valid source and destination IP and port addresses with false ones. It is often used in DoS attacks but is not considered a DoS attack itself. Teardrop, Smurf, and ping of death are all DoS attacks.

15. C. A SYN flood attack is waged by breaking the standard three-way handshake used by TCP/IP to initiate communication sessions. Exploiting a packet processing glitch in Windows 95 is a Win-Nuke attack. The use of an amplification network is a Smurf attack. Oversized ping packets are used in a ping of death attack.

16. A. In a land attack, the attacker sends a victim numerous SYN packets that have been spoofed to use the same source and destination IP address and port number as the victim's. The victim then thinks it sent a TCP/IP session-opening a packet to itself.

17. D. In a teardrop attack, an attacker exploits a bug in operating systems. The bug exists in the routines used to reassemble (i.e., resequence) fragmented packets. An attacker sends numerous specially formatted fragmented packets to the victim, which causes the system to freeze or crash.

18. C. Spoofing grants the attacker the ability to hide their identity through misdirection. It is therefore involved in most attacks.

19. B. A spamming attack is a type of denial of service attack. *Spam* is the term describing unwanted e-mail, newsgroup, or discussion forum messages. It can be an advertisement from a well-meaning vendor or a floods of unrequested messages with viruses or Trojan horses attached.

20. C. In a hijack attack, which is an offshoot of a man-in-the-middle attack, a malicious user is positioned between a client and server and then interrupts the session and takes it over.

Chapter 3

ISO Model, Network Security, and Protocols

THE CISSP EXAM TOPICS COVERED IN THIS CHAPTER INCLUDE:

- ✓ International Organization for Standardization/Open Systems Interconnection (ISO/OSI) Layers and Characteristics
- ✓ Communications and Network Security
- ✓ Internet/Intranet/Extranet Components
- ✓ Network Services

Computer systems and computer networks are complex entities. They combine hardware and software components to create a system that can perform operations and calculations beyond the capabilities of humans. From the integration of communication devices, storage devices, processing devices, security devices, input devices, output devices, operating systems, software, services, data, and people emerge computers and networks. The CISSP CBK states that a thorough knowledge of the hardware and software components a system comprises is an essential element of being able to implement and maintain security.

The Telecommunications and Network Security domain for the CISSP certification exam deals with topics related to network components (primarily network devices and protocols); specifically, how they function and how they are relevant to security. This domain is discussed in this chapter and in Chapter 4, "Communications Security and Countermeasures." Be sure to read and study the materials in both chapters to ensure complete coverage of the essential material for the CISSP certification exam.

OSI Model

Communications between computers over networks is made possible by the use of protocols. A *protocol* is a set of rules and restrictions that define how data is transmitted over a network medium (e.g., *twisted-pair* cable, wireless transmission, and so on). Protocols make computer-to-computer communications possible. In the early days of network development, many companies had their own proprietary protocols, which meant interaction between computers of different vendors was often difficult if not impossible. In an effort to eliminate this problem, the *International Organization for Standardization (ISO)* developed the *OSI model* for protocols in the early 1980s. ISO Standard 7498 defines the OSI Reference Model (also called the OSI model).

History of the OSI Model

The OSI model wasn't the first or only movement to streamline networking protocols or establish a common communications standard. In fact, the most widely used protocol today, the TCP/IP protocol (which was based upon the DARPA model, also known now as the TCP/IP model), was developed in the early 1970s.

The *Open Systems Interconnection (OSI)* protocol was developed to establish a common communication structure or standard for all computer systems. The actual OSI protocol was never widely adopted, but the theory behind the OSI protocol, the OSI model, was readily accepted. The OSI model serves as an abstract framework, or theoretical model, for how protocols should function in an ideal world on ideal hardware. Thus, the OSI model has become a common reference point against which all protocols can be compared and contrasted.

OSI Functionality

The OSI model divides networking tasks into seven distinct layers. Each layer is responsible for performing specific tasks or operations toward the ultimate goal of supporting data exchange (i.e., network communication) between two computers. The layers are always numbered from bottom to top (see Figure 3.1). They are referred to by either their name or their layer number. For example, *layer 3* is also known as the *Network layer*. The layers are ordered specifically to indicate how information flows through the various levels of communication. Layers are said to communicate with three other layers. Each layer communicates directly with the layer above it as well as the layer below it plus the peer layer on a communication partner system.

The OSI model is an open network architecture guide for network product vendors. This standard, or guide, provides a common foundation for the development of new protocols, networking services, and even hardware devices. By working from the OSI model, vendors are able to ensure that their products will integrate with products from other companies and be supported by a wide range of operating systems. If vendors developed their own networking framework, interoperability between products from different vendors would be next to impossible.

The real benefit of the OSI model is found in its expression of how networking actually functions. In the most basic sense, network communications occur over a physical connection. This is true even if wireless networking devices are employed. Physical devices establish channels through which electronic signals can pass from one computer to another. These physical device channels are only one type of the seven logical channel types defined by the OSI model. Each layer of the OSI model communicates via a logical channel with its peer layer on another computer. This enables protocols based on the OSI model to support a type of authentication by being able to identify the remote communication entity as well as authenticate the source of the received data.

FIGURE 3.1   A representation of the OSI model

Application	7
Presentation	6
Session	5
Transport	4
Network	3
Data Link	2
Physical	1

Encapsulation/Deencapsulation

Protocols based on the OSI model employ a mechanism called *encapsulation*. As the message is encapsulated at each layer, it grows in size. Encapsulation occurs as the data moves down through the OSI model layers from Application to Physical. The inverse action occurring as data moves up through the OSI model layers from the Physical to Application is known as deencapsulation. The encapsulation/deencapsulation process is as follows:

1. The Application layer creates a message.

2. The Application layer passes the message to the Presentation layer.

3. The Presentation layer encapsulates the message by adding information to it. Information is added at the beginning of the message (called a header) and at the end of the message (called a footer), as shown in Figure 3.2.

4. The process of passing the message down and adding layer-specific information continues until the message reaches the Physical layer.

5. At the Physical layer, the message is converted into electrical impulses that represent bits and is transmitted over the physical connection.

6. The receiving computer captures the bits from the physical connection and re-creates the message in the Physical layer.

7. The Physical layer strips off its information and sends the message up to the Data Link layer.

8. The Data Link layer strips its information off and sends the message up to the Network layer.

9. This process of deencapsulation is performed until the message reaches the Application layer.

10. When the message reaches the Application layer, the data in the message is sent to the intended software recipient.

The information removed by each layer contains instructions, checksums, and so on that can only be understood by the peer layer that originally added or created the information (see Figure 3.3). This information is what creates the logical channel that enables peer layers on different computers to communicate.

FIGURE 3.2   A representation of OSI model encapsulation

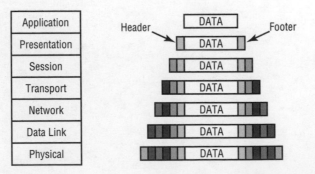

FIGURE 3.3   A representation of the OSI model peer layer logical channels

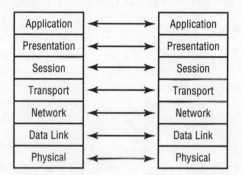

The message sent into the protocol stack at the Application layer (layer 7) is called the data or PDU (protocol data unit). Once it is encapsulated by the Presentation layer (layer 6), it is called a protocol data unit (PDU). It retains the label of PDU until it reaches the Transport layer (layer 4), where it is called a segment. In the Network layer (layer 3), it is called a packet or a datagram. In the Data Link layer (layer 2), it is called a frame. In the Physical layer (layer 1), the data has been converted into bits for transmission over the physical connection medium. Figure 3.4 shows how each layer changes the data through this process.

OSI Layers

Understanding the functions and responsibilities of each layer of the OSI model will help you understand how network communications function, how attacks can be perpetrated against network communications, and how security can be implemented to protect network communications. Each layer, starting with the bottom layer, is discussed in the following sections.

FIGURE 3.4   The OSI model data names

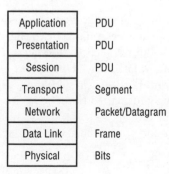

For more info on the TCP/IP stack, do a search for "TCP/IP" at Wikipedia (en.wikipedia.org).

Physical Layer

The *Physical layer (layer 1)* accepts the frame from the Data Link layer and converts the frame into bits for transmission over the physical connection medium. The Physical layer is also responsible for receiving bits from the physical connection medium and converting them back into a frame to be used by the Data Link layer.

The Physical layer contains the device drivers that tell the protocol how to employ the hardware for the transmission and reception of bits. Located within the Physical layer are electrical specifications, protocols, and interface standards such as the following:

- EIA/TIA-232 and EIA/TIA-449
- X.21
- High-Speed Serial Interface (HSSI)
- Synchronous Optical Network (SONET)
- V.24 and V.35

Through the device drivers and these standards, the Physical layer controls throughput rates, handles synchronization, manages line noise and medium access, and determines whether to use digital or analog signals or light pulses to transmit or receive data over the physical hardware interface.

Network hardware devices that function at layer 1, the Physical layer, are network interface cards (NICs), *hubs, repeaters, concentrators,* and *amplifiers*. These devices perform hardware-based signal operations, such as sending a signal from one *port* out on all other ports (a hub) or amplifying the signal to support greater transmission distances (a repeater).

Data Link Layer

The *Data Link layer (layer 2)* is responsible for formatting the packet from the Network layer into the proper format for transmission. The proper format is determined by the hardware and the technology of the network. There are numerous possibilities, such as *Ethernet* (IEEE 802.3), *Token Ring* (IEEE 802.5), *asynchronous transfer mode (ATM), Fiber Distributed Data Interface (FDDI),* and *Copper DDI (CDDI)*. Within the Data Link layer resides the technology-specific protocols that convert the packet into a properly formatted frame. Once the frame is formatted, it is sent to the Physical layer for transmission.

The following list includes some of the protocols found within the Data Link layer:

- Serial Line Internet Protocol (SLIP)
- Point-to-Point Protocol (PPP)
- Address Resolution Protocol (ARP)
- Reverse Address Resolution Protocol (RARP)

- Layer 2 Forwarding (L2F)
- Layer 2 Tunneling Protocol (L2TP)
- Point-to-Point Tunneling Protocol (PPTP)
- Integrated Services Digital Network (ISDN)

Part of the processing performed on the data within the Data Link layer includes adding the hardware source and destination addresses to the frame. The hardware address is the *Media Access Control (MAC) address,* which is a 6-byte address written in hexadecimal notation. The first 3 bytes of the address indicate the vendor or manufacturer of the physical network interface. The last 3 bytes represent a unique number assigned to that interface by the manufacturer. No two devices can have the same MAC address.

Among the protocols at the Data Link layer (layer 2) of the OSI model, the two you should be familiar with are Address Resolution Protocol (ARP) and Reverse Address Resolution Protocol (RARP). ARP is used to resolve IP addresses into MAC addresses. Traffic on a network segment (e.g., cables across a hub) is directed from its source system to its destination system using MAC addresses. RARP is used to resolve MAC addresses into IP addresses.

The Data Link layer contains two sublayers: the Logical Link Control (LLC) sublayer and the MAC sublayer. Details about these sublayers are not critical for the CISSP exam.

Network hardware devices that function at layer 2, the Data Link layer, are *switches* and bridges. These devices support MAC-based traffic routing. Switches receive a frame on one port and send it out another port based on the destination MAC address. MAC address destinations are used to determine whether a frame is transferred over the bridge from one network to another.

Network Layer

The *Network layer (layer 3)* is responsible for adding routing and addressing information to the data. The Network layer accepts the segment from the Transport layer and adds information to it to create a packet. The packet includes the source and destination IP addresses.

The routing protocols are located at this layer and include the following:

- Internet Control Message Protocol (ICMP)
- Routing Information Protocol (RIP)
- Open Shortest Path First (OSPF)
- Border Gateway Protocol (BGP)
- Internet Group Management Protocol (IGMP)
- Internet Protocol (IP)
- Internet Protocol Security (IPSec)
- Internetwork Packet Exchange (IPX)
- Network Address Translation (NAT)
- Simple Key Management for Internet Protocols (SKIP)

The Network layer is responsible for providing routing or delivery information, but it is not responsible for verifying guaranteed delivery (that is the responsibility of the Transport layer). The Network layer also manages error detection and node data traffic (i.e., traffic control).

Routers are among the network hardware devices that function at layer 3, along with *brouters*. Routers determine the best logical path for the transmission of packets based on speed, hops, preference, and so on. Routers use the destination IP address to guide the transmission of packets. A brouter, working primarily in layer 3 but in layer 2 when necessary, is a device that attempts to route first but if that fails defaults to bridging.

Transport Layer

The *Transport layer (layer 4)* is responsible for managing the integrity of a connection and controlling the session. It accepts a PDU from the *Session layer* and converts it into a segment. The Transport layer controls how devices on the network are addressed or referenced, establishes communication connections between nodes (also known as devices), and defines the rules of a session. Session rules specify how much data each segment can contain, how to verify the integrity of data transmitted, and how to determine if data has been lost. Session rules are established through a handshaking process. (You should recall the discussion of the SYN/ACK three-way handshake for TCP/IP from Chapter 2, "Attacks and Monitoring.")

The Transport layer establishes a logical connection between two devices and provides end-to-end transport services to ensure data delivery. This layer includes mechanisms for segmentation, sequencing, error checking, controlling the flow of data, error correction, multiplexing, and network service optimization. The following protocols operate within the Transport layer:

- *Transmission Control Protocol (TCP)*
- *User Datagram Protocol (UDP)*
- *Sequenced Packet Exchange (SPX)*

Session Layer

The *Session layer (layer 5)* is responsible for establishing, maintaining, and terminating communication sessions between two computers. It manages dialog discipline or dialog control (simplex, half-duplex, full-duplex), establishes checkpoints for grouping and recovery, and retransmits PDUs that have failed or been lost since the last verified checkpoint. The following protocols operate within the Session layer:

- Secure Sockets Layer (SSL)
- Transport Layer Security (TLS)
- Network File System (NFS)
- Structured Query Language (SQL)
- Remote Procedure Call (RPC)

Communication sessions can operate in one of three different discipline or control modes:

Simplex   One-way direction communication

Half-duplex   Two-way communication, but only one direction can send data at a time

Full-duplex   Two-way communication, in which data can be sent in both directions simultaneously

Presentation Layer

The *Presentation layer (layer 6)* is responsible for transforming data received from the *Application layer* into a format that any system following the OSI model can understand. It imposes common or standardized structure and formatting rules onto the data. The Presentation layer is also responsible for encryption and compression. Thus, it acts as an interface between the network and applications. It is what allows various applications to interact over a network, and it does so by ensuring that the data formats are supported by both systems. Most file or data formats operate within this layer. This includes formats for images, video, sound, documents, e-mail, web pages, control sessions, and so on. The following list includes some of the format standards that exist within the Presentation layer:

- American Standard Code for Information Interchange (ASCII)
- Extended Binary-Coded Decimal Interchange Mode (EBCDIC)
- Tagged Image File Format (TIFF)
- Joint Photographic Experts Group (JPEG)
- Moving Picture Experts Group (MPEG)
- Musical instrument digital interface (MIDI)

Application Layer

The *Application layer (layer 7)* is responsible for interfacing user applications, network services, or the operating system itself with the protocol stack. It allows applications to communicate with the protocol stack. The Application layer determines whether a remote communication partner is available and accessible. It also ensures that sufficient resources are available to support the requested communications.

The application itself is not located within this layer; rather, the protocols and services required to transmit files, exchange messages, connect to remote terminals, and so on are found here. Numerous application-specific protocols are found within this layer, such as the following:

- Hypertext Transfer Protocol (HTTP)
- File Transfer Protocol (FTP)
- Line Print Daemon (LPD)
- Simple Mail Transfer Protocol (SMTP)
- Telnet
- Trivial File Transfer Protocol (TFTP)
- Electronic Data Interchange (EDI)
- Post Office Protocol version 3 (POP3)
- Internet Message Access Protocol (IMAP)
- Simple Network Management Protocol (SNMP)
- Network News Transport Protocol (NNTP)
- Secure Remote Procedure Call (S-RPC)
- Secure Electronic Transaction (SET)

There is a network device (or service) that works at the Application layer, namely the gateway. However, an Application layer gateway is a very specific type of component. It serves as a protocol translation tool. For example, an IP-to-IPX gateway takes inbound communications from TCP/IP and translates them over to IPX/SPX for outbound transmission.

TCP/IP Model

The TCP/IP model (also called the DARPA or the DOD model) consists of only four layers, as opposed to the OSI Reference Model's seven. These four layers can be compared to the seven layers of the OSI model (refer to Figure 3.5). The four layers of the TCP/IP model are Application, Host-to-Host, Internet, and Network Access. The TCP/IP protocol suite was developed before the OSI Reference Model was created. The designers of the OSI Reference Model took care to ensure that the TCP/IP protocol suite fit their model due to its established deployment in networking.

The TCP/IP model's Application layer corresponds to layers 5, 6, and 7 of the OSI model. The TCP/IP model's Host-to-Host layer corresponds to layer 4 from the OSI model. The TCP/IP model's Internet layer corresponds to layer 3 from the OSI model. The TCP/IP model's Network Access layer corresponds to layers 1 and 2 from the OSI model.

It has become common practice (through confusion, misunderstanding, and probably laziness) to also call the TCP/IP model layers by their OSI model layer equivalent names. The TCP/IP model's Application layer is already using a name borrowed from the OSI, so that one's a snap. The TCP/IP model's Host-to-Host layer is sometimes called the Transport layer (the OSI model's fourth layer). The TCP/IP model's Internet layer is sometimes called the Network layer (the OSI model's third layer). And the TCP/IP model's Network Access layer is sometimes called the Data Link layer (the OSI model's second layer).

FIGURE 3.5   Comparing the OSI model with the TCP/IP model

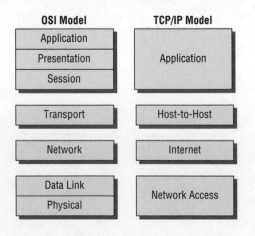

Since the TCP/IP model layer names and the OSI model layer names can be used interchangeably, it is important to know which model is being addressed in various contexts. Unless informed otherwise, always assume the OSI model provides the basis for discussion because it's the most widely used network reference model.

Communications and Network Security

Establishing security on a network involves more than just managing the OS and software. You must also address physical issues, including cabling, *topology*, and technology.

LANs vs. WANs

There are two basic types of networks: LANs and WANs. A *local area network (LAN)* is a self-enclosed network typically spanning a single floor or building. LANs usually employ low- to moderate-speed technologies. *Wide area network (WAN)* is the term usually assigned to the long-distance connections between geographically remote networks. WANs often employ high-speed connections, but they can also employ low-speed dial-up links as well as leased connection technologies.

WAN connections and communication links can include private circuit technologies and packet-switching technologies. Common private circuit technologies include dedicated or leased lines and PPP, SLIP, ISDN, and DSL connections. Packet-switching technologies include *X.25, Frame Relay,* asynchronous transfer mode (ATM), *Synchronous Data Link Control (SDLC),* and High-Level Data Link Control (HDLC). Packet-switching technologies use virtual circuits instead of dedicated circuits. A virtual circuit is created only when needed, which makes for efficient use of the medium and is extremely cost effective.

Network Cabling

The type of connectivity media employed in a network is important to the network's design, layout, and capabilities. Without the right cabling, a network may not be able to span your entire enterprise or it may not support the necessary traffic volume. In fact, the most common causes of network failure (i.e., violations of availability) are caused by cable failures or misconfigurations. So it is important for you to understand that different types of network devices and technologies are used with different types of cabling. Each cable type has unique useful lengths, throughput rates, and connectivity requirements.

Coaxial Cable

Coaxial cable, also called coax, was a popular networking cable type used throughout the 1970s and 1980s. In the early 1990s, its use quickly declined due to the popularity of twisted-pair wiring (explained in more detail later). Coaxial cable has a center core of copper wire surrounded by a layer of insulation, which is in turn surrounded by a conductive braided shielding and encased in a final insulation sheath.

The center copper core and the braided shielding layer act as two independent conductors, thus allowing two-way communications over a coaxial cable. The design of coaxial cable makes it fairly resistant to *electromagnetic interference (EMI)* and able to support high bandwidths (in comparison to other technologies of the time period), and it offers longer usable lengths than twisted-pair. It ultimately failed to retain its place as the popular networking cable technology due to twisted-pair's much lower cost and ease of installation. Coaxial cable requires the use of segment terminators, whereas twisted-pair does not. Coaxial cable is bulkier and has a larger minimum arc radius than twisted-pair. (The arc radius is the maximum distance the cable can be bent before damaging the internal conductors.) Additionally, with the widespread deployment of switched networks, the issues of cable distance became moot due to the implementation of hierarchical wiring patterns.

There are two main types of coaxial cable: *thinnet* and *thicknet.* Thinnet, also known as *10Base2,* was commonly used to connect systems to backbone trunks of thicknet cabling. Thinnet can span distances of 185 meters and provide throughput up to 10Mbps. Thicknet, also known as *10Base5,* can span 500 meters and provide throughput up to 10Mbps.

The most common problems with coax cable are as follows:

- Bending the coax cable past its maximum arc radius and thus breaking the center conductor
- Deploying the coax cable in a length greater than its maximum recommended length (e.g., 185 m for 10Base2 or 500 m for 10Base5)
- Not properly terminating the ends of the coax cable with a 50 ohm resistor

Baseband and Broadband

The naming convention used to label most network cable technologies follows the syntax *XXyyyyZZ. XX* represents the maximum speed the cable type offers, such as 10Mbps for a 10Base2 cable. *yyyy* represents the *baseband* or *broadband* aspect of the cable, such as baseband for a 10Base2 cable. Baseband cables can transmit only a single signal at a time. Broadband cables can transmit multiple signals simultaneously. Most networking cables are baseband cables. However, when used in specific configurations, coaxial cable can be used as a broadband connection, such as with cable modems. *ZZ* either represents the maximum distance the cable can be used or acts as shorthand to represent the technology of the cable, such as the approximately 200 meters for 10Base2 cable (actually 185 meters, but it's rounded up to 200), or T or TX for twisted-pair in *10Base-T* or *100Base-TX.* (Note that 100Base-TX is implemented using two CAT 5 UTP or STP cables, one issued for receiving, the other for transmitting.)

Table 3.1 shows the important characteristics for the most common network cabling types.

TABLE 3.1   Important Characteristics for Common Network Cabling Types

Type	Max Speed	Distance	Difficulty of Installation	Susceptibility to EMI	Cost
10Base2	10Mbps	185 m	Medium	Medium	Medium
10Base5	10Mbps	500 m	High	Low	High
10Base-T (UTP)	10Mbps	100 m	Low	High	Very low
STP	155Mbps	100 m	Medium	Medium	High
100Base-T/ 100Base-TX	100Mbps	100 m	Low	High	Low
1000Base-T	1Gbps	100 m	Low	High	Medium
Fiber-optic	2Gbps	2 k	Very high	None	Very high

Twisted-Pair

Twisted-pair cabling is extremely thin and flexible compared to coaxial cable. It is made up of four pairs of wires that are twisted around each other and then sheathed in a PVC insulator. If there is a metal foil wrapper around the wires underneath the external sheath, the wire is known as *shielded twisted-pair (STP)*. The foil provides additional protection from external EMI. Twisted-pair cabling without the foil is known as *unshielded twisted-pair (UTP)*. UTP is most often referred to as just 10Base-T.

The wires that make up UTP and STP are small, thin copper wires that are twisted in pairs. The twisting of the wires provides protection from external radio frequencies and electric and magnetic interference and reduces crosstalk between pairs. Crosstalk occurs when data transmitted over one set of wires is picked up by another set of wires due to radiating electromagnetic fields produced by the electrical current. Each wire pair within the cable is twisted at a different rate (i.e., twists per inch); thus, the signals traveling over one pair of wires cannot cross over onto another pair of wires. The tighter the twist (the more twists per inch), the more resistant the cable is to internal and external interference and crosstalk and thus the capacity for throughput (that is, higher bandwidth) is greater.

There are several classes of UTP cabling. The various categories are created through the use of tighter twists of the wire pairs, variations in the quality of the conductor, and variations in the quality of the external shielding. Table 3.2 shows the UTP categories.

TABLE 3.2   UTP Categories

UTP Category	Throughput	Notes
Cat 1	Voice only	Not suitable for networks, but usable by modems
Cat 2	4Mbps	Not suitable for most networks, often employed for host-to-terminal connections on mainframes
Cat 3	10Mbps	Primarily used in 10Base-T Ethernet networks (offers only 4Mpbs when used on Token Ring networks)
Cat 4	16Mbps	Primarily used in Token Ring networks
Cat 5	100Mbps	Used in 100Base-TX, FDDI, and ATM networks
Cat 6	155Mbps	Used in high-speed networks
Cat 7	1Gbps	Used on gigabit-speed networks

The following problems are the most common with twisted-pair cabling:

- Using the wrong category of twisted-pair cable for high-throughput networking
- Deploying a twisted-pair cable longer than its maximum recommended length (i.e., 100 m).
- Using UTP in environments with significant interference

Conductors

The distance limitations of conductor-based network cabling is due to the resistance of the metal used as a conductor. Copper, the most popular conductor, is one of the best and least expensive room-temperature conductors available. However, it is resistant to the flow of electrons. This resistance results in a degradation of signal strength and quality over the length of the cable.

> **NOTE** Plenum cable is a type of cabling sheathed with a special material that does not release toxic fumes when burned, as does traditional PVC coated wiring. Often plenum grade cable must be used to comply with building codes, especially if the building has enclosed spaces where people are likely to be found that could trap gases.

The maximum length defined for each cable type indicates the point at which the level of degradation could begin to interfere with the efficient transmission of data. This degradation of the signal is known as *attenuation*. It is often possible to use a cable segment that is longer than the cable is rated for, but the number of errors and retransmissions will be increased over that cable segment, ultimately resulting in poor network performance. Attenuation is more pronounced as the speed of the transmission increases. It is recommended to use shorter cable lengths as the speed of the transmission increases.

Long cable lengths can often be supplemented through the use of repeaters or concentrators. A repeater is just a signal amplification device, much like the amplifier for your car or home stereo. The repeater boosts the signal strength of an incoming data stream and rebroadcasts it through its second port. A concentrator does the same thing except it has more than just two ports. However, the use of more than four repeaters in a row is discouraged (see the sidebar "3-4-5 Rule").

3-4-5 Rule

The 3-4-5 rule is used whenever Ethernet or other IEEE 802.3 shared-access networks are deployed in a tree topology (i.e., a central trunk with various splitting branches). This rule defines the number of repeaters/concentrators and segments that can be used in a network design. The rule states that between any two nodes (a node can be any type of processing entity, such as a server, client, router), there can be a maximum of five segments connected by four repeaters/concentrators and that only three of those five segments can be populated (i.e., have additional or other user, server, or networking device connections).

The 3-4-5 rule does not apply to switched networks.

An alternative to conductor-based network cabling is *fiber-optic* cable. Fiber-optic cables transmit pulses of light rather than electricity. This has the advantage of being extremely fast and nearly impervious to tapping. However, it is difficult to install and expensive; thus, the security and performance it offers comes at a steep price.

Wireless

In addition to wire-based network connectivity media, we must include wireless connectivity. Wireless network interfaces are widely used as an alternative to running UTP cabling throughout a work area. Wireless networking is based on IEEE 802.11b and 802.11a standards. 802.11b devices can transmit data up to 11Mbps. 802.11a devices can transmit data up to 54Mbps. Wireless networking uses connection hubs that can support one to dozens of wireless NICs. The primary drawback of wireless networking is that the signals connecting the NICs to the hubs may not be encrypted. *Virtual private networks (VPNs)* or other traffic encryption mechanisms must be employed to provide security for the connections. A wireless link is more susceptible to eavesdropping because the signals can often be detected blocks away, whereas UTP cables require direct physical access to tap into the traffic.

LAN Technologies

There are three main types of local area network (LAN) technologies: Ethernet, Token Ring, and FDDI. There are a handful of other LAN technologies, but they are not as widely used as these three. Most of the differences between LAN technologies occurs at and below the Data Link layer.

Ethernet

Ethernet is a shared-media LAN technology (also known as a broadcast technology). That means it allows numerous devices to communicate over the same medium but requires that each device take turns communicating and perform collision detection and avoidance. Ethernet employs broadcast and collision domains. A *broadcast* domain is a physical grouping of systems in which all of the systems in the group receive a broadcast sent by a single system in the group. A broadcast is a message transmitted to a specific address that indicates that all systems are the intended recipients.

A collision domain consists of groupings of systems within which a data collision occurs if two systems transmit simultaneously. A data collision takes place when two transmitted messages attempt to use the network medium at the same time. It causes one or both of the messages to be corrupted.

Ethernet can support full-duplex communications (i.e., full two-way) and usually employs coaxial or twisted-pair cabling. Ethernet is most often deployed on star or bus topologies. Ethernet is based on the IEEE 802.3 standard. Individual units of Ethernet data are called frames. Fast Ethernet supports 100Mbps throughput. Gigabit Ethernet supports 1000Gbps throughput.

Token Ring

Token Ring employs a token-passing mechanism to control which systems can transmit data over the network medium. The *token* travels in a logical loop among all members of the LAN. Token Ring can be employed on ring or star network topologies. It is rarely used today due to its performance limitations, higher cost compared to Ethernet, and increased difficulty in deployment and management.

Fiber Distributed Data Interface (FDDI)

Fiber Distributed Data Interface (FDDI) is a high-speed token-passing technology that employs two rings with traffic flowing in opposite directions. FDDI is often used as a backbone for large enterprise networks. Its dual-ring design allows for self-healing by removing the failed segment from the loop and creating a single loop out of the remaining inner and outer ring portions. FDDI is expensive but was often used in campus environments before Fast Ethernet and Gigabit Ethernet were developed.

Sub-technologies

Most networks comprise numerous technologies rather than a single technology. For example, Ethernet is not just a single technology but a superset of sub-technologies that support its common and expected activity and behavior. Ethernet includes the technologies of digital communications, synchronous communications, and baseband communications, and it supports broadcast, multicast, and unicast communications and Carrier-Sense Multiple Access with Collision Detection (CSMA/CD). Many of the LAN technologies, such as Ethernet, Token Ring, and FDDI, may include many of the sub-technologies described in the following sections.

Analog and Digital

One sub-technology is the mechanism used to actually transmit communication signals over a physical medium, such as a cable. There are two types: analog and digital. Analog communications occur with a continuous signal that varies in frequency, amplitude, phase, voltage, and so on. The variances in the continuous signal produce a wave shape (as opposed to the square shape of a digital signal). The actual communication occurs by variances in the constant signal. Digital communications occur through the use of a discontinuous electrical signal and a state change or on-off pulses.

Synchronous and Asynchronous

Some communications are synchronized with some sort of clock or timing activity. Communications are either synchronous or asynchronous. Synchronous communications rely upon a timing or clocking mechanism based upon either an independent clock or a time stamp embedded in the data stream. Synchronous communications are typically able to support very high rates of data transfer. Asynchronous communications rely upon a stop and start delimiter bit to manage transmission of data. Due to the use of delimiter bits and the stop and start nature of its transmission, asynchronous communication is best suited for smaller amounts of data. Standard modems over normal telephone lines are good examples of asynchronous communication.

Baseband and Broadband

How many communications can occur simultaneously over a cable segment depends on whether you use baseband technology or broadband technology. Baseband technology can support only a single communication channel. It uses a direct current applied to the cable. A current that is on represents the binary signal of 1, and a current that is off represents the binary signal of 0. Ethernet is a baseband technology. Broadband technology can support multiple simultaneous signals. Broadband uses frequency modulation to support numerous channels, each supporting a distinct communication session. Broadband is suitable for high-throughput rates, especially when several channels are multiplexed. Cable television and cable modems, ISDN, DSL, T1, and T3 are examples of broadband technologies.

Broadcast, Multicast, and Unicast

Another sub-technology determines how many destinations a single transmission can reach. The options are broadcast, multicast, and unicast. A broadcast technology supports communications to all possible recipients. A multicast technology supports communications to multiple specific recipients. A unicast technology supports only a single communication to a specific recipient.

LAN Media Access

Finally, there are at least five LAN media access technologies that are used to avoid or prevent transmission collisions.

Carrier Sense Multiple Access (CSMA)   The LAN media access technology that performs communications using the following steps:

1. The host listens to the LAN media to determine if it is in use.
2. If the LAN media is not being used, the host transmits its communication.
3. The host waits for an acknowledgment.
4. If no acknowledgment is received after a timeout period, the host starts over at step 1.

Carrier-Sense Multiple Access with Collision Avoidance (CSMA/CA)   The LAN media access technology that performs communications using the following steps:

1. The host has two connections to the LAN media: inbound and outbound. The host listens on the inbound connection to determine if the LAN media is in use.
2. If the LAN media is not being used, the host requests permission to transmit.
3. If permission is not granted after a timeout period, the host starts over at step 1.
4. If permission is granted, the host transmits its communication over the outbound connection.
5. The host waits for an acknowledgment.
6. If no acknowledgment is received after a timeout period, the host starts over at step 1.

AppleTalk and 802.11 wireless networking are examples of networks that employ CSMA/CA technologies.

Carrier-Sense Multiple Access with Collision Detection (CSMA/CD)   The LAN media access technology that performs communications using the following steps:

1. The host listens to the LAN media to determine if it is in use.
2. If the LAN media is not being used, the host transmits its communication.
3. While transmitting, the host listens for collisions (i.e., two or more hosts transmitting simultaneously).
4. If a collision is detected, the host transmits a jam signal.
5. If a jam signal is received, all hosts stop transmitting. Each host waits a random period of time and then starts over at step 1.

Ethernet networks employ the CSMA/CD technology.

Token Passing   The LAN media access technology that performs communications using a digital token. Possession of the token allows a host to transmit data. Once its transmission is complete, it releases the token on to the next system. Token passing is used by Token Ring networks, such as FDDI.

Polling   The LAN media access technology that performs communications using a master-slave configuration. One system is labeled as the primary system. All other systems are labeled as secondary. The primary system polls or inquires of each secondary system in turn whether they have a need to transmit data. If a secondary system indicates a need, it is granted permission to transmit. Once its transmission is complete, the primary system moves on to poll the next secondary system. Synchronous Data Link Control (SDLC) uses polling.

Network Topologies

The physical layout and organization of computers and networking devices is known as the network topology. The logical topology is the grouping of networked systems into trusted collectives. The physical topology is not always the same as the logical topology. There are four basic topologies of the physical layout of a network: ring, bus, star, and mesh.

Ring Topology

A ring topology connects each system as points on a circle (see Figure 3.6). The connection medium acts as a unidirectional transmission loop. Only one system can transmit data at a time. Traffic management is performed by a token. A token is a digital hall pass that travels around the ring until a system grabs it. A system in possession of the token can transmit data. Data and the token are transmitted to a specific destination. As the data travels around the loop, each system checks to see if it is the intended recipient of the data. If not, it passes the token on. If so, it reads the data. Once the data is received, the token is released and returns to traveling around the loop until another system grabs it. If any one segment of the loop is broken, all communication around the loop ceases. Some implementations of ring topologies employ a fault tolerance mechanism, such as dual loops running in opposite directions, to prevent single points of failure.

FIGURE 3.6   A ring topology

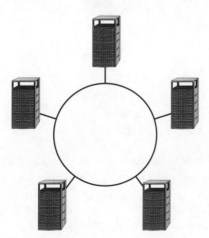

Bus Topology

A bus topology connects each system to a trunk or backbone cable. All systems on the bus can transmit data simultaneously, which can result in collisions. A collision occurs when two systems transmit data at the same time; the signals interfere with each other. To avoid this, the systems employ a collision avoidance mechanism that basically "listens" for any other currently occurring traffic. If traffic is heard, the system waits a few moments and listens again. If no traffic is heard, the system transmits its data. When data is transmitted on a bus topology, all systems on the network hear the data. If the data is not addressed to a specific system, that system just ignores the data. The benefit of a bus topology is that if a single segment fails, communications on all other segments continue uninterrupted. However, the central trunk line remains a single point of failure.

There are two types of bus topologies: linear and tree. A linear bus topology employs a single trunk line with all systems directly connected to it. A tree topology employs a single trunk line with branches that can support multiple systems. Figure 3.7 illustrates both types.

FIGURE 3.7   A linear topology and a tree bus topology

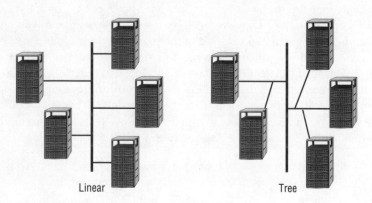

Linear   Tree

Star Topology

A star topology employs a centralized connection device. This device can be a simple hub or switch. Each system is connected to the central hub by a dedicated segment (see Figure 3.8). If any one segment fails, the other segments can continue to function. However, the central hub is a single point of failure. Generally, the star topology uses less cabling than other topologies and makes the identification of damaged cables easier.

A logical bus and a logical ring can be implemented as a physical star. Ethernet is a bus-based technology. It can be deployed as a physical star, but the hub device is actually a logical bus connection device. Likewise, Token Ring is a ring-based technology. It can be deployed as a physical star using a multistation access unit (MAU). An MAU allows for the cable segments to be deployed as a star while internally the device makes logical ring connections.

FIGURE 3.8   A star topology

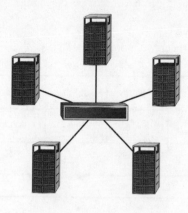

FIGURE 3.9   A mesh topology

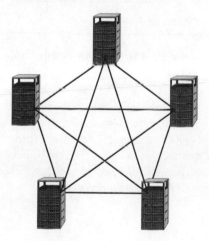

Mesh Topology

A mesh topology connects systems to other systems using numerous paths (see Figure 3.9). A full mesh topology connects each system to all other systems on the network. A partial mesh topology connects many systems to many other systems. Mesh topologies provide redundant connections to systems, allowing multiple segment failures without seriously affecting connectivity.

TCP/IP Overview

The most widely used protocol is TCP/IP, but it is not just a single protocol; rather, it is a protocol stack comprising dozens of individual protocols (see Figure 3.10). TCP/IP is a platform-independent protocol based on open standards. However, this is both a benefit and a drawback.

TCP/IP can be found in just about every available operating system, but it consumes a significant amount of resources and is relatively easy to hack into because it was designed for ease of use rather than for security.

FIGURE 3.10 The four layers of TCP/IP and its component protocols

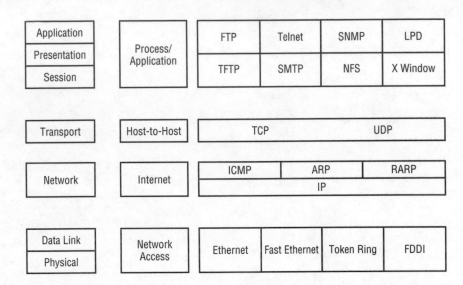

TCP/IP can be secured using VPN links between systems. VPN links are encrypted to add privacy, confidentiality, and authentication and to maintain data integrity. Protocols used to establish VPNs are Point-to-Point Tunneling Protocol (PPTP), Layer 2 Tunneling Protocol (L2TP), and Internet Protocol Security (IPSec). Another method is to employ TCP wrappers. A *TCP wrapper* is an application that can serve as a basic *firewall* by restricting access based on user IDs or system IDs. Using TCP wrappers is a form of port-based access control.

Transport Layer Protocols

The two primary Transport layer protocols of TCP/IP are TCP and UDP. TCP is a connection-oriented protocol, whereas UDP is a connectionless protocol. When a communication connection is established between two systems, it is done using ports. TCP and UDP each have 65,536 ports. Since port numbers are 16-digit binary numbers, the total number of ports is 2^{16}, or 65,536, numbered from 0 through 65,535. A port (also called a socket) is little more than an address number that both ends of the communication link agree to use when transferring data. Ports allow a single IP address to be able to support multiple simultaneous communications, each using a different port number.

The first 1,024 of these ports (0–1,023) are called the *well-known ports* or the *service ports*. This is because they have standardized assignments as to the services they support. For example, port 80 is the standard port for Web (HTTP) traffic, port 23 is the standard port for Telnet, and port 25 is the standard port for SMTP.

Transmission Control Protocol (TCP) operates at layer 4 (the Transport layer) of the OSI model. It supports full-duplex communications, is connection oriented, and employs reliable virtual circuits. TCP is connection-oriented because it employs a handshake process between two systems to establish a communication session. Upon completion of this handshake process, a communication session that can support data transmission between the client and server is established. The three-way handshake process is as follows:

1. The client sends a SYN (synchronize) packet to the server.

2. The server responds with a SYN/ACK (synchronize and acknowledge) packet back to the client.

3. The client responds with an ACK (acknowledge) packet back to the server.

The segments of a TCP transmission are sequenced. This allows the receiver to rebuild the original communication by reordering received segments back into their proper arrangement in spite of the order in which they were received. Data communicated through a TCP session is periodically verified with an acknowledgement signal. The acknowledgement is a hash value of all previously transmitted data. If the server's own hash of received data does not match the hash value sent by the client, the server asks the client to resend the last collection of data. The number of packets transmitted before an acknowledge packet is sent is known as the transmission window. Data flow is controlled through a mechanism called sliding windows. TCP is able to use different sizes of windows (i.e., a different number of transmitted packets) before sending an acknowledgement. Larger windows allow for faster data transmission, but they should be used only on reliable connections where lost or corrupted data is minimal. Smaller windows should be used when the communication connection is unreliable. TCP should be employed when delivery of data is required. The IP header protocol field value for TCP is 6. The protocol field value is the label or flag found in the header of every IP packet that tells the receiving system what type of packet it is. Think of it like the label on a mystery meat package wrapped in butcher paper you pull out of the deep freeze. Without the label, you would have to open it and inspect it to figure out what it was. But with the label, you can search or filter quickly to find items of interest.

User Datagram Protocol (UDP) also operates at layer 4 (the Transport layer) of the OSI model. It is a connectionless "best effort" communications protocol. It offers no error detection or correction, does not use sequencing, does not use flow control mechanisms, does not use a virtual circuit, and is considered unreliable. UDP has very low overhead and thus can transmit data quickly. However, UDP should be used only when delivery of data is not essential. UDP is often employed by real-time or streaming communications for audio or video. The IP header protocol field value for UDP is 17.

Network Layer Protocols

Another important protocol in the TCP/IP protocol suite operates at the Network layer of the OSI model—namely Internet Protocol (IP). IP provides route addressing for data packets. Similar to UDP, IP is connectionless and is an unreliable datagram service. IP does not offer guarantees that packets will be delivered or that packets will be delivered in the correct order, nor does it guarantee that packets will not be delivered more than once. Thus, you must employ TCP on IP to gain reliable and controlled communication sessions.

Other protocols at the OSI model Network layer include ICMP, IGMP, and NAT.

ICMP

Internet Control Message Protocol (ICMP) is used to determine the health of a network or a specific link. ICMP is utilized by ping, TRACEROUTE, PATHPING, and other network management tools. The ping utility employs ICMP echo packets and bounces them off remote systems. Thus, ping can be used to determine if the remote system is online, if the remote system is responding promptly, whether the intermediary systems are supporting communications, and the level of performance efficiency at which the intermediary systems are communicating. ping includes a redirect function that allows the echo responses to be sent to a different destination than the system of origin. Unfortunately, this ICMP capability is often exploited in various forms of bandwidth-based denial of service attacks. The IP header protocol field value for ICMP is 1.

IGMP

Internet Group Management Protocol (IGMP) allows systems to support multicasting. Multicasting is the transmission of data to multiple specific recipients. (RFC 1112 discusses the requirements to perform IGMP multicasting.) IGMP is used by IP hosts to register their dynamic multicast group membership. It is also used by connected routers to discover these groups. The IP header protocol field value for IGMP is 2.

ARP and Reverse ARP

Address Resolution Protocol (ARP) and *Reverse Address Resolution Protocol (RARP)* are two important protocols you need to be familiar with. ARP is used to resolve IP addresses (32-bit binary number for logical addressing) into MAC (Media Access Control) addresses. MAC addresses are the six-digit hexadecimal numbers (48-bit binary numbers for hardware addressing) assigned by manufacturers to network interface cards. Traffic on a network segment (e.g., cables across a hub) is directed from its source system to its destination system using MAC addresses. RARP is used to resolve MAC addresses into IP addresses.

NAT

Network Address Translation (NAT) was developed to allow private networks to use any IP address set without causing collisions or conflicts with public Internet hosts with the same IP addresses. In effect, NAT translates the IP addresses of your internal clients to leased addresses outside of your environment. Most often, a private network employs the private IP addresses defined in RFC 1918. The private IP address ranges are 10.0.0.0–10.255.255.255 (an entire Class A range), 172.16.0.0–172.31.255.255 (16 Class B ranges), and 192.168.0.0–192.168.255.255 (255 Class C ranges). These ranges of IP addresses are defined by default on routers as nonroutable. They are reserved for use by private networks. Attempting to use these addresses directly on the Internet is futile because all publicly accessible routers will drop data packets containing a source or destination IP address from these ranges.

Frequently, security professionals refer to NAT when they really mean PAT. By definition, NAT maps one internal IP address to one external IP address. However, *Port Address Translation (PAT)* maps one internal IP address to an external IP address and port number combination. Thus, PAT can theoretically support 65,536 (2^{32}) simultaneous communications from internal clients over a single external leased IP address. So with NAT, you must lease as many public IP addresses as simultaneous communications you wish to have, while with PAT you can lease fewer IP addresses and obtain a reasonable 100:1 ratio of internal clients to external leased IP addresses.

NAT can be used in two modes: static and dynamic. Static mode NAT is used when a specific internal client's IP address is assigned a permanent mapping to a specific external public IP address. This allows for external entities to communicate with systems inside of your network even if you are using the RFC 1918 IP addresses. Dynamic mode NAT is used to grant multiple internal clients access to a few leased public IP addresses. Thus, a large internal network can still access the Internet without having to lease a large block of public IP addresses. This keeps public IP address usage abuse to a minimum and helps keep Internet access costs to a minimum. In a dynamic mode NAT implementation, the NAT system maintains a database of mappings so that all response traffic from Internet services are properly routed back to the original internal requesting client. Often NAT is combined with a proxy server or proxy firewall to provide additional Internet access and content caching features. NAT is not directly compatible with IPSec because it modifies packet headers, which IPSec relies upon to prevent security violations.

Automatic Private IP Addressing (APIPA)

APIPA, or Automatic Private IP Addressing, not to be confused with RFC 1918, assigns an IP address to a system in the event of a DHCP assignment failure. APIPA is primarily a feature of Windows. APIPA assigns each failed DHCP client with an IP address from the range of 169.254.0.1 to 169.254.255.254 along with the default Class B subnet mask of 255.255.0.0. This allows the system to communicate with other APIPA configured clients within the same broadcast domain but not with any system across a router or with a correctly assigned IP address.

It is a good idea to know how to convert between decimal, binary, and even hexadecimal. Also, don't forget about how to covert from a dotted-decimal notation IP address (such as 172.16.1.1) to its binary equivalent (that is, 10101100000100000000000100000001). And it is probably not a bad idea to be able to convert the 32-bit binary number to a single decimal number (that is, 2886729985).

IP Classes

Basic knowledge of IP addressing and IP classes is a must for any security professional. If you are rusty on addressing, subnetting, classes, and other related topics, take the time to refresh yourself. Table 3.3 and Table 3.4 provide a quick overview of the key details of classes and default subnets.

The Loopback Address

Another IP address range that you should be careful not to confuse with RFC 1918 is the loopback address. The loopback address is purely a software entity. It is an IP address used to create a software interface that connects back to itself via the TCP/IP protocol. The loopback address allows for testing of local network settings in spite of missing, damaged, or nonfunctional network hardware and/or related device drivers. Technically, the entire 127.x.x.x network is reserved for loopback use. However, only the 127.0.0.1 address is widely used. Windows XP SP2 (and possibly other OS updates) recently restricted the client to use only 127.0.0.1 as the loopback address. This caused several applications that used other addresses in the upper ranges of the 127.x.x.x network services to fail. In restricting client use to only 127.0.0.1, Microsoft has attempted to open up a wasted Class A address. Even if this tactic is successful for Microsoft, it will only affect the modern Windows systems.

TABLE 3.3   IP Classes

Class	First Binary Digits	Decimal Range of First Octet
A	0	1–126
B	10	128–191
C	110	192–223
D	1110	224–239
E	1111	240–255

TABLE 3.4   IP Classes Default Subnet Masks

Class	Default Subnet Mask	CIDR Equivalent
A	255.0.0.0	/8
B	255.255.0.0	/16
C	255.255.255.0	/24
D	255.0.0.0	/8
E	255.0.0.0	/8

Another option for subnetting is to use Classless Inter-Domain Routing (CIDR). CIDR uses mask bits rather than a full dotted-decimal notation subnet mask. Thus, instead of 255.255.0.0, a CIDR is added to the IP address after a slash, e.g., 172.16.1.1/16.

Common Application Layer Protocols

In the Application layer of the TCP/IP model (which includes the Session, Presentation, and Application layers of the OSI model) reside numerous application- or service-specific protocols. A basic knowledge of these protocols and their relevant service ports is important for the CISSP exam:

Telnet, port 23   A terminal emulation network application that supports remote connectivity for executing commands and running applications but that does not support transfer of files.

File Transfer Protocol (FTP), ports 20, 21   A network application that supports an exchange of files that requires anonymous or specific authentication.

Trivial File Transfer Protocol (TFTP), port 69   A network application that supports an exchange of files that does not require authentication.

Simple Mail Transfer Protocol (SMTP), port 25   A protocol used to transmit e-mail messages from a client to an e-mail server and from one e-mail server to another.

Post Office Protocol (POP3), port 110   A protocol used to pull e-mail messages from an inbox on an e-mail server down to an e-mail client.

Internet Mail Authentication Protocol (IMAP 4), port 143   A protocol used to pull e-mail messages from an inbox on an e-mail server down to an e-mail client. IMAP is more secure than POP3 and offers the ability to pull headers down from the e-mail server as well as to delete messages directly off the e-mail server without having to download to the local client first.

Dynamic Host Configuration Protocol (DHCP), ports 67 and 68   DHCP uses port 67 for server point-to-point response and port 68 for client request broadcast. It is used to assign TCP/IP configuration settings to systems upon bootup. DHCP enables centralized control of network addressing.

HyperText Transport Protocol (HTTP), port 80   This is the protocol used to transmit web page elements from a web server to web browsers.

Secure Sockets Layer (SSL), port 443   A VPN-like security protocol that operates at the session layer. SSL was originally designed to support secured Web communications (HTTPS) but is capable of securing any Application-layer protocol communications.

Line Print Daemon (LPD)   A network service that is used to spool print jobs and to send print jobs to printers.

X Window   A GUI API for operating systems.

Bootstrap Protocol (BootP)   A protocol used to connect diskless workstations to a network through auto-assignment of IP configuration and download of basic OS elements. BootP is the forerunner to Dynamic Host Configuration Protocol (DHCP).

Network File System (NFS)   A network service used to support file sharing between dissimilar systems.

Simple Network Management Protocol (SNMP), port 161   A network service used to collect network health and status information by polling monitoring devices from a central monitoring station.

TCP/IP's vulnerabilities are numerous. Improperly implemented TCP/IP stacks in various operating systems are vulnerable to buffer overflows, SYN flood attacks, various DoS attacks, fragment attacks, over-sized packet attacks, spoofing attacks, man-in-the-middle attacks, hijack attacks, and coding error attacks.

In addition to these intrusive attacks, TCP/IP (as well as most protocols) is also subject to passive attacks via monitoring or sniffing. Network monitoring is the act of monitoring traffic patterns to obtain information about a network. Packet sniffing is the act of capturing packets from the network in hopes of extracting useful information from the packet contents. Effective packet sniffers can extract usernames, passwords, e-mail addresses, encryption keys, credit card numbers, IP addresses, system names, and so on.

Internet/Intranet/Extranet Components

The Internet is the global network of interconnected networks that provides the wealth of information we know as the World Wide Web. The Internet is host to countless information services and numerous applications, including the Web, e-mail, FTP, Telnet, newsgroups, chat, and so on. The Internet is also home to malicious persons whose primary goal is to locate your computer and extract valuable data from it, use it to launch further attacks, or damage it in some way. You should be familiar with the Internet and able to readily identify its benefits and drawbacks from your own online experiences. Due to the success and global use of the Internet, many of its technologies were adapted or integrated into the private business network. This created two new forms of networks: intranets and extranets.

An *intranet* is a private network that is designed to host the same information services found on the Internet. Networks that rely upon external servers (i.e., ones positioned on the public Internet) to provide information services internally are not considered intranets. Intranets provide users with access to the Web, e-mail, and other services on internal servers that are not accessible to anyone outside of the private network.

An *extranet* is a cross between the Internet and an intranet. An extranet is a section of an organization's network that has been sectioned off so that it acts as an intranet for the private network but also serves information out to the public Internet. An extranet is often reserved for use by specific partners or customers. It is rarely on a public network. An extranet for public consumption is typically labeled a demilitarized zone (DMZ), or perimeter network.

When you're designing a secure network (whether a private network, an intranet, or an extranet), there are numerous networking devices that must be evaluated. Not all of these components are necessary for a secure network, but they are all common network devices that may have an impact on network security.

Firewalls

Firewalls are essential tools in managing and controlling network traffic. A *firewall* is a network device used to filter traffic and is typically deployed between a private network and a link to the Internet, but it can be deployed between departments within an organization. Without firewalls, it would not be possible to restrict malicious traffic from the Internet from entering into your private network. Firewalls filter traffic based on a defined set of rules, also called filters or access control lists. They are basically a set of instructions that are used to distinguish authorized traffic from unauthorized and/or malicious traffic. Only authorized traffic is allowed to cross the security barrier provided by the firewall.

Firewalls are useful for blocking or filtering traffic. They are most effective against unrequested traffic and attempts to connect from outside the private network and for blocking known malicious data, messages, or packets based on content, application, protocol, port, or source address. They are capable of hiding the structure and addressing scheme of a private network from the public. Most firewalls offer extensive logging, auditing, and monitoring capabilities, as well as alarms and basic intrusion detection system (IDS) functions. Firewalls are unable to block viruses or malicious code transmitted through otherwise authorized communication channels, prevent unauthorized but accidental or intended disclosure of information by users, prevent attacks by malicious users already behind the firewall, or protect data after it passes out of or into the private network.

In addition to logging network traffic activity, firewalls should log several other events as well:

- Reboot of the firewall
- Proxies or dependencies that cannot or didn't start
- Proxies or other important services that have crashed or restarted
- Changes to the firewall configuration file
- A configuration or system error while the firewall is running

Firewalls are only one part of an overall security solution. With a firewall, many of the security mechanisms are concentrated in one place, and thus they may be a single point of failure. Firewall failure is most commonly caused by human error and misconfiguration. Firewalls provide protection only against traffic that crosses the firewall from one subnet to another. They offer no protection against traffic within a subnet (i.e., behind a firewall).

There are four basic types of firewalls: static packet-filtering firewalls, application-level gateway firewalls, circuit-level gateway firewalls, and stateful inspection firewalls. There are also ways to create hybrid or complex gateway firewalls by combining two or more of these firewall types into a single firewall solution. In most cases, having a multilevel firewall provides greater control over filtering traffic. Regardless, let's look at the various firewall types and discuss firewall deployment architectures as well.

Static Packet-Filtering Firewall

A *static packet-filtering firewall* filters traffic by examining data from a message header. Usually, the rules are concerned with source, destination, and port addresses. Using static filtering, a firewall is unable to provide user authentication or to tell whether a packet originated from inside or outside the private network, and it is easily fooled with spoofed packets. Static packet-filtering firewalls are known as first-generation firewalls; they operate at layer 3 (the Network layer) of the OSI model. They can also be called screening routers or common routers.

Application-Level Gateway Firewall

An *application-level gateway firewall* is also called a *proxy* firewall. A proxy is a mechanism that copies packets from one network into another; the copy process also changes the source and destination address to protect the identity of the internal or private network. An application-level gateway firewall filters traffic based on the Internet service (i.e., application) used to transmit or receive the data. Each type of application must have its own unique proxy server. Thus, an application-level gateway firewall comprises numerous individual proxy servers. This type of firewall negatively affects network performance because each packet must be examined and processed as it passes through the firewall. Application-level gateways are known as second-generation firewalls, and they operate at the Application layer (layer 7) of the OSI model.

Circuit-Level Gateway Firewalls

Circuit-level gateway firewalls are used to establish communication sessions between trusted partners. They operate at the Session layer (layer 5) of the OSI model. SOCKS (SOCKetS, as in TCP/IP ports) is a common implementation of a circuit-level gateway firewall. Circuit-level gateway firewalls, also known as circuit proxies, manage communications based on the circuit, not the content of traffic. They permit or deny forwarding decisions based solely on the endpoint designations of the communication circuit (i.e., the source and destination addresses and service port numbers). Circuit-level gateway firewalls are considered second-generation firewalls because they represent a modification of the *application-level gateway firewall* concept.

Stateful Inspection Firewalls

Stateful inspection firewalls evaluate the state or the context of network traffic. By examining source and destination addresses, application usage, source of origin, and the relationship between current packets and the previous packets of the same session, stateful inspection firewalls are able to grant a broader range of access for authorized users and activities and actively watch for and block unauthorized users and activities. Stateful inspection firewalls generally operate more efficiently than application-level gateway firewalls. They are known as third-generation firewalls, and they operate at Network and Transport layers (layers 3 and 4) of the OSI model.

Multihomed Firewalls

Some firewall systems have more than one interface. For instance, a multihomed firewall must have at least two interfaces to filter traffic (they're also known as dual-homed firewalls). All multihomed firewalls should have IP forwarding disabled to force the filtering rules to control all traffic rather than allowing a software-supported shortcut between one interface and another. A bastion host or a screened host is just a firewall system logically positioned between a private network and an untrusted network. Usually, the bastion host is located behind the router that connects the private network to the untrusted network. All inbound traffic is routed to the bastion host, which in turn acts as a proxy for all of the trusted systems within the private network. It is responsible for filtering traffic coming into the private network as well as for protecting the identity of the internal client. A screened subnet is similar to the screened host in concept, except a subnet is placed between two routers and the bastion host is located within that subnet. All inbound traffic is directed to the bastion host, and only traffic proxied by the bastion host can pass through the second router into the private network.

Firewall Deployment Architectures

There are three commonly recognized firewall deployment architectures: single-tier, two-tier, and three-tier (also known as multitier). As you can see in Figure 3.11, a single-tier deployment places the private network behind a firewall, which is then connected through a router to the Internet (or some other untrusted network). Single-tier deployments are useful against generic attacks only. This architecture offers only minimal protection.

A two-tier deployment architecture uses a firewall with three or more interfaces. This allows for a DMZ or a publicly accessible extranet. The DMZ is used to host information server systems to which external users should have access. The firewall routes traffic to the DMZ or the trusted network according to its strict filtering rules. This architecture introduces a moderate level of routing and filtering complexity.

FIGURE 3.11   Three firewall deployment architectures

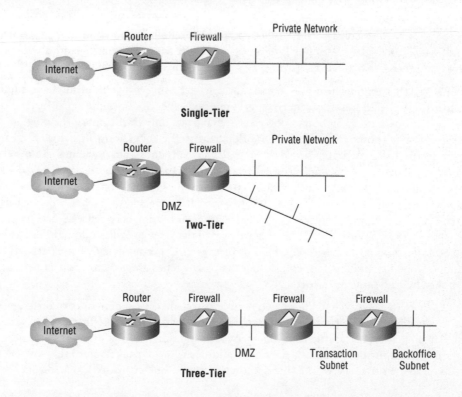

A three-tier deployment architecture is the deployment of multiple subnets between the private network and the Internet separated by firewalls. Each subsequent firewall has more stringent filtering rules to restrict traffic to only trusted sources. The outermost subnet is usually a DMZ. A middle subnet can serve as a transaction subnet where systems needed to support complex web applications in the DMZ reside. The third or back-end subnet can support the private network. This architecture is the most secure; however, it is also the most complex to design, implement, and manage.

Other Network Devices

There are numerous devices used in the construction of a network. Strong familiarity with the components of network building can assist you in designing an IT infrastructure that avoids single points of failure and provides strong support for availability.

Repeaters, concentrators, and amplifiers   Repeaters, concentrators, and amplifiers are used to strengthen the communication signal over a cable segment as well as connect network segments that use the same protocol. These devices can be used to extend the maximum length of a specific cable type by deploying one or more repeaters along a lengthy cable run. Repeaters, concentrators, and amplifiers operate at OSI layer 1. Systems on either side of a repeater, concentrator, or amplifier are part of the same collision domain and broadcast domain.

Hubs   Hubs are used to connect multiple systems in a star topology and connect network segments that use the same protocol. They repeat inbound traffic over all outbound ports. This ensures that the traffic will reach its intended host. A hub is a multiport repeater. Hubs operate at OSI layer 1. Systems on either side of a hub are part of the same collision and broadcast domains.

Switches   Rather than using a hub, you might consider using a switch, or intelligent hub. Switches know the addresses of the systems connected on each outbound port. Instead of repeating traffic on every outbound port, a switch repeats only traffic out of the port on which the destination is known to exist. Switches offer greater efficiency for traffic delivery, create separate collision domains, and improve the overall throughput of data. Switches can also create separate broadcast domains when used to create VLANs. In such configurations, broadcasts are allowed within a single VLAN but not allowed to cross unhindered from one VLAN to another. Switches operate primarily at OSI layer 2. When switches have additional features, such as routing, they can operate at OSI layer 3 as well (such as when routing between VLANs). Systems on either side of a switch operating at layer 2 are part of the same broadcast domain but are in different collision domains. Systems on either side of a switch operating at layer 3 are part of different broadcast domains and different collision domains. Switches are used to connect network segments that use the same protocol.

Bridges   A bridge is used to connect two networks together, even networks of different topologies, cabling types, and speeds, in order to connect network segments that use the same protocol. A bridge forwards traffic from one network to another. Bridges that connect networks using different transmission speeds may have a buffer to store packets until they can be forwarded on to the slower network. This is known as a store-and-forward device. Bridges operate at OSI layer 2. Systems on either side of a bridge are part of the same broadcast domain but are in different collision domains.

Routers   Routers are used to control traffic flow on networks and are often used to connect similar networks and control traffic flow between the two. They can function using statically defined routing tables or they can employ a dynamic routing system. There are numerous dynamic routing protocols, such as RIP, OSPF, and BGP. Routers operate at OSI layer 3. Systems on either side of a router are part of different broadcast domains and different collision domains. Routers are used to connect network segments that use the same protocol.

Brouter   Brouters are combination devices comprising a router and a bridge. A brouter attempts to route first, but if that fails it defaults to bridging. Thus, a brouter operates primarily at layer 3 but can operate at layer 2 when necessary. Systems on either side of a brouter operating at layer 3 are part of different broadcast domains and different collision domains. Systems on either side of a brouter operating at layer 2 are part of the same broadcast domain but are in different collision domains. Brouters are used to connect network segments that use the same protocol.

Gateways   A gateway connects networks that are using different network protocols. A gateway is responsible for transferring traffic from one network to another by transforming the format of that traffic into a form compatible with the protocol or transport method used by each network. Gateways, also known as protocol translators, can be stand-alone hardware devices or a software service. Systems on either side of a gateway are part of different broadcast domains and different collision domains. Gateway are used to connect network segments that use different protocols. There are many types of gateways, including data, mail, application, secure, and Internet. Gateways typically operate at OSI layer 7.

Proxies   A proxy is a form of gateway that does not translate across protocols. Instead, proxies serve as mediators, filters, caching servers, and even NAT/PAT servers for a network. A proxy performs a function or requests a service on behalf of another system and connects network segments that use the same protocol. Proxies are most often used in the context of providing clients on a private network with Internet access while protecting the identity of the clients. A proxy accepts requests from clients, alters the source address of the requester, maintains a mapping of requests to clients, and sends the altered request packets out. Once a reply is received, the proxy server determines which client it is destined for by reviewing its mappings and then sends the packets on to the client. Systems on either side of a proxy are part of different broadcast domains and different collision domains.

LAN extender   A LAN extender is a remote access, multilayer switch used to connect distant networks over WAN links. This is a strange beast of a device in that it creates WANs, but marketers of this device steer clear of the WAN term and use only the LAN or extended LAN terms. The idea behind this device was to make the terminology easier to understand and easier to sell than a normal WAN device with complex concepts and terms tied to it. Ultimately, it was the exact same product as a WAN switch or WAN router. (We agree with Douglas Adams, who believes the marketing people should be shipped out with the lawyers and phone sanitizers on the first ship to the far end of the universe.)

Remote Access Security Management

Telecommuting, or remote connectivity, has become a common feature of business computing. Remote access is the ability of a distant client to establish a communication session with a network. This can take the form of using a modem to dial up directly to a remote access server, connecting to a network over the Internet through a VPN, or even connecting to a terminal server system through a thin-client connection. The first two examples use fully capable clients. They establish connections just as if they were directly connected to the LAN. The last example, with terminal server, establishes a connection from a thin client. In such a situation, all computing activities occur on the terminal server system rather than on the distant client.

When remote access capabilities are deployed in any environment, security must be considered and implemented to provide protection for your private network against remote access complications. Remote access users should be strongly authenticated before being granted access. Only those users who specifically need remote access for their assigned work tasks should be granted permission to establish remote connections. All remote communications should be protected from interception and eavesdropping. This usually requires an encryption solution that provides strong protection for both the authentication traffic as well as all data transmission.

When outlining your remote access security management strategy, be sure to address the following issues:

Remote connectivity technology   Each type of connection has its own unique security issues. Fully examine every aspect of your connection options. This can include modems, DSL, ISDN, wireless networking, and cable modems.

Transmission protection   There are several forms of encrypted protocols, encrypted connection systems, and encrypted network services or applications. Use the appropriate combination of secured services for your remote connectivity needs. This can include VPNs, SSL, TLS, Secure Shell (SSH), IPSec, and L2TP.

Authentication protection   In addition to protecting data traffic, you must also ensure that all logon credentials are properly secured. This requires the use of an authentication protocol and may mandate the use of a centralized remote access authentication system. This can include Password Authentication Protocol (PAP), Challenge Handshake Authentication Protocol (CHAP), Extensible Authentication Protocol (EAP), Remote Authentication Dial-In User Service (RADIUS), and Terminal Access Controller Access Control System (TACACS).

Remote user assistance   Remote access users may periodically require technical assistance. You must have a means established to provide this as efficiently as possible. This can include addressing software and hardware issues, user training issues, and so on.

The ability to use remote access or establish a remote connection should be tightly controlled. As mentioned earlier, only those users who require remote access for their work tasks should be granted such access. You can control and restrict use of remote connectivity by using filters, rules, or access controls based on user identity, workstation identity, protocol, application, content, and time of day. To provide protection and restriction of remote access only to authorized users, you can use callback and caller ID. Callback is a mechanism that disconnects a remote user upon initial contact and then immediately attempts to reconnect to them using a predefined phone number (i.e., the number defined in the user account's security database). Callback does have a user-defined mode. However, this mode is not used for security; it is used to reverse toll charges to the company rather than charging the remote client. Caller ID verification can be used for the same purpose as callback—by verifying the physical location (via phone number) of the authorized user.

It should be a standard element in your security policy that no unauthorized modems be present on any system connected to the private network. You may need to further specify this policy by indicating that portable systems must either remove their modems before connecting to the network or boot with a hardware profile that disables the modem's device driver.

Network and Protocol Security Mechanisms

TCP/IP is the primary protocol used on most networks and on the Internet. It is a robust protocol, but it has numerous security deficiencies. In an effort to improve the security of TCP/IP, many subprotocols, mechanisms, or applications have been developed to protect the confidentiality, integrity, and availability of transmitted data. It is important to remember that even with the single foundational protocol of TCP/IP, there are literally hundreds, if not thousands, of individual protocols, mechanisms, and applications in use across the Internet. Some of them are designed to provide security services. Some protect integrity, others confidentiality, and others provide authentication and access control. In the next sections, some of the more common network and protocol security mechanisms are discussed.

VPN Protocols

A *virtual private network (VPN) protocol* is used to establish a secured tunnel for communications across an untrusted network. That network can be the Internet or a private network. The VPN can link two networks or two individual systems. VPNs can link clients, servers, routers, firewalls, and switches. VPNs are also helpful in providing security for legacy applications that rely upon risky or vulnerable communication protocols or methodologies, especially when communicating across a network.

Point-to-Point Tunneling Protocol (PPTP) is an enhancement of PPP that creates encrypted tunnels between communication endpoints. PPTP is used on VPNs, but it is often replaced by the *Layer 2 Tunneling Protocol (L2TP)*, which uses IPSec to provide traffic encryption for VPNs. L2TP was created by combining elements of PPTP and L2F (Layer 2 Forwarding), a VPN protocol from Cisco.

IP Security (IPSec) is a standards-based mechanism for providing encryption for point-to-point TCP/IP traffic. IPSec has two primary components or functions: *Authentication Header (AH)* and *Encapsulating Security Payload (ESP)*. AH provides authentication, integrity, and nonrepudiation. ESP provides encryption to protect the confidentiality of transmitted data, but it can also perform limited authentication. IPSec is often used in a VPN in either transport or tunnel mode. In *transport mode*, the IP packet data is encrypted but the header of the packet is not. In *tunnel mode*, the entire IP packet is encrypted and a new header is added to the packet to govern transmission through the tunnel. IPSec functions at layer 3 of the OSI model.

Table 3.5 illustrates the main characteristics of VPN protocols.

TABLE 3.5   VPN Characteristics

VPN Protocol	Native Authentication Protection	Native Data Encryption	Protocols Supported	Dial-Up Links Supported	Number of Simultaneous Connections
PPTP	Y	N	IP only	Y	Single point to point
L2F	Y	N	IP only	Y	Single point to point
L2TP	Y	N (Can use IPSec)	Any	Y	Single point to point
IPSec	Y	Y	IP only	N	Multiple

A VPN device is a network add-on device used to create VPN tunnels separately from server or client OSes. Use of VPN devices is transparent to networked systems.

Secure Communications Protocols

Protocols that provide security services for application-specific communication channels are called *secure communication protocols. Simple Key Management for IP (SKIP)* is an encryption tool used to protect sessionless datagram protocols. SKIP was designed to integrate with IPSec and functions at layer 3. SKIP is able to encrypt any subprotocol of the TCP/IP suite.

Software IP encryption (SWIPE) is another layer 3 security protocol for IP. It provides authentication, integrity, and confidentiality using an encapsulation protocol.

Secure Remote Procedure Call (S-RPC) is an authentication service and is simply a means to prevent unauthorized execution of code on remote systems.

Secure Sockets Layer (SSL) is an encryption protocol developed by Netscape to protect the communications between a web server and a web browser. SSL can be used to secure Web, e-mail, FTP, or even Telnet traffic. It is a session-oriented protocol that provides confidentiality and integrity. SSL is deployed using a 40-bit key or a 128-bit key.

E-Mail Security Solutions

E-mail is inherently insecure. Internet e-mail relies primarily upon Simple Mail Transfer Protocol (SMTP). SMTP provides no security services. In fact, all e-mail transmitted over the Internet is transmitted in cleartext. Thus, messages that are intercepted or subjected to eavesdropping attacks can be easily read. The only means to provide protection for e-mail is to add encryption to the client applications used. The following paragraphs describe four common e-mail security solutions.

Secure Multipurpose Internet Mail Extensions (S/MIME) secures the transmission of e-mail and attachments. S/MIME provides protection through public key encryption and digital signatures. Two types of messages can be formed using S/MIME—signed messages and enveloped messages. A signed message provides integrity and sender authentication. An enveloped message provides integrity, sender authentication, and confidentiality.

Secure Electronic Transaction (SET) is a security protocol for the transmission of transactions over the Internet. SET is based on Rivest, Shamir, and Adelman (RSA) encryption and Data Encryption Standard (DES). It has the support of major credit card companies, such as Visa and MasterCard.

Privacy Enhanced Mail (PEM) is an e-mail encryption mechanism that provides authentication, integrity, confidentiality, and nonrepudiation. PEM is a layer 7 protocol and uses RSA, DES, and X.509.

Pretty Good Privacy (PGP) is a public-private key system that uses the IDEA algorithm to encrypt files and e-mail messages. PGP is not a standard, but rather an independently developed product that has wide Internet grassroots support.

Dial-Up Protocols

When a remote connection link is established, some protocol must be used to govern how the link is actually created and to establish a common communication foundation for other protocols to work over. Dial-up protocols provide this function not only for true dial-up links but also for some VPN links.

One of the many proprietary dial-up protocols is Microcom Networking Protocol (MNP). MNP was found on Microcom modems in the 1990s. It supports its own form of error control called Echoplex.

Point-to-Point Protocol (PPP) is a full-duplex protocol used for the transmission of TCP/IP packets over various non-LAN connections, such as modems, ISDN, VPNs, Frame Relay, and so on. PPP is widely supported and is the transport protocol of choice for dial-up Internet connections. PPP authentication is protected through the use of various protocols, such as CHAP or PAP. PPP is a replacement for SLIP and can support any LAN protocol, not just TCP/IP.

Serial Line Internet Protocol (SLIP) is an older technology developed to support TCP/IP communications over asynchronous serial connections, such as serial cables or modem dial-up. SLIP is rarely used but is still supported on many systems. SLIP can support only IP, requires static IP addresses, offers no error detection or correction, and does not support compression.

Authentication Protocols

After a connection is initially established between a remote system and a server or a network, the first activity that should take place is to verify the identity of the remote user. This activity is known as authentication. There are several *authentication protocols* that control how the logon credentials are exchanged and whether or not those credentials are encrypted during transport.

Challenge Handshake Authentication Protocol (CHAP) is one of the authentication protocols used over PPP links. CHAP encrypts usernames and passwords. It performs authentication using a challenge-response dialog that cannot be replayed. CHAP also periodically reauthenticates the remote system throughout an established communication session to verify persistent identity of the remote client. This activity is transparent to the user.

Password Authentication Protocol (PAP) is a standardized authentication protocol for PPP. PAP transmits usernames and passwords in the clear. It offers no form of encryption; it simply provides a means to transport the logon credentials from the client to the authentication server.

Extensible Authentication Protocol (EAP) is a framework for authentication instead of an actual protocol. EAP allows customized authentication security solutions, such as supporting smart cards, tokens, and biometrics.

Centralized Remote Authentication Services

As remote access becomes a key element in an organization's business functions, it is often important to add additional layers of security between remote clients and the private network. Centralized remote authentication services, such as RADIUS and TACACS, provide this extra layer of protection. These mechanisms provide a separation of the authentication and authorization processes for remote clients from that performed for LAN or local clients. If the RADIUS or TACACS servers are ever compromised, then only remote connectivity is affected, not the rest of the network.

Remote Authentication Dial-In User Service (RADIUS) is used to centralize the authentication of remote dial-up connections. A network that employs a RADIUS server is configured so the remote access server passes dial-up user logon credentials to the RADIUS server for authentication. This process is similar to the process used by domain clients sending logon credentials to a domain controller for authentication.

Terminal Access Controller Access Control System (TACACS) is an alternative to RADIUS. TACACS is available in three versions: original TACACS, Extended TACACS (XTACACS), and TACACS+. TACACS integrates the authentication and authorization processes. XTACACS keeps the authentication, authorization, and accounting processes separate. TACACS+ improves XTACACS by adding two-factor authentication. TACACS operates similarly to RADIUS and provides the same functionality as RADIUS.

Network and Protocol Services

Another aspect of networking is the protocol services used to connect a LAN to WAN communication technologies. A basic knowledge of these services is important for anyone working in a security field or serving as a network manager. The following sections introduce some key issues about several WAN communication technologies.

Remote Access and Telecommuting Techniques

There are three main types of remote access techniques: service specific, remote control, and remote node operation. Service-specific remote access gives users the ability to remotely connect to and manipulate or interact with a single service, such as e-mail. Remote control remote access grants a remote user the ability to fully control another system that is physically distant from them. The monitor and keyboard act as if they are directly connected to the remote system. Remote node operation is just another name for dial-up connectivity. A remote system connects to a remote access server. That server provides the remote client with network services and possible Internet access.

Telecommuting is performing work at a location other than the primary office. In fact, there is a good chance that you perform some form of telecommuting as part of your current job. Telecommuting clients can use any or all of these remote access techniques to establish connectivity to the central office LAN.

Frame Relay

Frame Relay is a layer 2 connection mechanism that uses packet-switching technology to establish virtual circuits between communication endpoints. Unlike dedicated or leased lines, for which cost is based primarily on the distance between endpoints, Frame Relay's cost is primarily based on the amount of data transferred. The Frame Relay network is a shared medium across which virtual circuits are created to provide point-to-point communications. All virtual circuits are independent of and invisible to each other. Companies using Frame Relay establish a *Committed Information Rate (CIR)* contract that guarantees a minimum bandwidth for their communications at all times. However, if additional bandwidth is required and the Frame Relay network can support additional traffic, the virtual circuit can automatically expand to allow a higher throughput rate. Frame Relay is a connection-oriented service.

Frame Relay requires the use of *data terminal equipment (DTE)* and *data circuit-terminating equipment (DCE)* at each connection point. The customer owns the DTE, which acts like a router or a switch and provides the customer's network with access to the Frame Relay network. The Frame Relay service provider owns the DCE, which performs the actual transmission of data over the Frame Relay as well as establishing and maintaining the virtual circuit for the customer.

There are two types of virtual circuits: *permanent virtual circuit (PVC)* and *switched virtual circuit (SVC)*. A PVC is a predefined virtual circuit that is always available. The virtual circuit may be closed down when not in use, but it can be instantly reopened whenever needed. An SVC is more like a dial-up connection. Each time the customer needs to transmit data over Frame Relay, a new virtual circuit is established using the best paths currently available. A PVC is like a two-way radio or walkie-talkie. Whenever communication is needed, you press the button and start talking; the radio reopens the predefined frequency automatically (i.e., the virtual circuit). A SVC is more like a shortwave or ham radio. You must tune the transmitter and receiver to a new frequency every time you want to communicate with someone.

Other WAN Technologies

Switched Multimegabit Data Services (SMDS) is a connectionless network communication service. It provides bandwidth on demand and is a preferred connection mechanism for linking remote LANs that communicate infrequently. SMDS is often a competitor of Frame Relay.

X.25 is an older WAN protocol that uses a carrier switch to provide end-to-end connections over a shared network medium. It is the predecessor to Frame Relay and operates in much the same fashion. However, X.25 use is declining due to its lower performance and throughput rates when compared to Frame Relay or ATM.

Asynchronous transfer mode (ATM) is a cell-switching technology, as opposed to a packet-switching technology like Frame Relay. ATM uses virtual circuits much like Frame Relay, but because it uses fixed-size frames or cells, it can guarantee throughput. This makes ATM an excellent WAN technology for voice and video conferencing.

High Speed Serial Interface (HSSI) is a layer 1 protocol used to connect routers and multiplexers to ATM or Frame Relay connection devices.

Synchronous Data Link Control (SDLC) is a layer 2 protocol employed by networks with dedicated or leased lines. SDLC was developed by IBM for remote communications with SNA systems. SDLC is a bit-oriented synchronous protocol.

High-Level Data Link Control (HDLC) is a layer 2 protocol used to transmit data over synchronous communication lines. HDLC is an ISO standard based on IBM's SDLC. HDLC supports full-duplex communications and both point-to-point and multipoint connections, offers flow control, and includes error detection and correction.

Avoiding Single Points of Failure

Any element in your IT infrastructure, physical environment, or staff can be a single point of failure. A single point of failure is simply any element—such as a device, service, protocol, or communication link—that would cause total or significant downtime if compromised, violated, or destroyed, affecting the ability of members of your organization to perform essential work tasks. To avoid single points of failure, you must design your networks and your physical environment with redundancy and backups by doing such things as deploying dual network backbones. The use of systems, devices, and solutions with fault-tolerant capabilities is a means to improve resistance to single-point-of-failure vulnerabilities. Taking steps to establish a means to provide alternate processing, failover capabilities, and quick recovery will also aid in avoiding single points of failure.

Redundant Servers

Using redundant servers is one fault-tolerant deployment option. Redundant servers can take numerous forms. Server mirroring is the deployment of a backup system along with the primary system. Every change made to the primary system is immediately duplicated to the secondary system. Electronic vaulting is the collection of changes on a primary system into a transaction or change document. Periodically, the change document is sent to an offsite duplicate server where the changes are applied. This is also known as batch processing because changes are duplicated over intervals rather than in real time. Remote journaling is the same as electronic vaulting except that changes are sent immediately to the offsite duplicate server rather than in batches. This provides a more real-time server backup. Database shadowing is remote journaling to more than one destination duplicate server. There may be one or more local duplicates and one or more offsite duplicates.

Another type of redundant server is a cluster or server farm. Clustering means deploying two or more duplicate servers in such a way as to share the workload of a mission-critical application. Users see the clustered systems as a single entity. A cluster controller manages traffic to and among the clustered systems to balance the workload across all clustered servers. As changes occur on one of the clustered systems, they are immediately duplicated to all other cluster partners.

Failover Solutions

When backup systems or redundant servers exist, there needs to be a means by which you can switch over to the backup in the event the primary system is compromised or fails. Rollover, or failover, is redirecting workload or traffic to a backup system when the primary system fails. Rollover can be automatic or manual. Manual rollover, also known as cold rollover, requires an administrator to perform some change in software or hardware configuration to switch the traffic load over from the down primary to a secondary server. With automatic rollover, also known as hot rollover, the switch from primary to secondary system is performed automatically as soon as a problem is encountered. *Fail-secure, fail-safe,* and *fail-soft* are terms related to these issues. A system that is fail-secure is able to resort to a secure state when an error or security violation is encountered. Fail-safe is a similar feature, but human safety is protected in the event of a system failure. However, these two terms are often used interchangeably to mean a system that is secure after a failure. *Fail-soft* describes a refinement of the fail-secure capability: only the portion of a system that encountered or experienced the failure or security breach is disabled or secured, while the rest of the system continues to function normally.

A specific implementation of a fail-secure system would be the use of TFTP servers to store network device configurations. In the event of a system failure, configuration corruption, or power outage, most network devices (such as routers and switches) can be hard-coded to pull their configuration file from a TFTP server upon reboot. In this way, essential network devices can self-restore quickly.

Power failure is always a single point of failure. If electrical power is lost, all electronic devices will cease to function. Addressing this weakness is important if 24/7 uptime is essential to your organization. Ways to combat power failure or fluctuation issues include power conditioners (i.e., surge protectors), uninterruptible power supplies, and onsite electric generators.

RAID

Within individual systems, storage devices can be a single point of failure. Redundant Array of Independent Disks (RAID) is a storage device mechanism that uses multiple hard drives in unique combinations to produce a storage solution that provides better throughput as well as resistance to device failure. The two primary storage techniques employed by RAID are mirroring and striping. Striping can be further enhanced by storing parity information. Parity information enables on-the-fly recovery or reconstruction of data lost due to the failure of one or more drives. There are several levels or forms of RAID. Some of the more common RAID levels are listed in Table 3.6.

TABLE 3.6   Common RAID Levels

RAID Level	Description
0	Striping
1	Mirroring
2	Hamming code parity
3	Byte-level parity
4	Block-level parity
5	Interleave parity
6	Second parity data
10	RAID levels 1 + 0
15	RAID levels 1 + 5

RAID can be implemented in hardware or in software. Hardware-based RAID offers more reliable performance and fault tolerance protection. Hardware-based RAID performs all processing necessary for multidrive access on the drive controllers. Software-based RAID performs the processing as part of the operating system. Thus, system resources are consumed in managing and using RAID when it is deployed through software.

There are three forms of RAID drive swapping: hot, cold, and warm. Hot-swappable RAID allows for failed drives to be removed and replaced while the host server remains up and running. Cold-swappable RAID systems require the host server to be fully powered down before failed drives can be removed and replaced. Warm-swappable RAID allows for failed drives to be removed and replaced by disabling the RAID configuration via software, then replacing the drive, and then reenabling the RAID configuration. RAID is a specific technology example of Fault Resistant Disk Systems (FRDS).

No matter what fault-tolerant designs and mechanisms you employ to avoid single points of failure, no environment's security precautions are complete without a backup solution. Backups are the only means of providing reliable insurance against minor and catastrophic losses of your data. For a backup system to provide protection, it must be configured to store all data necessary to support your organization. It must perform the backup operation as quickly and efficiently as possible. The backups must be performed on a regular basis, such as daily, weekly, or in real time. And backups must be periodically tested to verify that they are functioning and that your restore processes are adequate. An untested backup cannot be assumed to work.

Summary

Designing, deploying, and maintaining security on a network requires intimate knowledge of the technologies involved in networking. This includes protocols, services, communication mechanisms, topologies, cabling, and networking devices.

The OSI model is a standard against which all protocols are evaluated. Understanding how the OSI model is used and how it applies to real-world protocols can help system designers and system administrators improve security.

There is a wide range of hardware components that can be used to construct a network, not the least of which is the cabling used to tie all the devices together. Understanding the strengths and weaknesses of each cabling type is part of designing a secure network.

There are three common LAN technologies: Ethernet, Token Ring, and FDDI. Each can be used to deploy a secure network. There are also several common network topologies: ring, bus, star, and mesh.

Most networks employ TCP/IP as the primary protocol. However, there are numerous subprotocols, supporting protocols, services, and security mechanisms that can be found in a TCP/IP network. A basic understanding of these various entities can aid in designing and deploying a secure network. These components include IPSec, SKIP, SWIPE, SSL, S/MIME, SET, PEM, PGP, PPP, SLIP, PPTP, L2TP, CHAP, PAP, RADIUS, TACACS, S-RPC, Frame Relay, SMDS, X.25, ATM, HSSI, SDLC, HDLC, and ISDN.

Remote access security management requires that security system designers address the hardware and software components of the implementation along with policy issues, work task issues, and encryption issues.

In addition to routers, hubs, switches, repeaters, gateways, and proxies, firewalls are an important part of a network's security. There are four primary types of firewalls: static packet-filtering, application-level gateway, circuit-level gateway, and stateful inspection.

Avoiding single points of failure includes incorporating fault-tolerant systems and solutions into an environment's design. When designing a fault-tolerant system, you should make sure you include redundant or mirrored systems, use TFTP servers, address power issues, use RAID, and maintain a backup solution.

Exam Essentials

Know the OSI model layers and what protocols are found in each.   The seven layers and protocols supported by each of the layers of the OSI model are as follows:

- Application: HTTP, FTP, LPD, SMTP, Telnet, TFTP, EDI, POP3, IMAP, SNMP, NNTP, S-RPC, and SET
- Presentation: encryption protocols, such as RSA and DES, and format types, such as ASCII, EBCDIC, TIFF, JPEG, MPEG, and MIDI
- Session: SSL, TLS, NFS, SQL, and RPC
- Transport: SPX, TCP, and UDP
- Network: ICMP, RIP, OSPF, BGP, IGMP, IP, IPSec, IPX, NAT, and SKIP
- Data Link: SLIP, PPP, ARP, RARP, L2F, L2TP, PPTP, FDDI, ISDN
- Physical: EIA/TIA-232, EIA/TIA-449, X.21, HSSI, SONET, V.24, and V.35

Know the TCP/IP model and how it relates to the OSI model.   The TCP/IP model has four layers: Application, Host-to-Host, Internet, and Network Access.

Know the different cabling types and their lengths and maximum throughput rates.   This includes STP, 10Base-T (UTP), 10Base2 (thinnet), 10Base5 (thicknet), 100Base-T, 1000Base-T, and fiber-optic. You should also be familiar with UTP categories 1 through 7.

Be familiar with the common LAN technologies.   These are Ethernet, Token Ring, and FDDI. Also be familiar with analog vs. digital communications; synchronous vs. asynchronous communications; baseband vs. broadband communications; broadcast, multicast, and unicast communications; CSMA, CSMA/CA, CSMA/CD, token passing, and polling.

Know the standard network topologies.   These are ring, bus, star, and mesh.

Have a thorough knowledge of TCP/IP.   Know the difference between TCP and UDP; be familiar with the four TCP/IP layers and how they correspond to the OSI model. In addition, understand the usage of the well-known ports and be familiar with the subprotocols.

Know the common network devices.   Common network devices are firewalls, routers, hubs, bridges, repeaters, switches, gateways, and proxies.

Understand the different types of firewalls.   There are four basic types of firewalls: static packet-filtering, application-level gateway, circuit-level gateway, and stateful inspection.

Understand the issues around remote access security management.   Remote access security management requires that security system designers address the hardware and software components of an implementation along with issues related to policy, work tasks, and encryption.

Be familiar with the various protocols and mechanisms that may be used on LANs and WANs.   These are IPSec, SKIP, SWIPE, SSL, S/MIME, SET, PEM, PGP, PPP, SLIP, PPTP, L2TP, CHAP, PAP, EAP, RADIUS, TACACS, and S-RPC.

Know the protocol services used to connect to LAN and WAN communication technologies.   These are Frame Relay, SMDS, X.25, ATM, HSSI, SDLC, HDLC, and ISDN.

Understand the issues around single points of failure.   Avoiding single points of failure includes incorporating fault-tolerant systems and solutions into an environment's design. Fault-tolerant systems include redundant or mirrored systems, TFTP servers, and RAID. You should also address power issues and maintain a backup solution.

Review Questions

1. What is layer 4 of the OSI model?

   A. Presentation

   B. Network

   C. Data Link

   D. Transport

2. What is encapsulation?

   A. Changing the source and destination addresses of a packet

   B. Adding a header and footer to data as it moves down the OSI stack

   C. Verifying a person's identity

   D. Protecting evidence until it has been properly collected

3. Which OSI model layer manages communications in simplex, half-duplex, and full-duplex modes?

   A. Application

   B. Session

   C. Transport

   D. Physical

4. Which of the following is the least resistant to EMI?

   A. Thinnet

   B. 10Base-T UTP

   C. 10Base5

   D. Coaxial cable

5. Which of the following cables has the most twists per inch?

   A. STP

   B. UTP

   C. 100Base-T

   D. 1000Base-T

6. Which of the following is not true?

   A. Fiber-optic cable offers very high throughput rates.

   B. Fiber-optic cable is difficult to install.

   C. Fiber-optic cable is expensive.

   D. Communications over fiber-optic cable can be tapped easily.

7. Which of the following is not one of the most common LAN technologies?

   A. Ethernet

   B. ATM

   C. Token Ring

   D. FDDI

8. Which networking technology is based on the IEEE 802.3 standard?

   A. Ethernet

   B. Token Ring

   C. FDDI

   D. HDLC

9. What is a TCP wrapper?

   A. An encapsulation protocol used by switches

   B. An application that can serve as a basic firewall by restricting access based on user IDs or system IDs

   C. A security protocol used to protect TCP/IP traffic over WAN links

   D. A mechanism to tunnel TCP/IP through non-IP networks

10. Which of the following protocols is connectionless?

    A. TCP

    B. UDP

    C. IP

    D. FTP

11. By examining source and destination address, application usage, source of origin, and the relationship between current packets with the previous packets of the same session, _____ firewalls are able to grant a broader range of access for authorized users and activities and actively watch for and block unauthorized users and activities.

    A. Static packet-filtering

    B. Application-level gateway

    C. Stateful inspection

    D. Circuit-level gateway

12. _____ firewalls are known as third-generation firewalls.

    A. Application-level gateway

    B. Stateful inspection

    C. Circuit-level gateway

    D. Static packet-filtering

13. Which of the following is not true regarding firewalls?

    A. They are able to log traffic information.

    B. They are able to block viruses.

    C. They are able to issue alarms based on suspected attacks.

    D. They are unable to prevent internal attacks.

14. Which of the following is not a routing protocol?

    A. OSPF

    B. BGP

    C. RPC

    D. RIP

15. A _____ is an intelligent hub because it knows the addresses of the systems connected on each outbound port. Instead of repeating traffic on every outbound port, it repeats only traffic out of the port on which the destination is known to exist.

    A. Repeater

    B. Switch

    C. Bridge

    D. Router

16. _____ is a standards-based mechanism for providing encryption for point-to-point TCP/IP traffic.

    A. UDP

    B. SSL

    C. IPSec

    D. SDLC

17. Which public-private key security system was developed independently of industry standards but has wide Internet grassroots support?

    A. SLIP

    B. PGP

    C. PPTP

    D. PAP

18. What authentication protocol offers no encryption or protection for logon credentials?

    A. PAP

    B. CHAP

    C. SSL

    D. RADIUS

19. _____ is a layer 2 connection mechanism that uses packet-switching technology to establish virtual circuits between the communication endpoints.

  A. ISDN

  B. Frame Relay

  C. SMDS

  D. ATM

20. Which of the following IP addresses is not a private IP address as defined by RFC 1918?

  A. 10.0.0.18

  B. 169.254.1.119

  C. 172.31.8.204

  D. 192.168.6.43

Answers to Review Questions

1. D. The Transport layer is layer 4. The Presentation layer is layer 6, the Data Link layer is layer 2, and the Network layer is layer 3.

2. B. Encapsulation is adding a header and footer to data as it moves through the Presentation layer down the OSI stack.

3. B. Layer 5, Session, manages simplex (one-direction), half-duplex (two-way, but only one direction can send data at a time), and full-duplex (two-way, in which data can be sent in both directions simultaneously) communications.

4. B. 10Base-T UTP is the least resistant to EMI because it is unshielded. Thinnet (10Base2) and thicknet (10Base5) are both a type of coaxial cable, which is shielded against EMI.

5. D. 1000Base-T offers 1000Mbps throughput and thus must have the greatest number of twists per inch. The tighter the twist (i.e., the number of twists per inch), the more resistant the cable is to internal and external interference and crosstalk and thus the greater the capacity is for throughput (i.e., higher bandwidth).

6. D. Fiber-optic cable is difficult to tap.

7. B. Ethernet, Token Ring, and FDDI are common LAN technologies. ATM is more common in a WAN environment.

8. A. Ethernet is based on the IEEE 802.3 standard.

9. B. A TCP wrapper is an application that can serve as a basic firewall by restricting access based on user IDs or system IDs.

10. B. UDP is a connectionless protocol.

11. C. Stateful inspection firewalls are able to grant a broader range of access for authorized users and activities and actively watch for and block unauthorized users and activities.

12. B. Stateful inspection firewalls are known as third-generation firewalls.

13. B. Most firewalls offer extensive logging, auditing, and monitoring capabilities as well as alarms and even basic IDS functions. Firewalls are unable to block viruses or malicious code transmitted through otherwise authorized communication channels, prevent unauthorized but accidental or intended disclosure of information by users, prevent attacks by malicious users already behind the firewall, or protect data after it passed out of or into the private network.

14. C. There are numerous dynamic routing protocols, including RIP, OSPF, and BGP, but RPC is not a routing protocol.

15. B. A switch is an intelligent hub. It is considered to be intelligent because it knows the addresses of the systems connected on each outbound port.

16. C. IPSec, or IP Security, is a standards-based mechanism for providing encryption for point-to-point TCP/IP traffic.

17. B. Pretty Good Privacy (PGP) is a public-private key system that uses the IDEA algorithm to encrypt files and e-mail messages. PGP is not a standard but rather an independently developed product that has wide Internet grassroots support.

18. A. PAP, or Password Authentication Protocol, is a standardized authentication protocol for PPP. PAP transmits usernames and passwords in the clear. It offers no form of encryption. It simply provides a means to transport the logon credentials from the client to the authentication server.

19. B. Frame Relay is a layer 2 connection mechanism that uses packet-switching technology to establish virtual circuits between the communication endpoints. The Frame Relay network is a shared medium across which virtual circuits are created to provide point-to-point communications. All virtual circuits are independent of and invisible to each other.

20. B. The 169.254.x.x. subnet is in the APIPA range, which is not part of RFC 1918. The addresses in RFC 1917 are 10.0.0.0–10.255.255.255, 172.16.0.0–172.31.255.255, and 192.168.0.0–192.168.255.255.

Chapter

4

Communications Security and Countermeasures

THE CISSP EXAM TOPICS COVERED IN THIS CHAPTER INCLUDE:

- ✓ Communications Security Techniques
- ✓ Packet and Circuit Switching
- ✓ WAN Technologies
- ✓ E-Mail Security
- ✓ Facsimlle Security
- ✓ Secure Voice Communications
- ✓ Security Boundaries
- ✓ Network Attacks and Countermeasures

Data residing in a static form on a storage device is fairly simple to secure. As long as physical access control is maintained and reasonable logical access controls are implemented, stored files remain confidential, retain their integrity, and are available to authorized users. However, once data is used by an application or transferred over a network connection, the process of securing it becomes much more difficult.

Communications security covers a wide range of issues related to the transportation of electronic information from one place to another. That transportation may be between systems on opposite sides of the planet or between systems on the same business network. Data becomes vulnerable to a plethora of threats to its confidentiality, integrity, and availability once it is involved in any means of transportation. Fortunately, many of these threats can be reduced or eliminated with the appropriate countermeasures.

Communications security is designed to detect, prevent, and even correct data transportation errors (i.e., integrity protection). This is done to sustain the security of networks while supporting the need to exchange and share data. This chapter takes a look at the many forms of communications security, vulnerabilities, and countermeasures.

The Telecommunications and Network Security domain for the CISSP certification exam deals with topics of communications security and vulnerability countermeasures. This domain is discussed in this chapter and in the preceding chapter (Chapter 3). Be sure to read and study the materials from both chapters to ensure complete coverage of the essential material for the CISSP certification exam.

Virtual Private Network (VPN)

A *virtual private network (VPN)* is simply a communication tunnel that provides point-to-point transmission of both authentication and data traffic over an intermediary network. Most VPNs use encryption to protect the encapsulated traffic, but encryption is not necessary for the connection to be considered a VPN. VPNs are most commonly associated with establishing secure communication paths through the Internet between two distant networks. However, VPNs can exist anywhere, including within private networks or between end-user systems connected to an ISP. VPNs provide confidentiality and integrity over insecure or untrusted intermediary networks. VPNs do not provide or guarantee availability.

Tunneling

Before you can truly understand VPNs, you must first understand tunneling. *Tunneling* is the network communications process that protects the contents of protocol packets by encapsulating them in packets of another protocol. The encapsulation is what creates the logical illusion of a communications tunnel over the untrusted intermediary network. This virtual path exists between the encapsulation and the deencapsulation entities located at the ends of the communication.

In fact, sending a letter to your grandmother involves the use of a tunneling system. You create the personal letter (the primary content protocol packet) and place it in an envelope (the tunneling protocol). The envelope is delivered through the postal service (the untrusted intermediary network) to its intended recipient.

The Need for Tunneling

Tunneling can be used in many situations, such as when you're bypassing firewalls, gateways, proxies, or other traffic control devices. The bypass is achieved by encapsulating the restricted content inside packets that are authorized for transmission. The tunneling process prevents the traffic control devices from blocking or dropping the communication because such devices don't know what the packets actually contain.

Tunneling is often used to enable communications between otherwise disconnected systems. If two systems are separated by a lack of network connectivity, a communication link can be established by a modem dial-up link or other remote access or wide area network (WAN) networking service. The actual LAN traffic is encapsulated in whatever communication protocol is used by the temporary connection, such as Point-to-Point Protocol (PPP) in the case of modem dial-up. If two networks are connected by a network employing a different protocol, the protocol of the separated networks can often be encapsulated within the intermediary network's protocol to provide a communication pathway.

Regardless of the actual situation, tunneling protects the contents of the inner protocol and traffic packets by encasing, or wrapping, it in an authorized protocol used by the intermediary network or connection. Tunneling can be used if the primary protocol is not routable and to keep the total number of protocols supported on the network to a minimum.

If the act of encapsulating a protocol involves encryption, tunneling can provide a means to transport sensitive data across untrusted intermediary networks without fear of losing confidentiality and integrity.

Tunneling Drawbacks

Tunneling is not without its problems. It is generally an inefficient means of communicating because all protocols include their own error detection, error handling, acknowledgment, and session management features, so using more than one protocol at a time compounds the overhead required to communicate a single message. Furthermore, tunneling creates either larger packets or more numerous packets that in turn consume additional network bandwidth. Tunneling can quickly saturate a network if sufficient bandwidth is not available. In addition, tunneling is a point-to-point communication mechanism and is not designed to handle broadcast traffic.

How VPNs Work

Now that you understand the basics of tunneling, let's discuss the details of VPNs. A VPN link can be established over any other network communication connection. This could be a typical LAN cable connection, a wireless LAN connection, a remote access dial-up connection, a WAN link, or even a client using an Internet connection for access to an office LAN. A VPN link acts just like a typical direct LAN cable connection; the only possible difference would be speed based on the intermediary network and on the connection types between the client system and the server system. Over a VPN link, a client can perform the exact same activities and access the same resources they could if they were directly connected via a LAN cable.

VPNs can be used to connect two individual systems or two entire networks. The only difference is that the transmitted data is protected only while it is within the VPN tunnel. Remote access servers or firewalls on the network's border act as the start points and endpoints for VPNs. Thus, traffic is unprotected within the source LAN, protected between the border VPN servers, and then unprotected again once it reaches the destination LAN.

VPN links through the Internet for connecting to distant networks are often inexpensive alternatives to direct links or leased lines. The cost of two high-speed Internet links to local ISPs to support a VPN is often significantly less than the cost of any other connection means available.

Implementing VPNs

VPNs can be implemented using software or hardware solutions. In either case, there are four common VPN protocols: PPTP, L2F, L2TP, and IPSec. PPTP, L2F, and L2TP operate at the Data Link layer (layer 2) of the OSI model. PPTP and IPSec are limited for use on IP networks, whereas L2F and L2TP can be used to encapsulate any LAN protocol.

Point-to-Point Tunneling Protocol (PPTP) is an encapsulation protocol developed from the dial-up protocol Point-to-Point Protocol (PPP). PPTP creates a point-to-point tunnel between two systems and encapsulates PPP packets. PPTP offers protection for authentication traffic through the same authentication protocols supported by PPP; namely, Microsoft Challenge Handshake Authentication Protocol (MS-CHAP), Challenge Handshake Authentication Protocol (CHAP), Password Authentication Protocol (PAP), Extensible Authentication Protocol (EAP), and Shiva Password Authentication Protocol (SPAP). The initial tunnel negotiation process used by PPTP is not encrypted. Thus, the session establishment packets that include the IP address of the sender and receiver—and can include usernames and hashed passwords—could be intercepted by a third party.

Cisco developed its own VPN protocol called *Layer 2 Forwarding (L2F)*, which is a mutual authentication tunneling mechanism. However, L2F does not offer encryption. L2F was not widely deployed and was soon replaced by L2TP.

Layer 2 Tunneling Protocol (L2TP) was derived by combining elements from both PPTP and L2F. L2TP creates a point-to-point tunnel between communication endpoints. It lacks a built-in encryption scheme, but it typically relies upon IPSec as its security mechanism. L2TP also supports TACACS+ and RADIUS, whereas PPTP does not.

The most commonly used VPN protocol is now IPSec. *IP Security (IPSec)* is both a stand-alone VPN protocol and the security mechanism for L2TP, and it can only be used for IP traffic.

IPSec provides for secured authentication as well as encrypted data transmission. It operates at the Network layer (layer 3) and can be used in transport mode or tunnel mode. In transport mode, the IP packet data is encrypted but the header of the packet is not. In tunnel mode, the entire IP packet is encrypted and a new header is added to the packet to govern transmission through the tunnel.

Network Address Translation

Hiding the identity of internal clients, masking the design of your private network, and keeping public IP address leasing costs to a minimum is made simple through the use of NAT. *Network Address Translation (NAT)* is a mechanism for converting the internal IP addresses found in packet headers into *public IP addresses* for transmission over the Internet. NAT offers numerous benefits, such as being able to connect an entire network to the Internet using only a single (or just a few) leased public IP addresses. NAT allows you to use the private IP addresses defined in *RFC 1918* in a private network while still being able to communicate with the Internet. NAT protects a network by hiding the IP addressing scheme and network topography from the Internet. It also provides protection by restricting connections so that only connections originating from the internal protected network are allowed back into the network from the Internet. Thus, most intrusion attacks are automatically repelled.

NAT can be found in a number of hardware devices and software products, including firewalls, routers, gateways, and proxies. It can only be used on IP networks and operates at the Network layer (layer 3).

Private IP Addresses

The use of NAT has proliferated recently due to the increased scarcity of public IP addresses and security concerns. With only roughly four billion addresses (2^{32}) available in IPv4, the world has simply deployed more devices using IP than there are unique IP addresses available. Fortunately, the early designers of the Internet and the TCP/IP protocol had good foresight and put aside a few blocks of addresses for private unrestricted use. These IP addresses, commonly called the private IP addresses, are defined in RFC 1918. They are as follows:

- 10.0.0.0–10.255.255.255 (a full Class A range)
- 172.16.0.0–172.31.255.255 (16 Class B ranges)
- 192.168.0.0–192.168.255.255 (255 Class C ranges)

All routers and traffic-directing devices are configured by default not to forward traffic to or from these IP addresses. In other words, the private IP addresses are not routed by default. Thus, they cannot be directly used to communicate over the Internet. However, they can be easily used on private networks where routers are not employed or where slight modifications to router configurations are made. The use of the private IP addresses in conjunction with NAT greatly reduces the cost of connecting to the Internet by allowing fewer public IP addresses to be leased from an ISP.

Stateful NAT

NAT operates by maintaining a mapping between requests made by internal clients, a client's internal IP address, and the IP address of the Internet service contacted. When a request packet is received by NAT from a client, it changes the source address in the packet from the client's to the NAT server's. This change is recorded in the NAT mapping database along with the destination address. Once a reply is received from the Internet server, NAT matches the reply's source address to an address stored in its mapping database and then uses the linked client address to redirect the response packet to its intended destination. This process is known as stateful NAT because it maintains information about the communication sessions between clients and external systems.

NAT can operate on a one-to-one basis with only a single internal client able to communicate over one of its leased public IP addresses at a time. This type of configuration can result in a bottleneck if more clients attempt Internet access than there are public IP addresses. For example, if there are only five leased public IP addresses, the sixth client must wait until an address is released before its communications can be transmitted out over the Internet. Other forms of NAT employ multiplexing techniques in which port numbers are used to allow the traffic from multiple internal clients to be managed on a single leased public IP address.

Switching Technologies

When two systems (individual computers or LANs) are connected over multiple intermediary networks, the task of transmitting data packets from one to the other is a complex process. To simplify this task, switching technologies were developed. The first switching technology is circuit switching.

Circuit Switching

Circuit switching was originally developed to manage telephone calls over the public switched telephone network. In circuit switching, a dedicated physical pathway is created between the two communicating parties. Once a call is established, the links between the two parties remain the same throughout the conversation. This provides for fixed or known transmission times, uniform level of quality, and little or no loss of signal or communication interruptions. Circuit-switching systems employ permanent, physical connections. However, the term *permanent* applies only to each communication session. The path is permanent throughout a single conversation. Once the path is disconnected, if the two parties communicate again, a different path may be assembled. During a single conversation, the same physical or electronic path is used throughout the communication and is used only for that one communication. Circuit switching grants exclusive use of a communication path to the current communication partners. Only after a session has been closed can a pathway be reused by another communication.

Packet Switching

Eventually, as computer communications increased as opposed to voice communications, a new form of switching was developed. Packet switching occurs when the message or communication is broken up into small segments (usually fixed-length packets, depending on the protocols and technologies employed) and sent across the intermediary networks to the destination. Each segment of data has its own header that contains source and destination information. The header is read by each intermediary system and is used to route each packet to its intended destination. Each channel or communication path is reserved for use only while a packet is actually being transmitted over it. As soon as the packet is sent, the channel is made available for other communications. Packet switching does not enforce exclusivity of communication pathways. Packet switching can be seen as a logical transmission technology because addressing logic dictates how communications traverse intermediary networks between communication partners. Table 4.1 shows a comparison between circuit switching and packet switching.

TABLE 4.1   Circuit Switching vs. Packet Switching

Circuit Switching	Packet Switching
Constant traffic	Bursty traffic
Fixed known delays	Variable delays
Connection oriented	Connectionless
Sensitive to connection loss	Sensitive to data loss
Used primarily for voice	Used for any type of traffic

Virtual Circuits

Within packet-switching systems are two types of communication paths, or virtual circuits. A virtual circuit is a logical pathway or circuit created over a packet-switched network between two specific endpoints. There are two types of virtual circuits: permanent virtual circuits (PVCs) and switched virtual circuits (SVCs). A PVC is like a dedicated leased line; the logical circuit always exists and is waiting for the customer to send data. An SVC is more like a dial-up connection because a virtual circuit has to be created before it can be used and then disassembled after the transmission is complete. In either type of virtual circuit, when a data packet enters point A of a virtual circuit connection, that packet is sent directly to point B or the other end of the virtual circuit. However, the actual path of one packet may be different than the path of another packet from the same transmission. In other words, multiple paths may exist between point A and point B as the ends of the virtual circuit, but any packet entering at point A will end up at point B.

WAN Technologies

WAN links and long-distance connection technologies can be divided into two primary categories: dedicated and nondedicated lines. A dedicated line is one that is indefinably and continually reserved for use by a specific customer. A dedicated line is always on and waiting for traffic to be transmitted over it. The link between the customer's LAN and the dedicated WAN link is always open and established. A dedicated line connects two specific endpoints and only those two endpoints together. A nondedicated line is one that requires a connection to be established before data transmission can occur. A nondedicated line can be used to connect with any remote system that uses the same type of nondedicated line.

The following list includes some examples of dedicated lines (also called leased lines or point-to-point links):

Technology	Connection Type	Speed
Digital Signal Level 0 (DS-0)	partial T1	64Kbps up to 1.544Mbps
Digital Signal Level 1 (DS-1)	T1	1.544Mbps
Digital Signal Level 3 (DS-3)	T3	44.736Mbps
European digital transmission format 1	El	2.108Mbps
European digital transmission format 3	E3	34.368Mbps
Cable modem or cable routers		up to 1.544Mbps

To obtain fault tolerance with leased lines or with connections to carrier networks (i.e., Frame Relay, ATM, SONET, SMDS, X.25, etc.), you must deploy two redundant connections. For even greater redundancy, purchase the connections from two different telcos or service providers. However, when you're using two different service providers, be sure they don't connect to the same regional backbone or share any major pipeline. If you cannot afford to deploy an exact duplicate of your primary leased line, consider a nondedicated DSL, ISDN, or cable modem connection. These less-expensive options may still provide partial availability in the event of a primary leased line failure.

Standard modems, DSL, and ISDN are examples of nondedicated lines. Digital subscriber line (DSL) is a technology that exploits the upgraded telephone network to grant consumers speeds from 144Kbps to 1.5Mbps. There are numerous formats of DSL, such as ADSL, xDSL, CDSL, HDSL, SDSL, RASDSL, IDSL, and VDSL. Each format varies as to the specific downstream and upstream bandwidth provided. The maximum distance a DSL line can be from a central office (i.e., a specific type of distribution node of the telephone network) is approximately 1,000 meters.

HDSL is the version of DSL that provides 1.544Mbps of full-duplex throughput (i.e., both upstream and downstream) over standard telephone wires (i.e., two pairs of twisted pair cabling).

Don't forget about satellite connections. Satellite connections may offer high-speed solutions even in locales that are inaccessible by cable-based, radio-wave-based, and line-of-sight-based communications. However, satellites are considered insecure because of their large surface footprint. Communications over a satellite can be intercepted by anyone. Just think of satellite radio. As long as you have a receiver, you can get the signal anywhere.

Integrated Services Digital Network (ISDN) is a fully digital telephone network that supports both voice and high-speed data communications. There are two standard classes or formats of ISDN service: BRI and PRI. Basic Rate Interface (BRI) offers customers a connection with 2 B channels and 1 D channel. The B channels support a throughput of 64Kbps and are used for data transmission. The D channel is used for call establishment, management, and teardown and has a bandwidth of 16Kbps. Even though the D channel was not designed to support data transmissions, a BRI ISDN is said to offer consumers 144Kbps of total throughput. Primary Rate Interface (PRI) offers consumers a connection with 2 to 23 64Kbps B channels and a single 64Kbps D channel. Thus, a PRI can be deployed with as little as 192Kbps and up to 1.544Mbps. However, remember that those numbers are bandwidth, not throughput, as they include the D channel, which cannot be used for actual data transmission (at least not in most normal commercial implementations).

WAN Connection Technologies

There are numerous WAN connection technologies available to companies that need communication services between multiple locations and even external partners. These WAN technologies vary greatly in cost and throughput. However, most share the common feature of being transparent to the connected LANs or systems. A WAN switch, specialized router, or border connection device provides all of the interfacing needed between the network carrier service and a company's LAN. The border connection devices are called channel service unit/data service unit (CSU/DSU). They convert LAN signals into the format used by the WAN carrier network and vice versa. The CSU/DSU contains data terminal equipment/data circuit-terminating equipment (DTE/DCE), which provides the actual connection point for the LAN's router (the DTE) and the WAN carrier network's switch (the DCE). The CSU/DSU acts as a translator, a store-and-forward device, and a link conditioner. A WAN switch is simply a specialized version of a LAN switch that is constructed with a built-in CSU/DSU for a specific type of carrier network. There are many types of carrier networks, or WAN connection technologies, such as X.25, Frame Relay, ATM, and SMDS:

X.25 WAN connections   X.25 is a packet-switching technology that is widely used in Europe. It uses permanent virtual circuits to establish specific point-to-point connections between two systems or networks.

Frame Relay connections   Like X.25, Frame Relay is a packet-switching technology that also uses PVCs. However, unlike X.25, Frame Relay supports multiple PVCs over a single WAN carrier service connection. A key concept related to Frame Relay is the Committed Information Rate (CIR). The CIR is the guaranteed minimum bandwidth a service provider grants to its customers. It is usually significantly less than the actual maximum capability of the provider network. Each customer may have a different CIR. The service network provider may allow customers to exceed their CIR over short intervals when additional bandwidth is available. Frame Relay operates at layer 2 (Data Link layer) of the OSI model. It is a connection-oriented packet-switching technology.

ATM   Asynchronous transfer mode (ATM) is a cell-switching WAN communication technology. It fragments communications into fixed-length 53-byte cells. The use of fixed-length cells allows ATM to be very efficient and offer high throughputs. ATM can use either PVCs or SVCs. ATM providers can guarantee a minimum bandwidth and a specific level of quality to their leased services. Customers can often consume additional bandwidth as needed when available on the service network for an additional pay-as-you-go fee; this is known as bandwidth on demand. ATM is a connection-oriented packet-switching technology.

SMDS   Switched Multimegabit Data Service (SMDS) is a packet-switching technology. Often, SMDS is used to connect multiple LANs to form a metropolitan area network (MAN) or a WAN. SMDS supports high-speed bursty traffic, is connectionless, and supports bandwidth on demand. SMDS has been mostly replaced by Frame Relay.

Some WAN connection technologies require additional specialized protocols to support various types of specialized systems or devices. Three of these protocols are SDLC, HDLC, and HSSI:

SDLC   Synchronous Data Link Control (SDLC) is used on permanent physical connections of dedicated leased lines to provide connectivity for mainframes, such as IBM Systems Network Architecture (SNA) systems. SDLC uses polling and operates at OSI layer 2 (the Data Link layer).

HDLC   High-Level Data Link Control (HDLC) is a refined version of SDLC designed specifically for serial synchronous connections. HDLC supports full-duplex communications and supports both point-to-point and multipoint connections. HDLC, like SDLC, uses polling and operates at OSI layer 2 (the Data Link layer).

HSSI   High Speed Serial Interface (HSSI) is a DTE/DCE interface standard that defines how multiplexors and routers connect to high-speed network carrier services such as ATM or Frame Relay. A multiplexor is a device that transmits multiple communications or signals over a single cable or virtual circuit. HSSI defines the electrical and physical characteristics of the interfaces or connection points and thus operates at OSI layer 1 (the Physical layer).

Encapsulation Protocols

The Point-to-Point Protocol (PPP) is an encapsulation protocol designed to support the transmission of IP traffic over dial-up or point-to-point links. PPP allows for multivendor interoperability of WAN devices supporting serial links. All dial-up and most point-to-point connections are serial in nature (as opposed to parallel). PPP includes a wide range of communication services, including assignment and management of IP addresses, management of synchronous communications, standardized encapsulation, multiplexing, link configuration, link quality testing, error detection, and feature or option negotiation (such as compression). PPP was originally designed to support CHAP and PAP for authentication. However, recent versions of PPP also support MS-CHAP, EAP, and SPAP. PPP can also be used to support Internetwork Packet Exchange (IPX) and DECnet protocols. PPP is an Internet standard documented in RFC 1661. It replaced the Serial Line Internet Protocol (SLIP). SLIP offered no authentication, supported only half-duplex communications, had no error detection capabilities, and required manual link establishment and teardown.

Miscellaneous Security Control Characteristics

When you're selecting or deploying security controls for network communications, there are numerous characteristics that should be evaluated in light of your circumstances, capabilities, and security policy. These issues are discussed in the following sections.

Transparency

Just as the name implies, *transparency* is the characteristic of a service, security control, or access mechanism that ensures that it is unseen by users. Transparency is often a desirable feature for security controls. The more transparent a security mechanism is, the less likely a user will be able to circumvent it or even be aware that it exists. With transparency, there is a lack of direct evidence that a feature, service, or restriction exists, and its impact on performance is minimal.

In some cases, transparency may need to function more as a configurable feature rather than as a permanent aspect of operation, such as when an administrator is troubleshooting, evaluating, or tuning a system's configurations.

Verifying Integrity

To verify the integrity of a transmission, you can use a checksum called a *hash total*. A hash function is performed on a message or a packet before it is sent over the communication pathway. The hash total obtained is added to the end of the message and is called the message digest. Once the message is received, the hash function is performed by the destination system and the result is compared to the original hash total. If the two hash totals match, then there is a high level of certainty that the message has not been altered or corrupted during transmission. Hash totals are similar to *cyclic redundancy checks (CRCs)* in that they both act as integrity tools. In most secure transaction systems, hash functions are used to guarantee communication integrity.

Record sequence checking is similar to a hash total check; however, instead of verifying content integrity, it verifies packet or message sequence integrity. Many communications services employ record sequence checking to verify that no portions of a message were lost and that all elements of the message are in their proper order.

Transmission Mechanisms

Transmission logging is a form of auditing focused on communications. Transmission logging records the particulars about source, destination, time stamps, identification codes, transmission status, number of packets, size of message, and so on. These pieces of information may be useful in troubleshooting problems and tracking down unauthorized communications or used against a system as a means to extract data about how it functions.

Transmission error correction is a capability built into connection- or session-oriented protocols and services. If it is determined that a message, in whole or in part, was corrupted, altered, or lost, a request can be made for the source to resend all or part of the message. Retransmission controls determine whether all or part of a message is retransmitted in the event that a transmission error correction system discovers a problem with a communication. Retransmission controls can also determine whether multiple copies of a hash total or CRC value are sent and whether multiple data paths or communication channels are employed.

Managing E-Mail Security

E-mail is one of the most widely and commonly used Internet services. The e-mail infrastructure employed on the Internet is primarily made up of e-mail servers using the *Simple Mail Transfer Protocol (SMTP)* to accept messages from clients, transport those messages to other servers, and deposit messages into a user's server-based inbox. In addition to e-mail servers, the infrastructure includes e-mail clients. Clients retrieve e-mail from their server-based inboxes using the *Post Office Protocol, version 3 (POP3)* or *Internet Message Access Protocol (IMAP)*. Clients communicate with e-mail servers using SMTP. All Internet compatible e-mail systems rely upon the X.400 standard for addressing and message handling.

Sendmail is the most common SMTP server for Unix systems, Exchange is the most common SMTP server for Microsoft systems, and GroupWise is the most common SMTP server for Novell systems. In addition to these three popular products, there are numerous alternatives, but they all share the same basic functionality and compliance with Internet e-mail standards.

If you deploy an SMTP server, it is imperative to properly configure authentication for both inbound and outbound mail. SMTP is designed to be a mail relay system. This means it relays mail from sender to intended recipient. However, you want to avoid turning your SMTP server into an open relay (also known as open relay agent, or relay agent),—an STMP server that does not authenticate senders before accepting and relaying mail. Open relays are prime targets for spammers because they allow spammers to send out floods of e-mails by piggybacking on an insecure e-mail infrastructure.

E-Mail Security Goals

For e-mail, the basic mechanism in use on the Internet offers efficient delivery of messages but lacks controls to provide for confidentiality, integrity, or even availability. In other words, basic e-mail is not secure. However, there are many ways to add security to e-mail. Adding security to e-mail may satisfy one or more of the following objectives:

- Provide for nonrepudiation
- Restrict access to messages to their intended recipients
- Maintain the integrity of messages
- Authenticate and verify the source of messages
- Verify the delivery of messages
- Classify sensitive content within or attached to messages

As with any aspect of IT security, e-mail security begins in a security policy approved by upper management. Within the security policy, several issues must be addressed:

- Acceptable use policies for e-mail
- Access control
- Privacy
- E-mail management
- E-mail backup and retention policies

Acceptable use policies define what activities can and cannot be performed over an organization's e-mail infrastructure. It is often stipulated that professional, business-oriented e-mail and a limited amount of personal e-mail can be sent and received. Specific restrictions are usually placed on performing personal business (i.e., work for another organization, including self-employment), illegal, immoral, or offensive communications, and any other activities that would have a detrimental effect on productivity, profitability, or public relations.

Access control over e-mail should be maintained so that users have access to only their specific inbox and e-mail archive databases. An extension of this rule implies that no other user, authorized or not, can gain access to an individual's e-mail. Access control should provide for both legitimate access and some level of privacy, at least from peer employees and unauthorized intruders.

The mechanisms and processes used to implement, maintain, and administer e-mail for an organization should be clarified. End users may not need to know the specifics of how e-mail is managed, but they do need to know whether e-mail is or is not considered private communication. E-mail has recently been the focus of numerous court cases in which archived messages were used as evidence. Often, this was to the chagrin of the author or recipient of those messages. If e-mail is to be retained (i.e., backed up and stored in archives for future use), users need to be made aware of this. If e-mail is to be reviewed for violations by an auditor, users need to be informed of this as well. Some companies have elected to retain only the last three months of e-mail archives before they are destroyed, whereas others have opted to retain e-mail for up to seven years.

Understanding E-Mail Security Issues

The first step in deploying e-mail security is to recognize the vulnerabilities specific to e-mail. The protocols used to support e-mail do not employ encryption. Thus, all messages are transmitted in the form in which they are submitted to the e-mail server, which is often plain text.

This makes interception and eavesdropping an easy task. However, the lack of native encryption is one of the least important security issues related to e-mail.

E-mail is the most common delivery mechanism for viruses, *worms,* Trojan horses, documents with destructive macros, and other malicious code. The proliferation of support for various scripting languages, auto-download capabilities, and auto-execute features has transformed hyperlinks within the content of e-mail and attachments into a serious threat to every system.

E-mail offers little in the way of source verification. Spoofing the source address of e-mail is a simple process for even the novice hacker. E-mail headers can be modified at their source or at any point during transit. Furthermore, it is also possible to deliver e-mail directly to a user's inbox on an e-mail server by directly connecting to the e-mail server's SMTP port. And speaking of in-transit modification, there are no native integrity checks to ensure that a message was not altered between its source and destination.

E-mail itself can be used as an attack mechanism. When sufficient numbers of messages are directed to a single user's inbox or through a specific STMP server, a denial of service (DoS) can result. This attack is often called *mailbombing* and is simply a DoS performed by inundating a system with messages. The DoS can be the result of storage capacity consumption or processing capability utilization. Either way the result is the same: legitimate messages cannot be delivered.

Like e-mail flooding and malicious code attachments, unwanted e-mail can be considered an attack. Sending unwanted, inappropriate, or irrelevant messages is called spamming. Spamming is often little more than a nuisance, but it does waste system resources both locally and over the Internet. It is often difficult to stop spam because the source of the messages is usually spoofed.

E-Mail Security Solutions

Imposing security on e-mail is possible, but the efforts should be in tune with the value and confidentiality of the messages being exchanged. There are several protocols, services, and solutions available to add security to e-mail without requiring a complete overhaul of the entire Internet-based SMTP infrastructure. These include S/MIME, MOSS, PEM, and PGP We'll discuss S/MIME further in Chapter 10, "PKI and Cryptographic Applications."

S/MIME   *Secure Multipurpose Internet Mail Extensions (S/MIME)* offers authentication and privacy to e-mail through secured attachments. Authentication is provided through X.509 digital certificates. Privacy is provided through the use of Public Key Cryptography Standard (PKCS) encryption. Two types of messages can be formed using S/MIME: signed messages and enveloped messages. A signed message provides integrity and sender authentication. An enveloped message provides integrity, sender authentication, and confidentiality.

MOSS   *MIME Object Security Services (MOSS)* can provide authenticity, confidentiality, integrity, and nonrepudiation for e-mail messages. MOSS employs Message Digest 2 (MD2) and MD5 algorithms; Rivest, Shamir, and Adelman (RSA) public key; and Data Encryption Standard (DES) to provide authentication and encryption services.

PEM   *Privacy Enhanced Mail (PEM)* is an e-mail encryption mechanism that provides authentication, integrity, confidentiality, and nonrepudiation. PEM uses RSA, DES, and X.509.

PGP   *Pretty Good Privacy (PGP)* is a public-private key system that uses the IDEA algorithm to encrypt files and e-mail messages. PGP is not a standard but rather an independently developed product that has wide Internet grassroots support.

Through the use of these and other security mechanisms for e-mail and communication transmissions, many of the vulnerabilities can be reduced or eliminated. Digital signatures can help eliminate impersonation. Encryption of messages reduces eavesdropping. And the use of e-mail filters keep spamming and mailbombing to a minimum.

Blocking attachments at the e-mail gateway system on your network can ease the threats from malicious attachments. You can have a 100-percent no-attachments policy or block only those attachments that are known or suspected to be malicious, such as attachments with extensions that are used for executable and scripting files. If attachments are an essential part of your e-mail communications, you'll need to rely upon the training of your users and your antivirus tools for protection. Training users to avoid contact with suspicious or unexpected attachments greatly reduces the risk of malicious code transference via e-mail. Antivirus software is generally effective against known viruses, but it offers little protection against new or unknown viruses.

Facsimile Security

Facsimile (fax) communications are waning in popularity due to the widespread use of e-mail. Electronic documents are easily exchanged as attachments to e-mail. Printed documents are just as easy to scan and e-mail as they are to fax. However, faxing must still be addressed in your overall security plan. Most modems give users the ability to connect to a remote computer system and send and receive faxes. Many operating systems include built-in fax capabilities, and there are numerous fax products for computer systems. Faxes sent from a computer's fax/modem can be received by another computer or by a normal fax machine.

Even with declining use, faxes still represent a communications path that is vulnerable to attack. Like any other telephone communication, faxes can be intercepted and are susceptible to eavesdropping. If an entire fax transmission is recorded, it can be played back by another fax machine to extract the transmitted documents.

Some of the mechanisms that can be deployed to improve the security of faxes include fax encryptors, link encryption, activity logs, and exception reports. A fax encryptor gives a fax machine the capability to use an encryption protocol to scramble the outgoing fax signal. The use of an encryptor requires that the receiving fax machine support the same encryption protocol so it can decrypt the documents. Link encryption is the use of an encrypted communication path, like a VPN link or a secured telephone link, over which to transmit the fax. Activity logs and exception reports can be used to detect anomalies in fax activity that could be symptoms of attack.

In addition to the security of a fax transmission, it is also important to consider the security of a received fax. Faxes that are automatically printed may sit in the out tray for a long period of time, therefore making them subject to viewing by unintended recipients. Studies have shown that adding banners of CONFIDENTIAL, PRIVATE, and so on have the opposite effect by spurring the curiosity of passersby. So, disable automatic printing. Also, avoid using faxes employing ribbons or duplication cartridges that retain images of the printed faxes. Consider integrating your fax system with your network so you can e-mail faxes to intended recipients instead of printing them to paper.

Securing Voice Communications

The vulnerability of voice communication is tangentially related to IT system security. However, as voice communication solutions move on to the network by employing digital devices and *Voice over IP (VoIP)*, securing voice communications becomes an increasingly important issue. When voice communications occur over the IT infrastructure, it is important to implement mechanisms to provide for authentication and integrity. Confidentially should be maintained by employing an encryption service or protocol to protect the voice communications while in transit.

Normal *private branch exchange (PBX)* or *plain old telephone service (POTS)* voice communications are vulnerable to interception, eavesdropping, tapping, and other exploitations. Often, physical security is required to maintain control over voice communications within the confines of your organization's physical locations. Security of voice communications outside of your organization is typically the responsibility of the phone company from which you lease services. If voice communication vulnerabilities are an important issue for sustaining your security policy, you should deploy an encrypted communication mechanism and use it exclusively.

Social Engineering

Malicious individuals can exploit voice communications through a technique known as social engineering. *Social engineering* is a means by which an unknown person gains the trust of someone inside of your organization. Adept individuals can convince employees that they are associated with upper management, technical support, the help desk, and so on. Once convinced, the victim is often encouraged to make a change to their user account on the system, such as reset their password. Other attacks include instructing the victim to open specific e-mail attachments, launch an application, or connect to a specific URL. Whatever the actual activity is, it is usually directed toward opening a back door that the attacker can use to gain network access.

The people within an organization make it vulnerable to social engineering attacks. With just a little information or a few facts, it is often possible to get a victim to disclose confidential information or engage in irresponsible activity. Social engineering attacks exploit human characteristics such as a basic trust in others and laziness. Overlooking discrepancies, being distracted, following orders, assuming others know more than they actually do, wanting to help others, and fearing reprimands can also lead to attacks. Attackers are often able to bypass extensive physical and logical security controls because the victim opens an access pathway from the inside, effectively punching a hole in the secured perimeter.

The only way to protect against social engineering attacks is to teach users how to respond and interact with voice-only communications. Here are some guidelines:

- Always err on the side of caution whenever voice communications seem odd, out of place, or unexpected.

- Always request proof of identity. This can be a driver's license number or Social Security number, which can be easily verified. It could also take the form of having a person in the office that would recognize the caller's voice take the call. For example, if the caller claims to be a department manager, you could confirm his identity by asking his administrative assistant to take the call.

- Require call-back authorizations on all voice-only requests for network alterations or activities.
- Classify information (usernames, passwords, IP addresses, manager names, dial-in numbers, etc.) and clearly indicate which information can be discussed or even confirmed using voice communications.
- If privileged information is requested over the phone by an individual who should know that giving out that particular information over the phone is against the company's security policy, ask why the information is needed and verify their identity again. This incident should also be reported to the security administrator.
- Never give out or change passwords based on voice-only communications.
- Always securely dispose of or destroy all office documentation, especially any paperwork or disposable media that contains information about the IT infrastructure or its security mechanisms.

Fraud and Abuse

Another voice communication threat is PBX fraud and abuse. Many PBX systems can be exploited by malicious individuals to avoid toll charges and hide their identity. Malicious attackers known as phreakers abuse phone systems in much the same way that crackers abuse computer networks. Phreakers may be able to gain unauthorized access to personal voice mailboxes, redirect messages, block access, and redirect inbound and outbound calls. Countermeasures to PBX fraud and abuse include many of the same precautions you would employ to protect a typical computer network: logical or technical controls, administrative controls, and physical controls. Here are several key points to keep in mind when designing a PBX security solution:

- Consider replacing remote access or long-distance calling through the PBX with a credit card or calling card system.
- Restrict dial-in and dial-out features to only authorized individuals who require such functionality for their work tasks.
- For your dial-in modems, use unpublished phone numbers that are outside of the prefix block range of your voice numbers.
- Block or disable any unassigned access codes or accounts.
- Define an acceptable use policy and train users on how to properly use the system.
- Log and audit all activities on the PBX and review the audit trails for security and use violations.
- Disable maintenance modems and accounts.
- Change all default configurations, especially passwords and capabilities related to administrative or privileged features.

- Block remote calling (i.e., allowing a remote caller to dial in to your PBX and then dial-out again, thus directing all toll charges to the PBX host).

- Deploy Direct Inward System Access (DISA) technologies to reduce PBX fraud by external parties.

- Keep the system current with vendor/service provider updates.

Additionally, maintaining physical access control to all PBX connection centers, phone portals, or wiring closets prevents direct intrusion from onsite attackers.

Phreaking

Phreaking is a specific type of hacking or cracking directed toward the telephone system. Phreakers use various types of technology to circumvent the telephone system to make free long-distance calls, to alter the function of telephone service, to steal specialized services, and even to cause service disruptions. Some phreaker tools are actual devices, whereas others are just particular ways of using a normal telephone. No matter what the tool or technology actually is, phreaker tools are referred to as colored boxes (black box, red box, etc.). Over the years, there have been many box technologies that were developed and widely used by phreakers, but only a few of them still work against today's telephone systems based on packet-switching. Here are a few of the phreaker tools you need to recognize for the exam:

- Black boxes are used to manipulate line voltages to steal long-distance services. They are often just custom-built circuit boards with a battery and wire clips.

- Red boxes are used to simulate tones of coins being deposited into a pay phone. They are usually just small tape recorders.

- Blue boxes are used to simulate 2600Hz tones to interact directly with telephone network trunk systems (i.e., backbones). This could be a whistle, a tape recorder, or a digital tone generator.

- White boxes are used to control the phone system. A white box is a DTMF or dual-tone multifrequency generator (i.e., a keypad). It can be a custom-built device or one of the pieces of equipment that most telephone repair personnel use.

Cell phone security is a growing concern. Captured electronic serial numbers (ESNs) and mobile identification numbers (MINs) can be burned into blank phones to create clones. When a clone is used, the charges are billed to the original owner's cell phone account. Furthermore, conversations and data transmission can be intercepted using radio frequency scanners. Also, anyone in the immediate vicinity can overhear at least one side of the conversation. So, don't talk about confidential, private, or sensitive topics in public places.

Security Boundaries

A security boundary is the line of intersection between any two areas, subnets, or environments that have different security requirements or needs. A security boundary exists between a high-security area and a low-security one, such as between a LAN and the Internet. It is important to recognize the security boundaries both on your network and in the physical world. Once you identify a security boundary, you need to deploy controls and mechanisms to control the flow of information across those boundaries.

Divisions between security areas can take many forms. For example, objects may have different classifications. Each classification defines what functions can be performed by which subjects on which objects. The distinction between classifications is a security boundary.

Security boundaries also exist between the physical environment and the logical environment. To provide logical security, security mechanisms that are different than those used to provide physical security must be employed. Both must be present to provide a complete security structure and both must be addressed in a security policy. However, they are different and must be assessed as separate elements of a security solution.

Security boundaries, such as a perimeter between a protected area and an unprotected one, should always be clearly defined. It's important to state in a security policy the point at which control ends or begins and to identify that point in both the physical and logical environments. Logical security boundaries are the points where electronic communications interface with devices or services for which your organization is legally responsible. In most cases, that interface is clearly marked and unauthorized subjects are informed that they do not have access and that attempts to gain access will result in prosecution.

The security perimeter in the physical environment is often a reflection of the security perimeter of the logical environment. In most cases, the area over which the organization is legally responsible determines the reach of a security policy in the physical realm. This can be the walls of an office, the walls of a building, or the fence around a campus. In secured environments, warning signs are posted indicating that unauthorized access is prohibited and attempts to gain access will be thwarted and result in prosecution.

When transforming a security policy into actual controls, you must consider each environment and security boundary separately. Simply deduce what available security mechanisms would provide the most reasonable, cost-effective, and efficient solution for a specific environment and situation. However, all security mechanisms must be weighed against the value of the objects they are to protect. Deploying countermeasures that cost more than the value of the protected objects is unwarranted.

Network Attacks and Countermeasures

Communication systems are vulnerable to attacks in much the same way any other aspect of the IT infrastructure is vulnerable. Understanding the threats and the possible countermeasures is an important part of securing an environment. Any activity or condition that can cause harm to data, resources, or personnel must be addressed and mitigated if possible. Keep in mind that harm includes more than just destruction or damage; it also includes disclosure, access delay, denial of access, fraud, resource waste, resource abuse, and loss. Common threats against communication systems security include denial of service, eavesdropping, impersonation, replay, and modification.

Eavesdropping

As the name suggests, *eavesdropping* is simply listening to communication traffic for the purpose of duplicating it. The duplication can take the form of recording the data to a storage device or to an extraction program that dynamically attempts to extract the original content from the traffic stream. Once a copy of traffic content is in the hands of a cracker, they can often extract many forms of confidential information, such as usernames, passwords, process procedures, data, and so on. Eavesdropping usually requires physical access to the IT infrastructure to connect a physical recording device to an open port or cable splice or to install a software recording tool onto the system. Eavesdropping is often facilitated by the use of a network traffic capture or monitoring program or a protocol analyzer system (often called a sniffer). Eavesdropping devices and software are usually difficult to detect because they are used in passive attacks. When eavesdropping or wiretapping is transformed into altering or injecting communications, the attack is considered an active attack.

You can combat eavesdropping by maintaining physical access security to prevent unauthorized personnel from accessing your IT infrastructure. As for protecting communications that occur outside of your network or protecting against internal attackers, the use of encryption (such as IPSec or SSH) and one-time authentication methods (i.e., one-time pads or token devices) on communication traffic will greatly reduce the effectiveness and timeliness of eavesdropping.

The common threat of eavesdropping is one of the primary motivations to maintain reliable communications security. While data is in transit, it is often easier to intercept than when it is in storage. Furthermore, the lines of communication may lie outside of your organization's control. Thus, reliable means to secure data while in transit outside of your internal infrastructure is of utmost importance. Some of the common network health and communication reliability evaluation and management tools, such as sniffers, can be used for nefarious purposes and thus require stringent controls and oversight to prevent abuse.

Second-Tier Attacks

Impersonation, replay, and modification attacks are all called second-tier attacks. A *second-tier attack* is an assault that relies upon information or data gained from eavesdropping or other similar data-gathering techniques. In other words, it is an attack that is launched only after some other attack is completed.

Impersonation/Masquerading

Impersonation, or *masquerading*, is the act of pretending to be someone or something you are not to gain unauthorized access to a system. Impersonation is often possible through the capture of usernames and passwords or of session setup procedures for network services.

Some solutions to prevent impersonation include the use of one-time pads and token authentication systems, the use of Kerberos, and the use of encryption to increase the difficulty of extracting authentication credentials from network traffic.

Replay Attacks

Replay attacks are an offshoot of impersonation attacks and are made possible through capturing network traffic via eavesdropping. Replay attacks attempt to reestablish a communication session by replaying captured traffic against a system. They can be prevented by using one-time authentication mechanisms and sequenced session identification.

Modification Attacks

Modification is an attack in which captured packets are altered and then played against a system. Modified packets are designed to bypass the restrictions of improved authentication mechanisms and session sequencing. Countermeasures to modification replay attacks include the use of digital signature verifications and packet checksum verification.

Address Resolution Protocol (ARP)

The *Address Resolution Protocol (ARP)* is a subprotocol of the TCP/IP protocol suite that operates at the Network layer (layer 3). ARP is used to discover the MAC address of a system by polling using its IP address. ARP functions by broadcasting a request packet with the target IP address. The system with that IP address (or some other system that already has an ARP mapping for it) will reply with the associated MAC address. The discovered IP-to-MAC mapping is stored in the ARP cache and is used to direct packets.

ARP mappings can be attacked through spoofing. Spoofing provides false MAC addresses for requested IP-addressed systems to redirect traffic to alternate destinations. ARP attacks are often an element in man-in-the-middle attacks. Such attacks involve an intruder's system spoofing its MAC address against the destination's IP address into the source's ARP cache. All packets received form the source system are inspected and then forwarded on to the actual intended destination system. You can take measures to fight ARP attacks, such as defining static ARP mappings for critical systems, monitoring ARP caches for MAC-to-IP address mappings, or using an IDS to detect anomalies in system traffic and changes in ARP traffic.

DNS Spoofing

An attack related to ARP is known as DNS spoofing. DNS spoofing occurs when an attacker alters the domain-name-to-IP-address mappings in a DNS system to redirect traffic to a rogue system or to simply perform a denial of service against a system. Protections against DNS spoofing include allowing only authorized changes to DNS, restricting zone transfers, and logging all privileged DNS activity.

Hyperlink Spoofing

Yet another related attack is hyperlink spoofing. Hyperlink spoofing is similar to DNS spoofing in that it is used to redirect traffic to a rogue or imposter system or to simply divert traffic away from its intended destination. Hyperlink spoofing can take the form of DNS spoofing or can simply be an alteration of the hyperlink URLs in the HTML code of documents sent to clients. Hyperlink spoofing attacks are usually successful because most users do not verify the domain name in a URL via DNS, rather, they assume the hyperlink is valid and just click it.

Protections against hyperlink spoofing include the same precautions used against DNS spoofing as well as keeping your system patched and using the Internet with caution.

Summary

Maintaining control over communication pathways is essential to supporting confidentiality, integrity, and availability for network, voice, and other forms of communication. Numerous attacks are focused on intercepting, blocking, or otherwise interfering with the transfer of data from one location to another. Fortunately, there are also reasonable countermeasures to reduce or even eliminate many of these threats.

Tunneling is a means by which messages in one protocol can be transported over another network or communications system using a second protocol. Tunneling, otherwise known as encapsulation, can be combined with encryption to provide security for the transmitted message. VPNs are based on encrypted tunneling.

NAT is used to hide the internal structure of a private network as well as enable multiple internal clients to gain Internet access through a few public IP addresses. NAT is often a native feature of border security devices, such as firewalls, routers, gateways, and proxies.

In circuit switching, a dedicated physical pathway is created between the two communicating parties. Packet switching occurs when the message or communication is broken up into small segments (usually fixed-length packets depending on the protocols and technologies employed) and sent across the intermediary networks to the destination. Within packet-switching systems are two types of communication paths or virtual circuits. A virtual circuit is a logical pathway or circuit created over a packet-switched network between two specific endpoints. There are two types of virtual circuits: permanent virtual circuits (PVCs) and switched virtual circuits (SVCs).

WAN links or long-distance connection technologies can be divided into two primary categories: dedicated and nondedicated lines. A dedicated line connects two specific endpoints and only those two endpoints together. A nondedicated line is one that requires a connection to be established before data transmission can occur. A nondedicated line can be used to connect with any remote system that uses the same type of nondedicated line. WAN connection technologies include X.25, Frame Relay, ATM, SMDS, SDLC, HDLC, and HSSI.

When selecting or deploying security controls for network communications, there are numerous characteristics that you should evaluate in light of your circumstances, capabilities, and security policy. Security controls should be transparent to users. Hash totals and CRC checks can be used to verify message integrity. Record sequences are used to ensure sequence integrity of a transmission. Transmission logging helps detect communication abuses.

Basic Internet-based e-mail is insecure, but there are steps you can take to secure it. To secure e-mail, you should provide for nonrepudiation, restrict access to authorized users, make sure integrity is maintained, authenticate the message source, verify delivery, and even classify sensitive content. These issues must be addressed in a security policy before they can be implemented in a solution. They often take the form of acceptable use policies, access controls, privacy declarations, e-mail management procedures, and backup and retention policies.

E-mail is a common delivery mechanism for malicious code. Filtering attachments, using anti-virus software, and educating users are effective countermeasures against that kind of attack. E-mail spamming or flooding is a form of denial of service, which can be deterred through filters and IDSs. E-mail security can be improved using S/MIME, MOSS, PEM, and PGP.

Using encryption to protect the transmission of documents and prevent eavesdropping improves fax and voice security. Training users effectively is a useful countermeasure against social engineering attacks.

A security boundary can be the division between one secured area and another secured area, or it can be the division between a secured area and an unsecured area. Both must be addressed in a security policy.

Communication systems are vulnerable to many attacks, including denial of service, eaves-dropping, impersonation, replay, modification, and ARP attacks. Fortunately, effective countermeasures exist for each of these. PBX fraud and abuse and phone phreaking are problems that must also be addressed.

Exam Essentials

Know what tunneling is.   Tunneling is the encapsulation of a protocol-deliverable message within a second protocol. The second protocol often performs encryption to protect the message contents.

Understand VPNs.   VPNs are based on encrypted tunneling. They can offer authentication and data protection as a point-to-point solution. Common VPN protocols are PPTP, L2F, L2TP, and IPSec.

Be able to explain NAT.   NAT protects the addressing scheme of a private network, allows the use of the private IP addresses, and enables multiple internal clients to obtain Internet access through a few public IP addresses. NAT is supported by many security border devices, such as firewalls, routers, gateways, and proxies.

Understand the difference between packet switching and circuit switching.   In circuit switching, a dedicated physical pathway is created between the two communicating parties. Packet switching occurs when the message or communication is broken up into small segments and sent across the intermediary networks to the destination. Within packet-switching systems are two types of communication paths or virtual circuits: permanent virtual circuits (PVCs) and switched virtual circuits (SVCs).

Understand the difference between dedicated and nondedicated links.   A dedicated line is one that is indefinably and continually reserved for use by a specific customer. A dedicated line is always on and waiting for traffic to be transmitted over it. The link between the customer's LAN and the dedicated WAN link is always open and established. A dedicated line connects two specific endpoints and only those two endpoints. Examples of dedicated lines include T1, T3, E1, E3, and cable modems. A nondedicated line is one that requires a connection to be established before data transmission can occur. A nondedicated line can be used to connect with any remote system that uses the same type of nondedicated line. Examples of nondedicated lines include standard modems, DSL, and ISDN.

Know the various types of WAN technologies.   Know that most WAN technologies require a channel service unit/data service unit (CSU/DSU). These can be referred to as WAN switches. There are many types of carrier networks and WAN connection technologies, such as X.25, Frame Relay, ATM, and SMDS. Some WAN connection technologies require additional specialized protocols to support various types of specialized systems or devices. Three of these protocols are SDLC, HDLC, and HSSI.

Understand the differences between PPP and SLIP.   The Point-to-Point Protocol (PPP) is an encapsulation protocol designed to support the transmission of IP traffic over dial-up or point-to-point links. PPP includes a wide range of communication services, including assignment and management of IP addresses, management of synchronous communications, standardized encapsulation, multiplexing, link configuration, link quality testing, error detection, and feature or option negotiation (such as compression). PPP was originally designed to support CHAP and PAP for authentication. However, recent versions of PPP also support MS-CHAP, EAP, and SPAP. PPP replaced the Serial Line Internet Protocol (SLIP). SLIP offered no authentication, supported only half-duplex communications, had no error detection capabilities, and required manual link establishment and teardown.

Understand common characteristics of security controls.   Security controls should be transparent to users. Hash totals and CRC checks can be used to verify message integrity. Record sequences are used to ensure sequence integrity of a transmission. Transmission logging helps detect communication abuses.

Understand how e-mail security works.   Internet e-mail is based on SMTP, POP3, and IMAP. It is inherently insecure. It can be secured, but the methods used must be addressed in a security policy. E-mail security solutions include using S/MIME, MOSS, PEM, or PGP.

Know how fax security works.   Fax security is primarily based on using encrypted transmissions or encrypted communication lines to protect the faxed materials. The primary goal is to prevent interception. Activity logs and exception reports can be used to detect anomalies in fax activity that could be symptoms of attack.

Know the threats associated with PBX systems and the countermeasures to PBX fraud. Countermeasures to PBX fraud and abuse include many of the same precautions you would employ to protect a typical computer network: logical or technical controls, administrative controls, and physical controls.

Recognize what a phreaker is.   Phreaking is a specific type of hacking or cracking in which various types of technology are used to circumvent the telephone system to make free long distance calls, to alter the function of telephone service, to steal specialized services, or even to cause service disruptions. Common tools of phreakers include black, red, blue, and white boxes.

Understand voice communications security.   Voice communications are vulnerable to many attacks, especially as voice communications become an important part of network services. Confidentiality can be obtained through the use of encrypted communications. Countermeasures must be deployed to protect against interception, eavesdropping, tapping, and other types of exploitation.

Be able to explain what social engineering is.   Social engineering is a means by which an unknown person gains the trust of someone inside of your organization by convincing employees that they are, for example, associated with upper management, technical support, or the help desk. The victim is often encouraged to make a change to their user account on the system, such as reset their password. The primary countermeasure for this sort of attack is user training.

Explain the concept of security boundaries.   A security boundary can be the division between one secured area and another secured area. It can also be the division between a secured area and an unsecured area. Both must be addressed in a security policy.

Understand the various attacks and countermeasures associated with communications security.   Communication systems are vulnerable to many attacks, including eavesdropping, impersonation, replay, modification, and ARP attacks. Be able to list effective countermeasures for each.

Review Questions

1. Which of the following is not true?

   A. Tunneling employs encapsulation.

   B. All tunneling uses encryption.

   C. Tunneling is used to transmit data over an intermediary network.

   D. Tunneling can be used to bypass firewalls, gateways, proxies, or other traffic control devices.

2. Tunnel connections can be established over all except for which of the following?

   A. WAN links

   B. LAN pathways

   C. Dial-up connections

   D. Stand-alone systems

3. What do most VPNs use to protect transmitted data?

   A. Obscurity

   B. Encryption

   C. Encapsulation

   D. Transmission logging

4. Which of the following is not an essential element of a VPN link?

   A. Tunneling

   B. Encapsulation

   C. Protocols

   D. Encryption

5. Which of the following cannot be linked over a VPN?

   A. Two distant LANs

   B. Two systems on the same LAN

   C. A system connected to the Internet and a LAN connected to the Internet

   D. Two systems without an intermediary network connection

6. Which of the following is not a VPN protocol?

   A. PPTP

   B. L2F

   C. SLIP

   D. IPSec

7. Which of the following VPN protocols do not offer encryption? (Choose all that apply.)

   A. L2F

   B. L2TP

   C. IPSec

   D. PPTP

8. At which OSI model layer does the IPSec protocol function?

   A. Data Link

   B. Transport

   C. Session

   D. Network

9. Which of the following is not defined in RFC 1918 as one of the private IP address ranges that are not routed on the Internet?

   A. 169.172.0.0–169.191.255.255

   B. 192.168.0.0–192.168.255.255

   C. 10.0.0.0–10.255.255.255

   D. 172.16.0.0–172.31.255.255

10. Which of the following is not a benefit of NAT?

    A. Hiding the internal IP addressing scheme

    B. Sharing a few public Internet addresses with a large number of internal clients

    C. Using the private IP addresses from RFC 1918 on an internal network

    D. Filtering network traffic to prevent brute force attacks

11. A significant benefit of a security control is when it goes unnoticed by users. What is this called?

    A. Invisibility

    B. Transparency

    C. Diversion

    D. Hiding in plain sight

12. When you're designing a security system for Internet-delivered e-mail, which of the following is least important?

    A. Nonrepudiation

    B. Availability

    C. Message integrity

    D. Access restriction

13. Which of the following is typically not an element that must be discussed with end users in regard to e-mail retention policies?

A. Privacy

B. Auditor review

C. Length of retainer

D. Backup method

14. What is it called when e-mail itself is used as an attack mechanism?

A. Masquerading

B. Mailbombing

C. Spoofing

D. Smurf attack

15. Why is spam so difficult to stop?

A. Filters are ineffective at blocking inbound messages.

B. The source address is usually spoofed.

C. It is an attack requiring little expertise.

D. Spam can cause denial of service attacks.

16. Which of the following security mechanisms for e-mail can provide two types of messages: signed and enveloped?

A. PEM

B. PGP

C. S/MIME

D. MOSS

17. In addition to maintaining an updated system and controlling physical access, which of the following is the most effective countermeasure against PBX fraud and abuse?

A. Encrypting communications

B. Changing default passwords

C. Using transmission logs

D. Taping and archiving all conversations

18. Which of the following can be used to bypass even the best physical and logical security mechanisms to gain access to a system?

A. Brute force attacks

B. Denial of service

C. Social engineering

D. Port scanning

19. Which of the following is not a denial of service attack?

    A. Exploiting a flaw in a program to consume 100 percent of the CPU

    B. Sending malformed packets to a system, causing it to freeze

    C. Performing a brute force attack against a known user account

    D. Sending thousands of e-mails to a single address

20. Which of the following is a digital end-to-end communications mechanism developed by telephone companies to support high-speed digital communications over the same equipment and infrastructure that is used to carry voice communications?

    A. ISDN

    B. Frame Relay

    C. SMDS

    D. ATM

Answers to Review Questions

1. B. Tunneling does not always use encryption. It does, however, employ encapsulation, is used to transmit data over an intermediary network, and is able to bypass firewalls, gateways, proxies, or other traffic control devices.

2. D. A stand-alone system has no need for tunneling because no communications between systems are occurring and no intermediary network is present.

3. B. Most VPNs use encryption to protect transmitted data. In and of themselves, obscurity, encapsulation, and transmission logging do not protect data as it is transmitted.

4. D. Encryption is not necessary for the connection to be considered a VPN, but it is recommended for the protection of that data.

5. D. An intermediary network connection is required for a VPN link to be established.

6. C. SLIP is a dial-up connection protocol, a forerunner of PPP. It is not a VPN protocol.

7. A, B. Layer 2 Forwarding (L2F) was developed by Cisco as a mutual authentication tunneling mechanism. However, L2F does not offer encryption. L2TP also lacks built-in encryption.

8. D. IPSec operates at the Network layer (layer 3).

9. A. The address range 169.172.0.0–169.191.255.255 is not listed in RFC 1918 as a public IP address range.

10. D. NAT does not protect against nor prevent brute force attacks.

11. B. When transparency is a characteristic of a service, security control, or access mechanism, it is unseen by users.

12. B. Although availability is a key aspect of security in general, it is the least important aspect of security systems for Internet-delivered e-mail.

13. D. The backup method is not an important factor to discuss with end users regarding e-mail retention.

14. B. Mailbombing is the use of e-mail as an attack mechanism. Flooding a system with messages causes a denial of service.

15. B. It is often difficult to stop spam because the source of the messages is usually spoofed.

16. C. Two types of messages can be formed using S/MIME: signed messages and enveloped messages. A signed message provides integrity and sender authentication. An enveloped message provides integrity, sender authentication, and confidentiality.

17. B. Changing default passwords on PBX systems provides the most effective increase in security.

18. C. Social engineering can often be used to bypass even the most effective physical and logical controls. Whatever the actual activity is that the attacker convinces the victim to perform, it is usually directed toward opening a back door that the attacker can use to gain access to the network.

19. C. A brute force attack is not considered a DoS.

20. A. ISDN, or Integrated Services Digital Network, is a digital end-to-end communications mechanism. ISDN was developed by telephone companies to support high-speed digital communications over the same equipment and infrastructure that is used to carry voice communications.

Chapter

5

Security Management Concepts and Principles

THE CISSP EXAM TOPICS COVERED IN THIS CHAPTER INCLUDE:

- ✓ Security Management Concepts and Principles
- ✓ Protection Mechanisms
- ✓ Change Control/Management
- ✓ Data Classification

The Security Management Practices domain of the Common Body of Knowledge (CBK) for the CISSP certification exam deals with the common elements of security solutions. These include elements essential to the design, implementation, and administration of security mechanisms.

This domain is discussed in this chapter and in Chapter 6, "Asset Value, Policies, and Roles." Be sure to read and study the materials from both chapters to ensure complete coverage of the essential material for the CISSP certification exam.

Security Management Concepts and Principles

Security management concepts and principles are inherent elements in a security policy and solution deployment. They define the basic parameters needed for a secure environment. They also define the goals and objectives that both policy designers and system implementers must achieve to create a secure solution. It is important for real-world security professionals, as well as CISSP exam students, to understand these items thoroughly.

The primary goals and objectives of security are contained within the *CIA Triad*. The CIA Triad is the name given to the three primary security principles: confidentiality, integrity, and availability. Security controls must address one or more of these three principles. Security controls are typically evaluated on whether or not they address all three of these core information security tenets. Vulnerabilities and risks are also evaluated based on the threat they pose against one or more of the CIA Triad principles. Thus, it is a good idea to be familiar with these principles and use them as guidelines and measuring sticks against which to judge all things related to security.

These three principles are considered the most important within the realm of security. However, how important each is to a specific organization depends upon the organization's security goals and requirements and on the extent to which its security might be threatened.

Confidentiality

The first principle from the CIA Triad is confidentiality. If a security mechanism offers *confidentiality,* it offers a high level of assurance that data, objects, or resources are not exposed to unauthorized subjects. If a threat exists against confidentiality, there is the possibility that unauthorized disclosure could take place.

In general, for confidentiality to be maintained on a network, data must be protected from unauthorized access, use, or disclosure while in storage, in process, and in transit. Unique and specific security controls are required for each of these states of data, resources, and objects to maintain confidentiality.

There are numerous attacks that focus on the violation of confidentiality. These include capturing network traffic and stealing password files as well as social engineering, port scanning, shoulder surfing, eavesdropping, sniffing, and so on.

Violations of confidentiality are not limited to directed intentional attacks. Many instances of unauthorized disclosure of sensitive or confidential information are due to human error, oversight, or ineptitude. Events that lead to confidentiality breaches include failing to properly encrypt a transmission, failing to fully authenticate a remote system before transferring data, leaving open otherwise secured access points, accessing malicious code that opens a back door, or even walking away from an access terminal while data is displayed on the monitor. Confidentiality violations can occur because of the actions of an end user or a system administrator. They can also occur due to an oversight in a security policy or a misconfigured security control.

There are numerous countermeasures to ensure confidentiality against possible threats. These include the use of *encryption*, network traffic padding, strict access control, rigorous authentication procedures, *data classification*, and extensive personnel training.

Confidentiality and integrity are dependent upon each other. Without object integrity, confidentiality cannot be maintained. Other concepts, conditions, and aspects of confidentiality include sensitivity, discretion, criticality, concealment, secrecy, privacy, seclusion, and isolation.

Integrity

The second principle from the CIA Triad is integrity. For integrity to be maintained, objects must retain their veracity and be intentionally modified by only authorized subjects. If a security mechanism offers integrity, it offers a high level of assurance that the data, objects, and resources are unaltered from their original protected state. This includes alterations occurring while the object is in storage, in transit, or in process. Thus, maintaining integrity means the object itself is not altered and the operating system and programming entities that manage and manipulate the object are not compromised.

Integrity can be examined from three perspectives:

- Unauthorized subjects should be prevented from making modifications.

- Authorized subjects should be prevented from making unauthorized modifications.

- Objects should be internally and externally consistent so that their data is a correct and true reflection of the real world and any relationship with any child, peer, or parent object is valid, consistent, and verifiable.

For integrity to be maintained on a system, controls must be in place to restrict access to data, objects, and resources. Additionally, activity logging should be employed to ensure that only authorized users are able to access their respective resources. Maintaining and validating object integrity across storage, transport, and processing requires numerous variations of controls and oversight.

There are numerous attacks that focus on the violation of integrity. These include viruses, logic bombs, unauthorized access, errors in coding and applications, malicious modification, intentional replacement, and system back doors.

As with confidentiality, integrity violations are not limited to intentional attacks. Many instances of unauthorized alteration of sensitive information are due to human error, oversight, or ineptitude. Events that lead to integrity breaches include accidentally deleting files; entering invalid data; altering configurations; including errors in commands, codes, and scripts; introducing a virus; and executing malicious code (such as a Trojan horse). Integrity violations can occur because of the actions of any user, including administrators. They can also occur due to an oversight in a security policy or a misconfigured security control.

There are numerous countermeasures to ensure integrity against possible threats. These include strict access control, rigorous authentication procedures, intrusion detection systems, object/data encryption, hash total verifications, interface restrictions, input/function checks, and extensive personnel training.

Integrity is dependent upon confidentiality. Without confidentiality, integrity cannot be maintained. Other concepts, conditions, and aspects of integrity include accuracy, truthfulness, authenticity, validity, nonrepudiation, accountability, responsibility, completeness, and comprehensiveness.

Availability

The third principle from the CIA Triad is *availability*, which means that authorized subjects are granted timely and uninterrupted access to objects. If a security mechanism offers availability, it offers a high level of assurance that the data, objects, and resources are accessible to authorized subjects. Availability includes efficient uninterrupted access to objects and prevention of denial of service (DoS) attacks. Availability also implies that the supporting infrastructure—including network services, communications, and access control mechanisms—is functional and allows authorized users to gain authorized access.

For availability to be maintained on a system, controls must be in place to ensure authorized access and an acceptable level of performance, to quickly handle interruptions, to provide for redundancy, to maintain reliable backups, and to prevent data loss or destruction.

There are numerous threats to availability. These include device failure, software errors, and environmental issues (heat, static, etc.). There are also some forms of attacks that focus on the violation of availability, including denial of service attacks, object destruction, and communications interruptions.

As with confidentiality and integrity, violations of availability are not limited to intentional attacks. Many instances of unauthorized alteration of sensitive information are due to human error, oversight, or ineptitude. Some events that lead to integrity breaches include accidentally deleting files, overutilizing a hardware or software component, under-allocating resources, and mislabeling or incorrectly classifying objects. Availability violations can occur because of the actions of any user, including administrators. They can also occur due to an oversight in a security policy or a misconfigured security control.

There are numerous countermeasures to ensure availability against possible threats. These include designing intermediary delivery systems properly, using access controls effectively, monitoring performance and network traffic, using firewalls and routers to prevent DoS attacks, implementing redundancy for critical systems, and maintaining and testing backup systems.

Availability is dependent upon both integrity and confidentiality. Without integrity and confidentiality, availability cannot be maintained. Other concepts, conditions, and aspects of availability include usability, accessibility, and timeliness.

Other Security Concepts

In addition to the CIA Triad, there is a plethora of other security-related concepts, principles, and tenets that should be considered and addressed when designing a security policy and deploying a security solution. This section discusses privacy, identification, authentication, authorization, accountability, nonrepudiation, and auditing.

Privacy

Privacy can be a difficult entity to define. The term is used frequently in numerous contexts without much quantification or qualification. Here are some possible partial definitions of privacy:

- Prevention of unauthorized access
- Freedom from unauthorized access to information deemed personal or confidential
- Freedom from being observed, monitored, or examined without consent or knowledge

When addressing privacy in the realm of IT, it usually becomes a balancing act between individual rights and the rights or activities of an organization. Some claim that individuals have the right to control whether or not information can be collected about them and what can be done with it. Others claim that any activity performed in public view, such as most activities performed over the Internet, can be monitored without the knowledge of or permission from the individuals being watched and that the information gathered from such monitoring can be used for whatever purposes an organization deems appropriate or desirable.

On one hand, protecting individuals from unwanted observation, direct marketing, and disclosure of private, personal, or confidential details is considered a worthy effort. Likewise, organizations profess that demographic studies, information gleaning, and focused marketing improve business models, reduce advertising waste, and save money for all parties.

Whatever your personal or organizational stance is on the issue of online privacy, it must be addressed in an organizational security policy. Privacy is an issue not just for external visitors to your online offerings, but also for your customers, employees, suppliers, and contractors. If you gather any type of information about any person or company, you must address privacy.

In most cases, especially when privacy is being violated or restricted, the individuals and companies must be informed; otherwise, you may face legal ramifications. Privacy issues must also be addressed when allowing or restricting personal use of e-mail, retaining e-mail, recording phone conversations, gathering information about surfing or spending habits, and so on.

Identification

Identification is the process by which a subject professes an identity and accountability is initiated. A subject must provide an identity to a system to start the process of authentication, authorization, and accountability. Providing an identity can be typing in a username; swiping a smart card; waving a token device; speaking a phrase; or positioning your face, hand, or finger for a camera or scanning device. Proving a process ID number also represents the identification process. Without an identity, a system has no way to correlate an authentication factor with the subject.

Once a subject has been identified (i.e., once the subject's identity has been recognized and verified), the identity is accountable for any further actions by that subject. IT systems track activity by identities, not by the subjects themselves. A computer doesn't know one human from another, but it does know that your user account is different from all other user accounts. A subject's identity is typically labeled as or considered to be public information.

Authentication

The process of verifying or testing that the claimed identity is valid is *authentication*. Authentication requires from the subject additional information that must exactly correspond to the identity indicated. The most common form of authentication is using a password. Authentication verifies the identity of the subject by comparing one or more factors against the database of valid identities (i.e., user accounts). The authentication factor used to verify identity is typically labeled as or considered to be private information. The capability of the subject and system to maintain the secrecy of the authentication factors for identities directly reflects the level of security of that system.

Identification and authentication are always used together as a single two-step process. Providing an identity is step one and providing the authentication factor(s) is step two. Without both, a subject cannot gain access to a system—neither element alone is useful.

There are several types of authentication information a subject can provide (e.g., something you know, something you have). Each authentication technique or factor has its unique benefits and drawbacks. Thus, it is important to evaluate each mechanism in light of the environment in which it will be deployed to determine viability. Authentication was discussed at length in Chapter 1, "Accountability and Access Control."

Authorization

Once a subject is authenticated, access must be authorized. The process of *authorization* ensures that the requested activity or access to an object is possible given the rights and privileges assigned to the authenticated identity. In most cases, the system evaluates an access control matrix that compares the subject, the object, and the intended activity. If the specific action is allowed, the subject is authorized. If the specific action is not allowed, the subject is not authorized.

Keep in mind that just because a subject has been identified and authenticated does not automatically mean they have been authorized. It is possible for a subject to be logged onto a network (i.e., identified and authenticated) but be blocked from accessing a file or printing to a printer (i.e., by not being authorized to perform that activity). Most network users are authorized to perform only a limited number of activities on a specific collection of resources. Identification and authentication are all-or-nothing aspects of access control. Authorization has a wide range of variations between all or nothing for each individual object within the environment. A user may be able to read a file but not delete it, print a document but not alter the print queue, or log on to a system but not access any resources.

Auditing

Auditing, or monitoring, is the programmatic means by which subjects are held accountable for their actions while authenticated on a system. Auditing is also the process by which unauthorized or abnormal activities are detected on a system. Auditing is recording activities of a subject and objects as well as recording the activities of core system functions that maintain the operating environment and the security mechanisms. The audit trails created by recording system events to logs can be used to evaluate the health and performance of a system. System crashes may indicate faulty programs, corrupt drivers, or intrusion attempts. The event logs leading up to a crash can often be used to discover the reason a system failed. Log files provide an audit trail for re-creating the history of an event, intrusion, or system failure. Auditing is needed to detect malicious actions by subjects, attempted intrusions, and system failures, and to reconstruct events, provide evidence for prosecution, and produce problem reports and analysis. Auditing is usually a native feature of an operating system and most applications and services. Thus, configuring the system to record information about specific types of events is fairly straightforward.

For more information on configuring and administrating auditing and logging, see Chapter 14, "Auditing and Monitoring."

Accountability

An organization's security policy can be properly enforced only if *accountability* is maintained. In other words, security can be maintained only if subjects are held accountable for their actions. Effective accountability relies upon the capability to prove a subject's identity and track their activities. Accountability is established by linking a human to the activities of an online identity through the security services and mechanisms of auditing, authorization, authentication, and identification.

Nonrepudiation

Nonrepudiation ensures that the subject of an activity or event cannot deny that the event occurred. Nonrepudiation prevents a subject from claiming not to have sent a message, not to have performed an action, or not to have been the cause of an event. It is made possible through identity, authentication, authorization, accountability, and auditing. Nonrepudiation can be established using digital certificates, session identifiers, transaction logs, and numerous other transactional and access control mechanisms.

Protection Mechanisms

Another aspect of security solution concepts and principles is the element of protection mechanisms. These are common characteristics of security controls. Not all security controls must have them, but many controls offer their protection for confidentiality, integrity, and availability through the use of these mechanisms.

Layering

Layering, also known as defense in depth, is simply the use of multiple controls in a series. No one specific control can protect against all possible threats. The use of a multilayered solution allows for numerous different and specific controls to be brought to bear against whatever threats come to pass. When security solutions are designed in layers, most threats are eliminated, mitigated, or thwarted.

Using layers in a series rather than in parallel is an important concept. Performing security restrictions in a series means to perform one after the other in a linear fashion. Only through a series configuration will each attack be scanned, evaluated, or mitigated by every security control. A single failure of a security control does not render the entire solution ineffective. If security controls were implemented in parallel, a threat could pass through a single checkpoint that did not address its particular malicious activity. Serial configurations are very narrow but very deep, whereas parallel configurations are very wide but very shallow. Parallel systems are useful in distributed computing applications, but parallelism is not a useful concept in the realm of security.

Think of physical entrances to buildings. A parallel configuration is used for shopping malls. There are many doors in many locations around the entire perimeter of the mall. A series configuration would most likely be used in a bank or an airport. A single entrance is provided and that entrance is actually several gateways or checkpoints that must be passed in sequential order to gain entry into active areas of the building.

Layering also includes the concept that networks comprise numerous separate entities, each with its own unique security controls and vulnerabilities. In an effective security solution, there is a synergy between all networked systems that creates a single security front. The use of separate security systems creates a layered security solution.

Abstraction

Abstraction is used for efficiency. Similar elements are put into groups, classes, or roles that are assigned security controls, restrictions, or permissions as a collective. Thus, the concept of abstraction is used when classifying objects or assigning roles to subjects. The concept of abstraction also includes the definition of object and subject types or of objects themselves (i.e., a data structure used to define a template for a class of entities). Abstraction is used to define what types of data an object can contain, what types of functions can be performed on or by that object, and what capabilities that object has. Abstraction simplifies security by enabling you to assign security controls to a group of objects collected by type or function.

Data Hiding

Data hiding is exactly what it sounds like: preventing data from being discovered or accessed by a subject. Keeping a database from being accessed by unauthorized visitors is a form of data hiding, as is restricting a subject at a lower classification level from accessing data at a higher classification level. Preventing an application from accessing hardware directly is also a form of data hiding. Data hiding is often a key element in security controls as well as in programming.

Encryption

Encryption is the art and science of hiding the meaning or intent of a communication from unintended recipients. Encryption can take many forms and be applied to every type of electronic communication, including text, audio, and video files, as well as applications themselves. Encryption is a very important element in security controls, especially in regard to the transmission of data between systems. There are various strengths of encryption, each of which is designed and/or appropriate for a specific use or purpose. Encryption is discussed at length in Chapters 9, "Cryptography and Private Key Algorithms," and 10, "PKI and Cryptographic Applications."

Change Control/Management

Another important aspect of security management is the control or management of change. Change in a secure environment can introduce loopholes, overlaps, missing objects, and oversights that can lead to new vulnerabilities. The only way to maintain security in the face of change is to systematically manage change. This usually involves extensive planning, testing, logging, auditing, and monitoring of activities related to security controls and mechanisms. The records of changes to an environment are then used to identify agents of change, whether those agents are objects, subjects, programs, communication pathways, or even the network itself.

The goal of *change management* is to ensure that any change does not lead to reduced or compromised security. Change management is also responsible for making it possible to roll back any change to a previous secured state. Change management is only a requirement for systems complying with the Information Technology Security Evaluation and Criteria (ITSEC) classifications of B2, B3, and A1. However, change management can be implemented on any system despite the level of security. Ultimately, change management improves the security of an environment by protecting implemented security from unintentional, tangential, or effected diminishments. While an important goal of change management is to prevent unwanted reductions in security, its primary purpose is to make all changes subject to detailed documentation and auditing and thus able to be reviewed and scrutinized by management.

Change management should be used to oversee alterations to every aspect of a system, including hardware configuration and OS and application software. Change management should be included in design, development, testing, evaluation, implementation, distribution, evolution, growth, ongoing operation, and modification. It requires a detailed inventory of every component and configuration. It also requires the collection and maintenance of complete documentation for every system component, from hardware to software and from configuration settings to security features.

The *change control* process of configuration or change management has several goals or requirements:

- Implement changes in a monitored and orderly manner. Changes are always controlled.

- A formalized testing process is included to verify that a change produces expected results.

- All changes can be reversed.
- Users are informed of changes before they occur to prevent loss of productivity.
- The effects of changes are systematically analyzed.
- Negative impact of changes on capabilities, functionality, and performance is minimized.

One example of a change management process is a *parallel run*, which is a type of new system deployment testing where the new system and the old system are run in parallel. Each major or significant user process is performed on each system simultaneously to ensure that the new system supports all required business functionality that the old system supported or provided.

Data Classification

Data classification is the primary means by which data is protected based on its need for secrecy, sensitivity, or confidentiality. It is inefficient to treat all data the same when designing and implementing a security system. Some data items need more security than others. Securing everything at a low security level means sensitive data is easily accessible. Securing everything at a high security level is too expensive and restricts access to unclassified, noncritical data. Data classification is used to determine how much effort, money, and resources are allocated to protect the data and control access to it.

The primary objective of data classification schemes is to formalize and stratify the process of securing data based on assigned labels of importance and sensitivity. Data classification is used to provide security mechanisms for the storage, processing, and transfer of data. It also addresses how data is removed from a system and destroyed.

The following are benefits of using a data classification scheme:

- It demonstrates an organization's commitment to protecting valuable resources and assets.
- It assists in identifying those assets that are most critical or valuable to the organization.
- It lends credence to the selection of protection mechanisms.
- It is often required for regulatory compliance or legal restrictions.
- It helps to define access levels, types of authorized uses, and parameters for declassification, and/or destruction of no longer valuable resources.

The criteria by which data is classified varies based on the organization performing the classification. However, there are numerous generalities that can be gleaned from common or standardized classification systems:

- Usefulness of the data
- Timeliness of the data
- Value or cost of the data
- Maturity or age of the data
- Lifetime of the data (or when it expires)

- Association with personnel
- Data disclosure damage assessment (i.e., how disclosure of the data would affect the organization)
- Data modification damage assessment (i.e., how modification of the data would affect the organization)
- National security implications of the data
- Authorized access to the data (i.e., who has access to the data)
- Restriction from the data (i.e., who is restricted from the data)
- Maintenance and monitoring of the data (i.e., who should maintain and monitor the data)
- Storage of the data

Using whatever criteria is appropriate for the organization, data is evaluated and an appropriate data classification label is assigned to it. In some cases, the label is added to the data object. In other cases, labeling is simply assigned by the placement of the data into a storage mechanism or behind a security protection mechanism.

To implement a classification scheme, there are seven major steps or phases that you must take:

1. Identify the custodian and define their responsibilities.

2. Specify the evaluation criteria of how the information will be classified and labeled.

3. Classify and label each resource. The owner conducts this step, but it should be reviewed by a supervisor.

4. Document any exceptions to the classification policy that are discovered and integrate them into the evaluation criteria.

5. Select the security controls that will be applied to each classification level to provide the necessary level of protection.

6. Specify the procedures for declassifying resources and the procedures for transferring custody of a resource to an external entity.

7. Create an enterprise-wide awareness program to instruct all personnel about the classification system.

Declassification is often overlooked when designing a classification system and documenting the usage procedures. Declassification is required once an asset no longer warrants or needs the protection of its currently assigned classification or sensitivity level. In other words, if the asset was new, it would be assigned a lower sensitivity label than it currently is assigned. When you fail to declassify assets as needed, you waste security resources and degrade the value and protection of the higher sensitivity levels.

The two common classification schemes are *government/military classification* and *commercial business/private sector classification*. There are five levels of government/military classification (listed highest to lowest):

Top secret   The highest level of classification. Unauthorized disclosure of top secret data will have drastic effects and cause grave damage to national security.

Secret   Used for data of a restricted nature. Unauthorized disclosure of data classified as secret will have significant effects and cause critical damage to national security.

Confidential   Used for data of a confidential nature. Unauthorized disclosure of data classified as confidential will have noticeable effects and cause serious damage to national security. This classification is used for all data between secret and sensitive but unclassified classifications.

Sensitive but unclassified   Used for data of a sensitive or private nature, but disclosure of this data would not cause significant damage.

Unclassified   The lowest level of classification. Used for data that is neither sensitive nor classified. Disclosure of unclassified data does not compromise confidentiality nor cause any noticeable damage.

An easy way to remember the names of the five levels of the government or military classification scheme in their correct order is with a memorization acronym: US Can Stop Terrorism. Notice that the five uppercase letters represent the five named classification levels and they appear in this phrase in the correct order from least secure on the left to most secure on the right (or bottom to top in the preceding list of items).

The classifications of confidential, secret, and top secret are collectively known or labeled as classified. Often, revealing the actual classification of data to unauthorized individuals is a violation of that data in and of itself. Thus, the term *classified* is generally used to refer to any data that is ranked above sensitive but unclassified. All classified data is exempt from the Freedom of Information Act as well as other laws and regulations. The U.S. military classification scheme is most concerned with the sensitivity of data and focuses on the protection of confidentiality (i.e., prevention of disclosure). You can roughly define each level or label of classification as to the level of damage that would be caused in the event of a confidentiality violation. Data from the Top Secret level would cause grave damage to national security, while data from the Unclassified level would not cause any serious damage to national or localized security.

There are four levels of commercial business/private sector classification (listed highest to lowest):

Confidential   The highest level of classification. Used for data that is extremely sensitive and for internal use only. A significant negative impact could occur for the company if confidential data is disclosed.

Private   Used for data that is of a private or personal nature and intended for internal use only. A significant negative impact could occur for the company or individuals if private data is disclosed.

Confidential and private data in a commercial business/private sector classification scheme both require roughly the same level of security protection. The real difference between the two labels is that confidential data is used for company data while private data is used only for data related to individuals, such as medical data.

Sensitive   Used for data that is more classified than public data. A negative impact could occur for the company if sensitive data is disclosed.

Public   The lowest level of classification. Used for all data that does not fit in one of the higher classifications. Its disclosure does not have a serious negative impact on the organization.

Another classification often used in the commercial business/private sector is proprietary. *Proprietary* data is a form of confidential information. If proprietary data is disclosed, it can have drastic affects on the competitive edge of an organization.

Summary

Security management concepts and principles are inherent elements in a security policy and in solution deployment. They define the basic parameters needed for a secure environment. They also define the goals and objectives that both policy designers and system implementers must achieve in order to create a secure solution. It is important for real-world security professionals as well as CISSP exam students to understand these items thoroughly.

The primary goals and objectives of security are contained within the CIA Triad: confidentiality, integrity, and availability. These three principles are considered the most important within the realm of security. Their importance to an organization depends on the organization's security goals and requirements and on how much of a threat to security exists in its environment.

The first principle from the CIA Triad is confidentiality, the principle that objects are not disclosed to unauthorized subjects. Security mechanisms that offer confidentiality offer a high level of assurance that data, objects, or resources are not exposed to unauthorized subjects. If a threat exists against confidentiality, there is the possibility that unauthorized disclosure could take place.

The second principle from the CIA Triad is integrity, the principle that objects retain their veracity and are intentionally modified by only authorized subjects. Security mechanisms that offer integrity offer a high level of assurance that the data, objects, and resources are unaltered from their original protected state. This includes alterations occurring while the object is in storage, in transit, or in process. Maintaining integrity means the object itself is not altered, nor are the operating system and programming entities that manage and manipulate the object compromised.

The third principle from the CIA Triad is availability, the principle that authorized subjects are granted timely and uninterrupted access to objects. Security mechanisms that offer availability offer a high level of assurance that the data, objects, and resources are accessible by authorized subjects. Availability includes efficient uninterrupted access to objects and prevention of denial of service attacks. It also implies that the supporting infrastructure is functional and allows authorized users to gain authorized access.

Other security-related concepts, principles, and tenets that should be considered and addressed when designing a security policy and deploying a security solution are privacy, identification, authentication, authorization, accountability, nonrepudiation, and auditing.

Yet another aspect of security solution concepts and principles is the elements of protection mechanisms: layering, abstraction, data hiding, and the use of encryption. These are common characteristics of security controls, and although not all security controls must have them, many controls use these mechanisms to protect confidentiality, integrity, and availability

The control or management of change is an important aspect of security management practices. When a secure environment is changed, loopholes, overlaps, missing objects, and oversights can lead to new vulnerabilities. You can, however, maintain security by systematically managing change. This typically involves extensive logging, auditing, and monitoring of activities related to security controls and security mechanisms. The resulting data is then used to identify agents of change, whether objects, subjects, programs, communication pathways, or even the network itself.

Data classification is the primary means by which data is protected based on its secrecy, sensitivity, or confidentiality. Because some data items need more security than others, it is inefficient to treat all data the same when designing and implementing a security system. If everything is secured at a low security level, sensitive data is easily accessible, but securing everything at a high security level is too expensive and restricts access to unclassified, noncritical data. Data classification is used to determine how much effort, money, and resources are allocated to protect the data and control access to it.

Exam Essentials

Understand the CIA Triad element confidentiality.   Confidentiality is the principle that objects are not disclosed to unauthorized subjects. Know why it is important, mechanisms that support it, attacks that focus on it, and effective countermeasures.

Understand the CIA Triad element integrity.   Integrity is the principle that objects retain their veracity and are intentionally modified by only authorized subjects. Know why it is important, mechanisms that support it, attacks that focus on it, and effective countermeasures.

Understand the CIA Triad element availability.   Availability is the principle that authorized subjects are granted timely and uninterrupted access to objects. Know why it is important, mechanisms that support it, attacks that focus on it, and effective countermeasures.

Know how privacy fits into the realm of IT security.   Know the multiple meanings/definitions of privacy, why it is important to protect, and the issues surrounding it, especially in a work environment.

Be able to explain how identification works.   Identification is the process by which a subject professes an identity and accountability is initiated. A subject must provide an identity to a system to start the process of authentication, authorization, and accountability.

Understand the process of authentication.   The process of verifying or testing that a claimed identity is valid is authentication. Authentication requires information from the subject that must exactly correspond to the identity indicated.

Know how authorization fits into a security plan.   Once a subject is authenticated, its access must be authorized. The process of authorization ensures that the requested activity or object access is possible given the rights and privileges assigned to the authenticated identity.

Be able to explain the auditing process. Auditing, or monitoring, is the programmatic means by which subjects are held accountable for their actions while authenticated on a system. Auditing is also the process by which unauthorized or abnormal activities are detected on a system. Auditing is needed to detect malicious actions by subjects, attempted intrusions, and system failures and to reconstruct events, provide evidence for prosecution, and produce problem reports and analysis.

Understand the importance of accountability. An organization's security policy can be properly enforced only if accountability is maintained. In other words, security can be maintained only if subjects are held accountable for their actions. Effective accountability relies upon the capability to prove a subject's identity and track their activities.

Be able to explain nonrepudiation. Nonrepudiation ensures that the subject of an activity or event cannot deny that the event occurred. It prevents a subject from claiming not to have sent a message, not to have performed an action, or not to have been the cause of an event.

Know how layering simplifies security. Layering is simply the use of multiple controls in series. Using a multilayered solution allows for numerous different and specific controls to be brought to bear against whatever threats come to pass.

Be able to explain the concept of abstraction. Abstraction is used to collect similar elements into groups, classes, or roles that are assigned security controls, restrictions, or permissions as a collective. It adds efficiency to carrying out a security plan.

Understand data hiding. Data hiding is exactly what it sounds like: preventing data from being discovered or accessed by a subject. It is often a key element in security controls as well as in programming.

Understand the need for encryption. Encryption is the art and science of hiding the meaning or intent of a communication from unintended recipients. It can take many forms and be applied to every type of electronic communication, including text, audio, and video files, as well as programs themselves. Encryption is a very important element in security controls, especially in regard to the transmission of data between systems.

Be able to explain the concepts of change control and change management. Change in a secure environment can introduce loopholes, overlaps, missing objects, and oversights that can lead to new vulnerabilities. The only way to maintain security in the face of change is to systematically manage change.

Know why and how data is classified. Data is classified to simplify the process of assigning security controls to groups of objects rather than to individual objects. The two common classification schemes are government/military and commercial business/private sector. Know the five levels of government/military classification and the four levels of commercial business/private sector classification.

Understand the importance of declassification. Declassification is required once an asset no longer warrants the protection of its currently assigned classification or sensitivity level.

Review Questions

1. Which of the following contains the primary goals and objectives of security?

   A. A network's border perimeter

   B. The CIA Triad

   C. A stand-alone system

   D. The Internet

2. Vulnerabilities and risks are evaluated based on their threats against which of the following?

   A. One or more of the CIA Triad principles

   B. Data usefulness

   C. Due care

   D. Extent of liability

3. Which of the following is a principle of the CIA Triad that means authorized subjects are granted timely and uninterrupted access to objects?

   A. Identification

   B. Availability

   C. Encryption

   D. Layering

4. Which of the following is not considered a violation of confidentiality?

   A. Stealing passwords

   B. Eavesdropping

   C. Hardware destruction

   D. Social engineering

5. Which of the following is not true?

   A. Violations of confidentiality include human error.

   B. Violations of confidentiality include management oversight.

   C. Violations of confidentiality are limited to direct intentional attacks.

   D. Violations of confidentiality can occur when a transmission is not properly encrypted.

6. Confidentiality is dependent upon which of the following?

   A. Accountability

   B. Availability

   C. Nonrepudiation

   D. Integrity

7. If a security mechanism offers availability, then it offers a high level of assurance that the data, objects, and resources are _____ by authorized subjects.

   A. Controlled

   B. Audited

   C. Accessible

   D. Repudiated

8. Which of the following describes the freedom from being observed, monitored, or examined without consent or knowledge?

   A. Integrity

   B. Privacy

   C. Authentication

   D. Accountability

9. All but which of the following items require awareness for all individuals affected?

   A. The restriction of personal e-mail

   B. Recording phone conversations

   C. Gathering information about surfing habits

   D. The backup mechanism used to retain e-mail messages

10. Which of the following is typically not used as an identification factor?

   A. Username

   B. Smart card swipe

   C. Fingerprint scan

   D. A challenge/response token device

11. What ensures that the subject of an activity or event cannot deny that the event occurred?

   A. CIA Triad

   B. Abstraction

   C. Nonrepudiation

   D. Hash totals

12. Which of the following is the most important and distinctive concept in relation to layered security?

   A. Multiple

   B. Series

   C. Parallel

   D. Filter

13. Which of the following is not considered an example of data hiding?

   A. Preventing an authorized reader of an object from deleting that object

   B. Keeping a database from being accessed by unauthorized visitors

   C. Restricting a subject at a lower classification level from accessing data at a higher classification level

   D. Preventing an application from accessing hardware directly

14. What is the primary goal of change management?

   A. Maintaining documentation

   B. Keeping users informed of changes

   C. Allowing rollback of failed changes

   D. Preventing security compromises

15. What is the primary objective of data classification schemes?

   A. To control access to objects for authorized subjects

   B. To formalize and stratify the process of securing data based on assigned labels of importance and sensitivity

   C. To establish a transaction trail for auditing accountability

   D. To manipulate access controls to provide for the most efficient means to grant or restrict functionality

16. Which of the following is typically not a characteristic considered when classifying data?

   A. Value

   B. Size of object

   C. Useful lifetime

   D. National security implications

17. What are the two common data classification schemes?

   A. Military and private sector

   B. Personal and government

   C. Private sector and unrestricted sector

   D. Classified and unclassified

18. Which of the following is the lowest military data classification for classified data?

   A. Sensitive

   B. Secret

   C. Sensitive but unclassified

   D. Private

19. Which commercial business/private sector data classification is used to control information about individuals within an organization?

A. Confidential

B. Private

C. Sensitive

D. Proprietary

20. Data classifications are used to focus security controls over all but which of the following?

A. Storage

B. Processing

C. Layering

D. Transfer

Answers to Review Questions

1. B. The primary goals and objectives of security are confidentiality, integrity, and availability, commonly referred to as the CIA Triad.

2. A. Vulnerabilities and risks are evaluated based on their threats against one or more of the CIA Triad principles.

3. B. Availability means that authorized subjects are granted timely and uninterrupted access to objects.

4. C. Hardware destruction is a violation of availability and possibly integrity. Violations of confidentiality include capturing network traffic, stealing password files, social engineering, port scanning, shoulder surfing, eavesdropping, and sniffing.

5. C. Violations of confidentiality are not limited to direct intentional attacks. Many instances of unauthorized disclosure of sensitive or confidential information are due to human error, oversight, or ineptitude.

6. D. Without integrity, confidentiality cannot be maintained.

7. C. Accessibility of data, objects, and resources is the goal of availability. If a security mechanism offers availability, then it is highly likely that the data, objects, and resources are accessible by authorized subjects.

8. B. Privacy is freedom from being observed, monitored, or examined without consent or knowledge.

9. D. Users should be aware that e-mail messages are retained, but the backup mechanism used to perform this operation does not need to be disclosed to them.

10. D. A challenge/response token device is almost exclusively used as an authentication factor, not an identification factor.

11. C. Nonrepudiation ensures that the subject of an activity or event cannot deny that the event occurred.

12. B. Layering is the deployment of multiple security mechanisms in a series. When security restrictions are performed in a series, they are performed one after the other in a linear fashion. Therefore, a single failure of a security control does not render the entire solution ineffective.

13. A. Preventing an authorized reader of an object from deleting that object is just an access control, not data hiding. If you can read an object, it is not hidden from you.

14. D. The prevention of security compromises is the primary goal of change management.

15. B. The primary objective of data classification schemes is to formalize and stratify the process of securing data based on assigned labels of importance and sensitivity.

16. B. Size is not a criteria for establishing data classification. When classifying an object, you should take value, lifetime, and security implications into consideration.

17. A. Military (or government) and private sector (or commercial business) are the two common data classification schemes.

18. B. Of the options listed, secret is the lowest classified military data classification.

19. B. The commercial business/private sector data classification of private is used to protect information about individuals.

20. C. Layering is a core aspect of security mechanisms, but it is not a focus of data classifications.

Chapter
6

Asset Value, Policies, and Roles

THE CISSP EXAM TOPICS COVERED IN THIS CHAPTER INCLUDE:

- ✓ Employment Policies and Practices
- ✓ Roles and Responsibilities
- ✓ Policies, Standards, Guidelines, and Procedures
- ✓ Risk Management
- ✓ Security Awareness Training
- ✓ Security Management Planning

The Security Management Practices domain of the Common Body of Knowledge (CBK) for the CISSP certification exam deals with hiring practices, security roles, formalizing security structure, risk management, awareness training, and management planning.

Because of the complexity and importance of hardware and software controls, security management for employees is often overlooked in overall security planning. This chapter explores the human side of security, from establishing secure hiring practices and job descriptions to developing an employee infrastructure. Additionally, employee training, management, and termination practices are considered an integral part of creating a secure environment. Finally, we examine how to assess and manage security risks.

Employment Policies and Practices

Humans are the weakest element in any security solution. No matter what physical or logical controls are deployed, humans can discover ways to avoid them, circumvent or subvert them, or disable them. Thus, it is important to take into account the humanity of your users when designing and deploying security solutions for your environment.

Issues, problems, and compromises related to humans occur at all stages of a security solution development. This is because humans are involved throughout the development, deployment, and ongoing administration of any solution. Therefore, you must evaluate the effect users, designers, programmers, developers, managers, and implementers have on the process.

Security Management for Employees

Hiring new staff typically involves several distinct steps: creating a job description, setting a classification for the job, screening candidates, and hiring and training the one best suited for the job. Without a *job description*, there is no consensus on what type of individual should be hired. Personnel should be added to an organization because there is a need for their specific skills and experience. Any job description for any position within an organization should address relevant security issues. You must consider items such as whether the position requires handling of sensitive material or access to classified information. In effect, the job description defines the roles to which an *employee* needs to be assigned to perform their work tasks. The job description should define the type and extent of access the position requires on the secured network. Once these issues have been resolved, assigning a security classification to the job description is fairly standard.

Important elements in constructing a job description include separation of duties, job responsibilities, and job rotation.

Separation of duties   *Separation of duties* is the security concept in which critical, significant, and sensitive work tasks are divided among several individuals. This prevents any one person from having the ability to undermine or subvert vital security mechanisms. This unwanted activity is called collusion.

Job responsibilities   *Job responsibilities* are the specific work tasks an employee is required to perform on a regular basis. Depending on their responsibilities, employees require access to various objects, resources, and services. On a secured network, users must be granted access privileges for those elements related to their work tasks. To maintain the greatest security, access should be assigned according to the principle of least privilege. The principle of least privilege states that in a secured environment, users should be granted the minimum amount of access necessary for them to complete their required work tasks or job responsibilities.

Job rotation   *Job rotation,* or rotating employees among numerous job positions, is simply a means by which an organization improves its overall security. Job rotation serves two functions. First, it provides a type of knowledge redundancy. When multiple employees are each capable of performing the work tasks required by several job positions, the organization is less likely to experience serious downtime or loss in productivity if an illness or other incident keeps one or more employees out of work for an extended period of time. Second, moving personnel around reduces the risk of fraud, data modification, theft, sabotage, and misuse of information. The longer a person works in a specific position, the more likely they are to be assigned additional work tasks and thus expand their privileges and access. As a person becomes increasingly familiar with their work tasks, they may abuse their privileges for personal gain or malice. If misuse or abuse is committed by one employee, it will be easier to detect by another employee who knows the job position and work responsibilities. Therefore, job rotation also provides a form of peer auditing.

When multiple people work together to perpetrate a crime, it's called *collusion*. The likelihood that a coworker will be willing to collaborate on an illegal or abusive scheme is reduced due to the higher risk of detection the combination of separation of duties, restricted job responsibilities, and job rotation provides.

Job descriptions are not used exclusively for the hiring process; they should be maintained throughout the life of the organization. Only through detailed job descriptions can a comparison be made between what a person should be responsible for and what they actually are responsible for. It is a managerial task to ensure that job descriptions overlap as little as possible and that one worker's responsibilities do not drift or encroach on those of another's. Likewise, managers should audit privilege assignments to ensure that workers do not obtain access that is not strictly required for them to accomplish their work tasks.

Screening and Background Checks

Screening candidates for a specific position is based on the sensitivity and classification defined by the job description. The sensitivity and classification of a specific position is dependent upon the level of harm that could be caused by accidental or intentional violations of security by a person in the position. Thus, the thoroughness of the screening process should reflect the security of the position to be filled.

Background checks and security clearances are essential elements in proving that a candidate is adequate, qualified, and trustworthy for a secured position. Background checks include obtaining a candidate's work and educational history; checking references; interviewing colleagues, neighbors, and friends; checking police and government records for arrests or illegal activities; verifying identity through fingerprints, driver's license, and birth certificate; and holding a personal interview. This process could also include a polygraph test, drug testing, and personality testing/evaluation.

Creating Employment Agreements

When a new employee is hired, they should sign an *employment agreement*. Such a document outlines the rules and restrictions of the organization, the security policy, the acceptable use and activities policies, details of the job description, violations and consequences, and the length of time the position is to be filled by the employee. Many of these items may be separate documents. In such a case, the employment agreement is used to verify that the employment candidate has read and understood the associated documentation for their perspective job position.

In addition to employment agreements, there may be other security-related documentation that must be addressed. One common document is a *nondisclosure agreement (NDA)*. An NDA is used to protect the confidential information within an organization from being disclosed by a former employee. When a person signs an NDA, they agree not to disclose any information that is defined as confidential to anyone outside of the organization. Violations of an NDA are often met with strict penalties.

Throughout the employment lifetime of personnel, managers should regularly audit the job descriptions, work tasks, privileges, and so on for every staff member. It is common for work tasks and privileges to drift over time. This can cause some tasks to be overlooked and others to be performed multiple times. Drifting can also result in security violations. Regularly reviewing the boundaries defined by each job description in relation to what is actually occurring aids in keeping security violations to a minimum. A key part of this review process is mandatory vacations. In many secured environments, *mandatory vacations* of one to two weeks are used to audit and verify the work tasks and privileges of employees. This removes the employee from the work environment and places a different worker in their position. This often results in easy detection of abuse, fraud, or negligence.

Employee Termination

When an employee must be terminated, there are numerous issues that must be addressed. A termination procedure *policy* is essential to maintaining a secure environment even in the face of a disgruntled employee who must be removed from the organization. The reactions of terminated employees can range from understanding acceptance to violent, destructive rage. A sensible procedure for handling terminations must be designed and implemented to reduce incidents.

The termination of an employee should be handled in a private and respectful manner. However, this does not mean that precautions should not be taken. Terminations should take place with at least one witness, preferably a higher-level manager and/or a security guard. Once the employee has been informed of their release, they should be escorted off the premises immediately. Before the employee is released, all organization-specific identification, access, or security badges as well as cards, keys, and access tokens should be collected.

When possible, an *exit interview* should be performed. However, this typically depends upon the mental state of the employee upon release and numerous other factors. If an exit interview is unfeasible immediately upon termination, it should be conducted as soon as possible. The primary purpose of the exit interview is to review the liabilities and restrictions placed on the former employee based on the employment agreement, nondisclosure agreement, and any other security-related documentation.

The following list includes some other issues that should be handled as soon as possible:

- Make sure the employee returns any organizational equipment or supplies from their vehicle or home.

- Remove or disable the employee's network user account.

- Notify human resources to issue a final paycheck, pay any unused vacation time, and terminate benefit coverage.

- Arrange for a member of the security department to accompany the released employee while they gather their personal belongings from the work area.

In most cases, you should disable or remove an employee's system access at the same time or just before they are notified of being terminated. This is especially true if that employee is capable of accessing confidential data or has the expertise or access to alter or damage data or services. Failing to restrict released employees' activities can leave your organization open to a wide range of vulnerabilities, including theft and destruction of both physical property and logical data.

Security Roles

A *security role* is the part an individual plays in the overall scheme of security implementation and administration within an organization. Security roles are not necessarily prescribed in job descriptions because they are not always distinct or static. Familiarity with security roles will help in establishing a communications and support structure within an organization. This structure will enable the deployment and enforcement of the security policy. (The following six roles are presented in the logical order in which they appear in a secured environment).

Senior manager   The *organizational owner* (senior manager) role is assigned to the person who is ultimately responsible for the security maintained by an organization and who should be most concerned about the protection of its assets. The senior manager must sign off on all policy issues. In fact, all activities must be approved by and signed off on by the senior manager before they can be carried out. There is no effective security policy if the senior manager does not authorize and support it. The senior manager's endorsement of the security policy indicates the accepted ownership of the implemented security within the organization. The senior manager is the person who will be held liable for the overall success or failure of a security solution and is responsible for exercising *due care* and *due diligence* in establishing security for an organization. Even though senior managers are ultimately responsible for security, they rarely implement security solutions. In most cases, that responsibility is delegated to security professionals within the organization.

Security professional   The *security professional*, information security officer, InfoSec officer, or CIRT (Computer Incident Response Team) role is assigned to a trained and experienced network, systems, and security engineer who is responsible for following the directives mandated by *senior management*. The security professional has the functional responsibility for security, for writing the security policy and implementing it. The role of security professional can be labeled as an IS/IT function role. The security professional role is often filled by a team that is responsible for designing and implementing security solutions based on the approved security policy. Security professionals are not decision makers; they are implementers. All decisions must be left to the senior manager.

Data owner   The *data owner* role is assigned to the person who is responsible for classifying information for placement and protection within the security solution. The data owner is typically a high-level manager who is ultimately responsible for data protection. However, the data owner usually delegates the responsibility of the actual data-management tasks to a data custodian.

Data custodian   The *data custodian* role is assigned to the user who is responsible for the tasks of implementing the prescribed protection defined by the security policy and *upper management*. The data custodian performs all activities necessary to provide adequate protection for the CIA of data and to fulfill the requirements and responsibilities delegated from upper management. These activities can include performing and testing backups, validating data integrity, deploying security solutions, and managing data storage based on classification.

User   The *user* (end user or operator) role is assigned to any person who has access to the secured system. A user's access is tied to their work tasks and is limited so they have only enough access to perform the tasks necessary for their job position (principle of least privilege). Users are responsible for understanding and upholding the security policy of an organization by following prescribed operational procedures and operating within defined security parameters.

Auditor   Another role is that of an *auditor*. An auditor is responsible for testing and verifying that the security policy is properly implemented and the derived security solutions are adequate. The auditor role may be assigned to a security professional or a trained user. The auditor produces compliance and effectiveness reports that are reviewed by the senior manager. Issues discovered through these reports are transformed into new directives assigned by the senior manager to security professionals or data custodians. However, the auditor is listed as the last or final role since the auditor needs users or operators to be working in an environment as the source of activity to audit and monitor.

All of these roles serve an important function within a secured environment. They are useful for identifying liability and responsibility as well as for identifying the hierarchical management and delegation scheme.

Security Management Planning

Security management planning ensures proper creation, implementation, and enforcement of a security policy. The most effective way to tackle security management planning is using a top-down approach. Upper, or senior, management is responsible for initiating and defining policies for the organization. Security policies provide direction for the lower levels of the organization's hierarchy. It is the responsibility of *middle management* to flesh out the security policy into standards, baselines, guidelines, and procedures. The operational managers or security professionals must then implement the configurations prescribed in the security management documentation. Finally, the end users must comply with all the security policies of the organization.

 The opposite of the top-down approach is the bottom-up approach. In a bottom-up approach environment, the IT staff makes security decisions directly without input from senior management. The bottom-up approach is rarely utilized in organizations and is considered problematic in the IT industry.

Security management is a responsibility of upper management, not of the IT staff, and is considered a business operations issue rather than an IT administration issue. The team or department responsible for security within an organization should be autonomous from all other departments. The InfoSec team should be lead by a designated chief security officer (CSO) who must report directly to senior management. Placing the autonomy of the CSO and his team outside of the typical hierarchical structure in an organization can improve security management across the entire organization. It also helps to avoid cross-department and internal political issues.

Elements of security management planning include defining security roles; prescribing how security will be managed, who will be responsible for security, and how security will be tested for effectiveness; developing security policies; performing risk analysis; and requiring security education for employees. These responsibilities are guided through the development of management plans.

The best laid security plan is useless without one key factor: approval by senior management. Without senior management's approval of and commitment to the security policy, the policy will not succeed. It is the responsibility of the policy development team to educate senior management sufficiently so it understands the risks, liabilities, and exposures that remain even after security measures prescribed in the policy are deployed. Developing and implementing a security policy is evidence of due care and due diligence on the part of senior management. If a company does not practice due care and due diligence, managers can be held liable for negligence and held accountable for both asset and financial losses.

A security management planning team should develop three types of plans:

Strategic plan   A *strategic plan* is a long-term plan that is fairly stable. It defines the organization's goals, mission, and objectives. It's useful for about five years if it is maintained and updated annually. The strategic plan also serves as the planning horizon. Long-term goals and visions for the future are discussed in a strategic plan. A strategic plan should include a risk assessment.

Tactical plan   The *tactical plan* is a midterm plan developed to provide more details on accomplishing the goals set forth in the strategic plan. A tactical plan is typically useful for about a year and often prescribes and schedules the tasks necessary to accomplish organizational goals. Some examples of tactical plans include project plans, acquisition plans, hiring plans, budget plans, maintenance plans, support plans, and system development plans.

Operational plan   An *operational plans* is a short-term and highly detailed plan based on the strategic and tactical plans. It is valid or useful only for a short time. Operational plans must be updated often (such as monthly or quarterly) to retain compliance with tactical plans. Operational plans are detailed plans that spell out how to accomplish the various goals of the organization. They include resource allotments, budgetary requirements, staffing assignments, scheduling, and step-by-step or implementation procedures. Operational plans include details on how the implementation processes are in compliance with the organization's security policy. Examples of operational plans include training plans, system deployment plans, and product design plans.

Security is a continuous process. Thus, the activity of security management planning may have a definitive initiation point, but its tasks and work is never fully accomplished or complete. Effective security plans focus attention on specific and achievable objectives, anticipate change and potential problems, and serve as a basis for decision making for the entire organization. Security documentation should be concrete, well defined, and clearly stated. For a security plan to be effective, it must be developed, maintained, and actually used.

Policies, Standards, Baselines, Guidelines, and Procedures

For most organizations, maintaining security is an essential part of ongoing business. If their security were seriously compromised, many organizations would fail. To reduce the likelihood of a security failure, the process of implementing security has been somewhat formalized. This formalization has greatly reduced the chaos and complexity of designing and implementing security solutions for IT infrastructures. The formalization of security solutions takes the form of a hierarchical organization of documentation. Each level focuses on a specific type or category of information and issues.

Security Policies

The top tier of the formalization is known as a security policy. A *security policy* is a document that defines the scope of security needed by the organization and discusses the assets that need protection and the extent to which security solutions should go to provide the necessary protection. The security policy is an overview or generalization of an organization's security needs. It defines the main security objectives and outlines the security framework of an organization. The security policy also identifies the major functional areas of data processing and clarifies and defines all relevant terminology. It should clearly define why security is important and what assets are valuable. It is a strategic plan for implementing security. It should broadly outline the security goals and practices that should be employed to protect the organization's vital interests. The document discusses the importance of security to every aspect of daily business operation and the importance of the support of the senior staff for the implementation of security. The security policy is used to assign responsibilities, define roles, specify audit requirements, outline enforcement processes, indicate compliance requirements, and define acceptable risk levels. This document is often used as the proof that senior management has exercised due care in protecting itself against *intrusion, attack,* and *disaster. Security policies are compulsory.*

Many organizations employ several types of security policies to define or outline their overall security strategy. An organizational security policy focuses on issues relevant to every aspect of an organization. An issue-specific security policy focuses on a specific network service, department, function, or other aspect that is distinct from the organization as a whole. A system-specific security policy focuses on individual systems or types of systems and prescribes approved hardware and software, outlines methods for locking down a system, and even mandates firewall or other specific security controls.

In addition to these focused types of security policies, there are three overall categories of security policies: regulatory, advisory, and informative. A *regulatory policy* is required whenever industry or legal standards are applicable to your organization. This policy discusses the regulations that must be followed and outlines the procedures that should be used to elicit compliance. An *advisory policy* discusses behaviors and activities that are acceptable and defines consequences of violations. It explains the senior management's desires for security and compliance within an organization. Most policies are advisory. An *informative policy* is designed to provide information or knowledge about a specific subject, such as company goals, mission statements, or how the organization interacts with partners and customers. An informative policy provides support, research, or background information relevant to the specific elements of the overall policy. An informative policy is nonenforceable.

From the security policies flow many other documents or sub-elements necessary for a complete security solution. Policies are broad overviews, whereas standards, baselines, guidelines, and procedures include more specific, detailed information on the actual security solution. Standards are the next level below security policies.

Security Policies and Individuals

As a rule of thumb, security policies (as well as standards, guidelines, and procedures) should not address specific individuals. Instead of assigning tasks and responsibilities to a person, the policy should define tasks and responsibilities to fit a role. That role is a function of administrative control or personnel management. Thus, a security policy does not define who is to do what but rather defines what must be done by the various roles within the security infrastructure. Then these defined security roles are assigned to individuals as a job description or an assigned work task.

Acceptable Use Policy

An acceptable use policy is a commonly produced document that exists as part of the overall security documentation infrastructure. The acceptable use policy is specifically designed to assign security roles within the organization as well as ensure the responsibilities tied to those roles. This policy defines a level of acceptable performance and expectation of behavior and activity. Failure to comply with the policy may result in job action warnings, penalties, or termination.

Security Standards, Baselines, and Guidelines

Standards define compulsory requirements for the homogenous use of hardware, software, technology, and security controls. They provide a course of action by which technology and procedures are uniformly implemented throughout an organization. Standards are tactical documents that define steps or methods to accomplish the goals and overall direction defined by security policies.

At the next level are baselines. A *baseline* defines a minimum level of security that every system throughout the organization must meet. All systems not complying with the baseline should be taken out of production until they can be brought up to the baseline. The baseline establishes a common foundational secure state upon which all additional and more stringent security measures can be built. Baselines are usually system specific and often refer to an industry or government standard, like the Trusted Computer System Evaluation Criteria (TCSEC) or Information Technology Security Evaluation and Criteria (ITSEC). For example, most military organizations require that all systems support the TCSEC C2 security level at a minimum.

Guidelines are the next element of the formalized security policy structure. A *guideline* offers recommendations on how standards and baselines are implemented and serves as operational guides for both security professionals and users. Guidelines are flexible so they can be customized for each unique system or condition and can be used in the creation of new procedures. They state which security mechanisms should be deployed instead of prescribing a specific product or control and detailing configuration settings. They outline methodologies, include suggested actions, and are not compulsory.

Security Procedures

Procedures are the final element of the formalized security policy structure. A *procedure* is a detailed, step-by-step how-to document that describes the exact actions necessary to implement a specific security mechanism, control, or solution. A procedure could discuss the entire system deployment operation or focus on a single product or aspect, such as deploying a firewall or updating virus definitions. In most cases, procedures are system and software specific. They must be updated as the hardware and software of a system evolve. The purpose of a procedure is to ensure the integrity of business processes. If everything is accomplished by following a detailed procedure, then all activities should be in compliance with policies, standards, and guidelines. Procedures help ensure standardization of security across all systems.

All too often, policies, standards, baselines, guidelines, and procedures are developed only as an afterthought at the urging of a consultant or auditor. If these documents are not used and updated, the administration of a secured environment will be unable to use them as guides. And without the planning, design, structure, and oversight provided by these documents, no environment will remain secure or represent proper diligent due care.

It is also common practice to develop a single document containing aspects of all of these elements. This should be avoided. Each of these structures must exist as a separate entity because each performs a different specialized function. At the top of the formalization structure (i.e., security policies), there are fewer documents because they contain general broad discussions of overview and goals. There are more documents further down the formalization structure (i.e., guidelines and procedures) because they contain details specific to a limited number of systems, networks, divisions, and areas.

Keeping these documents as separate entities provides several benefits:

- Not all users need to know the security standards, baselines, guidelines, and procedures for all security classification levels.

- When changes occur, it is easier to update and redistribute only the affected material rather than updating a monolithic policy and redistributing it throughout the organization.

Risk Management

Security is aimed at preventing loss or disclosure of data while sustaining authorized access. The possibility that something could happen to damage, destroy, or disclose data is known as *risk*. Managing risk is therefore an element of sustaining a secure environment. *Risk management* is a detailed process of identifying factors that could damage or disclose data, evaluating those factors in light of data value and *countermeasure* cost, and implementing cost-effective solutions for mitigating or reducing risk.

The primary goal of risk management is to reduce risk to an acceptable level. What that level actually is depends upon the organization, the value of its assets, and the size of its budget. It is impossible to design and deploy a totally risk-free environment; however, significant risk reduction is possible, often with little effort. Risks to an IT infrastructure are not all computer based. In fact, many risks come from non-computer sources. It is important to consider all possible risks when performing risk evaluation for an organization.

The process by which the primary goal of risk management is achieved is known as *risk analysis*. It includes analyzing an environment for risks, evaluating each risk as to its likelihood of occurring and the cost of the damage it would cause if it did occur, assessing the cost of various countermeasures for each risk, and creating a cost/benefit report for safeguards to present to upper management. In addition to these risk-focused activities, risk management also requires evaluation, assessment, and the assignment of value for all assets within the organization. Without proper asset valuations, it is not possible to prioritize and compare risks with possible losses.

Risk Terminology

Risk management employs a vast terminology that must be clearly understood, especially for the CISSP exam. This section defines and discusses all of the important risk-related terminology.

Asset   An *asset* is anything within an environment that should be protected. It can be a computer file, a network service, a system resource, a process, a program, a product, an IT infrastructure, a database, a hardware device, software, facilities, and so on. If an organization places any value on an item under its control and deems that item important enough to protect, it is labeled an asset for the purposes of risk management and analysis. The loss or disclosure of an asset could result in an overall security compromise, loss of productivity, reduction in profits, additional expenditures, discontinuation of the organization, and numerous intangible consequences.

Asset valuation   *Asset valuation* is a dollar value assigned to an asset based on actual cost and nonmonetary expenses. These can include costs to develop, maintain, administer, advertise, support, repair, and replace an asset; they can also include more elusive values, such as public confidence, industry support, productivity enhancement, knowledge equity, and ownership benefits. Asset valuation is discussed in detail later in this chapter.

Threats   Any potential occurrence that may cause an undesirable or unwanted outcome for an organization or for a specific asset is a *threat*. Threats are any action or inaction that could cause damage, destruction, alteration, loss, or disclosure of assets or that could block access to or prevent maintenance of assets. Threats can be large or small and result in large or small consequences. They may be intentional or accidental. They may originate from people, organizations, hardware, networks, structures, or nature. *Threat agents* intentionally exploit vulnerabilities. Threat agents are usually people, but they could also be programs, hardware, or systems. *Threat events* are accidental exploitations of vulnerabilities. Threat events include fire, earthquake, flood, system failure, human error (due to lack of training or ignorance), and power outages.

Vulnerability   The absence or the weakness of a safeguard or countermeasure is called a *vulnerability*. In other words, a vulnerability is a flaw, loophole, oversight, error, limitation, frailty, or susceptibility in the IT infrastructure or any other aspect of an organization. If a vulnerability is exploited, loss or damage to assets can occur.

Exposure   *Exposure* is being susceptible to asset loss due to a threat; there is the possibility that a vulnerability can or will be exploited by a threat agent or event. Exposure doesn't mean that a realized threat (an event that results in loss) is actually occurring (the exposure to a realized threat is called experienced exposure). It just means that if there is a vulnerability and a threat that can exploit it, there is the possibility that a threat event, or potential exposure, can occur.

Risk   Risk is the possibility or likelihood that a threat will exploit a vulnerability to cause harm to an asset. It is an assessment of probability, possibility, or chance. The more likely it is that a threat event will occur, the greater the risk. Every instance of exposure is a risk. When written as a formula, risk can be defined as risk = threat + vulnerability. Thus, reducing either the threat agent or the vulnerability directly results in a reduction in risk.

When a risk is realized, a threat agent or a threat event has taken advantage of a vulnerability and caused harm to or disclosure of one or more assets. The whole purpose of security is to prevent risks from becoming realized by removing vulnerabilities and blocking threat agents and threat events from jeopardizing assets. As a risk management tool, security is the implementation of safeguards.

Safeguards   A *safeguard,* or countermeasure, is anything that removes a vulnerability or protects against one or more specific threats. A safeguard can be installing a software patch, making a configuration change, hiring security guards, altering the infrastructure, modifying processes, improving the security policy, training personnel more effectively, electrifying a perimeter fence, installing lights, and so on. It is any action or product that reduces risk through the elimination or lessening of a threat or a vulnerability anywhere within an organization. Safeguards are the only means by which risk is *mitigated* or removed.

Attack   An attack is the exploitation of a vulnerability by a threat agent. In other words, an attack is any intentional attempt to exploit a vulnerability of an organization's security infrastructure to cause damage, loss, or disclosure of assets. An attack can also be viewed as any violation or failure to adhere to an organization's security policy.

Breach   A *breach* is the occurrence of a security mechanism being bypassed or thwarted by a threat agent. When a breach is combined with an attack, a penetration, or intrusion, can result. A *penetration* is the condition in which a threat agent has gained access to an organization's infrastructure through the circumvention of security controls and is able to directly imperil assets.

The elements asset, threat, vulnerability, exposure, risk, and safeguard are related, as shown in Figure 6.1. Threats exploit vulnerabilities, which results in exposure. Exposure is risk, and risk is mitigated by safeguards. Safeguards protect assets that are endangered by threats.

FIGURE 6.1   The elements of risk

Risk Assessment Methodologies

Risk management and analysis is primarily an exercise for upper management. It is their responsibility to initiate and support risk analysis and assessment by defining the scope and purpose of the endeavor. The actual processes of performing risk analysis are often delegated to security professionals or an evaluation team. However, all risk assessments, results, decisions, and outcomes must be understood and approved by upper management as an element in providing prudent due care.

All IT systems have risk. There is no way to eliminate 100 percent of all risks. Instead, upper management must decide which risks are acceptable and which are not. Determining which risks are acceptable requires detailed and complex asset and risk assessments.

Risk Analysis

Risk analysis is performed to provide upper management with the details necessary to decide which risks should be mitigated, which should be transferred, and which should be accepted. The result is a cost/benefit comparison between the expected cost of asset loss and the cost of deploying safeguards against threats and vulnerabilities. Risk analysis identifies risks, quantifies the impact of threats, and aids in budgeting for security. Risk analysis helps to integrate the needs and objectives of the security policy with the organization's business goals and intentions.

The first step in risk analysis is to appraise the value of an organization's assets. If an asset has no value, then there is no need to provide protection for it. A primary goal of risk analysis is to ensure that only cost-effective safeguards are deployed. It makes no sense to spend $100,000 protecting an asset that is worth only $1,000. The value of an asset directly affects and guides the level of safeguards and security deployed to protect it. As a rule, the annual costs of safeguards should not exceed the expected annual cost of asset loss.

Asset Valuation

When evaluating the cost of an asset, there are many aspects to consider. The goal of asset evaluation is to assign a specific dollar value to it. Determining an exact value is often difficult if not impossible, but nevertheless, a specific value must be established. (Note that the discussion of qualitative versus quantitative risk analysis in the next section may clarify this issue.) Improperly assigning value to assets can result in failing to properly protect an asset or implementing financially infeasible safeguards. The following list includes some of the issues that contribute to the valuation of assets:

Purchase cost	Development cost	Administrative or management cost
Maintenance or upkeep cost	Cost in acquiring asset	Cost to protect or sustain asset
Value to owners and users	Value to competitors	Intellectual property or equity value
Market valuation (sustainable price)	Replacement cost	Productivity enhancement or degradation
Operational costs of asset presence and loss	Liability of asset loss	Usefulness

Assigning or determining the value of assets to an organization can fulfill numerous requirements. It serves as the foundation for performing a cost/benefit analysis of asset protection through safeguard deployment. It serves as a means for selecting or evaluating safeguards and countermeasures. It provides values for insurance purposes and establishes an overall net worth or net value for the organization. It helps senior management understand exactly what is at risk within the organization. Understanding the value of assets also helps to prevent negligence of due care and encourages compliance with legal requirements, industry regulations, and internal security policies.

After asset valuation, threats must be identified and examined. This involves creating an exhaustive list of all possible threats for the organization and its IT infrastructure. The list should include threat agents as well as threat events. It is important to keep in mind that threats can come from anywhere. Threats to IT are not limited to IT sources. When compiling a list of threats, be sure to consider the following:

Viruses	Hackers	Processing errors, buffer overflows	Coding/programming errors
Cascade errors and dependency faults	User errors	Personnel privilege abuse	Intruders (physical and logical)
Criminal activities by authorized users	Natural disasters (earthquakes, floods, fire, volcanoes, hurricanes, tornadoes, tsunamis, etc.)	Temperature extremes	Environmental factors (presence of gases, liquids, organisms, etc.)
Movement (vibrations, jarring, etc.)	Physical damage (crushing, projectiles, cable severing, etc.)	Energy anomalies (static, EM pulses, radio frequencies [RFs], power loss, power surges, etc.)	Equipment failure
Intentional attacks	Misuse of data, resources, or services	Loss of data	Physical theft
Reorganization	Changes or compromises to data classification or security policies	Information warfare	Social engineering
Authorized user illness or epidemics	Government, political, or military intrusions or restrictions	Bankruptcy or alteration/ interruption of business activity	

In most cases, a team rather than a single individual should perform risk assessment and analysis. Also, the team members should be from various departments within the organization. It is not usually a requirement that all team members be security professionals or even network/ system administrators. The diversity of the team based on the demographics of the organization will help to exhaustively identify and address all possible threats and risks.

Once a list of threats is developed, each threat and its related risk must be individually evaluated. There are two risk assessment methodologies: quantitative and qualitative. *Quantitative risk analysis* assigns real dollar figures to the loss of an asset. *Qualitative risk analysis* assigns subjective and intangible values to the loss of an asset. Both methods are necessary for a complete risk analysis.

Quantitative Risk Analysis

The quantitative method results in concrete probability percentages. However, a purely quantitative analysis is not possible; not all elements and aspects of the analysis can be quantified because some are qualitative, subjective, or intangible. The process of quantitative risk analysis starts with asset valuation and threat identification. Next, you estimate the potential and frequency of each risk. This information is then used to calculate various cost functions that are used to evaluate safeguards.

The six major steps or phases in quantitative risk analysis are as follows:

1. Inventory assets and assign a value (AV).

2. Research each asset and produce a list of all possible threats of each individual asset. For each listed threat, calculate the exposure factor (EF) and single loss expectancy (SLE).

3. Perform a threat analysis to calculate the likelihood of each threat taking place within a single year, that is, the annualized rate of occurrence (ARO).

4. Derive the overall loss potential per threat by calculating the annualized loss expectancy (ALE).

5. Research countermeasures for each threat, and then calculate the changes to ARO and ALE based on an applied countermeasure.

6. Perform a cost/benefit analysis of each countermeasure for each threat for each asset. Select the most appropriate response to each threat.

Cost Functions

Some of the cost functions associated with quantitative risk analysis include exposure factor, single loss expectancy, annualized rate of occurrence, and annualized loss expectancy:

Exposure factor   The *exposure factor (EF)* represents the percentage of loss that an organization would experience if a specific asset were violated by a *realized risk*. The EF can also be called the loss potential. In most cases, a realized risk does not result in the total loss of an asset. The EF simply indicates the expected overall asset value loss due to a single realized risk. The EF is usually small for assets that are easily replaceable, such as hardware. It can be very large for assets that are irreplaceable or proprietary, such as product designs or a database of customers. The EF is expressed as a percentage.

Single loss expectancy The EF is needed to calculate the *single loss expectancy (SLE)*. The SLE is the cost associated with a single realized risk against a specific asset. It indicates the exact amount of loss an organization would experience if an asset were harmed by a specific threat. The SLE is calculated using the formula SLE = asset value (AV) * exposure factor (EF) (or SLE = AV * EF). The SLE is expressed in a dollar value. For example, if an asset is valued at $200,000 and it has an EF of 45% for a specific threat, then the SLE of the threat for that asset is $90,000.

Annualized rate of occurrence The *annualized rate of occurrence (ARO)* is the expected frequency with which a specific threat or risk will occur (i.e., become realized) within a single year. The ARO can range from a value of 0.0 (zero), indicating that the threat or risk will never be realized, to a very large number, indicating the threat or risk occurs often. Calculating the ARO can be complicated. It can be derived from historical records, statistical analysis, or guesswork. ARO calculation is also known as probability determination. The ARO for some threats or risks is calculated by multiplying the likelihood of a single occurrence by the number of users who could initiate the threat. For example, the ARO of an earthquake in Tulsa may be .00001, whereas the ARO of an e-mail virus in an office in Tulsa may be 10,000,000.

Annualized loss expectancy The *annualized loss expectancy (ALE)* is the possible yearly cost of all instances of a specific realized threat against a specific asset. The ALE is calculated using the formula ALE = single loss expectancy (SLE) * annualized rate of occurrence (ARO) (or ALE = SLE * ARO). For example, if the SLE of an asset is $90,000 and the ARO for a specific threat (such as total power loss) is .5, then the ALE is $45,000. On the other hand, if the ARO for a specific threat were 15 (such as compromised user account), then the ALE would be $1,350,000.

Table 6.1 illustrates the various formulas associated with quantitative risk analysis.

T A B L E 6 . 1   Quantitative Risk Analysis Formulas

Concept	Formula
Exposure factor (EF)	%
Single loss expectancy (SLE)	SLE = AV * EF
Annualized rate of occurrence (ARO)	# / year
Annualized loss expectancy (ALE)	ALE = SLE * ARO ALE = AV * EF * ARO
Annual cost of the safeguard (ACS)	$ / year
Value or benefit of a safeguard	[ALE1 – ALE2] – ACS

Threat/Risk Calculations

The task of calculating EF, SLE, ARO, and ALE for every asset and every threat/risk is a daunting one. Fortunately, there are quantitative risk assessment tools that simplify and automate much of this process. These tools are used to produce an asset inventory with valuations and then, using predefined AROs along with some customizing options (i.e., industry, geography, IT components, etc.), to produce risk analysis reports.

Calculating Annualized Loss Expectancy (ALE)

In addition to determining the annual cost of the safeguard, you must calculate the ALE for the asset if the safeguard is implemented. This requires a new EF and ARO specific to the safeguard. As mentioned earlier, the annual costs of safeguards should not exceed the expected annual cost of asset loss. To make the determination of whether the safeguard is financially equitable, use the following formula:

ALE before safeguard – ALE after implementing the safeguard – annual cost of safeguard = value of the safeguard to the company.

If the result is negative, the safeguard is not a financially responsible choice. If the result is positive, then that value is the annual savings your organization can reap by deploying the safeguard.

The annual savings or loss from a safeguard should not be the only element considered when evaluating safeguards. The issues of legal responsibility and prudent due care should also be considered. In some cases, it makes more sense to lose money in the deployment of a safeguard than to risk legal liability in the event of an asset disclosure or loss.

Calculating Safeguard Costs

For each specific risk, one or more safeguards or countermeasures must be evaluated on a cost/benefit basis. To perform this evaluation, you must first compile a list of safeguards for each threat. Then each safeguard must be assigned a deployment value. In fact, the deployment value or the cost of the safeguard must be measured against the value of the protected asset. The value of the protected asset therefore determines the maximum expenditures for protection mechanisms. Security should be cost effective, and thus it is not prudent to spend more (in terms of cash or resources) protecting an asset than its value to the organization. If the cost of the countermeasure is greater than the value of the asset (i.e., the cost of the risk), then the risk should be accepted.

There are numerous factors involved in calculating the value of a countermeasure:

- Cost of purchase, development, and licensing
- Cost of implementation and customization
- Cost of annual operation, maintenance, administration, and so on
- Cost of annual repairs and upgrades
- Productivity improvement or loss
- Changes to environment
- Cost of testing and evaluation

To perform the cost/benefit analysis of a safeguard, you must first calculate the following:

- The pre-countermeasure ALE for an asset-and-threat pairing
- The post-countermeasure ALE for an asset-and-threat pairing
- The annual cost of the safeguard (ACS)

Here is the cost/benefit formula:

[pre-countermeasure ALE – post-countermeasure ALE] – ACS.

The countermeasure with the greatest result from this cost/benefit formula makes the most economic sense to deploy against the specific asset-and-threat pairing.

Qualitative Risk Analysis

Qualitative risk analysis is more scenario based than it is calculator based. Rather than assigning exact dollar figures to possible losses, you rank threats on a scale to evaluate their risks, costs, and effects. The process of performing qualitative risk analysis involves judgment, intuition, and experience. There are many actual techniques and methods used to perform qualitative risk analysis:

- Brainstorming
- Delphi technique
- Storyboarding
- Focus groups
- Surveys
- Questionnaires
- Checklists
- One-on-one meetings
- Interviews

Determining which mechanism to employ is based on the culture of the organization and the types of risks and assets involved. It is common for several methods to be employed simultaneously and their results compared and contrasted in the final risk analysis report to upper management.

Scenarios

The basic process for all of these mechanisms involves the creation of scenarios. A scenario is a written description of a single major threat. The description focuses on how a threat would be instigated and what effects it could have on the organization, the IT infrastructure, and specific assets. Generally, the scenarios are limited to one page of text to keep them manageable. For each scenario, one or more safeguards that would completely or partially protect against the major threat discussed in the scenario are described. The analysis participants then assign a threat level to the scenario, a loss potential, and the advantages of each safeguard. These assignments can be grossly simple, such as using high, medium, and low or a basic number scale of

1 to 10, or they can be detailed essay responses. The responses from all participants are then compiled into a single report that is presented to upper management.

The usefulness and validity of a qualitative risk analysis is improved as the number and diversity of the participants in the evaluation increases. Whenever possible, include one or more persons from each level of the organizational hierarchy, from upper management to end user. It is also important to include a cross section from each major department, division, office, or branch.

Delphi Technique

The *Delphi technique* is probably the only mechanism on this list that is not immediately recognizable and understood. The Delphi technique is simply an anonymous feedback and response process. Its primary purpose is to elicit honest and uninfluenced responses from all participants. The participants are usually gathered into a single meeting room. To each request for feedback, each participant writes down their response on paper anonymously. The results are compiled and presented to the group for evaluation. The process is repeated until a consensus is reached.

Both the quantitative and qualitative risk analysis mechanisms offer useful results. However, each technique involves a unique method of evaluating the same set of assets and risks. Prudent due care requires that both methods be employed. The benefits and disadvantages of these two systems are displayed in Table 6.2.

TABLE 6.2 Comparison of Quantitative and Qualitative Risk Analysis

Characteristic	Qualitative	Quantitative
Employs complex functions	No	Yes
Uses cost/benefit analysis	No	Yes
Results in specific values	No	Yes
Requires guesswork	Yes	No
Supports automation	No	Yes
Involves a high volume of information	No	Yes
Is objective	No	Yes
Uses opinions	Yes	No
Requires significant time and effort	No	Yes
Offers useful and meaningful results	Yes	Yes

Handling Risk

The results of risk analysis are many:

- Complete and detailed valuation of all assets
- An exhaustive list of all threats and risks, rate of occurrence, and extent of loss if realized
- A list of threat-specific safeguards and countermeasures that identifies their effectiveness and ALE
- A cost/benefit analysis of each safeguard

This information is essential for management to make informed, educated, and intelligent decisions about safeguard implementation and security policy alterations.

Once the risk analysis is complete, management must address each specific risk. There are four possible responses to risk:

- Reduce
- Assign
- Accept
- Reject

Reducing risk, or risk mitigation, is the implementation of safeguards and countermeasures to eliminate vulnerabilities or block threats. Picking the most cost-effective or beneficial countermeasure is part of risk management, but it is not an element of risk assessment. In fact, countermeasure selection is a post-risk assessment or risk analysis activity.

Assigning risk, or *transferring risk,* is the placement of the cost of loss a risk represents onto another entity or organization. Purchasing insurance and outsourcing are common forms of assigning or transferring risk.

Accepting risk is the valuation by management of the cost/benefit analysis of possible safeguards and the determination that the cost of the countermeasure greatly outweighs the possible cost of loss due to a risk. It also means that management has agreed to accept the consequences and the loss if the risk is realized. In most cases, accepting risk requires a clearly written statement that indicates why a safeguard was not implemented, who is responsible for the decision, and who will be responsible for the loss if the risk is realized, usually in the form of a "sign off letter." An organization's decision to accept risk is based on its risk tolerance. *Risk tolerance* is the ability of an organization to absorb the losses associated with realized risks.

A final but unacceptable possible response to risk is to *reject risk* or *ignore risk.* Denying that a risk exists and hoping that by ignoring a risk it will never be realized are not valid prudent due care responses to risk.

Once countermeasures are implemented, the risk that remains is known as residual risk. *Residual risk* comprises any threats to specific assets against which upper management chooses not to implement a safeguard. In other words, residual risk is the risk that management has chosen to accept rather than mitigate. In most cases, the presence of residual risk indicates that the cost/benefit analysis showed that the available safeguards were not cost-effective deterrents.

Total risk is the amount of risk an organization would face if no safeguards were implemented. A formula for total risk is threats * vulnerabilities * asset value = total risk. The difference between total risk and residual risk is known as the *controls gap*. The controls gap is the amount of risk that is reduced by implementing safeguards. A formula for residual risk is total risk − controls gap = residual risk.

Countermeasure Selection

Selecting a countermeasure within the realm of risk management does rely heavily on the cost/benefit analysis results. However, there are several other factors that you should consider:

- The cost of the countermeasure should be less than the value of asset.

- The cost of the countermeasure should be less than the benefit of the countermeasure.

- The result of the applied countermeasure should make the cost of an attack greater for the perpetrator than the derived benefit from an attack.

- The countermeasure should provide a solution to a real and identified problem. (Don't install countermeasures just because they are available, are advertised, or sound cool.)

- The benefit of the countermeasure should not be dependent upon its secrecy. This means that "security through obscurity" is not a viable countermeasure and that any viable countermeasure can withstand public disclosure and scrutiny.

- The benefit of the countermeasure should be testable and verifiable.

- The countermeasure should provide consistent and uniform protection across all users, systems, protocols, and so on.

- The countermeasure should have few or no dependencies to reduce cascade failures.

- The countermeasure should require minimal human intervention after initial deployment and configuration.

- The countermeasure should be tamperproof.

- The countermeasure should have overrides accessible to privileged operators only.

- The countermeasure should provide fail-safe and/or fail-secure options.

Security Awareness Training

The successful implementation of a security solution requires changes in user behavior. These changes primarily consist of alterations in normal work activities to comply with the standards, guidelines, and procedures mandated by the security policy. Behavior modification involves some level of learning on the part of the user. There are three commonly recognized learning levels: awareness, training, and education.

A prerequisite to actual security training is *awareness*. The goal of creating awareness is to bring security into the forefront and make it a recognized entity for users. Awareness establishes a common baseline or foundation of security understanding across the entire organization. Awareness is not exclusively created through a classroom type of exercise but also through the work environment. There are many tools that can be used to create awareness, such as posters, notices, newsletter articles, screen savers, T-shirts, rally speeches by managers, announcements, presentations, mouse pads, office supplies, and memos as well as the traditional instructor-led training courses. Awareness focuses on key or basic topics and issues related to security that all employees, no matter which position or classification they have, must understand and comprehend.

Awareness is a tool to establish a minimum standard common denominator or foundation of security understanding. All personnel should be fully aware of their security responsibilities and liabilities. They should be trained to know what to do and what not to do.

The issues that users need to be aware of include avoiding waste, fraud, and unauthorized activities. All members of an organization, from senior management to temporary intern, need the same level of awareness. The awareness program in an organization should be tied in with its security policy, incident handling plan, and disaster recovery procedures. For an awareness-building program to be effective, it must be fresh, creative, and updated often. The awareness program should also be tied to an understanding of how the corporate culture will affect and impact security for individuals as well as the organization as a whole. If employees do not see enforcement of security policies and standards, especially at the awareness level, then they may not feel obligated to abide by them.

Training is teaching employees to perform their work tasks and to comply with the security policy. All new employees require some level of training so they will be able to comply with all standards, guidelines, and procedures mandated by the security policy. New users need to know how to use the IT infrastructure, where data is stored, and how and why resources are classified. Many organizations choose to train new employees before they are granted access to the network, whereas others will grant new users limited access until their training in their specific job position is complete. Training is an ongoing activity that must be sustained throughout the lifetime of the organization for every employee. It is considered an administrative security control.

Awareness and training are often provided in-house. That means these teaching tools are created and deployed by and within the organization itself. However, the next level of knowledge distribution is usually obtained from an external third-party source.

Education is a more detailed endeavor in which students/users learn much more than they actually need to know to perform their work tasks. Education is most often associated with users pursuing certification or seeking job promotion. It is typically a requirement for personnel seeking security professional positions. A security professional requires extensive knowledge of security and the local environment for the entire organization and not just their specific work tasks.

Summary

When planning a security solution, it's important to consider how humans are the weakest element. Regardless of the physical or logical controls deployed, humans can discover ways to avoid them, circumvent or subvert them, or disable them. Thus, it is important to take users into account when designing and deploying security solutions for your environment. The aspects of secure hiring practices, roles, policies, standards, guidelines, procedures, risk management, awareness training, and management planning all contribute to protecting assets. The use of these security structures provides some protection from the threat of humans.

Secure hiring practices require detailed job descriptions. Job descriptions are used as a guide for selecting candidates and properly evaluating them for a position. Maintaining security through job descriptions includes the use of separation of duties, job responsibilities, and job rotation.

A termination policy is needed to protect an organization and its existing employees. The termination procedure should include witnesses, return of company property, disabling network access, an exit interview, and an escort from the property.

Security roles determine who is responsible for the security of an organization's assets. Those assigned the senior management role are ultimately responsible and liable for any asset loss, and they are the ones who define security policy. Security professionals are responsible for implementing security policy, and users are responsible for complying with the security policy. The person assigned the data owner role is responsible for classifying information, and a data custodian is responsible for maintaining the secure environment and backing up data. An auditor is responsible for making sure a secure environment is properly protecting assets.

A formalized security policy structure consists of policies, standards, baselines, guidelines, and procedures. These individual documents are essential elements to the design and implementation of security in any environment.

The process of identifying, evaluating, and preventing or reducing risks is known as risk management. The primary goal of risk management is to reduce risk to an acceptable level. Determining this level depends upon the organization, the value of its assets, and the size of its budget. Although it is impossible to design and deploy a completely risk-free environment, it is possible to significantly reduce risk with little effort. Risk analysis is the process by which risk management is achieved and includes analyzing an environment for risks, evaluating each risk as to its likelihood of occurring and the cost of the resulting damage, assessing the cost of various countermeasures for each risk, and creating a cost/benefit report for safeguards to present to upper management.

To successfully implement a security solution, user behavior must change. Such changes primarily consist of alterations in normal work activities to comply with the standards, guidelines, and procedures mandated by the security policy. Behavior modification involves some level of learning on the part of the user. There are three commonly recognized learning levels: awareness, training, and education.

An important aspect of security management planning is the proper implementation of a security policy. To be effective, the approach to security management must be a top-down approach. The responsibility of initiating and defining a security policy lies with upper or senior management. Security policies provide direction for the lower levels of the organization's hierarchy. Middle management is responsible for fleshing out the security policy into standards, baselines, guidelines, and procedures. It is the responsibility of the operational managers or security professionals to implement the configurations prescribed in the security management documentation. Finally, the end users' responsibility is to comply with all security policies of the organization.

Security management planning includes defining security roles, developing security policies, performing risk analysis, and requiring security education for employees. These responsibilities are guided by the developments of management plans. Strategic, tactical, and operational plans should be developed by a security management team.

Exam Essentials

Understand the security implications of hiring new employees.   To properly plan for security, you must have standards in place for job descriptions, job classification, work tasks, job responsibilities, preventing collusion, candidate screening, background checks, security clearances, employment agreements, and nondisclosure agreements. By deploying such mechanisms, you ensure that new hires are aware of the required security standards, thus protecting your organization's assets.

Be able to explain separation of duties.   Separation of duties is the security concept of dividing critical, significant, sensitive work tasks among several individuals. By separating duties in this manner, you ensure that no one person can compromise system security.

Understand the principle of least privilege.   The principle of least privilege states that, in a secured environment, users should be granted the minimum amount of access necessary for them to complete their required work tasks or job responsibilities. By limiting user access only to those items that they need to complete their work tasks, you limit the vulnerability of sensitive information.

Know why job rotation and mandatory vacations are necessary.   Job rotation serves two functions: It provides a type of knowledge redundancy, and moving personnel around reduces the risk of fraud, data modification, theft, sabotage, and misuse of information. Mandatory vacations of one to two weeks are used to audit and verify the work tasks and privileges of employees. This often results in easy detection of abuse, fraud, or negligence.

Be able to explain proper termination policies.   A termination policy defines the procedure for terminating employees. It should include items such as always having a witness, disabling the employee's network access, and performing an exit interview. A termination policy should also include escorting the terminated employee off of the premises and requiring the return of security tokens and badges and company property.

Understand key security roles.   The primary security roles are senior manager, organizational owner, upper management, security professional, user, data owner, data custodian, and auditor. By creating a security role hierarchy, you limit risk overall.

Know the elements of a formalized security policy structure.   To create a comprehensive security plan, you need the following items in place: security policy, standards, baselines, guidelines, and procedures. Such documentation clearly states security requirements and creates due diligence on the part of the responsible parties.

Be able to define overall risk management.   The process of identifying factors that could damage or disclose data, evaluating those factors in light of data value and countermeasure cost, and implementing cost-effective solutions for mitigating or reducing risk is known as risk management. By performing risk management, you lay the foundation for reducing risk overall.

Understand risk analysis and the key elements involved.   Risk analysis is the process by which upper management is provided with details to make decisions about which risks are to be mitigated, which should be transferred, and which should be accepted. To fully evaluate risks and subsequently take the proper precautions, you must analyze the following: assets, asset valuation, threats, vulnerability, exposure, risk, realized risk, safeguards, countermeasures, attacks, and breaches.

Know how to evaluate threats.   Threats can originate from numerous sources, including IT, humans, and nature. Threat assessment should be performed as a team effort to provide the widest range of perspective. By fully evaluating risks from all angles, you reduce your system's vulnerability.

Understand quantitative risk analysis.   Quantitative risk analysis focuses on hard values and percentages. A complete quantitative analysis is not possible due to intangible aspects of risk. The process involves asset valuation and threat identification and then determining a threat's potential frequency and the resulting damage; the result is a cost/benefit analysis of safeguards.

Be able to explain the concept of an exposure factor (EF).   An exposure factor is an element of quantitative risk analysis that represents the percentage of loss that an organization would experience if a specific asset were violated by a realized risk. By calculating exposure factors, you are able to implement a sound risk management policy.

Know what single loss expectancy (SLE) is and how to calculate it.   SLE is an element of quantitative risk analysis that represents the cost associated with a single realized risk against a specific asset. The formula is SLE = asset value (AV) * exposure factor (EF).

Understand annualized rate of occurrence (ARO).   ARO is an element of quantitative risk analysis that represents the expected frequency with which a specific threat or risk will occur (i.e., become realized) within a single year. Understanding AROs further enables you to calculate the risk and take proper precautions.

Know what annualized loss expectancy (ALE) is and how to calculate it.   ALE is an element of quantitative risk analysis that represents the possible yearly cost of all instances of a specific realized threat against a specific asset. The formula is ALE = single loss expectancy (SLE) * annualized rate of occurrence (ARO).

Know the formula for safeguard evaluation.   In addition to determining the annual cost of a safeguard, you must calculate the ALE for the asset if the safeguard is implemented. To do so, use the formula ALE before safeguard – ALE after implementing the safeguard – annual cost of safeguard = value of the safeguard to the company.

Understand qualitative risk analysis.   Qualitative risk analysis is based more on scenarios than calculations. Exact dollar figures are not assigned to possible losses; instead, threats are ranked on a scale to evaluate their risks, costs, and effects. Such an analysis assists those responsible in creating proper risk management policies.

Understand the Delphi technique.   The Delphi technique is simply an anonymous feedback and response process used to arrive at a consensus. Such a consensus gives the responsible parties the opportunity to properly evaluate risks and implement solutions.

Know the options for handling risk.   Reducing risk, or risk mitigation, is the implementation of safeguards and countermeasures. Assigning risk or transferring a risk places the cost of loss a risk represents onto another entity or organization. Purchasing insurance is one form of assigning or transferring risk. Accepting risk means the management has evaluated the cost/benefit analysis of possible safeguards and has determined that the cost of the countermeasure greatly outweighs the possible cost of loss due to a risk. It also means that management has agreed to accept the consequences and the loss if the risk is realized.

Be able to explain total risk, residual risk, and controls gap.   Total risk is the amount of risk an organization would face if no safeguards were implemented. To calculate total risk, use the formula threats * vulnerabilities * asset value = total risk. Residual risk is the risk that management has chosen to accept rather than mitigate. The difference between total risk and residual risk is known as the controls gap. The controls gap is the amount of risk that is reduced by implementing safeguards. To calculate residual risk, use the formula total risk – controls gap = residual risk.

Know how to implement security awareness training.   Before actual training can take place, awareness of security as a recognized entity must be created for users. Once this is accomplished, training, or teaching employees to perform their work tasks and to comply with the security policy, can begin. All new employees require some level of training so they will be able to comply with all standards, guidelines, and procedures mandated by the security policy. Education is a more detailed endeavor in which students/users learn much more than they actually need to know to perform their work tasks. Education is most often associated with users pursuing certification or seeking job promotion.

Understand security management planning.   Security management is based on three types of plans: strategic, tactical, and operational. A strategic plan is a long-term plan that is fairly stable. It defines the organization's goals, mission, and objectives. The tactical plan is a midterm plan developed to provide more details on accomplishing the goals set forth in the strategic plan. Operational plans are short-term and highly detailed plans based on the strategic and tactical plans.

Review Questions

1. Which of the following is the weakest element in any security solution?

   A. Software products

   B. Internet connections

   C. Security policies

   D. Humans

2. When seeking to hire new employees, what is the first step?

   A. Create a job description.

   B. Set position classification.

   C. Screen candidates.

   D. Request resumes.

3. What is the primary purpose of an exit interview?

   A. To return the exiting employee's personal belongings

   B. To review the nondisclosure agreement

   C. To evaluate the exiting employee's performance

   D. To cancel the exiting employee's network access accounts

4. When an employee is to be terminated, which of the following should be done?

   A. Inform the employee a few hours before they are officially terminated.

   B. Disable the employee's network access just before they are informed of the termination.

   C. Send out a broadcast e-mail informing everyone that a specific employee is to be terminated.

   D. Wait until you and the employee are the only people remaining in the building before announcing the termination.

5. Who is liable for failing to perform prudent due care?

   A. Security professionals

   B. Data custodian

   C. Auditor

   D. Senior management

6. Which of the following is a document that defines the scope of security needed by an organization, lists the assets that need protection, and discusses the extent to which security solutions should go to provide the necessary protection?

   A. Security policy

   B. Standard

   C. Guideline

   D. Procedure

7. Which of the following policies is required when industry or legal standards are applicable to your organization?

    A. Advisory

    B. Regulatory

    C. Baseline

    D. Informative

8. Which of the following is not an element of the risk analysis process?

    A. Analyzing an environment for risks

    B. Creating a cost/benefit report for safeguards to present to upper management

    C. Selecting appropriate safeguards and implementing them

    D. Evaluating each risk as to its likelihood of occurring and cost of the resulting damage

9. Which of the following would not be considered an asset in a risk analysis?

    A. A development process

    B. An IT infrastructure

    C. A proprietary system resource

    D. Users' personal files

10. Which of the following represents accidental exploitations of vulnerabilities?

    A. Threat events

    B. Risks

    C. Threat agents

    D. Breaches

11. When a safeguard or a countermeasure is not present or is not sufficient, what is created?

    A. Vulnerability

    B. Exposure

    C. Risk

    D. Penetration

12. Which of the following is not a valid definition for risk?

    A. An assessment of probability, possibility, or chance

    B. Anything that removes a vulnerability or protects against one or more specific threats

    C. Risk = threat + vulnerability

    D. Every instance of exposure

13. When evaluating safeguards, what is the rule that should be followed in most cases?

   A. Expected annual cost of asset loss should not exceed the annual costs of safeguards.

   B. Annual costs of safeguards should equal the value of the asset.

   C. Annual costs of safeguards should not exceed the expected annual cost of asset loss.

   D. Annual costs of safeguards should not exceed 10 percent of the security budget.

14. How is single loss expectancy (SLE) calculated?

   A. Threat + vulnerability

   B. Asset value ($) * exposure factor

   C. Annualized rate of occurrence * vulnerability

   D. Annualized rate of occurrence * asset value * exposure factor

15. How is the value of a safeguard to a company calculated?

   A. ALE before safeguard – ALE after implementing the safeguard – annual cost of safeguard

   B. ALE before safeguard * ARO of safeguard

   C. ALE after implementing safeguard + annual cost of safeguard – controls gap

   D. Total risk – controls gap

16. What security control is directly focused on preventing collusion?

   A. Principle of least privilege

   B. Job descriptions

   C. Separation of duties

   D. Qualitative risk analysis

17. Which security role is responsible for assigning the sensitivity label to objects?

   A. Users

   B. Data owner

   C. Senior management

   D. Data custodian

18. When you are attempting to install a new security mechanism for which there is not a detailed step-by-step guide on how to implement that specific product, which element of the security policy should you turn to?

   A. Policies

   B. Procedures

   C. Standards

   D. Guidelines

19. While performing a risk analysis, you identify a threat of fire and a vulnerability because there are no fire extinguishers. Based on this information, which of the following is a possible risk?

    A. Virus infection

    B. Damage to equipment

    C. System malfunction

    D. Unauthorized access to confidential information

20. You've performed a basic quantitative risk analysis on a specific threat/vulnerability/risk relation. You select a possible countermeasure. When re-performing the calculations, which of the following factors will change?

    A. Exposure factor

    B. Single loss expectancy

    C. Asset value

    D. Annualized rate of occurrence

Answers to Review Questions

1. D. Regardless of the specifics of a security solution, humans are the weakest element.

2. A. The first step in hiring new employees is to create a job description. Without a job description, there is no consensus on what type of individual needs to be found and hired.

3. B. The primary purpose of an exit interview is to review the nondisclosure agreement (NDA).

4. B. You should remove or disable the employee's network user account immediately before or at the same time they are informed of their termination.

5. D. Senior management is liable for failing to perform prudent due care.

6. A. The document that defines the scope of an organization's security requirements is called a security policy. The policy lists the assets to be protected and discusses the extent to which security solutions should go to provide the necessary protection.

7. B. A regulatory policy is required when industry or legal standards are applicable to your organization. This policy discusses the rules that must be followed and outlines the procedures that should be used to elicit compliance.

8. C. Risk analysis includes analyzing an environment for risks, evaluating each risk as to its likelihood of occurring and the cost of the damage it would cause, assessing the cost of various countermeasures for each risk, and creating a cost/benefit report for safeguards to present to upper management. Selecting safeguards is a task of upper management based on the results of risk analysis. It is a task that falls under risk management, but it is not part of the risk analysis process.

9. D. The personal files of users are not assets of the organization and thus not considered in a risk analysis.

10. A. Threat events are accidental exploitations of vulnerabilities.

11. A. A vulnerability is the absence or weakness of a safeguard or countermeasure.

12. B. Anything that removes a vulnerability or protects against one or more specific threats is considered a safeguard or a countermeasure, not a risk.

13. C. The annual costs of safeguards should not exceed the expected annual cost of asset loss.

14. B. SLE is calculated using the formula SLE = asset value ($) * exposure factor.

15. A. The value of a safeguard to an organization is calculated by ALE before safeguard – ALE after implementing the safeguard – annual cost of safeguard.

16. C. The likelihood that a coworker will be willing to collaborate on an illegal or abusive scheme is reduced due to the higher risk of detection created by the combination of separation of duties, restricted job responsibilities, and job rotation.

17. B. The data owner is responsible for assigning the sensitivity label to new objects and resources.

18. D. If no detailed step-by-step instructions or procedures exist, then turn to the guidelines for general principles to follow for the installation.

19. B. The threat of a fire and the vulnerability of a lack of fire extinguishers leads to the risk of damage to equipment.

20. D. A countermeasure directly affects the annualized rate of occurrence, primarily because the countermeasure is designed to prevent the occurrence of the risk, thus reducing its frequency per year.

Chapter

7

Data and Application Security Issues

THE CISSP EXAM TOPICS COVERED IN THIS CHAPTER INCLUDE:

- ✓ Application Issues
- ✓ Databases and Data Warehousing
- ✓ Data/Information Storage
- ✓ Knowledge-Based Systems
- ✓ Systems Development Controls

All too often, security administrators are unaware of system vulnerabilities caused by applications with security flaws (either intentional or unintentional). Security professionals often have a background in system administration and don't have an in-depth understanding of the application development process, and therefore of application security. This can be a critical error. As you will learn in Chapter 14, "Auditing and Monitoring," organization insiders (i.e., employees, contractors, and trusted visitors) are the most likely candidates to commit computer crimes. Security administrators must be aware of all threats to ensure that adequate checks and balances exist to protect against a malicious insider or application vulnerability.

This chapter examines some of the common threats applications pose to both traditional and distributed computing environments. Next, we explore how to protect data. Finally, we take a look at some of the systems development controls that can help ensure the accuracy, reliability, and integrity of internal application development processes.

Application Issues

As technology marches on, application environments are becoming much more complex than they were in the days of simple stand-alone DOS systems running precompiled code. Organizations are now faced with challenges that arise from connecting their systems to networks of all shapes and sizes (from the office LAN to the global Internet) as well as from distributed computing environments. These challenges come in the form of malicious code threats such as mobile code objects, viruses, worms and denial of service attacks. In this section, we'll take a brief look at a few of these issues.

Local/Nondistributed Environment

In a traditional, nondistributed computing environment, individual computer systems store and execute programs to perform functions for the local user. Such tasks generally involve networked applications that provide access to remote resources, such as web servers and remote file servers, as well as other interactive networked activities, such as the transmission and reception of electronic mail. The key characteristic of a nondistributed system is that all user-executed code is stored on the local machine (or on a file system accessible to that machine, such as a file server on the machine's LAN) and executed using processors on that machine.

The threats that face local/nondistributed computing environments are some of the more common malicious code objects that you are most likely already familiar with, at least in passing. This section contains a brief description of those objects to introduce them from an application security standpoint. They are covered in greater detail in Chapter 8, "Malicious Code and Application Attacks."

Viruses

Viruses are the oldest form of malicious code objects that plague cyberspace. Once they are in a system, they attach themselves to legitimate operating system and user files and applications and normally perform some sort of undesirable action, ranging from the somewhat innocuous display of an annoying message on the screen to the more malicious destruction of the entire local file system.

Before the advent of networked computing, viruses spread from system to system through infected media. For example, suppose a user's hard drive is infected with a virus. That user might then format a floppy disk and inadvertently transfer the virus to it along with some data files. When the user inserts the disk into another system and reads the data, that system would also become infected with the virus. The virus might then get spread to several other users, who go on to share it with even more users in an exponential fashion.

Macro viruses are among the most insidious viruses out there. They're extremely easy to write and take advantage of some of the advanced features of modern productivity applications to significantly broaden their reach.

In this day and age, more and more computers are connected to some type of network and have at least an indirect connection to the Internet. This greatly increases the number of mechanisms that can transport viruses from system to system and expands the potential magnitude of these infections to epidemic proportions. After all, an e-mail macro virus that can automatically propagate itself to every contact in your address book can inflict far more widespread damage than a boot sector virus that requires the sharing of physical storage media to transmit infection. The various types of viruses and their propagation techniques are discussed in Chapter 8.

Trojan Horses

During the Trojan War, the Greek military used a false horse filled with soldiers to gain access to the fortified city of Troy. The Trojans fell prey to this deception because they believed the horse to be a generous gift and were unaware of its insidious payload. Modern computer users face a similar threat from today's electronic version of the Trojan horse. A *Trojan horse* is a malicious code object that appears to be a benevolent program—such as a game or simple utility. When a user executes the application, it performs the "cover" functions, as advertised; however, electronic Trojan horses also carry an unknown payload. While the computer user is using the new program, the Trojan horse performs some sort of malicious action—such as opening a security hole in the system for hackers to exploit, tampering with data, or installing keystroke monitoring software.

Logic Bombs

Logic bombs are malicious code objects that lie dormant until events occur that satisfy one or more logical conditions. At that time, they spring into action, delivering their malicious payload to unsuspecting computer users. They are often planted by disgruntled employees or other individuals who want to harm an organization but for one reason or another might want to delay the malicious activity for a period of time. Many simple logic bombs operate based solely upon the system date or time. For example, an employee who was terminated might set a logic bomb to destroy critical business data on the first anniversary of their termination. Other logic bombs operate using more complex criteria. For example, a programmer who fears termination might plant a logic bomb that alters payroll information after the programmer's account is locked out of the system.

Worms

Worms are an interesting type of malicious code that greatly resemble viruses, with one major distinction. Like viruses, worms spread from system to system bearing some type of malicious payload. However, whereas viruses must be shared to propagate, worms are self-replicating. They remain resident in memory and exploit one or more networking vulnerabilities to spread from system to system under their own power. Obviously, this allows for much greater propagation and can result in a denial of service attack against entire networks. Indeed, the famous Internet Worm launched by Robert Morris in November 1988 (technical details of this worm are presented in Chapter 8) actually crippled the entire Internet for several days.

Distributed Environment

The previous section discussed how the advent of networked computing facilitated the rapid spread of malicious code objects between computing systems. This section examines how distributed computing (an offshoot of networked computing) introduces a variety of new malicious code threats that information system security practitioners must understand and protect their systems against.

Essentially, distributed computing allows a single user to harness the computing power of one or more remote systems to achieve a single goal. A very common example of this is the client/server interaction that takes place when a computer user browses the World Wide Web. The client uses a web browser, such as Microsoft Internet Explorer or Netscape Navigator, to request information from a remote server. The remote server's web hosting software then receives and processes the request. In many cases, the web server fulfills the request by retrieving an HTML file from the local file system and transmitting it to the remote client. In the case of dynamically generated web pages, that request might involve generating custom content tailored to the needs of the individual user (real-time account information is a good example of this). In effect, the web user is causing remote server(s) to perform actions on their behalf.

Agents

Agents (also known as *bots*) are intelligent code objects that perform actions on behalf of a user. Agents typically take initial instructions from the user and then carry on their activity in an unattended manner for a predetermined period of time, until certain conditions are met, or for an indefinite period.

The most common type of intelligent agent in use today is the web bot. These agents continuously crawl a variety of websites retrieving and processing data on behalf of the user. For example, a user interested in finding a low airfare between two cities might program an intelligent agent to scour a variety of airline and travel websites and continuously check fare prices. Whenever the agent detects a fare lower than previous fares, it might send the user an e-mail message, pager alert, or other notification of the cheaper travel opportunity. More adventurous bot programmers might even provide the agent with credit card information and instruct it to actually order a ticket when the fare reaches a certain level.

Although agents can be very useful computing objects, they also introduce a variety of new security concerns that must be addressed. For example, what if a hacker programs an agent to continuously probe a network for security holes and report vulnerable systems in real time? How about a malicious individual who uses a number of agents to flood a website with bogus requests, thereby mounting a denial of service attack against that site? Or perhaps a commercially available agent accepts credit card information from a user and then transmits it to a hacker at the same time that it places a legitimate purchase.

Applets

Recall that agents are code objects sent from a user's system to query and process data stored on remote systems. *Applets* perform the opposite function; these code objects are sent from a server to a client to perform some action. In fact, applets are actually self-contained miniature programs that execute independently of the server that sent them.

This process is best explained through the use of an example. Imagine a web server that offers a variety of financial tools to Web users. One of these tools might be a mortgage calculator that processes a user's financial information and provides a monthly mortgage payment based upon the loan's principal and term and the borrower's credit information. Instead of processing this data and returning the results to the client system, the remote web server might send to the local system an applet that enables it to perform those calculations itself. This provides a number of benefits to both the remote server and the end user:

- The processing burden is shifted to the client, freeing up resources on the web server to process requests from more users.

- The client is able to produce data using local resources rather than waiting for a response from the remote server. In many cases, this results in a quicker response to changes in the input data.

- In a properly programmed applet, the web server does not receive any data provided to the applet as input, therefore maintaining the security and privacy of the user's financial data.

However, just as with agents, applets introduce a number of security concerns. They allow a remote system to send code to the local system for execution. Security administrators must take steps to ensure that this code is safe and properly screened for malicious activity. Also, unless the code is analyzed line by line, the end user can never be certain that the applet doesn't contain a Trojan horse component. For example, the mortgage calculator might indeed transmit sensitive financial information back to the web server without the end user's knowledge or consent.

The following sections explore two common applet types: Java applets and ActiveX controls.

Java Applets

Java is a platform-independent programming language developed by Sun Microsystems. Most programming languages use compilers that produce applications custom-tailored to run under a specific operating system. This requires the use of multiple compilers to produce different versions of a single application for each platform it must support. Java overcomes this limitation by inserting the Java Virtual Machine (JVM) into the picture. Each system that runs Java code downloads the version of the JVM supported by its operating system. The JVM then takes the Java code and translates it into a format executable by that specific system. The great benefit of this arrangement is that code can be shared between operating systems without modification. Java applets are simply short Java programs transmitted over the Internet to perform operations on a remote system.

Security was of paramount concern during the design of the Java platform and Sun's development team created the "sandbox" concept to place privilege restrictions on Java code. The sandbox isolates Java code objects from the rest of the operating system and enforces strict rules about the resources those objects can access. For example, the sandbox would prohibit a Java applet from retrieving information from areas of memory not specifically allocated to it, preventing the applet from stealing that information.

ActiveX Controls

ActiveX controls are Microsoft's answer to Sun's Java applets. They operate in a very similar fashion, but they are implemented using any one of a variety of languages, including Visual Basic, C, C++, and Java. There are two key distinctions between Java applets and ActiveX controls. First, ActiveX controls use proprietary Microsoft technology and, therefore, can execute only on systems running Microsoft operating systems. Second, ActiveX controls are not subject to the sandbox restrictions placed on Java applets. They have full access to the Windows operating environment and can perform a number of privileged actions. Therefore, special precautions must be taken when deciding which ActiveX controls to download and execute. Many security administrators have taken the somewhat harsh position of prohibiting the download of any ActiveX content from all but a select handful of trusted sites.

Object Request Brokers

To facilitate the growing trend toward distributed computing, the Object Management Group (OMG) set out to develop a common standard for developers around the world. The results of their work, known as the *Common Object Request Broker Architecture (CORBA),* defines an international standard (sanctioned by the International Organization for Standardization) for distributed computing. It defines the sequence of interactions between client and server shown in Figure 7.1.

In this model, clients do not need specific knowledge of a server's location or technical details to interact with it. They simply pass their request for a particular object to a local Object Request Broker (ORB) using a well-defined interface. These interfaces are created using the OMG's Interface Definition Language (IDL). The ORB, in turn, invokes the appropriate object, keeping the implementation details transparent to the original client.

FIGURE 7.1   Common Object Request Broker Architecture (CORBA)

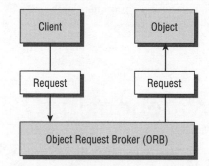

 Object Request Brokers (ORBs) are an offshoot of object-oriented programming, a topic discussed later in this chapter.

 The discussion of CORBA and ORBs presented here is, by necessity, an oversimplification designed to provide security professionals with an overview of the process. CORBA extends well beyond the model presented in Figure 7.1 to facilitate ORB-to-ORB interaction, load balancing, fault tolerance, and a number of other features. If you're interested in learning more about CORBA, the OMG has an excellent tutorial on their website at www.omg.org/getting-started/index.htm.

Microsoft Component Models

The driving force behind OMG's efforts to implement CORBA was the desire to create a common standard that enabled non-vendor-specific interaction. However, as such things often go, Microsoft decided to develop its own proprietary standards for object management: COM and DCOM.

The *Component Object Model (COM)* is Microsoft's standard architecture for the use of components within a process or between processes running on the same system. It works across the range of Microsoft products, from development environments to the Office productivity suite. In fact, Office's *object linking and embedding (OLE)* model that allows users to create documents that utilize components from different applications uses the COM architecture.

Although COM is restricted to local system interactions, the *Distributed Component Object Model (DCOM)* extends the concept to cover distributed computing environments. It replaces COM's interprocess communications capability with an ability to interact with the network stack and invoke objects located on remote systems.

Although DCOM and CORBA are competing component architectures, Microsoft and OMG agreed to allow some interoperability between ORBs utilizing different models.

Databases and Data Warehousing

Almost every modern organization maintains some sort of *database* that contains information critical to operations—be it customer contact information, order tracking data, human resource and benefits information, or sensitive trade secrets. It's likely that many of these databases contain personal information that users hold secret, such as credit card usage activity, travel habits, grocery store purchases, and telephone records. Because of the growing reliance on database systems, information security professionals must ensure that adequate security controls exist to protect them against unauthorized access, tampering, or destruction of data.

In the following sections, we'll discuss database management system (DBMS) architecture, the various types of DBMSs, and their features. Then we'll discuss database security features, polyinstantiation, ODBS, aggregation, inference, and data mining. They're loaded sections, so pay attention.

Database Management System (DBMS) Architecture

Although there is variety of *database management system (DBMS)* architectures available today, the vast majority of contemporary systems implement a technology known as relational database management systems (RDBMSs). For this reason, the following sections focus primarily on *relational databases*. However, first we'll discuss two other important DBMS architectures: hierarchical and distributed.

Hierarchical and Distributed Databases

A *hierarchical data model* combines records and fields that are related in a logical tree structure. This is done so that each field can have one child, many, or no children, but each field can have only a single parent, resulting in a consistent data mapping relationship of one-to-many. The hierarchical database model is not considered to be as flexible as the model for relational databases (which uses a data mapping relationship of one-to-one). This is due to the hierarchical database's tree structure created by its linkages of data elements. Changing a single leaf or field is easy, but altering an entire branch (called pruning) is difficult. A great example of the hierarchical data model is the DNS system or the forked competition maps used in sports tournaments.

The *distributed data model* has data stored in more than one database, but those databases are logically connected. The user perceives the database as a single entity, even though it comprises numerous parts interconnected over a network. Each field can have numerous children as well as numerous parents. Thus, the data mapping relationship for distributed databases is many-to-many.

Relational Databases

A relational database is a flat two-dimensional table made up of rows and columns. The row and column structure provides for one-to-one data mapping relationships. The main building block of the relational database is the *table* (also known as a relation). Each table contains a set of related *records*. For example, a sales database might contain the following tables:

- Customers table that contains contact information for all of the organization's clients
- Sales Reps table that contains identity information on the organization's sales force
- Orders table that contains records of orders placed by each customer

---

Object-Oriented Programming and Databases

When relational databases are combined with object-oriented programming environments, *object-relational databases* are produced. True Object Oriented DataBases (OODBs) benefit from the ease of code reuse, ease of troubleshooting analysis, and reduced overall maintenance. OODBs are also better suited for supporting complex applications involving multimedia, CAD, video, graphics, and expert systems than other types of databases.

Each of these tables contains a number of *attributes*, or fields. They are typically represented as the columns of a table. For example, the Customers table might contain columns for the company name, address, city, state, zip code, and telephone number. Each customer would have its own record, or tuple, represented by a row in the table. The number of rows in the relation is referred to as *cardinality* and the number of columns is the *degree*. The domain of a relation is the set of allowable values that the attribute can take.

To remember cardinality, think of a deck of cards on a desk, each card (i.e., the first four letters of this term!) is a row. To remember degree, think of a wall thermometer as a column (i.e., the temperature in degrees as measured on a thermometer!).

Relationships between the tables are defined to identify related records. In this example, relationships would probably exist between the Customers table and the Sales Reps table because each customer is assigned a sales representative and each sales representative is assigned to one or more customers. Additionally, a relationship would probably exist between the Customers table and the Orders table because each order must be associated with a customer and each customer is associated with one or more product orders.

Records are identified using a variety of keys. Quite simply, keys are a subset of the fields of a table used to uniquely identify records. There are three types of keys with which you should be familiar:

Candidate keys Subsets of attributes that can be used to uniquely identify any record in a table. No two records in the same table will ever contain the same values for all attributes composing a candidate key. Each table may have one or more candidate keys, which are chosen from column headings.

Primary keys   Selected from the set of candidate keys for a table to be used to uniquely identify the records in a table. Each table has only one primary key, selected by the database designer from the set of candidate keys. The RDBMS enforces the uniqueness of primary keys by disallowing the insertion of multiple records with the same primary key.

Foreign keys   Used to enforce relationships between two tables (also known as *referential integrity*). Referential integrity ensures that if one table contains a foreign key, it actually corresponds to a still existing primary key in the other table in the relationship. It makes certain that no record/tuple/row contains a reference to a primary key of a nonexistent record/tuple/row.

Modern relational databases use a standard language, the *Structured Query Language (SQL)*, to provide users with a consistent interface for the storage, retrieval, and mo;dification of data and for administrative control of the DBMS. Each DBMS vendor implements a slightly different version of SQL (like Microsoft's Transact-SQL and Oracle's PL/SQL), but all support a core feature set. SQL's primary security feature is its granularity of authorization. However, SQL supports a myriad of ways to execute or phrase the same query. In fact, the six basic SQL commands (Select, Update, Delete, Insert, Grant, and Revoke) can be used in various ways to perform the same activity.

Database Normalization

Database developers strive to create well-organized and efficient databases. To assist with this effort, they've created several defined levels of database organization known as normal forms. The process of bringing a database table into compliance with the normal forms is known as *normalization.*

Although there is a number of normal forms out there, the three most common are the First Normal Form (1NF), the Second Normal Form (2NF), and the Third Normal Form (3NF). Each of these forms adds additional requirements to reduce redundancy in the table, eliminating misplaced data and performing a number of other housekeeping tasks. The normal forms are cumulative; to be in 2NF, a table must first be 1NF compliant. Before making a table 3NF compliant, it must first be in 2NF.

The details of normalizing a database table are beyond the scope of the CISSP exam, but there is a large number of resources available on the Web to help you understand the requirements of the normal forms in greater detail.

A *bind variable* is a placeholder for SQL literal values, such as numbers or character strings. When a SQL query containing bind variables is passed to the server, the server expects you to follow up the query later to pass on the actual literals to put into the placeholders.

SQL provides the complete functionality necessary for administrators, developers, and end users to interact with the database. In fact, most of the GUI interfaces popular today merely wrap some extra bells and whistles around a simple SQL interface to the DBMS. SQL itself is divided into two distinct components: the *Data Definition Language (DDL)*, which allows for the creation and modification of the database's structure (known as the *schema*), and the *Data Manipulation Language (DML)*, which allows users to interact with the data contained within that schema.

Database Transactions

Relational databases support the explicit and implicit use of transactions to ensure data integrity. Each transaction is a discrete set of SQL instructions that will either succeed or fail as a group. It's not possible for part of a transaction to succeed while part fails. Consider the example of a transfer between two accounts at a bank. We might use the following SQL code to first add $250 to account 1001 and then subtract $250 from account 2002:

```
BEGIN TRANSACTION

UPDATE accounts
SET balance = balance + 250
WHERE account_number = 1001

UPDATE accounts
SET balance = balance - 250
WHERE account_number = 2002

END TRANSACTION
```

Imagine a case where these two statements were not executed as part of a transaction, but were executed separately. If the database failed during the moment between completion of the first transaction and completion of the second transaction, $250 would have been added to account 1001 but there would have been no corresponding deduction from account 2002. The $250 would have appeared out of thin air! This simple example underscores the importance of transaction-oriented processing.

When a transaction successfully completes, it is said to be committed to the database and can not be undone. Transaction committing may be explicit, using SQL's COMMIT command, or implicit if the end of the transaction is successfully reached. If a transaction must be aborted, it may be rolled back explicitly using the ROLLBACK command or implicitly if there is a hardware or software failure. When a transaction is rolled back, the database restores itself to the condition it was in before the transaction began.

There are four required characteristics of all database transactions: *atomicity, consistency, isolation,* and *durability*. Together, these attributes are known as the *ACID model,* which is a critical concept in the development of database management systems. Let's take a brief look at each of these requirements:

Atomicity   Database transactions must be atomic—that is, they must be an "all or nothing" affair. If any part of the transaction fails, the entire transaction must be rolled back as if it never occurred.

Consistency   All transactions must begin operating in an environment that is consistent with all of the database's rules (for example, all records have a unique primary key). When the transaction is complete, the database must again be consistent with the rules, regardless of whether those rules were violated during the processing of the transaction itself. No other transaction should ever be able to utilize any inconsistent data that might be generated during the execution of another transaction.

Isolation   The isolation principle requires that transactions operate separately from each other. If a database receives two SQL transactions that modify the same data, one transaction must be completed in its entirety before the other transaction is allowed to modify the same data. This prevents one transaction from working with invalid data generated as an intermediate step by another transaction.

Durability   Database transactions must be durable. That is, once they are committed to the database, they must be preserved. Databases ensure durability through the use of backup mechanisms, such as transaction logs.

In the following sections, we'll discuss a variety of specific security issues of concern to database developers and administrators.

Security for Multilevel Databases

As you learned in Chapter 5, "Security Management Concepts and Principles," many organizations use data classification schemes to enforce access control restrictions based upon the security labels assigned to data objects and individual users. When mandated by an organization's security policy, this classification concept must also be extended to the organization's databases.

Multilevel security databases contain information at a number of different classification levels. They must verify the labels assigned to users and, in response to user requests, provide only information that's appropriate. However, this concept becomes somewhat more complicated when considering security for a database.

When multilevel security is required, it's essential that administrators and developers strive to keep data with different security requirements separate. The mixing of data with different classification levels and/or need-to-know requirements is known as database *contamination* and is a significant security risk. Often, administrators will deploy a trusted front end to add multilevel security to a legacy or insecure DBMS.

> ### Restricting Access with Views
>
> Another way to implement multilevel security in a database is through the use of database *views*. Views are simply SQL statements that present data to the user as if they were tables themselves. They may be used to collate data from multiple tables, aggregate individual records, or restrict a user's access to a limited subset of database attributes and/or records.
>
> Views are stored in the database as SQL commands rather than as tables of data. This dramatically reduces the space requirements of the database and allows views to violate the rules of normalization that apply to tables. On the other hand, retrieving data from a complex view can take significantly longer than retrieving it from a table because the DBMS may need to perform calculations to determine the value of certain attributes for each record.
>
> Due to the flexibility of views, many database administrators use them as a security tool—allowing users to interact only with limited views rather than with the raw tables of data underlying them.

Concurrency

Concurrency, or edit control, is a preventative security mechanism that endeavors to make certain that the information stored in the database is always correct or at least has its integrity and availability protected. This feature can be employed whether the database is multilevel or single level. Concurrency uses a "lock" feature to allow an authorized user to make changes but deny other users access to view or make changes to data elements at the same time. Then, after the changes have been made, an "unlock" feature allows other users the access they need. In some instances, administrators will use concurrency with auditing mechanisms to track document and/or field changes. When this recorded data is reviewed, concurrency becomes a detective control.

Other Security Mechanisms

There are several other security mechanisms that administrators may deploy when using a DBMS. These features are relatively easy to implement and are common in the industry. The mechanisms related to *semantic integrity,* for instance are common security features of a DBMS. Semantic integrity ensures that no structural and semantic rules are violated due to any queries or updates by any user. It also checks that all stored data types are within valid domain ranges, ensures that only logical values exist, and confirms that the system complies with any and all uniqueness constraints.

Administrators may employ time and date stamps to maintain data integrity and availability. Time and date stamps often appear in distributed database systems. When a time stamp is placed on all change transactions and those changes are distributed or replicated to the other database members, all changes are applied to all members but they are implemented in correct chronological order.

Another common security feature of DBMS is that objects can be controlled granularly within the database; this can also improve security control. *Content-dependent access control* is an example of *granular object control*. Content-dependent access control focuses on control based upon the contents or payload of the object being accessed. Since decisions must be made on an object-by-object basis, content-dependent control increases processing overhead. Another form of granular control is cell suppression. *Cell suppression* is the concept of hiding or imposing more security restrictions on individual database fields or cells.

Context-dependent access control is often discussed alongside content-dependent access control due to the similarity of their names. Context-dependent access control evaluates the big picture to make its access control decisions. The key factor in context-dependent access control is how each object or packet or field relates to the overall activity or communication. Any single element may look innocuous by itself, but in a larger context that element may be revealed to be benign or malign.

Administrators may employ *database partitioning* to subvert aggregation, inferencing, and contamination vulnerabilities. Database partitioning is the process of splitting a single database into multiple parts, each with a unique and distinct security level or type of content.

Polyinstantiation occurs when two or more rows in the same relational database table appear to have identical primary key elements but contain different data for use at differing classification levels. It is often used as a defense against some types of inference attacks (we'll discuss inference in just a moment).

Consider a database table containing the location of various naval ships on patrol. Normally, this database contains the exact position of each ship stored at the level with secret classification. However, one particular ship, the USS *UpToNoGood,* is on an undercover mission to a top-secret location. Military commanders do not want anyone to know that the ship deviated from its normal patrol. If the database administrators simply change the classification of the *UpToNoGood*'s location to top secret, a user with a secret clearance would know that something unusual was going on when they couldn't query the location of the ship. However, if polyinstantiation is used, two records could be inserted into the table. The first one, classified at the top secret level, would reflect the true location of the ship and be available only to users with the appropriate top secret security clearance. The second record, classified at the secret level, would indicate that the ship was on routine patrol and would be returned to users with a secret clearance.

Finally, administrators can utilize noise and perturbation to insert false or misleading data into a DBMS in order to redirect or thwart information confidentiality attacks.

ODBC

Open Database Connectivity (ODBC) is a database feature that allows applications to communicate with different types of databases without having to be directly programmed for interaction with every type of database. ODBC acts as a proxy between applications and back-end database drivers, giving application programmers greater freedom in creating solutions without having to worry about the back-end database system. Figure 7.2 illustrates the relationship between ODBC and DBMS.

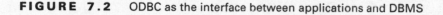

FIGURE 7.2 ODBC as the interface between applications and DBMS

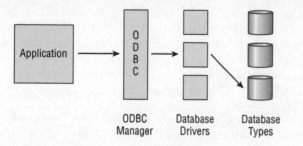

Aggregation

SQL provides a number of functions that combine records from one or more tables to produce potentially useful information. This process is called *aggregation*. Some of the functions, known as the *aggregate functions,* are listed here:

COUNT( )   Returns the number of records that meet specified criteria

MIN( )   Returns the record with the smallest value for the specified attribute or combination of attributes

MAX( )   Returns the record with the largest value for the specified attribute or combination of attributes

SUM( )   Returns the summation of the values of the specified attribute or combination of attributes across all affected records

AVG( )   Returns the average value of the specified attribute or combination of attributes across all affected records

These functions, although extremely useful, also pose a significant risk to the security of information in a database. For example, suppose a low-level military records clerk is responsible for updating records of personnel and equipment as they are transferred from base to base. As part of their duties, this clerk may be granted the database permissions necessary to query and update personnel tables. Aggregation is not without its security vulnerabilities. Aggregation attacks are used to collect numerous low-level security items or low-value items and combine them together to create something of a higher security level or value.

The military might not consider an individual transfer request (i.e., Sgt. Jones is being moved from Base X to Base Y) to be classified information. The records clerk has access to that information, but most likely, Sgt. Jones has already informed his friends and family that he will be moving to Base Y. However, with access to aggregate functions, the records clerk might be able to count the number of troops assigned to each military base around the world. These force levels are often closely guarded military secrets, but the low-ranking records clerk was able to deduce them by using aggregate functions across a large amount of unclassified data.

Inference

The database security issues posed by inference attacks are very similar to those posed by the threat of data aggregation. As with aggregation, *inference* attacks involve the combination of several pieces of nonsensitive information used to gain access to information that should be classified at a higher level. However, inference makes use of the human mind's deductive capacity rather than the raw mathematical ability of modern database platforms.

A commonly cited example of an inference attack is that of the accounting clerk at a large corporation who is allowed to retrieve the total amount the company spends on salaries for use in a top-level report but is not allowed to access the salaries of individual employees. The accounting clerk often has to prepare those reports with effective dates in the past and so is allowed to access the total salary amounts for any day in the past year. Say, for example, that this clerk must also know the hiring and termination dates of various employees and has access to this information. This opens the door for an inference attack. If an employee was the only person hired on a specific date, the accounting clerk can now retrieve the total salary amount on that date and the day before and deduce the salary of that particular employee—sensitive information that the user would not be permitted to access directly.

As with aggregation, the best defense against inference attacks is to maintain constant vigilance over the permissions granted to individual users. Furthermore, intentional blurring of data may be used to prevent the inference of sensitive information. For example, if the accounting clerk were able to retrieve only salary information rounded to the nearest million, they would probably not be able to gain any useful information about individual employees.

For this reason, it's especially important for database security administrators to strictly control access to aggregate functions and adequately assess the potential information they may reveal to unauthorized individuals.

Data Mining

Many organizations use large databases, known as *data warehouses,* to store large amounts of information from a variety of databases for use in specialized analysis techniques. These data warehouses often contain detailed historical information not normally stored in production databases due to storage limitations or data security concerns.

An additional type of storage, known as a *data dictionary,* is commonly used for storing critical information about data, including usage, type, sources, relationships, and formats. DBMS software reads the data dictionary to determine access rights for users attempting to access data.

Data mining techniques allow analysts to comb through these data warehouses and look for potential correlated information amid the historical data. For example, an analyst might discover that the demand for light bulbs always increases in the winter months and then use this information when planning pricing and promotion strategies. The information that is discovered during a data mining operation is called *metadata,* or data about data, and is stored in a *data mart.* A data mart is a more secure storage environment than a data warehouse.

Data warehouses and data mining are significant to security professionals for two reasons. First, as previously mentioned, data warehouses contain large amounts of potentially sensitive information vulnerable to aggregation and inference attacks, and security practitioners must ensure that adequate access controls and other security measures are in place to safeguard this data. Second, data mining can actually be used as a security tool when it's used to develop baselines for statistical anomaly-based intrusion detection systems (see Chapter 2, "Attacks and Monitoring," for more information on the various types and functionality of intrusion detection systems).

Data/Information Storage

Database management systems have helped harness the power of data and gain some modicum of control over who can access it and the actions they can perform on it. However, security professionals must keep in mind that DBMS security covers access to information through only the traditional "front door" channels. Data is also processed through a computer's storage resources—both memory and physical media. Precautions must be in place to ensure that these basic resources are protected against security vulnerabilities as well. After all, you would never incur a lot of time and expense to secure the front door of your home and then leave the back door wide open, would you?

Types of Storage

Modern computing systems use several types of storage to maintain system and user data. The systems strike a balance between the various storage types to satisfy an organization's computing requirements. There are several common storage types:

Primary (or "real") memory   Consists of the main memory resources directly available to a system's CPU. Primary memory normally consists of volatile random access memory (RAM) and is usually the most high-performance storage resource available to a system.

Secondary storage   Consists of more inexpensive, nonvolatile storage resources available to a system for long-term use. Typical *secondary storage* resources include magnetic and optical media, such as tapes, disks, hard drives, and CD/DVD storage.

Virtual memory   Allows a system to simulate additional primary memory resources through the use of secondary storage. For example, a system low on expensive RAM might make a portion of the hard disk available for direct CPU addressing.

Virtual storage   Allows a system to simulate secondary storage resources through the use of *primary storage.* The most common example of virtual storage is the "RAM disk" that presents itself to the operating system as a secondary storage device but is actually implemented in volatile RAM. This provides an extremely fast file system for use in various applications but provides no recovery capability.

Random access storage   Allows the operating system to request contents from any point within the media. RAM and hard drives are examples of random access storage.

Sequential access storage   Requires scanning through the entire media from the beginning to reach a specific address. A magnetic tape is a common example of sequential access storage.

Volatile storage   Loses its contents when power is removed from the resource. RAM is the most common type of *volatile storage*.

Nonvolatile storage   Does not depend upon the presence of power to maintain its contents. Magnetic/optical media and nonvolatile RAM (NVRAM) are typical examples of *nonvolatile storage*.

Storage Threats

Information security professionals should be aware of two main threats posed against data storage systems. First, the threat of illegitimate access to storage resources exists no matter what type of storage is in use. If administrators do not implement adequate file system access controls, an intruder might stumble across sensitive data simply by browsing the file system. In more sensitive environments, administrators should also protect against attacks that involve bypassing operating system controls and directly accessing the physical storage media to retrieve data. This is best accomplished through the use of an encrypted file system, which is accessible only through the primary operating system. Furthermore, systems that operate in a multilevel security environment should provide adequate controls to ensure that shared memory and storage resources provide fail-safe controls so that data from one classification level is not readable at a lower classification level.

Covert channel attacks pose the second primary threat against data storage resources. Covert storage channels allow the transmission of sensitive data between classification levels through the direct or indirect manipulation of shared storage media. This may be as simple as writing sensitive data to an inadvertently shared portion of memory or physical storage. More complex covert storage channels might be used to manipulate the amount of free space available on a disk or the size of a file to covertly convey information between security levels. For more information on covert channel analysis, see Chapter 12, "Principles of Security Models."

Knowledge-Based Systems

Since the advent of computing, engineers and scientists have worked toward developing systems capable of performing routine actions that would bore a human and consume a significant amount of time. The majority of the achievements in this area focused on relieving the burden of computationally intensive tasks. However, researchers have also made giant strides toward developing systems that have an "artificial intelligence" that can simulate (to some extent) the purely human power of reasoning.

The following sections examine two types of knowledge-based artificial intelligence systems: expert systems and neural networks. We'll also take a look at their potential applications to computer security problems.

Expert Systems

Expert systems seek to embody the accumulated knowledge of mankind on a particular subject and apply it in a consistent fashion to future decisions. Several studies have shown that expert systems, when properly developed and implemented, often make better decisions than some of their human counterparts when faced with routine decisions.

There are two main components to every expert system. The *knowledge base* contains the rules known by an expert system. The knowledge base seeks to codify the knowledge of human experts in a series of "if/then" statements. Let's consider a simple expert system designed to help homeowners decide if they should evacuate an area when a hurricane threatens. The knowledge base might contain the following statements (these statements are for example only):

- If the hurricane is a Category 4 storm or higher, then flood waters normally reach a height of 20 feet above sea level.

- If the hurricane has winds in excess of 120 miles per hour (mph), then wood-frame structures will fail.

- If it is late in the hurricane season, then hurricanes tend to get stronger as they approach the coast.

In an actual expert system, the knowledge base would contain hundreds or thousands of assertions such as those just listed.

The second major component of an expert system—the *inference engine*—analyzes information in the knowledge base to arrive at the appropriate decision. The expert system user utilizes some sort of user interface to provide the inference engine with details about the current situation, and the inference engine uses a combination of logical reasoning and fuzzy logic techniques to draw a conclusion based upon past experience. Continuing with the hurricane example, a user might inform the expert system that a Category 4 hurricane is approaching the coast with wind speeds averaging 140 mph. The inference engine would then analyze information in the knowledge base and make an evacuation recommendation based upon that past knowledge.

Expert systems are not infallible—they're only as good as the data in the knowledge base and the decision-making algorithms implemented in the inference engine. However, they have one major advantage in stressful situations—their decisions do not involve judgment clouded by emotion. Expert systems can play an important role in analyzing situations such as emergency events, stock trading, and other scenarios in which emotional investment sometimes gets in the way of a logical decision. For this reason, many lending institutions now utilize expert systems to make credit decisions instead of relying upon loan officers who might say to themselves, "Well, Jim hasn't paid his bills on time, but he seems like a perfectly nice guy."

Fuzzy Logic

As previously mentioned, inference engines commonly use a technique known as fuzzy logic. This technique is designed to more closely approximate human thought patterns than the rigid mathematics of set theory or algebraic approaches that utilize "black and white" categorizations of data. Fuzzy logic replaces them with blurred boundaries, allowing the algorithm to think in the "shades of gray" that dominate human thought. Fuzzy logic as used by an expert system has four steps or phases: fuzzification, inference, composition, and defuzzification.

Neural Networks

In *neural networks,* chains of computational units are used in an attempt to imitate the biological reasoning process of the human mind. In an expert system, a series of rules is stored in a knowledge base, whereas in a neural network, a long chain of computational decisions that feed into each other and eventually sum to produce the desired output is set up.

Keep in mind that no neural network designed to date comes close to having the actual reasoning power of the human mind. That notwithstanding, neural networks show great potential to advance the artificial intelligence field beyond its current state. Benefits of neural networks include linearity, input-output mapping, and adaptivity. These benefits are evident in the implementations of neural networks for voice recognition, face recognition, weather prediction, and the exploration of models of thinking and consciousness.

Typical neural networks involve many layers of summation, each of which requires weighting information to reflect the relative importance of the calculation in the overall decision-making process. These weights must be custom-tailored for each type of decision the neural network is expected to make. This is accomplished through the use of a training period during which the network is provided with inputs for which the proper decision is known. The algorithm then works backward from these decisions to determine the proper weights for each node in the computational chain. This activity is known as the *Delta rule* or *learning rule.* Through the use of the Delta rule, neural networks are able to learn from experience.

Decision Support Systems

A Decision Support System (DSS) is a knowledge-based application that analyzes business data and presents it in such a way as to make business decisions easier for users. It is considered more of an informational application than an operational application. Often a DSS is employed by knowledge workers (such as help desk or customer support personnel) and by sales services (such as phone operators). This type of application may present information in a graphical manner so as to link concepts and content and guide the script of the operator. Often a DSS is backed by an expert system controlling a database.

Security Applications

Both expert systems and neural networks have great applications in the field of computer security. One of the major advantages offered by these systems is their capability to rapidly make consistent decisions. One of the major problems in computer security is the inability of system administrators to consistently and thoroughly analyze massive amounts of log and audit trail data to look for anomalies. It seems like a match made in heaven!

One successful application of this technology to the computer security arena is the Next-Generation Intrusion Detection Expert System (NIDES) developed by Philip Porras and his team at the Information and Computing Sciences System Design Laboratory of SRI International. This system provides an inference engine and knowledge base that draws information from a variety of audit logs across a network and provides notification to security administrators when the activity of an individual user varies from their standard usage profile.

Systems Development Controls

Many organizations use custom-developed hardware and software systems to achieve flexible operational goals. As you will learn in Chapter 8 and Chapter 12, these custom solutions can present great security vulnerabilities as a result of malicious and/or careless developers who create trap doors, buffer overflow vulnerabilities, or other weaknesses that can leave a system open to exploitation by malicious individuals.

To protect against these vulnerabilities, it's vital to introduce security concerns into the entire systems development life cycle. An organized, methodical process helps ensure that solutions meet functional requirements as well as security guidelines. The following sections explore the spectrum of systems development activities with an eye toward security concerns that should be foremost on the mind of any information security professional engaged in solutions development.

Software Development

Security should be a consideration at every stage of a system's development, including the software development process. Programmers should strive to build security into every application they develop, with greater levels of security provided to critical applications and those that process sensitive information. It's extremely important to consider the security implications of a software development project from the early stages because it's much easier to build security into a system than it is to add security onto an existing system.

Assurance

To ensure that the security control mechanisms built into a new application properly implement the security policy throughout the life cycle of the system, administrators use *assurance procedures*. Assurance procedures are simply formalized processes by which trust is built into the life cycle of a system. The Trusted Computer System Evaluation Criteria (TCSEC) Orange Book refers to this process as life cycle assurance. We'll discuss this further in Chapter 13, "Administrative Management."

Avoiding System Failure

No matter how advanced your development team, your systems will likely fail at some point in time. You should plan for this type of failure when you put the software and hardware controls in place, ensuring that the system will respond appropriately. You can employ many methods to avoid failure, including using limit checks and creating fail-safe or fail-open procedures. Let's talk about these in more detail.

Limit Checks

Environmental controls and hardware devices cannot prevent problems created by poor program coding. It is important to have proper software development and coding practices to ensure that security is a priority during product development. To avoid buffer overflow attacks, you must perform limit checks by managing data types, data formats, and data length when accepting input from a user or another application. Limit checks ensure that data does not exceed maximum allowable values. Depending on the application, you may also need to include sequence checks to ensure that data input is properly ordered.

In most organizations, security professionals come from a system administration background and don't have professional experience in software development. If your background doesn't include this type of experience, don't let that stop you from learning about it and educating your organization's developers on the importance of secure coding.

Fail-Secure and Fail-Open

In spite of the best efforts of programmers, product designers, and project managers, developed applications will be placed into situations and environments that were neither predicted nor fully understood. Some of these conditions will cause failures. Since failures are unpredictable, programmers should design into their code a general sense of how to respond to and handle failures.

There are two basic choices when planning for system failure: *fail-secure* (also called fail-safe) or *fail-open*. The fail-secure failure state puts the system into a high level of security (and possibly even disables it entirely) until an administrator can diagnose the problem and restore the system to normal operation. In the vast majority of environments, fail-secure is the appropriate failure state because it prevents unauthorized access to information and resources.

Software should revert to a fail-secure condition. This may mean closing just the application or possibly stopping the operation of the entire host system. An example of such failure response is seen in the Windows OS with the appearance of the Blue Screen of Death (BSOD), but it is really called a *STOP error*. A STOP error occurs when an insecure and illegal activity occurs in spite of the OS's efforts to prevent it. This could include an application gaining direct access to hardware, bypassing a security access check, or one process interfering with the memory space of another. Once an illegal operation occurs, the environment itself is no longer trustworthy. So, rather than continuing to support an unreliable and insecure operating environment, the OS initiates a STOP error as its fail-secure response. Once a fail-secure operation occurs, the programmer should consider the activities that occur afterward. The options are to remain in a fail-secure state or to automatically reboot the system. The former option requires an administrator to manually reboot the system and oversee the process. This action can be enforced by using a boot password. The latter option does not require human intervention for the system to restore itself to a functioning state, but it has its own unique issues. First, it is subject to initial program load (IPL) vulnerabilities (for more information on IPL, review Chapter 14, "Auditing and Monitoring"). Second, it must restrict the system to reboot into a nonprivileged state. In other words, the system should not reboot and perform an automatic logon; instead, it should prompt the user for authorized access credentials.

In limited circumstances, it may be appropriate to implement a fail-open failure state, which allows users to bypass security controls when a system fails. This is sometimes appropriate for lower-layer components of a multilayered security system. Fail-open systems should be used with extreme caution. Before deploying a system using this failure mode, clearly validate the business requirement for this move. If it is justified, ensure that adequate alternative controls are in place to protect the organization's resources should the system fail. It's extremely rare that you'd want all of your security controls to utilize a fail-open approach.

Even when security is properly designed and embedded in software, that security is often disabled in order to support easier installation. Thus, it is common for the IT administrator to have the responsibility of turning on and configuring security to match the needs of their specific environment. Maintaining security is often a trade-off with user-friendliness and functionality, as you can see from Figure 7.3. Additionally, as you add or increase security, you will also increase costs, increase administrative overhead, and reduce productivity/throughput.

FIGURE 7.3   Security vs. user-friendliness vs. functionality

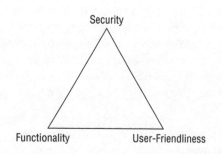

Programming Languages

As you probably know, software developers use programming languages to develop software code. You might not know that there are several types of languages that can be used simultaneously by the same system. This section takes a brief look at the different types of programming languages and the security implications of each.

Computers understand binary code. They speak a language of 1s and 0s and that's it! The instructions that a computer follows are made up of a long series of binary digits in a language known as *machine language*. Each CPU chipset has its own machine language and it's virtually impossible for a human being to decipher anything but the most simple machine language code without the assistance of specialized software. *Assembly language* is a higher-level alternative that uses mnemonics to represent the basic instruction set of a CPU but still requires hardware-specific knowledge of a relatively obscure assembly language. It also requires a large amount of tedious programming; a task as simple as adding two numbers together could take five or six lines of assembly code!

Programmers, of course, don't want to write their code in either machine language or assembly language. They prefer to use *high-level languages,* such as C++, Java, and Visual Basic. These languages allow programmers to write instructions that better approximate human communication, decrease the length of time needed to craft an application, may decrease the number of programmers needed on a project, and also allow some portability between different operating systems and hardware platforms. Once programmers are ready to execute their programs, there are two options available to them, depending upon the language they've chosen.

Some languages (such as C++, Java, and FORTRAN) are *compiled languages.* When using a compiled language, the programmer uses a tool known as the compiler to convert the higher-level language into an executable file designed for use on a specific operating system. This executable is then distributed to end users who may use it as they see fit. Generally speaking, it's not possible to view or modify the software instructions in an executable file.

Other languages (such as JavaScript and VBScript) are *interpreted languages.* When these languages are used, the programmer distributes the source code, which contains instructions in the higher-level language. End users then use an interpreter to execute that source code on their system. They're able to view the original instructions written by the programmer.

There are security advantages and disadvantages to each approach. Compiled code is generally less prone to manipulation by a third party. However, it's also easier for a malicious (or unskilled) programmer to embed back doors and other security flaws in the code and escape detection because the original instructions can't be viewed by the end user. Interpreted code, however, is less prone to the insertion of malicious code by the original programmer because the end user may view the code and check it for accuracy. On the other hand, everyone who touches the software has the ability to modify the programmer's original instructions and possibly embed malicious code in the interpreted software.

Reverse engineering is considered an unethical form of engineering, whereby programmers decompile vendor code in order to understand the intricate details of its functionality. Ethics come in to play because such efforts most often presage creating a similar, competing, or compatible product of their own.

Object-Oriented Programming

Many of the latest programming languages, such as C++ and Java, support the concept of *object-oriented programming (OOP)*. Older programming styles, such as functional programming, focused on the flow of the program itself and attempted to model the desired behavior as a series of steps. Object-oriented programming focuses on the *objects* involved in an interaction. It can be thought of as a group of objects that can be requested to perform certain operations or exhibit certain behaviors. Objects work together to provide a system's functionality or capabilities. OOP has the potential to be more reliable and able to reduce the propagation of program change errors. As a type of programming method, it is better suited to modeling or mimicking the real world. For example, a banking program might have three object classes that correspond to accounts, account holders, and employees. When a new account is added to the system, a new *instance,* or copy, of the appropriate object is created to contain the details of that account.

Each object in the OOP model has *methods* that correspond to specific actions that can be taken on the object. For example, the account object can have methods to add funds, deduct funds, close the account, and transfer ownership.

Objects can also be subclasses of other objects and *inherit* methods from their parent class. For example, the account object may have subclasses that correspond to specific types of accounts, such as savings, checking, mortgages, and auto loans. The subclasses can use all of the methods of the parent class and have additional class-specific methods. For example, the checking object might have a method called `write_check()` whereas the other subclasses do not.

Computer Aided Software Engineering (CASE)

The advent of object-oriented programming has reinvigorated a movement toward applying traditional engineering design principles to the software engineering field. One such movement has been toward the use of computer aided software engineering (CASE) tools to help developers, managers, and customers interact through the various stages of the software development life cycle.

One popular CASE tool, Middle CASE, is used in the design and analysis phase of software engineering to help create screen and report layouts.

From a security point of view, object-oriented-programming provides a black-box approach to abstraction. Users need to know the details of an object's interface (generally the inputs, outputs, and actions that correspond to each of the object's methods) but don't necessarily need to know the inner workings of the object to use it effectively. To provide the desired characteristics of object-oriented systems, the objects are encapsulated (self-contained) and they can be accessed only through specific messages (i.e., input). Objects can also exhibit the substitution property, which allows different objects providing compatible operations to be substituted for each other.

Here is a list of common object-oriented programming terms you might come across in your work:

Message   A *message* is a communication to or input of an object.

Method   A *method* is internal code that defines the actions an object performs in response to a message.

Behavior   The results or output exhibited by an object is a *behavior*. Behaviors are the results of a message being processed through a method.

Class   A collection of the common methods from a set of objects that defines the behavior of those objects is called a *class*.

Instance   Objects are *instances* of or examples of classes that contain their method.

Inheritance   Inheritance is the occurance when methods from a class (parent or superclass) are *inherited* by another subclass (child).

Delegation   *Delegation* is the forwarding of a request by an object to another object or delegate. An object delegates if it does not have a method to handle the message.

Polymorphism   A *polymorphism* is the characteristic of an object to provide different behaviors based upon the same message and methods owing to changes in external conditions.

Cohesive   An object is highly *cohesive* if it can perform a task with little or no help from others. Highly cohesive objects are not as dependent upon other objects as objects that are less cohesive. Highly cohesive objects are often better. Objects that have high cohesion perform tasks alone and have low coupling.

Coupling   *Coupling* is the level of interaction between objects. Lower coupling means less interaction. Lower coupling provides better software design because objects are more independent. Lower coupling is easier to troubleshoot and update. Objects that have low cohesion require lots of assistance from other objects to perform tasks and have high coupling.

Systems Development Life Cycle

Security is most effective if it is planned and managed throughout the life cycle of a system or application. Administrators employ project management to keep a development project on target and moving toward the goal of a completed product. Often project management is structured using life cycle models to direct the development process. The use of formalized life cycle models helps to ensure good coding practices and the embedding of security in every stage of product development.

There are several activities that all systems development processes should have in common. Although they may not necessarily share the same names, these core activities are essential to the development of sound, secure systems. The section "Life Cycle Models" later in this chapter examines two life cycle models and shows how these activities are applied in real-world software engineering environments.

It's important to note at this point that the terminology used in system development life cycles varies from model to model and from publication to publication. Don't spend too much time worrying about the exact terms used in this book or any of the other literature you may come across. When taking the CISSP examination, it's much more important that you have an understanding of how the process works and the fundamental principles underlying the development of secure systems. That said, as with any rule, there are several exceptions.

Conceptual Definition

The conceptual definition phase of systems development involves creating the basic concept statement for a system. Simply put, it's a simple statement agreed upon by all interested stakeholders (the developers, customers, and management) that states the purpose of the project as well as the general system requirements. The conceptual definition is a very high-level statement of purpose and should not be longer than one or two paragraphs. If you were reading a detailed summary of the project, you might expect to see the concept statement as an abstract or introduction that enables an outsider to gain a top-level understanding of the project in a short period of time.

It's very helpful to refer to the concept statement at all phases of the systems development process. Often, the intricate details of the development process tend to obscure the overarching goal of the project. Simply reading the concept statement periodically can assist in refocusing a team of developers.

Functional Requirements Determination

Once all stakeholders have agreed upon the concept statement, it's time for the development team to sit down and begin the functional requirements process. In this phase, specific system functionalities are listed and developers begin to think about how the parts of the system should interoperate to meet the functional requirements. The deliverable from this phase of development is a functional requirements document that lists the specific system requirements.

As with the concept statement, it's important to ensure that all stakeholders agree on the functional requirements document before work progresses to the next level. When it's finally completed, the document shouldn't be simply placed on a shelf to gather dust—the entire development team should constantly refer to this document during all phases to ensure that the project is on track. In the final stages of testing and evaluation, the project managers should use this document as a checklist to ensure that all functional requirements are met.

Protection Specifications Development

Security-conscious organizations also ensure that adequate protections are designed into every system from the earliest stages of development. It's often very useful to have a protection specifications development phase in your life cycle model. This phase takes place soon after the development of functional requirements and often continues as the design and design review phases progress.

During the development of protection specifications, it's important to analyze the system from a number of security perspectives. First, adequate access controls must be designed into every system to ensure that only authorized users are allowed to access the system and that they are not permitted to exceed their level of authorization. Second, the system must maintain the confidentiality of vital data through the use of appropriate encryption and data protection technologies. Next, the system should provide both an audit trail to enforce individual accountability and a detective mechanism for illegitimate activity. Finally, depending upon the criticality of the system, availability and fault-tolerance issues should be addressed.

Keep in mind that designing security into a system is not a one-shot process and it must be done proactively. All too often, systems are designed without security planning and then developers attempt to retrofit the system with appropriate security mechanisms. Unfortunately, these mechanisms are an afterthought and do not fully integrate with the system's design, which leaves gaping security vulnerabilities. Also, the security requirements should be revisited each time a significant change is made to the design specification. If a major component of the system changes, it's very likely that the security requirements will change as well.

Design Review

Once the functional and protection specifications are complete, let the system designers do their thing! In this often lengthy process, the designers determine exactly how the various parts of the system will interoperate and how the modular system structure will be laid out. Also during this phase, the design management team commonly sets specific tasks for various teams and lays out initial timelines for completion of coding milestones.

After the design team completes the formal design documents, a review meeting with the stakeholders should be held to ensure that everyone's in agreement that the process is still on track for successful development of a system with the desired functionality.

Code Review Walk-Through

Once the stakeholders have given the software design their blessing, it's time for the software developers to start writing code. Project managers should schedule several code review walk-though meetings at various milestones throughout the coding process. These technical meetings usually involve only development personnel who sit down with a copy of the code for a specific module and walk through it, looking for problems in logical flow or other design/security flaws. The meetings play an instrumental role in ensuring that the code produced by the various development teams performs according to specification.

System Test Review

After many code reviews and a lot of long nights, there will come a point at which a developer puts in that final semicolon and declares the system complete. As any seasoned software engineer knows, the system is never complete. Now it's time to begin the system test review phase. Initially, most organizations perform the initial system tests using development personnel to seek out any obvious errors. Once this phase is complete, a series of beta test deployments takes place to ensure that customers agree that the system meets all functional requirements and performs according to the original specification. As with any critical development process, it's important that you maintain a copy of the written system test plan and test results for future review.

Maintenance

Once a system is operational, a variety of *maintenance* tasks are necessary to ensure continued operation in the face of changing operational, data processing, storage, and environmental requirements. It's essential that you have a skilled support team in place to handle any routine or unexpected maintenance. It's also important that any changes to the code be handled through a formalized change request/control process, as described in Chapter 5.

Life Cycle Models

One of the major complaints you'll hear from practitioners of the more established engineering disciplines (such as civil, mechanical, and electrical engineering) is that software engineering is not an engineering discipline at all. In fact, they contend, it's simply a combination of chaotic processes that somehow manage to scrape out workable solutions from time to time. Indeed, some of the "software engineering" that takes place in today's development environments is nothing but bootstrap coding held together by "duct tape and chicken wire."

However, the adoption of more formalized life cycle management processes is being seen in mainstream software engineering as the industry matures. After all, it's hardly fair to compare the processes of an age-old discipline such as civil engineering to those of an industry that's barely a few decades old. In the 1970s and 1980s, pioneers like Winston Royce and Barry Boehm proposed several software development life cycle (SDLC) models to help guide the practice toward formalized processes. In 1991, the Software Engineering Institute introduced the Capability Maturity Model, which described the process organizations undertake as they move toward incorporating solid engineering principles into their software development processes. In this section, we'll take a look at the work produced by these studies.

Having a management model in place should improve the resultant products. However, if the SDLC methodology is inadequate, the project may fail to meet business and user needs. Thus, it is important to verify that the SDLC model is properly implemented and is appropriate for your environment. Furthermore, one of the initial steps of implementing an SDLC should include management approval.

Waterfall Model

Originally developed by Winston Royce in 1970, the waterfall model seeks to view the systems development life cycle as a series of iterative activities. As shown in Figure 7.4, the traditional waterfall model has seven stages of development. As each stage is completed, the project moves into the next phase. As illustrated by the backward arrows, the modern waterfall model does allow development to return to the previous phase to correct defects discovered during the subsequent phase. This is often known as the feedback loop characteristic of the waterfall model.

The waterfall model was one of the first comprehensive attempts to model the software development process while taking into account the necessity of returning to previous phases to correct system faults. However, one of the major criticisms of this model is that it allows the developers to step back only one phase in the process. It does not make provisions for the later discovery of errors.

FIGURE 7.4   The waterfall life cycle model

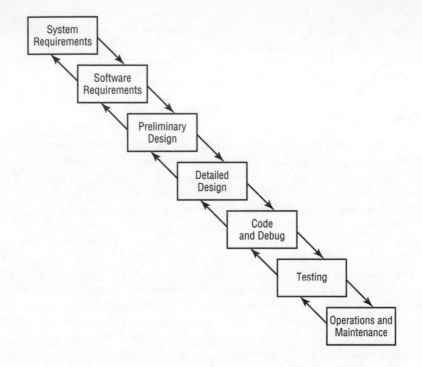

 More recently, the waterfall model has been improved by adding validation and verification steps to each phase. Verification evaluates the product against specifications, while validation evaluates how well the product satisfies real-world requirements. The improved model was labeled the modified waterfall model. However, it did not gain widespread use before the spiral model dominated the project management scene.

Spiral Model

In 1988, Barry Boehm of TRW proposed an alternative life cycle model that allows for multiple iterations of a waterfall-style process. An illustration of this model is shown in Figure 7.5. Because the spiral model encapsulates a number of iterations of another model (the waterfall model), it is known as a *metamodel,* or a "model of models."

Notice that each "loop" of the spiral results in the development of a new system prototype (represented by P1, P2, and P3 in the illustration). Theoretically, system developers would apply the entire waterfall process to the development of each prototype, thereby incrementally working toward a mature system that incorporates all of the functional requirements in a fully validated fashion. Boehm's spiral model provides a solution to the major criticism of the water-fall model—it allows developers to return to the planning stages as changing technical demands and customer requirements necessitate the evolution of a system.

FIGURE 7.5 The spiral life cycle model

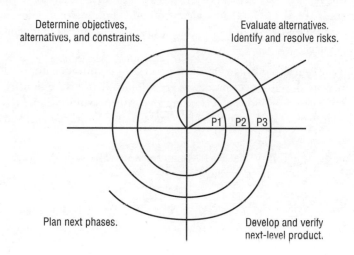

Determine objectives, alternatives, and constraints.

Evaluate alternatives. Identify and resolve risks.

P1 P2 P3

Plan next phases.

Develop and verify next-level product.

Software Capability Maturity Model

The Software Engineering Institute (SEI) at Carnegie Mellon University introduced the Capability Maturity Model for Software (or Software Capability Maturity Model) (SW-CMM or CMM or SCMM), which contends that all organizations engaged in software development move through a variety of maturity phases in sequential fashion. The SW-CMM describes the principles and practices underlying software process maturity. It is intended to help software organizations improve the maturity and quality of their software processes by implementing an evolutionary path from ad hoc, chaotic processes to mature, disciplined software processes. The idea behind the SW-CMM is that the quality of software is dependent on the quality of its development process.

The stages of the SW-CMM are as follows:

Level 1: Initial In this phase, you'll often find hard-working people charging ahead in a disorganized fashion. There is usually little or no defined software development process.

Level 2: Repeatable In this phase, basic life cycle management processes are introduced. Reuse of code in an organized fashion begins to enter the picture and repeatable results are expected from similar projects. SEI defines the key process areas for this level as Requirements Management, Software Project Planning, Software Project Tracking and Oversight, Software Subcontract Management, Software Quality Assurance, and Software Configuration Management.

Level 3: Defined In this phase, software developers operate according to a set of formal, documented software development processes. All development projects take place within the constraints of the new standardized management model. SEI defines the key process areas for this level as Organization Process Focus, Organization Process Definition, Training Program, Integrated Software Management, Software Product Engineering, Intergroup Coordination, and Peer Reviews.

Level 4: Managed   In this phase, management of the software process proceeds to the next level. Quantitative measures are utilized to gain a detailed understanding of the development process. SEI defines the key process areas for this level as Quantitative Process Management and Software Quality Management.

Level 5: Optimizing   In the optimized organization, a process of continuous improvement occurs. Sophisticated software development processes are in place that ensure that feedback from one phase reaches back to the previous phase to improve future results. SEI defines the key process areas for this level as Defect Prevention, Technology Change Management, and Process Change Management.

For more information on the Capability Maturity Model for Software, visit the Software Engineering Institute's website at www.sei.cmu.edu.

IDEAL Model

The Software Engineering Institute also developed the IDEAL model for software development, which implements many of the CMM attributes. The IDEAL model, illustrated in Figure 7.6, has five phases:

I: Initiating   In the initiating phase of the IDEAL model, the business reasons behind the change are outlined, support is built for the initiative, and the appropriate infrastructure is put in place.

D: Diagnosing   During the diagnosing phase, engineers analyze the current state of the organization and make general recommendations for change.

E: Establishing   In the establishing phase, the organization takes the general recommendations from the diagnosing phase and develops a specific plan of action that helps achieve those changes.

A: Acting   In the acting phase, it's time to stop "talking the talk" and "walk the walk." The organization develops solutions and then tests, refines, and implements them.

L: Learning   As with any quality improvement process, the organization must continuously analyze their efforts to determine whether they've achieved the desired goals and, when necessary, propose new actions to put the organization back on course.

Gantt Charts and PERT

A *Gantt chart* is a type of bar chart that shows the interrelationships over time between projects and schedules. It provides a graphical illustration of a schedule that helps to plan, coordinate, and track specific tasks in a project. An example of a Gantt chart is shown in Figure 7.7.

FIGURE 7.6   The IDEAL Model

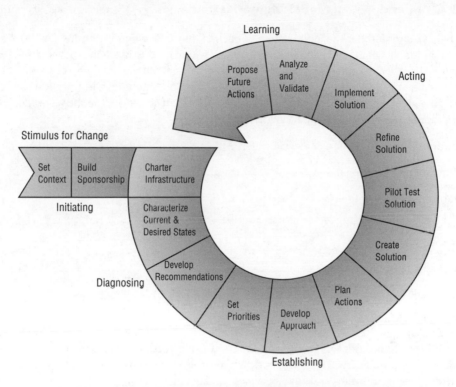

Special permission to reproduce "IDEAL Model," ©2004 by Carnegie Mellon University, is granted by the Carnegie Mellon Software Engineering Institute.

FIGURE 7.7   A Gantt chart

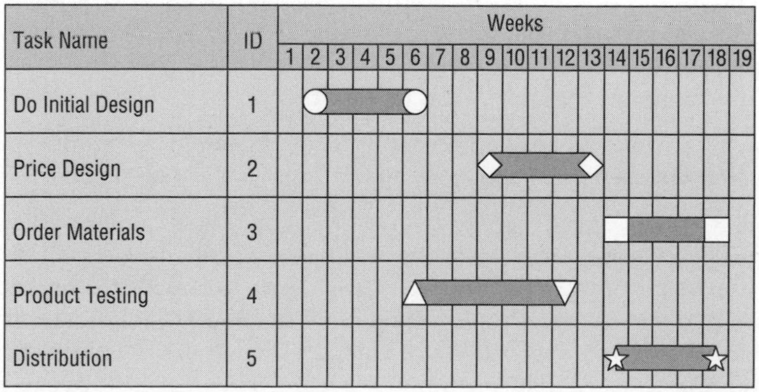

Task Name	ID	Weeks																		
		1	2	3	4	5	6	7	8	9	10	11	12	13	14	15	16	17	18	19
Do Initial Design	1		⬭━━━━⬭																		
Price Design	2									◇━━◇											
Order Materials	3														▭━━▭						
Product Testing	4					△━━━━▽															
Distribution	5														☆━━☆						

SW-CMM and IDEAL Model Memorization

To help you remember the initial letters of each of the 10 level names of the SW-CMM and IDEAL model (II DR ED AM LO), imagine yourself sitting on the couch in a psychiatrist's office saying, "I ... I, Dr. Ed, am lo(w)." If you can remember that phrase, then you can extract the 10 initial letters of the level names. If you write the letters out into two columns, you can reconstruct the level names in order of the two systems. The left column is the IDEAL model and the right represents the levels of the SW-CMM.

Initiating	Initiating
Diagnosing	Repeatable
Establishing	Defined
Acting	Managed
Learning	Optimized

Program Evaluation Review Technique (PERT) is a project scheduling tool used to judge the size of a software product in development and calculate the Standard Deviation (SD) for risk assessment. PERT relates the estimated lowest possible size, the most likely size, and the highest possible size of each component. PERT is used to direct improvements to project management and software coding in order to produce more efficient software. As the capabilities of programming and management improve, the actual produced size of software should be smaller.

Change Control and Configuration Management

Once software has been released into a production environment, users will inevitably request the addition of new features, correction of bugs, and other modifications to the code. Just as the organization developed a regimented process for developing software, they must also put a procedure in place to manage changes in an organized fashion.

The *change control* process has three basic components:

Request control   The request control process provides an organized framework within which users can request modifications, managers can conduct cost/benefit analysis, and developers can prioritize tasks.

Change control   The change control process is used by developers to re-create the situation encountered by the user and analyze the appropriate changes to remedy the situation. It also provides an organized framework within which multiple developers can create and test a solution prior to rolling it out into a production environment. Change control includes conforming to quality control restrictions, developing tools for update or change deployment, properly documenting any coded changes, and restricting the effects of new code to minimize diminishment of security.

Release control   Once the changes are finalized, they must be approved for release through the release control procedure. An essential step of the release control process is to double-check and ensure that any code inserted as a programming aid during the change process (such as debugging code and/or back doors) is removed before releasing the new software to production. Release control should also include acceptance testing to ensure that any alterations to end-user work tasks are understood and functional.

In addition to the change control process, security administrators should be aware of the importance of *configuration management*. This process is used to control the version(s) of software used throughout an organization and formally track and control changes to the software configuration. It has four main components:

Configuration identification   During the configuration identification process, administrators document the configuration of covered software products throughout the organization.

Configuration control   The configuration control process ensures that changes to software versions are made in accordance with the change control and configuration management policies. Updates can be made only from authorized distributions in accordance with those policies.

Configuration status accounting   Formalized procedures are used to keep track of all authorized changes that take place.

Configuration Audit   A periodic configuration audit should be conducted to ensure that the actual production environment is consistent with the accounting records and that no unauthorized configuration changes have taken place.

Together, change control and configuration management techniques form an important part of the software engineer's arsenal and protect the organization from development-related security issues.

Software Testing

As part of the development process, your organization should thoroughly test any software before distributing it internally (or releasing it to market). The best time to address testing is as the modules are designed. In other words, the mechanisms you use to test a product and the data sets you use to explore that product should be designed in parallel with the product itself. Your programming team should develop special test suites of data that exercise *all* paths of the software to the fullest extent possible and know the correct resulting outputs beforehand. This extensive test suite process is known as a reasonableness check. Furthermore, while conducting stress tests, you should check how the product handles normal and valid input data, incorrect types, out-of-range values, and other bounds and/or conditions. Live workloads provide the best stress testing possible. However, you should not use live or actual field data for testing, especially in the early development stages, since a flaw or error could result in the violation of integrity or confidentiality of the test data.

When testing software, you should apply the same rules of separation of duties that you do for other aspects of your organization. In other words, you should assign the testing of your software to someone other than the programmer(s) to avoid a conflict of interest and assure a more successful finished product. When a third party tests your software, you are assured that the third party performs an objective and nonbiased examination. The third-party test allows for a broader and more thorough test and prevents the bias and inclinations of the programmers from affecting the results of the test.

You can utilize three testing methods or ideologies for software testing:

White box testing   *White box testing* examines the internal logical structures of a program.

Black box testing   *Black box testing* examines the input and output of a program without focusing on the internal logical structures.

Test data method   *Test data method* examines the extent of the system testing in order to locate untested program logic.

Proper software test implementation is a key element in the project development process. Many of the common mistakes and oversights often found in commercial and in-house software can be eliminated. Keep the test plan and results as part of the system's permanent documentation.

Security Control Architecture

All secure systems implement some sort of security control architecture. At the hardware and operating system levels, controls should ensure enforcement of basic security principles. The following sections examine several basic control principles that should be enforced in a secure computing environment.

Process Isolation

Process isolation is one of the fundamental security procedures put into place during system design. Basically, using process isolation mechanisms (whether part of the operating system or part of the hardware itself) ensures that each process has its own isolated memory space for storage of data and the actual executing application code itself. This guarantees that processes cannot access each other's reserved memory areas and protects against confidentiality violations or intentional/unintentional modification of data by an unauthorized process. *Hardware segmentation* is a technique that implements process isolation at the hardware level by enforcing memory access constraints.

Protection Rings

The ring-oriented protection scheme provides for several modes of system operation, thereby facilitating secure operation by restricting processes to running in the appropriate security ring. An illustration of the four-layer ring protection scheme supported by Intel microprocessors appears in Figure 7.8.

FIGURE 7.8   Ring protection scheme

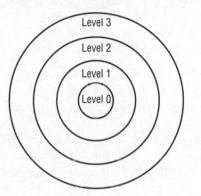

In this scheme, each of the rings has a separate and distinct function:

Level 0   Represents the ring where the operating system itself resides. This ring contains the *security kernel*—the core set of operating system services that handles all user/application requests for access to system resources. The kernel also implements the *reference monitor,* an operating system component that validates all user requests for access to resources against an access control scheme. Processes running at Level 0 are often said to be running in *supervisory mode,* also called privileged mode. Level 0 processes have full control of all system resources, so it's essential to ensure that they are fully verified and validated before implementation.

Levels 1 and 2   Contain device drivers and other operating system services that provide higher-level interfaces to system resources. However, in practice, most operating systems do not implement either one of these layers.

Level 3   Represents the security layer where user applications and processes reside. This layer is commonly referred to as *user mode,* or protected mode, and applications running here are not permitted direct access to system resources. In fact, when an application running in protected mode attempts to access an unauthorized resource, the commonly seen General Protection Fault (GPF) occurs.

The security kernel and reference monitor are extremely important computer security topics that must be understood by any information security practitioner.

The reference monitor component (present at Level 0) is an extremely important element of any operating system offering multilevel secure services. This concept was first formally described in the Department of Defense Trusted Computer System Evaluation Criteria (commonly referred to as the "Orange Book" due to the color of its cover). The DoD set forth the following three requirements for an operational reference monitor:

- It must be tamperproof.

- It must always be invoked.

- It must be small enough to be subject to analysis and tests, the completeness of which can be assured.

Abstraction

Abstraction is a valuable tool drawn from the object-oriented software development model that can be extrapolated to apply to the design of all types of information systems. In effect, abstraction states that a thorough understanding of a system's operational details is not often necessary to perform day-to-day activities. For example, a system developer might need to know that a certain procedure, when invoked, writes information to disk, but it's not necessary for the developer to understand the underlying principles that enable the data to be written to disk or the exact format that the disk procedures use to store and retrieve data. The process of developing increasingly sophisticated objects that draw upon the abstracted methods of lower-level objects is known as *encapsulation*. The deliberate concealment of lower levels of functionality from higher-level processes is known as *data hiding* or *information hiding*.

Security Modes

In a secure environment, information systems are configured to process information in one of four security modes. These modes are set out by the Department of Defense as follows:

- Systems running in *compartmented security mode* may process two or more types of compartmented information. All system users must have an appropriate clearance to access all information processed by the system but do not necessarily have a need to know all of the information in the system. Compartments are subcategories or compartments within the different classification levels, and extreme care is taken to preserve the information within the different compartments. The system may be classified at the secret level but contain five different compartments, all classified secret. If a user has the need to know about only two of the five different compartments to do their job, that user can access the system but can access only the two compartments.

- Systems running in *dedicated security mode* are authorized to process only a specific classification level at a time, and all system users must have clearance and a need to know that information.

- Systems running in *multilevel security mode* are authorized to process information at more than one level of security even when all system users do not have appropriate clearances or a need to know for all information processed by the system.

- Systems running in *system-high security mode* are authorized to process only information that all system users are cleared to read and have a valid need to know. These systems are not trusted to maintain separation between security levels, and all information processed by these systems must be handled as if it were classified at the same level as the most highly classified information processed by the system.

Service Level Agreements

Using *service level agreements (SLAs)* is an increasingly popular way to ensure that organizations providing services to internal and/or external customers maintain an appropriate level of service agreed upon by both the service provider and the vendor. It's a wise move to put SLAs in place for any data circuits, applications, information processing systems, databases, or other critical components that are vital to your organization's continued viability. The following issues are commonly addressed in SLAs:

- System uptime (as a percentage of overall operating time)
- Maximum consecutive downtime (in seconds/minutes/etc.)
- Peak load
- Average load
- Responsibility for diagnostics
- Failover time (if redundancy is in place)

Service level agreements also often commonly include financial and other contractual remedies that kick in if the agreement is not maintained. For example, if a critical circuit is down for more than 15 minutes, the service provider might agree to waive all charges on that circuit for one week.

Summary

As we continue our journey into the Information Age, data is quickly becoming the most valuable resource many organizations possess. Therefore, it's critical that information security practitioners understand the necessity of safeguarding the data itself and the systems and applications that assist in the processing of that data. Protections against malicious code, database vulnerabilities, and system/application development flaws must be implemented in every technology-aware organization.

There is number of malicious code objects that can pose a threat to the computing resources of organizations. In the nondistributed environment, such threats include viruses, logic bombs, Trojan horses, and worms. Chapter 8 delves more deeply into specific types of malicious code objects, as well as other attacks commonly used by hackers. We'll also explore some effective defense mechanisms to safeguard your network against their insidious effects.

By this point, you no doubt recognize the importance of placing adequate access controls and audit trails on these valuable information resources. Database security is a rapidly growing field; if databases play a major role in your security duties, take the time to sit down with database administrators, courses, and textbooks and learn the underlying theory. It's a valuable investment.

Finally, there are various controls that can be put into place during the system and application development process to ensure that the end product of these processes is compatible with operation in a secure environment. Such controls include process isolation, hardware segmentation abstraction, and service level agreements (SLAs). Security should always be introduced in the early planning phases of any development project and continually monitored throughout the design, development, deployment, and maintenance phases of production.

Exam Essentials

Understand the application threats present in a local/nondistributed environment. Describe the functioning of viruses, worms, Trojan horses, and logic bombs. Understand the impact each type of threat may have on a system and the methods they use to propagate.

Understand the application threats unique to distributed computing environments. Know the basic functioning of agents and the impact they may have on computer/network security. Understand the functionality behind Java applets and ActiveX controls and be able to determine the appropriate applet security levels for a given computing environment.

Explain the basic architecture of a relational database management system (RDBMS). Know the structure of relational databases. Be able to explain the function of tables (relations), rows (records/tuples), and columns (fields/attributes). Know how relationships are defined between tables.

Understand the various types of keys used to identify information stored in a database. You should be familiar with the basic types of keys. Understand that each table has one or more candidate keys that are chosen from a column heading in a database and that uniquely identify rows within a table. The database designer selects one candidate key as the primary key for the table. Foreign keys are used to enforce referential integrity between tables participating in a relationship.

Recognize the various common forms of DBMS safeguards. The common DBMS safeguards include concurrency, edit control, semantic integrity mechanisms, use of time and date stamps, granular control of objects, content-dependant access control, context-dependant access control, cell suppression, database partitioning, noise, perturbation, and polyinstantiation.

Explain the database security threats posed by aggregation and inference. Aggregation utilizes specialized database functions to draw conclusions about a large amount of data based on individual records. Access to these functions should be restricted if aggregate information is considered more sensitive than the individual records. Inference occurs when database users can deduce sensitive facts from less-sensitive information.

Know the various types of storage. Explain the differences between primary memory and virtual memory, secondary storage and virtual storage, random access storage and sequential access storage, and volatile storage and nonvolatile storage.

Explain how expert systems function. Expert systems consist of two main components: a knowledge base that contains a series of "if/then" rules and an inference engine that uses that information to draw conclusions about other data.

Describe the functioning of neural networks. Neural networks simulate the functioning of the human mind to a limited extent by arranging a series of layered calculations to solve problems. Neural networks require extensive training on a particular problem before they are able to offer solutions.

Understand the waterfall and spiral models of systems development.   Know that the waterfall model describes a sequential development process that results in the development of a finished product. Developers may step back only one phase in the process if errors are discovered. The spiral model uses several iterations of the waterfall model to produce a number of fully specified and tested prototypes.

Explain the ring protection scheme.   Understand the four rings of the ring protection scheme and the activities that typically occur within each ring. Know that most operating systems only implement Level 0 (privileged or supervisory mode) and Level 3 (protected or user mode).

Describe the function of the security kernel and reference monitor.   The security kernel is the core set of operating system services that handles user requests for access to system resources. The reference monitor is a portion of the security kernel that validates user requests against the system's access control mechanisms.

Understand the importance of testing.   Software testing should be designed as part of the development process. Testing should be used as a management tool to improve the design, development, and production processes.

Understand the four security modes approved by the Department of Defense.   Know the differences between compartmented security mode, dedicated security mode, multilevel security mode, and system-high security mode. Understand the different types of classified information that can be processed in each mode and the types of users that can access each system.

Written Lab

Answer the following questions about data and application security issues.

1. How does a worm travel from system to system?

2. Describe three benefits of using applets instead of server-side code for web applications.

3. What are the three requirements set for an operational reference monitor in a secure computing system?

4. What operating systems are capable of processing ActiveX controls posted on a website?

5. What type of key is selected by the database developer to uniquely identify data within a relational database table?

6. What database security technique appears to permit the insertion of multiple rows sharing the same uniquely identifying information?

7. What type of storage is commonly referred to as a RAM disk?

8. How far backward does the waterfall model allow developers to travel when a development flaw is discovered?

Review Questions

1. Which one of the following malicious code objects might be inserted in an application by a disgruntled software developer with the purpose of destroying system data upon the deletion of the developer's account (presumably following their termination)?

   A. Virus

   B. Worm

   C. Trojan horse

   D. Logic bomb

2. What term is used to describe code objects that act on behalf of a user while operating in an unattended manner?

   A. Agent

   B. Worm

   C. Applet

   D. Browser

3. Which form of DBMS primarily supports the establishment of one-to-many relationships?

   A. Relational

   B. Hierarchical

   C. Mandatory

   D. Distributed

4. Which of the following characteristics can be used to differentiate worms from viruses?

   A. Worms infect a system by overwriting data in the Master Boot Record of a storage device.

   B. Worms always spread from system to system without user intervention.

   C. Worms always carry a malicious payload that impacts infected systems.

   D. All of the above.

5. What programming language(s) can be used to develop ActiveX controls for use on an Internet site?

   A. Visual Basic

   B. C

   C. Java

   D. All of the above

6. What form of access control is concerned with the data stored by a field rather than any other issue?

   A. Content-dependent

   B. Context-dependent

   C. Semantic integrity mechanisms

   D. Perturbation

7. Which one of the following key types is used to enforce referential integrity between database tables?

    A. Candidate key

    B. Primary key

    C. Foreign key

    D. Super key

8. Richard believes that a database user is misusing his privileges to gain information about the company's overall business trends by issuing queries that combine data from a large number of records. What process is the database user taking advantage of?

    A. Inference

    B. Contamination

    C. Polyinstantiation

    D. Aggregation

9. What database technique can be used to prevent unauthorized users from determining classified information by noticing the absence of information normally available to them?

    A. Inference

    B. Manipulation

    C. Polyinstantiation

    D. Aggregation

10. Which one of the following terms cannot be used to describe the main RAM of a typical computer system?

    A. Nonvolatile

    B. Sequential access

    C. Real memory

    D. Primary memory

11. What type of information is used to form the basis of an expert system's decision-making process?

    A. A series of weighted layered computations

    B. Combined input from a number of human experts, weighted according to past performance

    C. A series of "if/then" rules codified in a knowledge base

    D. A biological decision-making process that simulates the reasoning process used by the human mind

12. Which one of the following intrusion detection systems makes use of an expert to detect anomalous user activity?

    A. PIX

    B. IDIOT

    C. AAFID

    D. NIDES

13. Which of the following acts as a proxy between two different systems to support interaction and simplify the work of programmers?

    A. SDLC

    B. ODBC

    C. DSS

    D. Abstraction

14. Which software development life cycle model allows for multiple iterations of the development process, resulting in multiple prototypes, each produced according to a complete design and testing process?

    A. Software Capability Maturity Model

    B. Waterfall model

    C. Development cycle

    D. Spiral model

15. In systems utilizing a ring protection scheme, at what level does the security kernel reside?

    A. Level 0

    B. Level 1

    C. Level 2

    D. Level 3

16. Which database security risk occurs when data from a higher classification level is mixed with data from a lower classification level?

    A. Aggregation

    B. Inference

    C. Contamination

    D. Polyinstantiation

17. Which of the following programming languages is least prone to the insertion of malicious code by a third party?

    A. C++

    B. Java

    C. VBScript

    D. FORTRAN

18. Which one of the following is not part of the change control process?

    A. Request control

    B. Release control

    C. Configuration audit

    D. Change control

19. What transaction management principle ensures that two transactions do not interfere with each other as they operate on the same data?

   A. Atomicity

   B. Consistency

   C. Isolation

   D. Durability

20. Which subset of the Structured Query Language is used to create and modify the database schema?

   A. Data Definition Language

   B. Data Structure Language

   C. Database Schema Language

   D. Database Manipulation Language

Answers to Review Questions

1. D. Logic bombs are malicious code objects programmed to lie dormant until certain logical conditions, such as a certain date, time, system event, or other criteria, are met. At that time, they spring into action, triggering their malicious payload.

2. A. Intelligent agents are code objects programmed to perform certain operations on behalf of a user in their absence. They are also often referred to as bots.

3. B. Hierarchical DBMS supports one-to-many relationships. Relational DBMS supports one-to-one. Distributed DBMS supports many-to-many. Mandatory is not a DBMS but an access control model.

4. B. The major difference between viruses and worms is that worms are self-replicating whereas viruses require user intervention to spread from system to system. Infection of the Master Boot Record is a characteristic of a subclass of viruses known as MBR viruses. Both viruses and worms are capable of carrying malicious payloads.

5. D. Microsoft's ActiveX technology supports a number of programming languages, including Visual Basic, C, C++, and Java. On the other hand, only the Java language may be used to write Java applets.

6. A. Content-dependent access control is focused on the internal data of each field.

7. C. Foreign keys are used to enforce referential integrity constraints between tables that participate in a relationship.

8. D. In this case, the process the database user is taking advantage of is aggregation. Aggregation attacks involve the use of specialized database functions to combine information from a large number of database records to reveal information that may be more sensitive than the information in individual records would reveal.

9. C. Polyinstantiation allows the insertion of multiple records that appear to have the same primary key values into a database at different classification levels.

10. B. Random access memory (RAM) allows for the direct addressing of any point within the resource. A sequential access storage medium, such as a magnetic tape, requires scanning through the entire media from the beginning to reach a specific address.

11. C. Expert systems utilize a knowledge base consisting of a series of "if/then" statements to form decisions based upon the previous experience of human experts.

12. D. The Next-Generation Intrusion Detection Expert System (NIDES) system is an expert system-based intrusion detection system. PIX is a firewall, and IDIOT and AAFID are intrusion detection systems that do not utilize expert systems.

13. B. ODBC acts as a proxy between applications and the back-end DBMS.

14. D. The spiral model allows developers to repeat iterations of another life cycle model (such as the waterfall model) to produce a number of fully tested prototypes.

15. A. The security kernel and reference monitor reside at Level 0 in the ring protection scheme, where they have unrestricted access to all system resources.

16. C. Contamination is the mixing of data from a higher classification level and/or need-to-know requirement with data from a lower classification level and/or need-to-know requirement.

17. C. Of the languages listed, VBScript is the least prone to modification by third parties because it is an interpreted language whereas the other three languages (C++, Java, and FORTRAN) are compiled languages.

18. C. Configuration audit is part of the configuration management process rather than the change control process.

19. C. The isolation principle states that two transactions operating on the same data must be temporally separated from each other such that one does not interfere with the other.

20. A. The Data Manipulation Language (DML) is used to make modifications to a relational database's schema.

Answers to Written Lab

Following are answers to the questions in this chapter's written lab:

1. Worms travel from system to system under their own power by exploiting flaws in networking software.

2. The processing burden is shifted from the server to the client, allowing the web server to handle a greater number of simultaneous requests. The client uses local resources to process the data, usually resulting in a quicker response. The privacy of client data is protected because information does not need to be transmitted to the web server.

3. It must be tamperproof, it must always be invoked, and it must be small enough to be subject to analysis and tests, the completeness of which can be assured.

4. Microsoft Windows platforms only.

5. Primary key.

6. Polyinstantiation.

7. Virtual storage.

8. One phase.

Chapter

8

Malicious Code and Application Attacks

THE CISSP EXAM TOPICS COVERED IN THIS CHAPTER INCLUDE:

- ✓ Malicious Code
- ✓ Methods of Attack

In previous chapters, you learned about many general security principles and the policy and procedure mechanisms that help security practitioners develop adequate protection against malicious individuals. This chapter takes an in-depth look at some of the specific threats faced on a daily basis by administrators in the field.

This material is not only critical for the CISSP exam, it's also some of the most basic information a computer security professional must understand to effectively practice their trade. We'll begin this chapter by looking at the risks posed by malicious code objects—viruses, worms, logic bombs, and Trojan horses. We'll then take a look at some of the other security exploits used by someone attempting to gain unauthorized access to a system or to prevent legitimate users from gaining such access.

Malicious Code

Malicious code objects include a broad range of programmed computer security threats that exploit various network, operating system, software, and physical security vulnerabilities to spread malicious payloads to computer systems. Some malicious code objects, such as computer viruses and Trojan horses, depend upon irresponsible computer use by human beings to spread from system to system with any success. Other objects, such as worms, spread rapidly among vulnerable systems under their own power.

All computer security practitioners must be familiar with the risks posed by the various types of malicious code objects so they can develop adequate countermeasures to protect the systems under their care as well as implement appropriate responses if their systems are compromised.

Sources

Where does malicious code come from? In the early days of computer security, malicious code writers were extremely skilled (albeit misguided) software developers who took pride in carefully crafting innovative malicious code techniques. Indeed, they actually served a somewhat useful function by exposing security holes in popular software packages and operating systems, raising the security awareness of the computing community. For an example of this type of code writer, see the sidebar in this chapter entitled "RTM and the Internet Worm."

Modern times have given rise to the script kiddie—the malicious individual who doesn't understand the technology behind security vulnerabilities but downloads ready-to-use software (or scripts) from the Internet and uses them to launch attacks against remote systems. This trend gave birth to a new breed of virus creation software that allows anyone with a minimal level of technical expertise to create a virus and unleash it upon the Internet. This is reflected in the large number of viruses documented by antivirus authorities to date. These amateur malicious code developers are usually just experimenting with the new tool they downloaded or attempting to cause problems for one or two enemies. Unfortunately, these objects sometimes spread rapidly and cause problems for Internet users in general.

Viruses

The computer *virus* is perhaps the earliest form of malicious code to plague security administrators. Indeed, viruses are so prevalent nowadays that major outbreaks receive attention from the mass media and provoke mild hysteria among average computer users. According to Symantec, one of the major antivirus software vendors, there were approximately 65,000 strains of viruses roaming the global network in early 2004. Hundreds of thousands of variations of these viruses strike unsuspecting computer users each day. Many carry malicious payloads that cause damage ranging in scope from displaying a profane message on the screen all the way to causing complete destruction of all data stored on the local hard drive.

As with biological viruses, computer viruses have two main functions—propagation and destruction. Miscreants who create viruses carefully design code to implement these functions in new and innovative methods that they hope escape detection and bypass increasingly sophisticated antivirus technology. It's fair to say that an arms race has developed between virus writers and antivirus technicians, each hoping to develop technology one step ahead of the other. The propagation function defines how the virus will spread from system to system, infecting each machine it leaves in its wake. A virus's payload delivers the destructive power by implementing whatever malicious activity the virus writer had in mind.

Virus Propagation Techniques

By definition, a virus must contain technology that enables it to spread from system to system, sometimes aided by unsuspecting computer users seeking to share data by exchanging disks, sharing networked resources, sending electronic mail, or using some other means. Once they've "touched" a new system, they use one of several propagation techniques to infect the new victim and expand their reach. In the following sections, we'll look at three common propagation techniques: Master Boot Record infection, file infection, and macro infection.

Master Boot Record (MBR) Viruses

The Master Boot Record (MBR) virus is one of the earliest known forms of virus infection. These viruses attack the MBR, the portion of a hard drive or floppy disk that the computer uses to load the operating system during the boot process. Because the MBR is extremely small (usually 512 bytes), it can't contain all of the code required to implement the virus's propagation and destructive functions. To bypass this space limitation, MBR viruses store the majority of their code on another portion of the storage media. When the system reads the infected MBR, the virus instructs it to read and execute the code stored in this alternate location, thereby loading the entire virus into memory and potentially triggering the delivery of the virus's payload.

The Boot Sector and the Master Boot Record

You'll often see the terms *boot sector* and *Master Boot Record* used interchangeably to describe the portion of a storage device used to load the operating system and the types of viruses that attack that process. This is not technically correct. The MBR is a single disk sector, normally the first sector of the media that is read in the initial stages of the boot process. The MBR determines which media partition contains the operating system and then directs the system to read that partition's boot sector to load the operating system.

Viruses can attack both the MBR and the boot sector, with substantially similar results. MBR viruses act by redirecting the system to an infected boot sector, which loads the virus into memory before loading the operating system from the legitimate boot sector. Boot sector viruses actually infect the legitimate boot sector and are loaded into memory during the operating system load process.

Most MBR viruses are spread between systems through the use of an infected floppy disk inadvertently shared between users. If the infected disk is in the drive during the boot process, the target system reads the floppy's infected MBR and the virus loads into memory, infects the MBR on the target system's hard drive, and spreads its infection to yet another machine.

File Infector Viruses

Many viruses infect different types of executable files and trigger when the operating system attempts to execute them. For Windows-based systems, these files end with .EXE and .COM extensions. The propagation routines of *file infector* viruses may slightly alter the code of an executable program, therefore implanting the technology the virus needs to replicate and damage the system. In some cases, the virus might actually replace the entire file with an infected version. Standard file infector viruses that do not use cloaking techniques like stealth or encryption (see the section titled "Virus Technologies" later in this chapter) are often easily detected by comparing file characteristics (such as size and modification date) before and after infection or by comparing *hash values*. The section titled "Antivirus Mechanisms" provides technical details behind these techniques.

A variation of the file infector virus is the *companion virus*. These viruses are self-contained executable files that escape detection by using a filename similar to, but slightly different from, a legitimate operating system file. They rely on the default extensions that DOS-based operating systems append to commands when executing program files (.COM, .EXE, and .BAT, in that order). For example, if you had a program on your hard disk named GAME.EXE, a companion virus might use the name GAME.COM. If you then open up a DOS prompt and simply type GAME, the operating system would execute the virus file, GAME.COM, instead of the file you actually intended to execute, GAME.EXE. This is a very good reason to avoid shortcuts and fully specify the name of the file you want to execute when working at the DOS prompt.

Macro Viruses

Many common software applications implement some sort of scripting functionality to assist with the automation of repetitive tasks. These functionalities often use simple, yet powerful, programming languages like Visual Basic for Applications (VBA). Although macros do indeed offer great productivity-enhancing opportunities to computer users, they also expose systems to yet another avenue of infection—*macro viruses*.

Macro viruses first appeared on the scene in the mid-1990s, utilizing crude technologies to infect documents created in the popular Microsoft Word environment. Although they were relatively unsophisticated, these viruses spread rapidly because the antivirus community didn't anticipate them and, therefore, antivirus applications didn't provide any defense against them. Macro viruses quickly became more and more commonplace, and vendors rushed to modify their antivirus platforms to scan application documents for malicious macros. In 1999, the Melissa virus spread through the use of a Word document that exploited a security vulnerability in Microsoft Outlook to replicate. The infamous I Love You virus quickly followed on its heels, exploiting similar vulnerabilities in early 2000.

WARNING   Macro viruses proliferate because of the ease of writing code in the scripting languages (such as VBA) utilized by modern productivity applications.

Although the vast majority of macro viruses infect documents created by applications belonging to the Microsoft Office suite (including Word, Excel, PowerPoint, Access, and Outlook), users of other applications are not immune. Viruses exist that infect Lotus, AmiPro, WordPerfect, and more.

Platforms

Just as most macro viruses infect systems running the popular Microsoft Office suite of applications, most computer viruses are designed to disrupt activity on systems running versions of the world's most popular operating system—Microsoft Windows. It's estimated that less than one percent of the viruses in the wild today are designed to impact other operating systems, such as Unix and MacOS. This may be the result of two influencing factors.

First, there really is no "Unix" operating system. Rather, there is a series of many similar operating systems that implement the same functions in a similar fashion and that are independently designed by a large number of developers. Large-scale corporate efforts, like Sun's Solaris and SCO Unix, compete with the myriad of freely available versions of the Linux operating system developed by the public at large. The sheer number of Unix versions and the fact that they are developed on entirely different kernels (the core code of an operating system) make it difficult to write a virus that would impact a large portion of Unix systems.

Second, according to a National Computer Security Association (NCSA) Virus Prevalence Study, 80 percent of all viruses are macro viruses, all but a slim percentage of which target Microsoft Office applications. There simply isn't a software package for non-Windows platforms that is anywhere near as prevalent as Office is among PC users, making it difficult to develop effective macro viruses for non-Windows platforms.

That said, Macintosh and Unix users should not rest on their laurels. The fact that there are only a few viruses out there that pose a risk to their system does not mean that one of those viruses couldn't affect their system at any moment. Anyone responsible for the security of a computer system should implement adequate antivirus mechanisms to ensure the continued safety of their resources.

Antivirus Mechanisms

Almost every desktop computer in service today runs some sort of antivirus software package. Popular desktop titles include McAfee VirusScan and Norton AntiVirus, but there are a plethora of other products on the market today offering protection for anything from a single system to an entire enterprise, as well as packages designed to protect against specific common types of virus invasion vectors, such as inbound e-mail.

The vast majority of these packages utilize a method known as *signature-based detection* to identify potential virus infections on a system. Essentially, an antivirus package maintains an extremely large database that contains the telltale characteristics of all known viruses. Depending upon the antivirus package and configuration settings, it scans storage media periodically, checking for any files that contain data matching those criteria. If any are detected, the antivirus package takes one of the following actions:

- If the software can eradicate the virus, it disinfects the affected files and restores the machine to a safe condition.

- If the software recognizes the virus but doesn't know how to disinfect the files, it may quarantine the files until the user or an administrator can examine them manually.

- If security settings/policies do not provide for quarantine or the files exceed a predefined danger threshold, the antivirus package may delete the infected files in an attempt to preserve system integrity.

When using a signature-based antivirus package, it's essential to remember that the package is only as effective as the virus definition file it's based upon. If you don't frequently update your virus definitions (usually requiring an annual subscription fee), your antivirus software will not be able to detect newly created viruses. With thousands of viruses appearing on the Internet each year, an outdated definition file will quickly render your defenses ineffective.

Most of the modern antivirus software products are able to detect, remove, and clean a system for a wide variety of types of malicious code. In other words, antivirus solutions are rarely limited to just viruses. These tools are often able to provide protection against worms, Trojan horses, logic bombs, and various other forms of e-mail or Web-borne code. In the event that you suspect new malicious code is sweeping the Internet, your best course of action is to contact your antivirus software vendor to inquire about your state of protection against the new threat. Don't wait until the next scheduled or automated signature dictionary update. Furthermore, never accept the word of any third party about protection status offered by an antivirus solution. Always contact the vendor directly. Most responsible antivirus vendors will send alerts to their customers as soon as new, substantial threats are identified, so be sure to register for such notifications as well.

Other security packages, such as the popular Tripwire data integrity assurance package, also provide a secondary antivirus functionality. Tripwire is designed to alert administrators of unauthorized file modifications. It's often used to detect web server defacements and similar attacks, but it also may provide some warning of virus infections if critical system executable files, such as COMMAND.COM, are modified unexpectedly. These systems work by maintaining a database of hash values for all files stored on the system (see Chapter 9, "Cryptography and Private Key Algorithms," for a full discussion of the hash functions used to create these values). These archived hash values are then compared to current computed values to detect any files that were modified between the two periods.

Virus Technologies

As virus detection and eradication technology rises to meet new threats programmed by malicious developers, new kinds of viruses designed to defeat those systems emerge. The following sections examine four specific types of viruses that use sneaky techniques in an attempt to escape detection—multipartite viruses, stealth viruses, polymorphic viruses, and encrypted viruses.

Multipartite Viruses

Multipartite viruses use more than one propagation technique in an attempt to penetrate systems that defend against only one method or the other. For example, the Marzia virus discovered in 1993 infects critical .COM and .EXE files, most notably the COMMAND.COM system file, by adding 2,048 bytes of malicious code to each file. This characteristic qualifies it as a file infector virus. In addition, two hours after it infects a system, it writes malicious code to the system's Master Boot Record, qualifying it as a boot sector virus.

Stealth Viruses

Stealth viruses hide themselves by actually tampering with the operating system to fool antivirus packages into thinking that everything is functioning normally. For example, a stealth boot sector virus might overwrite the system's Master Boot Record with malicious code but then also modify the operating system's file access functionality to cover its tracks. When the antivirus package requests a copy of the MBR, the modified operating system code provides it with exactly what the antivirus package expects to see—a clean version of the MBR free of any virus signatures. However, when the system boots, it reads the infected MBR and loads the virus into memory.

Polymorphic Viruses

Polymorphic viruses actually modify their own code as they travel from system to system. The virus's propagation and destruction techniques remain exactly the same, but the signature of the virus is somewhat different each time it infects a new system. It is the hope of polymorphic virus creators that this constantly changing signature will render signature-based antivirus packages useless. However, antivirus vendors have "cracked the code" of many polymorphism techniques and current versions of antivirus software are able to detect known polymorphic viruses. The only concern that remains is that it takes vendors longer to generate the necessary signature files to stop a polymorphic virus in its tracks, resulting in a lengthened period that the virus can run free on the Internet.

Encrypted Viruses

Encrypted viruses use cryptographic techniques, such as those described in Chapter 9, to avoid detection. In their outward appearance, they are actually quite similar to polymorphic viruses—each infected system has a virus with a different signature. However, they do not generate these modified signatures by changing their code; instead, they alter the way they are stored on the disk. Encrypted viruses use a very short segment of code, known as the virus decryption routine, that contains the cryptographic information necessary to load and decrypt the main virus code stored elsewhere on the disk. Each infection utilizes a different cryptographic key, causing the main code to appear completely different on each system. However, the virus decryption routines often contain telltale signatures that render them vulnerable to updated antivirus software packages.

Hoaxes

No discussion of viruses is complete without mentioning the nuisance and wasted resources caused by virus hoaxes. Almost every e-mail user has, at one time or another, received a message forwarded by a friend or relative that warns of the latest virus threat to roam the Internet. Invariably, this purported "virus" is the most destructive virus ever unleashed and no antivirus package is able to detect and/or eradicate it. One famous example of such a hoax is the Good Times virus warning that first surfaced on the Internet in 1994 and still circulates today.

For more information on this topic, the renowned virus hoax expert Rob Rosenberger edits a website that contains a comprehensive repository of virus hoaxes. You can find it at `www.vmyths.com`.

Logic Bombs

As you learned in Chapter 7, *logic bombs* are malicious code objects that infect a system and lie dormant until they are triggered by the occurrence of one or more conditions such as time, program launch, website logon, and so on. The vast majority of logic bombs are programmed into custom-built applications by software developers seeking to ensure that their work is destroyed if they unexpectedly leave the company. The previous chapter provided several examples of this type of logic bomb.

However, it's important to remember that, like any malicious code object, logic bombs come in many shapes and sizes. Indeed, many viruses and Trojan horses contain a logic bomb component. The famous Michelangelo virus caused a media frenzy when it was discovered in 1991 due to the logic bomb trigger it contained. The virus infects a system's Master Boot Record through the sharing of infected floppy disks and then hides itself until March 6—the birthday of the famous Italian artist Michelangelo Buonarroti. On that date, it springs into action, reformatting the hard drives of infected systems and destroying all of the data they contain.

Trojan Horses

System administrators constantly warn computer users not to download and install software from the Internet unless they are absolutely sure it comes from a trusted source. In fact, many companies strictly prohibit the installation of any software not prescreened by the IT department. These policies serve to minimize the risk that an organization's network will be compromised by a *Trojan horse*—a software program that appears benevolent but carries a malicious, behind-the-scenes payload that has the potential to wreak havoc on a system or network.

Trojans differ very widely in functionality. Some will destroy all of the data stored on a system in an attempt to cause a large amount of damage in as short a time frame as possible. Some are fairly innocuous. For example, a series of Trojans appeared on the Internet in mid-2002 that claimed to provide PC users with the ability to run games designed for the Microsoft Xbox gaming system on their computers. When users ran the program, it simply didn't work. However, it also inserted a value into the Windows Registry that caused a specific web page to open each time the computer booted. The Trojan creators hoped to cash in on the advertising revenue generated by the large number of page views their website received from the Xbox Trojan horses. Unfortunately for them, antivirus experts quickly discovered their true intentions and the website was shut down.

Back Orifice is a well-known Trojan horse that affects various versions of the Windows operating system. To install Back Orifice on the systems of unsuspecting users, malicious individuals place it within the installation package for legitimate software. When a victim installs the legitimate software, they unknowingly install Back Orifice at the same time. The package then runs in the background and gives the miscreant the ability to remotely access the target computer and gain administrative access.

Worms

Worms pose an unparalleled risk to network security. They contain the same destructive potential as other malicious code objects with an added twist—they propagate themselves without requiring any human intervention.

The Internet Worm was the first major computer security incident to occur on the Internet. Since that time, hundreds of new worms (with thousands of variant strains) have unleashed their destructive power on the Internet.

The Code Red worm received a good deal of media attention in the summer of 2001 when it rapidly spread among web servers running unpatched versions of Microsoft's Internet Information Server (IIS). Code Red performed three malicious actions on the systems it penetrated:

- It randomly selected hundreds of IP addresses and then probed those hosts to see if they were running a vulnerable version of IIS. Any systems it found were quickly compromised. This greatly magnified Code Red's reach as each host it infected sought many new targets.

- It defaced HTML pages on the local web server, replacing normal content with the text
  ```
  Welcome to http://www.worm.com!
  Hacked By Chinese!
  ```

- It planted a logic bomb that would initiate a *denial of service (DoS) attack* against the IP address 198.137.240.91, which at that time belonged to the web server hosting the White House's home page. Quick-thinking government web administrators changed the White House's IP address before the attack actually began.

The destructive power of the Internet Worm, Code Red, and their many variants poses an extreme risk to the modern Internet. This presents a strong argument that system administrators simply must ensure that they apply appropriate security patches to their Internet-connected systems as software vendors release them. A security fix for IIS vulnerability exploited by Code Red was available from Microsoft over a month before the worm attacked the Internet. Had security administrators applied it promptly, Code Red would have been a miserable failure.

RTM and the Internet Worm

In November 1988, a young computer science student named Robert Tappan Morris brought the fledgling Internet to its knees with a few lines of computer code. A malicious worm he claimed to have created as an experiment and accidentally released onto the Internet spread quickly and crashed a large number of systems.

This worm spread by exploiting four specific security holes in the Unix operating system:

Sendmail debug mode   Then-current versions of the popular sendmail software package used to route electronic mail messages across the Internet contained a security vulnerability. This vulnerability allowed the worm to spread itself by sending a specially crafted e-mail message that contained the worm's code to the sendmail program on a remote system. When the remote system processed the message, it became infected.

Password attack   The worm also used a *dictionary attack* to attempt to gain access to remote systems by utilizing the username and password of a valid system user (you'll find more on dictionary attacks later in this chapter).

Finger vulnerability   The popular Internet utility finger allowed users to determine who was logged on to a remote system. Then-current versions of the finger software contained a *buffer overflow* vulnerability that allowed the worm to spread (there is a detailed discussion of buffer overflows later in this chapter). The finger program has since been removed from most Internet-connected systems.

Trust relationships   After the worm infected a system, it analyzed any existing trust relationships with other systems on the network and attempted to spread itself to those systems through the trusted path.

This multipronged approach made the Internet Worm extremely dangerous. Fortunately, the (then-small) computer security community quickly put together a crack team of investigators who disarmed the worm and patched the affected systems. Their efforts were facilitated by several inefficient routines in the worm's code that limited the rate of its spread.

Due to the lack of experience among law enforcement authorities and the court system in dealing with computer crimes, Morris received only a slap on the wrist for his transgression. He was sentenced to three years' probation, 400 hours of community service, and a $10,000 fine under the Computer Fraud and Abuse Act of 1986. Ironically, Morris's father, Robert Morris, was serving as director of the National Security Agency's (NSA's) National Computer Security Center (NCSC) at the time of the incident.

Active Content

The increasing demand of web users for more and more dynamic content on the sites they visit has created a dilemma for web administrators. Delivery of this dynamic content requires the use of web applications that can place an enormous computational burden on the server and increased demand for them requires commitment of a large number of resources.

In an effort to solve this problem, software developers created the concept of *active content,* web programs that are downloaded to users' own computers for execution rather than consuming server-side resources. These programs, utilizing technologies like Java *applets* and ActiveX controls, greatly reduce the load on the server and client waiting time. Most web browsers allow users to choose to have the active content automatically downloaded, installed, and executed from trusted sites.

Unfortunately, this very technology can pose a major threat to client systems. Unsuspecting users may download active content from an untrusted source and allow it to execute on their systems, creating a significant security vulnerability. This vulnerability led to the creation of a whole new type of malicious code—the *hostile applet.* Like other forms of malware, hostile applets have a variety of intentions, from causing a denial of service attack that merely consumes system resources to more insidious goals, such as theft of data.

Countermeasures

The primary means of defense against malicious code is the use of antivirus filtering software. These packages are primarily signature-based systems, designed to detect known viruses running on a system. It's wise to consider implementing antivirus filters in at least three key areas:

 Removal is often possible within hours after new malicious code is discovered. Removal removes the malicious code but does not repair the damage caused by it. Cleaning capabilities are usually made available within a few days after a new malicious code is discovered. Cleaning not only removes the code, it also repairs any damage it causes.

Client systems   Every workstation on a network should have updated antivirus software searching the local file system for malicious code.

Server systems   Servers should have similar protections. This is even more critical than protecting client systems because a single virus on a common server could quickly spread throughout an entire network.

Content filters   The majority of viruses today are exchanged over the Internet. It's a wise move to implement on your network content filtering that scans inbound and outbound electronic mail and web traffic for signs of malicious code.

WARNING

Remember, most antivirus filters are signature based. Therefore, they're only as good as the most recent update to their virus definition files. It's critical that you update these files frequently, especially when a new piece of high-profile malicious code appears on the Internet.

Signature-based filters rely upon the descriptions of known viruses provided by software developers. Therefore, there is a period of time between when any given virus first appears "in the wild" and when updated filters are made available. There are two solutions to this problem commonly used today:

- Integrity checking software, such as Tripwire (an open-source version is available at `www.tripwire.org`), scans your file system for unexpected modifications and reports to you on a periodic basis.

- Access controls should be strictly maintained and enforced to limit the ability of malicious code to damage your data and spread on your network.

There are two additional techniques used specifically to prevent systems from being infected by malicious code embedded in active content:

- Java's *sandbox* provides applets with an isolated environment in which they can run safely without gaining access to critical system resources.

- ActiveX control signing utilizes a system of digital signatures to ensure that the code originates from a trusted source. It is up to the end user to determine whether the authenticated source should be trusted.

For an in-depth explanation of digital signature technology, see Chapter 10, "PKI and Cryptographic Applications."

NOTE

These techniques provide added protection against hostile applets. Most content filtering solutions also scan active content for malicious code as well.

Password Attacks

One of the simplest techniques hackers use to gain illegitimate access to a system is to learn the username and password of an authorized system user. Once they've gained access as a regular user, they have a foothold into the system. At that point, they can use other techniques, including automated rootkit packages, to gain increased levels of access to the system (see the section "Rootkits" later in this chapter). They may also use the compromised system as a jumping-off point for attacks on other, more attractive targets on the same network.

The following sections examine three methods hackers use to learn the passwords of legitimate users and access a system: password guessing attacks, dictionary attacks, and social engineering attacks. Many of these attacks rely upon weak password storage mechanisms. For example, many Unix operating systems store encrypted versions of a user's password in the `/etc/passwd` file.

Password Guessing

In the most basic type of password attack, hackers simply attempt to guess a user's password. No matter how much security education users receive, they often use extremely weak passwords. If hackers are able to obtain a list of authorized system users, they can often quickly figure out the correct usernames. (On most networks, usernames consist of the first initial of the user's first name followed by a portion of their last name.) With this information, they can begin making some educated guesses about the user's password. The most commonly used password is some form of the user's last name, first name, or username. For example, the user mchapple might use the weak password elppahcm because it's easy to remember. Unfortunately, it's also easy to guess.

If that attempt fails, hackers turn to widely available lists of the most common passwords on the Internet. Some of these are shown in the sidebar "Most Common Passwords."

Most Common Passwords

Hackers often use the Internet to distribute lists of commonly used passwords based on data gathered during system compromises. Many of these are no great surprise. Here are just a very few of the 815 passwords contained in a hacker list retrieved from the Internet in July 2002:

password	secret	sex	money	love
computer	football	hello	morning	ibm
work	office	online	terminal	internet

Along with these common words, the password list contained over 300 first names, 70 percent of which were female names.

Finally, a little knowledge about a person can provide extremely good clues to their password. Many people use the name of a spouse, child, family pet, relative, or favorite entertainer. Common passwords also include birthdays, anniversaries, Social Security numbers, phone numbers, and (believe it or not!) ATM PINs.

Dictionary Attacks

As mentioned previously, many Unix systems store encrypted versions of user passwords in an /etc/passwd file accessible to all system users. To provide some level of security, the file doesn't contain the actual user passwords; it contains an encrypted value obtained from a one-way encryption function (see Chapter 9 for a discussion of encryption functions). When a user attempts to log on to the system, access verification routines use the same encryption function to encrypt the password entered by the user and then compare it with the encrypted version of the actual password stored in the /etc/passwd file. If the values match, the user is allowed access.

Password hackers use automated tools like the Crack program to run automated dictionary attacks that exploit a simple vulnerability in this mechanism. They take a large dictionary file that contains thousands of words and then run the encryption function against all of those words to obtain their encrypted equivalents. Crack then searches the password file for any encrypted values for which there is a match in the encrypted dictionary. When a match is found, it reports the username and password (in plain text) and the hacker gains access to the system.

It sounds like simple security mechanisms and education would prevent users from using passwords that are easily guessed by Crack, but the tool is surprisingly effective at compromising live systems. As new versions of Crack are released, more advanced features are introduced to defeat common techniques used by users to defeat password complexity rules. Some of these are included in the following list:

- Rearranging the letters of a dictionary word
- Appending a number to a dictionary word
- Replacing each occurrence of the letter *O* in a dictionary word with the number *0* (or the letter *l* with the number *1*)
- Combining two dictionary words in some form

Social Engineering

Social engineering is one of the most effective tools hackers use to gain access to a system. In its most basic form, a *social engineering* attack consists of simply calling the user and asking for their password, posing as a technical support representative or other authority figure that needs the information immediately. Fortunately, most contemporary computer users are aware of these scams and the effectiveness of simply asking a user for a password is somewhat diminished today.

However, social engineering still poses a significant threat to the security of passwords (and networks in general). Hackers can often obtain sensitive personal information by "chatting up" computer users, office gossips, and administrative personnel. This information can provide excellent ammunition when mounting a password guessing attack. Furthermore, hackers can sometimes obtain sensitive network topography or configuration data that is useful when planning other types of electronic attacks against an organization.

Countermeasures

The cornerstone of any security program is education. Security personnel should continually remind users of the importance of choosing a secure password and keeping it secret. Users should receive training when they first enter an organization, and they should receive periodic refresher training, even if it's just an e-mail from the administrator reminding them of the threats.

Provide users with the knowledge they need to create secure passwords. Tell them about the techniques hackers use when guessing passwords and give them advice on how to create a strong password. One of the most effective password techniques is to use a mnemonic device such as thinking of an easy-to-remember sentence and creating a password out of the first letter of each word. For example, "My son Richard likes to eat 4 pies" would become MsRlte4p—an extremely strong password.

One of the most common mistakes made by overzealous security administrators is to create a series of strong passwords and then assign them to users (who are then prevented from changing their password). At first glance, this seems to be a sound security policy. However, the first thing a user will do when they receive a password like 1mf0A8flt is write it down on a Post-It note and stick it under the computer keyboard. Whoops! Security just went out the window (or under the keyboard)!

If your network includes Unix operating systems that implement the /etc/passwd file, consider using some other access verification mechanism to increase security. One popular technique available in many versions of Unix and Linux is the use of a shadow password file, /etc/shadow. This file contains the true encrypted passwords of each user, but it is not accessible to anyone but the administrator. The publicly accessible /etc/passwd file then simply contains a list of usernames without the data necessary to mount a dictionary attack.

Denial of Service Attacks

As you learned in Chapter 2, malicious individuals often use denial of service (DoS) attacks in an attempt to prevent legitimate users from accessing resources. This is often a "last ditch" effort when a hacker realizes that they can't penetrate a system—"If I can't have it, then nobody can." In the following sections, we'll take a look at five specific denial of service attacks and the mechanisms they use to disable computing systems. In some of these attacks, a *brute force attack* is used, simply overwhelming a targeted system with so many requests that it can't possibly sort out the legitimate ones from those that are part of the attack. Others include elegantly crafted commands that cause vulnerable systems to crash or hang indefinitely.

SYN Flood

Recall from Chapter 2 that the TCP/IP protocol utilizes a three-way *handshaking* process to set up connections between two hosts. In a typical connection, the originating host sends a single *packet* with the SYN flag enabled, attempting to open one side of the communications channel. The destination host receives this packet and sends a reply with the ACK flag enabled (confirming that the first side of the channel is open) and the SYN flag enabled (attempting to open the reverse channel). Finally, the originating host transmits a packet with the ACK flag enabled, confirming that the reverse channel is open and the connection is established. If, for some reason, the process is not completed, the communicating hosts leave the connection in a half-open state for a predetermined period of time before aborting the attempt. The standard handshaking process is illustrated in Figure 8.1.

In a *SYN flood attack,* hackers use special software that sends a large number of fake packets with the SYN flag set to the targeted system. The victim then reserves space in memory for the connection and attempts to send the standard SYN/ACK reply but never hears back from the originator. This process repeats hundreds or even thousands of times, and the targeted computer eventually becomes overwhelmed and runs out of available resources for the half-opened connections. At that time, it either crashes or simply ignores all inbound connection requests because it can't possibly handle any more half-open connections. This prevents everyone—both hackers and legitimate users—from connecting to the machine and results in an extremely effective denial of service attack. The SYN flood modified handshaking process is shown in Figure 8.2.

The SYN flood attack crippled many computing systems in the late 1990s and the year 2000. Web servers were especially vulnerable to this type of attack. Fortunately, modern firewalls contain specialized technology designed to prevent successful SYN flood attacks in the future. For example, Checkpoint Software's popular Firewall-1 package contains the SYNDefender functionality that acts as a proxy for SYN requests and shelters the destination system from any barrage of requests.

FIGURE 8.1 Standard TCP/IP three-way handshaking

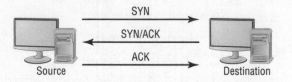

FIGURE 8.2 SYN flood modified handshaking process

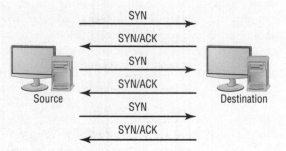

Distributed DoS Toolkits

Distributed denial of service (DDoS) attacks allow hackers to harness the power of many third-party systems to attack the ultimate target. In many DDoS attacks, a hacker will first use some other technique to compromise a large number of systems. They then install on those compromised systems software that enables them to participate in the main attack, effectively enlisting those machines into an army of attackers.

Trinoo and the Tribal Flood Network (TFN) are two commonly used DDoS toolkits. Hackers compromise third-party systems and install Trinoo/TFN clients that lie dormant waiting for instructions to begin an attack. When the hacker is satisfied that enough clients are lying in wait, they use a Trinoo/TFN master server to "wake up" the clients and initiate a coordinated attack against a single destination system or network from many directions. The current versions of Trinoo and TFN allow the master server to initiate many common DoS attacks, including SYN floods and Smurf attacks, from the third-party client machines.

Distributed denial of service attacks using these toolkits pose extreme risk to Internet-connected systems and are very difficult to defend against. In February 2000, hackers launched a week-long DDoS campaign against a number of high-profile websites, including those of Yahoo!, CNN, and Amazon.com. The attacks rendered these sites virtually inaccessible to legitimate users for an extended period of time. In fact, many security practitioners consider DDoS attacks the single greatest threat facing the Internet today.

Smurf

The *Smurf attack* takes the distributed denial of service attack to the next level by harnessing the power of many unwitting third-party hosts to attack a system. Attacks that are like Smurf and are amplified using third-party networks are known as *distributed reflective denial of service (DRDoS)* attacks.

The Smurf DRDoS attack in particular exploits a vulnerability in the implementation of the Internet Control Message Protocol (ICMP)'s *ping* functionality. The intended use of ping allows users to send single "Are you there?" packets to other systems. If the system is alive and responding, it sends back a single "Yes, I am" packet. It offers a very efficient way to check network connectivity and diagnose potential networking issues. The typical exchange involves only two packets transiting the network and consumes minimal computer/network resources.

In a Smurf attack, the originating system creates a false ping packet that appears to be from the target of the attack. The destination of the packet is the *broadcast address* of the third-party network. Therefore, each machine on the third-party network receives a copy of the ping request. According to the request they received, the originator is the victim system and each machine on the network sends a "Yes, I'm alive" packet to the victim. The originator repeats this process by rapidly sending a large number of these requests through different intermediary networks and the victim quickly becomes overwhelmed by the number of requests. The Smurf attack data flow is illustrated in Figure 8.3. A similar attack, the *Fraggle* attack, works in the same manner as Smurf but uses User Datagram Protocol (UDP) instead of ICMP.

Prevention of Smurf attacks depends upon the use of responsible filtering rules by networks across the entire Internet. System administrators should set rules at the router and/or firewall that prohibit inbound ping packets sent to a broadcast address (or perhaps even prohibit inbound pings entirely!). Furthermore, administrators should use egress filtering—a technique that prohibits systems on a network from transmitting packets with IP addresses that do not belong to the network. This prevents a network from being utilized by malicious individuals seeking to initiate a Smurf attack or any type of *masquerading* attack aimed at a remote network (see the section "Masquerading Attacks" for more information on this topic).

Fraggle

Fraggle is another distributed reflective denial of service (DRDoS) attack that works in a manner very similar to that of Smurf attacks. However, rather than using ICMP packets, Fraggle takes advantage of the uncommonly used *chargen* and *echo* UDP services. An easy way to prevent Fraggle attacks on your network is to disable these services. It's more than likely that you'll never have a legitimate use for them.

FIGURE 8.3 Smurf attack data flow

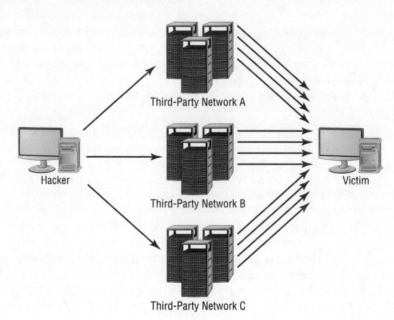

Teardrop

The *teardrop attack* is a member of a subclass of DoS attacks known as *fragmentation attacks*, which exploit vulnerabilities in the *fragment* reassembly functionality of the TCP/IP protocol stack. System administrators can configure the maximum size allowed for TCP/IP packets that traverse each network that carries them. They usually choose this value based upon the available hardware, quality of service, and typical network traffic parameters to maximize network efficiency and throughput.

When a network receives a packet larger than its maximum allowable packet size, it breaks it up into two or more fragments. These fragments are each assigned a size (corresponding to the length of the fragment) and an offset (corresponding to the starting location of the fragment). For example, if a packet is 250 bytes long and the maximum packet size for the network is 100 bytes, it will require fragmentation. In a correctly functioning TCP/IP stack, the packet would be broken up into three fragments, as shown in Figure 8.4.

In the teardrop attack, hackers use software that sends out packet fragments that don't conform to the protocol specification. Specifically, they send two or more overlapping fragments. This process is illustrated in Figure 8.5. The malicious individual might send out fragment 1, a perfectly normal packet fragment of length 100. Under normal conditions, this fragment would be followed by a second fragment with offset 100 (correlating to the length of the first fragment). However, in the teardrop attack, the hacker sends a second fragment with an offset value that is too low, placing the second fragment right in the middle of the first fragment. When the receiving system attempts to reassemble the fragmented packet, it doesn't know how to properly handle the overlapping fragments and freezes or crashes.

As with many of the attacks described in this book, the teardrop attack is a well-known exploit, and most operating system vendors have released security patches that prevent this type of attack from crippling updated systems. However, attacks like teardrop continue to cause damage on a daily basis due to the neglect of system administrators who fail to apply appropriate patches, leaving their systems vulnerable to attack.

FIGURE 8.4   Standard packet fragmentation

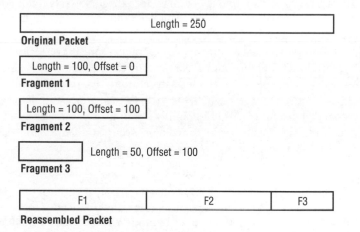

FIGURE 8.5   Teardrop attack

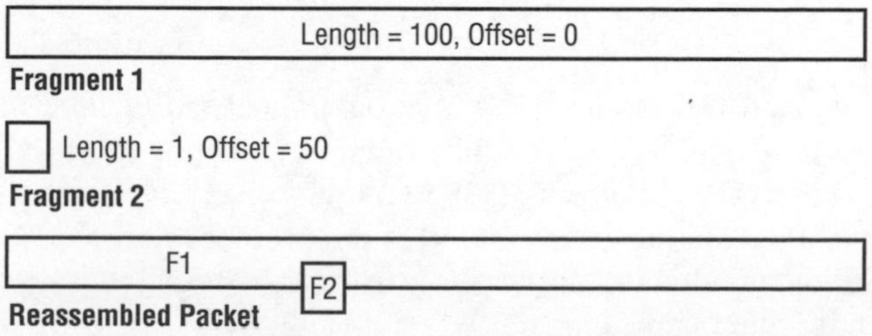

Land

The Land denial of service attack causes many older operating systems (such as Windows NT 4, Windows 95, and SunOS 4.1.4) to freeze and behave in an unpredictable manner. It works by creating an artificial TCP packet that has the SYN flag set. The attacker sets the destination IP address to the address of the victim machine and the destination port to an open port on that machine. Next, the attacker sets the source IP address and source port to the same values as the destination IP address and port. When the targeted host receives this unusual packet, the operating system doesn't know how to process it and freezes, crashes, or behaves in an unusual manner as a result.

DNS Poisoning

Another DoS attack, *DNS poisoning*, works without ever touching the targeted host. Instead, it exploits vulnerabilities in the Domain Name System (DNS) protocol and attempts to redirect traffic to an alternative server without the knowledge of the targeted victim.

Consider an example—suppose a hacker wants to redirect all legitimate traffic headed for www.whitehouse.gov to an alternative site, say www.youvebeenhacked.com. We can assume that the White House site, as a frequent target of hackers, is highly secure. Instead of attempting to directly penetrate that site, the hacker might try to insert into the DNS system false data that provides the IP address of www.youvebeenhacked.com when users query for the IP address of www.whitehouse.gov.

How can this happen? When you create a domain name, you use one of several domain name registrars that serve as central clearinghouses for DNS registrations. If a hacker is able to gain access to your registrar account (or the registrar's infrastructure itself), they might be able to alter your DNS records without your knowledge. In the early days of DNS, authentication was weak and users could change DNS information by simply sending an unauthenticated e-mail message. Fortunately, registrars have since implemented more secure authentication techniques that use cryptographic technology to verify user identities.

WARNING   DNS authentication techniques will protect you only if you use them! Ensure that you've enabled all of the security features offered by your registrar. Also, when an administrator leaves your organization, remember to change the passwords for any accounts used to manage DNS information. DNS poisoning is an easy way for a disgruntled former employee to get revenge!

Ping of Death

The final denial of service attack we'll examine is the infamous *ping of death attack* that plagued systems in the mid-1990s. This exploit is actually quite simple. According to the ICMP specification, the largest permissible ICMP packet is 65,536 bytes. However, many early operating system developers simply relied upon the assumption that the protocol stacks of sending machines would never exceed this value and did not build in error-handling routines to monitor for packets that exceeded this maximum.

Hackers seeking to exploit the ping of death vulnerability simply use a packet generation program to create a ping packet destined for the victim host with a size of at least 65,537 bytes. If the victim's operating system doesn't check the length of the packet and attempts to process it, unpredictable results occur. Some operating systems may hang or crash.

After this exploit was discovered, operating system manufacturers quickly updated their ICMP algorithms to prevent future occurrences. However, machines running older versions of certain operating systems may still be vulnerable to this attack. Some notable versions include Windows 3.11 and MacOS 7, along with unpatched versions of Windows 95, Windows NT 4, and Solaris 2.4–2.5.1. If you're running any of those operating systems on your network, update them to the appropriate patch level or version to protect yourself against this exploit.

Application Attacks

In Chapter 7, you learned about the importance of utilizing solid software engineering processes when developing operating systems and applications. In the following sections, we'll take a brief look at some of the specific techniques hackers use to exploit vulnerabilities left behind by sloppy coding practices.

Buffer Overflows

When creating software, developers must pay special attention to variables that allow user input. Many programming languages do not enforce size limits on variables intrinsically—they rely on the programmer to perform this bounds checking in the code. This is an inherent vulnerability because many programmers feel that parameter checking is an unnecessary burden that slows down the development process. As a security practitioner, it's your responsibility to ensure that developers in your organization are aware of the risks posed by buffer overflow vulnerabilities and take appropriate measures to protect their code against this type of attack.

Any time a program variable allows user input, the programmer should take steps to ensure that each of the following conditions are met:

- The user can't enter a value longer than the size of any buffer that will hold it (e.g., a 10-letter word into a 5-letter string variable).

- The user can't enter an invalid value for the variable types that will hold it (e.g., a character into a numeric variable).

- The user can't enter a value that will cause the program to operate outside of its specified parameters (e.g., answer a "Yes or No" question with "Maybe").

Failure to perform simple checks to make sure these conditions are met can result in a buffer overflow vulnerability that may cause the system to crash or even allow the user to execute shell commands and gain access to the system. Buffer overflow vulnerabilities are especially prevalent in code developed rapidly for the Web using CGI or other languages that allow unskilled programmers to quickly create interactive web pages.

Time-of-Check-to-Time-of-Use

The *time-of-check-to-time-of-use (TOCTTOU or TOC/TOU)* issue is a timing vulnerability that occurs when a program checks access permissions too far in advance of a resource request. For example, if an operating system builds a comprehensive list of access permissions for a user upon logon and then consults that list throughout the logon session, a TOCTTOU vulnerability exists. If the system administrator revokes a particular permission, that restriction would not be applied to the user until the next time they log on. If the user is logged on when the access revocation takes place, they will have access to the resource indefinitely. The user simply needs to leave the session open for days and the new restrictions will never be applied.

Trap Doors

Trap doors are undocumented command sequences that allow software developers to bypass normal access restrictions. They are often used during the development and debugging process to speed up the workflow and avoid forcing developers to continuously authenticate to the system. Occasionally, developers leave these trap doors in the system after it reaches a production state, either by accident or so they can "take a peek" at their system when it is processing sensitive data to which they should not have access.

Obviously, the undocumented nature of trap doors makes them a significant threat to the security of any system that contains them, especially when they are undocumented and forgotten. If a developer leaves the firm, they could later use the trap door to access the system and retrieve confidential information or participate in industrial sabotage.

Rootkits

Rootkits are specialized software packages that have only one purpose—to allow hackers to gain expanded access to a system. Rootkits are freely available on the Internet and exploit known vulnerabilities in various operating systems. Hackers often obtain access to a standard system user account through the use of a password attack or social engineering and then use a rootkit to increase their access to the *root* (or administrator) level.

There is one simple measure administrators can take to protect their systems against the vast majority of rootkit attacks—and it's nothing new. Administrators must keep themselves informed about new security patches released for operating systems used in their environment and apply these corrective measures consistently. This straightforward step will fortify a network against almost all rootkit attacks as well as a large number of other potential vulnerabilities.

Reconnaissance Attacks

As with any attacking force, hackers require solid intelligence to effectively focus their efforts against the targets most likely to yield the best results. To assist with this targeting, hacker tool developers have created a number of automated tools that perform network reconnaissance. In the following sections, we'll examine three of those automated techniques—IP probes, port scans, and vulnerability scans—and then look at how these techniques can be supplemented by the more physically intensive dumpster-diving technique.

IP Probes

IP probes (also called IP sweeps) are often the first type of network reconnaissance carried out against a targeted network. With this technique, automated tools simply attempt to ping each address in a range. Systems that respond to the ping request are logged for further analysis. Addresses that do not produce a response are assumed to be unused and are ignored.

IP probes are extremely prevalent on the Internet today. Indeed, if you configure a system with a public IP address and connect it to the Internet, you'll probably receive at least one IP probe within hours of booting up. The widespread use of this technique makes a strong case for disabling ping functionality, at least for users external to a network.

Port Scans

After a hacker performs an IP probe, they are left with a list of active systems on a given network. The next task is to select one or more systems to target with additional attacks. Often, hackers have a type of target in mind—web servers, file servers, or other critical operations are prime targets.

To narrow down their search, hackers use *port scan* software to probe all of the active systems on a network and determine what public services are running on each machine. For example, if the hacker wants to target a web server, they might run a port scan to locate any systems with a service running on port 80, the default port for HTTP services.

Vulnerability Scans

The third technique is the *vulnerability scan*. Once the hacker determines a specific system to target, they need to discover in that system a specific vulnerability that can be exploited to gain the desired access permissions. A variety of tools available on the Internet assist with this task. Two of the more popular ones are the Satan and Saint vulnerability scanners. These packages contain a database of known vulnerabilities and probe targeted systems to locate security flaws. They then produce very attractive reports that detail every vulnerability detected. From that point, it's simply a matter of locating a script that exploits a specific vulnerability and launching an attack against the victim.

It's important to note that vulnerability scanners are highly automated tools. They can be used to launch an attack against a specific system, but it's just as likely that a hacker used a series of IP probes, port scans, and vulnerability scans to narrow down a list of potential victims. However, chances are an intruder will run a vulnerability scanner against an entire network to probe for any weakness that could be exploited.

Once again, simply updating operating systems to the most recent security patch level can repair almost every weakness reported by a vulnerability scanner. Furthermore, wise system administrators learn to think like the enemy—they download and run these vulnerability scanners against their own networks (with the permission of upper management) to see what security holes might be pointed out to a potential hacker. This allows them to quickly focus their resources on fortifying the weakest points on their networks.

Dumpster Diving

Every organization generates trash—often significant amounts on a daily basis. Have you ever taken the time to sort through your trash and look at the sensitivity of the materials that hit the recycle bin? Give it a try—the results may frighten you. When you're analyzing the working papers thrown away each day, look at them from a hacker's perspective. What type of intelligence could you glean from them that might help you launch an attack? Is there sensitive data about network configurations or installed software versions? A list of employees' birthdays from a particular department that might be used in a social engineering attack? A policy manual that contains detailed procedures on the creation of new accounts? Discarded floppy disks or other storage media?

Dumpster diving is one of the oldest hacker tools in the book and it's still used today. The best defense against these attacks is quite simple—make them more difficult. Purchase shredders for key departments and encourage employees to use them. Keep the trash locked up in a secure area until the garbage collectors arrive. A little common sense goes a long way in this area.

Masquerading Attacks

One of the easiest ways to gain access to resources you're not otherwise entitled to use is to impersonate someone who does have the appropriate access permissions. In the offline world, teenagers often borrow the driver's license of an older sibling to purchase alcohol—the same thing happens in the computer security world. Hackers borrow the identities of legitimate users and systems to gain the trust of third parties. In the following sections, we'll take a look at two common masquerading attacks—IP spoofing and session hijacking.

IP Spoofing

In an *IP spoofing* attack, the malicious individual simply reconfigures their system so that it has the IP address of a trusted system and then attempts to gain access to other external resources. This is surprisingly effective on many networks that don't have adequate filters installed to prevent this type of traffic from occurring. System administrators should configure filters at the perimeter of each network to ensure that packets meet at least the following criteria:

- Packets with internal source IP addresses don't enter the network from the outside.
- Packets with external source IP addresses don't exit the network from the inside.
- Packets with private IP addresses don't pass through the router in either direction (unless specifically allowed as part of an intranet configuration).

These three simple filtering rules can eliminate the vast majority of IP spoofing attacks and greatly enhance the security of a network.

Session Hijacking

Session hijacking attacks occur when a malicious individual intercepts part of the communication between an authorized user and a resource and then uses a hijacking technique to take over the session and assume the identity of the authorized user. The following list includes some common techniques:

- Capturing details of the authentication between a client and server and using those details to assume the client's identity

- Tricking the client into thinking the hacker's system is the server, acting as the middleman as the client sets up a legitimate connection with the server, and then disconnecting the client

- Accessing a web application using the cookie data of a user who did not properly close the connection

All of these techniques can have disastrous results for the end user and must be addressed with both administrative controls (such as anti-replay authentication techniques) and application controls (such as expiring cookies within a reasonable period of time).

Decoy Techniques

Hackers aren't the only ones with tricks up their sleeves—security administrators have also mastered sleight-of-hand tricks and use them to lure hackers into a sense of false security. After they've had the opportunity to observe hackers and trace their actions back to the source, they send law enforcement or other authorities to swoop in and stop the malicious activity cold. In the following sections, we'll examine two such techniques used by creative system administrators: honey pots and pseudo-flaws.

Honey Pots

Administrators often create *honey pot* systems that appear to be extremely lucrative hacker targets. They may contain files that appear to be sensitive and/or valuable or run false services (like a web server) that appear to be critical to an organization's operations. In reality, these systems are nothing but decoys set up to lure hackers away from truly critical resources and allow administrators to monitor and trace their activities.

Pseudo-Flaws

Pseudo-flaws are false vulnerabilities or apparent loopholes intentionally implanted into a system in an attempt to detect hackers. They are often used on honey-pot systems and on critical resources to emulate well-known operating system vulnerabilities. Hackers seeking to exploit a known flaw might stumble across a pseudo-flaw and think that they have successfully penetrated a system. More sophisticated pseudo-flaw mechanisms actually simulate the penetration and convince the hacker that they have gained additional access privileges to a system. However, while the hacker is exploring the bounds of these newfound rights, monitoring and alerting mechanisms trigger in the background to alert administrators to the threat and increase the defensive posture surrounding critical network resources.

Summary

Throughout history, criminals have always been extremely creative. No matter what security mechanisms have been put in place to deter them, criminals have found methods to bypass them and reach their ultimate goals. This is no less true in the realm of computer security than in any other aspect of criminal psychology. Hackers use a number of automated tools to perform network reconnaissance so they can focus their efforts on the targets most likely to yield the best results. Examples include IP probes, port scans, malicious code, password attacks, denial of service attacks, application attacks, reconnaissance attacks, masquerading attacks, and decoy techniques.

By no means was this a comprehensive look at all possible hacking methods—that would be an impossible task. New tools and techniques appear in the hacking subculture almost on a daily basis. However, you should now have a good feeling for the types of weapons hackers have at their disposal as well as some of the best defense mechanisms security administrators can use to fortify their protected systems and networks against hacker intrusions.

Remember the following key actions you can take to increase your security posture:

- Use strong passwords.

- Update operating systems and applications with security patches as they are released by vendors.

- Use common-sense filtering techniques to ensure that traffic on your network is what it appears to be.

Pay particular attention to the technical details of the attacks presented in this chapter. Be familiar with the technology underlying each attack and be prepared to identify them in a multiple-choice format. Just as important, understand the countermeasures system administrators can apply to prevent each one of those attacks from occurring on protected networks.

Exam Essentials

Understand the propagation techniques used by viruses.   Viruses use three main propagation techniques—file infection, boot sector infection, and macro infection—to penetrate systems and spread their malicious payloads.

Know how antivirus software packages detect known viruses.   Most antivirus programs use signature-based detection algorithms to look for telltale patterns of known viruses. This makes it essential to periodically update virus definition files in order to maintain protection against newly authored viruses as they emerge.

Be able to explain the techniques viruses use to escape detection.   Viruses use polymorphism and encryption to avoid leaving behind signature footprints. Multipartite viruses use more than one propagation technique to infiltrate systems. Stealth viruses alter operating systems to trick antivirus packages into thinking everything is normal.

Understand the basic principles behind logic bombs, Trojan horses, and worms.   Logic bombs remain dormant until one or more conditions are met. At that time, they trigger their malicious payload. Trojan horses penetrate systems by masquerading as a benevolent program while unleashing their payload in the background. Worms spread from system to system under their own power, potentially consuming massive amounts of resources.

Be familiar with common password attacks and understand how to develop strong passwords.   Hackers attempting to gain access to a system use straightforward guessing in combination with dictionary attacks and social engineering techniques to learn user passwords. System administrators should implement security education programs and operating system controls to ensure that users choose strong passwords.

Understand common denial of service attacks and appropriate countermeasures.   Hackers use standard denial of service attacks like SYN flooding, teardrop fragmentation attacks, and the ping of death to cripple targeted systems. They also harness the power of the global computing grid through the use of Smurf attacks and other distributed denial of service attacks.

Be familiar with the various types of application attacks hackers use to exploit poorly written software.   Buffer overflow vulnerabilities are one of the greatest threats to modern computing. Hackers also exploit trap doors, time-of-check-to-time-of-use vulnerabilities, and rootkits to gain illegitimate access to a system.

Know the network reconnaissance techniques used by hackers preparing to attack a network.   Before launching an attack, hackers use IP sweeps to search out active hosts on a network. These hosts are then subjected to port scans and other vulnerability probes to locate weak spots that might be attacked in an attempt to compromise the network.

Understand decoy techniques used by system administrators seeking to lure hackers into a trap.   System administrators use honey-pot systems that appear to be lucrative, easy-to-hit targets for hackers in attempts to draw them away from critical systems and track their activities. These systems might contain pseudo-flaws—apparent vulnerabilities that don't really exist—in an attempt to lull malicious individuals into a false sense of security.

Written Lab

Answer the following questions about malicious code and application attacks:

1. What is the major difference between a virus and a worm?

2. Explain the four propagation methods used by Robert Tappan Morris's Internet Worm.

3. Describe how the normal TCP/IP handshaking process works and how the SYN flood attack exploits this process to cause a denial of service.

4. What are the actions an antivirus software package might take when it discovers an infected file?

5. Explain how a data integrity assurance package like Tripwire provides some secondary virus detection capabilities.

Review Questions

1. What is the size of the Master Boot Record on a system installed with a typical configuration?

    A. 256 bytes

    B. 512 bytes

    C. 1,024 bytes

    D. 2,048 bytes

2. How many steps take place in the standard TCP/IP handshaking process?

    A. One

    B. Two

    C. Three

    D. Four

3. Which one of the following types of attacks relies upon the difference between the timing of two events?

    A. Smurf

    B. TOCTTOU

    C. Land

    D. Fraggle

4. What propagation technique does the Good Times virus use to spread infection?

    A. File infection

    B. Boot sector infection

    C. Macro infection

    D. None of the above

5. What advanced virus technique modifies the malicious code of a virus on each system it infects?

    A. Polymorphism

    B. Stealth

    C. Encryption

    D. Multipartitism

6. Which one of the following files might be modified or created by a companion virus?

    A. COMMAND.EXE

    B. CONFIG.SYS

    C. AUTOEXEC.BAT

    D. WIN32.DLL

7. What is the best defensive action that system administrators can take against the threat posed by brand new malicious code objects that exploit known software vulnerabilities?

    A. Update antivirus definitions monthly

    B. Install anti-worm filters on the proxy server

    C. Apply security patches as they are released

    D. Prohibit Internet use on the corporate network

8. Which one of the following passwords is least likely to be compromised during a dictionary attack?

    A. mike

    B. elppa

    C. dayorange

    D. dlayna

9. What file is instrumental in preventing dictionary attacks against Unix systems?

    A. /etc/passwd

    B. /etc/shadow

    C. /etc/security

    D. /etc/pwlog

10. Which one of the following tools can be used to launch a distributed denial of service attack against a system or network?

    A. Satan

    B. Saint

    C. Trinoo

    D. Nmap

11. Which one of the following network attacks takes advantages of weaknesses in the fragment reassembly functionality of the TCP/IP protocol stack?

    A. Teardrop

    B. Smurf

    C. Ping of death

    D. SYN flood

12. What type of reconnaissance attack provides hackers with useful information about the services running on a system?

    A. Session hijacking

    B. Port scan

    C. Dumpster diving

    D. IP sweep

13. A hacker located at IP address 12.8.0.1 wants to launch a Smurf attack on a victim machine located at IP address 129.74.15.12 utilizing a third-party network located at 141.190.0.0/16. What would be the source IP address on the single packet the hacker transmits?

A. 12.8.0.1

B. 129.74.15.12

C. 141.190.0.0

D. 141.190.255.255

14. What type of virus utilizes more than one propagation technique to maximize the number of penetrated systems?

A. Stealth virus

B. Companion virus

C. Polymorphic virus

D. Multipartite virus

15. What is the minimum size a packet can be to be used in a ping of death attack?

A. 2,049 bytes

B. 16,385 bytes

C. 32,769 bytes

D. 65,537 bytes

16. Jim recently downloaded an application from a website that ran within his browser and caused his system to crash by consuming all available resources. Of what type of malicious code was Jim most likely the victim of?

A. Virus

B. Worm

C. Trojan horse

D. Hostile applet

17. Alan is the security administrator for a public network. In an attempt to detect hacking attempts, he installed a program on his production servers that imitates a well-known operating system vulnerability and reports exploitation attempts to the administrator. What is this type of technique called?

A. Honey pot

B. Pseudo-flaw

C. Firewall

D. Bear trap

18. What technology does the Java language use to minimize the threat posed by applets?

   A. Confidentiality

   B. Encryption

   C. Stealth

   D. Sandbox

19. Renee is the security administrator for a research network. She's attempting to convince her boss that they should disable two unused services—chargen and echo. What attack is the network more vulnerable to with these services running?

   A. Smurf

   B. Land

   C. Fraggle

   D. Ping of death

20. Which one of the following attacks uses a TCP packet with the SYN flag set and identical source/destination IP addresses and ports?

   A. Smurf

   B. Land

   C. Fraggle

   D. Ping of death

Answers to Review Questions

1.   B. The Master Boot Record is a single sector of a floppy disk or hard drive. Each sector is normally 512 bytes. The MBR contains only enough information to direct the proper loading of the operating system.

2.   C. The TCP/IP handshake consists of three phases: SYN, SYN/ACK, and ACK. Attacks like the SYN flood abuse this process by taking advantage of weaknesses in the handshaking protocol to mount a denial of service attack.

3.   B. The time-of-check-to-time-of-use (TOCTTOU) attack relies upon the timing of the execution of two events.

4.   D. The Good Times virus is a famous hoax that does not actually exist.

5.   A. In an attempt to avoid detection by signature-based antivirus software packages, polymorphic viruses modify their own code each time they infect a system.

6.   A. Companion viruses are self-contained executable files with filenames similar to those of existing system/program files but with a modified extension. The virus file is executed when an unsuspecting user types the filename without the extension at the command prompt.

7.   C. The vast majority of new malicious code objects exploit known vulnerabilities that were already addressed by software manufacturers. The best action administrators can take against new threats is to maintain the patch level of their systems.

8.   D. All of the other choices are forms of common words that might be found during a dictionary attack. *mike* is a name and would be easily detected. *elppa* is simply *apple* spelled backwards, and *dayorange* combines two dictionary words. Crack and other utilities can easily see through these "sneaky" techniques. *dlayna* is simply a random string of characters that a dictionary attack would not uncover.

9.   B. Shadow password files move encrypted password information from the publicly readable /etc/passwd file to the protected /etc/shadow file.

10.   C. Trinoo and the Tribal Flood Network (TFN) are the two most commonly used distributed denial of service (DDoS) attack toolkits. The other three tools mentioned are reconnaissance techniques used to map networks and scan for known vulnerabilities.

11.   A. The teardrop attack uses overlapping packet fragments to confuse a target system and cause the system to reboot or crash.

12.   B. Port scans reveal the ports associated with services running on a machine and available to the public.

13.   B. The single packet would be sent from the hacker to the third-party network. The source address of this packet would be the IP address of the victim (129.74.15.12), and the destination address would be the broadcast address of the third-party network (141.190.255.255).

14. D. Multipartite viruses use two or more propagation techniques (e.g., file infection and boot sector infection) to maximize their reach.

15. D. The maximum allowed ping packet size is 65,536 bytes. To engage in a ping of death attack, an attacker must send a packet that exceeds this maximum. Therefore, the smallest packet that might result in a successful attack would be 65,537 bytes.

16. D. Hostile applets are a type of malicious code that users download from a remote website and run within their browsers. These applets, written using technologies like ActiveX and Java, may then perform a variety of malicious actions.

17. B. Alan has implemented pseudo-flaws in his production systems. Honey pots often use pseudo-flaws, but they are not the technology used in this case because honey pots are stand-alone systems dedicated to detecting hackers.

18. D. The Java sandbox isolates applets and allows them to run within a protected environment, limiting the effect they may have on the rest of the system.

19. C. The Fraggle attack utilizes the uncommonly used UDP services chargen and echo to implement a denial of service attack.

20. B. The Land attack uses a TCP packet constructed with the SYN flag set and identical source and destination sockets. It causes older operating systems to behave in an unpredictable manner.

Answers to Written Lab

Following are answers to the questions in this chapter's written lab:

1. Viruses and worms both travel from system to system attempting to deliver their malicious payloads to as many machines as possible. However, viruses require some sort of human intervention, such as sharing a file, network resource, or e-mail message, to propagate. Worms, on the other hand, seek out vulnerabilities and spread from system to system under their own power, thereby greatly magnifying their reproductive capability, especially in a well-connected network.

2. The Internet Worm used four propagation techniques. First, it exploited a bug in the sendmail utility that allowed the worm to spread itself by sending a specially crafted e-mail message that contained the worm's code to the sendmail program on a remote system. Second, it used a dictionary-based password attack to attempt to gain access to remote systems by utilizing the username and password of a valid system user. Third, it exploited a buffer overflow vulnerability in the finger program to infect systems. Finally, it analyzed any existing trust relationships with other systems on the network and attempted to spread itself to those systems through the trusted path.

3. In a typical connection, the originating host sends a single packet with the SYN flag enabled, attempting to open one side of the communications channel. The destination host receives this packet and sends a reply with the ACK flag enabled (confirming that the first side of the channel is open) and the SYN flag enabled (attempting to open the reverse channel). Finally, the originating host transmits a packet with the ACK flag enabled, confirming that the reverse channel is open and the connection is established. In a SYN flood attack, hackers use special software that sends a large number of fake packets with the SYN flag set to the targeted system. The victim then reserves space in memory for the connection and attempts to send the standard SYN/ACK reply but never hears back from the originator. This process repeats hundreds or even thousands of times and the targeted computer eventually becomes overwhelmed and runs out of available memory for the half-opened connections.

4. If possible, it may try to disinfect the file, removing the virus's malicious code. If that fails, it might either quarantine the file for manual review or automatically delete it to prevent further infection.

5. Data integrity assurance packages like Tripwire compute checksum values for each file stored on a protected system. If a file infector virus strikes the system, this would result in a change in the affected file's checksum value and would, therefore, trigger a file integrity alert.

Chapter
9

Cryptography and Private Key Algorithms

THE CISSP EXAM TOPICS COVERED IN THIS CHAPTER INCLUDE:

- ✓ Use of Cryptography to Achieve Confidentiality, Integrity, Authentication, and Nonrepudiation
- ✓ Cryptographic Concepts, Methodologies, and Practices
- ✓ Private Key Algorithms

Cryptography provides added levels of security to data during processing, storage, and communications. Over the years, mathematicians and computer scientists developed a series of increasingly complex algorithms designed to ensure confidentiality, integrity, authentication, and nonrepudiation. During that same period, hackers and governments alike devoted significant resources to undermining those cryptographic algorithms. This led to an "arms race" in cryptography and resulted in the development of the extremely sophisticated algorithms in use today. This chapter takes a look at the history of cryptography, the basics of cryptographic communications, and the fundamental principles of private key cryptosystems. The next chapter continues the discussion of cryptography by examining public key cryptosystems and the various techniques attackers use to defeat cryptography.

History

Since the beginning of mankind, human beings devised various systems of written communication, ranging from ancient hieroglyphics written on cave walls to CD-ROMs stuffed with encyclopedias full of information in modern English. As long as mankind has been communicating, it has also used secretive means to hide the true meaning of those communications from the uninitiated. Ancient societies used a complex system of secret symbols to represent safe places to stay during times of war. Modern civilizations use a variety of codes and ciphers to facilitate private communication between individuals and groups. In the following sections, we'll take a brief look at the evolution of modern cryptography and several famous attempts to covertly intercept and decipher encrypted communications.

Caesar Cipher

One of the earliest known cipher systems was used by Julius Caesar to communicate with Cicero in Rome while he was conquering Europe. Caesar knew that there were several risks when sending messages—the messengers themselves might be an enemy spy or they might be ambushed while en route to the deployed forces. For that reason, he developed a cryptographic system now known as the Caesar cipher. The system itself is extremely simple. To encrypt a message, you simply shift each letter of the alphabet three places to the right. For example, *A* would become *D* and *B* would become *E*. If you reach the end of the alphabet during this process, you simply wrap around to the beginning so that *X* becomes *A*, *Y* becomes *B*, and *Z* becomes *C*. For this reason, the Caesar cipher also became known as the ROT3 (or Rotate 3) cipher. The Caesar cipher is a substitution cipher that is monoalphabetic; it's also known as a C3 cipher.

Here's an example of the Caesar cipher in action. The first line contains the original sentence, and the second line shows what the sentence looks like when it is encrypted using the Caesar cipher:

```
THE DIE HAS BEEN CAST
WKH GLH KDV EHHQ FDVW
```

To decrypt the message, you simply shift each letter three places to the left.

> Although the Caesar cipher is relatively easy to use, it's also relatively easy to crack. It's vulnerable to a type of attack known as *frequency analysis*. As you may know, the most common letters in the English language are *E, T, A, O, N, R, I, S,* and *H*. An attacker seeking to break a Caesar-style cipher merely needs to find the most common letters in the encrypted text and experiment with substitutions of the letters above to help determine the pattern.

American Civil War

Between the time of Caesar and the early years of the United States, scientists and mathematicians made significant advances beyond the early ciphers used by ancient civilizations. During the American Civil War, Union and Confederate troops both used relatively advanced cryptographic systems to secretly communicate along the front lines, due to the fact that both sides were tapping into the telegraph lines to spy on the other side. These systems used complex combinations of word substitutions and transposition (see the section on ciphers for more details) to attempt to defeat enemy decryption efforts. Another system used widely during the Civil War was a series of flag signals developed by army doctor Albert Myer.

> Photos of many of the items discussed in this chapter are available online at www.nsa.gov/museum/tour.html.

Ultra vs. Enigma

Americans weren't the only ones who expended significant resources in the pursuit of superior code making machines. Prior to World War II, the German military-industrial complex adapted a commercial code machine nicknamed Enigma for government use. This machine used a series of three to six rotors to implement an extremely complicated substitution cipher. The only possible way to decrypt the message with contemporary technology was to use a similar machine with the same rotor settings used by the transmitting device. The Germans recognized the importance of safeguarding these devices and made it extremely difficult for the Allies to acquire one.

The Allied forces began a top-secret effort known by the code name Ultra to attack the Enigma codes. Eventually, their efforts paid off when the Polish military successfully reconstructed an Enigma prototype and shared their findings with British and American cryptology experts. The Allies successfully broke the Enigma code in 1940, and historians credit this triumph as playing a significant role in the eventual defeat of the Axis powers.

The Japanese used a similar machine, known as the Japanese Purple Machine, during World War II. A significant American attack on this cryptosystem resulted in the breaking of the Japanese code prior to the end of the war. The Americans were aided by the fact that Japanese communicators used very formal message formats that resulted in a large amount of similar text in multiple messages, easing the cryptanalytic effort.

Cryptographic Basics

The study of any science must begin with a discussion of some of the fundamental principles it is built upon. The following sections lay this foundation with a review of the goals of cryptography, an overview of the basic concepts of cryptographic technology, and a look at the major mathematical principles utilized by cryptographic systems.

Goals of Cryptography

Security practitioners utilize cryptographic systems to meet four fundamental goals: confidentiality, integrity, authentication, and nonrepudiation. Achieving each of these goals requires the satisfaction of a number of design requirements, and not all cryptosystems are intended to achieve all four goals. In the following sections, we'll examine each goal in detail and give a brief description of the technical requirements necessary to achieve it.

Confidentiality

Confidentiality ensures that a message remains private during transmission between two or more parties. This is perhaps the most widely cited goal of cryptosystems—the facilitation of secret communications between individuals and groups. There are two main types of cryptosystems that enforce confidentiality. Symmetric key cryptosystems make use of a shared secret key available to all users of the cryptosystem. Public key cryptosystems utilize individual combinations of public and private keys for each user of the system. Both of these concepts are explored in the section "Modern Cryptography" later in this chapter.

Integrity

Integrity ensures that a message is not altered while in transit. If integrity mechanisms are in place, the recipient of a message can be certain that the message received is identical to the message that was sent. This protects against all forms of alteration: intentional alteration by a third party attempting to insert false information and unintentional alteration by faults in the transmission process. Message integrity is enforced through the use of digitally signed message digests created upon transmission of a message. The recipient of the message simply verifies that the message's digest and signature is valid, ensuring that the message was not altered in transit. Integrity can be enforced by both public and secret key cryptosystems. This concept is discussed in detail in the section "Digital Signatures" in Chapter 10, "PKI and Cryptographic Applications."

Authentication

Authentication verifies the claimed identity of system users and is a major function of cryptosystems. For example, suppose that Jim wants to establish a communications session with Bob and they are both participants in a shared secret communications system. Jim might use a challenge-response authentication technique to ensure that Bob is who he claims to be.

Figure 9.1 shows how this challenge-response protocol might work in action. In this example, the shared-secret code used by Jim and Bob is quite simple—the letters of each word are simply reversed. Bob first contacts Jim and identifies himself. Jim then sends a challenge message to Bob, asking him to encrypt a short message using the secret code known only to Jim and Bob. Bob replies with the encrypted message. After Jim verifies that the encrypted message is correct, he trusts that Bob himself is truly on the other end of the connection.

FIGURE 9.1 Challenge-response authentication protocol

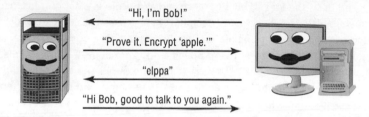

Nonrepudiation

Nonrepudiation provides assurance to the recipient that the message was actually originated by the sender and not someone masquerading as the sender. It prevents the sender from claiming that they never sent the message in the first place (also known as repudiating the message). Secret key, or symmetric key, cryptosystems (such as the ROT3 cipher) do not provide this guarantee of nonrepudiation. If Jim and Bob participate in a secret key communication system, they can both produce the same encrypted message using their shared secret key. Nonrepudiation is offered only by public key, or asymmetric, cryptosystems, a topic discussed in greater detail in Chapter 10.

Cryptography Concepts

As with any science, you must be familiar with certain terminology before studying cryptography. Let's take a look at a few of the key terms used to describe codes and ciphers. Before a message is put into a coded form, it is known as a *plaintext* message and is represented by the letter P when encryption functions are described. The sender of a message uses a cryptographic algorithm to *encrypt* the plaintext message and produce a *ciphertext* message, represented by the letter C. This message is transmitted by some physical or electronic means to the recipient. The recipient then uses a predetermined algorithm to *decrypt* the ciphertext message and retrieve the plaintext version.

All cryptographic algorithms rely upon *keys* to maintain their security. For the most part, a key is nothing more than a number. It's usually a very large binary number, but a number nonetheless. Every algorithm has a specific key space. The key space is the range of values that are valid for use as a key for a specific algorithm. A key space is defined by its bit size. Bit size is nothing more than the number of binary bits or digits in the key. The key space is the range between the key that has all 0s and the key that has all 1s. Or to state it another way, the key space is the range of numbers from 0 to 2^n, where n is the bit size of the key. So a 128-bit key can have a value from 0 to 2^{128} (which is roughly $3.40282367 * 10^{38}$, that is, very big number!). Even though a key is just a number, it is a very important number. In fact, if the algorithm is known, then the all security you gain from cryptography rests on your ability to keep the keys used private.

Kerchoff's Principle

All cryptography is based upon the idea of an algorithm. An algorithm is a set of rules, usually mathematical, that dictates how enciphering and deciphering processes are to take place. Most algorithms are dictated by the Kerchoff principle, a concept that makes algorithms known and public, allowing anyone to examine and test them. Specifically, the Kerchoff principle (also known as Kerchoff's assumption) is that all algorithms should be public but all keys should remain private. A large number of cryptologists adhere to this principle, but not all of them do. In fact, a significant group adheres to the opposite view and believes better overall security can be maintained by keeping both the algorithm and the key private. Kerchoff's adherents retort that the opposite approach includes the practice of "security through obscurity" and believe that public exposure produces more activity and exposes more weaknesses more readily, leading to the abandonment of insufficiently strong algorithms and quicker adoption of suitable ones.

As you'll learn in this chapter and the next, different types of algorithms require different types of keys. In private key (or secret key) cryptosystems, all participants use a single shared key. In public key cryptosystems, each participant has their own pair of keys. Cryptographic keys are sometimes referred to as *cryptovariables*.

The art of creating and implementing secret codes and ciphers is known as *cryptography*. This practice is paralleled by the art of *cryptanalysis*—the study of methods to defeat codes and ciphers. Together, cryptography and cryptanalysis are commonly referred to as *cryptology*. Specific implementations of a code or cipher in hardware and software are known as *cryptosystems*. Federal Information Processing Standards-140 (FIPS-140), "Security Requirements for Cryptographic Modules," defines the hardware and software requirements for cryptographic modules that the federal government uses.

Be sure to understand the meanings of these terms before continuing your study of this chapter and the following chapter. They are essential to understanding the technical details of the cryptographic algorithms presented in the following sections.

Cryptographic Mathematics

Cryptography is no different than most computer science disciplines in that it finds its foundations in the science of mathematics. To fully understand cryptography, you must first understand the basics of binary mathematics and the logical operations used to manipulate binary values. The following sections present a brief look at some of the most fundamental concepts with which you should be familiar.

Binary Mathematics

Binary mathematics defines the rules used for the bits and bytes that form the nervous system of any computer. You're most likely familiar with the decimal system. It is a base 10 system in which an integer from 0 to 9 is used in each place and each place value is a multiple of 10. It's likely that our reliance upon the decimal system has biological origins—human beings have 10 fingers that can be used to count.

Binary math can be very confusing at first, but it's well worth the investment of time to learn how the various logical operations work, specifically logical functions. More important, you need to understand these concepts to truly understand the inner workings of cryptographic algorithms.

Similarly, the computer's reliance upon the binary system has electrical origins. In an electrical circuit, there are only two possible states—on (representing the presence of electrical current) and off (representing the absence of electrical current). All computation performed by an electrical device must be expressed in these terms, giving rise to the use of binary computation in modern electronics. In general, computer scientists refer to the on condition as a true value and the off condition as a false value.

Logical Operations

The binary mathematics of cryptography utilizes a variety of logical functions to manipulate data. We'll take a brief look at several of these operations.

AND

The *AND* operation (represented by the ∧ symbol) checks to see whether two values are both true. The truth table that follows illustrates all four possible outputs for the AND function. Remember, the AND function takes only two variables as input. In binary math, there are only two possible values for each of these variables, leading to four possible inputs to the AND function. It's this finite number of possibilities that makes it extremely easy for computers to implement logical functions in hardware. Notice in the following truth table that only one combination of inputs (where both inputs are true) produces an output value of true:

X	Y	X ∧ Y
0	0	0
0	1	0
1	0	0
1	1	1

Logical operations are often performed on entire binary words rather than single values. Take a look at the following example:

```
X:    0 1 1 0 1 1 0 0
Y:    1 0 1 0 0 1 1 1
_____

X ∧ Y:  0 0 1 0 0 1 0 0
```

Notice that the AND function is computed by comparing the values of *X* and *Y* in each column. The output value is true only in columns where both *X* and *Y* are true.

OR

The *OR* operation (represented by the ∨ symbol) checks to see whether at least one of the input values is true. Refer to the following truth table for all possible values of the OR function. Notice that the only time the OR function returns a false value is when both of the input values are false:

X	Y	X ∨ Y
0	0	0
0	1	1
1	0	1
1	1	1

We'll use the same example we used in the previous section to show you what the output would be if X and Y were fed into the OR function rather than the AND function:

```
X:      0 1 1 0 1 1 0 0
Y:      1 0 1 0 0 1 1 1
_____
X ∨ Y:  1 1 1 0 1 1 1 1
```

NOT

The *NOT* operation (represented by the ~ or ! symbol) simply reverses the value of an input variable. This function operates on only one variable at a time. Here's the truth table for the NOT function:

X	~X
0	1
1	0

In this example, we take the value of X from the previous examples and run the NOT function against it:

```
X:      0 1 1 0 1 1 0 0
_____
~X:     1 0 0 1 0 0 1 1
```

Exclusive OR

The final logical function we'll examine in this chapter is perhaps the most important and most commonly used in cryptographic applications—the exclusive OR (XOR) function. It's referred to in mathematical literature as the *XOR* function and is commonly represented by the ⊕ symbol. The XOR function returns a true value when only one of the input values is true. If both values are false or both values are true, the output of the XOR function is false. Here is the truth table for the XOR operation:

X	Y	X ⊕ Y
0	0	0
0	1	1
1	0	1
1	1	0

The following operation shows the X and Y values when they are used as input to the XOR function:

```
X:     0 1 1 0 1 1 0 0
Y:     1 0 1 0 0 1 1 1
```
_____
```
X ⊕ Y:   1 1 0 0 1 0 1 1
```

Modulo Function

The *modulo* function is extremely important in the field of cryptography. Think back to the early days when you first learned division. At that time, you weren't familiar with decimal numbers and compensated by showing a remainder value each time you performed a division operation. Computers don't naturally understand the decimal system either, and these remainder values play a critical role when computers perform many mathematical functions. The modulo function is, quite simply, the remainder value left over after a division operation is performed.

The modulo function is just as important to cryptography as the logical operations are. Be sure you're familiar with its functionality and can perform simple modular math.

The modulo function is usually represented in equations by the abbreviation *mod*, although it's also sometimes represented by the % operator. Here are several inputs and outputs for the modulo function:

```
8 mod 6 = 2
6 mod 8 = 6
10 mod 3 = 1
10 mod 2 = 0
32 mod 8 = 0
```

Hopefully, this introduction gives you a good understanding of how the modulo function works. We'll revisit this function in Chapter 10 when we explore the RSA public key encryption algorithm (named after Rivest, Shamir, and Adleman, its inventors).

One-Way Functions

In theory, a *one-way function* is a mathematical operation that easily produces output values for each possible combination of inputs but makes it impossible to retrieve the input values. Public key cryptosystems are all based upon some sort of one-way function. In practice, however, it's never been proven that any specific known function is truly one way. Cryptographers rely upon functions that they suspect may be one way, but it's theoretically possible that they might be broken by future cryptanalysts.

Here's an example. Imagine you have a function that multiplies three numbers together. If you restrict the input values to single-digit numbers, it's a relatively straightforward matter to reverse-engineer this function and determine the possible input values by looking at the numerical output. For example, the output value 15 was created by using the input values 1, 3, and 5. However, suppose you restrict the input values to five-digit prime numbers. It's still quite simple to obtain an output value by using a computer or a good calculator, but reverse-engineering is not quite so simple. Can you figure out what three prime numbers were used to obtain the output value 10,718,488,075,259? Not so simple, eh? (That number is the product of the prime numbers 17093, 22441, and 27943.) There are actually 8,363 five-digit prime numbers, so this problem might be attacked using a computer and a brute force algorithm, but there's no easy way to figure it out in your head, that's for sure!

Confusion and Diffusion

Cryptographic algorithms rely upon two basic operations to obscure plaintext messages—*confusion* and *diffusion*. *Confusion* occurs when the relationship between the plaintext and the key is so complicated that an attacker can't merely continue altering the plaintext and analyzing the resulting ciphertext to determine the key. *Diffusion* occurs when a change in the plaintext results in multiple changes spread out throughout the ciphertext.

Nonce

Cryptography often gains strength by adding randomness to the encryption process. One method by which this is accomplished is through the use of a nonce. A nonce is a random number generator. It acts as a placeholder variable in mathematical functions. When the function is executed, the nonce is replaced with a random number generated at the moment of processing. The nonce produces a unique number each time it is used. One of the more recognizable examples of a nonce is an initialization vector (IV), a random bit string that is the same length as the block size and is XORed with the message. IVs are used to create unique ciphertext every time the same message is encrypted using the same key.

Least and Most Significant String Bit

When striving to provide protection via cryptography, it is often important to know which portion of a message is the most vulnerable or, if compromised, provides the attacker with the greatest advantage. If a cryptography attack can successfully extract the original data from the most significant part of an encrypted message, the rest of the message is often easily obtained. However, if all the attacker can break is the least significant portion, they don't gain any leverage against the remainder of the encrypted communication. The least significant bit in a string is the rightmost bit. The most significant bit in a string is the leftmost bit. This means that there is more information present in the leftmost bit in a string, especially in encrypted material, than in the rightmost bit. There is an easy way to remember this concept: just think about how you would like to see the five digits of 0,0,0,0, and 1 arranged on a check made out to you. Obviously, placing the 1 in the leftmost position is most significant (and valuable) because that would make the check worth $10,000! Any other arrangement, in fact, puts less money into your account.

Zero Knowledge Proof

One of the benefits of cryptography is found in the mechanism to prove an individual's or organization's identity digitally. This is often accomplished using zero knowledge proof. Zero knowledge proof is a concept of communication whereby a specific type of information is exchanged but no real data is transferred. Great examples of this idea includes digital signatures and digital certificates. With either system, the recipient is able to prove the sender's identity. However, neither digital signatures nor digital certificates provide the recipient with any actual data. There is nothing for the recipient to save to a hard drive or transmit to someone else. Thus, they get proof of identity but zero knowledge about anything else.

Split Knowledge

When the information or privilege required to perform an operation is divided among multiple users, no single person has sufficient privileges to compromise the security of an environment. This separation of duties and two-man control contained in a single solution is called *split knowledge*. Split knowledge is mentioned in Chapter 13, "Administrative Management," but it makes most sense as it relates to cryptography.

The best example of split knowledge is seen in the concept of key escrow when the security practice of M of N Control is enforced (we'll explain M of N Control in a second). Using *key escrow* cryptographic keys, digital signatures and even digital certificates can be stored or backed up in a special database called the key escrow database. In the event a user loses or damages their key, that key can be extracted from the backup. However, if only a single key escrow recovery agent exists, there is opportunity for fraud and abuse of this privilege. So, M of N Control requires that a minimum number of agents (M) out of the total number of agents (N) work together to perform high-security tasks. So, implementing 3 of 8 control would require 3 people out of the 8 with the assigned work task of Key Escrow Recovery Agent to work together to pull a single key out of the key escrow database (thereby also illustrating that M is always less than or equal to N).

Work Function

You can measure the strength of a cryptography system by measuring the effort in terms of cost and/or time using a *work function* or *work factor*. Usually the time and effort required to perform a complete brute force attack against an encryption system is what the work function represents. The security and protection offered by a cryptosystem is directly proportional to the value of the work function/factor. The size of the work function should be matched against the relative value of the protected asset. The work function need be only slightly greater than the time value of that asset. In other words, all security, including cryptography, should be cost effective and cost efficient. Spend no more effort to protect an asset than it warrants, but be sure to provide sufficient protection. Thus, if information loses its value over time, the work function needs to be only large enough to ensure protection until the value of the data is gone.

Clustering

Cryptography is not without its drawbacks. *Clustering* (a.k.a. key clustering) is a weakness in cryptography where a plaintext message generates identical ciphertext messages using the same algorithm but using different keys. One of the often underemphasized truisms of cryptography is that repetition is bad. Whenever two duplicate cryptography elements exist, you halve the difficulty of breaking the protection. This is the inverse of the binary law of keys, which states that for every additional binary bit added to a key, you double its work factor/function. Thus, never encrypt the exact same message twice. Never use the same key twice (for encryption purposes, not for authentication and nonrepudiation purposes). Don't use a cryptography system that produces duplicate ciphertext outputs (i.e., different messages may use different keys yet still produce the same ciphertext); that admonition applies to symmetric and asymmetric keys as well as hashing techniques.

Ciphers

Cipher systems have long been used by individuals and governments interested in preserving the confidentiality of their communications. In the following sections, we'll take a brief look at the definition of a cipher and several common cipher types that form the basis of modern ciphers. It's important to remember that these concepts seem somewhat basic, but when used in combination, they can be formidable opponents and cause cryptanalysts many hours of frustration.

Codes vs. Ciphers

People often use the words *code* and *cipher* interchangeably, but technically, they aren't interchangeable. There are important distinctions between the two concepts. *Codes,* which are cryptographic systems of symbols that represent words or phrases, are sometime secret but they are not necessarily meant to provide confidentiality. A common example of a code is the "10 system" of communications used by law enforcement agencies. Under this system, the sentence "I received your communication and understand the contents" is represented by the code phrase "10-4." This code is commonly known by the public, but it does provide for ease of communication. Some codes are secret. They may use mathematical functions or a secret dictionary to convey confidential messages by representing words, phrases, or sentences. For example, a spy might transmit the sentence "the eagle has landed" to report the arrival of an enemy aircraft.

Ciphers, on the other hand, are always meant to hide the true meaning of a message. They use a variety of techniques to alter and/or rearrange the characters or bits of a message to achieve confidentiality. Ciphers convert messages from plaintext to ciphertext on a bit basis (i.e., a single digit of a binary code), character basis (i.e., a single character of an ASCII message), or block basis (i.e., a fixed-length segment of a message, usually expressed in number of bits). The following sections look at several common ciphers in use today.

An easy way to keep the difference between codes and ciphers straight is to remember that codes work on words and phrases whereas ciphers work on individual characters and bits.

Transposition Ciphers

Transposition ciphers use an encryption algorithm to rearrange the letters of a plaintext message, forming the ciphertext message. The decryption algorithm simply reverses the encryption transformation to retrieve the original message.

In the challenge-response protocol example in the section "Authentication" earlier in this chapter, a simple transposition cipher was used to simply reverse the letters of the message so that *apple* became *elppa*. Transposition ciphers can be much more complicated than this. For example, you can use a keyword to perform a columnar transposition. In this example, we're attempting to encrypt the message "The fighters will strike the enemy bases at noon" using the secret key *attacker*. Our first step is to take the letters of the keyword and number them in alphabetical order. The first appearance of the letter *A* receives the value 1; the second appearance is numbered 2. The next letter in sequence, *C*, is numbered 3, and so on. This results in the following sequence:

```
A T T A C K E R
1 7 8 2 3 5 4 6
```

Next, the letters of the message are written in order underneath the letters of the keyword:

```
A T T A C K E R
1 7 8 2 3 5 4 6
T H E F I G H T
E R S W I L L S
T R I K E T H E
E N E M Y B A S
E S A T N O O N
```

Finally, the sender enciphers the message by reading down each column; the order in which the columns are read corresponds to the numbers assigned in the first step. This produces the following ciphertext:

```
T E T E E F W K M T I I E Y N H L H A O G L T B O T S E S
 N H R R N S E S I C A
```

On the other end, the recipient reconstructs the eight-column matrix using the ciphertext and the same keyword and then simply reads the plaintext message across the rows.

Substitution Ciphers

Substitution ciphers use the encryption algorithm to replace each character or bit of the plaintext message with a different character. The Caesar cipher discussed in the beginning of this chapter is a good example of a substitution cipher. Now that you've learned a little bit about cryptographic math, we'll take another look at the Caesar cipher. Recall that we simply shifted each letter three places to the right in the message to generate the ciphertext. However, we ran into a problem when we got to the end of the alphabet and ran out of letters. We solved this by wrapping around to the beginning of the alphabet so that the plaintext character *Z* became the ciphertext character *C*.

You can express the ROT3 cipher in mathematical terms by converting each letter to its decimal equivalent (where *A* is 0 and *Z* is 25). You can then add three to each plaintext letter to determine the ciphertext. You account for the wrap-around by using the modulo function discussed in the section "Cryptographic Mathematics." The final encryption function for the Caesar cipher is then this:

```
C = (P + 3) mod 26
```

The corresponding decryption function is as follows:

```
P = (C - 3) mod 26
```

As with transposition ciphers, there are many substitution ciphers that are more sophisticated than the examples provided in this chapter. *Polyalphabetic substitution* ciphers make use of multiple alphabets in the same message to hinder decryption efforts. One of the most notable examples of a polyalphabetic substitution cipher system is the *Vigenere cipher*. The Vigenere cipher uses a single encryption/decryption chart shown here:

```
A B C D E F G H I J K L M N O P Q R S T U V W X Y Z
A B C D E F G H I J K L M N O P Q R S T U V W X Y Z
B C D E F G H I J K L M N O P Q R S T U V W X Y Z A
C D E F G H I J K L M N O P Q R S T U V W X Y Z A B
D E F G H I J K L M N O P Q R S T U V W X Y Z A B C
E F G H I J K L M N O P Q R S T U V W X Y Z A B C D
F G H I J K L M N O P Q R S T U V W X Y Z A B C D E
G H I J K L M N O P Q R S T U V W X Y Z A B C D E F
H I J K L M N O P Q R S T U V W X Y Z A B C D E F G
I J K L M N O P Q R S T U V W X Y Z A B C D E F G H
J K L M N O P Q R S T U V W X Y Z A B C D E F G H I
K L M N O P Q R S T U V W X Y Z A B C D E F G H I J
L M N O P Q R S T U V W X Y Z A B C D E F G H I J K
M N O P Q R S T U V W X Y Z A B C D E F G H I J K L
N O P Q R S T U V W X Y Z A B C D E F G H I J K L M
O P Q R S T U V W X Y Z A B C D E F G H I J K L M N
P Q R S T U V W X Y Z A B C D E F G H I J K L M N O
Q R S T U V W X Y Z A B C D E F G H I J K L M N O P
R S T U V W X Y Z A B C D E F G H I J K L M N O P Q
S T U V W X Y Z A B C D E F G H I J K L M N O P Q R
T U V W X Y Z A B C D E F G H I J K L M N O P Q R S
U V W X Y Z A B C D E F G H I J K L M N O P Q R S T
V W X Y Z A B C D E F G H I J K L M N O P Q R S T U
W X Y Z A B C D E F G H I J K L M N O P Q R S T U V
X Y Z A B C D E F G H I J K L M N O P Q R S T U V W
Y Z A B C D E F G H I J K L M N O P Q R S T U V W X
Z A B C D E F G H I J K L M N O P Q R S T U V W X Y
```

Notice that the chart is simply the alphabet written repeatedly (26 times) under the master heading shifting by one letter each time. You need a key to use the Vigenere system. For example, the key could be *secret*. Then, you would perform the following encryption process:

1. Write out the plaintext followed by the key.

2. Repeat the key as many times as needed to establish a line of text that is the same length as the plaintext.

3. Convert each letter position from plaintext to ciphertext.

    a. Locate the column headed by the first plaintext character (*a*).

    b. Next, locate the row headed by the first key word character (*s*).

    c. Finally, locate where these two items intersect and write down the letter that appears there (*s*). This is the ciphertext for that letter position.

4. Repeat steps 1 through 3 for each letter in the plaintext.

Plaintext: a t t a c k a t d a w n

Key Word: s e c r e t s e c r e t

Ciphertext: s x v r g d s x f r a g

While polyalphabetic substitution protects against direct frequency analysis, it is vulnerable to a second-order form of frequency analysis called *period analysis,* which is an examination of frequency based upon the repeated use of the key.

One-Time Pads

A *one-time pad* is an extremely powerful type of substitution cipher. One-time pads use a different alphabet for each letter of the plaintext message. They can be represented by the following encryption function, where K is the encryption key for the letter represented by C:

```
C = (P + K) mod 26
```

Normally, one-time pads are written as a very long series of numbers to be plugged into the function.

 One-time pads are also known as *Vernam ciphers,* after the name of their inventor—Gilbert Sandford Vernam of AT&T.

The great advantage of one-time pads is that, when used properly, they are an unbreakable encryption scheme. There is no repeating pattern of alphabetic substitution, rendering cryptanalytic efforts useless. However, several requirements must be met to ensure the integrity of the algorithm:

- The encryption key must be randomly generated. Using a phrase or a passage from a book would introduce the possibility of cryptanalysts breaking the code.

- The one-time pad must be physically protected against disclosure. If the enemy has a copy of the pad, they can easily decrypt the enciphered messages.

- Each one-time pad must be used only once. If pads are reused, cryptanalysts can compare similarities in multiple messages encrypted with the same pad and possibly determine the key values used.

- The key must be at least as long as the message to be encrypted. This is because each key element is used to encode only one character of the message.

> These one-time pad security requirements are essential knowledge for any network security professional. All too often, people attempt to implement a one-time pad cryptosystem but fail to meet one or more of these fundamental requirements. Read on for an example of how an entire Soviet code system was broken due to carelessness in this area.

If any one of these requirements is not met, the impenetrable nature of the one-time pad instantly breaks down. In fact, one of the major intelligence successes of the United States resulted when cryptanalysts broke a top-secret Soviet cryptosystem that relied upon the use of one-time pads. In this project, code-named VENONA, a pattern in the way the Soviets generated the key values used in their pads was discovered. The existence of this pattern violated the first requirement of a one-time pad cryptosystem: the keys must be randomly generated without the use of any recurring pattern. The entire VENONA project was recently declassified and is publicly available on the National Security Agency website at www.nsa.gov/docs/venona/index.html.

One-time pads have been used throughout history to protect extremely sensitive communications. The major obstacle to their widespread use is the difficulty of generating, distributing, and safeguarding the lengthy keys required. One-time pads can realistically be used only for short messages, due to key lengths.

Running Key Ciphers

Many cryptographic vulnerabilities surround the limited length of the cryptographic key. As you learned in the previous section, the one-time pad avoids these vulnerabilities by using separate alphabets for each cryptographic transformation during encryption and decryption. However, one-time pads are awkward to implement because they require physical exchange of pads.

One common solution to this dilemma is the use of a *running key cipher* (also known as a book cipher). In this cipher, the encryption key is as long as the message itself and is often chosen from a common book. For example, the sender and recipient might agree in advance to use the text of a chapter from *Moby Dick,* beginning with the third paragraph, as the key. They would both simply use as many consecutive characters as necessary to perform the encryption and decryption operations.

Let's look at an example. Suppose you wanted to encrypt the message "Richard will deliver the secret package to Matthew at the bus station tomorrow" using the key just described. This message is 66 characters in length, so you'd use the first 66 characters of the running key: "With much interest I sat watching him. Savage though he was, and hideously marred." Any algorithm could then be used to encrypt the plaintext message using this key. Let's look at the example of modulo 26 addition, which converts each letter to a decimal equivalent, then adds the plaintext to the key, and then performs a modulo 26 operation to yield the ciphertext. If you assign the letter *A* the value 1 and the letter *Z* the value 26, you have the following encryption operation for the first two words of the ciphertext:

Plaintext	R	I	C	H	A	R	D	W	I	L	L
Key	W	I	T	H	M	U	C	H	I	N	T
Decimal Plaintext	17	8	2	7	0	17	3	22	8	11	11
Decimal Key	22	8	19	7	12	20	2	7	8	13	19
Decimal Ciphertext	13	16	21	14	12	11	5	3	16	24	4
Ciphertext	N	Q	V	O	M	L	F	D	Q	Y	E

When the recipient receives the ciphertext, they use the same key and then subtract the key from the ciphertext, perform a modulo 26 operation, and then convert the resulting plaintext back to alphabetic characters.

Block Ciphers

Block ciphers operate on "chunks," or blocks, of a message and apply the encryption algorithm to an entire message block at the same time. The transposition ciphers are examples of block ciphers. The simple algorithm used in the challenge-response algorithm takes an entire word and reverses its letters. The more complicated columnar transposition cipher works on an entire message (or a piece of a message) and encrypts it using the transposition algorithm and a secret keyword. Most modern encryption algorithms implement some type of block cipher.

Stream Ciphers

Stream ciphers are ciphers that operate on each character or bit of a message (or data stream) one character/bit at a time. The Caesar cipher is an example of a stream cipher. The one-time pad is also a stream cipher because the algorithm operates on each letter of the plaintext message independently. Stream ciphers can also function as a type of block cipher. In such operations there is a buffer that fills up to real-time data that is then encrypted as a block and transmitted to the recipient.

Modern Cryptography

Modern cryptosystems utilize computationally complex algorithms and long cryptographic keys to meet the cryptographic goals of confidentiality, integrity, authentication, and nonrepudiation. The following sections take a look at the roles cryptographic keys play in the world of data security and examines three types of algorithms commonly used today: symmetric encryption algorithms, asymmetric encryption algorithms, and hashing algorithms.

Cryptographic Keys

In the early days of security, one of the predominant principles was "security through obscurity." Security professionals felt that the best way to keep an encryption algorithm secure was to hide the details of the algorithm from outsiders. Old cryptosystems required communicating parties to keep the algorithm used to encrypt and decrypt messages secret from third parties. Any disclosure of the algorithm could lead to compromise of the entire system by an adversary.

Modern cryptosystems do not rely upon the secrecy of their algorithms. In fact, the algorithms for most cryptographic systems are widely available for public review in the accompanying literature and on the Internet. This actually improves the security of algorithms by opening them to public scrutiny. Widespread analysis of algorithms by the computer security community allows practitioners to discover and correct potential security vulnerabilities and ensure that the algorithms they use to protect their communications are as secure as possible.

Instead of relying upon secret algorithms, modern cryptosystems rely upon the secrecy of one or more cryptographic keys used to personalize the algorithm for specific users or groups of users. Recall from the discussion of transposition ciphers that a keyword is used with the columnar transposition to guide the encryption and decryption efforts. The algorithm used to perform columnar transposition is well known—you just read the details of it in this book! However, columnar transposition can be used to securely communicate between parties as long as a keyword that would not be guessed by an outsider is chosen. As long as the security of this keyword is maintained, it doesn't matter that third parties know the details of the algorithm. (Note, however, that columnar transposition possesses several inherent weaknesses that make it vulnerable to cryptanalysis and therefore make it an inadequate technology for use in modern secure communication.)

Key Length

In the discussion of one-time pads earlier in this chapter, you learned that the main strength of the one-time pad algorithm is derived from the fact that it uses an extremely long key. In fact, for that algorithm, the key is at least as long as the message itself. Most modern cryptosystems do not use keys quite that long, but the length of the key is still an extremely important factor in determining the strength of the cryptosystem and the likelihood that the encryption will not be compromised through cryptanalytic techniques.

The rapid increase in computing power allows you to use increasingly long keys in your cryptographic efforts. However, this same computing power is also in the hands of cryptanalysts attempting to defeat the algorithms you use. Therefore, it's essential that you outpace adversaries by using sufficiently long keys that will defeat contemporary cryptanalysis efforts. Additionally, if you are concerned that your data remains safe from cryptanalysis some time into the future, you must strive to use keys that will outpace the projected increase in cryptanalytic capability during the entire time period the data must be kept safe.

Several decades ago, when the Data Encryption Standard (DES) was created, a 56-bit key was considered sufficient to maintain the security of any data. However, there is now widespread agreement that the 56-bit DES algorithm is no longer secure due to advances in cryptanalysis techniques and supercomputing power. Modern cryptographic systems use at least a 128-bit key to protect data against prying eyes.

Symmetric Key Algorithms

Symmetric key algorithms rely upon a "shared secret" encryption key that is distributed to all members who participate in the communications. This key is used by all parties to both encrypt and decrypt messages, so the sender and the receiver both possess a copy of the shared key. The same key on both ends of the communication is used to encrypt and decrypt messages. When large-sized keys are used, symmetric encryption is very difficult to break. It is primarily employed to perform bulk encryption and only provides for the security service of confidentiality. Symmetric key cryptography can also be called secret key cryptography and private key cryptography. The symmetric key encryption and decryption processes are illustrated in Figure 9.2.

The use of the term *private key* can be tricky because it is part of three different terms that have two different meanings. The term *private key* always means the private key from the key pair of public key cryptography (a.k.a. asymmetric). However, both *private key cryptography* and *shared private key* refer to symmetric cryptography. The meaning of the word *private* is stretched to mean when two people share a secret that they keep confidential instead of its true meaning that only a single person has a secret that's kept confidential. Be sure to keep these confusing terms straight in your studies.

FIGURE 9.2   Symmetric key cryptography

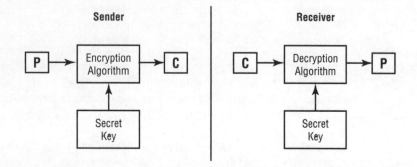

Symmetric key cryptography has several weaknesses:

Key distribution is a major problem.   Parties must have a secure method of exchanging the secret key before establishing communications with the symmetric key protocol. If a secure electronic channel is not available, an offline key distribution method must often be used (i.e., out-of-band exchange).

Symmetric key cryptography does not implement nonrepudiation.   Because any communicating party can encrypt and decrypt messages with the shared secret key, there is no way to tell where a given message originated.

The algorithm is not scalable.   It is extremely difficult for large groups to communicate using symmetric key cryptography. Secure private communication between individuals in the group could be achieved only if each possible combination of users shared a private key.

Keys must be regenerated often.   Each time a participant leaves the group, all keys that involved that participant must be discarded.

The major strength of symmetric key cryptography is the great speed at which it can operate. Symmetric keying is very fast, often 1,000 to 10,000 times faster than asymmetric. By nature of the mathematics involved, symmetric key cryptography also naturally lends itself to hardware implementations, creating the opportunity for even higher-speed operations.

The section "Symmetric Cryptography" later in this chapter provides a detailed look at the major secret key algorithms in use today.

Asymmetric Key Algorithms

Asymmetric key algorithms, also known as public key algorithms, provide a solution to the weaknesses of symmetric key encryption. In these systems, each user has two keys: a public key, which is shared with all users, and a private key, which is kept secret and known only to the user. But here's a twist: opposite and related keys must be used in tandem to encrypt and decrypt. In other words, if the public key encrypts a message, then only the private key can decrypt it and vice versa.

The algorithm used to encrypt and decrypt messages in a public key cryptosystem is shown in Figure 9.3. Consider this example: If Alice wants to send a message to Bob using public key cryptography, she creates the message and then encrypts it using Bob's public key. The only possible way to decrypt this ciphertext is to use Bob's private key and the only user with access to that key is Bob. Therefore, Alice can't even decrypt the message herself after she encrypts it. If Bob wants to send a reply to Alice, he simply encrypts the message using Alice's public key and then Alice reads the message by decrypting it with her private key.

FIGURE 9.3   Asymmetric key cryptography

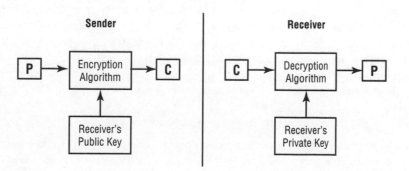

Key Requirements

The fact that symmetric cryptosystems require each pair of potential communicators to have a shared private key makes the algorithm nonscalable. The total number of keys required to completely connect n parties is given by the following formula:

```
Number of Keys = [n * (n - 1)]/2
```

Now, this might not sound so bad (and it's not for small systems), but consider the following figures:

Number of Participants	Number of Keys Required
2	1
3	2
4	6
5	10
10	45
100	4,950
1,000	499,500
10,000	49,995,000

Obviously, the larger the population, the less likely a symmetric cryptosystem will be suitable to meet its needs.

Asymmetric key algorithms also provide support for digital signature technology. Basically, if Bob wants to assure other users that a message with his name on it was actually sent by him, he first creates a message digest by using a hashing algorithm (there is more on hashing algorithms in the next section). Bob then encrypts that digest using his private key. Any user who wants to verify the signature simply decrypts the message digest using Bob's public key and then verifies that the decrypted message digest is accurate. This process is explained in greater detail in Chapter 10.

The following is a list of the major strengths of asymmetric key cryptography:

The addition of new users requires the generation of only one public-private key pair.   This same key pair is used to communicate with all users of the asymmetric cryptosystem. This makes the algorithm extremely scalable.

Users can be removed far more easily from asymmetric systems.   Asymmetric algorithms provide a *key revocation* mechanism that allows a key to be canceled, effectively removing a user from the system.

Key regeneration is required only when a user's private key is compromised.   If a user leaves the community, the system administrator simply needs to invalidate that user's keys. No other keys are compromised and therefore key regeneration is not required for any other user.

Asymmetric key encryption can provide integrity, authentication, and nonrepudiation.   If a user does not share their private key with other individuals, a message signed by that user can be shown to be accurate and from a specific source and cannot be later repudiated.

Key distribution is a simple process.   Users who want to participate in the system simply make their public key available to anyone with whom they want to communicate. There is no method by which the private key can be derived from the public key.

No preexisting communication link needs to exist.   Two individuals can begin communicating securely from the moment they start communicating. Asymmetric cryptography does not require a preexisting relationship to provide a secure mechanism for data exchange.

The major weakness of public key cryptography is its slow speed of operation. For this reason, many applications that require the secure transmission of large amounts of data use public key cryptography to establish a connection and then exchange a symmetric secret key. The remainder of the session then uses symmetric cryptography. Table 9.1 compares the symmetric and asymmetric cryptography systems. Close examination of this table reveals that a weakness in one system is matched by a strength in the other.

   Chapter 10, "PKI and Cryptographic Applications," provides technical details on modern public key encryption algorithms and some of their applications.

TABLE 9.1   Comparison of Symmetric and Asymmetric

Symmetric	Asymmetric
Single shared key	Key pair sets
Out-of-band exchange	In-band exchange
Not scalable	Scalable
Fast	Slow
Bulk encryption	Small blocks of data, digital signatures, digital envelopes, digital certificates
Confidentiality	Integrity, authenticity, nonrepudiation

Hashing Algorithms

In the previous section, you learned that public key cryptosystems can provide digital signature capability when used in conjunction with a message digest. Message digests are summaries of a message's content (not unlike a file checksum) produced by a hashing algorithm. It's extremely difficult, if not impossible, to derive a message from an ideal *hash* function, and it's very unlikely that two messages will produce the same hash value.

The following are some of the more common hashing algorithms in use today:

- Message Digest 2 (MD2)

- Message Digest 4 (MD4)

- Message Digest 5 (MD5)

- Secure Hash Algorithm (SHA)

- Hash-Based Message Authentication Code (HMAC)

Chapter 10 provides details on these contemporary hashing algorithms and explains how they are used to provide digital signature capability, which helps meet the cryptographic goals of integrity and nonrepudiation.

Symmetric Cryptography

You've learned the basic concepts underlying symmetric key cryptography, asymmetric key cryptography, and hashing functions. In the following sections, we'll take an in-depth look at several common symmetric cryptosystems: the Data Encryption Standard (DES), Triple DES (3DES), International Data Encryption Algorithm (IDEA), Blowfish, Skipjack, and the Advanced Encryption Standard (AES).

Data Encryption Standard (DES)

The United States government published the *Data Encryption Standard (DES)* in 1977 as a proposed standard cryptosystem for all government communications. Indeed, many government entities continue to use DES for cryptographic applications today, despite the fact that it was superseded by the *Advanced Encryption Standard (AES)* in December 2001. DES is a 64-bit block cipher that has four modes of operation: Electronic Codebook (ECB) mode, Cipher Block Chaining (CBC) mode, Cipher Feedback (CFB) mode, and Output Feedback (OFB) mode. These modes are explained in the following sections. All of the DES modes operate on 64 bits of plaintext at a time to generate 64-bit blocks of ciphertext. The key used by DES is 56 bits long.

DES utilizes a long series of exclusive OR (XOR) operations to generate the ciphertext. This process is repeated 16 times for each encryption/decryption operation. Each repetition is commonly referred to as a "round" of encryption, explaining the statement that DES performs 16 rounds of encryption. In the following sections, we'll take a look at each of the four modes utilized by DES.

As mentioned in the text, DES uses a 56-bit key to drive the encryption and decryption process. However, you may read in some literature that DES uses a 64-bit key. This is not an inconsistency—there's a perfectly logical explanation. The DES specification calls for a 64-bit key. However, of those 64 bits, only 56 actually contain keying information. The remaining 8 bits are supposed to contain parity information to ensure that the other 56 bits are accurate. In practice, however, those parity bits are rarely used. You should commit the 56-bit figure to memory.

Electronic Codebook (ECB) Mode

Electronic Codebook (ECB) mode is the simplest mode to understand and the least secure. Each time the algorithm processes a 64-bit block, it simply encrypts the block using the chosen secret key. This means that if the algorithm encounters the same block multiple times, it will produce the exact same encrypted block. If an enemy were eavesdropping on the communications, they could simply build a "codebook" of all of the possible encrypted values. After a sufficient number of blocks were gathered, cryptanalytic techniques could be used to decipher some of the blocks and break the encryption scheme.

This vulnerability makes it impractical to use ECB mode on all but the shortest transmissions. In everyday use, ECB is used only for the exchange of small amounts of data, such as keys and parameters used to initiate other DES modes and well as the cells in a database.

Cipher Block Chaining (CBC) Mode

In *Cipher Block Chaining (CBC)* mode, each block of unencrypted text is XORed with the block of ciphertext immediately preceding it before it is encrypted using the DES algorithm. The decryption process simply decrypts the ciphertext and reverses the XOR operation. CBC implements an IV and XORs it with the first block of the message, producing a unique output every time the operation is performed. The IV must be sent to the recipient, perhaps by tacking the IV onto the front of the completed ciphertext in plain form or by protecting it with ECB mode encryption using the same key used for the message. One important consideration when using CBC mode is that errors propagate—if one block is corrupted during transmission, it becomes impossible to decrypt that block and the next block as well.

Cipher Feedback (CFB) Mode

Cipher Feedback (CFB) mode is the streaming cipher version of CBC. In other words, CFB operates against data produced in real time. However, instead of breaking a message into blocks, it uses memory buffers of the same block size. As the buffer becomes full, it is encrypted and then sent to the recipient(s). Then the system waits for the next buffer to be filled as the new data is generated before it is in turn encrypted and then transmitted. Other than the change from pre-existing data to real-time data, CFB operates in the same fashion as CBC. It uses an IV and it uses chaining.

CBC and CFB are best suited for authentication encryption.

Output Feedback (OFB) Mode

In *Output Feedback (OFB)* mode, DES operates in almost the same fashion as it does in CFB mode. However, instead of XORing an encrypted version of the previous preceding block of ciphertext, DES XORs the plaintext with a seed value. For the first encrypted block, an initialization vector is used to create the seed value. Future seed values are derived by running the DES algorithm on the previous preceding seed value. The major advantages of OFB mode are that there is no chaining function and transmission errors do not propagate to affect the decryption of future blocks.

Triple DES (3DES)

As mentioned in previous sections, the Data Encryption Standard's 56-bit key is no longer considered adequate in the face of modern cryptanalytic techniques and supercomputing power. However, an adapted version of DES, *Triple DES (3DES)*, uses the same algorithm to produce a more secure encryption

There are four versions of 3DES. The first simply encrypts the plaintext three times, using three different keys: K_1, K_2, and K_3. It is known as DES-EEE3 mode (the Es indicate that there are three encryption operations, whereas the numeral 3 indicates that three different keys are used). DES-EEE3 can be expressed using the following notation, where $E(K,P)$ represents the encryption of plaintext P with key K:

$E(K_1,E(K_2,E(K_3,P)))$

DES-EEE3 has an effective key length of 168 bits.

The second variant (DES-EDE3) also uses three keys but replaces the second encryption operation with a decryption operation:

$E(K_1,D(K_2,E(K_3,P)))$

The third version of 3DES (DES-EEE2) uses only two keys, K_1 and K_2, as follows:

$E(K_1,E(K_2,E(K_1,P)))$

The fourth variant of 3DES (DES-EDE2) also uses two keys but uses a decryption operation in the middle:

$E(K_1,D(K_2,E(K_1,P)))$

Both the third and fourth variants have an effective key length of 112 bits.

Technically, there is a fifth variant of 3DES, DES-EDE1, which uses only one cryptographic key. However, it results in the exact same algorithm (and strength) as standard DES and is only provided for backward compatibility purposes.

These four variants of 3DES were developed over the years because several cryptologists put forth theories that one variant was more secure than the others. However, the current belief is that all modes are equally secure.

Take some time to understand the variants of 3DES. Sit down with a pencil and paper and be sure you understand the way each variant uses two or three keys to achieve stronger encryption.

This discussion begs an obvious question—what happened to Double DES (2DES)? You'll read in Chapter 10 that Double DES was tried but quickly abandoned when it was proven that an attack existed that rendered 2DES no more secure than standard DES.

International Data Encryption Algorithm (IDEA)

The *International Data Encryption Algorithm (IDEA)* block cipher was developed in response to complaints about the insufficient key length of the DES algorithm. Like DES, IDEA operates on 64-bit blocks of plain-/ciphertext. However, it begins its operation with a 128-bit key. This key is then broken up in a series of operations into 52 16-bit subkeys. The subkeys then act on the input text using a combination of XOR and modulus operations to produce the encrypted/decrypted version of the input message. IDEA is capable of operating in the same four modes utilized by DES: ECB, CBC, CFB, and OFB.

All of this material on key length block size and the number of rounds of encryption may seem dreadfully boring; however, it's very important material, so be sure to brush up on it while preparing for the exam.

The IDEA algorithm itself is patented by its Swiss developers. However, they have granted an unlimited license to anyone who wants to use IDEA for noncommercial purposes. IDEA provides the cryptographic functionality in Phil Zimmerman's popular Pretty Good Privacy (PGP) secure e-mail package. Chapter 10 covers PGP in further detail.

Blowfish

Bruce Schneier's *Blowfish* block cipher is another alternative to DES and IDEA. Like its predecessors, Blowfish operates on 64-bit blocks of text. However, it extends IDEA's key strength even further by allowing the use of variable-length keys ranging from a relatively insecure 32 bits to an extremely strong 448 bits. Obviously, the longer keys will result in a corresponding increase in encryption/decryption time. However, time trials have established Blowfish as a much faster algorithm than both IDEA and DES. Also, Mr. Schneier released Blowfish for public use with no license required. Blowfish encryption is built into a number of commercial software products and operating systems. There are also a number of Blowfish libraries available for software developers.

Skipjack

The *Skipjack* algorithm was approved for use by the U.S. government in Federal Information Processing Standard (FIPS) 185, the Escrowed Encryption Standard (EES). Like many block ciphers, Skipjack operates on 64-bit blocks of text. It uses an 80-bit key and supports the same four modes of operation supported by DES. Skipjack was quickly embraced by the U.S. government and provides the cryptographic routines supporting the Clipper and Capstone high-speed encryption chips designed for mainstream commercial use.

However, Skipjack has an added twist—it supports the escrow of encryption keys. Two government agencies, the National Institute of Standards and Technology (NIST) and the Department of the Treasury, each holds a portion of the information required to reconstruct a Skipjack key. When law enforcement authorities obtain legal authorization, they contact the two agencies, obtain the pieces of the key, and are able to decrypt communications between the affected parties.

Skipjack and the Clipper chip have not been embraced by the cryptographic community at large because of its mistrust of the escrow procedures in place within the U.S. government. In fact, it's unlikely that any key escrow arrangement will succeed given the proliferation of inexpensive, powerful encryption technology on the Internet and the fact that Skipjack's 80-bit key is relatively insecure.

Rivest Cipher 5 (RC5)

Rivest Cipher 5, or RC5, is a symmetric algorithm patented by Rivest, Shamir, and Adleman (RSA) Data Security, the people who developed the RSA asymmetric algorithm. RC5 is a block cipher of variable block sizes (32, 64 or 128 bit) that uses keys sizes between 0 (zero) length and 2048 bits.

Advanced Encryption Standard (AES)

In October 2000, the National Institute of Standards and Technology (NIST) announced that the *Rijndael block cipher* (pronounced "rhine-doll") had been chosen as the replacement for DES. In December of that same year, the secretary of commerce approved FIPS 197, which mandated the use of AES/Rijndael for the encryption of all sensitive but unclassified data by the U.S. government.

The Rijndael cipher allows the use of three key strengths: 128 bits, 192 bits, and 256 bits. The original specification for AES called for the processing of 128-bit blocks, but Rijndael exceeded this specification, allowing cryptographers to use a block size equal to the key length. The number of encryption rounds depends upon the key length chosen:

- 128-bit keys require 9 rounds of encryption.
- 192-bit keys require 11 rounds of encryption.
- 256-bit keys require 13 rounds of encryption.

Twofish

The Twofish algorithm developed by Bruce Schneier (also the creator of Blowfish) was another one of the AES finalists. Like Rijndael, Twofish is a block cipher. It operates on 128-bit blocks of data and is capable of using cryptographic keys up to 256 bits in length.

Twofish utilizes two techniques not found in other algorithms. Prewhitening involves XORing the plaintext with a separate subkey before the 1st round of encryption. Postwhitening uses a similar operation after the 16th round of encryption.

 By the way, two of the other AES finalists were MARS and SERPENT.

The Rijndael algorithm uses three layers of transformations to encrypt/decrypt blocks of message text:

- Linear Mix Transform
- Nonlinear Transform
- Key Addition Transform

The total number of round key bits needed is equal to the following:
Block length * number of rounds + 1
For example, with a block length of 128 bits and 13 rounds of encryption, 1,792 round key bits are needed.

The operational details of these layers are beyond the scope of this book. Interested readers can obtain a complete copy of the 45-page Rijndael algorithm description at the Rijndael website: www.rijndael.com.

AES is just one of the many symmetric encryption algorithms you need to be familiar with. Table 9.2 lists several common and well-known symmetric encryption algorithms along with their block size and key size.

TABLE 9.2   Symmetric Memorization Chart

Name	Block Size	Key Size
Data Encryption Standard (DES)	64	56
Triple DES (3DES)	64	168
Advanced Encryption Standard (AES), Rijndael	variable	128, 192, 256
Twofish	128	1–256
Blowfish (often used in SSH)	variable	1– 448
IDEA (used in PGP)	64	128
Rivest Cipher 5 (RC5), based on RSA	32, 64, 128	0–2048
Rivest Cipher 4 (RC4), based on RSA	streaming	128
Rivest Cipher 2 (RC2), based on RSA	64	128
Skipjack		80

Key Distribution

As previously mentioned, one of the major problems underlying symmetric encryption algorithms is the secure distribution of the secret keys required to operate the algorithms. In the following sections, we'll examine the three main methods used to exchange secret keys securely: offline distribution, public key encryption, and the Diffie-Hellman key exchange algorithm.

Offline Distribution

The most technically simple method involves the physical exchange of key material. One party provides the other party with a sheet of paper or piece of storage media containing the secret key. In many hardware encryption devices, this key material comes in the form of an electronic device that resembles an actual key that is inserted into the encryption device. If participants recognize each other's voice, they might use the (tedious) process of reading keying material over the telephone. However, each one of these methods has its own inherent flaws. If keying material is sent through the mail, it might be intercepted. Telephones can be wiretapped. Papers containing keys might be inadvertently thrown in the trash or lost.

Public Key Encryption

Many communicators want to obtain the speed benefits of secret key encryption without the hassles of key distribution. For this reason, many people use public key encryption to set up an initial communications link. Once the link is successfully established and the parties are satisfied as to each other's identity, they exchange a secret key over the secure public key link. They then switch communications from the public key algorithm to the secret key algorithm and enjoy the increased processing speed. In general, secret key encryption is 1,000 times faster than public key encryption.

Diffie-Hellman

In some cases, neither public key encryption nor offline distribution is sufficient. Two parties might need to communicate with each other but they have no physical means to exchange key material and there is no public key infrastructure in place to facilitate the exchange of secret keys. In situations like this, key exchange algorithms like the *Diffie-Hellman algorithm* prove to be extremely useful mechanisms.

The Diffie-Hellman algorithm represented a major advance in the state of cryptographic science when it was released in 1976. It's still in use today.

The Diffie-Hellman algorithm works as follows:

1. The communicating parties (we'll call them Richard and Sue) agree on two large numbers: p (which is a prime number) and g (which is an integer) such that $1 < g < p$.

2. Richard chooses a random large integer r and performs the following calculation:

    R = gr mod p

3. Sue chooses a random large integer s and performs the following calculation:

    S = gs mod p

4. Richard sends R to Sue and Sue sends S to Richard.

5. Richard then performs the following calculation:

    K = Sr mod p

6. Sue then performs the following calculation:

    K = Rs mod p

At this point, Richard and Sue both have the same value, K, and can use this for secret key communication between the two parties.

Secure RPC (SRPC) employs Diffie-Hellman for key exchange.

Key Escrow

Cryptography is a powerful tool. Like most tools, it can be used for a number of beneficent purposes, but it can also be used with malicious intent. To gain a handle on the explosive growth of cryptographic technologies, governments around the world have floated ideas to implement a *key escrow system.* These systems allow the government, under limited circumstances such as a court order, to obtain the cryptographic key used for a particular communication from a central storage facility.

There are two major approaches to key escrow that have been proposed over the past decade:

- In the *Fair Cryptosystems* escrow approach, the secret keys used in a communication are divided into two or more pieces, each of which is given to an independent third party. Each of these pieces is useless on its own but may be recombined to obtain the secret key. When the government obtains legal authority to access a particular key, it provides evidence of the court order to each of the third parties and then reassembles the secret key.

- The *Escrowed Encryption Standard* takes a different approach by providing the government with a technological means to decrypt ciphertext. This standard is the basis behind the Skipjack algorithm discussed earlier in this chapter.

It's highly unlikely that government regulators will ever overcome the legal and privacy hurdles necessary to implement key escrow on a widespread basis. The technology is certainly available, but the general public will likely never accept the potential government intrusiveness it facilitates.

Summary

Cryptographers and cryptanalysts are in a never-ending race to develop more secure cryptosystems and advanced cryptanalytic techniques designed to circumvent those systems. Cryptography dates back as early as Caesar and has been an ongoing study for many years. In this chapter, you learned some of the fundamental concepts underlying the field of cryptography, gained a basic understanding of the terminology used by cryptographers, and looked at some historical codes and ciphers used in the early days of cryptography. This chapter also examined the similarities and differences between symmetric key cryptography (where communicating parties use the same key) and asymmetric key cryptography (where each communicator has a pair of public and private keys).

We wrapped up the chapter by analyzing some of the symmetric algorithms currently available and their strengths and weaknesses as well as some solutions to the key exchange dilemma that plagues secret key cryptographers. The next chapter expands this discussion to cover contemporary public key cryptographic algorithms. Additionally, some of the common cryptanalytic techniques used to defeat both types of cryptosystems will be explored.

Exam Essentials

Understand the role confidentiality plays in cryptosystems. Confidentiality is one of the major goals of cryptography. It ensures that messages remain protected from disclosure to unauthorized individuals and allows encrypted messages to be transmitted freely across an open network. Confidentiality can be assured by both symmetric and asymmetric cryptosystems.

Understand the role integrity plays in cryptosystems. Integrity provides the recipient of a message with the assurance that the message was not altered (intentionally or unintentionally) between the time it was created by the sender and the time it was received by the recipient. Integrity can be assured by both symmetric and asymmetric cryptosystems.

Understand the importance of providing nonrepudiation capability in cryptosystems. Nonrepudiation provides undeniable proof that the sender of a message actually authored it. It prevents the sender from subsequently denying that they sent the original message. Nonrepudiation is only possible with asymmetric cryptosystems.

Know how cryptosystems can be used to achieve authentication goals. Authentication provides assurances as to the identity of a user. One possible scheme that uses authentication is the challenge-response protocol, in which the remote user is asked to encrypt a message using a key known only to the communicating parties. Authentication can be achieved with both symmetric and asymmetric cryptosystems.

Be familiar with the basic terminology of cryptography. When a sender wants to transmit a private message to a recipient, the sender takes the plaintext (unencrypted) message and encrypts it using an algorithm and a key. This produces a ciphertext message that is transmitted to the recipient. The recipient then uses a similar algorithm and key to decrypt the ciphertext and re-create the original plaintext message for viewing.

Be able to explain how the binary system works and know the basic logical and mathematical functions used in cryptographic applications. Binary mathematics uses only the numbers 0 and 1 to represent false and true states, respectively. You use logical operations such as AND, OR, NOT, and XOR on these values to perform computational functions. The modulo function returns the remainder of integer division and is critical in implementing several cryptographic algorithms. Public key cryptography relies upon the use of one-way functions that are difficult to reverse.

Understand the difference between a code and a cipher and explain the basic types of ciphers. Codes are cryptographic systems of symbols that operate on words or phrases and are sometimes secret but don't always provide confidentiality. Ciphers, however, are always meant to hide the true meaning of a message. Know how the following types of ciphers work: transposition ciphers, substitution ciphers (including one-time pads), stream ciphers, and block ciphers.

Know the requirements for successful use of a one-time pad. For a one-time pad to be successful, the key must be generated randomly without any known pattern. The key must be at least as long as the message to be encrypted. The pads must be protected against physical disclosure and each pad must be used only one time and then discarded.

Understand what an initialization vector (IV) is.   An initialization vector (IV) is a random bit string (a nonce) that is the same length as the block size that is XORed with the message. IVs are used to create a unique ciphertext every time the same message is encrypted with the same key.

Understand the concept of zero knowledge proof.   Zero knowledge proof is a communication concept. A specific type of information is exchanged but no real data is transferred, as with digital signatures and digital certificates.

Understand split knowledge.   Split knowledge means that the information or privilege required to perform an operation is divided among multiple users. This ensures that no single person has sufficient privileges to compromise the security of the environment. M of N Control is an example of split knowledge.

Understand work function or work factor.   Work function or work factor is a way to measure the strength of a cryptography system by measuring the effort in terms of cost and/or time to decrypt messages. Usually the time and effort required to perform a complete brute force attack against an encryption system is what a work function rating represents. The security and protection offered by a cryptosystem is directly proportional to the value of its work function/factor.

Understand the importance of key security.   Cryptographic keys provide the necessary element of secrecy to a cryptosystem. Modern cryptosystems utilize keys that are at least 128 bits long to provide adequate security. It's generally agreed that the 56-bit key of the Data Encryption Standard (DES) is no longer sufficiently long enough to provide security.

Know the differences between symmetric and asymmetric cryptosystems.   Symmetric key cryptosystems (or secret key cryptosystems) rely upon the use of a shared secret key. They are much faster than asymmetric algorithms but they lack support for scalability, easy key distribution, and nonrepudiation. Asymmetric cryptosystems use public-private key pairs for communication between parties but operate much more slowly than symmetric algorithms.

Be able to explain the basic operational modes of the Data Encryption Standard (DES) and Triple DES (3DES).   The Data Encryption Standard operates in four modes: Electronic Codebook (ECB) mode, Cipher Block Chaining (CBC) mode, Cipher Feedback (CFB) mode, and Output Feedback (OFB) mode. ECB mode is considered the least secure and is used only for short messages. 3DES uses three iterations of DES with two or three different keys to increase the effective key strength to 112 bits.

Know the Advanced Encryption Standard (AES) and the Rijndael algorithm.   The Advanced Encryption Standard (AES) utilizes the Rijndael algorithm and is the new U.S. government standard for the secure exchange of sensitive but unclassified data. AES uses key lengths and block sizes of 128, 192, and 256 bits to achieve a much higher level of security than that provided by the older DES algorithm.

Written Lab

Answer the following questions about cryptography and private key algorithms.

1. What is the major hurdle preventing the widespread adoption of one-time pad cryptosystems to ensure data confidentiality?

2. Encrypt the message "I will pass the CISSP exam and become certified next month" using columnar transposition with the keyword SECURE.

3. Decrypt the message "F R Q J U D W X O D W L R Q V B R X J R W L W" using the Caesar ROT3 substitution cipher.

Review Questions

1. Which one of the following is not a goal of cryptographic systems?

   A. Nonrepudiation

   B. Confidentiality

   C. Availability

   D. Integrity

2. John recently received an electronic mail message from Bill. What cryptographic goal would need to be met to convince John that Bill was actually the sender of the message?

   A. Nonrepudiation

   B. Confidentiality

   C. Availability

   D. Integrity

3. What is the length of the cryptographic key used in the Data Encryption Standard (DES) cryptosystem?

   A. 56 bits

   B. 128 bits

   C. 192 bits

   D. 256 bits

4. What type of cipher relies upon changing the location of characters within a message to achieve confidentiality?

   A. Stream cipher

   B. Transposition cipher

   C. Block cipher

   D. Substitution cipher

5. Which one of the following is *not* a possible key length for the Advanced Encryption Standard Rijndael cipher?

   A. 56 bits

   B. 128 bits

   C. 192 bits

   D. 256 bits

6. Which one of the following is a cryptographic goal that cannot be achieved by a secret key cryptosystem?

   A. Nonrepudiation

   B. Confidentiality

   C. Availability

   D. Integrity

7. When correctly implemented, what is the only cryptosystem known to be unbreakable?

   A. Transposition cipher

   B. Substitution cipher

   C. Advanced Encryption Standard

   D. One-time pad

8. What is the output value of the mathematical function 16 mod 3?

   A. 0

   B. 1

   C. 3

   D. 5

9. In the 1940s, a team of cryptanalysts from the United States successfully broke a Soviet code based upon a one-time pad in a project known as VENONA. What rule did the Soviets break that caused this failure?

   A. Key values must be random.

   B. Key values must be the same length as the message.

   C. Key values must be used only once.

   D. Key values must be protected from physical disclosure.

10. Which one of the following cipher types operates on large pieces of a message rather than individual characters or bits of a message?

    A. Stream cipher

    B. Caesar cipher

    C. Block cipher

    D. ROT3 cipher

11. What is the minimum number of cryptographic keys required for secure two-way communications in symmetric key cryptography?

    A. One

    B. Two

    C. Three

    D. Four

12. What is the minimum number of cryptographic keys required for secure two-way communications in asymmetric key cryptography?

    A. One

    B. Two

    C. Three

    D. Four

13. Which one of the following Data Encryption Standard (DES) operating modes can be used for large messages with the assurance that an error early in the encryption/decryption process won't spoil results throughout the communication?

    A. Cipher Block Chaining (CBC)

    B. Electronic Codebook (ECB)

    C. Cipher Feedback (CFB)

    D. Output Feedback (OFB)

14. What encryption algorithm is used by the Clipper chip, which supports the Escrowed Encryption Standard sponsored by the U.S. government?

    A. Data Encryption Standard (DES)

    B. Advanced Encryption Standard (AES)

    C. Skipjack

    D. IDEA

15. What is the minimum number of cryptographic keys required to achieve a higher level of security than DES with the Triple DES algorithm?

    A. 1

    B. 2

    C. 3

    D. 4

16. What approach to key escrow divides the secret key into several pieces that are distributed to independent third parties?

    A. Fair Cryptosystems

    B. Key Escrow Standard

    C. Escrowed Encryption Standard

    D. Fair Escrow

17. What kind of attack makes the Caesar cipher virtually unusable?

    A. Meet-in-the-middle attack

    B. Escrow attack

    C. Frequency attack

    D. Transposition attack

18. What type of cryptosystem commonly makes use of a passage from a well-known book for the encryption key?

    A. Vernam cipher

    B. Running key cipher

    C. Skipjack cipher

    D. Twofish cipher

19. Which AES finalist makes use of prewhitening and postwhitening techniques?

    A. Rijndael

    B. Twofish

    C. Blowfish

    D. Skipjack

20. Matthew and Richard wish to communicate using symmetric cryptography but do not have a prearranged secret key. What algorithm might they use to resolve this situation?

    A. DES

    B. AES

    C. Diffie-Hellman

    D. Skipjack

Answers to Review Questions

1. C. The four goals of cryptographic systems are confidentiality, integrity, authentication, and nonrepudiation.

2. A. Nonrepudiation prevents the sender of a message from later denying that they sent it.

3. A. DES uses a 56-bit key. This is considered one of the major weaknesses of this cryptosystem.

4. B. Transposition ciphers use a variety of techniques to reorder the characters within a message.

5. A. The Rijndael cipher allows users to select a key length of 128, 192, or 256 bits, depending upon the specific security requirements of the application.

6. A. Nonrepudiation requires the use of a public key cryptosystem to prevent users from falsely denying that they originated a message.

7. D. Assuming that it is used properly, the one-time pad is the only known cryptosystem that is not vulnerable to attacks.

8. B. Option B is correct because 16 divided by 3 equals 5, with a remainder value of 1.

9. A. The cryptanalysts from the United States discovered a pattern in the method the Soviets used to generate their one-time pads. After this pattern was discovered, much of the code was eventually broken.

10. C. Block ciphers operate on message "chunks" rather than on individual characters or bits. The other ciphers mentioned are all types of stream ciphers that operate on individual bits or characters of a message.

11. A. Symmetric key cryptography uses a shared secret key. All communicating parties utilize the same key for communication in any direction.

12. D. In asymmetric (public key) cryptography, each communicating party must have a pair of public and private keys. Therefore, two-way communication between parties requires a total of four cryptographic keys (a public and private key for each user).

13. D. Cipher Block Chaining and Cipher Feedback modes will carry errors throughout the entire encryption/decryption process. Electronic Codebook (ECB) operation is not suitable for large amounts of data. Output Feedback (OFB) mode does not allow early errors to interfere with future encryption/decryption.

14. C. The Skipjack algorithm implemented the key escrow standard supported by the U.S. government.

15. B. To achieve added security over DES, 3DES must use at least two cryptographic keys.

16. A. The Fair Cryptosystems approach would have independent third parties each store a portion of the secret key and then provide them to the government upon presentation of a valid court order.

17. C. The Caesar cipher (and other simple substitution ciphers) are vulnerable to frequency attacks that analyze the rate at which specific letters appear in the ciphertext.

18. B. Running key (or "book") ciphers often use a passage from a commonly available book as the encryption key.

19. B. The Twofish algorithm, developed by Bruce Schneier, uses prewhitening and postwhitening.

20. C. The Diffie-Hellman algorithm allows for the secure exchange of symmetric keys over an insecure medium.

Answers to Written Lab

Following are answers to the questions in this chapter's written lab:

1. The major obstacle to the widespread adoption of one-time pad cryptosystems is the difficulty in creating and distributing the very lengthy keys that the algorithm depends on.

2. The first step in encrypting this message requires the assignment of numeric column values to the letters of the secret keyword:

```
S E C U R E
5 2 1 6 4 3
```

Next, the letters of the message are written in order underneath the letters of the keyword:

```
S E C U R E
5 2 1 6 4 3
I W I L L P
A S S T H E
C I S S P E
X A M A N D
B E C O M E
C E R T I F
I E D N E X
T M O N T H
```

Finally, the sender enciphers the message by reading down each column; the order in which the columns are read correspond to the numbers assigned in the first step. This produces the following ciphertext:

```
I S S M C R D O W S I A E E E M P E E D E F X H L H P N
 M I E T I A C X B C I T L T S A O T N N
```

3. This message is decrypted by using the following function:

```
P = (C - 3) mod 26
C: F R Q J U D W X O D W L R Q V B R X J R W L W
P: C O N G R A T U L A T I O N S Y O U G O T I T
```

And the hidden message is "Congratulations You Got It." Congratulations, you got it!

Chapter

10

PKI and Cryptographic Applications

THE CISSP EXAM TOPICS COVERED IN THIS CHAPTER INCLUDE:

- ✓ Cryptographic Concepts, Methodologies, and Practices
- ✓ Public Key Algorithms
- ✓ Public Key Infrastructure
- ✓ System Architecture for Implementing Cryptographic Functions
- ✓ Methods of Attack

In Chapter 9, we introduced basic cryptography concepts and explored a variety of private key cryptosystems. These symmetric cryptosystems offer fast, secure communication but introduce the substantial challenge of key exchange between previously unrelated parties. This chapter explores the world of asymmetric (or public key) cryptography and the public key infrastructure (PKI) that supports worldwide secure communication between parties that don't necessarily know each other prior to the communication. We'll also explore several practical applications of cryptography: securing electronic mail, web communications, electronic commerce, and networking. This chapter concludes with an examination of a variety of attacks malicious individuals might use to compromise weak cryptosystems.

Asymmetric Cryptography

The section "Modern Cryptography" in Chapter 9 introduced the basic principles behind both private (symmetric) and public (asymmetric) key cryptography. You learned that symmetric key cryptosystems require both communicating parties to have the same shared secret key, creating the problem of secure key distribution. You also learned that asymmetric cryptosystems avoid this hurdle by using pairs of public and private keys to facilitate secure communication without the overhead of complex key distribution systems. The security of these systems relies upon the difficulty of reversing a one-way function.

The terms *asymmetric cryptography* and *public key cryptography* are often (acceptably) used interchangeably. However, when you get down to brass tacks, they can be different systems. Without getting too technical or straying outside the bounds of this book, suffice it to say that some asymmetric cryptography systems are not public-key based. Thinking asymmetric cryptography and public key cryptography are similar is fine for day-to-day use, but if you formally study mathematics or cryptography, you'll soon learn otherwise.

In the following sections, we'll explore the concepts of public key cryptography in greater detail and look at three of the more common public key cryptosystems in use today: RSA, El Gamal, and the Elliptic Curve Cryptosystem.

Public and Private Keys

Recall from Chapter 9 that *public key* cryptosystems rely on pairs of keys assigned to each user of the cryptosystem. Every user maintains both a public key and a private key. As the names imply, public key cryptosystem users make their public keys freely available to anyone with whom they want to communicate. The mere possession of the public key by third parties does not introduce any weaknesses into the cryptosystem. The *private key,* on the other hand, is reserved for the sole use of the individual. It is never shared with any other cryptosystem user.

Normal communication between public key cryptosystem users is quite straightforward. The general process is shown in Figure 10.1.

FIGURE 10.1   Asymmetric key cryptography

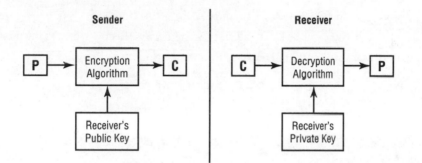

Notice that the process does not require the sharing of private keys. The sender encrypts the plaintext message (P) with the recipient's public key to create the ciphertext message (C). When the recipient opens the ciphertext message, they decrypt it using their private key to re-create the original plaintext message. Once the sender encrypts the message with the recipient's public key, no user (including the sender) can decrypt that message without knowledge of the recipient's private key (the second half of the public-private key pair used to generate the message). This is the beauty of public key cryptography—public keys can be freely shared using unsecured communications and then used to create secure communications channels between users previously unknown to each other.

You also learned in the previous chapter that public key cryptography entails a higher degree of computational complexity. Keys used within public key systems must be longer than those used in private key systems to produce cryptosystems of equivalent strengths.

RSA

The most famous public key cryptosystem is named after its creators. In 1977, Ronald Rivest, Adi Shamir, and Leonard Adleman proposed the *RSA* public key algorithm that remains a worldwide standard today. They patented their algorithm and formed a commercial venture known as RSA Security to develop mainstream implementations of their security technology.

Today, the RSA algorithm forms the security backbone of a large number of well-known security infrastructures produced by companies like Microsoft, Nokia, and Cisco.

The RSA algorithm depends upon the computational difficulty inherent in factoring large prime numbers. Each user of the cryptosystem generates a pair of public and private keys using the algorithm described in the following steps:

1. Choose two large prime numbers (approximately 200 digits each), labeled p and q.

2. Compute the product of those two numbers, $n = p * q$.

3. Select a number, e, that satisfies the following two requirements:

   a. e is less than n.

   b. e and $(n-1)(q-1)$ are relatively prime—that is, the two numbers have no common factors other than 1.

4. Find a number, d, such that $(ed - 1) \bmod (p-1)(q-1) = 0$.

5. Distribute e and n as the public key to all cryptosystem users. Keep d secret as the private key.

If Alice wants to send an encrypted message to Bob, she generates the ciphertext (C) from the plaintext (P) using the following formula (where e is Bob's public key and n is the product of p and q created during the key generation process):

```
C = Pe mod n
```

When Bob receives the message, he performs the following calculation to retrieve the plaintext message:

```
P = Cd mod n
```

Merkle-Hellman Knapsack

Another early asymmetric algorithm, the Merkle-Hellman Knapsack algorithm, was developed the year after RSA was publicized. Like RSA, it's also based upon the difficulty of performing factoring operations, but it relies upon a component of set theory known as superincreasing sets rather than on large prime numbers. Merkle-Hellman was proven ineffective when it was broken in 1984.

El Gamal

In Chapter 9, you learned how the Diffie-Hellman algorithm uses large integers and modular arithmetic to facilitate the secure exchange of secret keys over insecure communications channels. In 1985, Dr. T. El Gamal published an article describing how the mathematical principles behind the Diffie-Hellman key exchange algorithm could be extended to support an entire public key cryptosystem used for the encryption and decryption of messages.

Importance of Key Length

The length of the cryptographic key is perhaps the most important security parameter that can be set at the discretion of the security administrator. It's important to understand the capabilities of your encryption algorithm and choose a key length that provides an appropriate level of protection. This judgment can be made by weighing the difficulty of defeating a given key length (measured in the amount of processing time required to defeat the cryptosystem) against the importance of the data.

Generally speaking, the more critical your data, the stronger the key you use to protect it should be. Timeliness of the data is also an important consideration. You must take into account the rapid growth of computing power—the famous Moore's Law states that computing power doubles approximately every 18 months. If it takes current computers one year of processing time to break your code, it will take only three months if the attempt is made with contemporary technology three years down the road. If you expect that your data will still be sensitive at that time, you should choose a much longer cryptographic key that will remain secure well into the future.

The strengths of various key lengths also vary greatly according to the cryptosystem you're using. According to a white paper published by Certicom, a provider of wireless security solutions, the key lengths shown in the following table for three asymmetric cryptosystems all provide equal protection:

Cryptosystem	Key Length
RSA	1,088 bits
DSA	1,024 bits
Elliptic curve	160 bits

One of the major advantages of *El Gamal* over the RSA algorithm is that it was released into the public domain. Dr. El Gamal did not obtain a patent on his extension of Diffie-Hellman and it is freely available for use, unlike the commercialized patented RSA technology.

However, El Gamal also has a major disadvantage—the algorithm doubles the length of any message it encrypts. This presents a major hardship when encrypting long messages or data that will be transmitted over a narrow bandwidth communications circuit.

Elliptic Curve

Also in 1985, two mathematicians, Neil Koblitz from the University of Washington and Victor Miller from International Business Machines (IBM), independently proposed the application of *elliptic curve cryptography* theory to develop secure cryptographic systems.

The mathematical concepts behind elliptic curve cryptography are quite complex and well beyond the scope of this book. However, you should be generally familiar with the elliptic curve algorithm and its potential applications when preparing for the CISSP exam. If you are interested in learning the detailed mathematics behind elliptic curve cryptosystems, an excellent tutorial exists at www.certicom.com/research/online.html.

Any elliptic curve can be defined by the following equation:

```
y2 = x3 + ax + b
```

In this equation, *x*, *y*, *a*, and *b* are all real numbers. Each elliptic curve has a corresponding *elliptic curve group* made up of the points on the elliptic curve along with the point *O*, located at infinity. Two points within the same elliptic curve group (*P* and *Q*) can be added together with an elliptic curve addition algorithm. This operation is expressed, quite simply, as follows:

```
P + Q
```

This problem can be extended to involve multiplication by assuming that *Q* is a multiple of *P*, meaning that

```
Q = xP
```

Computer scientists and mathematicians believe that it is extremely hard to find *x*, even if *P* and *Q* are already known. This difficult problem, known as the elliptic curve discrete logarithm problem, forms the basis of elliptic curve cryptography. It is widely believed that this problem is harder to solve than both the prime factorization problem that the RSA cryptosystem is based upon and the standard discrete logarithm problem utilized by Diffie-Hellman and El Gamal. This is illustrated by the data shown in the table in the sidebar "Importance of Key Length," which noted that a 1,024-bit RSA key is cryptographically equivalent to a 160-bit elliptic curve cryptosystem key.

Hash Functions

Later in this chapter, you'll learn how cryptosystems implement digital signatures to provide proof that a message originated from a particular user of the cryptosystem and to ensure that the message was not modified while in transit between the two parties. Before you can completely understand that concept, we must first explain the concept of *hash functions*. This section explores the basics of hash functions and looks at several common hash functions used in modern digital signature algorithms.

Hash functions have a very simple purpose—they take a potentially long message and generate a unique output value derived from the content of the message. This value is commonly referred to as the *message digest*. Message digests can be generated by the sender of a message and transmitted to the recipient along with the full message for two reasons. First, the recipient can use the same hash function to recompute the message digest from the full message. They can then compare the computed message digest to the transmitted one to ensure that the message sent by the originator is the same one received by the recipient. If the message digests do not match, it indicates that the message was somehow modified while in transit. Second, the message digest can be used to implement a digital signature algorithm. This concept is covered in "Digital Signatures" later in this chapter.

> The term *message digest* can be used interchangeably with a wide variety of other synonyms, including *hash, hash value, hash total, CRC, fingerprint, checksum,* and *digital ID.*

In most cases, a message digest is 128 bits or larger. However, a single-digit value can be used to perform the function of parity, a low-level or single-digit checksum value used to provide a single individual point of verification. In most cases, the longer the message digest, the more reliable its verification of integrity.

According to RSA Security, there are five basic requirements for a cryptographic hash function:

- The input can be of any length.
- The output has a fixed length.
- The hash function is relatively easy to compute for any input.
- The hash function is one-way (meaning that it is extremely hard to determine the input when provided with the output). One-way functions and their usefulness in cryptography are described in Chapter 9.
- The hash function is collision free (meaning that it is extremely hard to find two messages that produce the same hash value).

In the following sections, we'll look at four common hashing algorithms: SHA, MD2, MD4, and MD5. HMAC is also discussed later in this chapter.

> There are numerous hashing algorithms not addressed in this exam. In addition to SHA, MDx, and HMAC, you should also recognize HAVAL. HAVAL (HAsh of VAriable Length) is a modification of MD5. HAVAL uses 1,024-bit blocks and produces hash values of 128, 160, 192, 224, and 256 bits.

SHA

The *Secure Hash Algorithm (SHA)* and its successor, SHA-1, are government standard hash functions developed by the National Institute of Standards and Technology (NIST) and are specified in an official government publication—the Secure Hash Standard (SHS), also known as Federal Information Processing Standard (FIPS) 180.

SHA-1 takes an input of virtually any length (in reality, there is an upper bound of approximately 2,097,152 terabytes on the algorithm) and produces a 160-bit message digest. Due to the mathematical structure of the hashing algorithm, this provides 80 bits of protection against collision attacks. The SHA-1 algorithm processes a message in 512-bit blocks. Therefore, if the message length is not a multiple of 512, the SHA algorithm pads the message with additional data until the length reaches the next highest multiple of 512.

Although SHA-1 is the current official standard for federal government applications, it is not quite strong enough. It was designed to work with the old Data Encryption Standard (DES) and its follow-on, Triple DES (3DES). The new Advanced Encryption Standard (described in the preceding chapter) supports key lengths of up to 256 bits. Therefore, the government is currently evaluating three new hash functions to replace SHA-1 in the near future:

- SHA-256 produces a 256-bit message digest and provides 128 bits of protection against collision attacks.

- SHA-512 produces a 512-bit message digest and provides 256 bits of protection against collision attacks.

- SHA-384 uses a truncated version of the SHA-512 hash to produce a 384-bit digest that supports 192 bits of protection against collision attacks.

Although it might seem trivial, take the time to memorize the size of the message digests produced by each one of the hash algorithms described in this chapter.

MD2

The *MD2 (Message Digest 2)* hash algorithm was developed by Ronald Rivest (the same Rivest of Rivest, Shamir, and Adleman fame) in 1989 to provide a secure hash function for 8-bit processors. MD2 pads the message so that its length is a multiple of 16 bytes. It then computes a 16-byte checksum and appends it to the end of the message. A 128-bit message digest is then generated by using the entire original message along with the appended checksum.

Cryptanalytic attacks exist against improper implementations of the MD2 algorithm. Specifically, Nathalie Rogier and Pascal Chauvaud discovered that if the checksum is not appended to the message before digest computation, collisions may occur.

MD4

The next year, in 1990, Rivest enhanced his message digest algorithm to support 32-bit processors and increase the level of security. This enhanced algorithm is known as *MD4*. It first pads the message to ensure that the message length is 64 bits smaller than a multiple of 512 bits. For example, a 16-bit message would be padded with 432 additional bits of data to make it 448 bits, which is 64 bits smaller than a 512-bit message.

The MD4 algorithm then processes 512-bit blocks of the message in three rounds of computation. The final output is a 128-bit message digest.

The MD4 algorithm is no longer accepted as a suitable hashing function.

Several mathematicians have published papers documenting flaws in the full version of MD4 as well as improperly implemented versions of MD4. In particular, Hans Dobbertin published a paper in 1996 outlining how a modern PC could be used to find collisions for MD4 message digests in less than one minute. For this reason, MD4 is no longer considered to be a secure hashing algorithm and its use should be avoided if at all possible.

MD5

In 1991, Rivest released the next version of his message digest algorithm, which he called *MD5*. It also processes 512-bit blocks of the message, but it uses four distinct rounds of computation to produce a digest of the same length as the MD2 and MD4 algorithms (128 bits). MD5 has the same padding requirements as MD4—the message length must be 64 bits less than a multiple of 512 bits.

MD5 implements additional security features that reduce the speed of message digest production significantly. Cryptanalysts have not yet proven that the full MD5 algorithm is vulnerable to collisions, but many experts suspect that such a proof may not be far away. However, MD5 is the strongest of Rivest's algorithms and remains in use today. MD5 is commonly seen in use in relation to file downloads, such as updates and patches, so the recipient can verify the integrity of a file after downloading and before installing or applying it to any system.

Table 10.1 lists well-known hashing algorithms and their resultant hash value lengths in bits. Earmark this page for memorization.

TABLE 10.1   Hash Algorithm Memorization Chart

Name	Hash Value Length
Secure Hash Algorithm (SHA-1)	160
Message Digest 5 (MD5)	128
Message Digest 4 (MD4)	128
Message Digest 2 (MD2)	128
HMAC (Hash Message Authenticating Code)	variable
HAVAL (Hash of Variable Length) —an MD5 variant	128, 160, 192, 224, and 256 bits

Digital Signatures

Once you have chosen a cryptographically sound hashing algorithm, you can use it to implement a *digital signature* system. Digital signature infrastructures have two distinct goals:

- Digitally signed messages assure the recipient that the message truly came from the claimed sender and enforce nonrepudiation (that is, they preclude the sender from later claiming that the message is a forgery).

- Digitally signed messages assure the recipient that the message was not altered while in transit between the sender and recipient. This protects against both malicious modification (a third party wanting to alter the meaning of the message) and unintentional modification (due to faults in the communications process, such as electrical interference).

Digital signature algorithms rely upon a combination of the two major concepts already covered in this chapter—public key cryptography and hashing functions. If Alice wants to digitally sign a message she's sending to Bob, she performs the following actions:

1. Alice generates a message digest of the original plaintext message using one of the cryptographically sound hashing algorithms, such as SHA-1, MD2, or MD5.

2. Alice then encrypts only the message digest using her private key.

3. Alice appends the signed message digest to the plaintext message.

4. Alice transmits the appended message to Bob.

 Digital signatures are used for more than just messages. Software vendors often use digital signature technology to authenticate code distributions that you download from the Internet, such as applets and software patches.

When Bob receives the digitally signed message, he reverses the procedure, as follows:

1. Bob decrypts the message digest using Alice's public key.

2. Bob uses the same hashing function to create a message digest of the full plaintext message received from Alice.

3. Bob then compares the decrypted message digest he received from Alice with the message digest he computed himself. If the two digests match, he can be assured that the message he received was sent by Alice. If they do not match, either the message was not sent by Alice or the message was modified while in transit.

Note that the digital signature process does not provide any privacy in and of itself. It only ensures that the cryptographic goals of integrity and nonrepudiation are met. However, if Alice wanted to ensure the privacy of her message to Bob, she would add an additional step to the message creation process. After appending the signed message digest to the plaintext message, Alice could encrypt the entire message with Bob's public key. When Bob received the message, he would decrypt it with his own private key before following the steps just outlined.

HMAC

The *Hashed Message Authentication Code (HMAC)* algorithm implements a partial digital signature—it guarantees the integrity of a message during transmission, but it does not provide for nonrepudiation.

Real World Scenario

Which Key Should I Use?

If you're new to public key cryptography, selection of the correct key for various applications can be quite confusing. Encryption, decryption, message signing, and signature verification all use the same algorithm with different key inputs. Here are a few simple rules to help keep these concepts straight in your mind when preparing for the CISSP exam:

- If you want to encrypt a message, use the sender's public key.

- If you want to decrypt a message sent to you, use your private key.

- If you want to digitally sign a message you are sending to someone else, use your private key.

- If you want to verify the signature on a message sent by someone else, use the sender's public key.

These four rules are the core principles of public key cryptography and digital signatures. If you understand each of them, you're off to a great start!

HMAC can be combined with any standard message digest generation algorithm, such as MD5 or SHA-1. It can be combined with these algorithms by using a shared secret key. Therefore, only communicating parties who know the key can generate or verify the digital signature. If the recipient decrypts the message digest but cannot successfully compare it to a message digest generated from the plaintext message, the message was altered in transit.

Because HMAC relies on a shared secret key, it does not provide any nonrepudiation functionality (as previously mentioned). However, it operates in a more efficient manner than the digital signature standard described in the following section and may be suitable for applications in which symmetric key cryptography is appropriate. In short, it represents a halfway point between unencrypted use of a message digest algorithm and computationally expensive digital signature algorithms based upon public key cryptography.

Digital Signature Standard

The National Institute of Standards and Technology specifies the digital signature algorithms acceptable for federal government use in Federal Information Processing Standard (FIPS) 186-2, also known as the *Digital Signature Standard (DSS)*. This document specifies that all federally approved digital signature algorithms must use the SHA-1 hashing function (recall from our discussion of hash functions that this specification is currently under review and will likely be revised to support longer message digests).

DSS also specifies the encryption algorithms that can be used to support a digital signature infrastructure. There are three currently approved standard encryption algorithms:

- The Digital Signature Algorithm (DSA) as specified in FIPS 186-2
- The Rivest, Shamir, Adleman (RSA) algorithm as specified in ANSI X9.31
- The Elliptic Curve DSA (ECDSA) as specified in ANSI X9.62

Two other digital signature algorithms you should recognize, at least by name, are Schnorr's signature algorithm and Nybergrueppel's signature algorithm. Also, DES and SHA appear from time to time as algorithms employed in digital signature systems.

Public Key Infrastructure

The major strength of public key encryption is its ability to facilitate communication between parties previously unknown to each other. This is made possible by the *public key infrastructure (PKI)* hierarchy of trust relationships. In the following sections, you'll learn the basic components of the public key infrastructure and the cryptographic concepts that make global secure communications possible. You'll learn the composition of a digital certificate, the role of certificate authorities, and the process used to generate and destroy certificates.

Certificates

Digital *certificates* provide communicating parties with the assurance that they are communicating with people who truly are who they claim to be. Digital certificates are essentially endorsed copies of an individual's public key. This prevents malicious individuals from distributing false public keys on behalf of another party and then convincing third parties that they are communicating with someone else.

Digital certificates contain specific identifying information, and their construction is governed by an international standard—X.509. Certificates that conform to X.509 contain the following data:

- Version of X.509 to which the certificate conforms
- Serial number (from the certificate creator)
- Signature algorithm identifier (specifies the technique used by the certificate authority to digitally sign the contents of the certificate)
- Issuer name (identification of the certificate authority that issued the certificate)

- Validity period (specifies the dates and times—a starting date and time and an ending date and time—during which the certificate is valid)
- Subject's name (contains the distinguished name, or DN, of the entity that owns the public key contained in the certificate)
- Subject's public key (the meat of the certificate—the actual public key the certificate owner used to set up secure communications)

The current version of X.509 (version 3) supports certificate extensions—customized variables containing data inserted into the certificate by the certificate authority to support tracking of certificates or various applications.

> If you're interested in building your own X.509 certificates or just want to explore the inner workings of the public key infrastructure, you can purchase the complete official X.509 standard from the International Telecommunications Union. It's part of the Open Systems Interconnection (OSI) series of communication standards and can be purchased electronically on the ITU website at www.itu.int.

X.509 has not been officially accepted as a standard, and implementations can vary from vendor to vendor. However, both Microsoft and Netscape have adopted X.509 as their de facto standard for *Secure Sockets Layer (SSL)* communication between their web clients and servers. SSL is covered in greater detail in the section "Applied Cryptography" later in this chapter.

Certificate Authorities

Certificate authorities (CAs) are the glue that binds the public key infrastructure together. These neutral organizations offer notarization services for digital certificates. In order to obtain a digital certificate from a reputable CA, you must appear in front of one of their agents in person and present appropriate identifying documents. The following list includes the major CAs:

- VeriSign
- Thawte Consulting
- Società per i Servizi Bancari-SSB S.p.A.
- Internet Publishing Services
- Certisign Certification Digital Ltda
- BelSign

There's nothing preventing any organization from simply setting up shop as a CA. However, the certificates issued by a CA are only as good as the trust placed in the organization that issued them. This is an important item to consider when receiving a digital certificate from a third party. If you don't recognize and trust the name of the CA that issued the certificate, you shouldn't place any trust in the certificate at all.

Registration authorities (RAs) assist CAs with the burden of verifying users' identities prior to issuing digital certificates. They do not directly issue certificates themselves, but they play an important role in the certification process, allowing CAs to outsource some of their workload. Basically, you can think of an RA as a read-only CA. The RA's primary work task is to distribute the CRL to any clients that request it.

> **TIP**
>
> You may have heard of Certificate Path Validation (CPV) in your studies of certificate authorities. CPV means that each certificate in a certificate path from original start or root of trust down to the server or client in question is valid and legitimate. CPV can be important if you need to verify that every link between "trusted" endpoints remains current, valid, and trustworthy. This issue arises from time to time when intermediary systems' certificates expire or are replaced; this can break the chain of trust or the verification path. By forcing a reverification of all stages of trust, you can reestablish all trust links and prove that the assumed trust remains assured.

Certificate Generation and Destruction

The technical concepts behind the public key infrastructure are relatively simple. In the following sections, we'll look at the processes used by certificate authorities to create, validate, and revoke client certificates.

Enrollment

When you want to obtain a digital certificate, you must first prove your identity to the certificate authority (CA) in some manner; this process is called *enrollment*. As mentioned in the previous section, this often involves physically appearing before an agent of the certification authority with appropriate identification documents. Some certificate authorities provide other means of verification, including the use of credit report data and identity verification by trusted community leaders.

Once you've satisfied the certificate authority regarding your identity, you provide them with your public key. The CA next creates an X.509 digital certificate containing your identifying information and a copy of your public key. The CA then digitally signs the certificate using the CA's private key and provides you with a copy of your signed digital certificate. You may then safely distribute this certificate to anyone with whom you want to communicate securely.

Verification

When you receive a digital certificate from someone with whom you want to communicate, you verify the certificate by checking the CA's digital signature using the CA's public key. Next, you must check and ensure that the certificate was not published on a *certificate revocation list* (CRL). At this point, you may assume that the public key listed in the certificate is authentic, provided that it satisfies the following requirements:

- The digital signature of the CA is authentic.

- You trust the CA.

- The certificate is not listed on a CRL.
- The certificate actually contains the data you are trusting.

The last point is a subtle but extremely important item. Before you trust an identifying piece of information about someone, be sure that it is actually contained within the certificate. If a certificate contains the e-mail address (`billjones@foo.com`) but not the individual's name, you can only be certain that the public key contained therein is associated with that e-mail address. The CA is not making any assertions about the actual identity of the `billjones@foo.com` e-mail account. However, if the certificate contains the name Bill Jones along with an address and telephone number, the CA is also vouching for that information as well.

Digital certificate verification algorithms are built in to a number of popular web browsing and e-mail clients, so you won't often need to get involved in the particulars of the process. However, it's important to have a solid understanding of the technical details taking place behind the scenes to make appropriate security judgments for your organization.

Revocation

Occasionally, a certificate authority needs to revoke a certificate. This might occur for one of the following reasons:

- The certificate was compromised (e.g., the certificate owner accidentally gave away the private key).
- The certificate was erroneously issued (e.g., the CA mistakenly issued a certificate without proper verification).
- The details of the certificate changed (e.g., the subject's name changed).
- The security association changed (e.g., the subject is no longer employed by the organization sponsoring the certificate).

Revocation request grace period is the maximum response time within which a CA will perform any requested revocation. This is defined in the Certificate Practice Statement (CPS). The CPS states the practices a CA employs when issuing or managing certificates.

There are two techniques used to verify the authenticity of certificates and identify revoked certificates:

Certificate revocation lists Certificate revocation lists (CRLs) are maintained by the various certification authorities and contain the serial numbers of certificates that have been issued by a CA and have been revoked, along with the date and time the *revocation* went into effect. The major disadvantage to certificate revocation lists is that they must be downloaded and cross-referenced periodically, introducing a period of latency between the time a certificate is revoked and the time end users are notified of the revocation. However, CRLs remain the most common method of checking certificate status in use today.

Online Certificate Status Protocol (OCSP)   This protocol eliminates the latency inherent in the use of certificate revocation lists by providing a means for real-time certificate verification. When a client receives a certificate, it sends an OCSP request to the CA's OCSP server. The server then responds with a status of valid, invalid, or unknown.

Key Management

When working within the public key infrastructure, it's important that you comply with several best practice requirements to maintain the security of your communications.

First, choose your encryption system wisely. As you learned earlier, "security through obscurity" is not an appropriate approach. Choose an encryption system with an algorithm in the public domain that has been thoroughly vetted by industry experts. Be wary of systems that use a "black box" approach and maintain that the secrecy of their algorithm is critical to the integrity of the cryptosystem.

You must also select your keys in an appropriate manner. Use a key length that balances your security requirements with performance considerations. Also, ensure that your key is truly random. Any patterns within the key increase the likelihood that an attacker will be able to break your encryption and degrade the security of your cryptosystem.

When using public key encryption, keep your secret key secret! Do not, under any circumstances, allow anyone else to gain access to your private key. Remember, allowing someone access even once permanently compromises all communications that take place (past, present, or future) using that key and allows the third party to successfully impersonate you.

Retire keys when they've served a useful life. Many organizations have mandatory key rotation requirements to protect against undetected key compromise. If you don't have a formal policy that you must follow, select an appropriate interval based upon the frequency with which you use your key. You might want to change your key pair every few months, if practical.

Back up your key! If you lose the file containing your secret key due to data corruption, disaster, or other circumstances, you'll certainly want to have a backup available. You may wish to either create your own backup or use a key escrow service that maintains the backup for you. In either case, ensure that the backup is handled in a secure manner. After all, it's just as important as your primary key file!

Applied Cryptography

Up to this point, you've learned a great deal about the foundations of cryptography, the inner workings of various cryptographic algorithms, and the use of the public key infrastructure to distribute identity credentials using digital certificates. You should now feel comfortable with the basics of cryptography and prepared to move on to higher-level applications of this technology to solve everyday communications problems. In the following sections, we'll examine the use of cryptography to secure electronic mail, web communications services, electronic commerce, and networking.

Electronic Mail

We have mentioned several times that security should be cost effective. When it comes to electronic mail, simplicity is the most cost-effective option, but sometimes cryptography functions provide specific security services that you can't avoid using. Since ensuring security is also cost effective, here are some simple rules about encrypting e-mail:

- If you need confidentiality when sending an e-mail message, then encrypt the message.
- If your message must maintain integrity, then you must hash the message.
- If your message needs authentication and integrity, then you should digitally sign the message.
- If your message requires confidentiality, integrity, authentication, and nonrepudiation, then you should encrypt and digitally sign the message.

It is always the responsibility of the sender to ensure that proper mechanisms are in place to ensure that the security (i.e., confidentiality, integrity, authenticity, and nonrepudiation) and privacy of a message or transmission are maintained.

One of the most demanded applications of cryptography is the encryption and signing of electronic mail messages. Until recently, encrypted e-mail required the use of complex, awkward software that required manual intervention and complicated key exchange procedures. An increased emphasis on security in recent years resulted in the implementation of strong encryption technology in mainstream electronic mail packages. Next, we'll look at some of the secure electronic mail standards in widespread use today.

Pretty Good Privacy

Phil Zimmerman's *Pretty Good Privacy (PGP)* secure e-mail system appeared on the computer security scene in 1991. It is based upon the "web of trust" concept, where you must become trusted by one or more PGP users to begin using the system. You then accept their judgment regarding the validity of additional users and, by extension, trust a multilevel "web" of users descending from your initial trust judgments. PGP initially encountered a number of hurdles to widespread use. The most difficult obstruction was the U.S. government export regulations, which treated encryption technology as munitions and prohibited the distribution of strong encryption technology outside of the United States. Fortunately, this restriction has since been repealed and PGP may be freely distributed to most countries.

PGP is available in two versions. The commercial version uses RSA for key exchange, IDEA for encryption/decryption, and MD5 for message digest production. The freeware version uses Diffie-Hellman key exchange, the Carlisle Adams/Stafford Tavares (CAST) 128-bit encryption/decryption algorithm, and the SHA-1 hashing function.

Privacy Enhanced Mail

The *Privacy Enhanced Mail (PEM)* standard addresses implementation guidelines for secure electronic mail in a variety of Internet Request for Comments (RFC) documents. RFC 1421 outlines an architecture that provides the following services:

- Disclosure protection
- Originator authenticity

- Message integrity
- Nonrepudiation (if asymmetric cryptography is used)

However, the same RFC also notes that PEM is not intended to provide the following services:

- Access control
- Traffic flow confidentiality
- Address list accuracy
- Routing control
- Assurance of message receipt and nondeniability of receipt
- Automatic association of acknowledgments with the messages to which they refer
- Replay protection

Security administrators who desire any of the services just listed should implement additional controls over and above those provided by a PEM-compliant electronic mail system. An important distinction between PEM and PGP is that PEM uses a CA-managed hierarchy of digital certificates whereas PGP relies upon the "web of trust" between system users.

MOSS

Another Request for Comments document, RFC 1848, specifies the *MIME Object Security Services (MOSS),* yet another standard for secure electronic mail, designed to supersede Privacy Enhanced Mail. Like PGP, MOSS does not require the use of digital certificates and provides easy associations between certificates and e-mail addresses. It also allows the secure exchange of attachments to e-mail messages. However, MOSS does not provide any interoperability with PGP or PEM.

S/MIME

The *Secure Multipurpose Internet Mail Extensions (S/MIME)* protocol has emerged as a likely standard for future encrypted electronic mail efforts. S/MIME utilizes the RSA encryption algorithm and has received the backing of major industry players, including RSA Security. S/MIME has already been incorporated in a large number of commercial products, including these:

- Microsoft Outlook and Outlook Express
- Netscape Communicator
- Lotus Notes
- VeriSign Digital ID
- Eudora WorldSecure

S/MIME relies upon the use of X.509 certificates for the exchange of cryptographic keys. The public keys contained in these certificates are used for digital signatures and for the exchange of symmetric keys used for longer communications sessions. RSA is the only public key cryptographic protocol supported by S/MIME. The protocol supports the following symmetric encryption algorithms:

- DES
- 3DES
- RC2

The strong industry support for the S/MIME standard makes it likely that S/MIME will be widely adopted and approved as an Internet standard for secure electronic mail by the Internet Engineering Task Force (IETF) in the near future.

Web

Although secure electronic mail is still in its early days, secure web browsing has achieved widespread acceptance in recent years. This is mainly due to the strong movement toward electronic commerce and the desire of both e-commerce vendors and consumers to securely exchange financial information (such as credit card information) over the Web. We'll look at the two technologies that are responsible for the small lock icon at the bottom of web browsers—Secure Sockets Layer (SSL) and Secure HTTP (S-HTTP).

Secure Sockets Layer

Secure Sockets Layer (SSL) was developed by Netscape to provide client/server encryption for web traffic. SSL operates above the TCP/IP protocol in the network stack. *Hypertext Transfer Protocol over Secure Sockets Layer (HTTPS)* uses port 443 to negotiate encrypted communications sessions between web servers and browser clients. Although SSL originated as a standard for Netscape browsers, Microsoft also adopted it as a security standard for its popular Internet Explorer browser. The incorporation of SSL into both of these products made it the de facto Internet standard.

SSL relies upon the exchange of server digital certificates to negotiate RSA encryption/decryption parameters between the browser and the web server. SSL's goal is to create secure communications channels that remain open for an entire web browsing session.

SSL forms the basis for a new security standard, the Transport Layer Security (TLS) protocol, specified in RFC 2246. TLS is expected to supersede SSL as it gains in popularity. SSL and TLS both support server authentication (mandatory) and client authentication (optional).

Be certain to know the differences between HTTP over SSL (HTTPS) and Secure HTTP (S-HTTP).

Secure HTTP

Secure HTTP (S-HTTP) is the second major protocol used to provide security on the World Wide Web. S-HTTP is not nearly as popular as SSL, but it has two major differences:

- S-HTTP secures individual messages between a client and server rather than creating a secure communications channel as SSL does.

- S-HTTP supports two-way authentication between a client and a server rather than the server-only authentication supported by SSL.

Steganography

Steganography is the art of using cryptographic techniques to embed secret messages within another message. Steganographic algorithms work by making alterations to the least significant bits of the many bits that make up image files. The changes are so minor that there is no appreciable effect on the viewed image. This technique allows communicating parties to hide messages in plain sight—such as embedding a secret message within an illustration on an otherwise innocent web page.

Steganographers often embed their secret messages within images or WAV files. These files are often so large that the secret message would easily be missed by even the most observant inspector.

E-Commerce

As mentioned in the previous section, the rapid growth of electronic commerce led to the widespread adoption of SSL and HTTPS as standards for the secure exchange of information through web browsers. Recently, industry experts have recognized the added security necessary for electronic transactions. In the next section, we'll explore the Secure Electronic Transaction (SET) protocol designed to add this enhanced security.

Secure Electronic Transactions

The *Secure Electronic Transaction (SET)* standard was originally developed jointly by Visa and MasterCard—the two largest providers of credit cards in the United States—as a means for securing e-commerce transactions. When they outlined the business case for SET, the two vendors identified the following seven requirements:

- Provide confidentiality of payment information and enable confidentiality of order information transmitted along with the payment information.

- Ensure the integrity of all transmitted data.

- Provide authentication that a cardholder is a legitimate user of a branded payment card account.

- Provide authentication that a merchant can accept branded payment card transactions through its relationship with an acquiring financial institution.

- Ensure the use of the best security practices and system design techniques to protect all legitimate parties in an electronic commerce transaction.

- Create a protocol that neither depends on transport security mechanisms nor prevents their use.

- Facilitate and encourage interoperability among software and network providers.

Material on SET is disappearing from the Internet since the original site, www.setco.org, is no longer active. For more information on SET, try visiting www.ectag.org.

SET utilizes a combination of RSA public key cryptography and DES private key cryptography in conjunction with digital certificates to secure electronic transactions. The original SET standard was published in 1997.

MONDEX

The *MONDEX* payment system, owned by MasterCard International, uses cryptographic technology to allow electronic commerce users to store value on smart chips in proprietary payment cards. The value can then be instantly transferred to a vendor at the point of purchase.

Networking

The final application of cryptography we'll explore in this chapter is the use of cryptographic algorithms to provide secure networking services. In the following sections, we'll take a brief look at two methods used to secure communications circuits, as well as IPSec and the ISAKMP protocol. We'll also look at some of the security issues surrounding wireless networking.

Circuit Encryption

Security administrators use two types of encryption techniques to protect data traveling over networks—*link encryption* and *end-to-end encryption*.

Link encryption protects entire communications circuits by creating a secure tunnel between two points using either a hardware or a software solution that encrypts all traffic entering one end of the tunnel and decrypts all traffic entering the other end of the tunnel. For example, a company with two offices connected via a data circuit might use link encryption to protect against attackers monitoring at a point in between the two offices.

End-to-end encryption protects communications between two parties (e.g., a client and a server) and is performed independently of link encryption. An example of end-to-end encryption would be the use of Privacy Enhanced Mail to pass a message between a sender and a receiver. This protects against an intruder who might be monitoring traffic on the secure side of an encrypted link or traffic sent over an unencrypted link.

The critical difference between link and end-to-end encryption is that in link encryption, *all* the data, including the header, trailer, address, and routing data, is also encrypted. Therefore, each packet has to be decrypted at each hop so it can be properly routed to the next hop and then reencrypted before it can be sent along its way, which slows the routing. End-to-end encryption does not encrypt the header, trailer, address, and routing data, so it moves faster from point to point but is more susceptible to sniffers and eavesdroppers. When encryption happens at the higher OSI layers, it is usually end-to-end encryption, and if encryption is done at the lower layers of the OSI model, it is usually link encryption.

Secure Shell (SSH) is a good example of an end-to-end encryption technique. This suite of programs provide encrypted alternatives to common Internet applications like FTP, Telnet, and rlogin. There are actually two versions of SSH. SSH1 (which is now considered insecure) supports the DES, 3DES, IDEA, and Blowfish algorithms. SSH2 drops support for DES and IDEA but adds support for several other algorithms.

IPSec

There are various security architectures in use today, each one designed to address security issues in different environments. One such architecture that supports secure communications is the Internet Protocol Security (IPSec) standard. IPSec is a standard architecture set forth by the Internet Engineering Task Force (IETF) for setting up a secure channel to exchange information between two entities. The two entities could be two systems, two routers, two gateways, or any combination of entities. Although generally used to connect two networks, IPSec can be used to connect individual computers, such as a server and a workstation or a pair of workstations (sender and receiver, perhaps). IPSec does not dictate all implementation details but is an open, modular framework that allows many manufacturers and software developers to develop IPSec solutions that work well with products from other vendors.

IPSec uses public key cryptography to provide encryption, access control, nonrepudiation, and message authentication, all using IP protocols. The primary use of IPSec is for virtual private networks (VPNs), so IPSec operates in either transport or tunnel mode. Tunnel mode is most often used when you set up VPNs between network gateways. In tunnel mode, the message and the original IP header are encrypted. Then a new IP header that addresses the destination's gateway is added. In contrast, in transport mode, only the message is encrypted, not the IP header.

The *IP Security (IPSec) protocol* provides a complete infrastructure for secured network communications. IPSec has gained widespread acceptance and is now offered in a number of commercial operating systems out of the box. IPSec relies upon security associations, and there are four main components:

- The *Authentication Header (AH)* provides assurances of message integrity and nonrepudiation. AH also provides authentication and access control and prevents replay attacks.

- The *Encapsulating Security Payload (ESP)* provides confidentiality and integrity of packet contents. It provides encryption and limited authentication and prevents replay attacks.

ESP also provides some limited authentication, but not to the degree of the AH. Though ESP is sometimes used without AH, it's rare to see AH used without ESP.

- The *IP Payload Compression (IPcomp) protocol* allows IPSec users to achieve enhanced performance by compressing packets prior to the encryption operation.

- The *Internet Key Exchange (IKE)* protocol provides for the secure exchange of cryptographic keys between IPSec participants. IKE establishes a shared security policy between communication partners and authenticates and/or produces keys for key-dependent services. All communication partners (e.g., router/firewall/host) must be identified before traffic is sent. This is accomplished through manual pre-shared keys or by a CA-controlled key distribution service (ISAKMP).

OAKLEY is a key establishment protocol that was proposed for IPsec but was superseded by IKE. OAKLEY is based on the Diffie-Hellman algorithm and designed to be a compatible component of ISAKMP.

IPSec provides for two discrete modes of operation. When IPSec is used in *transport mode,* only the packet payload is encrypted. This mode is designed for peer-to-peer communication. When it's used in *tunnel mode,* the entire packet, including the header, is encrypted. This mode is designed for gateway-to-gateway communication.

IPSec is an extremely important concept in modern computer security. Be certain that you're familiar with the four component protocols and the two modes of IPSec operation.

At runtime, you set up an IPSec session by creating a *security association (SA).* The SA represents the communication session and records any configuration and status information about the connection. The SA represents a simplex connection. If you want a two-way channel, you need two SAs, one for each direction. Also, if you want to support a bidirectional channel using both AH and ESP, you will need to set up four SAs. Some of IPSec's greatest strengths comes from being able to filter or manage communications on a per-SA basis so that clients or gateways between which security associations exist can be rigorously managed in terms of what kinds of protocols or services can use an IPSec connection. Also, without a valid security association defined, pairs of users or gateways cannot establish IPSec links.

Further details of the IPSec algorithm are provided in Chapter 3, "ISO Model, Network Security, and Protocols."

ISAKMP

The *Internet Security Association and Key Management Protocol (ISAKMP)* provides background security support services for IPSec by negotiating, establishing, modifying, and deleting security associations. As you learned in the previous section, IPSec relies upon a system of security associations (SAs). These SAs are managed through the use of ISAKMP. There are four basic requirements for ISAKMP, as set forth in Internet RFC 2408:

- Authenticate communicating peers.
- Create and manage security associations.
- Provide key generation mechanisms.
- Protect against threats (e.g., replay and denial of service attacks).

Wireless Networking

The widespread rapid adoption of wireless networks poses a tremendous security risk. Many traditional networks do not implement encryption for routine communications between hosts on the local network and rely upon the assumption that it would be too difficult for an attacker to gain physical access to the network wire inside a secure location to eavesdrop on the network. However, wireless networks transmit data through the air, leaving them extremely vulnerable to interception.

The security community responded with the introduction of *Wired Equivalent Privacy (WEP)*, which provides 40-, 64-, and 128-bit encryption options to protect communications within the wireless LAN. WEP is described in IEEE 802.11 as an optional component of the wireless networking standard. Unfortunately, there are several vulnerabilities in this protocol that make it a less than desirable choice for many security administrators.

WARNING   Remember that WEP is not an end-to-end security solution. It encrypts traffic only between a mobile computer and the nearest wireless access point. Once the traffic hits the wired network, it's in the clear again.

Another commonly used wireless security standard, IEEE 802.1x, provides a flexible framework for authentication and key management in wireless networks. It greatly reduces the burden inherent in changing WEP encryption keys manually and supports a number of diverse authentication techniques.

Wireless Application Protocol (WAP)

Unlike WEP, Wireless Application Protocol (WAP) is not used for 802.11 wireless networking. Instead, WAP is used by portable devices like cell phones and PDAs to support Internet connectivity via your telco or carrier provider. WAP is not a single protocol, but rather a suite of protocols:

- Wireless Markup Language (WML) and Script
- Wireless Application Environment (WAE)
- Wireless Transaction Protocol (WTP)
- Wireless Transport Layer Security Protocol (WTLS; provides three classes of security)
- Wireless Datagram Protocol (WDP)

Wireless Transport Layer Security Protocol (WTLS) provides the authentication mechanism for WAP. It is a wireless version of TLS, which is a derivative of SSL v.3.0. WTLS provides for three types of authentication:

- Class 1 (Anonymous authentication)
- Class 2 (Server authentication)
- Class 3 (Two-way client and server authentication)

The biggest problem with WAP is known as the "gap in wap." This means that WAP is used to protect data from the handheld device to the receiving station at the telco, but once on the telco's servers, data returns to its pre-WAP state (i.e., decrypted into plain text) before being reencoded or reencrypted into SSL for secured transmission from the telco's servers to the ultimate Internet-based destination. This temporary state of insecurity grants the telco (and other potential eavesdroppers) the ability to gain direct access to your data.

Cryptographic Attacks

As with any security mechanism, malicious individuals have found a number of attacks to defeat cryptosystems. It's important that you, as a security administrator, understand the threats posed by various cryptographic attacks to minimize the risks posed to your systems:

Analytic attack   This is an algebraic manipulation that attempts to reduce the complexity of the algorithm. *Analytic attacks* focus on the logic of the algorithm itself.

Implementation attack   This is a type of attack that exploits weaknesses in the implementation of a cryptography system. It focuses on exploiting the software code, not just errors and flaws but methodology employed to program the encryption system.

Statistical attack   A statistical attack exploits statistical weaknesses in a cryptosystem, such as inability to produce random numbers and floating point errors. *Statistical attacks* attempt to find a vulnerability in the hardware or operating system hosting the cryptography application.

Brute force   *Brute force attacks* are quite straightforward. Such an attack attempts every possible valid combination for a key or password. They involve using massive amounts of processing power to methodically guess the key used to secure cryptographic communications. For a non-flawed protocol, the average amount of time required to discover the key through a brute force attack is directly proportional to the length of the key. A brute force attack will always be successful given enough time. However, enough time is relative to the length of the key. For example, a computer that could brute force a DES 56-bit key in 1 second would take 149 trillion years to brute force an AES 128-bit key. Every additional bit of key length doubles the time to perform a brute force attack because the number of potential keys is doubled.

Known plaintext   In the *known plaintext attack*, the attacker has a copy of the encrypted message along with the plaintext message used to generate the ciphertext (the copy). This knowledge greatly assists the attacker in breaking weaker codes. For example, imagine the ease with which you could break the Caesar cipher described in Chapter 9 if you had both a plaintext and a ciphertext copy of the same message.

Chosen ciphertext   In a *chosen ciphertext attack*, the attacker has the ability to decrypt chosen portions of the ciphertext message and use the decrypted portion of the message to discover the key.

Chosen plaintext   In a *chosen plaintext attack*, the attacker has the ability to encrypt plaintext messages of their choosing and can then analyze the ciphertext output of the encryption algorithm.

Meet-in-the-middle   Attackers might use a *meet-in-the-middle attack* to defeat encryption algorithms that use two rounds of encryption. This attack is the reason that Double DES (2DES) was quickly discarded as a viable enhancement to the DES encryption in favor of Triple DES (3DES). In the meet-in-the-middle attack, the attacker uses a known plaintext message. The plaintext is then encrypted using every possible key (k1), while the equivalent ciphertext is decrypted using all possible keys (k2). When a match is found, the corresponding pair (k1, k2) represents both portions of the double encryption. This type of attack generally takes only double the time necessary to break a single round of encryption (or 2^n rather than the anticipated $2^n * 2^n$), offering minimal added protection.

Man-in-the-middle   In the *man-in-the-middle attack*, a malicious individual sits between two communicating parties and intercepts all communications (including the setup of the cryptographic session). The attacker responds to the originator's initialization requests and sets up a secure session with the originator. The attacker then establishes a second secure session with the intended recipient using a different key and posing as the originator. The attacker can then "sit in the middle" of the communication and read all traffic as it passes between the two parties.

 Be careful not to confuse the meet-in-the-middle attack with the man-in-the-middle attack. They sound very similar!

Birthday   The *birthday attack* (also known as a *collision attack* or *reverse hash matching* (see our discussion of brute force and dictionary attacks in Chapter 2)) seeks to find flaws in the one-to-one nature of hashing functions. In this attack, the malicious individual seeks to substitute in a digitally signed communication a different message that produces the same message digest, thereby maintaining the validity of the original digital signature.

Replay   The *replay attack* is used against cryptographic algorithms that don't incorporate temporal protections. In this attack, the malicious individual intercepts an encrypted message between two parties (often a request for authentication) and then later "replays" the captured message to open a new session. This attack can be defeated by incorporating a time stamp and expiration period into each message.

Summary

Public key encryption provides an extremely flexible infrastructure, facilitating simple, secure communication between parties that do not necessarily know each other prior to initiating the communication. It also provides the framework for the digital signing of messages to ensure nonrepudiation and message integrity. This chapter explored public key encryption, which is made possible by the *public key infrastructure (PKI)* hierarchy of trust relationships. We also described some popular cryptographic algorithms, such as *link encryption* and *end-to-end encryption*. Finally, we introduced you to the public key infrastructure, which uses certificate authorities (CAs) to generate digital certificates containing the public keys of system users and digital signatures, which rely upon a combination of public key cryptography and hashing functions.

We also looked at some of the common applications of cryptographic technology in solving everyday problems. You learned how cryptography can be used to secure electronic mail (using PGP, PEM, MOSS, and S/MIME), web communications (using SSL and S-HTTP), electronic commerce (using steganography and SET), and both peer-to-peer and gateway-to-gateway networking (using IPSec and ISAKMP) as well as wireless communications (using WEP).

Finally, we looked at some of the more common attacks used by malicious individuals attempting to interfere with or intercept encrypted communications between two parties. Such attacks include birthday, cryptanalytic, replay, brute force, known plaintext, chosen plaintext, chosen ciphertext, meet-in-the-middle, man-in-the-middle, and birthday attacks. It's important for you to understand these attacks in order to provide adequate security against them.

Exam Essentials

Understand the key types used in asymmetric cryptography.   Public keys are freely shared among communicating parties, whereas private keys are kept secret. To encrypt a message, use the recipient's public key. To decrypt a message, use your own private key. To sign a message, use your own private key. To validate a signature, use the sender's public key.

Be familiar with the three major public key cryptosystems.   RSA is the most famous public key cryptosystem; it was developed by Rivest, Shamir, and Adleman in 1977. It depends upon the difficulty of factoring the product of prime numbers. El Gamal is an extension of the Diffie-Hellman key exchange algorithm that depends upon modular arithmetic. The elliptic curve algorithm depends upon the elliptic curve discrete logarithm problem and provides more security than other algorithms when both are used with keys of the same length.

Know the fundamental requirements of a hash function.   Good hash functions have five requirements. They must allow input of any length, provide fixed-length output, make it relatively easy to compute the hash function for any input, provide one-way functionality, and be collision free.

Be familiar with the four major hashing algorithms.   The Secure Hash Algorithm (SHA) and its successor SHA-1 make up the government standard message digest function. SHA-1 produces a 160-bit message digest. MD2 is a hash function that is designed for 8-bit processors and provides a 16-byte hash. MD4 and MD5 both produce a 128-bit hash, but MD4 has proven vulnerabilities and is no longer accepted.

Understand how digital signatures are generated and verified.   To digitally sign a message, first use a hashing function to generate a message digest. Then encrypt the digest with your private key. To verify the digital signature on a message, decrypt the signature with the sender's public key and then compare the message digest to one you generate yourself. If they match, the message is authentic.

Know the components of the Digital Signature Standard (DSS).   The Digital Signature Standard uses the SHA-1 message digest function along with one of three encryption algorithms: the Digital Signature Algorithm (DSA), the Rivest, Shamir, Adleman (RSA) algorithm, or the Elliptic Curve DSA (ECDSA) algorithm.

Understand the public key infrastructure (PKI)   In the public key infrastructure, certificate authorities (CAs) generate digital certificates containing the public keys of system users. Users then distribute these certificates to people with whom they wish to communicate. Certificate recipients verify a certificate using the CA's public key.

Know the common applications of cryptography to secure electronic mail.   The emerging standard for encrypted messages is the S/MIME protocol. Other popular e-mail security protocols include Phil Zimmerman's Pretty Good Privacy (PGP), Privacy Enhanced Mail (PEM), and MIME Object Security Services (MOSS).

Know the common applications of cryptography to secure web activity.   The de facto standard for secure web traffic is the use of HTTP over Secure Sockets Layer (SSL), otherwise known as HTTPS. Secure HTTP (S-HTTP) also plays an important role in protecting individual messages. Most web browsers support both standards.

Know the common applications of cryptography to secure electronic commerce.   The Secure Electronic Transaction (SET) protocol was developed jointly by Visa and MasterCard to provide end-to-end security for electronic commerce transactions.

Know the common applications of cryptography to secure networking.   The IPSec protocol standard provides a common framework for encrypting network traffic and is built in to a number of common operating systems. In IPSec transport mode, packet contents are encrypted for peer-to-peer communication. In tunnel mode, the entire packet, including header information, is encrypted for gateway-to-gateway communications.

Describe IPSec.   IPSec is a security architecture framework that supports secure communication over IP. IPSec establishes a secure channel in either transport mode or tunnel mode. It can be used to establish direct communication between computers or to set up a VPN between networks. IPSec uses two protocols: Authentication Header (AH) and Encapsulating Security Payload (ESP).

Explain common cryptographic attacks   Brute force attacks are attempts to randomly find the correct cryptographic key. Known plaintext, chosen ciphertext, and chosen plaintext attacks require the attacker to have some extra information in addition to the ciphertext. The meet-in-the-middle attack exploits protocols that use two rounds of encryption. The man-in-the-middle attack fools both parties into communicating with the attacker instead of directly with each other. The birthday attack is an attempt to find collisions in hash functions. The replay attack is an attempt to reuse authentication requests.

Review Questions

1. In the RSA public key cryptosystem, which one of the following numbers will always be largest?

   A. e

   B. n

   C. p

   D. q

2. Which cryptographic algorithm forms the basis of the El Gamal cryptosystem?

   A. RSA

   B. Diffie-Hellman

   C. 3DES

   D. IDEA

3. If Richard wants to send an encrypted message to Sue using a public key cryptosystem, which key does he use to encrypt the message?

   A. Richard's public key

   B. Richard's private key

   C. Sue's public key

   D. Sue's private key

4. If a 2,048-bit plaintext message was encrypted with the El Gamal public key cryptosystem, how long would the resulting ciphertext message be?

   A. 1,024 bits

   B. 2,048 bits

   C. 4,096 bits

   D. 8,192 bits

5. Acme Widgets currently uses a 1,024-bit RSA encryption standard companywide. The company plans to convert from RSA to an elliptic curve cryptosystem. If it wishes to maintain the same cryptographic strength, what ECC key length should it use?

   A. 160 bits

   B. 512 bits

   C. 1,024 bits

   D. 2,048 bits

6. John would like to produce a message digest of a 2,048-byte message he plans to send to Mary. If he uses the SHA-1 hashing algorithm, what size will the message digest for this particular message be?

   A. 160 bits

   B. 512 bits

   C. 1,024 bits

   D. 2,048 bits

7. Which one of the following message digest algorithms is considered flawed and should no longer be used?

   A. SHA-1

   B. MD2

   C. MD4

   D. MD5

8. Which one of the following message digest algorithms is the current U.S. government standard in use by secure federal information processing systems?

   A. SHA-1

   B. MD2

   C. MD4

   D. MD5

9. Richard received an encrypted message sent to him from Sue. Which key should he use to decrypt the message?

   A. Richard's public key

   B. Richard's private key

   C. Sue's public key

   D. Sue's private key

10. Richard would like to digitally sign a message he's sending to Sue so that Sue can be sure the message came from him without modification while in transit. Which key should he use to encrypt the message digest?

   A. Richard's public key

   B. Richard's private key

   C. Sue's public key

   D. Sue's private key

11. Which one of the following algorithms is *not* supported by the Digital Signature Standard?

   A. Digital Signature Algorithm

   B. RSA

   C. El Gamal DSA

   D. Elliptic Curve DSA

12. Which International Telecommunications Union (ITU) standard governs the creation and endorsement of digital certificates for secure electronic communication?

    A. X.500

    B. X.509

    C. X.900

    D. X.905

13. What cryptosystem provides the encryption/decryption technology for the commercial version of Phil Zimmerman's Pretty Good Privacy secure e-mail system?

    A. DES/3DES

    B. IDEA

    C. ECC

    D. El Gamal

14. What TCP/IP communications port is utilized by Secure Sockets Layer traffic?

    A. 80

    B. 220

    C. 443

    D. 559

15. What type of cryptographic attack rendered Double DES (2DES) no more effective than standard DES encryption?

    A. Birthday

    B. Chosen ciphertext

    C. Meet-in-the-middle

    D. Man-in-the-middle

16. Which of the following security systems was created to support the use of stored-value payment cards?

    A. SET

    B. IPSec

    C. MONDEX

    D. PGP

17. Which of the following links would be protected by WEP encryption?

    A. Firewall to firewall

    B. Router to firewall

    C. Client to wireless access point

    D. Wireless access point to router

18. What is the major disadvantage of using certificate revocation lists?

   A. Key management

   B. Latency

   C. Record keeping

   D. Vulnerability to brute force attacks

19. Which one of the following encryption algorithms is now considered insecure?

   A. El Gamal

   B. RSA

   C. Skipjack

   D. Merkle-Hellman Knapsack

20. What does IPSec define?

   A. All possible security classifications for a specific configuration

   B. A framework for setting up a secure communication channel

   C. The valid transition states in the Biba model

   D. TCSEC security categories

Answers to Review Questions

1. B. The number n is generated as the product of the two large prime numbers p and q. Therefore, n must always be greater than both p and q. Furthermore, it is an algorithm constraint that e must be chosen such that e is smaller than n. Therefore, in RSA cryptography n is always the largest of the four variables shown in the options to this question.

2. B. The El Gamal cryptosystem extends the functionality of the Diffie-Hellman key exchange protocol to support the encryption and decryption of messages.

3. C. Richard must encrypt the message using Sue's public key so that Sue can decrypt it using her private key. If he encrypted the message with his own public key, the recipient would need to know Richard's private key to decrypt the message. If he encrypted it with his own private key, any user could decrypt the message using Richard's freely available public key. Richard could not encrypt the message using Sue's private key because he does not have access to it. If he did, any user could decrypt it using Sue's freely available public key.

4. C. The major disadvantage of the El Gamal cryptosystem is that it doubles the length of any message it encrypts. Therefore, a 2,048-bit plaintext message would yield a 4,096-bit ciphertext message when El Gamal is used for the encryption process.

5. A. The elliptic curve cryptosystem requires significantly shorter keys to achieve encryption that would be the same strength as encryption achieved with the RSA encryption algorithm. A 1,024-bit RSA key is cryptographically equivalent to a 160-bit elliptic curve cryptosystem key.

6. A. The SHA-1 hashing algorithm always produces a 160-bit message digest, regardless of the size of the input message. In fact, this fixed-length output is a requirement of any secure hashing algorithm.

7. C. The MD4 algorithm has documented flaws that produce collisions, rendering it useless as a hashing function for secure cryptographic applications.

8. A. SHA-1 is the current U.S. government standard, as defined in the Secure Hashing Standard (SHS), also known as Federal Information Processing Standard (FIPS) 180. Several newer algorithms (such as SHA-256, SHA-384, and SHA-512) are being considered to replace SHA-1 and make it cryptographically compatible with the stronger Advanced Encryption Standard.

9. B. Sue would have encrypted the message using Richard's public key. Therefore, Richard needs to use the complementary key in the key pair, his private key, to decrypt the message.

10. B. Richard should encrypt the message digest with his own private key. When Sue receives the message, she will decrypt the digest with Richard's public key and then compute the digest herself. If the two digests match, she can be assured that the message truly originated from Richard.

11. C. The Digital Signature Standard allows federal government use of the Digital Signature Algorithm, RSA, or the Elliptic Curve DSA in conjunction with the SHA-1 hashing function to produce secure digital signatures.

12. B. X.509 governs digital certificates and the public key infrastructure (PKI). It defines the appropriate content for a digital certificate and the processes used by certificate authorities to generate and revoke certificates.

13. B. Pretty Good Privacy uses a "web of trust" system of digital signature verification. The encryption technology is based upon the IDEA private key cryptosystem.

14. C. Secure Sockets Layer utilizes TCP port 443 for encrypted client/server communications.

15. C. The meet-in-the-middle attack demonstrated that it took relatively the same amount of computation power to defeat 2DES as it does to defeat standard DES. This led to the adoption of Triple DES (3DES) as a standard for government communication.

16. C. The MONDEX payment system, owned by MasterCard International, provides the cryptographic technology necessary to support stored-value payment cards.

17. C. The Wired Equivalent Privacy protocol encrypts traffic passing between a mobile client and the wireless access point. It does not provide end-to-end encryption.

18. B. Certificate revocation lists (CRLs) introduce an inherent latency to the certificate expiration process due to the time lag between CRL distributions.

19. D. The Merkle-Hellman Knapsack algorithm, which relies upon the difficulty of factoring superincreasing sets, has been broken by cryptanalysts.

20. B. IPSec is a security protocol that defines a framework for setting up a secure channel to exchange information between two entities.

Chapter

11

Principles of Computer Design

THE CISSP EXAM TOPICS COVERED IN THIS CHAPTER INCLUDE:

✓ **Principles of Common Computer and Network Organizations, Architectures, and Designs**

In previous chapters of this book, we've taken a look at basic security principles and the protective mechanisms put in place to prevent violation of them. We've also examined some of the specific types of attacks used by malicious individuals seeking to circumvent those protective mechanisms. Until this point, when discussing preventative measures we have focused on policy measures and the software that runs on a system. However, security professionals must also pay careful attention to the system itself and ensure that their higher-level protective controls are not built upon a shaky foundation. After all, the most secure firewall configuration in the world won't do a bit of good if the computer it runs on has a fundamental security flaw that allows malicious individuals to simply bypass the firewall completely.

In this chapter, we'll take a look at those underlying security concerns by conducting a brief survey of a field known as computer architecture: the physical design of computers from various components. We'll examine each of the major physical components of a computing system—hardware and firmware—looking at each from a security perspective. Obviously, the detailed analysis of a system's hardware components is not always a luxury available to you due to resource and time constraints. However, all security professionals should have at least a basic understanding of these concepts in case they encounter a security incident that reaches down to the system design level.

The federal government takes an active interest in the design and specification of the computer systems used to process classified national security information. Government security agencies have designed elaborate controls, such as the TEMPEST program used to protect against unwanted electromagnetic emanations and the Orange Book security levels that define acceptable parameters for secure systems.

This chapter also introduces two key concepts: security models and security modes, both of which tie into computer architectures and system designs. A security model defines basic approaches to security that sit at the core of any security policy implementation. Security models address such basic questions as: What basic entities or operations need security? What is a security principal? What is an access control list? Security models covered in this chapter include state machine, Bell-LaPadula, Biba, Clark-Wilson, information flow, noninterference, Take-Grant, access control matrix, and Brewer and Nash models.

Security modes represent ways in which systems can operate, depending on various elements such as the sensitivity or security classification of the data involved, the clearance level of the user involved, and the type of data operations requested. A security mode describes the conditions under which a system runs. Four such modes are recognized: dedicated security, system high security, compartmented security, and multilevel security modes, all covered in detail in this chapter.

The next chapter, "Principles of Security Models," examines how security models and security modes condition system behavior and capabilities and explores security controls and the criteria used to evaluate compliance with them.

Computer Architecture

Computer architecture is an engineering discipline concerned with the design and construction of computing systems at a logical level. Many college-level computer engineering and computer science programs find it difficult to cover all the basic principles of computer architecture in a single semester, so this material is often divided into two one-semester courses for undergraduates. Computer architecture courses delve into the design of central processing unit (CPU) components, memory devices, device communications, and similar topics at the bit level, defining processing paths for individual logic devices that make simple "0 or 1" decisions. Most security professionals do not need that level of knowledge, which is well beyond the scope of this book. However, if you will be involved in the security aspects of the design of computing systems at this level, you would be well advised to conduct a more thorough study of this field.

The more complex a system, the less assurance it provides. More complexity means more areas for vulnerabilities exist and more areas must be secured against threats. More vulnerabilities and more threats mean that the subsequent security provided by the system is less trustworthy.

Hardware

Any computing professional is familiar with the concept of hardware. As in the construction industry, hardware is the physical "stuff" that makes up a computer. The term *hardware* encompasses any tangible part of a computer that you can actually reach out and touch, from the keyboard and monitor to its CPU(s), storage media, and memory chips. Take careful note that although the physical portion of a storage device (such as a hard disk or SIMM) may be considered hardware, the contents of those devices—the collections of 0s and 1s that make up the software and data stored within them—may not. After all, you can't reach inside the computer and pull out a handful of bits and bytes!

Processor

The central processing unit (CPU), generally called the *processor,* is the computer's nerve center—it is the chip, or chips in a multiprocessor system, that governs all major operations and either directly performs or coordinates the complex symphony of calculations that allows a computer to perform its intended tasks. Surprisingly, the CPU is actually capable of performing only a limited set of computational and logical operations, despite the complexity of the tasks it allows the computer to perform. It is the responsibility of the operating system and compilers to translate high-level programming languages used to design software into simple assembly language instructions that a CPU understands. This limited range of functionality is intentional—it allows a CPU to perform computational and logical operations at blazing speeds, often measured in units known as MIPS (million instructions per second). To give you an idea of the magnitude of the progress in computing technology over the years, consider this: The original Intel 8086 processor introduced in 1978 operated at a rate of 0.33 MIPS (that's 330,000 calculations per second). A reasonably current 3.2GHz Pentium 4 processor introduced in 2003 operates at a blazing speed of 3,200 MIPS, or 3,200,000,000 calculations per second, almost 10,000 times as fast!

Execution Types

As computer processing power increased, users demanded more advanced features to enable these systems to process information at greater rates and to manage multiple functions simultaneously. Computer engineers devised several methods to meet these demands.

At first blush, the terms *multitasking, multiprocessing, multiprogramming,* and *multithreading* may seem nearly identical. However, they describe very different ways of approaching the "doing two things at once" problem. We strongly advise that you take the time to review the distinctions between these terms until you feel comfortable with them.

MULTITASKING

In computing, *multitasking* means handling two or more tasks simultaneously. In reality, most systems do not truly multitask; they rely upon the operating system to simulate multitasking by carefully structuring the sequence of commands sent to the CPU for execution. After all, when your processor is humming along at 3,200 MIPS, it's hard to tell that it's switching between tasks rather than actually working on two tasks at once.

MULTIPROCESSING

In a *multiprocessing* environment, a multiprocessor computing system (that is, one with more than one CPU) harnesses the power of more than one processor to complete the execution of a single application. For example, a database server might run on a system that contains three processors. If the database application receives a number of separate queries simultaneously, it might send each query to a separate processor for execution.

Two types of multiprocessing are most common in modern systems with multiple CPUs. The scenario just described, where a single computer contains more than one processor controlled by a single operating system, is called *symmetric multiprocessing (SMP)*. In SMP, processors share not only a common operating system, but also a common data bus and memory resources. In this type of arrangement, systems may use a large number of processors. Fortunately, this type of computing power is more than sufficient to drive most systems.

Some computationally intensive operations, such as those that support the research of scientists and mathematicians, require more processing power than a single operating system can deliver. Such operations may be best served by a technology known as *massively parallel processing (MPP)*. MPP systems house hundreds or even thousands of processors, each of which has its own operating system and memory/bus resources. When the software that coordinates the entire system's activities and schedules them for processing encounters a computationally intensive task, it assigns responsibility for the task to a single processor. This processor in turn breaks the task up into manageable parts and distributes them to other processors for execution.

Those processors return their results to the coordinating processor where they are assembled and returned to the requesting application. MPP systems are extremely powerful (not to mention extremely expensive!) and are the focus of a good deal of computing research.

Both types of multiprocessing provide unique advantages and are suitable for different types of situations. SMP systems are adept at processing simple operations at extremely high rates, whereas MPP systems are uniquely suited for processing very large, complex, computationally intensive tasks that lend themselves to decomposition and distribution into a number of subordinate parts.

MULTIPROGRAMMING

Multiprogramming is similar to multitasking. It involves the pseudo-simultaneous execution of two tasks on a single processor coordinated by the operating system as a way to increase operational efficiency. Multiprogramming is considered a relatively obsolete technology and is rarely found in use today except in legacy systems. There are two main differences between multiprogramming and multitasking:

- Multiprogramming usually takes place on large-scale systems, such as mainframes, whereas multitasking takes place on PC operating systems, such as Windows and Linux.

- Multitasking is normally coordinated by the operating system, whereas multiprogramming requires specially written software that coordinates its own activities and execution through the operating system.

MULTITHREADING

Multithreading permits multiple concurrent tasks to be performed within a single process. Unlike multitasking, where multiple tasks occupy multiple processes, multithreading permits multiple tasks to operate within a single process. Multithreading is often used in applications where frequent context switching between multiple active processes consumes excessive overhead and reduces efficiency. In multithreading, switching between threads incurs far less overhead and is therefore more efficient. In modern Windows implementations, for example, the overhead involved in switching from one thread to another within a single process is on the order of 40 to 50 instructions, with no substantial memory transfers needed. Whereas switching from one process to another involves 1,000 instructions or more and requires substantial memory transfers as well.

A good example of multithreading occurs when multiple documents are opened at the same time in a word processing program. In that situation, you do not actually run multiple instances of the word processor—this would place far too great a demand on the system. Instead, each document is treated as a single thread within a single word processor process, and the software chooses which thread it works on at any given moment.

Symmetric multiprocessing systems actually make use of threading at the operating system level. As in the word processing example just described, the operating system also contains a number of threads that control the tasks assigned to it. In a single-processor system, the OS sends one thread at a time to the processor for execution. SMP systems send one thread to each available processor for simultaneous execution.

Processing Types

Many high-security systems control the processing of information assigned to various security levels, such as the classification levels of unclassified, confidential, secret, and top secret the U.S. government assigns to information related to national defense. Computers must be designed so that they do not—ideally, so that they cannot—inadvertently disclose information to unauthorized recipients.

Computer architects and security policy administrators have attacked this problem at the processor level in two different ways. One is through a policy mechanism, whereas the other is through a hardware solution. The next two sections explore each of those options.

SINGLE STATE

Single state systems require the use of policy mechanisms to manage information at different levels. In this type of arrangement, security administrators approve a processor and system to handle only one security level at a time. For example, a system might be labeled to handle only secret information. All users of that system must then be approved to handle information at the secret level. This shifts the burden of protecting the information being processed on a system away from the hardware and operating system and onto the administrators who control access to the system.

MULTISTATE

Multistate systems are capable of implementing a much higher level of security. These systems are certified to handle multiple security levels simultaneously by using specialized security mechanisms such as those described in the next section "Protection Mechanisms." These mechanisms are designed to prevent information from crossing between security levels. One user might be using a multistate system to process secret information while another user is processing top secret information at the same time. Technical mechanisms prevent information from crossing between the two users and thereby crossing between security levels.

In actual practice, multistate systems are relatively uncommon owing to the expense of implementing the necessary technical mechanisms. This expense is sometimes justified; however, when dealing with a very expensive resource, such as a massively parallel system, the cost of obtaining multiple systems far exceeds the cost of implementing the additional security controls necessary to enable multistate operation on a single such system.

Protection Mechanisms

If a computer isn't running, it's an inert lump of plastic, silicon, and metal doing nothing. When a computer is running, it operates a runtime environment that represents the combination of the operating system and whatever applications may be active. When running, the computer also has the capability to access files and other data as the user's security permissions allow. Within that runtime environment it's necessary to integrate security information and controls to protect the integrity of the operating system itself, to manage which users are allowed to access specific data items, to authorize or deny operations requested against such data, and so forth. The ways in which running computers implement and handle security at runtime may be broadly described as a collection of protection mechanisms. In the following sections, we describe various protection mechanisms that include protection rings, operational states, and security modes.

Because the ways in which computers implement and use protection mechanisms are so important to maintaining and controlling security, you should
understand how all three mechanisms covered here—rings, operational states,
and security modes—are defined and how they behave. Don't be surprised to
see exam questions about specifics in all three areas, because this is such
important stuff!

PROTECTION RINGS

The ring protection scheme is an oldie but a goodie: it dates all the way back to work on the
Multics operating system. This experimental operating system was designed and built between
1963 and1969 with the collaboration of Bell Laboratories, MIT, and General Electric. Though
it did see commercial use in implementations from Honeywell, Multics has left two enduring
legacies in the computing world: one, it inspired the creation of a simpler, less intricate operating system called Unix (a play on the word *multics*), and two, it introduced the idea of protection rings to operating system design.

From a security standpoint, protection rings organize code and components in an operating
system (as well as applications, utilities, or other code that runs under the operating system's
control) into concentric rings, as shown in Figure 11.1. The deeper inside the circle you go, the
higher the privilege level associated with the code that occupies a specific ring. Though the original Multics implementation allowed up to seven rings (numbered 0 through 6), most modern
operating systems use a four-ring model (numbered 0 through 3).

As the innermost ring, 0 has the highest level of privilege and can basically access any resource,
file, or memory location. The part of an operating system that always remains resident in memory
(so that it can run on demand at any time) is called the *kernel*. It occupies ring 0 and can preempt
code running at any other ring. The remaining parts of the operating system—those that come and
go as various tasks are requested, operations performed, processes switched, and so forth—occupy
ring 1. Ring 2 is also somewhat privileged in that it's where I/O drivers and system utilities reside;
these are able to access peripheral devices, special files, and so forth that applications and other programs cannot themselves access directly. Those applications and programs occupy the outermost
ring, ring 3.

The essence of the ring model lies in priority, privilege, and memory segmentation. Any process that wishes to execute must get in line (a pending process queue). The process associated
with the lowest ring number always runs before processes associated with higher-numbered
rings. Processes in lower-numbered rings can access more resources and interact with the operating system more directly than those in higher-numbered rings. Those processes that run in
higher-numbered rings must generally ask a handler or a driver in a lower-numbered ring for
services they need; this is sometimes called a mediated-access model. In its strictest implementation, each ring has its own associated memory segment. Thus, any request from a process in
a higher-numbered ring for an address in a lower-numbered ring must call on a helper process
in the ring associated with that address. In practice, many modern operating systems break
memory into only two segments: one for system-level access (rings 0 through 2) and one for
user-level programs and applications (ring 3).

From a security standpoint, the ring model enables an operating system to protect and insulate itself from users and applications. It also permits the enforcement of strict boundaries between highly privileged operating system components (like the kernel) and less-privileged parts of the operating system (like other parts of the operating system, plus drivers and utilities). Within this model, direct access to specific resources is possible only within certain rings; likewise, certain operations (such as process switching, termination, scheduling) are only allowed within certain rings as well.

FIGURE 11.1   In the commonly used four-ring model, protection rings segregate the operating system into kernel, components, and drivers in rings 0–2 and applications and programs run at ring 3.

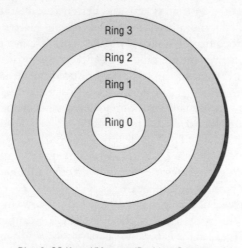

Ring 3

Ring 2

Ring 1

Ring 0

Ring 0: OS Kernel/Memory (Resident Components)
Ring 1: Other OS Components
Ring 2: Drivers, Protocols, etc.
Ring 3: User-Level Programs and Applications

Rings 0– 2 run in supervisory or privileged mode.
Ring 3 runs in user mode.

The ring that a process occupies, therefore, determine its access level to system resources (and determines what kinds of resources it must request from processes in lower-numbered, more-privileged rings). Processes may access objects directly only if they reside within their own ring or within some ring outside its current boundaries (in numerical terms, for example, this means a process at ring 1 can access its own resources directly, plus any associated with rings 2 and 3, but it can't access any resources associated only with ring 0). The mechanism whereby mediated access occurs—that is, the driver or handler request mentioned in a previous paragraph—is usually known as a *system call* and usually involves invocation of a specific system or programming interface designed to pass the request to an inner ring for service. Before any such request can be honored, however, the called ring must check to make sure that the calling process has the right credentials and authorization to access the data and to perform the operation(s) involved in satisfying the request.

PROCESS STATES

Also known as operating states, process states are various forms of execution in which a process may run. Where the operating system is concerned, it can be in one of two modes at any given moment: operating in a privileged, all-access mode known as *supervisor state* or operating in what's called the *problem state* associated with user mode, where privileges are low and all access requests must be checked against credentials for authorization before they are granted or denied. The latter is called the problem state not because problems are guaranteed to occur, but because the unprivileged nature of user access means that problems can occur and the system must take appropriate measures to protect security, integrity, and confidentiality.

Processes line up for execution in an operating system in a processing queue, where they will be scheduled to run as a processor becomes available. Because many operating systems allow processes to consume processor time only in fixed increments or chunks, when a new process is created, it enters the processing queue for the first time; should a process consume its entire chunk of processing time (called a *time slice*) without completing, it returns to the processing queue for another time slice the next time its turn comes around. Also, the process scheduler usually selects the highest-priority process for execution, so reaching the front of the line doesn't always guarantee access to the CPU (because a process may be preempted at the last instant by another process with higher priority).

According to whether a process is running or not, it can operate in one of several states:

Ready   In the *ready* state, a process is ready to resume or begin processing as soon as it is scheduled for execution. If the CPU is available when the process reaches this state, it will transition directly into the running state; otherwise, it sits in the ready state until its turn comes up. This means the process has all the memory and other resources it needs to begin executing immediately.

Waiting   *Waiting* can also be understood as "waiting for a resource"—that is, the process is ready for continued execution but is waiting for a device or access request (an interrupt of some kind) to be serviced before it can continue processing (for example, a database application that asks to read records from a file must wait for that file to be located and opened and for the right set of records to be found).

Running   The *running* process executes on the CPU and keeps going until it finishes, its time slice expires, or it blocks for some reason (usually because it's generated an interrupt for access to a device or the network and is waiting for that interrupt to be serviced). If the time slice ends and the process isn't completed, it returns to the ready state (and queue); if the process blocks while waiting for a resource to become available, it goes into the waiting state (and queue).

The running state is also often called the problem state. However, don't associate *problem* with *error*. Instead, think of the problem state as you would think of a math problem being solved to obtain the answer.

Supervisory   The *supervisory state* is used when the process must perform an action that requires greater than normal privileges, including modifying system configuration, installing device drivers, or modifying security settings.

Stopped   When a process finishes or must be terminated (because an error occurs, a required resource is not available, or a resource request can't be met), it goes into a *stopped* state. At this point, the operating system can recover all memory and other resources allocated to the process and reuse them for other processes as needed.

Figure 11.2 shows a diagram of how these various states relate to one another. New processes always transition into the ready state. From there, ready processes always transition into the running state. While running, a process can transition into the stopped state if it completes or is terminated, return to the ready state for another time slice, or transition to the waiting state until its pending resource request is met. When the operating system decides which process to run next, it checks the waiting queue and the ready queue and takes the highest-priority job that's ready to run (so that only waiting jobs whose pending requests have been serviced, or are ready to service, are eligible in this consideration). A special part of the kernel, called the program executive or the process scheduler, is always around (waiting in memory) so that when a process state transition must occur, it can step in and handle the mechanics involved.

FIGURE 11.2   The process scheduler

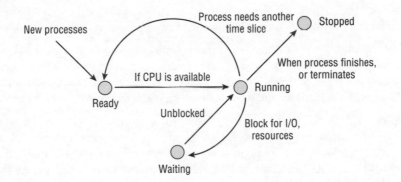

In Figure 11.2, the process scheduler manages the processes awaiting execution in the ready and waiting states and decides what happens to running processes when they transition into another state (ready, waiting, or stopped).

SECURITY MODES

The U.S. government has designated four approved security modes for systems that process classified information. These are described in the following sections. In Chapter 5, "Security Management Concepts and Principles," we reviewed the classification system used by the federal government and the concepts of security clearances and access approval. The only new term in this context is *need-to-know*, which refers to an access authorization scheme in which a subject's right to access an object takes into consideration not just a privilege level, but also the relevance of the data involved to the role the subject plays (or the job they perform). Need-to-know indicates that the subject requires access to the object to perform their job properly, or to fill some specific role. Those with no need-to-know may not access the object, no matter what level of privilege they hold. If you need a refresher on those concepts, please review them before proceeding.

Three specific elements must exist before the security modes themselves can be deployed:

- A hierarchical MAC environment
- Total physical control over which subjects can access the computer console
- Total physical control over which subjects can enter into the same room as the computer console

You will rarely, if ever, encounter the following modes outside of the world of government agencies and contractors. However, you may discover this terminology in other contexts, so you'd be well advised to commit the terms to memory.

DEDICATED MODE

Dedicated mode systems are essentially equivalent to the single state system described in the section "Processing Types" earlier in this chapter. There are three requirements for users of dedicated systems:

- Each user must have a security clearance that permits access to all information processed by the system.
- Each user must have access approval for all information processed by the system.
- Each user must have a valid need-to-know for all information processed by the system.

In the definitions of each of these modes, we use the phrase "all information processed by the system" for brevity. The official definition is more comprehensive and uses the phrase "all information processed, stored, transferred, or accessed."

SYSTEM HIGH MODE

System high mode systems have slightly different requirements that must be met by users:

- Each user must have a valid security clearance that permits access to all information processed by the system.
- Each user must have access approval for all information processed by the system.
- Each user must have a valid need-to-know for some information processed by the system.

Note that the major difference between the dedicated mode and the system high mode is that all users do not necessarily have a need-to-know for all information processed on a system high mode computing device.

COMPARTMENTED MODE

Compartmented mode systems weaken these requirements one step further:

- Each user must have a valid security clearance that permits access to all information processed by the system.
- Each user must have access approval for all information they will have access to on the system.
- Each user must have a valid need-to-know for all information they will have access to on the system.

Notice that the major difference between compartmented mode systems and system high mode systems is that users of a compartmented mode system do not necessarily have access approval for all of the information on the system. However, as with system high and dedicated systems, all users of the system must still have appropriate security clearances. In a special implementation of this mode called *compartmented mode workstations (CMWs)*, users with the necessary clearances can process multiple compartments of data at the same time.

CMWs require that two forms of security labels be placed on objects: sensitivity levels and information labels. Sensitivity levels describe the levels at which objects must be protected. These are common among all four of the modes. Information labels prevent data overclassification and associate additional information with the objects, which assists in proper and accurate data labeling not related to access control.

MULTILEVEL MODE

The government's definition of *multilevel mode* systems pretty much parallels the technical definition given in the previous section. However, for consistency, we'll express it in terms of clearance, access approval, and need-to-know:

- Some users do not have a valid security clearance for all information processed by the system. Thus access is controlled by whether the subject's clearance level dominates the object's sensitivity label.

- Each user must have access approval for all information they will have access to on the system.

- Each user must have a valid need-to-know for all information they will have access to on the system.

As you look through the requirements for the various modes of operation approved by the federal government, you'll notice that the administrative requirements for controlling the types of users that access a system decrease as we move from dedicated systems down to multilevel systems. However, this does not decrease the importance of limiting individual access so that users may obtain only information that they are legitimately entitled to access. As discussed in the previous section, it's simply a matter of shifting the burden of enforcing these requirements from administrative personnel—who physically limit access to a computer—to the hardware and software—which control what information can be accessed by each user of a multiuser system.

Multilevel security mode can also be called the controlled security mode.

Table 11.1 summarizes and compares these four security modes according to security clearances required, need-to-know, and the ability to process data from multiple clearance levels (abbreviated PDMCL). When comparing all four security modes, it is generally understood that the multilevel mode is exposed to the highest level of risk.

Operating Modes

Modern processors and operating systems are designed to support multiuser environments in which individual computer users might not be granted access to all components of a system or all of the information stored on it. For that reason, the processor itself supports two modes of operation, user mode and privileged mode. These two modes are discussed in the following sections.

TABLE 11.1 Comparing Security Modes

Mode	Clearance	Need-to-Know	PDMCL
Dedicated	Same	None	None
System-high	Same	Yes	None
Compartmented	Same	Yes	Yes
Multilevel	Different	Yes	Yes

Clearance is **Same** if all users must have the same security clearances, **Different** if otherwise.

Need-to-know is **None** if it does not apply and not used or if it is used but all users have the need to know all data present on the system, **Yes** if access is limited by need-to-know restrictions.

Applies if and when CMW implementations are used (**Yes**); otherwise, PDMCL is **None**.

USER

User mode is the basic mode used by the CPU when executing user applications. In this mode, the CPU allows the execution of only a portion of its full instruction set. This is designed to protect users from accidentally damaging the system through the execution of poorly designed code or the unintentional misuse of that code. It also protects the system and its data from a malicious user who might try to execute instructions designed to circumvent the security measures put in place by the operating system or who might mistakenly perform actions that could result in unauthorized access or damage to the system or valuable information assets.

Often processes within user mode are executed within a controlled environment called a virtual machine (VM) or a virtual subsystem machine. A virtual machine is a simulated environment created by the OS to provide a safe and efficient place for programs to execute. Each VM is isolated from all other VMs and each VM has its own assigned memory address space that can be used by the hosted application. It is the responsibility of the elements in privileged mode (a.k.a. kernel mode) to create and support the VMs and prevent the processes in one VM from interfering with the processes in other VMs.

PRIVILEGED

CPUs also support *privileged mode,* which is designed to give the operating system access to the full range of instructions supported by the CPU. This mode goes by a number of names, and the exact terminology varies according to the CPU manufacturer. Some of the more common monikers are included in the following list:

- Privileged mode
- Supervisory mode
- System mode
- Kernel mode

No matter which term you use, the basic concept remains the same—this mode grants a wide range of permissions to the process executing on the CPU. For this reason, well-designed operating systems do not let any user applications execute in privileged mode. Only those processes that are components of the operating system itself are allowed to execute in this mode, for both security and system integrity purposes.

> Don't confuse processor modes with any type of user access permissions. The fact that the high-level processor mode is sometimes called privileged or supervisory mode has no relationship to the role of a user. All user applications, including those of system administrators, run in user mode. When system administrators use system tools to make configuration changes to the system, those tools also run in user mode. When a user application needs to perform a privileged action, it passes that request to the operating system using a system call, which evaluates it and either rejects the request or approves it and executes it using a privileged mode process outside the user's control.

Memory

The second major hardware component of a system is *memory,* the storage bank for information that the computer needs to keep readily available. There are many different kinds of memory, each suitable for different purposes, and we'll take a look at each in the sections that follow.

Read-Only Memory (ROM)

Read-only memory (ROM) works like the name implies—it's memory the PC can read but can't change (no writing allowed). The contents of a standard ROM chip are burned in at the factory and the end user simply cannot alter it. ROM chips often contain "bootstrap" information that computers use to start up prior to loading an operating system from disk. This includes the familiar power-on self-test (POST) series of diagnostics that run each time you boot a PC.

ROM's primary advantage is that it can't be modified. There is no chance that user or administrator error will accidentally wipe out or modify the contents of such a chip. This attribute makes ROM extremely desirable for orchestrating a computer's innermost workings. There is a type of ROM that may be altered by administrators to some extent. It is known as programmable read-only memory (PROM) and comes in several subtypes, described in the following sections.

PROGRAMMABLE READ-ONLY MEMORY (PROM)

A basic *programmable read-only memory (PROM)* chip is very similar to a ROM chip in functionality, but with one exception. During the manufacturing process, a PROM chip's contents aren't "burned in" at the factory as with standard ROM chips. Instead, a PROM incorporates special functionality that allows an end user to burn in the chip's contents later on. However, the burning process has a similar outcome—once data is written to a PROM chip, no further changes are possible. After it's burned it, a PROM chip essentially functions like a ROM chip.

PROM chips provide software developers with an opportunity to store information permanently on a high-speed, customized memory chip. PROMs are commonly used for hardware applications where some custom functionality is necessary, but seldom changes once programmed.

ERASABLE PROGRAMMABLE READ-ONLY MEMORY (EPROM)

Combine the relatively high cost of PROM chips and software developers' inevitable desires to tinker with their code once it's written and you've got the rationale that led to the development of *erasable PROM (EPROM)*. These chips have a small window that, when illuminated with a special ultraviolet light, causes the contents of the chip to be erased. After this process is complete, end users can burn new information into the EPROM as if it had never been programmed before.

ELECTRONICALLY ERASABLE PROGRAMMABLE READ-ONLY MEMORY (EEPROM)

Although it's better than no erase function at all, EPROM erasure is pretty cumbersome. It requires physical removal of the chip from the computer and exposure to a special kind of ultraviolet light. A more flexible, friendly alternative is *electronically erasable PROM (EEPROM)*, which uses electric voltages delivered to the pins of the chip to force erasure. EEPROMs can be erased without removing them from the computer, which makes them much more attractive than standard PROM or EPROM chips.

One well-known type of EEPROM is the CompactFlash cards often used in modern computers, PDAs, MP3 players, and digital cameras to store files, data, music, and images. These cards can be erased without removing them from the devices that use them, but they retain information even when the device is not powered on.

Random Access Memory (RAM)

Random access memory (RAM) is readable and writeable memory that contains information a computer uses during processing. RAM retains its contents only when power is continuously supplied to it. Unlike with ROM, when a computer is powered off, all data stored in RAM disappears. For this reason, RAM is useful only for temporary storage. Any critical data should never be stored solely in RAM; a backup copy should always be kept on another storage device to prevent its disappearance in the event of a sudden loss of electrical power.

REAL MEMORY

Real memory (also known as main memory or primary memory) is typically the largest RAM storage resource available to a computer. It is normally composed of a number of dynamic RAM chips and, therefore, must be refreshed by the CPU on a periodic basis (see the sidebar "Dynamic vs. Static RAM" for more information on this subject).

CACHE RAM

Computer systems contain a number of caches that improve performance by taking data from slower devices and temporarily storing it in faster devices when repeated use is likely; this is called *cache RAM*. The processor normally contains an onboard cache of extremely fast memory used to hold data on which it will operate. This on-chip, or level 1 cache, is often backed up by a static RAM cache on a separate chip, called a level 2 cache, that holds data from the computer's main bank of real memory. Likewise, real memory often contains a cache of information stored on magnetic media. This chain continues down through the memory/storage hierarchy to enable computers to improve performance by keeping data that's likely to be used next closer at hand (be it for CPU instructions, data fetches, file access, or what have you).

Many peripherals also include onboard caches to reduce the storage burden they place on the CPU and operating system. For example, many higher-end printers include large RAM caches so that the operating system can quickly spool an entire job to the printer. After that, the processor can forget about the print job; it won't be forced to wait for the printer to actually produce the requested output, spoon-feeding it chunks of data one at a time. The printer can preprocess information from its onboard cache, thereby freeing the CPU and operating system to work on other tasks.

🌐 Real World Scenario

Dynamic vs. Static RAM

There are two main types of RAM: dynamic RAM and static RAM. Most computers contain a combination of both types and use them for different purposes.

To store data, dynamic RAM uses a series of capacitors, tiny electrical devices that hold a charge. These capacitors either hold a charge (representing a 1 bit in memory) or do not hold a charge (representing a 0 bit). However, because capacitors naturally lose their charges over time, the CPU must spend time refreshing the contents of dynamic RAM to ensure that 1 bits don't unintentionally change to 0 bits, thereby altering memory contents.

Static RAM uses more sophisticated technology—a logical device known as a flip-flop, which to all intents and purposes is simply an on/off switch that must be moved from one position to another to change a 0 to 1 or vice versa. More important, static memory maintains its contents unaltered so long as power is supplied and imposes no CPU overhead for periodic refresh operations.

That said, dynamic RAM is cheaper than static RAM because capacitors are cheaper than flip-flops. However, static RAM runs much faster than dynamic RAM. This creates a trade-off for system designers, who combine static and dynamic RAM modules to strike the right balance of cost versus performance.

Registers

The CPU also includes a limited amount of onboard memory, known as *registers,* that provide it with directly accessible memory locations that the brain of the CPU, the arithmetic-logical unit (or ALU), uses when performing calculations or processing instructions. In fact, any data that the ALU is to manipulate must be loaded into a register unless it is directly supplied as part of the instruction. The main advantage of this type of memory is that it is part of the ALU itself and, therefore, operates in lockstep with the CPU at typical CPU speeds.

Memory Addressing

When utilizing memory resources, the processor must have some means of referring to various locations in memory. The solution to this problem is known as *addressing*, and there are several different addressing schemes used in various circumstances. We'll look at five of the more common addressing schemes.

REGISTER ADDRESSING

As you learned in the previous section, registers are small memory locations directly in the CPU. When the CPU needs information from one of its registers to complete an operation, it uses a *register address* (e.g., "register 1") to access its contents.

IMMEDIATE ADDRESSING

Immediate addressing is not technically a memory addressing scheme per se, but rather a way of referring to data that is supplied to the CPU as part of an instruction. For example, the CPU might process the command "Add 2 to the value in register 1." This command uses two addressing schemes. The first is immediate addressing—the CPU is being told to add the value 2 and does not need to retrieve that value from a memory location—it's supplied as part of the command. The second is register addressing—it's instructed to retrieve the value from register 1.

DIRECT ADDRESSING

In *direct addressing,* the CPU is provided with an actual address of the memory location to access. The address must be located on the same *memory page* as the instruction being executed.

INDIRECT ADDRESSING

Indirect addressing uses a scheme similar to direct addressing. However, the memory address supplied to the CPU as part of the instruction doesn't contain the actual value that the CPU is to use as an operand. Instead, the memory address contains another memory address (perhaps located on a different page). The CPU reads the indirect address to learn the address where the desired data resides and then retrieves the actual operand from that address.

BASE+OFFSET ADDRESSING

Base+Offset addressing uses a value stored in one of the CPU's registers as the base location from which to begin counting. The CPU then adds the offset supplied with the instruction to that base address and retrieves the operand from that computed memory location.

Secondary Memory

Secondary memory is a term commonly used to refer to magnetic/optical media or other storage devices that contain data not immediately available to the CPU. For the CPU to access data in secondary memory, the data must first be read by the operating system and stored in real memory. However, secondary memory is much more inexpensive than primary memory and can be used to store massive amounts of information. In this context, hard disks, floppy drives, and optical media like CD-ROMs or DVDs can all function as secondary memory.

VIRTUAL MEMORY

Virtual memory is a special type of secondary memory that the operating system manages to make look and act just like real memory. The most common type of virtual memory is the pagefile that most operating systems manage as part of their memory management functions. This specially formatted file contains data previously stored in memory but not recently used. When the operating system needs to access addresses stored in the pagefile, it checks to see if the page is memory-resident (in which case it can access it immediately) or if it's been swapped to disk, in which case it reads the data from disk back into real memory (this process is called paging). Using virtual memory is an inexpensive way to make a computer operate as if it had more real memory than is physically installed. Its major drawback is that the paging operations that occur when data is exchanged between primary and secondary memory are relatively slow (memory functions in microseconds, disk systems in milliseconds; usually, this means four orders of magnitude difference!) and consume significant computer overhead, slowing down the entire system.

Memory Security Issues

Memory stores and processes your data—some of which may be extremely sensitive. It's essential that you understand the various types of memory and know how they store and retain data. Any memory devices that may retain data should be purged before they are allowed to leave your organization for any reason. This is especially true for secondary memory and ROM/PROM/EPROM/EEPROM devices designed to retain data even after the power is turned off.

However, memory data retention issues are not limited to those types of memory designed to retain data. Remember that static and dynamic RAM chips store data through the use of capacitors and flip-flops (see the sidebar "Dynamic vs. Static RAM"). It is technically possible that those electrical components could retain some of their charge for a limited period of time after power is turned off. A technically sophisticated individual could theoretically take electrical measurements of those components and retrieve small portions of the data stored on such devices. However, this requires a good deal of technical expertise and is not a likely threat unless you have entire governments as your adversary.

WARNING   The greatest security threat posed by RAM chips is a simple one. They are highly pilferable and are quite often stolen. After all, who checks to see how much memory is in their computer at the start of each day? Someone could easily remove a single memory module from each of a large number of systems and walk out the door with a small bag containing valuable chips. Today, this threat is diminishing as the price of memory chips continues to fall ($70 for 512MB DDR400 static RAM as we write).

One of the most important security issues surrounding memory is controlling who may access data stored in memory while a computer is in use. This is primarily the responsibility of the operating system and is the main memory security issue underlying the various processing modes described in previous sections in this chapter. In the section "Security Protection Mechanisms" later in this chapter, you'll learn how the principle of process isolation can be used to ensure that processes don't have access to read or write to memory spaces not allocated to them. If you're operating in a multilevel security environment, it's especially important to ensure that adequate protections are in place to prevent the unwanted leakage of memory contents between security levels, through either direct memory access or covert channels (a full discussion of covert channels appears in Chapter 12).

Storage

Data storage devices make up the third class of computer system components we'll discuss. These devices are used to store information that may be used by a computer any time after it's written. We'll first examine a few common terms that relate to storage devices and then look at some of the security issues related to data storage.

Primary vs. Secondary

The concepts of primary and secondary storage can be somewhat confusing, especially when compared to primary and secondary memory. There's an easy way to keep it straight—they're the same thing! *Primary memory,* also known as *primary storage,* is the RAM that a computer uses to keep necessary information readily available to the CPU while the computer is running. *Secondary memory* (or *secondary storage*) includes all the familiar long-term storage devices that you use every day. Secondary storage consists of magnetic and optical media such as hard drives, floppy disks, magnetic tapes, compact discs (CDs), digital video disks (DVDs), flash memory cards, and the like.

Volatile vs. Nonvolatile

You're already familiar with the concept of volatility from our discussion of memory, although you may not have heard it described using that term before. The volatility of a storage device is simply a measure of how likely it is to lose its data when power is turned off. Devices designed to retain their data (such as magnetic media) are classified as *nonvolatile,* whereas devices such as static or dynamic RAM modules, which are designed to lose their data, are classified as *volatile.* Recall from the discussion in the previous section that sophisticated technology may sometimes be able to extract data from volatile memory after power is removed, so the lines between the two may sometimes be blurry.

Random vs. Sequential

Storage devices may be accessed in one of two fashions. *Random access storage* devices allow an operating system to read (and sometimes write) immediately from any point within the device by using some type of addressing system. Almost all primary storage devices are random access devices. You can use a memory address to access information stored at any point within a RAM chip without reading the data that is physically stored before it. Most secondary storage devices are also random access. For example, hard drives use a movable head system that allows you to move directly to any point on the disk without spinning past all of the data stored on previous tracks; likewise, CD-ROM and DVD devices use an optical scanner that can position itself anywhere on the platter surface as well.

Sequential storage devices, on the other hand, do not provide this flexibility. They require that you read (or speed past) all of the data physically stored prior to the desired location. A common example of a sequential storage device is a magnetic tape drive. To provide access to data stored in the middle of a tape, the tape drive must physically scan through the entire tape (even if it's not necessarily processing the data that it passes in fast forward mode) until it reaches the desired point.

Obviously, sequential storage devices operate much slower than random access storage devices. However, here again you're faced with a cost/benefit decision. Many sequential storage devices can hold massive amounts of data on relatively inexpensive media. This property makes tape drives uniquely suited for backup tasks associated with a disaster recovery/business continuity plan (see Chapters 15 and 16 for more on Business Continuity Planning and Disaster

Recovery Planning). In a backup situation, you often have extremely large amounts of data that need to be stored and you infrequently need to access that stored information. The situation just begs for a sequential storage device!

Storage Media Security

We discussed the security problems that surround primary storage devices in the previous section. There are three main concerns when it comes to the security of secondary storage devices; all of them mirror concerns raised for primary storage devices:

- Data may remain on secondary storage devices even after it has been erased. This condition is known as data remanence. Most technically savvy computer users know that utilities are available that can retrieve files from a disk even after they have been deleted. It's also technically possible to retrieve data from a disk that has been reformatted. If you truly want to remove data from a secondary storage device, you must use a specialized utility designed to destroy all traces of data on the device or damage or destroy it beyond possible repair.

- Secondary storage devices are also prone to theft. Economic loss is not the major factor (after all, how much does a floppy disk cost?), but the loss of confidential information poses great risks. If someone copies your trade secrets onto a floppy disk and walks out the door with it, it's worth a lot more than the cost of the disk itself.

- Access to data stored on secondary storage devices is one of the most critical issues facing computer security professionals. For hard disks, data can often be protected through a combination of operating system access controls. Floppy disks and other removable media pose a greater challenge, so securing them often requires encryption technologies.

Input and Output Devices

Input and output devices are often seen as basic, primitive peripherals and usually don't receive much attention until they stop working properly. However, even these basic devices can present security risks to a system. Security professionals should be aware of these risks and ensure that appropriate controls are in place to mitigate them. The next four sections examine some of the risks posed by specific input and output devices.

Monitors

Monitors seem fairly innocuous. After all, they simply display the data presented by the operating system. When you turn them off, the data disappears from the screen and can't be recovered. However, a technology known as TEMPEST can compromise the security of data displayed on a monitor.

TEMPEST truly is an extremely interesting technology. If you'd like to learn more, there are a number of very good Web resources on TEMPEST protection and exploitation. A good starting point is the article "The Computer Spyware Uncle Sam Won't Let You Buy" posted on InfoWar.com at http://www.hackemate.com.ar/ezines/swat/swat26/Swt26-00.txt.

TEMPEST is a technology that allows the electronic emanations that every monitor produces (known as Van Eck radiation) to be read from a distance and even from another location. The technology is also used to protect against such activity. Various demonstrations have shown that you can easily read the screens of monitors inside an office building using gear housed in a van parked outside on the street. Unfortunately, the protective controls required to prevent Van Eck radiation (lots and lots of copper!) are expensive to implement and cumbersome to use.

Printers

Printers also may represent a security risk, albeit a simpler one. Depending upon the physical security controls used at your organization, it may be much easier to walk out with sensitive information in printed form than to walk out with a floppy disk or other magnetic media. Also, if printers are shared, users may forget to retrieve their sensitive printouts, leaving them vulnerable to prying eyes. These are all issues that are best addressed by an organization's security policy.

Keyboards/Mice

Keyboards, mice, and similar input devices are not immune from security vulnerabilities either. All of these devices are vulnerable to TEMPEST monitoring. Also, keyboards are vulnerable to less-sophisticated bugging. A simple device can be placed inside a keyboard to intercept all of the keystrokes that take place and transmit them to a remote receiver using a radio signal. This has the same effect as TEMPEST monitoring but can be done with much less-expensive gear.

Modems

Nowadays, modems are extremely cheap and most computer systems ship from manufacturers with a high-speed modem installed as part of the basic configuration. This is one of the greatest woes of a security administrator. Modems allow users to create uncontrolled access points into your network. In the worst case, if improperly configured, they can create extremely serious security vulnerabilities that allow an outsider to bypass all of your perimeter protection mechanisms and directly access your network resources. At best, they create an alternate egress channel that insiders can use to funnel data outside of your organization.

You should seriously consider an outright ban on modems in your organization's security policy unless they are truly needed for business reasons. In those cases, security officials should know the physical and logical locations of all modems on the network, ensure that they are correctly configured, and make certain that appropriate protective measures are in place to prevent their illegitimate use.

Input/Output Structures

Certain computer activities related to general input/output (I/O) operations, rather than individual devices, also have security implications. Some familiarity with manual input/output device configuration is required to integrate legacy peripheral devices (those that do not auto-configure or support Plug and Play, or PnP, setup) in modern PCs as well. Three types of operations that require manual configuration on legacy devices are involved here:

Memory-mapped I/O   For many kinds of devices, *memory-mapped I/O* is a technique used to manage input/output. That is, a part of the address space that the CPU manages functions to provide access to some kind of device through a series of mapped memory addresses or locations. Thus, by reading mapped memory locations, you're actually reading the input from the corresponding device (which is automatically copied to those memory locations at the system level when the device signals that input is available). Likewise, by writing to those mapped memory locations, you're actually sending output to that device (automatically handled by copying from those memory locations to the device at the system level when the CPU signals that the output is available). From a configuration standpoint, it's important to make sure that only one device maps into a specific memory address range and that the address range is used for no other purpose than to handle device I/O. From a security standpoint, access to mapped memory locations should be mediated by the operating system and subject to proper authorization and access controls.

Interrupt (IRQ)   *Interrupt (IRQ)* is an abbreviation for Interrupt ReQuest line, a technique for assigning specific signal lines to specific devices through a special interrupt controller. When a device wishes to supply input to the CPU, it sends a signal on its assigned IRQ (which usually falls in a range of 0–16 on older PCs for two cascaded 8-line interrupt controllers and 0–23 on newer ones with three cascaded 8-line interrupt controllers). Where newer PnP-compatible devices may actually share a single interrupt (IRQ number), older legacy devices must generally have exclusive use of a unique IRQ number (a well-known pathology called interrupt conflict occurs when two or more devices are assigned the same IRQ number and is best recognized by an inability to access all affected devices). From a configuration standpoint, finding unused IRQ numbers that will work with legacy devices can be a sometimes trying exercise. From a security standpoint, only the operating system should be able to mediate access to IRQs at a sufficiently high level of privilege to prevent tampering or accidental misconfiguration.

Direct Memory Access (DMA)   *Direct Memory Access (DMA)* works as a channel with two signal lines, where one line is a DMA request (DMQ) line, the other a DMA acknowledgment (DACK) line. Devices that can exchange data directly with real memory (RAM) without requiring assistance from the CPU use DMA to manage such access. Using its DRQ line, a device signals the CPU that it wants to make direct access (which may be read or write, or some combination of the two) to another device, usually real memory. The CPU authorizes access and then allows the access to proceed independently while blocking other access to the memory locations involved. When the access is complete, the device uses the DACK line to signal that the CPU may once again permit access to previously blocked memory locations. This is faster than requiring the CPU to mediate such access and permits the CPU to move on to other tasks while the memory access is underway. DMA is used most commonly to permit disk drives, optical drives, display cards, and multimedia cards to manage large-scale data transfers to and from real memory. From a configuration standpoint, it's important to manage DMA addresses to keep device addresses unique and to make sure such addresses are used only for DMA signaling. From a security standpoint, only the operating system should be able to mediate DMA assignment and use of DMA to access I/O devices.

If you understand common IRQ assignments, how memory-mapped I/O and DMA work, and related security concerns, you know enough to tackle the CISSP exam. If not, some additional reading may be warranted. In that case, PC Guide's excellent overview of system memory (`www.pcguide.com/ref/ram/`) should tell you everything you need to know.

Firmware

Firmware (also known as *microcode* in some circles) is a term used to describe software that is stored in a ROM chip. This type of software is changed infrequently (actually, never, if it's stored on a true ROM chip as opposed to an EPROM/EEPROM) and often drives the basic operation of a computing device.

BIOS

The *Basic Input/Output System (BIOS)* contains the operating-system independent primitive instructions that a computer needs to start up and load the operating system from disk. The BIOS is contained in a firmware device that is accessed immediately by the computer at boot time. In most computers, the BIOS is stored on an EEPROM chip to facilitate version updates. The process of updating the BIOS is known as "flashing the BIOS."

Device Firmware

Many hardware devices, such as printers and modems, also need some limited processing power to complete their tasks while minimizing the burden placed on the operating system itself. In many cases, these "mini" operating systems are entirely contained in firmware chips onboard the devices they serve. As with a computer's BIOS, device firmware is frequently stored on an EEPROM device so it can be updated as necessary.

Security Protection Mechanisms

The need for security mechanisms within an operating system is due to one simple fact: software is not trusted. Third-party software is untrustworthy, no matter who it comes from. The OS must employ protection mechanisms to keep the computing environment stable and to keep processes isolated from each other. Without these efforts, the security of data could never be reliable or even possible.

There are a number of common protection mechanisms that computer system designers should adhere to when designing secure systems. These principles are specific instances of more general security rules that govern safe computing practices. We'll divide our discussion into two areas: technical mechanisms and policy mechanisms.

Technical Mechanisms

Technical mechanisms are the controls that system designers can build right into their systems. We'll look at five: layering, abstraction, data hiding, process isolation, and hardware segmentation.

Layering

By *layering* processes, you implement a structure similar to the ring model used for operating modes (and discussed earlier in this chapter) and apply it to each operating system process. It puts the most-sensitive functions of a process at the core, surrounded by a series of increasingly larger concentric circles with correspondingly lower sensitivity levels (using a slightly different approach, this is also sometimes explained in terms of upper and lower layers, where security and privilege decrease when climbing up from lower to upper layers).

Communication between layers takes place only through the use of well-defined, specific interfaces to provide necessary security. All inbound requests from outer (less-sensitive) layers are subject to stringent authentication and authorization checks before they're allowed to proceed (or denied, if they fail such checks). As you'll understand more completely later in this chapter, using layering for security is similar to using security domains and lattice-based security models in that security and access controls over certain subjects and objects are associated with specific layers and privileges and access increase as one moves from outer to inner layers.

In fact, separate layers can only communicate with one another through specific interfaces designed to maintain a system's security and integrity. Even though less-secure outer layers depend on services and data from more-secure inner layers, they only know how to interface with those layers and are not privy to those inner layers' internal structure, characteristics, or other details. To maintain layer integrity, inner layers neither know about nor depend on outer layers. No matter what kind of security relationship may exist between any pair of layers, neither can tamper with the other (so that each layer is protected from tampering by any other layer). Finally, outer layers cannot violate or override any security policy enforced by an inner layer.

Abstraction

Abstraction is one of the fundamental principles behind the field known as object-oriented programming. It is the "black box" doctrine that says that users of an object (or operating system component) don't necessarily need to know the details of how the object works; they just need to know the proper syntax for using the object and the type of data that will be returned as a result. This is very much what's involved in mediated access to data or services, as when user mode applications use system calls to request administrator mode service or data (and where such requests may be granted or denied depending on the requester's credentials and permissions) rather than obtaining direct, unmediated access.

Another way in which abstraction applies to security is in the introduction of object groups, sometimes called classes, where access controls and operation rights are assigned to groups of objects rather than on a per-object basis. This approach allows security administrators to define and name groups easily (often related to job roles or responsibilities) and helps make administration of rights and privileges easier (adding an object to a class confers rights and privileges rather than having to manage rights and privileges for each individual object separately).

Data Hiding

Data hiding is an important characteristic in multilevel secure systems. It ensures that data existing at one level of security is not visible to processes running at different security levels. Chapter 7, "Data and Application Security Issues," covers a number of data hiding techniques used to prevent users from deducing even the very existence of a piece of information. The key concept behind data hiding is a desire to make sure those who have no need to know the details involved in accessing and processing data at one level have no way to learn or observe those details covertly or illicitly. From a security perspective, data hiding relies on placing objects in different security containers from those that subjects occupy so as to hide object details from those with no need to know about them.

Process Isolation

Process isolation requires that the operating system provide separate memory spaces for each process's instructions and data. It also requires that the operating system enforce those boundaries, preventing one process from reading or writing data that belongs to another process. There are two major advantages to using this technique:

- It prevents unauthorized data access. Process isolation is one of the fundamental requirements in a multilevel security mode system.

- It protects the integrity of processes. Without such controls, a poorly designed process could go haywire and write data to memory spaces allocated to other processes, causing the entire system to become unstable rather than only affecting execution of the errant process. In a more malicious vein, processes could attempt (and perhaps even succeed) at reading or writing to memory spaces outside their scopes, intruding upon or attacking other processes.

Many modern operating systems address the need for process isolation by implementing so-called *virtual machines* on a per-user or per-process basis. A virtual machine presents a user or process with a processing environment—including memory, address space, and other key system resources and services—that allows that user or process to behave as though they have sole, exclusive access to the entire computer. This allows each user or process to operate independently without requiring it to take cognizance of other users or processes that might actually be active simultaneously on the same machine. As part of the mediated access to the system that the operating system provides, it maps virtual resources and access in user mode so that they use supervisory mode calls to access corresponding real resources. This not only makes things easier for programmers, it also protects individual users and processes from one another.

Hardware Segmentation

Hardware segmentation is similar to process isolation in purpose—it prevents the access of information that belongs to a different process/security level. The main difference is that hardware segmentation enforces these requirements through the use of physical hardware controls rather than the logical process isolation controls imposed by an operating system. Such implementations are rare, and they are generally restricted to national security implementations where the extra cost and complexity is offset by the sensitivity of the information involved and the risks inherent in unauthorized access or disclosure.

Security Policy and Computer Architecture

Just as security policy guides the day-to-day security operations, processes, and procedures in organizations, it has an important role to play when designing and implementing systems. This is equally true whether a system is entirely hardware based, entirely software based, or a combination of both. In this case, the role of a security policy is to inform and guide the design, development, implementation, testing, and maintenance of some particular system. Thus, this kind of security policy tightly targets a single implementation effort (though it may be adapted from other, similar efforts, it should reflect the target as accurately and completely as possible).

For system developers, a security policy is best encountered in the form of a document that defines a set of rules, practices, and procedures that describe how the system should manage, protect, and distribute sensitive information. Security policies that prevent information flow from higher security levels to lower security levels are called multilevel security policies. As a system is developed, the security policy should be designed, built, implemented, and tested as it relates to all applicable system components or elements, including any or all of the following: physical hardware components, firmware, software, and how the organization interacts with and uses the system.

Policy Mechanisms

As with any security program, policy mechanisms should also be put into place. These mechanisms are extensions of basic computer security doctrine, but the applications described in this section are specific to the field of computer architecture and design.

Principle of Least Privilege

In Chapter 1, "Accountability and Access Control," you learned about the general security *principle of least privilege* and how it applies to users of computing systems. This principle is also very important to the design of computers and operating systems, especially when applied to system modes. When designing operating system processes, you should always ensure that they run in user mode whenever possible. The greater the number of processes that execute in privileged mode, the higher the number of potential vulnerabilities that a malicious individual could exploit to gain supervisory access to the system. In general, it's better to use APIs to ask for supervisory mode services or to pass control to trusted, well-protected supervisory mode processes as they're needed from within user mode applications than it is to elevate such programs or processes to supervisory mode altogether.

Separation of Privilege

The principle of *separation of privilege* builds upon the principle of least privilege. It requires the use of granular access permissions; that is, different permissions for each type of privileged operation. This allows designers to assign some processes rights to perform certain supervisory functions without granting them unrestricted access to the system. It also allows individual requests for services or access to resources to be inspected, checked against access controls, and granted or denied based on the identity of the user making the requests or on the basis of groups to which the user belongs or security roles that the user occupies.

Accountability

Accountability is an essential component in any security design. Many high-security systems contain physical devices (such as pen registers and non-modifiable audit trails) that enforce individual accountability for privileged functionality. In general, however, such capability relies on a system's ability to monitor activity on and interactions with a system's resources and configuration data and to protect resulting logs from unwanted access or alteration so that they provide an accurate and reliable record of activity and interaction that documents every user's (including administrators or other trusted individuals with high levels of privilege) history on that system.

Distributed Architecture

As computing has evolved from a host/terminal model, where users could be physically distributed but all functions, activity, data, and resources resided on a single centralized system, to a client/server model, where users operate independent fully functional desktop computers but also access services and resources on networked servers, security controls and concept have had to evolve to follow suit. This means that clients have computing and storage capabilities and, typically, that multiple servers do likewise. Thus, security must be addressed everywhere instead of at a single centralized host. From a security standpoint, this means that, because processing and storage are distributed on multiple clients and servers, all those computers must be properly secured and protected. It also means that the network links between clients and servers (and in some cases, these links may not be purely local) must also be secured and protected.

Vulnerabilities

Distributed architectures are prone to vulnerabilities unthinkable in monolithic host/terminal systems. Desktop systems can contain sensitive information that may be at some risk of being exposed and must therefore be protected. Individual users may lack general security savvy or awareness, and therefore the underlying architecture has to compensate for those lacks. Desktop PCs, workstations, and laptops can provide avenues of access into critical information systems elsewhere in a distributed environment because users require access to networked servers and services to do their jobs. By permitting user machines to access a network and its distributed resources, organizations must also recognize that those user machines can become threats if they are misused or compromised.

Communications equipment can also provide unwanted points of entry into a distributed environment. For example, modems attached to a desktop machine that's also attached to an organization's network can make that network vulnerable to dial-in attack. Likewise, users who download data from the Internet increase the risk of infecting their own and other systems with malicious code, Trojan horses, and so forth. Desktops, laptops, and workstations—and associated disks or other storage devices—may not be secure from physical intrusion or theft. Finally, when data resides only on client machines, it may not be secured with a proper backup (it's often the case that while servers are backed up routinely, the same is not true for client computers).

Safeguards

Hopefully the foregoing litany of potential vulnerabilities in distributed architectures argues strongly that such environments require numerous safeguards to implement appropriate security and to ensure that such vulnerabilities are eliminated, mitigated, or remedied. Clients must be subjected to policies that impose safeguards on their contents and their users' activities. These include the following:

- E-mail must be screened so that it cannot become a vector for infection by malicious software; e-mail should also be subject to policies that govern appropriate use and limit potential liability.

- Download/upload policies must be created so that incoming and outgoing data is screened and suspect materials blocked.

- Systems must be subject to robust access controls, which may include multifactor authentication and/or biometrics to restrict access to desktops and to prevent unauthorized access to servers and services.

- Graphical user interface mechanisms and database management systems should be installed, and their use required, to restrict and manage access to critical information.

- File encryption may be appropriate for files and data stored on client machines (indeed, drive-level encryption is a good idea for laptops and other mobile computing gear that is subject to loss or theft outside an organization's premises).

- It's essential to separate and isolate processes that run in user and supervisory mode so that unauthorized and unwanted access to high-privilege processes and capabilities is prevented.

- Protection domains should be created so that compromise of a client won't automatically compromise an entire network.

- Disks and other sensitive materials should be clearly labeled as to their security classification or organizational sensitivity; procedural processes and system controls should combine to help protect sensitive materials from unwanted or unauthorized access.

- Files on desktop machines should be backed up, as well as files on servers—ideally, using some form of centralized backup utility that works with client agent software to identify and capture files from clients stored in a secure backup storage archive.

- Desktop users need regular security awareness training to maintain proper security awareness; they also need to be notified about potential threats and instructed on how to deal with them appropriately.

- Desktop computers and their storage media require protection against environmental hazards (temperature, humidity, power loss/fluctuation, and so forth).

- Desktop computers should be included in disaster recovery and business continuity planning because they're potentially as important (if not more important) to getting their users back to work as other systems and services within an organization.

- Developers of custom software built in and for distributed environments also need to take security into account, including use of formal methods for development and deployment, such as code libraries, change control mechanisms, configuration management, and patch and update deployment.

In general, safeguarding distributed environments means understanding the vulnerabilities to which they're subject and applying appropriate safeguards. These can (and do) range from technology solutions and controls to policies and procedures that manage risk and seek to limit or avoid losses, damage, unwanted disclosure, and so on.

Security Models

In information security, models provide a way to formalize security policies. Such models can be abstract or intuitive (some are decidedly mathematical), but all are intended to provide an explicit set of rules that a computer can follow to implement the fundamental security concepts, processes, and procedures that make up a security policy. These models offer a way to deepen your understanding of how a computer operating system should be designed and developed to support a specific security policy. You'll explore nine security models in the following sections; all of them can shed light on how security enters into computer architectures and operating system design:

- State machine model
- Information flow model
- Noninterference model
- Take-Grant model
- Access control matrix
- Bell-LaPadula
- Biba
- Clark-Wilson
- Brewer and Nash model (a.k.a. Chinese Wall)

While it is understood that no system can be totally secure, it is possible to design and build reasonably secure systems. In fact, if a secured system complies with a specific set of security criteria, it can be said to exhibit a level of trust. Therefore, trust can be built into a system and then evaluated, certified, and accredited. In the remainder of this chapter and into Chapter 12, "Principles of Security Models," this flow of thought will be followed through from design to final accreditation.

State Machine Model

The *state machine model* describes a system that is always secure no matter what state it is in. It's based on the computer science definition of a finite state machine (FSM). An FSM combines an external input with an internal machine state to model all kinds of complex systems, including parsers, decoders, and interpreters. Given an input and a state, an FSM transitions to another state and may create an output. Mathematically, the next state is a function of the current state and the input next state = G(input, current state). Likewise, the output is also a function of the input and the current state output = F(input, current state).

Many security models are based on the secure state concept. According to the state machine model, a *state* is a snapshot of a system at a specific moment in time. If all aspects of a state meet the requirements of the security policy, that state is considered secure. A transition occurs when accepting input or producing output. A transition always results in a new state (also called a state transition). All state transitions must be evaluated. If each possible state transitions results in another secure state, the system can be called a secure state machine. A secure state machine model system always boots into a secure state, maintains a secure state across all transitions, and allows subjects to access resources only in a secure manner compliant with the security policy. The secure state machine model is the basis for many other security models.

Information Flow Model

The *information flow model* focuses on the flow of information. Information flow models are based on a state machine model. The Bell-LaPaduss and Biba models, which we will discuss in detail in a moment, are both information flow models. Bell-LaPadula is concerned with preventing information from flowing from a high security level to a low security level. Biba is concerned with preventing information from flowing from a low security level to a high security level. Information flow models don't necessarily deal with only the direction of information flow; they can also address the type of flow.

Information flow models are designed to prevent unauthorized, insecure, or restricted information flow. Information flow can be between subjects and objects at the same classification level as well as between subjects and objects at different classification levels. An information flow model allows all authorized information flows, whether within the same classification level or between classification levels. It prevents all unauthorized information flows, whether within the same classification level or between classification levels.

Another interesting perspective on the information flow model is that it is used to establish a relationship between two versions or states of the same object when those two versions or states exist at different points in time. Thus, information flow dictates the transformation of an object from one state at one point in time to another state at another point in time.

Noninterference Model

The *noninterference model* is loosely based on the information flow model. However, instead of being concerned about the flow of information, the noninterference model is concerned with how the actions of a subject at a higher security level affect the system state or actions of a subject at a lower security level. Basically, the actions of subject A (high) should not affect the actions of subject B (low) or even be noticed by subject B. The real concern is to prevent the actions of subject A at a high level of security classification from affecting the system state at a lower level. If this occurs, subject B may be placed into an insecure state or be able to deduce or infer information about a higher level of classification. This is a type of information leakage and implicitly creates a covert channel. Thus, the noninterference model can be imposed to provide a form of protection against damage caused by malicious programs such as Trojan horses.

Take-Grant Model

The *Take-Grant model* employs a directed graph to dictate how rights can be passed from one subject to another or from a subject to an object. Simply put, a subject with the grant right can grant another subject or another object any other right they possess. Likewise, a subject with the take right can take a right from another subject.

Access Control Matrix

An access control matrix is a table of subjects and objects that indicates the actions or functions that each subject can perform on each object. Each column of the matrix is an ACL. Each row of the matrix is a *capability list*. An ACL is tied to the object; it lists valid actions each subject can perform. A capability list is tied to the subject; it lists valid actions that can be taken on each object. From an administration perspective, using only capability lists for access control is a management nightmare. A capability list method of access control can be accomplished by storing on each subject a list of rights the subject has for every object. This effectively gives each user a key ring of accesses and rights to objects within the security domain. To remove access to a particular object, every user (subject) that has access to it must be individually manipulated. Thus, managing access on each user account is much more difficult than managing access on each object (i.e., via ACLs).

Implementing an access control matrix model usually involves constructing an environment that can create and manage lists of subjects and objects and a function that can return the type associated with whatever object is supplied to that function as input (this is important because an object's type determines what kinds of operations may be applied to it).

The access control matrix shown in Table 11.2 is for a discretionary access control system. A mandatory or rule-based matrix can be constructed simply by replacing the subject names with classifications or roles. Access control matrixes are used by systems to quickly determine whether the requested action by a subject for an object is authorized.

TABLE 11.2   An Access Control Matrix

	Objects (Categorized by Type)		
Subjects	**Document File**	**Printer**	**Network Folder Share**
Bob	Read	No Access	No Access
Mary	No Access	No Access	Read
Amanda	Read, Write	Print	No Access
Mark	Read, Write	Print	Read, Write
Kathryn	Read, Write	Print, Manage Print Queue	Read, Write, Execute
Colin	Read, Write, Change Permissions	Print, Manage Print Queue, Change Permissions	Read, Write, Execute, Change Permissions

Bell-LaPadula Model

The *Bell-LaPadula model* was developed out of the U.S. Department of Defense (DoD) multilevel security policy. The DoD's policy includes four levels of classification, from most sensitive to least: top secret, secret, confidential, and unclassified. The policy states that a subject with any level of clearance can access resources at or below its clearance level. However, within the clearances of confidential, secret, and top secret, access is granted only on a need-to-know basis. In other words, access to a specific object is granted to the classified levels only if a specific work task requires such access. With these restrictions, the Bell-LaPadula model is focused on maintaining the confidentiality of objects. Bell-LaPadula does not address the aspects of integrity or availability for objects. Bell-LaPadula is the first mathematical model of a multilevel security policy.

By design, the Bell-LaPadula model prevents the leaking or transfer of classified information to less-secure clearance levels. This is accomplished by blocking lower-classified subjects from accessing higher-classified objects.

In its conception, the Bell-LaPadula model is based on the state machine model and information flow model. It also employs mandatory access controls and the lattice model. The lattice tiers are the *classification levels* used by the security policy of the organization. In this model, secure states are circumscribed by two rules, or properties:

Simple Security Property   The *Simple Security Property (SS Property)* states that a subject at a specific classification level cannot read data with a higher classification level. This is often shortened to "no read up."

* Security Property   The ** (star) Security Property (* Property), also known as the confinement property,* states that a subject at a specific classification level cannot write data to a lower classification level. This is often shortened to "no write down."

These two rules define the states into which the system can transition. No other transitions are allowed. All states accessible through these two rules are secure states. Thus, Bell-LaPadula–modeled systems offer state machine model security (see Figure 11.3).

FIGURE 11.3   The Bell-LaPadula model

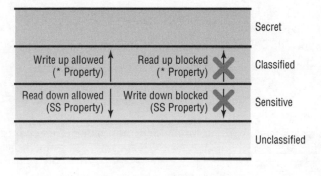

Secret

Write up allowed (* Property)   Read up blocked (* Property)   Classified

Read down allowed (SS Property)   Write down blocked (SS Property)   Sensitive

Unclassified

Real World Scenario

Lattice-Based Access Control

This general category for nondiscretionary access controls was introduced in Chapter 1. Here's a quick refresher on the subject (which drives the underpinnings for most access control security models): Subjects under lattice-based access controls are assigned positions in a lattice. These positions fall between defined security labels or classifications. Subjects can access only objects that fall into the range between the least upper bound (the nearest security label or classification higher than their lattice position) and the highest lower bound (the nearest security label or classification lower than their lattice position) of the labels or classifications for their lattice position. Thus, a subject that falls between the private and sensitive labels in a commercial scheme that reads bottom up as public, sensitive, private, proprietary, and confidential can access only private and sensitive data but not public, proprietary, or confidential data. See Figure 1.3 for an illustration. Lattice-based access controls also fit into the general category of information flow models and deal primarily with confidentiality (hence the connection to Bell-LaPadula).

There is an exception in the Bell-LaPadula model that states that a "trusted subject" is not constrained by the * Property. A trusted subject is defined as "a subject that is guaranteed not to consummate a security-breaching information transfer even if it is possible." This means that a trusted subject is allowed to violate the * Property and perform a write down.

The Bell-LaPadula efficiently manages confidentiality, but it fails to address or manage numerous other important issues:

- It does not address integrity or availability.

- It does not address access control management, nor does it provide a way to assign or change an object's or subject's classification level.

- It does not prevent covert channels. *Covert channels,* discussed in Chapter 12, "Principles of Security Models," are means by which data can be communicated outside of normal, expected, or detectable methods.

- It does not address file sharing (a common feature on networked systems).

Biba

For many nonmilitary organizations, integrity is more important than confidentiality. Out of this need, several integrity-focused security models were developed, such those developed by Biba and Clark-Wilson.

The *Biba model* was derived as a direct analogue to the Bell-LaPadula model. Biba is also based on the state machine model and the information flow model. Biba is likewise based on a classification lattice with mandatory access controls. Biba was designed to address three integrity issues:

- Prevent modification of objects by unauthorized subjects.

- Prevent unauthorized modification of objects by authorized subjects.

- Protect internal and external object consistency.

As with Bell-LaPadula, Biba requires that all subjects and objects have a classification label. Thus, data integrity protection is dependent upon data classification.

Biba has two integrity axioms:

Simple Integrity Axiom   The *Simple Integrity Axiom (SI Axiom)* states that a subject at a specific classification level cannot read data with a lower classification level. This is often shortened to "no read down."

* Integrity Axiom   The ** (star) Integrity Axiom (* Axiom)* states that a subject at a specific classification level cannot write data to a higher classification level. This is often shortened to "no write up."

These Biba model axioms are illustrated in Figure 11.4.

Critiques of the Biba model mention a few drawbacks:

- It only addresses integrity, not confidentiality or availability.

- It focuses on protecting objects from external threats; it assumes that internal threats are handled programmatically.

- It does not address access control management, nor does it provide a way to assign or change an object's or subject's classification level.

- It does not prevent covert channels (see Chapter 12).

FIGURE 11.4   The Biba model

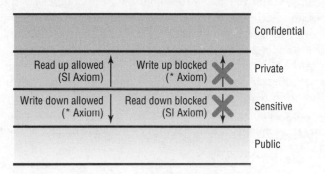

Confidential

Read up allowed (SI Axiom)   Write up blocked (* Axiom)   Private

Write down allowed (* Axiom)   Read down blocked (SI Axiom)   Sensitive

Public

Clark-Wilson

The *Clark-Wilson model* is also an integrity-protecting model. The Clark-Wilson model was developed after Biba and approaches integrity protection from a different perspective. Rather than employing a lattice structure, it uses a three-part relationship of subject/program/object (or subject/transaction/object) known as a triple or an access control triple. Subjects do not have direct access to objects. Objects can be accessed only through programs. Through the use of two principles—well-formed transactions and separation of duties—the Clark-Wilson model provides an effective means to protect integrity.

Well-formed transactions take the form of programs. A subject is able to access objects only by using a program. Each program has specific limitations on what it can and cannot do to an object. This effectively limits the subject's capabilities. If the programs are properly designed, then the triple relationship provides a means to protect the integrity of the object.

Separation of duties takes the form of dividing critical functions into two or more parts. A different subject must complete each part. This prevents authorized subjects from making unauthorized modifications to objects. This further protects the integrity of the object.

In addition to these two principles, auditing is required. Auditing tracks changes and access to objects as well as inputs from outside the system.

The Clark-Wilson model can also be called a *restricted interface model*. A restricted interface model uses classification-based restrictions to offer only subject-specific authorized information and functions. One subject at one classification level will see one set of data and have access to one set of functions, whereas another subject at a different classification level will see a different set of data and have access to a different set of functions.

Brewer and Nash Model (a.k.a. Chinese Wall)

This model was created to permit access controls to change dynamically based on a user's previous activity (making it a kind of state machine model as well). This model applies to a single integrated database; it seeks to create security domains that are sensitive to the notion of conflict of interest (for example, someone who works at Company C who has access to proprietary data for Company A should not also be allowed access to similar data for Company B if those two companies compete with one another). This model is known as the Chinese wall because it creates a class of data that defines which security domains are potentially in conflict and prevents any subject with access to one domain that belongs to a specific conflict class from accessing any other domain that belongs to the same conflict class. Metaphorically, this puts a wall around all other information in any conflict class and explains the terminology. Thus, this model also uses the principle of data isolation within each conflict class to keep users out of potential conflict-of-interest situations (e.g., management of company datasets). Because company relationships change all the time, this explains the importance of dynamic update to members of and definitions for conflict classes.

Classifying and Comparing Models

Careful reading of the preceding sections on access control models will reveal that they fall into three broad categories, as follows:

Information flow   Information flow models deal with how information moves or how changes at one security level affect other security levels. They include the information flow and noninterference models and composition theories.

Integrity   Because integrity models are concerned with how information moves from one level to another, they are a special type of information flow models. That is, they enforce security by enforcing integrity constraints. Two examples of integrity models are the Biba and Clark-Wilson models. To maintain integrity, the goals are to establish and maintain internal and external consistency, to prevent authorized users from making improper or illegal modifications, and to block unauthorized users from making any modifications whatsoever. Whereas Clark-Wilson delivers on all three goals, Biba only blocks unauthorized users from making modifications. This explains why Clark-Wilson is used far more frequently than Biba in real-world applications.

Access control   Access control models attempt to enforce security using formal access controls, which determine whether or not subjects can access objects they request. They include the state machine, access matrix, Take-Grant, Bell-LaPadula, and Brewer and Nash models.

When it comes to anticipating questions and coverage of the various models mentioned, the following items recur repeatedly in all of the practice exams we reviewed for this chapter:

- Biba and Clark-Wilson versus Bell-LaPadula: Biba or Clark-Wilson is used to enforce integrity, Bell-LaPadula to enforce confidentiality. Biba uses integrity levels and Clark-Wilson uses access triples where subjects must use programs to access objects (all subject to integrity constraints), whereas Bell-LaPadula uses security levels. Because Bell-LaPadula focuses on confidentiality, it's most often used in military applications; likewise, because Biba and Clark-Wilson focus on integrity, they're most often used in commercial applications.

- Of all security models, Bell-LaPadula and Biba are best known.

- Of all security models, Bell-LaPadula is used most often in military applications, Clark-Wilson in commercial ones.

- Bell-LaPadula defines access permissions using an access control matrix.

- Access control models provide a formal description of a security policy (one that's designed to make sense to a computer, in fact).

- The Clark-Wilson access triple involves an object (a constrained data item), a subject (an integrity verification procedure or a certification rule), and a program (a transformation procedure or an enforcement rule). Because these same access triples include a program element as well as a subject, Clark-Wilson also supports separation of duties, which divides operations into disconnected parts and also requires different users to perform each part to prevent fraud or misuse.

- The access matrix model is most commonly implemented using access control lists (ACLs).

- Brewer and Nash (a.k.a. Chinese wall) manages how subjects access datasets according to their assignments to conflict-of-interest classes.

Summary

Designing secure computing systems is a complex task, and many security engineers have dedicated their entire careers to understanding the innermost workings of information systems and ensuring that they support the core security functions required to safely operate in the current environment. Many security professionals don't necessarily require an in-depth knowledge of these principles, but they should have at least a broad understanding of the basic fundamentals that drive the process to enhance security within their own organizations.

Such understanding begins with an investigation of hardware, software, and firmware and how those pieces fit into the security puzzle. It's important to understand the principles of common computer and network organizations, architectures, and designs, including addressing (both physical and symbolic), the difference between address space and memory space, and machine types (real, virtual, multistate, multitasking, multiprogramming, multiprocessing, multiprocessor, and multiuser).

Additionally, a security professional must have a solid understanding of operating states (single state, multistate), operating modes (user, supervisor, privileged), storage types (primary, secondary, real, virtual, volatile, nonvolatile, random, sequential), and protection mechanisms (layering, abstraction, data hiding, process isolation, hardware segmentation, principle of least privilege, separation of privilege, accountability).

All of this understanding must culminate into an effective system security implementation in terms of preventive, detective, and corrective controls. That's why you must also know the access control models and their functions. This includes the state machine model, Bell-LaPadula, Biba, Clark-Wilson, the information flow model, the noninterference model, the Take-Grant model, the access control matrix model, and the Brewer and Nash model.

Exam Essentials

Be able to explain the differences between multitasking, multithreading, multiprocessing, and multiprogramming. Multitasking is the simultaneous execution of more than one application on a computer and is managed by the operating system. Multithreading permits multiple concurrent tasks to be performed within a single process. Multiprocessing is the use of more than one processor to increase computing power. Multiprogramming is similar to multitasking but takes place on mainframe systems and requires specific programming.

Understand the differences between single state processors and multistate processors. Single state processors are capable of operating at only one security level at a time, whereas multistate processors can simultaneously operate at multiple security levels.

Describe the four security modes approved by the federal government for processing classified information. Dedicated systems require that all users have appropriate clearance, access permissions, and need-to-know for all information stored on the system. System high mode removes the need-to-know requirement. Compartmented mode removes the need-to-know requirement and the access permission requirement. Multilevel mode removes all three requirements.

Explain the two layered operating modes used by most modern processors. User applications operate in a limited instruction set environment known as user mode. The operating system performs controlled operations in privileged mode, also known as system mode, kernel mode, and supervisory mode.

Describe the different types of memory used by a computer. ROM is nonvolatile and can't be written to by the end user. PROM chips allow the end user to write data once. EPROM chips may be erased through the use of ultraviolet light and then rewritten. EEPROM chips may be erased with electrical current and then rewritten. RAM chips are volatile and lose their contents when the computer is powered off.

Know the security issues surrounding memory components. There are three main security issues surrounding memory components: the fact that data may remain on the chip after power is removed, the fact that memory chips are highly pilferable, and the control of access to memory in a multiuser system.

Describe the different characteristics of storage devices used by computers. Primary storage is the same as memory. Secondary storage consists of magnetic and optical media that must be first read into primary memory before the CPU can use the data. Random access storage devices can be read at any point, whereas sequential access devices require scanning through all the data physically stored before the desired location.

Know the security issues surrounding secondary storage devices. There are three main security issues surrounding secondary storage devices: removable media can be used to steal data, access controls and encryption must be applied to protect data, and data can remain on the media even after file deletion or media formatting.

Understand security risks that input and output devices can pose.   Input/output devices can be subject to eavesdropping and tapping, used to smuggle data out of an organization, or used to create unauthorized, insecure points of entry into an organization's systems and networks. Be prepared to recognize and mitigate such vulnerabilities.

Understand I/O addresses, configuration, and setup.   Working with legacy PC devices requires some understanding of IRQs, DMA, and memory-mapped I/O. Be prepared to recognize and work around potential address conflicts and misconfigurations and to integrate legacy devices with Plug and Play (PnP) counterparts.

Know the purpose of firmware.   Firmware is software stored on a ROM chip. At the computer level, it contains the basic instructions needed to start a computer. Firmware is also used to provide operating instructions in peripheral devices such as printers.

Be able to describe process isolation, layering, abstraction, data hiding, and hardware segmentation.   Process isolation ensures that individual processes can access only their own data. Layering creates different realms of security within a process and limits communication between them. Abstraction creates "black box" interfaces without requiring knowledge of an algorithm's or device's inner workings. Data hiding prevents information from being read from a different security level. Hardware segmentation enforces process isolation with physical controls.

Understand how a security policy drives system design, implementation, testing, and deployment.   The role of a security policy is to inform and guide the design, development, implementation, testing, and maintenance of some particular system.

Understand how the principle of least privilege, separation of privilege, and accountability apply to computer architecture.   The principle of least privilege ensures that only a minimum number of processes are authorized to run in supervisory mode. Separation of privilege increases the granularity of secure operations. Accountability ensures that an audit trail exists to trace operations back to their source.

Know details about each of the access control models.   Know the access control models and their functions. The state machine model ensures that all instances of subjects accessing objects are secure. Bell-LaPadula subjects have a clearance level that allows them to access only objects with corresponding classification levels. Biba prevents subjects with lower security levels from writing to objects at higher security levels. Clark-Wilson is an integrity model that relies on auditing to ensure that unauthorized subjects cannot access objects and that authorized users access objects properly. The information flow model is designed to prevent unauthorized, insecure, or restricted information flow. The noninterference model prevents the actions of one subject from affecting the system state or actions of another subject. The Take-Grant model dictates how rights can be passed from one subject to another or from a subject to an object. Finally, an access control matrix is a table of subjects and objects that indicates the actions or functions that each subject can perform on each object.

Review Questions

1. Many PC operating systems provide functionality that enables them to support the simultaneous execution of multiple applications on single-processor systems. What term is used to describe this capability?

    A. Multiprogramming

    B. Multithreading

    C. Multitasking

    D. Multiprocessing

2. Which one of the following devices is most susceptible to TEMPEST monitoring of its emanations?

    A. Floppy drive

    B. Monitor

    C. CD-ROM

    D. Keyboard

3. You have three applications running on a single-processor system that supports multitasking. One of those applications is a word processing program that is managing two threads simultaneously. The other two applications are using only one thread of execution. How many application threads are running on the processor at any given time?

    A. 1

    B. 2

    C. 3

    D. 4

4. What type of federal government computing system requires that all individuals accessing the system have a need-to-know all of the information processed by that system?

    A. Dedicated

    B. System high

    C. Compartmented

    D. Multilevel

5. What term describes the processor mode used to run the system tools used by administrators seeking to make configuration changes to a machine?

    A. User mode

    B. Supervisory mode

    C. Kernel mode

    D. Privileged mode

6. What type of memory chip allows the end user to write information to the memory only one time and then preserves that information indefinitely without the possibility of erasure?

   A. ROM

   B. PROM

   C. EPROM

   D. EEPROM

7. Which type of memory chip can be erased only when it is removed from the computer and exposed to a special type of ultraviolet light?

   A. ROM

   B. PROM

   C. EPROM

   D. EEPROM

8. Which one of the following types of memory might retain information after being removed from a computer and, therefore, represent a security risk?

   A. Static RAM

   B. Dynamic RAM

   C. Secondary memory

   D. Real memory

9. What is the single largest security threat RAM chips pose to your organization?

   A. Data retention

   B. Fire

   C. Theft

   D. Electronic emanations

10. What type of electrical component serves as the primary building block for dynamic RAM chips?

   A. Capacitor

   B. Resistor

   C. Flip-flop

   D. Transistor

11. Which one of the following storage devices is *most likely* to require encryption technology in order to maintain data security in a networked environment?

   A. Hard disk

   B. Backup tape

   C. Floppy disk

   D. RAM

12. In which of the following security modes can you be assured that all users have access permissions for all information processed by the system but will not necessarily have a need-to-know all of that information?

    A. Dedicated

    B. System high

    C. Compartmented

    D. Multilevel

13. Which one of the following security modes does not require that all users have a security clearance for the highest level of information processed by the system?

    A. Dedicated

    B. System high

    C. Compartmented

    D. Multilevel

14. What type of memory device is normally used to contain a computer's BIOS?

    A. PROM

    B. EEPROM

    C. ROM

    D. EPROM

15. What type of memory is directly available to the CPU and does not need to be loaded?

    A. RAM

    B. ROM

    C. Register memory

    D. Virtual memory

16. In what type of addressing scheme is the data actually supplied to the CPU as an argument to the instruction?

    A. Direct addressing

    B. Immediate addressing

    C. Base+Offset addressing

    D. Indirect addressing

17. What type of addressing scheme supplies the CPU with a location that contains the memory address of the actual operand?

    A. Direct addressing

    B. Immediate addressing

    C. Base+Offset addressing

    D. Indirect addressing

18. What security principle helps prevent users from accessing memory spaces assigned to applications being run by other users?

   A. Separation of privilege

   B. Layering

   C. Process isolation

   D. Least privilege

19. Which security principle mandates that only a minimum number of operating system processes should run in supervisory mode?

   A. Abstraction

   B. Layering

   C. Data hiding

   D. Least privilege

20. Which security principle takes the concept of process isolation and implements it using physical controls?

   A. Hardware segmentation

   B. Data hiding

   C. Layering

   D. Abstraction

Answers to Review Questions

1. C. Multitasking is processing more than one task at the same time. In most cases, multitasking is actually simulated by the operating system even when not supported by the processor.

2. B. Although all electronic devices emit some unwanted emanations, monitors are the devices most susceptible to this threat.

3. A. A single-processor system can operate on only one thread at a time. There would be a total of four application threads (ignoring any threads created by the operating system), but the operating system would be responsible for deciding which single thread is running on the processor at any given time.

4. A. In a dedicated system, all users must have a valid security clearance for the highest level of information processed by the system, they must have access approval for all information processed by the system, and they must have a valid need-to-know all information processed by the system.

5. A. All user applications, regardless of the security permissions assigned to the user, execute in user mode. *Supervisory mode, kernel mode,* and *privileged mode* are all terms that describe the mode used by the processor to execute instructions that originate from the operating system itself.

6. B. Programmable read-only memory (PROM) chips may be written once by the end user but may never be erased. The contents of ROM chips are burned in at the factory and the end user is not allowed to write data. EPROM and EEPROM chips both make provisions for the end user to somehow erase the contents of the memory device and rewrite new data to the chip.

7. C. EPROMs may be erased through exposure to high-intensity ultraviolet light. ROM and PROM chips do not provide erasure functionality. EEPROM chips may be erased through the application of electrical currents to the chip pins and do not require removal from the computer prior to erasure.

8. C. *Secondary memory* is a term used to describe magnetic and optical media. These devices will retain their contents after being removed from the computer and may be later read by another user.

9. C. RAM chips are highly pilferable items and the single greatest threat they pose is the economic loss that would result from their theft.

10. A. Dynamic RAM chips are built from a large number of capacitors, each of which holds a single electrical charge. These capacitors must be continually refreshed by the CPU in order to retain their contents. The data stored in the chip is lost when power is removed.

11. C. Floppy disks are easily removed and it is often not possible to apply operating system access controls to them. Therefore, encryption is often the only security measure short of physical security that can be afforded to them. Backup tapes are most often well controlled through physical security measures. Hard disks and RAM chips are often secured through operating system access controls.

12. C. In system high mode, all users have appropriate clearances and access permissions for all information processed by the system but have a need-to-know for only *some* of the information processed by that system.

13. D. In a multilevel security mode system, there is no requirement that all users have appropriate clearances to access all of the information processed by the system.

14. B. BIOS and device firmware are often stored on EEPROM chips in order to facilitate future firmware updates.

15. C. Registers are small memory locations that are located directly on the CPU chip itself. The data stored within them is directly available to the CPU and can be accessed extremely quickly.

16. B. In immediate addressing, the CPU does not need to actually retrieve any data from memory. The data is contained in the instruction itself and can be immediately processed.

17. D. In indirect addressing, the location provided to the CPU contains a memory address. The CPU retrieves the operand by reading it from the memory address provided (hence the use of the term *indirect*).

18. C. Process isolation provides separate memory spaces to each process running on a system. This prevents processes from overwriting each other's data and ensures that a process can't read data from another process.

19. D. The principle of least privilege states that only processes that absolutely need kernel-level access should run in supervisory mode. The remaining processes should run in user mode to reduce the number of potential security vulnerabilities.

20. A. Hardware segmentation achieves the same objectives as process isolation but takes them to a higher level by implementing them with physical controls in hardware.

Chapter

12

Principles of Security Models

THE CISSP EXAM TOPICS COVERED IN THIS CHAPTER INCLUDE:

- ✓ Principles of Common Security Models, Architectures, and Evaluation Criteria
- ✓ Common Flaws and Security Issues Associated with System Architectures and Designs

Increasing the security level of information systems is a challenging task for any organization. Ideally, security is something that is planned and integrated from the very inception of a system's architecture and considered at each stage of its development, testing, deployment, and day-to-day use. The first step in this endeavor is to evaluate an organization's current levels of security exposure by carefully examining its information systems and checking for vulnerability to threats or attack. Next, one must decide what steps to take to remedy any such exposures as may be discovered during the examination process. Making decisions about which solutions will work well can be the most difficult part of the process when seeking to secure information systems properly. If this is not to become a constant case of discovering vulnerabilities and applying relevant security patches or fixes—as is so common with systems like Windows, Unix, and Linux today—the level of security consciousness and attention during initial system design and implementation must be substantially increased.

Understanding the philosophy behind security solutions helps to limit one's search for the best security controls for a specific situation and for specific security needs. In this chapter, we discuss methods to evaluate the levels of security that a system provides. We also refer back to the general security models (originally introduced in Chapter 11, "Principles of Computer Design") upon which many security controls are constructed. Next, we talk about Common Criteria and other methods that governments and corporations alike use to evaluate information systems from a security perspective, with particular emphasis on U.S. Department of Defense and international security evaluation criteria. We finish off this chapter by discussing commonly encountered design flaws and other security-related issues that can make information systems susceptible to attack.

Common Security Models, Architectures, and Evaluation Criteria

The process of determining how secure a system is can be difficult and time consuming. Organizations need methods to evaluate given systems, to assign general security ratings, and to determine if a system meets a security policy's requirements. Further, any such security rating should be general enough to enable meaningful comparison among multiple systems, along with their relative levels of security. The following sections describe the process involved in evaluating a computer system's level of security. We begin by introducing and explaining basic concepts and terminology used to describe information system security and talk about secure computing, secure perimeters, security and access monitors, and kernel code. We turn to security models to explain how access and security controls may be implemented. We also briefly explain how system security may be categorized as either open or closed; describe a set of standard security techniques used to ensure confidentiality, integrity, and availability of data; discuss security controls; and introduce a standard suite of secure networking protocols.

Trusted Computing Base (TCB)

An old U.S. Department of Defense standard known colloquially as "the Orange Book" (DoD Standard 5200.28, covered in more detail later in this chapter in the "Rainbow Series" section) describes a *trusted computing base (TCB)* as a combination of hardware, software, and controls that works together to form a trusted base to enforce your security policy. The TCB is a subset in a complete information system. It should be as small as possible so that a detailed analysis can reasonably ensure that the system meets design specifications and requirements. The TCB is the only portion of that system that can be trusted to adhere to and enforce the security policy. It is not necessary that every component of a system be trusted. But anytime you consider a system from a security standpoint, your evaluation should include all trusted components that define that system's TCB.

In general, TCB components in a system are responsible for controlling access to the system. The TCB must provide methods to access resources both inside and outside the TCB itself. TCB components commonly restrict the activities of components outside the TCB. It is the responsibility of TCB components to ensure that a system behaves properly in all cases and that it adheres to the security policy under all circumstances.

Security Perimeter

The *security perimeter* of your system is an imaginary boundary that separates the TCB from the rest of the system. For the TCB to communicate with the rest of the system, it must create secure channels, also called trusted paths. A *trusted path* is a channel established with strict standards to allow necessary communication to occur without exposing the TCB to security vulnerabilities. A trusted path also protects system users (sometimes known as subjects) from compromise as a result of a TCB interchange. As you learn more about formal security guidelines and evaluation criteria later in this chapter, you'll also learn that trusted paths are required in systems that seek to deliver high levels of security to their users. According to the TCSEC guidelines described later in this chapter, trusted paths are required in B2 and higher systems.

Reference Monitors and Kernels

When the time comes to implement a secure system, it's essential to develop some part of the TCB to enforce access controls on system assets and resources (sometimes known as objects). The part of the TCB that validates access to every resource prior to granting access requests is called the *reference monitor*. The reference monitor stands between every subject and object, verifying that a requesting subject's credentials meet the object's access requirements before any requests are allowed to proceed. If such access requirements aren't met, access requests are turned down. The reference monitor may be a conceptual part of the TCB; it need not be an actual, stand-alone or independent working system component.

The collection of components in the TCB that work together to implement reference monitor functions is called the *security kernel*. The purpose of the security kernel is to launch appropriate components to enforce reference monitor functionality and resist all known attacks. The security kernel uses a trusted path to communicate with subjects. It also mediates all resource access requests, granting only those requests that match the appropriate access rules in use for a system.

The reference monitor requires descriptive information about each resource that it protects. Such information normally includes its classification and designation. When a subject requests access to an object, the reference monitor consults the object's descriptive information to discern whether access should be granted or denied (see the sidebar "Tokens, Capabilities, and Labels" for more information on how this works).

Security Models

A security model provides a framework inside which one can implement a security policy. Where a security policy is an abstract statement of security intentions, a security model represents exactly how the policy should be implemented. A good model accurately represents each facet of the security policy and how to implement some control to enforce the facet. The following sections discuss three well-known security models, originally introduced in Chapter 11, and their basic features and functions. Each security model shares similarities with the others but also has its own unique characteristics.

A security model provides a way for designers to map abstract statements in a security policy into the algorithms and data structures necessary to build software. Thus, a security model gives software designers something against which to measure their design and implementation. That model, of course, must support each part of the security policy. In this way, developers can be sure their security implementation supports the security policy.

Tokens, Capabilities, and Labels

There are several different methods in use to describe the necessary security attributes for an object. A security *token* is a separate object that is associated with a resource and describes its security attributes. This token can communicate security information about an object prior to requesting access to the actual object. In other implementations, various lists are used to store security information about multiple objects. A *capabilities list* maintains a row of security attributes for each controlled object. Although not as flexible as the token approach, capabilities lists generally offer quicker lookups when a subject requests access to an object. A third common type of attribute storage is called a security label. A *security label* is generally a permanent part of the object to which it's attached. Once a security label is set, it normally cannot be altered. This permanence provides another safeguard against tampering that neither tokens nor capabilities lists provide.

Bell-LaPadula Model

The *Bell-LaPadula model* was developed by the U.S. Department of Defense (DoD) in the 1970s to address concerns about protecting classified information. The DoD stores multiple levels of classified documents. The classifications the DoD uses are unclassified, sensitive but unclassified, confidential, secret, and top secret. Any person with a secret security clearance can access secret, confidential, sensitive but unclassified, and unclassified documents but not top secret documents. Also, to access a document, the person seeking access must also have a need-to-know for that document.

The complexities involved in ensuring the confidentiality of documents are addressed in the Bell-LaPadula model. This model is built on a state machine concept. The state machine supports multiple states with explicit transitions between any two states; this concept is used because the correctness of the machine, and guarantees of document confidentiality, can be proven mathematically. There are three basic properties of this state machine:

- The *Simple Security Property* states that a subject may not read information at a higher sensitivity level (no read up).

- The * *(star) Security Property* states that a subject may not write information to an object at a lower sensitivity level (no write down).

- The *Discretionary Security Property* states that the system uses an access matrix to enforce discretionary access control.

The Bell-LaPadula properties are in place to protect data confidentiality. A subject cannot read an object that is classified at a higher level than the subject is cleared for. Because objects at one level have data that is more sensitive or secret than data at a lower level, a subject cannot write data from one level to an object at a lower level (with the exception of a trusted subject). That action would be similar to pasting a top secret memo into an unclassified document file. The third property enforces a subject's "need-to-know" in order to access an object.

The Bell-LaPadula model addresses only the confidentiality of data. It does not address its integrity or availability. Because it was designed in the 1970s, it does not support many operations that are common today, such as file sharing. It also assumes secure transitions between security layers and does not address covert channels (covered later in this chapter). Bell-LaPadula does handle confidentiality well, so it is often used in combination with other models that provide mechanisms to handle integrity and availability.

Biba Model

The *Biba model* was designed after the Bell-LaPadula model. Where the Bell-LaPadula model addresses confidentiality, the Biba model addresses integrity. The Biba model is also built on a state machine concept. In fact, Biba appears to be pretty similar to the Bell-LaPadula model. Both use states and transitions. Both have basic properties. The biggest difference is their primary focus: Biba primarily protects data integrity. Here are the basic properties of the Biba model state machine:

- The *Simple Integrity Property* states that a subject cannot read an object at a lower integrity level (no read down).

- The * *(star) Integrity Property* states that a subject cannot modify an object at a higher integrity level (no write up).

When you compare Biba to Bell-LaPadula, you will notice that they look like they are opposite. That's because they focus on different areas of security. Where Bell-LaPadula model ensures data confidentiality, Biba ensures data integrity.

Consider both Biba properties. The second property of the Biba model is pretty straightforward. A subject cannot write to an object at a higher integrity level. That makes sense. What about the first property? Why can't a subject read an object at a lower integrity level? The answer takes a little thought. Think of integrity levels as being like the purity level of air. You would not want to pump air from the smoking section into the clean room environment. The same applies to data. When integrity is important, you do not want unvalidated data read into validated documents. The potential for data contamination is too great to permit such access.

Because the Biba model focuses on data integrity, it is a more common choice for commercial security models than the Bell-LaPadula model. Most commercial organizations are more concerned with the integrity of their data than its confidentiality.

Clark-Wilson Model

Although the Biba model works in commercial applications, another model was designed in 1987 specifically for the commercial environment. The *Clark-Wilson model* uses a multifaceted approach to enforcing data integrity. Instead of defining a formal state machine, the Clark-Wilson model defines each data item and allows modifications through only a small set of programs. Clark-Wilson defines the following items and procedures:

- A constrained data item (CDI) is any data item whose integrity is protected by the security model.

- An unconstrained data item (UDI) is any data item that is not controlled by the security model. Any data that is to be input and hasn't been validated or any output would be considered an unconstrained data item.

- An integrity verification procedure (IVP) is a procedure that scans data items and confirms their integrity.

- Transformation procedures (TPs) are the only procedures that are allowed to modify a CDI. The limited access to CDIs through TPs forms the backbone of the Clark-Wilson integrity model.

The Clark-Wilson model uses security labels to grant access to objects, but only through transformation procedures. The model also enforces separation of duties to further protect the integrity of data. Through these mechanisms, the Clark-Wilson model ensures that data is protected from unauthorized changes from any user. The Clark-Wilson design makes it a very good model for commercial applications.

Objects and Subjects

Controlling access to any resource in a secure system involves two entities. The *subject* of the access is the user or process that makes a request to access a resource. Access can mean reading from or writing to a resource. The *object* of an access is the resource a user or process wants to access. Keep in mind that the subject and object refer to some specific access request, so the same resource can serve as a subject and an object in different access requests.

For example, process A may ask for data from process B. To satisfy process A's request, process B must ask for data from process C. In this example, process B is the object of the first request and the subject of the second request:

First request   process A (subject)   process B (object)

Second request   process B (subject)   process C (object)

Closed and Open Systems

Systems are designed and built according to two differing philosophies. A closed system is designed to work well with a narrow range of other systems, generally all from the same manufacturer. The standards for closed systems are often proprietary and not normally disclosed. Open systems, on the other hand, are designed using agreed-upon industry standards. Open systems are much easier to integrate with systems from different manufacturers that support the same standards.

Closed systems are harder to integrate with unlike systems, but they can be more secure. A closed system often comprises proprietary hardware and software that does not incorporate industry standards. This lack of integration ease means that attacks on many generic system components either will not work or must be customized to be successful. In many cases, attacking a closed system is harder than launching an attack on an open system. Many software and hardware components with known vulnerabilities may not exist on a closed system. In addition to the lack of known vulnerable components on a closed system, it is often necessary to possess more in-depth knowledge of the specific target system to launch a successful attack.

Open systems are generally far easier to integrate with other open systems. It is easy, for example, to create a LAN with a Microsoft Windows 2000 machine, a Linux machine, and a Macintosh machine. Although all three computers use different operating systems and represent at least two different hardware architectures, each supports industry standards and makes it easy for networked (or other) communications to occur. This ease comes at a price, however. Because standard communications components are incorporated into each of these three open systems, there are far more entry points and methods for launching attacks. In general, their openness makes them more vulnerable to attack, and their widespread availability makes it possible for attackers to find (and even to practice on) plenty of potential targets. Also, open systems are more popular than closed systems and attract more attention. An attacker who develops basic cracking skills will find more targets on open systems than on closed ones. This larger "market" of potential targets normally means that there is more emphasis on targeting open systems. Inarguably, there's a greater body of shared experience and knowledge on how to attack open systems than there is for closed systems.

Techniques for Ensuring Confidentiality, Integrity, and Availability

To guarantee the confidentiality, integrity, and availability of data, you must ensure that all components that have access to data are secure and well behaved. Software designers use different techniques to ensure that programs do only what is required and nothing more. Suppose a program writes to and reads from an area of memory that is being used by another program. The first program could potentially violate all three security tenets: confidentiality, integrity, and availability. If an affected program is processing sensitive or secret data, that data's confidentiality is no longer guaranteed. If that data is overwritten or altered in an unpredictable way (a common problem when multiple readers and writers inadvertently access the same shared data), there is no guarantee of integrity. And, if data modification results in corruption or outright loss, it could become unavailable for future use. Although the concepts we discuss in this section all relate to software programs, they are also commonly used in all areas of security. For example, physical confinement guarantees that all physical access to hardware is controlled.

Confinement

Software designers use process confinement to restrict the actions of a program. Simply put, process *confinement* allows a process to read from and write to only certain memory locations and resources. The operating system, or some other security component, disallows illegal read/write requests. If a process attempts to initiate an action beyond its granted authority, that action will be denied. In addition, further actions, such as logging the violation attempt, may be taken. Systems that must comply with higher security ratings most likely record all violations and respond in some tangible way. Generally, the offending process is terminated.

Bounds

Each process that runs on a system is assigned an authority level. The authority level tells the operating system what the process can do. In simple systems, there may be only two authority levels: user and kernel. The authority level tells the operating system how to set the bounds for a process. The *bounds* of a process consist of limits set on the memory addresses and resources it can access. The bounds state the area within which a process is confined. In most systems, these bounds segment logical areas of memory for each process to use. It is the responsibility of the operating system to enforce these logical bounds and to disallow access to other processes. More secure systems may require physically bounded processes. Physical bounds require each bounded process to run in an area of memory that is physically separated from other bounded processes, not just logically bounded in the same memory space. Physically bounded memory can be very expensive, but it's also more secure than logical bounds.

Isolation

When a process is confined through enforcing access bounds, that process runs in *isolation*. Process isolation ensures that any behavior will affect only the memory and resources associated with the isolated process. These three concepts (confinement, bounds, and isolation) make designing secure programs and operating systems more difficult, but they also make it possible to implement more secure systems.

Controls

We introduced the concept of security controls in Chapter 1, "Accountability and Access Control." To ensure the security of a system, you need to allow subjects to access only authorized objects. A *control* uses access rules to limit the access by a subject to an object. Access rules state which objects are valid for each subject. Further, an object might be valid for one type of access and be invalid for another type of access. One common control is for file access. A file can be protected from modification by making it read-only for most users but read-write for a small set of users who have the authority to modify it.

Recall from Chapter 1 that there are both mandatory and discretionary access controls, often called MAC and DAC, respectively. With mandatory controls, static attributes of the subject and the object are considered to determine the permissibility of an access. Each subject possesses attributes that define its clearance, or authority to access resources. Each object possesses attributes that define its classification. Different types of security methods classify resources in different ways. For example, subject A is granted access to object B if the security system can find a rule that allows a subject with subject A's clearance to access an object with object B's classification. This is called rule-based access control. The predefined rules state which subjects can access which objects.

Discretionary controls differ from mandatory controls in that the subject has some ability to define the objects to access. Within limits, discretionary access controls allow the subject to define a list of objects to access as needed. This access control list (often called an ACL) serves as a dynamic access rule set that the subject can modify. The constraints imposed on the modifications often relate to the subject's identity. Based on the identity, the subject may be allowed to add or modify the rules that define access to objects.

Both mandatory and discretionary access controls limit the access to objects by subjects. The primary goals of controls are to ensure the confidentiality and integrity of data by disallowing unauthorized access by authorized or unauthorized subjects.

Trust and Assurance

Proper security concepts, controls, and mechanisms must be integrated before and during the design and architectural period in order to produce a reliably secure product. Security issues should not be added on as an afterthought; this causes oversights, increased costs, and less reliability. Once security is integrated into the design, it must be engineered, implemented, tested, audited, evaluated, certified, and finally accredited.

A *trusted system* is one in which all protection mechanisms work together to process sensitive data for many types of users while maintaining a stable and secure computing environment. *Assurance* is simply defined as the degree of confidence in satisfaction of security needs. Assurance must be continually maintained, updated, and reverified. This is true whether the trusted system experiences a known change or a significant amount of time has passed. In either case, change has occurred at some level. Change is often the antithesis of security; it often diminishes security. So, whenever change occurs, the system needs to be reevaluated to verify that the level of security it provided previously is still intact. Assurance varies from one system to another and must be established on individual systems. However, there are grades or levels of assurance that can be placed across numerous systems of the same type, systems that support the same services, or systems that are deployed in the same geographic location.

Understanding System Security Evaluation

Those who purchase information systems for certain kinds of applications—think, for example, about national security agencies where sensitive information may be extremely valuable (or dangerous in the wrong hands) or central banks or securities traders where certain data may be worth billions of dollars—often want to understand their security strengths and weaknesses. Such buyers are often willing to consider only systems that have been subjected to formal evaluation processes in advance and received some kind of security rating so that they know what they're buying (and, usually, also what steps they must take to keep such systems as secure as possible).

When formal evaluations are undertaken, systems are usually subjected to a two-step process. In the first step, a system is tested and a technical evaluation is performed to make sure that the system's security capabilities meet criteria laid out for its intended use. In the second step, the system is subjected to a formal comparison of its design and security criteria and its actual capabilities and performance, and individuals responsible for the security and veracity of such systems must decide whether to adopt them, reject them, or make some changes to their criteria and try again. Very often, in fact, trusted third parties (such as TruSecure Corporation, well known for its security testing laboratories) are hired to perform such evaluations; the most important result from such testing is their "seal of approval" that the system meets all essential criteria. Whether or not the evaluations are conducted inside an organization or out of house, the adopting organization must decide to accept or reject the proposed systems. An organization's management must take formal responsibility if and when systems are adopted and be willing to accept any risks associated with its deployment and use.

Rainbow Series

Since the 1980s, governments, agencies, institutions, and business organizations of all kinds have had to face the risks involved in adopting and using information systems. This led to a historical series of information security standards that attempted to specify minimum acceptable security criteria for various categories of use. Such categories were important as purchasers attempted to obtain and deploy systems that would protect and preserve their contents or that would meet various mandated security requirements (such as those that contractors must routinely meet to conduct business with the government). The first such set of standards resulted in the creation of the Trusted Computer System Evaluation Criteria in the 1980s, as the U.S. Department of Defense (DoD) worked to develop and impose security standards for the systems it purchased and used. In turn, this led to a whole series of such publications through the mid-1990s. Since these publications were routinely identified by the color of their covers, they are known collectively as the "rainbow series."

Following in the DoD's footsteps, other governments or standards bodies created computer security standards that built and improved on the rainbow series elements. Significant standards in this group include a European model called the Information Technology Security Evaluation Criteria (ITSEC) which was developed in 1999 and used through 1998. They also include the so-called Common Criteria, adopted by the U.S., Canada, France, Germany, and the U.K. in 1998, but more formally known as the "Arrangement on the Recognition of Common Criteria Certificates in the Field of IT Security." Both of these standards will be discussed in later sections as well.

When governments or other security conscious agencies evaluate information systems, they make use of various standard evaluation criteria. In 1985, the National Computer Security Center (NCSC) developed the Trusted Computer System Evaluation Criteria (TCSEC), usually called the "Orange Book" because of the color of this publication's covers. The TCSEC established guidelines to be used when evaluating a stand-alone computer from the security perspective. These guidelines address basic security functionality and allow evaluators to measure and rate a system's functionality and trustworthiness. In the TSCEC, in fact, functionality and security assurance are combined and not separated as they are in security criteria developed later. TCSEC guidelines were designed to be used when evaluating vendor products or by vendors to ensure that they build all necessary functionality and security assurance into new products.

Next, we'll take a look at some of the details in the Orange Book itself and then talk about some of the other important elements in the rainbow series.

TCSEC Classes and Required Functionality

TCSEC combines the functionality and assurance rating of a system into four major categories. These categories are then subdivided into additional subcategories. TCSEC defines the following major categories:

Category A   Verified protection

Category B   Mandatory protection

Category C   Discretionary protection

Category D   Minimal protection

Category D is reserved for systems that have been evaluated but do not meet requirements to belong to any other category. In this scheme, category A systems have the highest level of security and category D represents systems with the lowest level of security. The sections that follow next include brief discussions of categories A through C along with numeric suffixes that represent any applicable subcategories.

Discretionary Protection (Categories C1, C2)

Discretionary protection systems provide basic access control. Systems in this category do provide some security controls but are lacking in more sophisticated and stringent controls that address specific needs for secure systems. C1 and C2 systems provide basic controls and complete documentation for system installation and configuration.

Discretionary Security Protection (C1)   A discretionary security protection system controls access by user IDs and/or groups. Although there are some controls in place that limit object access, systems in this category only provide weak protection.

Controlled Access Protection (C2)   Controlled access protection systems are stronger than C1 systems. Users must be identified individually to gain access to objects. C2 systems must also enforce media cleansing. With media cleansing, any media that is reused by another user must first be thoroughly cleansed so that no remnant of the previous data remains available for inspection or use. Additionally, strict logon procedures must be enforced that restrict access for invalid or unauthorized users.

Mandatory Protection (Categories B1, B2, B3)

Mandatory protection systems provide more security controls than category D or C systems. More granularity of control is mandated, so security administrators can apply specific controls that allow only very limited sets of subject/object access. This category of systems is based on the Bell-LaPadula model. Mandatory access is based on security labels.

Labeled Security (B1) In a labeled security system, each subject and each object has a security label. A B1 system grants access by matching up the subject and object labels and comparing their permission compatibility. B1 systems support sufficient security to house classified data.

Structured Protection (B2) In addition to the requirement for security labels (as in B1 systems), B2 systems must ensure that no covert channels exist. Operator and administrator functions are separated and process isolation is maintained. B2 systems are sufficient for classified data that requires more security functionality than a B1 system can deliver.

Security Domains (B3) Security domain systems provide more secure functionality by further increasing the separation and isolation of unrelated processes. Administration functions are clearly defined and separate from functions available to other users. The focus of B3 systems shifts to simplicity to reduce any exposure to vulnerabilities in unused or extra code. The secure state of B3 systems must also be addressed during the initial boot process. B3 systems are difficult to attack successfully and provide sufficient secure controls for very sensitive or secret data.

Verified Protection (Category A1)

Verified protection systems are similar to B3 systems in the structure and controls they employ. The difference is in the development cycle. Each phase of the development cycle is controlled using formal methods. Each phase of the design is documented, evaluated, and verified before the next step is taken. This forces extreme security consciousness during all steps of development and deployment and is the only way to formally guarantee strong system security.

A verified design system starts with a design document that states how the resulting system will satisfy the security policy. From there, each development step is evaluated in the context of the security policy. Functionality is crucial, but assurance becomes more important than in lower security categories. A1 systems represent the top level of security and are designed to handle top secret data. Every step is documented and verified, from the design all the way through to delivery and installation.

Other Colors in the Rainbow Series

Altogether, there are nearly 30 titles in the collection of DoD documents that either add to or further elaborate on the Orange Book. Although the colors don't necessarily mean anything, they're used to describe publications in this series. Other important elements in this collection of documents include the following (for a more complete list, please consult Table 12.1):

Red Book Because the Orange Book applies only to stand-alone computers not attached to a network and so many systems were used on networks (even in the 1980s), the Red Book was developed to interpret the TCSEC in a networking context. In fact, the official title of the Red Book is the *Trusted Network Interpretation (TNI)*, so it could be considered an interpretation of the Orange Book with a bent on networking. Quickly, the Red Book became more relevant and important to system buyers and builders than the Orange Book. The following list includes a few other functions of the Red Book:

- Rates confidentiality and integrity
- Addresses communications integrity
- Addresses denial of service protection
- Addresses compromise (i.e., intrusion) protection and prevention
- Is restricted to a limited class of networks that are labeled as "centralized networks with a single accreditation authority"
- Uses only 4 rating levels: None, C1 (Minimum), C2 (Fair), B2 (Good)

TABLE 12.1   Important Rainbow Series Elements

Pub#	Title	Book Name
5200.28-STD	*DoD Trusted Computer System Evaluation Criteria*	Orange Book
CSC-STD-002-85	*DoD Password Management Guidelines*	Green Book
CSC-STD-003-85	*Guidance for Applying TCSEC in Specific Environments*	Yellow Book
NCSC-TG-001	*A Guide to Understanding Audit in Trusted Systems*	Tan Book
NCSC-TG-002	*Trusted Product Evaluation—A Guide for Vendors*	Bright Blue Book
NCSC-TG-002-85	*PC Security Considerations*	Light Blue Book
NCSC-TG-003	*A Guide to Understanding Discretionary Access Controls in Trusted Systems*	Neon Orange Book
NCSC-TG-005	*Trusted Network Interpretation*	Red Book
NCSC-TG-004	*Glossary of Computer Security Terms*	Aqua Book
NCSC-TG-006	*A Guide to Understanding Configuration Management in Trusted Systems*	Amber Book
NCSC-TG-007	*A Guide to Understanding Design Documentation in Trusted Systems*	Burgundy Book
NCSC-TG-008	*A Guide to Understanding Trusted Distribution in Trusted Systems*	Lavender Book
NCSC-TG-009	*Computer Security Subsystem Interpretation of the TCSEC*	Venice Blue Book

For more information, please consult **http://csrc.ncsl.nist.gov/secpubs/rainbow/**, download links available.

Green Book   The Green Book, or the *Department of Defense Password Management Guidelines,* provides password creation and management guidelines; it's important for those who configure and manage trusted systems.

Given all the time and effort that went into formulating the TCSEC, it's not unreasonable to wonder why evaluation criteria have evolved to newer, more advanced standards. The relentless march of time and technology aside, these are the major critiques of TCSEC and help to explain why newer standards are now in use worldwide:

- Although the TCSEC put considerable emphasis on controlling user access to information, they don't exercise control over what users do with information once access is granted. This can be a problem in both military and commercial applications alike.

- Given their origins at the U.S. Department of Defense, it's understandable that the TCSEC focus their concerns entirely on confidentiality, which assumes that controlling how users access data means that concerns about data accuracy or integrity are irrelevant. This doesn't work in commercial environments where concerns about data accuracy and integrity can be more important than concerns about confidentiality.

- Outside their own emphasis on access controls, the TCSEC do not carefully address the kinds of personnel, physical, and procedural policy matters or safeguards that must be exercised to fully implement security policy. They don't deal much with how such matters can impact system security either.

- The Orange Book, per se, doesn't deal with networking issues (though the Red Book, developed later in 1987, does).

To some extent, these criticisms reflect the unique security concerns of the military, which developed the TCSEC. Then, too, the prevailing computing tools and technologies widely available at the time (networking was really just getting started in 1985) had an impact as well. Certainly, an increasingly sophisticated and holistic view of security within organizations helps to explain why and where the TCSEC also fell short, procedurally and policy-wise. But because ITSEC has been largely superseded by the Common Criteria, coverage in the next section explains ITSEC as a step along the way toward the Common Criteria (covered in the section after that).

ITSEC Classes and Required Assurance and Functionality

The Information Technology Security Evaluation Criteria (ITSEC) represents an initial attempt to create security evaluation criteria in Europe. It was developed as an alternative to the TCSEC guidelines. The ITSEC guidelines evaluate the functionality and assurance of a system using separate ratings for each category. In this context, the functionality of a system measures its utility value for users. The functionality rating of a system states how well the system performs all necessary functions based on its design and intended purpose. The assurance rating represents the degree of confidence that the system will work properly in a consistent manner.

ITSEC refers to any system being evaluated as a target of evaluation (TOE). All ratings are expressed as TOE ratings in two categories. ITSEC uses two scales to rate functionality and assurance. The functionality of a system is rated from F-D through F-B3 (which is used twice; there is no F-A1). The assurance of a system is rated from E0 through E6. Most ITSEC ratings generally correspond with TCSEC ratings (for example, a TCSEC C1 system corresponds to an

ITSEC F-C1, E1 system). See Table 12.3 (at the end of the next section) for a comparison of TCSEC, ITSEC, and Common Criteria ratings.

Differences between TCSEC and ITSEC are many and varied. Some of the most important differences between the two standards include the following:

- Although the TCSEC concentrates almost exclusively on confidentiality, ITSEC addresses concerns about the loss of integrity and availability in addition to confidentiality, thereby covering all three elements so important to maintaining complete information security.

- ITSEC does not rely on the notion of a TCB, nor does it require that a system's security components be isolated within a TCB.

- Unlike TCSEC, which required any changed systems to be reevaluated anew—be it for operating system upgrades, patches or fixes; application upgrades or changes; and so forth—ITSEC includes coverage for maintaining targets of evaluation (TOEs) after such changes occur without requiring a new formal evaluation.

For more information on ITSEC (now largely supplanted by the Common Criteria, covered in the next section), please visit the official ITSEC website at www.cesg.gov.uk/site/iacs/, then click on the link labeled "ITSEC & Common Criteria."

Common Criteria

The Common Criteria represent a more or less global effort that involves everybody who worked on TCSEC and ITSEC as well as other global players. Ultimately, it results in the ability to purchase CC-evaluated products (where CC, of course, stands for Common Criteria). The Common Criteria define various levels of testing and confirmation of systems' security capabilities, where the number of the level indicates what kind of testing and confirmation has been performed. Nevertheless, it's wise to observe that even the highest CC ratings do not equate to a guarantee that such systems are completely secure, nor that they are entirely devoid of vulnerabilities or susceptibility to exploit.

Recognition of Common Criteria

Caveats and disclaimers aside, a document entitled "Arrangement on the Recognition of Common Criteria Certificates in the Field of IT Security" was signed by representatives from government organizations in Canada, France, Germany, the United Kingdom, and the United States in 1998, making it an international standard. This document was converted by ISO into an official standard, namely IS 15408 "Evaluation Criteria for Information Technology Security." The objectives of the CC are as follows:

- To add to buyer's confidence in the security of evaluated, rated IT products.

- To eliminate duplicate evaluations (among other things, this means that if one country, agency, or validation organizations follows the CC in rating specific systems and configurations, others elsewhere need not repeat this work).

- To keep making security evaluations and the certification process more cost effective and efficient.

- To make sure evaluations of IT products adhere to high and consistent standards.

- To promote evaluation, and increase availability of evaluated, rated IT products.

- To evaluate the functionality (i.e., what the system does) and assurance (i.e., how much can you trust the system) of the TOE.

The Common Criteria are available at many locations online. In the United States, the National Institute of Standards and Technology (NIST) maintains a CC web page at `http://csrc.nist.gov/cc/`. Visit here to get information on the current version of the CC (2.1 as of this writing) and guidance on using the CC, along with lots of other useful, relevant information.

The Common Criteria process is based on two key elements: protection profiles and security targets. *Protection profiles (PPs)* specify the security requirements and protections of a product that is to be evaluated (the TOE), which are considered the security desires or the "I want" from a customer. *Security targets (STs)* specify the claims of security from the vendor that are built into a TOE. STs are considered the implemented security measures or the "I will provide" from the vendor. In addition to offering security targets, vendors may also offer packages of additional security features. A *package* is an intermediate grouping of security requirement components that can be added or removed from a TOE (like the option packages when purchasing a new vehicle).

The PP is compared to various STs from the selected vendor's TOEs. The closest or best match is what the client purchases. The client initially selects a vendor based on published or marketed Evaluation Assurance Levels, or EALs (see the next section for more details on EALs), for currently available systems. Using common criteria to choose a vendor allows clients to request exactly what they need for security rather than having to use static fixed security levels. It also allows vendors more flexibility on what they design and create. A well-defined set of common criteria supports subjectivity and versatility and it automatically adapts to changing technology and threat conditions. Furthermore, the EALs provide a method for comparing vendor systems that is more standardized (like the old TCSEC).

Structure of the Common Criteria

The CC are divided into three topical areas, as follows (complete text for version 2.1 is available at NIST at `http://csrc.nist.gov/cc/CC-v2.1.html`, along with links to earlier versions):

Part 1 Introduction and General Model: Describes the general concepts and underlying model used to evaluate IT security and what's involved in specifying targets of evaluation (TOEs). It's useful introductory and explanatory material for those unfamiliar with the workings of the security evaluation process or who need help reading and interpreting evaluation results.

Part 2 Security Functional Requirements: Describes various functional requirements in terms of security audits, communications security, cryptographic support for security, user data protection, identification and authentication, security management, TOE security functions (TSFs), resource utilization, system access, and trusted paths. Covers the complete range of security functions as envisioned in the CC evaluation process, with additional appendices (called annexes) to explain each functional area.

Part 3 Security Assurance: Covers assurance requirements for TOEs in the areas of configuration management, delivery and operation, development, guidance documents, and life cycle support plus assurance tests and vulnerability assessments. Covers the complete range of security assurance checks and protects profiles as envisioned in the CC evaluation process, with information on evaluation assurance levels (EALs) that describe how systems are designed, checked, and tested.

Most important of all the information that appears in these various CC documents (worth at least a cursory read-through), are the evaluation assurance packages or levels commonly known as EALs. Table 12.2 summarizes EALs 1 through 7.

TABLE 12.2   CC Evaluation Assurance Levels

Level	Assurance Level	Description
EAL1	Functionally tested	Applies when some confidence in correct operation is required but where threats to security are not serious. Of value when independent assurance that due care has been exercised in protecting personal information.
EAL2	Structurally tested	Applies when delivery of design information and test results are in keeping with good commercial practices. Of value when developers or users require low to moderate levels of independently assured security. Especially relevant when evaluating legacy systems.
EAL3	Methodically tested and checked	Applies when security engineering begins at the design stage and is carried through without substantial subsequent alteration. Of value when developers or users require moderate level of independently assured security, including thorough investigation of TOE and its development.
EAL4	Methodically designed, tested, and reviewed	Applies when rigorous, positive security engineering and good commercial development practices are used. Does not require substantial specialist knowledge, skills, or resources. Involves independent testing of all TOE security functions.
EAL5	Semi-formally designed and tested	Uses rigorous security engineering and commercial development practices, including specialist security engineering techniques, for semi-formal testing. Applies when developers or users require a high level of independently assured security in a planned development approach, followed by rigorous development.
EAL6	Semi-formally verified, designed, and tested	Uses direct, rigorous security engineering techniques at all phase of design, development, and testing to produce a premium TOE. Applies when TOEs for high-risk situations are needed, where the value of protected assets justifies additional cost. Extensive testing reduce risks of penetration, probability of cover channels, and vulnerability to attack.
EAL7	Formally verified, designed, and tested	Used only for highest-risk situations or where high-value assets are involved. Limited to TOEs where tightly focused security functionality is subject to extensive formal analysis and testing.

For a complete description of EALs, consult Chapter 6 in part 3 of the CC documents; page 54 is especially noteworthy since it explains all EALs in terms of the CC's assurance criteria.

Though the CC are flexible and accommodating enough to capture most security needs and requirements, they are by no means perfect. As with other evaluation criteria, the CC do nothing to make sure that how users act on data is also secure. The CC also does not address administrative issues outside the specific purview of security. As with other evaluation criteria, the CC does not include evaluation of security in situ—that is, it does not address controls related to personnel, organizational practices and procedures, or physical security. Likewise, controls over electromagnetic emissions are not addressed, nor are the criteria for rating the strength of cryptographic algorithms explicitly laid out. Nevertheless, the CC represent some of the best techniques whereby systems may be rated for security. To conclude this discussion of security evaluation standards, Table 12.3 summarizes how various ratings from the TCSEC, ITSEC, and the CC may be compared.

TABLE 12.3 Comparing Security Evaluation Standards

TCSEC	ITSEC	CC	Designation
D	F-D+E0	EAL0, EAL1	Minimal/no protection
C1	F-C1+E1	EAL2	Discretionary security mechanisms
C2	F-C2+E2	EAL3	Controlled access protection
B1	F-B1+E3	EAL4	Labeled security protection
B2	F-B2+E4	EAL5	Structured security protection
B3	F-B3+E5	EAL6	Security domains
A1	F-B3+E6	EAL7	Verified security design

Certification and Accreditation

Organizations that require secure systems need one or more methods to evaluate how well a system meets their security requirements. The formal evaluation process is divided into two phases, called certification and accreditation. The actual steps required in each phase depend on the evaluation criteria an organization chooses. A CISSP candidate must understand the need for each phase and the criteria commonly used to evaluate systems. The two evaluation phases are discussed in the next two sections, and then we present various evaluation criteria and considerations you must address when assessing the security of a system.

The process of evaluation provides a way to assess how well a system measures up to a desired level of security. Because each system's security level depends on many factors, all of them must be taken into account during the evaluation. Even though a system is initially described as secure, the installation process, physical environment, and general configuration details all contribute to its true general security. Two identical systems could be assessed at different levels of security due to configuration or installation differences.

The terms *certification, accreditation,* and *maintenance* used in the following sections are official terms used by the defense establishment and you should be familiar with them.

Certification and accreditation are additional steps in the software and IT systems development process normally required from defense contractors and others working in a military environment. The official definitions of these terms as used by the U.S. government are from Department of Defense Instruction 5200.40, Enclosure 2.

Certification

The first phase in a total evaluation process is *certification*. Certification is the comprehensive evaluation of the technical and nontechnical security features of an IT system and other safeguards made in support of the accreditation process to establish the extent to which a particular design and implementation meets a set of specified security requirements.

System certification is the technical evaluation of each part of a computer system to assess its concordance with security standards. First, you must choose evaluation criteria (we will present criteria alternatives in later sections). Once you select criteria to use, you analyze each system component to determine whether or not it satisfies the desired security goals. The certification analysis includes testing the system's hardware, software, and configuration. All controls are evaluated during this phase, including administrative, technical, and physical controls.

After you assess the entire system, you can evaluate the results to determine the security level the system supports in its current environment. The environment of a system is a critical part of the certification analysis, so a system can be more or less secure depending on its surroundings. The manner in which you connect a secure system to a network can change its security standing. Likewise, the physical security surrounding a system can affect the overall security rating. You must consider all factors when certifying a system.

You complete the certification phase when you have evaluated all factors and determined the level of security for the system. Remember that the certification is only valid for a system in a specific environment and configuration. Any changes could invalidate the certification. Once you have certified a security rating for a specific configuration, you are ready to seek acceptance of the system. Management accepts the certified security configuration of a system through the accreditation process.

Accreditation

In the certification phase, you test and document the security capabilities of a system in a specific configuration. With this information in hand, the management of an organization compares the capabilities of a system to the needs of the organization. It is imperative that the security policy clearly states the requirements of a security system. Management reviews the certification information and decides if the system satisfies the security needs of the organization. If management decides the certification of the system satisfies their needs, the system is *accredited*. Accreditation is the formal declaration by the Designated Approving Authority (DAA) that an IT system is approved to operate in a particular security mode using a prescribed set of safeguards at an acceptable level of risk. Once accreditation is performed, management can formally accept the adequacy of the overall security performance of an evaluated system.

The process of certification and accreditation is often an iterative process. In the accreditation phase, it is not uncommon to request changes to the configuration or additional controls to address security concerns. Remember that whenever you change the configuration, you must recertify the new configuration. Likewise, you need to recertify the system when a specific time period elapses or when you make any configuration changes. Your security policy should specify what conditions require recertification. A sound policy would list the amount of time a certification is valid along with any changes that would require you to restart the certification and accreditation process.

Certification and Accreditation Systems

There are two government standards currently in place for the certification and accreditation of computing systems: The DoD standard is the Defense Information Technology Security Certification and Accreditation Process (DITSCAP), and the standard for all U.S. government executive branch departments, agencies, and their contractors and consultants is the National Information Assurance Certification and Accreditation Process (NIACAP). Both of these processes are divided into four phases:

Phase 1: Definition Involves the assignment of appropriate project personnel; documentation of the mission need; and registration, negotiation, and creation of a System Security Authorization Agreement (SSAA) that guides the entire certification and accreditation process

Phase 2: Verification Includes refinement of the SSAA, systems development activities, and a certification analysis

Phase 3: Validation Includes further refinement of the SSAA, certification evaluation of the integrated system, development of a recommendation to the DAA, and the DAA's accreditation decision

Phase 4: Post Accreditation Includes maintenance of the SSAA, system operation, change management, and compliance validation

 These phases are adapted from Department of Defense Instruction 5200.40, Enclosure 3.

The NIACAP process, administered by the Information Systems Security Organization of the National Security Agency, outlines three different types of accreditation that may be granted. The definitions of these types of accreditation (from National Security Telecommunications and Information Systems Security Instruction 1000) are as follows:

- For a system accreditation, a major application or general support system is evaluated.

- For a site accreditation, the applications and systems at a specific, self-contained location are evaluated.

- For a type accreditation, an application or system that is distributed to a number of different locations is evaluated.

Common Flaws and Security Issues

No security architecture is complete and totally secure. There are weaknesses and vulnerabilities in every computer system. The goal of security models and architectures is to address as many known weaknesses as possible. This section presents some of the more common security issues that affect computer systems. You should understand each of the issues and how they can degrade the overall security of your system. Some issues and flaws overlap one another and are used in creative ways to attack systems. Although the following discussion covers the most common flaws, the list is not exhaustive. Attackers are very clever.

Covert Channels

A *covert channel* is a method that is used to pass information and that is not normally used for communication. Because the path is not normally used for communication, it may not be protected by the system's normal security controls. Usage of a covert channel provides a means to violate, bypass, or circumvent a security policy undetected. As you might imagine, a covert channel is the opposite of an *overt channel*. An overt channel is a known, expected, authorized, designed, monitored, and controlled method of communication.

There are two basic types of covert channels:

- A *covert timing channel* conveys information by altering the performance of a system component or modifying a resource's timing in a predictable manner. Using a covert timing channel is generally a more sophisticated method to covertly pass data and is very difficult to detect.

- A *covert storage channel* conveys information by writing data to a common storage area where another process can read it. Be diligent for any process that writes to any area of memory that another process can read.

Both types of covert channels rely on the use of communication techniques to exchange information with otherwise unauthorized subjects. Because the nature of the covert channel is that it is unusual and outside the normal data transfer environment, detecting it can be difficult. The best defense is to implement auditing and analyze log files for any covert channel activity.

The lowest level of security that addresses covert channels is B2 (F4+E4 for ITSEC, EAL5 for CC). All levels at or above level B2 must contain controls that detect and prohibit covert channels.

Attacks Based on Design or Coding Flaws and Security Issues

Certain attacks may result from poor design techniques, questionable implementation practices and procedure, or poor or inadequate testing. Some attacks may result from deliberate design decisions when special points of entry built into code to circumvent access controls, login, or other security checks often added to code while under development is not removed when that code is put into production. For what we hope are obvious reasons, such points of egress are properly called back doors because they avoid security measures by design (they're covered in a later section in this chapter, titled "Maintenance Hooks and Privileged Programs"). Extensive testing and code review is required to uncover such covert means of access, which are incredibly easy to remove during final phases of development but can be incredibly difficult to detect during testing or maintenance phases.

Although functionality testing is commonplace for commercial code and applications, separate testing for security issues has only been gaining attention and credibility in the past few years, courtesy of widely publicized virus and worm attacks and occasional defacements of or disruptions to widely used public sites online. In the sections that follow, we cover common sources of attack or security vulnerability that can be attributed to failures in design, implementation, pre-release code cleanup, or out-and-out coding mistakes. While avoidable, finding and fixing such flaws requires rigorous security-conscious design from the beginning of a development project and extra time and effort spent in testing and analysis. While this helps to explain the often lamentable state of software security, it does not excuse it!

Initialization and Failure States

When an unprepared system crashes and subsequently recovers, two opportunities to compromise its security controls may arise during that process. Many systems unload security controls as part of their shutdown procedures. *Trusted recovery* ensures that all controls remain intact in the event of a crash. During a trusted recovery, the system ensures that there are no opportunities for access to occur when security controls are disabled. Even the recovery phase runs with all controls intact.

For example, suppose a system crashes while a database transaction is being written to disk for a database classified as top secret. An unprotected system might allow an unauthorized user to access that temporary data before it gets written to disk. A system that supports trusted recovery ensures that no data confidentiality violations occur, even during the crash. This process requires careful planning and detailed procedures for handling system failures. Although automated recovery procedures may make up a portion of the entire recovery, manual intervention may still be required. Obviously, if such manual action is needed, appropriate identification and authentication for personnel performing recovery is likewise essential.

Input and Parameter Checking

One of the most notorious security violations is called a buffer overflow. This violation occurs when programmers fail to validate input data sufficiently, particularly when they do not impose a limit on the amount of data their software will accept as input. Because such data is usually stored in an input buffer, when the normal maximum size of the buffer is exceeded, the extra data is called *overflow*. Thus, the type of attack that results when someone attempts to supply malicious instructions or code as part of program input is called a *buffer overflow*. Unfortunately, in many systems such overflow data is often executed directly by the system under attack at a high level of privilege or at whatever level of privilege attaches to the process accepting such input. For nearly all types of operating systems, including Windows, Unix, Linux, and others, buffer overflows expose some of the most glaring and profound opportunities for compromise and attack of any kind of known security vulnerability.

The party responsible for a buffer overflow vulnerability is always the programmer who wrote the offending code. Due diligence from programmers can eradicate buffer overflows completely, but only if programmers check all input and parameters before storing them in any data structure (and limit how much data can be proffered as input). Proper data validation is the only way to do away with buffer overflows. Otherwise, discovery of buffer overflows leads to a familiar pattern of critical security updates that must be applied to affected systems to close the point of attack.

Checking Code for Buffer Overflows

In early 2002, Bill Gates acted in his traditional role as the archetypal Microsoft spokesperson when he announced something he called the "Trustworthy Computing Initiative," a series of design philosophy changes intended to beef up the often questionable standing of Microsoft's operating systems and applications when viewed from a security perspective. As discussion on this subject continued through 2002 and 2003, the topic of buffer overflows occurred repeatedly (more often, in fact, than Microsoft Security Bulletins reported security flaws related to this kind of problem, which is among the most serious yet most frequently reported types of programming errors with security implications). As is the case for many other development organizations and also for the builders of software development environments (the software tools that developers use to create other software), increased awareness of buffer overflow exploits has caused changes at many stages during the development process:

- Designers must specify bounds for input data or state acceptable input values and set hard limits on how much data will be accepted, parsed, and handled when input is solicited.

- Developers must follow such limitations when building code that solicits, accepts, and handles input.

- Testers must check to make sure that buffer overflows can't occur and attempt to circumvent or bypass security settings when testing input handling code.

In his book *Secrets & Lies*, noted information security expert Bruce Schneier makes a great case that security testing is in fact quite different from standard testing activities like unit testing, module testing, acceptance testing, and quality assurance checks (see the glossary) that software companies have routinely performed as part of the development process for years and years. What's not yet clear at Microsoft (and at other development companies as well, to be as fair to the colossus of Redmond as possible) is whether this change in design and test philosophy equates to the right kind of rigor necessary to foil all buffer overflows or not (some of the most serious security holes that Microsoft reports as recently as April 2005 clearly invoke "buffer overruns" or identify the cause of the vulnerability as an "unchecked buffer").

Maintenance Hooks and Privileged Programs

Maintenance hooks are entry points into a system that are known by only the developer of the system. Such entry points are also called *back doors*. Although the existence of maintenance hooks is a clear violation of security policy, they still pop up in many systems. The original purpose of back doors was to provide guaranteed access to the system for maintenance reasons or if regular access was inadvertently disabled. The problem is that this type of access bypasses all security controls and provides free access to anyone who knows that the back doors exist. It is imperative that you explicitly prohibit such entry points and monitor your audit logs to uncover any activity that may indicate unauthorized administrator access.

Another common system vulnerability is the practice of executing a program whose security level is elevated during execution. Such programs must be carefully written and tested so they do not allow any exit and/or entry points that would leave a subject with a higher security rating. Ensure that all programs that operate at a high security level are accessible only to appropriate users and that they are hardened against misuse.

Incremental Attacks

Some forms of attack occur in slow, gradual increments rather than through obvious or recognizable attempts to compromise system security or integrity. Two such forms of attack are called data diddling and the salami attack. *Data diddling* occurs when an attacker gains access to a system and makes small, random, or incremental changes to data during storage, processing, input, output, or transaction rather than obviously altering file contents or damaging or deleting entire files. Such changes can be difficult to detect unless files and data are protected by encryption or some kind of integrity check (such as a checksum or message digest) is routinely performed and applied each time a file is read or written. Encrypted file systems, file-level encryption techniques, or some form of file monitoring (which includes integrity checks like those performed by applications like TripWire) usually offer adequate guarantees that no data diddling is underway. Data diddling is often considered an attack performed more often by insiders rather than outsiders (i.e., external intruders). It should be obvious that since data diddling is an attack that alters data, it is considered an active attack.

The *salami attack* is more apocryphal, by all published reports. The name of the attack refers to a systematic whittling at assets in accounts or other records with financial value, where very small amounts are deducted from balances regularly and routinely. Metaphorically, the attack may be explained as stealing a very thin slice from a salami each time it's put on the slicing machine when it's being accessed by a paying customer. In reality, though no documented examples of such an attack are available, most security experts concede that salami attacks are possible, especially when organizational insiders could be involved. Only by proper separation of duties and proper control over code can organizations completely prevent or eliminate such an attack. Setting financial transaction monitors to track very small transfers of funds or other items of value should help to detect such activity; regular employee notification of the practice should help to discourage attempts at such attacks.

If you'd like an entertaining method of learning about the salami attack or the salami technique, view the movies *Office Space, Sneakers,* and *Superman III.*

Programming

We have already mentioned the biggest flaw in programming. The buffer overflow comes from the programmer failing to check the format and/or the size of input data. There are other potential flaws with programs. Any program that does not handle any exception gracefully is in danger of exiting in an unstable state. It is possible to cleverly crash a program after it has increased its security level to carry out a normal task. If an attacker is successful in crashing the program at the right time, they can attain the higher security level and cause damage to the confidentiality, integrity, and availability of your system.

All programs that are executed directly or indirectly must be fully tested to comply with your security model. Make sure you have the latest version of any software installed and be aware of any known security vulnerabilities. Because each security model, and each security policy, is different, you must ensure that the software you execute does not exceed the authority you allow. Writing secure code is difficult, but it's certainly possible. Make sure all programs you use are designed to address security concerns.

Timing, State Changes, and Communication Disconnects

Computer systems perform tasks with rigid precision. Computers excel at repeatable tasks. Attackers can develop attacks based on the predictability of task execution. The common sequence of events for an algorithm is to check that a resource is available and then access it if you are permitted. The *time-of-check (TOC)* is the time at which the subject checks on the status of the object. There may be several decisions to make before returning to the object to access it. When the decision is made to access the object, the procedure accesses it at the *time-of-use (TOU)*. The difference between the TOC and the TOU is sometimes large enough for an attacker to replace the original object with another object that suits their own needs. *Time-of-check-to-time-of-use (TOCTTOU)* attacks are often called race conditions because the attacker is racing with the legitimate process to replace the object before it is used.

A classic example of a TOCTTOU attack is replacing a data file after its identity has been verified but before data is read. By replacing one authentic data file with another file of the attacker's choosing and design, an attacker can potentially direct the actions of a program in many ways. Of course, the attacker would have to have in-depth knowledge of the program and system under attack.

Likewise, attackers can attempt to take action between two known states when the state of a resource or the entire system changes. Communication disconnects also provide small windows that an attacker might seek to exploit. Any time a status check of a resource precedes action on the resource, a window of opportunity exists for a potential attack in the brief interval between check and action. These attacks must be addressed in your security policy and in your security model.

Electromagnetic Radiation

Simply because of the kinds of electronic components from which they're built, many computer hardware devices emit electromagnetic radiation during normal operation. The process of communicating with other machines or peripheral equipment creates emanations that can be intercepted. It's even possible to re-create keyboard input or monitor output by intercepting and processing electromagnetic radiation from the keyboard and computer monitor. You can also detect and read network packets passively (that is, without actually tapping into the cable) as they pass along a network segment. These emanation leaks can cause serious security issues but are generally easy to address.

The easiest way to eliminate electromagnetic radiation interception is to reduce emanation through cable shielding or conduit and block unauthorized personnel and devices from getting too close to equipment or cabling by applying physical security controls. By reducing the signal strength and increasing the physical buffer around sensitive equipment, you can dramatically reduce the risk of signal interception.

Summary

Secure systems are not just assembled. They are designed to support security. Systems that must be secure are judged for their ability to support and enforce the security policy. This process of evaluating the effectiveness of a computer system is called certification. The certification process is the technical evaluation of a system's ability to meet its design goals. Once a system has satisfactorily passed the technical evaluation, the management of an organization begins the formal acceptance of the system. The formal acceptance process is called accreditation.

The entire certification and accreditation process depends on standard evaluation criteria. Several criteria exist for evaluating computer security systems. The earliest criteria, TCSEC, was developed by the U.S. Department of Defense. TCSEC, also called the Orange Book, provides criteria to evaluate the functionality and assurance of a system's security components. ITSEC is an alternative to the TCSEC guidelines and is used more often in European countries. Regardless of which criteria you use, the evaluation process includes reviewing each security control for compliance with the security policy. The better a system enforces the good behavior of subjects' access to objects, the higher the security rating.

When security systems are designed, it is often helpful to create a security model to represent the methods the system will use to implement the security policy. We discussed three security models in this chapter. The earliest model, the Bell-LaPadula model, supports data confidentiality only. It was designed for the military and satisfies military concerns. The Biba model and the Clark-Wilson model address the integrity of data and do so in different ways. The latter two security models are appropriate for commercial applications.

No matter how sophisticated a security model is, flaws exist that attackers can exploit. Some flaws, such as buffer overflows and maintenance hooks, are introduced by programmers, whereas others, such as covert channels, are architectural design issues. It is important to understand the impact of such issues and modify the security architecture when appropriate to compensate.

Exam Essentials

Know the definitions of certification and accreditation.   Certification is the technical evaluation of each part of a computer system to assess its concordance with security standards. Accreditation is the process of formal acceptance of a certified configuration.

Be able to describe open and closed systems.   Open systems are designed using industry standards and are usually easy to integrate with other open systems. Closed systems are generally proprietary hardware and/or software. Their specifications are not normally published and they are usually harder to integrate with other systems.

Know what confinement, bounds, and isolation are.   Confinement restricts a process to reading from and writing to certain memory locations. Bounds are the limits of memory a process cannot exceed when reading or writing. Isolation is the mode a process runs in when it is confined through the use of memory bounds.

Be able to define *object* and *subject* in terms of access.   The subject of an access is the user or process that makes a request to access a resource. The object of an access request is the resource a user or process wishes to access.

Know how security controls work and what they do.   Security controls use access rules to limit the access by a subject to an object.

Be able to list the classes of TCSEC, ITSEC, and the Common Criteria.   The classes of TCSEC include A: Verified protection; B: Mandatory protection; C: Discretionary protection and D: Minimal protection. Table 12.3 covers and compares equivalent and applicable rankings for TCSEC, ITSEC, and the CC (remember that functionality ratings from F7 to F10 in ITSEC have no corresponding ratings in TCSEC).

Define a trusted computing base (TCB).   A TCB is the combination of hardware, software, and controls that form a trusted base that enforces the security policy.

Be able to explain what a security perimeter is.   A security perimeter is the imaginary boundary that separates the TCB from the rest of the system. TCB components communicate with non-TCB components using trusted paths.

Know what the reference monitor and the security kernel are.   The reference monitor is the logical part of the TCB that confirms whether a subject has the right to use a resource prior to granting access. The security kernel is the collection of the TCB components that implement the functionality of the reference monitor.

Describe the Bell-LaPadula security model.   The Bell-LaPadula security model was developed in the 1970s to address military concerns over unauthorized access to secret data. It is built on a state machine model and ensures the confidentiality of protected data.

Describe the Biba integrity model.   The Biba integrity model was designed to ensure the integrity of data. It is very similar to the Bell-LaPadula model, but its properties ensure that data is not corrupted by subjects accessing objects at different security levels.

Describe the Clark-Wilson security model.   The Clark-Wilson security model ensures data integrity as the Biba model does, but it does so using a different approach. Instead of being built on a state machine, the Clark-Wilson model uses object access restrictions to allow only specific programs to modify objects. Clark-Wilson also enforces the separation of duties, which further protects the data integrity.

Describe the difference between certification and accreditation and the various types of accreditation.   Understand the certification and accreditation processes used by the U.S. Department of Defense and all other executive government agencies. Describe the differences between system accreditation, site accreditation, and type accreditation.

Be able to explain what covert channels are.   A covert channel is any method that is used to pass information but that is not normally used for information.

Understand what buffer overflows and input checking are.   A buffer overflow occurs when the programmer fails to check the size of input data prior to writing the data into a specific memory location. In fact, any failure to validate input data could result in a security violation.

Describe common flaws to security architectures.   In addition to buffer overflows, programmers can leave back doors and privileged programs on a system after it is deployed. Even well-written systems can be susceptible to time-of-check-to-time-of-use (TOCTTOU) attacks. Any state change could be a potential window of opportunity for an attacker to compromise a system.

Review Questions

1. What is system certification?

    A. Formal acceptance of a stated system configuration

    B. A technical evaluation of each part of a computer system to assess its compliance with security standards

    C. A functional evaluation of the manufacturer's goals for each hardware and software component to meet integration standards

    D. A manufacturer's certificate stating that all components were installed and configured correctly

2. What is system accreditation?

    A. Formal acceptance of a stated system configuration

    B. A functional evaluation of the manufacturer's goals for each hardware and software component to meet integration standards

    C. Acceptance of test results that prove the computer system enforces the security policy

    D. The process to specify secure communication between machines

3. What is a closed system?

    A. A system designed around final, or closed, standards

    B. A system that includes industry standards

    C. A proprietary system that uses unpublished protocols

    D. Any machine that does not run Windows

4. Which best describes a confined process?

    A. A process that can run only for a limited time

    B. A process that can run only during certain times of the day

    C. A process that can access only certain memory locations

    D. A process that controls access to an object

5. What is an access object?

    A. A resource a user or process wishes to access

    B. A user or process that wishes to access a resource

    C. A list of valid access rules

    D. The sequence of valid access types

6. What is a security control?

    A. A security component that stores attributes that describe an object

    B. A document that lists all data classification types

    C. A list of valid access rules

    D. A mechanism that limits access to an object

7. For what type of information system security accreditation are the applications and systems at a specific, self-contained location evaluated?

    A. System accreditation

    B. Site accreditation

    C. Application accreditation

    D. Type accreditation

8. How many major categories do the TCSEC criteria define?

    A. Two

    B. Three

    C. Four

    D. Five

9. What is a trusted computing base (TCB)?

    A. Hosts on your network that support secure transmissions

    B. The operating system kernel and device drivers

    C. The combination of hardware, software, and controls that work together to enforce a security policy

    D. The software and controls that certify a security policy

10. What is a security perimeter? (Choose all that apply.)

    A. The boundary of the physically secure area surrounding your system

    B. The imaginary boundary that separates the TCB from the rest of the system

    C. The network where your firewall resides

    D. Any connections to your computer system

11. What part of the TCB validates access to every resource prior to granting the requested access?

    A. TCB partition

    B. Trusted library

    C. Reference monitor

    D. Security kernel

12. What is the best definition of a security model?

    A. A security model states policies an organization must follow.

    B. A security model provides a framework to implement a security policy.

    C. A security model is a technical evaluation of each part of a computer system to assess its concordance with security standards.

    D. A security model is the process of formal acceptance of a certified configuration.

13. Which security models are built on a state machine model?

    A. Bell-LaPadula and Take-Grant

    B. Biba and Clark-Wilson

    C. Clark-Wilson and Bell-LaPadula

    D. Bell-LaPadula and Biba

14. Which security model(s) address(es) data confidentiality?

    A. Bell-LaPadula

    B. Biba

    C. Clark-Wilson

    D. Both A and B

15. Which Bell-LaPadula property keeps lower-level subjects from accessing objects with a higher security level?

    A. * (star) Security Property

    B. No write up property

    C. No read up property

    D. No read down property

16. What is a covert channel?

    A. A method that is used to pass information and that is not normally used for communication

    B. Any communication used to transmit secret or top secret data

    C. A trusted path between the TCB and the rest of the system

    D. Any channel that crosses the security perimeter

17. What term describes an entry point that only the developer knows about into a system?

    A. Maintenance hook

    B. Covert channel

    C. Buffer overflow

    D. Trusted path

18. What is the time-of-check?

    A. The length of time it takes a subject to check the status of an object

    B. The time at which the subject checks on the status of the object

    C. The time at which a subject accesses an object

    D. The time between checking and accessing an object

19. How can electromagnetic radiation be used to compromise a system?

   A. Electromagnetic radiation can be concentrated to disrupt computer operation.

   B. Electromagnetic radiation makes some protocols inoperable.

   C. Electromagnetic radiation can be intercepted.

   D. Electromagnetic radiation is necessary for some communication protocol protection schemes to work.

20. What is the most common programmer-generated security flaw?

   A. TOCTTOU vulnerability

   B. Buffer overflow

   C. Inadequate control checks

   D. Improper logon authentication

Answers to Review Questions

1. B. A system certification is a technical evaluation. Option A describes system accreditation. Options C and D refer to manufacturer standards, not implementation standards.

2. A. Accreditation is the formal acceptance process. Option B is not an appropriate answer because it addresses manufacturer standards. Options C and D are incorrect because there is no way to prove that a configuration enforces a security policy and accreditation does not entail secure communication specification.

3. C. A closed system is one that uses largely proprietary or unpublished protocols and standards. Options A and D do not describe any particular systems, and Option B describes an open system.

4. C. A constrained process is one that can access only certain memory locations. Options A, B, and D do not describe a constrained process.

5. A. An object is a resource a user or process wishes to access. Option A describes an access object.

6. D. A control limits access to an object to protect it from misuse from unauthorized users.

7. B. The applications and systems at a specific, self-contained location are evaluated for DITSCAP and NIACAP site accreditation.

8. C. TCSEC defines four major categories: Category A is verified protection, category B is mandatory protection, category C is discretionary protection, and category D is minimal protection.

9. C. The TCB is the part of your system you can trust to support and enforce your security policy.

10. A, B. Although the most correct answer in the context of this chapter is B, option A is also a correct answer in the context of physical security.

11. C. Options A and B are not valid TCB components. Option D, the security kernel, is the collection of TCB components that work together to implement the reference monitor functions.

12. B. Option B is the only option that correctly defines a security model. Options A, C, and D define part of a security policy and the certification and accreditation process.

13. D. The Bell-LaPadula and Biba models are built on the state machine model.

14. A. Only the Bell-LaPadula model addresses data confidentiality. The other models address data integrity.

15. C. The no read up property, also called the Simple Security Policy, prohibits subjects from reading a higher security level object.

16. A. A covert channel is any method that is used to secretly pass data and that is not normally used for communication. All of the other options describe normal communication channels.

17. A. An entry point that only the developer knows about into a system is a maintenance hook, or back door.

18. B. Option B defines the time-of-check (TOC), which is the time at which a subject verifies the status of an object.

19. C. If a receiver is in close enough proximity to an electromagnetic radiation source, it can be intercepted.

20. B. By far, the buffer overflow is the most common, and most avoidable, programmer-generated vulnerability.

Chapter

13

Administrative Management

All companies must take into account the issues that can make day-to-day operations susceptible to breaches in security. *Personnel management* is a form of administrative control, or administrative management, and is an important factor in maintaining operations security. Clearly defined personnel management practices must be included in your security policy and subsequent formalized security structure documentation (i.e., standards, guidelines, and procedures).

Operations security topics are related to personnel management because personnel management can directly affect security and daily operations. They are included in the Operations Security domain of the Common Body of Knowledge (CBK) for the CISSP certification exam, which deals with topics and issues related to maintaining an established secure IT environment. Operations security is concerned with maintaining the IT infrastructure after it has been designed and deployed and involves using hardware controls, media controls, and subject (user) controls that are designed to protect against asset threats.

This domain is discussed in this chapter and further in the following chapter (Chapter 14, "Auditing and Monitoring"). Be sure to read and study both chapters to ensure your understanding of the essential antivirus and operations material.

Operations Security Concepts

The primary purpose of operations security is to safeguard information assets that are resident in a system on a day-to-day basis, to identify and safeguard any vulnerabilities there are in the system, and finally, to prevent any exploitation of threats. Administrators often consider the relationship between assets, vulnerabilities, and threats an *operations security triple*. The trick from here is how to tackle the operations security triple.

The Operations Security domain is a broad collection of many concepts that are both distinct and interrelated, including antivirus management, operational assurance, backup maintenance, changes in location, privileges, trusted recovery, configuration and *change management control*, due care and due diligence, privacy, security, and operations controls.

The following sections highlight these important day-to-day issues that affect company operations by discussing them in relation to maintaining security.

Antivirus Management

Viruses are the most common form of security breach in the IT world. Any communications pathway can be and is being exploited as a delivery mechanism for a virus or other malicious code. Viruses are distributed via e-mail (the most common means), websites, and documents and even within commercial software. Antivirus management is the design, deployment, and maintenance of an antivirus solution for your IT environment.

If users are allowed to install and execute software without restriction, then the IT infrastructure is more vulnerable to virus infections. To provide a more virus-free environment, you should make sure software is rigidly controlled. Users should be able to install and execute only company approved and distributed software. All new software should be thoroughly tested and scanned before it is distributed on a production network. Even commercial software has become an inadvertent carrier of viruses.

Users should be trained in the skills of safe computing, especially if they are granted Internet access or have any form of e-mail. In areas where technical controls cannot prevent virus infections, users should be trained to prevent them. User awareness training should include information about handling attachments or downloads from unknown sources and unrequested attachments from known sources. Users should be told to never test an executable by executing it. All instances of suspect software should be reported immediately to the security administrator.

Antivirus software should be deployed on multiple levels of a network. All traffic—including internal, inbound, and outbound—should be scanned for viruses. A virus scanning tool should be present on all border connection points, on all servers, and on all clients. Installing products from different vendors on each of these three arenas will provide a more thorough and foolproof scanning gauntlet.

Never install more than one virus scanning tool on a single system. It will cause an unrecoverable system failure in most cases.

Endeavor to have 100-percent virus-free servers and 100-percent virus-free backups. To accomplish the former, you must scan every single bit of data before it is allowed into or onto a server for processing or storage. To accomplish the latter, you must scan every bit of data before it is stored onto the backup media. Having virus-free systems and backups will enable you to recover from a virus infection in an efficient and timely manner.

In addition to using a multilevel or concentric circle antivirus strategy, you must maintain the system. A concentric circle strategy basically consists of multiple layers of antivirus scanning throughout the environment to ensure that all current data and backups are free from viruses. Regular updates to the virus signature and definitions database should be performed. However, distribution of updates should occur only after verifying that the update is benign. It is possible for virus lists and engine updates to crash a system.

Maintain vigilance by joining notification newsletters, mailing lists, and vendor sites. When a new virus epidemic breaks out, take appropriate action by shutting down your e-mail service or Internet connectivity (if at all possible) until a solution/repair/inoculation is available.

Operational Assurance and Life Cycle Assurance

Assurance is the degree of confidence you can place in the satisfaction of security needs of a computer, network, solution, and so on. It is based on how well a specific system complies with stated security needs and how well it upholds the security services it provides. Assurance was discussed in Chapter 12, "Principles of Security Models," but there is another element of assurance that applies to the Operation Security domain.

The Trusted Computer System Evaluation Criteria (TCSEC) is used to assign a level of assurance to systems. TCSEC, or the Orange Book, also defines two additional types or levels of assurance: operational assurance and life cycle assurance. As you are aware, TCSEC was replaced by Common Criteria in December 2000. It is, however, important to be aware of TCSEC-related material simply as a means to convey concepts and theories about security evaluation. Thus, you don't need to know the complete details of these two assurance levels, but there are a few specific issues that you should be familiar with.

Operational assurance focuses on the basic features and architecture of a system that lend themselves to supporting security. There are five requirements or elements of operation assurance:

- System architecture (We discussed system architecture in Chapter 7.)

- System integrity (For more information, see Chapters 11 and 12.)

- Covert channel analysis (For more information, see Chapter 12.)

- Trusted facility management (Check out Chapter 19 for information about trusted facility management.)

- Trusted recovery (We discussed this in Chapter 13.)

Life cycle assurance focuses on the controls and standards that are necessary for designing, building, and maintaining a system. The following are the four requirements or elements of life cycle assurance (these are all covered in detail in Chapter 7):

- Security testing

- Design specification and testing

- Configuration management

- Trusted distribution

Backup Maintenance

Backing up critical information is a key part of maintaining the availability and integrity of data. Systems fail for various reasons, such as hardware failure, physical damage, software corruption, and malicious destruction from intrusions and attacks. Having a reliable backup is the best form of insurance that the data on the affected system is not permanently lost. Backups are the only form of insurance available against data loss. Without a backup, it is often impossible to restore data to its pre-disaster state. A backup can be considered reliable only if it is periodically tested. Testing a backup involves restoring files from backup media and then checking them to make sure they're readable and correct.

Backups are an essential part of maintaining operations security and are discussed further in Chapter 16, "Disaster Recovery Planning."

Changes in Workstation/Location

Changes in a user's workstation or in their physical location within an organization can be used as a means to improve or maintain security. Similar to job rotation, changing a user's workstation prevents a user from altering the system or installing unapproved software because the next person to use the system would most likely be able to discover it. Having nonpermanent workstations encourages users to keep all materials stored on network servers where it can be easily protected, overseen, and audited. It also discourages the storage of personal information on the system as a whole. A periodic change in the physical location of a user's workspace can also be a deterrent to collusion because they are less likely to be able to convince employees with whom they're not familiar to perform unauthorized or illegal activities.

Need-to-Know and the Principle of Least Privilege

Need-to-know and the principle of least privilege are two standard axioms of high-security environments. A user must have a need-to-know to gain access to data or resources. Even if that user has an equal or greater security classification than the requested information, if they do not have a need-to-know, they are denied access. A *need-to-know* is the requirement to have access to, knowledge about, or possession of data or a resource to perform specific work tasks. The *principle of least privilege* is the notion that users should be granted the least amount of access to the secure environment as possible for them to be able to complete their work tasks.

Periodic Reviews of User Account Management

Many administrators utilize periodic reviews of user account management to revisit and maintain processes and procedures employed by the administrative staff in their support of users. Such reviews should include examination of how well the principle of least privilege is being enforced, whether active accounts are still in use, if out-of-use accounts have been disabled or deleted, and whether all current practices are approved by management.

Review of user account management typically does not address whether a specific user's password conforms to the stated company password policy. That issue is covered by the enrollment tools, password policies, and periodic penetration testing/ethical hacking activities.

It is also important to note that the action of adding, removing, and managing the settings of user accounts are the purview of the account administrators or operations administrators, not that of a security administrator. However, it is the responsibility of security administrators to set the clearances of users in a MAC-based environment.

Privileged Operations Functions

Privileged operations functions are activities that require special access or privileges to perform within a secured IT environment. In most cases, these functions are restricted to administrators and system operators. Maintaining privileged control over these functions is an essential part of sustaining the system's security. Many of these functions could be easily exploited to violate the confidentiality, integrity, or availability of the system's assets.

The following list includes some examples of privileged operations functions:

- Using operating system control commands
- Configuring interfaces
- Accessing audit logs
- Managing user accounts
- Configuring security mechanism controls
- Running script/task automation tools
- Backing up and restoring the system
- Controlling communication
- Using database recovery tools and log files
- Controlling system reboots

Managing privileged access is an important part of keeping security under control. In addition to restricting privileged operations functions, you should also employ separation of duties. Separation of duties ensures that no single person has total control over a system's or environment's security mechanisms. This is necessary to ensure that no single person can compromise the system as a whole. It can also be called a form of split knowledge. In deployment, separation of duties is enforced by dividing the top- and mid-level administrative capabilities and functions among multiple trusted users.

Further control and restriction of privileged capabilities can be implemented by using two-man controls and rotation of duties. Two-man controls is the configuration of privileged activities so that they require two administrators to work in conjunction in order to complete the task. The necessity of two operators also gives you the benefits of peer review and reduced likelihood of collusion and fraud. Rotation of duties is the security control that involves switching several privileged security or operational roles among several users on a regular basis. For example, if an organization has divided its administrative activities into six distinct roles or job descriptions, then six or seven people need to be cross-trained for those distinct roles. Each person would work in a specific role for two to three months, and then everyone in this group would be switched or rotated to a new role. When the organization has more than the necessary minimum number of trained administrators, every rotation leaves out one person, who can take some vacation time and serve as a fill-in when necessary. The rotation of duties security control provides for peer review, reduces collusion and fraud, and provides for cross-training. Cross-training makes your environment less dependent on any single individual.

Trusted Recovery

For a secured system, trusted recovery is recovering securely from operation failures or system crashes. The purpose of trusted recovery is to provide assurance that after a failure or crash, the rebooted system is no less secure than it was before the failure or crash. You must address two elements of the process to implement a trusted recovery solution. The first element is failure preparation. In most cases, this is simply the deployment of a reliable backup solution that keeps a current backup of all data. A reliable backup solution also implies that there is a means by which data on the backup media can be restored in a protected and efficient manner. The second element is the process of system recovery. The system should be forced to reboot into a single-user nonprivileged state. This means that the system should reboot so that a normal user account can be used to log in and that the system does not grant unauthorized access to users. System recovery also includes the restoration of all affected files and services active or in use on the system at the time of the failure or crash. Any missing or damaged files are restored, any changes to classification labels are corrected, and the settings on all security critical files is verified.

Trusted recovery is a security mechanism discussed in the Common Criteria. The Common Criteria defines three types or hierarchical levels of trusted recovery:

Manual Recovery   An administrator is required to manually perform the actions necessary to implement a secured or trusted recovery after a failure or system crash.

Automated Recovery   The system itself is able to perform trusted recovery activities to restore a system, but only against a single failure.

Automated Recovery without Undue Loss   The system itself is able to perform trusted recovery activities to restore a system. This level of trusted recovery allows for additional steps to provide verification and protection of classified objects. These additional protection mechanisms may include restoring corrupted files, rebuilding data from transaction logs, and verifying the integrity of key system and security components.

What happens when a systems suffers from an uncontrolled TCB or media failure? Such failures may compromise the stability and security of the environment, and the only possible response is to terminate the current environment and re-create the environment through rebooting. Related to trusted recovery, an emergency system restart is the feature of a security system that forces an immediate reboot once the system goes down.

Configuration and Change Management Control

Once a system has been properly secured, it is important to keep that security intact. Change in a secure environment can introduce loopholes, overlaps, missing objects, and oversights that can lead to new vulnerabilities. The only way to maintain security in the face of change is to systematically manage change. Typically, this involves extensive logging, auditing, and monitoring of activities related to security controls and mechanisms. The resulting data is then used to identify agents of change, whether objects, subjects, programs, communication pathways, or even the network itself. The means to provide this function is to deploy *configuration management* control or change management control. These mechanisms ensure that any alterations or changes to a system do not result in diminished security. Configuration/change management controls provide a process by which all system changes are tracked, audited, controlled, identified, and approved. It requires that all system changes undergo a rigorous testing procedure before being deployed onto the production environment. It also requires documentation of any changes to user work tasks and the training of any affected users. Configuration/change management controls should minimize the effect on security from any alteration to the system. They often provide a means to roll back a change if it is found to cause a negative or unwanted effect on the system or on security.

There are five steps or phases involved in configuration/change management control:

1. Applying to introduce a change
2. Cataloging the intended change
3. Scheduling the change
4. Implementing the change
5. Reporting the change to the appropriate parties

When a configuration/change management control solution is enforced, it creates complete documentation of all changes to a system. This provides a trail of information if the change needs to be removed. It also provides a roadmap or procedure to follow if the same change is implemented on other systems. When a change is properly documented, that documentation can assist administrators in minimizing the negative effects of the change throughout the environment.

Configuration/change management control is a mandatory element of the TCSEC ratings of B2, B3, and A1 but it is recommended for all other TCSEC rating levels. Ultimately, change management improves the security of an environment by protecting implemented security from unintentional, tangential, or effected diminishments. Those in charge of change management should oversee alterations to every aspect of a system, including hardware configuration and system and application software. It should be included in design, development, testing, evaluation, implementation, distribution, evolution, growth, ongoing operation, and application of modifications. Change management requires a detailed inventory of every component and configuration. It also requires the collection and maintenance of complete documentation for every system component (including hardware and software) and for everything from configuration settings to security features.

Standards of Due Care and Due Diligence

Due care is using reasonable care to protect the interests of an organization. *Due diligence* is practicing the activities that maintain the due care effort. For example, due care is developing a formalized security structure containing a security policy, standards, baselines, guidelines, and procedures. Due diligence is the continued application of this security structure onto the IT infrastructure of an organization. Operational security is the ongoing maintenance of continued due care and due diligence by all responsible parties within an organization.

In today's business environment, showing prudent due care and due diligence is the only way to disprove negligence in an occurrence of loss. Senior management must show reasonable due care and due diligence to reduce their culpability and liability when a loss occurs. Senior management could be responsible for monetary damages up to $290 million for nonperformance of due diligence in accordance with the U.S. Federal Sentencing Guidelines of 1991.

Privacy and Protection

Privacy is the protection of personal information from disclosure to any unauthorized individual or entity. In today's online world, the line between public information and private information is often blurry. For example, is information about your web surfing habits private or public? Can that information be gathered legally without your consent? And can the gathering organization sell that information for a profit that you don't share in? However, your personal information includes more than information about your online habits; it also includes who you are (name, address, phone, race, religion, age, etc.), your health and medical records, your financial records, and even your criminal or legal records.

Dealing with privacy is a requirement for any organization that has people as employees. Thus, privacy is a central issue for all organizations. The protection of privacy should be a core mission or goal set forth in the security policy of an organization. Privacy issues are discussed at greater length in Chapter 17, "Law and Investigations."

Legal Requirements

Every organization operates within a certain industry and country. Both of these entities impose legal requirements, restrictions, and regulations on the practices of organizations that fall within their realm. These legal requirements can apply to licensed use of software, hiring restrictions, handling of sensitive materials, and compliance with safety regulations. Complying with all applicable legal requirements is a key part of sustaining security. The legal requirements of an industry and of a country (and often of a state and city) should be considered the baseline or foundation upon which the remainder of the security infrastructure must be built.

Illegal Activities

Illegal activities are actions that violate a legal restriction, regulation, or requirement. They include fraud, misappropriation, unauthorized disclosure, theft, destruction, espionage, entrapment, and so on. A secure environment should provide mechanisms to prevent the committal of illegal activities and the means to track illegal activities and maintain accountability from the individuals perpetrating the crimes.

Preventative control mechanisms include identification and authentication, access control, separation of duties, job rotation, mandatory vacations, background screening, awareness training, least privilege, and many more. Detective mechanisms include auditing, intrusion detection systems, and more.

Record Retention

Record retention is the organizational policy that defines what information is maintained and for how long. In most cases, the records in question are audit trails of user activity. This may include file and resource access, logon patterns, e-mail, and the use of privileges. Note that in some legal jurisdictions, users must be made aware that their activities are being tracked.

Depending upon your industry and your relationship with the government, you may need to retain records for three years, seven years, or indefinitely. In most cases, a separate backup mechanism is used to create archived copies of sensitive audit trails and accountability information. This allows for the main data backup system to periodically reuse its media without violating the requirement to retain audit trails and the like.

If data about individuals is being retained by your organization (such as a conditional employment agreement or a use agreement), the employees and customers need to be made aware of it. In many cases, the notification requirement is a legal issue; in others, it is simply a courtesy. In either case, it is a good idea to discuss the issue with appropriate legal counsel.

Sensitive Information and Media

Managing information and media properly—especially in a high-security environment in which sensitive, confidential, and proprietary data is processed—is crucial to the security and stability of an organization. Because the value of the stored data is momentous in comparison with the cost of the storage media, always purchase media of the highest quality. In addition to media selection, there are several key areas of information and media management: marking, handling, storage, life span, reuse, and destruction. Marking, handling, storage, and observance of life span ensure the viability of data on a storage media. Reuse and destruction focus on destroying the hosted data, not retaining it.

Marking and Labeling Media

The marking of media is the simple and obvious activity of clearly and accurately defining its contents. The most important aspect of marking is to indicate the security classification of the data stored on the media so that the media itself can be handled properly. Tapes with unclassified data do not need as much security in their storage and transport as do tapes with classified data. Data labels should be created automatically and stored as part of the backup set on the media. Additionally, a physical label should be applied to the media and maintained for the lifetime of the media. Media used to store classified information should never be reused to store less-sensitive data. Media labels help to ensure proper handling of hosted sensitive, classified, or confidential data. All removable media, including tapes, USB drives, floppies, CDs, hard drives, and printouts, should be labeled.

Handling Media

Handling refers to the secured transportation of media from the point of purchase through storage and finally to destruction. Media must be handled in a manner consistent with the classification of the data it hosts. The environment within which media is stored can significantly affect its useful lifetime. For example, very warm environments or very dusty environments can cause damage to tape media, shortening its life span. Here are some useful guidelines for handling media:

- Keep new media in its original sealed packaging until it's needed to keep it isolated from the environment's dust and dirt.

- When opening a media package, take extra caution not to damage the media in any way. This includes avoiding sharp objects and not twisting or flexing the media.

- Avoid exposing the media to temperature extremes; it shouldn't be stored too close to heaters, radiators, air conditioners, or anything else that could cause extreme temperatures.

- Do not use media that has been damaged in any way, exposed to abnormal levels of dust and dirt, or dropped.

- Media should be transported from one site to another in a temperature-controlled vehicle.

- Media should be protected from exposure to the outside environment; avoid sunlight, moisture, humidity, heat, and cold. Always transport media in an airtight, waterproof, secured container.

- Media should be acclimated for 24 hours before use.

- Appropriate security should be maintained over media from the point of departure from the backup device to the secured offsite storage facility. Media is vulnerable to damage and theft at any point during transportation.

- Appropriate security should be maintained over media at all other times (including when it's reused) throughout the lifetime of the media until destruction.

Storing Media

Media should be stored only in a secured location in which the temperature and humidity is controlled, and it should not be exposed to magnetic fields, especially tape media. Elevator motors, printers, and CRT monitors all have strong electric fields. The cleanliness of the storage area will directly affect the life span and usefulness of media. Access to the storage facility should be controlled at all times. Physical security is essential to maintaining the confidentiality, integrity, and availability of backup media.

Managing Media Life Span

All media has a useful life span. Reusable media will have a *mean time to failure (MTTF)* that is usually represented in the number of times it can be reused. Most tape backup media can be reused 3 to 10 times. When media is reused, it must be properly cleared. *Clearing* is a method of sufficiently deleting data on media that will be reused in the same secured environment. *Purging* is *erasing* the data so the media can be reused in a less-secure environment. Unless absolutely necessary, do not employ media purging. The cost of supplying each classification level with its own media is insignificant compared to the damage that can be caused by disclosure. If media is not to be archived or reused within the same environment, it should be securely destroyed.

Once a backup media has reached its MTTF, it should be destroyed. Secure destruction of media that contained confidential and sensitive data is just as important as the storage of such media. When destroying media, it should be erased properly to remove data remanence. Once properly purged, media should be physically destroyed to prevent easy reuse and attempted data gleaning through casual (keyboard attacks) or high-tech (laboratory attacks) means. Physical crushing is often sufficient, but incineration may be necessary.

Preventing Disclosure via Reused Media

Preventing disclosure of information from backup media is an important aspect of maintaining operational security. Disclosure prevention must occur at numerous instances in the life span of media. It must be addressed upon every reuse in the same secure environment, upon every reuse in a different or less-secure environment, upon removal from service, and upon destruction. Addressing this issue can take many forms, including erasing, clearing, purging, declassification, sanitization, overwriting, degaussing, and destruction.

Erasing media is simply performing a delete operation against a file, a selection of files, or the entire media. In most cases, the deletion or removal process only removes the directory or catalog link to the data. The actual data remains on the drive. The data will remain on the drive until it is overwritten by other data or properly removed from the media.

Clearing, or *overwriting,* is a process of preparing media for reuse and assuring that the cleared data cannot be recovered by any means. When media is cleared, unclassified data is written over specific locations or over the entire media where classified data was stored. Often, the unclassified data is strings of 1s and 0s. The clearing process typically prepares media for reuse in the same secure environment, not for transfer to other environments.

Purging is a more intense form of clearing that prepares media for reuse in less-secure environments. Depending on the classification of the data and the security of the environment, the purging process is repeated 7 to 10 times to provide assurance against data recovery via laboratory attacks.

Declassification involves any process that clears media for reuse in less-secure environments. In most cases, purging is used to prepare media for declassification, but most of the time, the efforts required to securely declassify media are significantly greater than the cost of new media for a less-secure environment.

Sanitization is any number of processes that prepares media for destruction. It ensures that data cannot be recovered by any means from destroyed or discarded media. Sanitization can also be the actual means by which media is destroyed. Media can be sanitized by purging or degaussing without physically destroying the media. *Degaussing* magnetic media returns it to its original pristine, unused state. Sanitization methods that result in the physical destruction of the media include incineration, crushing, and shredding.

Care should be taken when performing any type of sanitization, clearing, or purging process. It is possible that the human operator or the tool involved in the activity will not properly perform the task of removing data from the media. Software can be flawed, magnets can be faulty, and either can be used improperly. Always verify that the desired result is achieved after performing a sanitization process.

Destruction is the final stage in the life cycle of backup media. Destruction should occur after proper sanitization or as a means of sanitization. When media destruction takes place, you must ensure that the media cannot be reused or repaired and that data cannot be extracted from the destroyed media by any possible means. Methods of destruction can include incineration, crushing, shredding, and dissolving using caustic or acidic chemicals.

 You might also consider demagnetizing the hard drive. However, in practice this activity is a function of degaussing, which is itself unreliable. When donating or selling used computer equipment, it is usually recommended to remove and destroy storage devices rather than attempting to purge or sanitize them.

Security Control Types

There are several methods used to classify security controls. The classification can be based on the nature of the control, such as administrative, technical/logical, or physical. It can also be based on the action or objective of the control, such as directive, preventative, detective, corrective, and recovery. Some controls can have multiple action/objective classifications.

A *directive control* is a security tool used to guide the security implementation of an organization. Examples of directive controls include security policies, standards, guidelines, procedures, laws, and regulations. The goal or objective of directive controls is to cause or promote a desired result.

A *preventive control* is a security mechanism, tool, or practice that can deter or mitigate undesired actions or events. Preventive controls are designed to stop or reduce the occurrence of various crimes, such as fraud, theft, destruction, embezzlement, espionage, and so on. They are also designed to avert common human failures such as errors, omissions, and oversights. Preventative controls are designed to reduce risk. Although not always the most cost effective, they are preferred over detective or corrective controls from a perspective of maintaining security. Stopping an unwanted or unauthorized action before it occurs results in a more secure environment than detecting and resolving problems after they occur does. Examples of preventive controls include firewalls, authentication methods, access controls, antivirus software, data classification, separation of duties, job rotation, risk analysis, encryption, warning banners, data validation, prenumbered forms, checks for duplications, and account lockouts.

A *detective control* is a security mechanism used to verify whether the directive and preventative controls have been successful. Detective controls actively search for both violations of the security policy and actual crimes. They are used to identify attacks and errors so that appropriate action can be taken. Examples of detective controls include audit trails, logs, closed-circuit television (CCTV), intrusion detection systems, antivirus software, penetration testing, password crackers, performance monitoring, and cyclical redundancy checks (CRCs).

Corrective controls are instructions, procedures, or guidelines used to reverse the effects of an unwanted activity, such as attacks and errors. Examples of corrective controls include manuals, procedures, logging and journaling, incident handling, and fire extinguishers.

A *recovery control* is used to return affected systems back to normal operations after an attack or an error has occurred. Examples of recovery controls include system restoration, backups, rebooting, key escrow, insurance, redundant equipment, fault-tolerant systems, failover, checkpoints, and contingency plans.

Operations Controls

Operations controls are the mechanisms and daily procedures that provide protection for systems. They are typically security controls that must be implemented or performed by people rather than automated by the system. Most operations controls are administrative in nature, but they also include some technical or logical controls.

When possible, operations controls should be invisible or transparent to users. The less a user sees the security controls, the less likely they will feel that security is hampering their productivity. Likewise, the less users know about the security of the system, the less likely they will be able to circumvent it.

Resource Protection

The operations controls for resource protection are designed to provide security for the resources of an IT environment. Resources are the hardware, software, and data assets that an organization's IT infrastructure comprises. To maintain confidentiality, integrity, and availability of the hosted assets, the resources themselves must be protected. When designing a protection scheme for resources, it is important to keep the following aspects or elements of the IT infrastructure in mind:

- Communication hardware/software
- Boundary devices
- Processing equipment
- Password files
- Application program libraries
- Application source code
- Vendor software
- Operating system
- System utilities
- Directories and address tables
- Proprietary packages
- Main storage
- Removable storage
- Sensitive/critical data
- System logs/audit trails
- Violation reports
- Backup files and media
- Sensitive forms and printouts
- Isolated devices, such as printers and faxes
- Telephone network

Privileged Entity Controls

Another aspect of operations controls is *privileged entity controls*. A *privileged entity* is an administrator or system operator who has access to special, higher-order functions and capabilities that normal users don't have access to. Privileged entity access is required for many administrative and control job tasks, such as creating new user accounts, adding new routes to a router table, or altering the configuration of a firewall. Privileged entity access can include system commands, system control interfaces, system log/audit files, and special control parameters. Access to privileged entity controls should be restricted and audited to prevent usurping of power by unauthorized users.

Hardware Controls

Hardware controls are another part of operations controls. Hardware controls focus on restricting and managing access to the IT infrastructure hardware. In many cases, periodic maintenance, error/attack repair, and system configuration changes require direct physical access to hardware. An operations control to manage access to hardware is a form of physical access control. All personnel who are granted access to the physical components of the system must have authorization. It is also a good idea to provide supervision while hardware operations are being performed by third parties.

Other issues related to hardware controls include management of maintenance accounts and port controls. Maintenance accounts are predefined default accounts that are installed on hardware (and in software) and have preset and widely known passwords. These accounts should be renamed and a strong password assigned. Many hardware devices have diagnostic or configuration/console ports. They should be accessible only to authorized personnel, and if possible, they should disabled when not in use for approved maintenance operations.

Input/Output Controls

Input and output controls are mechanisms used to protect the flow of information into and out of a system. These controls also protect applications and resources by preventing invalid, oversized, or malicious input from causing errors or security breaches. Output controls restrict the data that is revealed to users by restricting content based on subject classification and the security of the communication's connection. Input and output controls are not limited to technical mechanisms; they can also be physical controls (for example, restrictions against bringing memory flashcards, printouts, floppy disks, CD-Rs, and so on into or out of secured areas).

Application Controls

Application controls are designed into software applications to minimize and detect operational irregularities. They limit end users' use of applications in such a way that only particular screens, records, and data are visible and only specific authorized functions are enabled. Particular uses of application can be focused on for monitoring and auditing. Application controls are transparent to the endpoint applications, so changes are not required to the applications involved.

Some applications include integrity verification controls, much like those employed by DMBS. These controls look for evidence of data manipulation, errors, and omissions. These types of controls are considered to be application controls (i.e., internal controls) rather than software management controls (i.e., external controls).

Media Controls

Media controls are similar to the topics discussed in the section "Sensitive Information and Media" earlier in this chapter. Media controls should encompass the marking, handling, storage, transportation, and destruction of media such as floppies, memory cards, hard drives, backup tapes, CD-Rs, CD-RWs, and so on. A tracking mechanism should be used to record and monitor the location and uses of media. Secured media should never leave the boundaries of the secured environment. Likewise, any media brought into a secured environment should not contain viruses, malicious code, or other unwanted code elements, nor should that media ever leave the secured environment except after proper sanitization or destruction.

Administrative Controls

Operations controls include many of the administrative controls that we have already discussed numerous times, such as separation of duties and responsibilities, rotation of duties, least privilege, and so on. However, in addition to these controls we must consider how the maintenance of hardware and software is performed.

When assessing the controls used to manage and sustain hardware and software maintenance, here are some key issues to ponder:

- Are program libraries properly restricted and controlled?

- Is version control or configuration management enforced?

- Are all components of a new product properly tested, documented, and approved prior to release to production?

- Are the systems properly hardened? Hardening a system involves removing unnecessary processes, segregating interprocess communications, and reducing executing privileges to increase system security.

Personnel Controls

No matter how much effort, expense, and expertise you put into physical access control and logical/technical security mechanisms, you will always have to deal with people. In fact, people are both your last line of defense and your worse security management issue. People are vulnerable to a wide range of attacks, plus they can intentionally violate security policy and attempt to circumvent physical and logical/technical security controls. Because of this, you must endeavor to employ only those people who are the most trustworthy.

Security controls to manage personnel are considered a type of administrative controls. These controls and issues should be clearly outlined in your security policy and followed as closely as possible. Failing to employ strong personnel controls may render all of your other security efforts worthless.

The first type of personnel controls are used in the hiring process. To hire a new employee, you must first know what position needs to be filled. This requires the creation of a detailed job description. The job description should outline the work tasks and responsibilities of the position, which will in turn dictate the access and privileges needed in the environment. Furthermore, the job description defines the knowledge, skill, and experience level required by the position. Only after the job description has been created is it possible to begin screening applicants for the position.

The next step in using personnel controls is selecting the best person for the job. In terms of security, this means the most trustworthy. Often trustworthiness is determined through background and reference checks, employment history verification, and education and certification verification. This process could even include credit checks and FBI background checks.

Once a person has been hired, personnel controls should be deployed to continue to monitor and evaluate their work. Personnel controls monitoring activity should be deployed for all employees, not just new ones. These controls can include access audit and review, validation of security clearances, periodic skills assessment, supervisory employee ratings, and supervisor oversight and review. Often companies will employ a policy of mandatory vacations in one or two week increments. Such a tool removes the employee from the environment and allows another cross-trained employee to perform their work tasks during the interim. This activity serves as a form of peer review, providing a means to detect fraud and collusion. At any time, if an employee is found to be in violation of security policy, they should be properly reprimanded and warned. If the employee continues to commit security policy violations, they should be terminated.

Finally, there are personnel controls that govern the termination process. When an employee is to be fired, an exit interview should be conducted. For the exit interview, the soon-to-be-released employee is brought to a manager's office for a private meeting. This meeting is designed to remove them from their workspace and to minimize the effect of the firing activity on other employees. The meeting usually consists of the employee, a manager, and a security guard. The security guard acts as a witness and as a protection agent. The exit interview should be coordinated with the security administration staff so that just as the exit interview begins, the employee's network and building access is revoked. During the exit interview, the employee is reminded of his legal obligations to comply with any nondisclosure agreements and not to disclose any confidential data. The employee must return all badges, keys, and other company equipment on their person. Once the exit interview is complete, the security guard escorts the terminated employee out of the facility and possibly even off of the grounds. If the ex-employee has any company equipment at home or at some other location, the security guard should accompany the ex-employee to recover those items. The purpose of an exit interview is primarily to reinforce the nondisclosure issue, but it also serves the purpose of removing the ex-employee from the environment, having all access removed and devices returned, and preventing or minimizing any retaliatory activities because of the termination.

Summary

There are many areas of day-to-day operations that are susceptible to security breaches. Therefore, all standards, guidelines, and procedures should clearly define personnel management practices. Important aspects of personnel management include antivirus management and operations security.

Personnel management is a form of administrative control or administrative management. You must include clearly defined personnel management practices in your security policy and subsequent formalized security documentation. From a security perspective, personnel management focuses on three main areas: hiring practices, ongoing job performance, and termination procedures.

Operations security consists of controls to maintain security in an office environment from design to deployment. Such controls include hardware, media, and subject (user) controls that are designed to protect against asset threats. Because viruses are the most common form of security breach in the IT world, managing a system's antivirus protection is one of the most important aspect of operations security. Any communications pathway, such as e-mail, websites, and documents, and even commercial software, can and will be exploited as a delivery mechanism for a virus or other malicious code. Antivirus management is the design, deployment, and maintenance of an antivirus solution for your IT environment.

Backing up critical information is a key part of maintaining the availability and integrity of data and an essential part of maintaining operations security. Having a reliable backup is the best form of insurance that the data on the affected system is not permanently lost.

Changes in a user's workstation or their physical location within an organization can be used as a means to improve or maintain security. When a user's workstation is changed, the user is less likely to alter the system or install unapproved software because the next person to use the system would most likely be able to discover it.

The concepts of need-to-know and the principle of least privilege are two important aspects of a high-security environment. A user must have a need-to-know to gain access to data or resources. To comply with the principle of least privilege, users should be granted the least amount of access to the secure environment as possible for them to be able to complete their work tasks.

Activities that require special access or privilege to perform within a secured IT environment are considered privileged operations functions. Such functions should be restricted to administrators and system operators.

Due care is performing reasonable care to protect the interest of an organization. Due diligence is practicing the activities that maintain the due care effort. Operational security is the ongoing maintenance of continued due care and due diligence by all responsible parties within an organization.

Another central issue for all organizations is privacy, which means providing protection of personal information from disclosure to any unauthorized individual or entity. The protection of privacy should be a core mission or goal set forth in an organization's security policy.

It's also important that an organization operate within the legal requirements, restrictions, and regulations of its country and industry. Complying with all applicable legal requirements is a key part of sustaining security.

Illegal activities are actions that violate a legal restriction, regulation, or requirement. Fraud, misappropriation, unauthorized disclosure, theft, destruction, espionage, and entrapment are all examples of illegal activities. A secure environment should provide mechanisms to prevent the committal of illegal activities and the means to track illegal activities and maintain accountability from the individuals perpetrating the crimes.

In a high-security environment where sensitive, confidential, and proprietary data is processed, managing information and media properly is crucial to the environment's security and stability. There are four key areas of information and media management: marking, handling, storage, and destruction. Record retention is the organizational policy that defines what information is maintained and for how long. If data about individuals is being retained by your organization, the employees and customers need to be made aware of it.

The classification of security controls can be based on their nature, such as administrative, technical/logical, or physical. It can also be based on the action or objective of the control, such as directive, preventative, detective, corrective, and recovery.

Operations controls are the mechanisms and daily procedures that provide protection for systems. They are typically security controls that must be implemented or performed by people rather than automated by the system. Most operations controls are administrative in nature, but as you can see from the following list, they also include some technical or logical controls:

- Resource protection
- Privileged-entity controls
- Change control management
- Hardware controls
- Input/output controls
- Media controls
- Administrative controls
- Trusted recovery process

Exam Essentials

Understand that personnel management is a form of administrative control, also called administrative management.   You must clearly define personnel management practices in your security policy and subsequent formalized security structure documentation. Personnel management focuses on three main areas: hiring practices, ongoing job performance, and termination procedures.

Understand antivirus management.   Antivirus management includes the design, deployment, and maintenance of an antivirus solution for your IT environment.

Know how to prevent unrestricted installation of software.   To provide a virus-free environment, installation of software should be rigidly controlled. This includes allowing users to install and execute only company-approved and -distributed software as well as thoroughly testing and scanning all new software before it is distributed on a production network. Even commercial software has become an inadvertent carrier of viruses.

Understand backup maintenance.   A key part of maintaining the availability and integrity of data is a reliable backup of critical information. Having a reliable backup is the only form of insurance that the data on a system that has failed or has been damaged or corrupted is not permanently lost.

Know how changes in workstation or location promote a secure environment.   Changes in a user's workstation or their physical location within an organization can be used as a means to improve or maintain security. Having a policy of changing users' workstations prevents them from altering the system or installing unapproved software and encourages them to keep all material stored on network servers where it can be easily protected, overseen, and audited.

Understand the need-to-know concept and the principle of least privilege.   Need-to-know and the principle of least privilege are two standard axioms of high-security environments. To gain access to data or resources, a user must have a need to know. If users do not have a need to know, they are denied access. The principle of least privilege means that users should be granted the least amount of access to the secure environment as possible for them to be able to complete their work tasks.

Understand privileged operations functions.   Privileged operations functions are activities that require special access or privilege to perform within a secured IT environment. For maximum security, such functions should be restricted to administrators and system operators.

Know the standards of due care and due diligence.   Due care is using reasonable care to protect the interest of an organization. Due diligence is practicing the activities that maintain the due care effort. Senior management must show reasonable due care and due diligence to reduce their culpability and liability when a loss occurs.

Understand how to maintain privacy.   Maintaining privacy means protecting personal information from disclosure to any unauthorized individual or entity. In today's online world, the line between public information and private information is often blurry. The protection of privacy should be a core mission or goal set forth in the security policy of an organization.

Know the legal requirements in your region and field of expertise.   Every organization operates within a certain industry and country, both of which impose legal requirements, restrictions, and regulations on its practices. Legal requirements can involve licensed use of software, hiring restrictions, handling of sensitive materials, and compliance with safety regulations.

Understand what constitutes an illegal activity.   An illegal activity is an action that violates a legal restriction, regulation, or requirement. A secure environment should provide mechanisms to prevent illegal activities from being committed and the means to track illegal activities and maintain accountability from the individuals perpetrating the crimes.

Know the proper procedure for record retention.   Record retention is the organizational policy that defines what information is maintained and for how long. In most cases, the records in question are audit trails of user activity. This can include file and resource access, logon patterns, e-mail, and the use of privileges.

Understand the elements of securing sensitive media.   Managing information and media properly, especially in a high-security environment where sensitive, confidential, and proprietary data is processed, is crucial to the security and stability of an organization. In addition to media selection, there are several key areas of information and media management: marking, handling, storage, life-span, reuse, and destruction.

Know and understand the security control types.   There are several methods used to classify security controls. The classification can be based on the nature of the control (administrative, technical/logical, or physical) or on the action or objective of the control (directive, preventative, detective, corrective, and recovery).

Know the importance of control transparency.   When possible, operations controls should be invisible or transparent to users to prevent users from feeling that security is hampering their productivity. Likewise, the less users know about the security of the system, the less likely they will be able to circumvent it.

Understand how to protect resources.   The operations controls for resource protection are designed to provide security for the IT environment's resources, including hardware, software, and data assets. To maintain confidentiality, integrity, and availability of the hosted assets, the resources themselves must be protected.

Be able to explain change and configuration control management.   Change in a secure environment can introduce loopholes, overlaps, misplaced objects, and oversights that can lead to new vulnerabilities. Therefore, you must systematically manage change by logging, auditing, and monitoring activities related to security controls and security mechanisms. The resulting data is then used to identify agents of change, whether they are objects, subjects, programs, communication pathways, or even the network itself. The goal of change management is to ensure that any change does not lead to reduced or compromised security.

Understand the trusted recovery process.   The trusted recovery process ensures that a system is not breached during a crash, failure, or reboot and that every time they occur, the system returns to a secure state.

Review Questions

1. Personnel management is a form of what type of control?

    A. Administrative

    B. Technical

    C. Logical

    D. Physical

2. What is the most common means of distribution for viruses?

    A. Unapproved software

    B. E-mail

    C. Websites

    D. Commercial software

3. Which of the following causes the vulnerability of being affected by viruses to increase?

    A. Length of time the system is operating

    B. The classification level of the primary user

    C. Installation of software

    D. Use of roaming profiles

4. In areas where technical controls cannot be used to prevent virus infections, what should be used to prevent them?

    A. Security baselines

    B. Awareness training

    C. Traffic filtering

    D. Network design

5. Which of the following is not true?

    A. Complying with all applicable legal requirements is a key part of sustaining security.

    B. It is often possible to disregard legal requirements if complying with regulations would cause a reduction in security.

    C. The legal requirements of an industry and of a country should be considered the baseline or foundation upon which the remainder of the security infrastructure must be built.

    D. Industry and governments impose legal requirements, restrictions, and regulations on the practices of an organization.

6. Which of the following is not an illegal activity that can be performed over a computer network?

   A. Theft

   B. Destruction of assets

   C. Waste of resources

   D. Espionage

7. Who does not need to be informed when records about their activities on a network are being recorded and retained?

   A. Administrators

   B. Normal users

   C. Temporary guest visitors

   D. No one

8. What is the best form of antivirus protection?

   A. Multiple solutions on each system

   B. A single solution throughout the organization

   C. Concentric circles of different solutions

   D. One-hundred-percent content filtering at all border gateways

9. Which of the following is an effective means of preventing and detecting the installation of unapproved software?

   A. Workstation change

   B. Separation of duties

   C. Discretionary access control

   D. Job responsibility restrictions

10. What is the requirement to have access to, knowledge about, or possession of data or a resource to perform specific work tasks commonly known as?

    A. Principle of least privilege

    B. Prudent man theory

    C. Need-to-know

    D. Role-based access control

11. Which are activities that require special access to be performed within a secured IT environment?

    A. Privileged operations functions

    B. Logging and auditing

    C. Maintenance responsibilities

    D. User account management

12. Which of the following requires that archives of audit logs be kept for long periods of time?
    A. Data remanence
    B. Record retention
    C. Data diddling
    D. Data mining

13. What is the most important aspect of marking media?
    A. Date labeling
    B. Content description
    C. Electronic labeling
    D. Classification

14. Which operation is performed on media so it can be reused in a less-secure environment?
    A. Erasing
    B. Clearing
    C. Purging
    D. Overwriting

15. Sanitization can be unreliable due to which of the following?
    A. No media can be fully swept clean of all data remnants.
    B. Even fully incinerated media can offer extractable data.
    C. The process can be performed improperly.
    D. Stored data is physically etched into the media.

16. Which security tool is used to guide the security implementation of an organization?
    A. Directive control
    B. Preventive control
    C. Detective control
    D. Corrective control

17. Which security mechanism is used to verify whether the directive and preventative controls have been successful?
    A. Directive control
    B. Preventive control
    C. Detective control
    D. Corrective control

18. When possible, operations controls should be _____ .

   A. Simple

   B. Administrative

   C. Preventative

   D. Transparent

19. What is the primary goal of change management?

   A. Personnel safety

   B. Allowing rollback of changes

   C. Ensuring that changes do not reduce security

   D. Auditing privilege access

20. What type of trusted recovery process requires the intervention of an administrator?

   A. Restricted

   B. Manual

   C. Automated

   D. Controlled

Answers to Review Questions

1. A. Personnel management is a form of administrative control. Administrative controls also include separation of duties and responsibilities, rotation of duties, least privilege, and so on.

2. B. E-mail is the most common distribution method for viruses.

3. C. As more software is installed, more vulnerabilities are added to the system, thus adding more avenues of attack for viruses.

4. B. In areas where technical controls cannot prevent virus infections, users should be trained on how to prevent them.

5. B. Laws and regulations must be obeyed and security concerns must be adjusted accordingly.

6. C. Although wasting resources is considered inappropriate activity, it is not actually a crime in most cases.

7. D. Everyone should be informed when records about their activities on a network are being recorded and retained.

8. C. Concentric circles of different solutions is the best form of antivirus protection.

9. A. Workstation change is an effective means of preventing and detecting the presence of unapproved software.

10. C. Need-to-know is the requirement to have access to, knowledge about, or possession of data or a resource to perform specific work tasks.

11. A. Privileged operations functions are activities that require special access to perform within a secured IT environment. They may include auditing, maintenance, and user account management.

12. B. To use record retention properly, archives of audit logs must be kept for long periods of time.

13. D. Classification is the most important aspect of marking media because it determines the precautions necessary to ensure the security of the hosted content.

14. C. Purging of media is erasing media so it can be reused in a less-secure environment. The purging process may need to be repeated numerous times depending on the classification of the data and the security of the environment.

15. C. Sanitization can be unreliable because the purging, degaussing, or other processes can be performed improperly.

16. A. A directive control is a security tool used to guide the security implementation of an organization.

17. C. A detective control is a security mechanism used to verify whether the directive and preventative controls have been successful.

18. D. When possible, operations controls should be invisible, or transparent, to users. This keeps users from feeling hampered by security and reduces their knowledge of the overall security scheme, thus further restricting the likelihood that users will violate system security deliberately.

19. C. The goal of change management is to ensure that any change does not lead to reduced or compromised security.

20. B. A manual recovery type of trusted recovery process requires the intervention of an administrator.

Chapter

14

Auditing and Monitoring

THE CISSP EXAM TOPICS COVERED IN THIS CHAPTER INCLUDE:

- ✓ Auditing and Audit Trails
- ✓ Monitoring
- ✓ Penetration Testing
- ✓ Inappropriate Activities
- ✓ Indistinct Threats and Countermeasures

The Operations Security domain of the Common Body of Knowledge (CBK) for the CISSP certification exam deals with the activities and efforts directed at maintaining operational security and includes the primary concerns of auditing and monitoring. Auditing and monitoring prompt IT departments to make efforts at detecting intrusions and unauthorized activities. Vigilant administrators must sort through a selection of countermeasures and perform penetration testing that helps to limit, restrict, and prevent inappropriate activities, crimes, and other threats.

We discussed the Operations Security domain in some detail in Chapter 13, "Administrative Management," and we will be finishing up coverage on this domain in this chapter. Be sure to read and study the materials from both chapters to ensure complete coverage of the essential operations security material for the CISSP certification exam.

Auditing

Auditing is a methodical examination or review of an environment to ensure compliance with regulations and to detect abnormalities, unauthorized occurrences, or outright crimes. Secure IT environments rely heavily on auditing. Overall, auditing serves as the primary type of detective control used in a secure environment.

Auditing Basics

Auditing encompasses a wide variety of different activities, including the recording of event/ occurrence data, examination of data, data reduction, the use of event/occurrence alarm triggers, and log analysis. These activities are also known as, for example, logging, monitoring, examining alerts, analysis, and even intrusion detection. *Logging* is the activity of recording information about events or occurrences to a log file or database. *Monitoring* is the activity of manually or programmatically reviewing logged information looking for something specific. *Alarm triggers* are notifications sent to administrators when a specific event occurs. *Log analysis* is a more detailed and systematic form of monitoring in which the logged information is analyzed in detail for trends and patterns as well as abnormal, unauthorized, illegal, and policy-violating activities. *Intrusion detection* is a specific form of monitoring both recorded information and real-time events to detect unwanted system access.

Accountability

Auditing and monitoring are required factors for sustaining and enforcing accountability. Monitoring is the programmatic means by which subjects are held accountable for their actions while authenticated on a system. Without an electronic account of a subject's actions, it is not possible to correlate IT activities, events, and occurrences with subjects. Monitoring is also the process by which unauthorized or abnormal activities are detected on a system. It is needed to detect malicious actions by subjects, attempted intrusions, and system failures and to reconstruct events, provide evidence for prosecution, and produce problem reports and analysis. Auditing and logging are usually native features of an operating system and most applications and services. Thus, configuring the system to record information about specific types of events is fairly straightforward.

Auditing is also used to monitor the health and performance of a system through recording the activities of subjects and objects as well as core system functions that maintain the operating environment and the security mechanisms. The audit trails created by recording system events to logs can be used to evaluate the health and performance of a system. System crashes can indicate faulty programs, corrupt drivers, or intrusion attempts. The event logs leading up to a crash can often be used to discover the reason a system failed. Log files provide an audit trail for re-creating step-by-step the history of an event, intrusion, or system failure.

In most cases, when sufficient logging and auditing is enabled to monitor a system, so much data is collected that the important details get lost in the bulk. The art of data reduction is crucial when working with large volumes of monitoring data. There are numerous tools to search through log files for specific events or ID codes. However, for true automation and even real-time analysis of events, an intrusion detection system (IDS) is required. IDS solutions are discussed in Chapter 2, "Attacks and Monitoring."

Compliance

Auditing is also commonly used for *compliance testing,* or *compliance checking.* Verification that a system complies with laws, regulations, baselines, guidelines, standards, and policies is an important part of maintaining security in any environment. Compliance testing ensures that all of the necessary and required elements of a security solution are properly deployed and functioning as expected. Compliance checks can take many forms, such as vulnerability scans and penetration testing. They can also be performed using log analysis tools to determine if any vulnerabilities for which countermeasures have been deployed have been realized on the system.

Audits can be performed from one of two perspectives: internal or external. Organizational employees from inside the IT environment who are aware of the implemented security solutions perform internal audits. Independent auditors from outside the IT environment who are not familiar with the implemented security solutions perform external audits. Insurance agencies, accounting firms, or even the organization itself hire external auditors to test the validity of security claims. The goal of both internal and external auditing is to measure the effectiveness of the deployed security solution.

Audit Time Frames

The frequency of an IT infrastructure security audit or security review is based on risk. When performing risk analysis, it must be determined whether sufficient risk exists to warrant the expense of and interruption caused by a security audit on a more or less frequent basis. In any case, the frequency of audit reviews should be clearly defined in the security guidelines or standards of an organization. Once defined in the formalized security infrastructure, it should be adhered to. Without regular assessments of the state of security of an IT infrastructure, there is no way to know how secure the environment is until an attack is either successful or thwarted. Waiting until the battle to determine whether or not you will succeed is a very poor business strategy.

As with many other aspects of deploying and maintaining security, security audits and effectiveness reviews are often viewed as key elements in displaying due care. If senior management fails to enforce compliance with regular periodic security reviews, then they will be held accountable and liable for any asset losses that occur due to security breaches or policy violations.

Audit Trails

Audit trails are the records created by recording information about events and occurrences into a database or log file. They are used to reconstruct an event, to extract information about an incident, to prove or disprove culpability, and much more. They allow events to be examined or traced in forward or reverse order. This flexibility is useful when tracking down problems, coding errors, performance issues, attacks, intrusions, security breaches, and other security policy violations. Using audit trails is a passive form of detective security control. They serve as a deterrent in the same manner closed-circuit television (CCTV) or security guards do: if the attacker knows they are being watched and their activities recorded, they are less likely to perform the illegal, unauthorized, or malicious activity. Audit trails are also essential as evidence in the prosecution of criminals. They can often be used to produce a before-and-after picture of the state of resources, systems, and assets. This in turn helps to identify whether the change or alteration is the result of the action of a user or an action of the OS or software or caused by some other sources (such as hardware failure).

Accountability is maintained for individual subjects through the use of audit trails. When activities of users and events caused by the actions of users while online are recorded, individuals can be held accountable for their actions. This directly promotes good user behavior and compliance with the organization's security policy. Users who are aware that their IT activities are being recorded are less likely to attempt to circumvent security controls or to perform unauthorized or restricted activities.

Audit trails give system administrators the ability to reconstruct events long after they have passed. When a security violation is detected, the conditions and system state leading up to the event, during the event, and after the event can be reconstructed through a close examination of the audit trail.

Audit trails offer details about recorded events. A wide range of information can be recorded in log files, including time, date, system, user, process, and type of error/event. Log files can even capture the memory state or the contents of memory. This information can help pinpoint the cause of the event. Using log files for this purpose is often labeled as problem identification.

Once a problem is identified, performing problem resolution is little more than following up on the disclosed information. Audit trails record system failures, OS bugs, and software errors as well as abuses of access, violations of privileges, attempted intrusions, and many forms of attacks. Intrusion detection is a specialized form of problem identification through the use of audit trails.

 If auditing records or logs are transmitted across a network from a sentry agent to a collector warehouse, the transaction should be encrypted. Log and audit information should never be allowed on the network in cleartext.

Once a security policy violation or a breach occurs, the source of that violation should be determined. If it is possible to track the individual who perpetrated the activity, they should be reprimanded or terminated (if an employee) or prosecuted (if an external intruder). In every case where a true security policy violation or breach has occurred (especially if a loss can be pinpointed), you should report the incident to your local authorities, possibly the FBI, and if the violation occurred online, to one or more Internet incident tracking organizations.

 You should time-synchronize all systems against a centralized or trusted public time server. This ensures that all audit logs are in sync so you can perform dependable and secure logging activities.

Reporting Concepts

The actual formats used by an organization to produce reports from audit trails will vary greatly. However, the reports should all address a few basic or central concepts: the purpose of the audit, the scope of the audit, and the results discovered or revealed by the audit. In addition to these basic foundational concepts, audit reports often include many details specific to the environment, such as time, date, specific systems, and so on. Audit reports can include a wide range of content that focuses on problems/events/conditions, standards/criteria/baselines, causes/reasons, impact/effect, or solutions/recommendations/safeguards.

Reporting Format

Audit reports should have a structure or design that is clear, concise, and objective. It is common for the auditor to include opinions or recommendations for response to the content of a report, but the actual findings of the audit report should be based on fact and evidence from audit trails. Audit reports include sensitive information and should be assigned a classification label and handled appropriately. Within the hierarchy of the organization, only those people with sufficient privilege should have access to audit reports. An audit report may also be prepared in various forms according to the hierarchy of the organization. They should provide only the details relevant to the position of the staff members who have access to them. For example, senior management does not need to know all of the minute details of an audit report. Therefore, the audit report for senior management is much more concise and offers more of an overview or summary of the findings. An audit report for the IT manager or the security administrator should be very detailed and include all available information on the events contained in it.

Reporting Time Frames

The frequency of producing audit reports is based on the value of the assets and the level of risk. The more valuable the asset and the higher the risk, the more often an audit report should be produced. Once an audit report is completed, it should be submitted to the assigned recipient (as defined in the security policy documentation) and a signed confirmation of receipt should be filed. When an audit report contains information about serious security violations or performance issues, the report should be escalated to higher levels of management for review, notification, and assignment of a response. Keep in mind that, in a formalized security infrastructure, only the higher levels of management have any decision-making power. All entities at the lower end of the structure must follow prescribed procedures and follow instruction.

Sampling

Sampling, or *data extraction,* is the process of extracting elements from a large body of data in order to construct a meaningful representation or summary of the whole. In other words, sampling is a form of data reduction that allows an auditor to quickly determine the important issues or events from an audit trail. There are two forms of sampling: statistical and nonstatistical. An auditing tool using precise mathematical functions to extract meaningful information from a large volume of data performs statistical sampling. There is always a risk that sampled data is not an accurate representation of the whole body of data and that it may mislead auditors and managers, and statistical sampling can be used to measure that risk.

Clipping, a form of sampling, selects only those error events that cross the clipping level threshold. *Clipping levels* are widely used in the process of auditing events to establish baseline of system or user activity that is considered routine activity. If this baseline is exceeded, an unusual event alarm is triggered. This works especially well when individuals exceed their authority, when there are too many people with unrestricted access, and for serious intrusion patterns.

Clipping levels are often associated with a form of mainframe auditing known as *violation analysis.* In violation analysis, an older form of auditing, the environment is monitored for occurrences of errors. A baseline of errors is expected and known, and this level of common errors is labeled as the clipping level. Any errors that exceed the clipping level threshold trigger a violation and details about such events are recorded into a violation record for later analysis.

Nonstatistical sampling can be described as random sampling or sampling at the auditor's discretion. It offers neither assurance of an accurate representation of the whole body of data nor a gauge of the sampling risk. Nonstatistical sampling is less expensive, requires less training, and does not require computer facilities.

Both statistical and nonstatistical sampling are accepted as valid mechanisms to create summaries or overviews of large bodies of audit data. However, statistical sampling is more reliable.

Record Retention

As the term implies, *record retention* involves retaining and maintaining important information. An organization should have a policy that defines what information is maintained and for how long. As it applies to the security infrastructure, in most cases, the records in question are audit trails of user activity, which may include file and resource access, logon patterns, e-mail, and the use of privileges.

Retention Time Frames

Depending upon your industry and your relationship with the government, you may need to retain records for three years, seven years, or indefinitely. In most cases, a separate backup mechanism is used to create archived copies of sensitive audit trails and accountability information. This allows for the main data backup system to periodically reuse its media without violating the requirement to retain audit trails and the like.

If data about individuals is being retained by your organization, the employees and customers need to be made aware of it (such as in a conditional employment agreement or a use agreement). In many cases, the notification requirement is a legal issue, whereas in others it is a simply a courtesy. In either case, it is a good idea to discuss the issue with a lawyer.

Media, Destruction, and Security

The media used to store or retain audit trails must be properly maintained. This includes taking secure measures for the marking, handling, storage, and destruction of media. For details on handling sensitive media, please see the section titled "Sensitive Information and Media" in Chapter 13, "Administrative Management."

Retained records should be protected against unauthorized and untimely destruction, against alteration, and against hindrances to availability. Many of the same security controls used to protect online resources and assets can be imposed to protect audit logs, audit trails, audit reports, and backup media containing audit information.

Access to audit information should be strictly controlled. Audit information can be used in inference attacks to discover information about higher classifications of data, thus the audit logs containing records about highly confidential assets should be handled in the same secure manner as the actual assets. Another way of stating this is that when an audit log is created, you are creating another asset entity with the same security needs as the original audited asset.

As the value of assets and the audit data goes up and risk increases, so does the need for an increase in security and frequency of backups for the audit information. Audit data should be treated with the same security precautions as all other high-classification data within an IT environment. It should be protected by physical and logical security controls, it should be audited, it should be regularly backed up, and the backup media should be stored off site in a controlled facility. The backup media hosting audit data should be protected from loss, destruction, alteration, and unauthorized physical and logical access. The integrity of audit data must be maintained and protected at all times. If audit data is not accurate, it is useless.

External Auditors

It is often necessary to test or verify the security mechanisms deployed in an environment. The test process is designed to ensure that the requirements dictated by the security policy are followed and that no significant holes or weaknesses exist in the deployed security solution. Many organizations conduct independent audits by hiring outside or external security auditors to check the security of their environment. External audits provide a level of objectivity that an internal audit cannot.

An external auditor is given access to the company's security policy and the authorization to inspect every aspect of the IT and physical environment. Thus the auditor must be a trusted entity. The goal of the audit activity is to obtain a final report that details any findings and suggests countermeasures when appropriate. However, an audit of this type can take a considerable amount of time to complete—weeks or months, in fact. During the course of the audit, the auditor may issue interim reports. An interim report is a written or verbal report given to the organization about a discovered security weakness that needs immediate attention. Interim reports are issued whenever a problem or issue is too severe to wait until the final audit report is issued.

Once the auditor completes their investigations, an exit conference is held. During the exit conference, the auditor presents and discusses their findings and discusses resolution issues with the affected parties. However, only after the exit conference is over and the auditor has left the premises does the auditor write and submit the final audit report to the organization. This allows the final audit report to be as unaffected as possible by office politics and coercion. After the final audit report is received, the internal auditors should verify whether or not the recommendations in the report are carried out. However, it is the responsibility of senior management to select which recommendations to follow and to delegate the implementation to the security team.

Monitoring

Monitoring is a form of auditing that focuses on the active review of the audited information or the audited asset. For example, you would audit the activity of failed logons, but you would *monitor* CPU performance. Monitoring is most often used in conjunction with performance, but it can be used in a security context as well. Monitoring can focus on events, subsystems, users, hardware, software, or any other object within the IT environment.

A common implementation of monitoring is known as illegal software monitoring. This type of monitoring is used to watch for attempted or successful installation of unapproved software, use of unauthorized software, or unauthorized use of approved software (i.e., attempts to bypass the restrictions of the security classification hierarchy). Monitoring in this fashion reduces the likelihood of a virus or Trojan horse being installed or of software circumventing the security controls imposed.

Monitoring Tools and Techniques

The actual tools and techniques used to perform monitoring vary greatly between environments and system platforms. However, there are several common forms found in most environments. These include warning banners, keystroke monitoring, traffic analysis, and trend analysis, and other monitoring tools.

Warning Banners

Warning banners are used to inform would-be intruders or those who attempt to violate security policy that their intended activities are restricted and that any further activities will be audited and monitored. A warning banner is basically an electronic equivalent of a no trespassing sign. In most situations, the wording of the banners is important from a legal standpoint. Be sure to consult with your attorneys about the proper wording for your banners. Only through valid warnings (i.e., clear explanations that unauthorized access is prohibited and that any such activity will be monitored and recorded) can most intrusions and attacks be prosecuted. Both authorized and unauthorized users should be informed when their activities are being logged. Most authorized users should assume such, and often their employment agreements will include specific statements indicating that any and all activity on the IT infrastructure may be recorded.

Keystroke Monitoring

Keystroke monitoring is the act of recording the key presses a user performs on a physical keyboard. The act of recording can be visual (such as with a video recorder) or logical/technical (such as with a capturing hardware device or a software program). In most cases, keystroke monitoring is used for malicious purposes. Only in extreme circumstances and highly secured environments is keystroke monitoring actually employed as a means to audit and analyze the activity of users at the keyboard. Keystroke monitoring can be extremely useful to track the keystroke-by-keystroke activities of physical intruders in order to learn the kinds of attacks and methods used to infiltrate a system.

Keystroke monitoring is often compared to wiretapping. There is some debate about whether keystroke monitoring should be restricted and controlled in the same manner as telephone wiretaps. Because there is no legal precedent set yet, many organizations that employ keystroke monitoring notify authorized and unauthorized users of such monitoring through employment agreements, security policies, and warning banners.

Traffic Analysis and Trend Analysis

Traffic analysis and *trend analysis* are forms of monitoring that examine the flow of packets rather than the actual content of packets. Traffic and trend analysis can be used to infer a large amount of information, such as primary communication routes, sources of encrypted traffic, location of primary servers, primary and backup communication pathways, amount of traffic supported by the network, typical direction of traffic flow, frequency of communications, and much more.

Other Monitoring Tools

There is a wide range of available tools to perform monitoring. Many are automated and perform the monitoring activities in real time. Some monitoring tools are developed in-house and are ad hoc implementations focusing on a single type of observation. Most monitoring tools are passive. This means they cause no effect on the monitored activity, event, or traffic and make no original transmissions of their own.

A common example of a tool for monitoring physical access is the use of closed-circuit television (CCTV). CCTV can be configured to automatically record the viewed events onto tape for later review, or personnel who watch for unwanted, unauthorized, and illegal activities in real time can watch it.

Failure recognition and response is an important part of monitoring and auditing. Otherwise, what is the point of performing the monitoring and auditing activities? On systems that use manual review, failure recognition is the responsibility of the observer or auditor. In order to recognize a failure, one must understand what is normal and expected. When the monitored or audited events stray from this standard baseline, then a failure, breach, intrusion, error, or problem has occurred and a response must be initiated.

Automated monitoring and auditing systems are usually programmed to recognize failures. Failure recognition can be based on signatures or be knowledge based. For a discussion of these two mechanisms, please see the intrusion detection discussion in Chapter 2.

In either case of a manual or automated recognition, the first step in a response is to notify the authority responsible for sustaining security and handling the problem or breach. Often this is the local administrator, the local manager, or the local security professional. The notification usually takes the form of an alarm or warning message. Once notification is performed, the responsible personnel (i.e., the administrator, manager, or security professional) or the automated tool can perform a response. When a person is responsible for the response, they can adapt the response to the specific condition and situation. For this reason, personnel-controlled responses are often the most effective. Automated tool responses are typically predefined response scripts that are usually much broader in scope than necessary. Automated tools are excellent for quick and efficient lockdown, but often the countermeasure or response imposed by a tool will significantly affect the ability of the system to continue to support and perform productive work. Whenever an automated tool response is deployed, personnel should be notified so the response can be fine-tuned and the network can be returned to normal as soon as possible.

Penetration Testing Techniques

In security terms, a penetration occurs when an attack is successful and an intruder is able to breach the perimeter of your environment. The breach can be as small as reading a few bits of data from your network or as big as logging in as a user with unrestricted privileges. One of the primary goals of security is to prevent penetrations.

One common method to test the strength of your security measures is to perform penetration testing. *Penetration testing* is a vigorous attempt to break into a protected network using any means necessary. It is common for organizations to hire external consultants to perform the penetration testing so the testers are not privy to confidential elements of the security's configuration, network design, and other internal secrets.

Planning Penetration Testing

Penetration testing is the art and science of evaluating implemented safeguards. It is just another name for launching intrusion attempts and attacks against a network. The activity in either is exactly the same, but penetration testing is performed with the approval and knowledge of senior management by security professionals in a controlled and monitored environment. Malicious users intent on violating the security of your IT environment perform intrusion attacks. If an internal user performs a test against a security measure without authorization, then it will be viewed as an attack rather than as a penetration test.

 Penetration testing will typically include social engineering attacks, network and system configuration review, and environment vulnerability assessment. Vulnerability analysis or vulnerability assessment is an element or phase within penetration testing where networks or hosts are evaluated or tested to determine whether or not they are vulnerable to known attacks.

Penetration testing can be performed using automated attack tools or manually. Automated attack tools range from professional vulnerability scanners to wild, underground cracker/hacker tools discovered on the Internet. Manual attacks often employ tools, such as penetration suites like ISS, Ballista and SATAN, but much more onus is placed on the attacker to know the details involved in perpetrating an attack.

 It is generally considered unethical and a poor business practice to hire ex-hackers, especially those with a criminal record, for any security activity including security assessment, penetration testing, or ethical hacking.

Penetration testing should be performed only with the consent and knowledge of the management staff. Performing unapproved security testing could result in productivity loss, trigger emergency response teams, or even cost you your job. However, even with full consent of senior management, your security assessment activities should fall short of actual damage to the target systems. Subversion or target destruction is never a valid or ethical activity of a penetration test. Furthermore, demonstration of the effect or flaws, weaknesses, and vulnerabilities should not be included as part of a penetration test. If such evidence is required, it should be performed only on a dedicated and isolated lab system created for the sole purpose of exploit demonstration.

Regularly staged penetration attempts are a good way to accurately judge the security mechanisms deployed by an organization. Penetration testing may also reveal areas where patches or security settings are insufficient and where new vulnerabilities have developed.

Penetration Testing Teams

Penetration testing teams can have various levels of knowledge about the environment to be evaluated. The three commonly recognized knowledge levels are zero, partial, and full. Zero knowledge teams know nothing about the site except for basic information, such as domain name and company address. An attack by a zero knowledge team most closely resembles a real external hacker attack because all information about the environment must be obtained from scratch. A partial knowledge team is given an inventory of hardware and software used at the site and possibly network design and configuration details. The team is then able to focus its efforts on attacks and vulnerabilities specific to actual hardware and software in use at the site. A full knowledge team is completely aware of every aspect of the environment, down to patch and upgrades installed and exact security configurations. The normal security administration staff can be considered a full knowledge team. Unfortunately, a full knowledge team is the least preferred type of penetration testing team because its members are often biased and may have blind spots. A full knowledge team knows what has been secured, so it may fail to properly test every possibility.

The TCSEC has several suggestions on how to conduct penetration testing with teams. In the NCSC/DOD/NIST Orange Book, the TCSEC recommends that appropriate personnel be well versed in the *Flaw Hypothesis Methodology of Penetration Testing*. With flaw hypothesis, general-purpose OSes are assessed using an open box testing technique. Team members are required to document and analyze potential flaws in the system—essentially to hypothesize any flaws that may exist. Using a system of probability, team members prioritize the list of potential flaws based on whether flaws exist, the vulnerability and exploitability of those flaws (if they do indeed exist), and the amount of control or compromise those flaws may inflict on the system. This list of priorities becomes the basis for the team's testing initiative.

Ethical Hacking

Ethical hacking is often used as another name for penetration testing. However, ethical hacking is not exactly the same as penetration testing. *Ethical hacking* is a security assessment process whereby hacking techniques and tools are employed. When an ethical hacker is engaged as part of your assessment tactics, it is important to ensure that the person does not have a conflict of interest. This would be a person who also is a provider, reseller, or consultant for security products or add-in or value-add services. An ethical hacker should not exploit discovered vulnerabilities. Writing to, altering, or damaging a target of evaluation is a violation of the concept of ethical hacking and bleeds into the realm of unethical (and often criminal) hacking.

War Dialing

War dialing is the act of using a modem to search for a system that will accept inbound connection attempts. A war dialer can be a typical computer with a modem attached and a war dialer program running or it can be a stand-alone device. In either case, they are used to systematically dial phone numbers and listen for a computer carrier tone. When a computer carrier tone is detected, the war dialer adds this number to its report that is generated at the end of the search process. A war dialer can be used to search any range of numbers, such as all 10,000 numbers within a specific prefix or all 10,000,000 within a specific area code.

War dialing is often used to locate unauthorized modems that have been installed on client systems within an otherwise secured network and have been inadvertently configured to answer inbound calls. An attacker can guess a relatively small range of phone numbers to scan by learning one or more of the phone numbers used by the organization. In most cases, the prefix is the same for all numbers within the organization if located within the same building or within a small geographic area. Thus, the war dialing search could be limited to 10,000 numbers. If several of the organization's phone numbers are sequentially close, the attacker may focus the war dialing search on a group of only a few hundred numbers.

War dialing as a penetration test is a useful tool to ensure that no unauthorized answering modems are present within your organization. In most cases, you will have a definitive list of the phone numbers controlled by or assigned to your organization. Such a list provides a focused plan of testing for war dialing.

Countermeasures against malicious war dialing include imposing strong remote access security (primarily in the arena of authentication), ensuring that no unauthorized modems are present, and using callback security, protocol restriction, and call logging.

Sniffing and Eavesdropping

Sniffing is a form of network traffic monitoring. Sniffing often involves the capture or duplication of network traffic for examination, re-creation, and extraction. It can be used both as a penetration test mechanism and as a malicious attack method. Sniffing is often an effective tool in capturing or extracting data from nonencrypted network traffic streams. Passwords, usernames, IP addresses, message contents, and much more can be captured using software or hardware-based sniffers.

Sniffers can capture either only the traffic directed to their host system's IP address or all traffic passing over the local network segment. To capture all traffic on a local network segment, the sniffer's NIC must be placed into promiscuous mode. Placing a NIC into promiscuous mode grants the operator the ability to obtain a complete statistical understanding of network activity.

There are many commercial, freeware, and hacker-ware sniffers available. These include Etherpeek, WinDump, Ethereal, sniffit, and Snmpsniff.

The primary countermeasure to sniffing attacks is to use encrypted traffic. Sniffing can also be thwarted by preventing unwanted software from being installed, by locking down all unused ports, and by using an IDS or a vulnerability scanner that is able to detect the telltale signs of a sniffer product.

Eavesdropping is just another term for sniffing. However, eavesdropping can include more than just capturing and recording network traffic. Eavesdropping also includes recording or listening to audio communications, faxes, radio signals, and so on. In other words, eavesdropping is listening in on, recording, capturing, or otherwise becoming aware of the contents of any form of communication.

Radiation Monitoring

Radiation monitoring is a specific form of sniffing or eavesdropping that involves the detection, capture, and recording of radio frequency signals and other radiated communication methods, including sound and light. Radiation monitoring can be as simple as using a hidden microphone in a room to record voices or as sophisticated as using a camera to record the light reflections in a room to reconstruct the contents of a visual computer display that is otherwise hidden from direct viewing. Radiation monitoring also includes the tapping of radio frequencies often used by cell phones, wireless network interfaces, two-way radios, radio and television broadcastings, short-wave radios, and CBs. In addition, it includes the tapping of a wide range of electrical signal variations that may not directly offer information but can be used in inference attacks. These include the change in electrical usage by an entire computer system, a hard drive, a modem, a network interface, a switch, and a router. Depending on the device, the electromagnetic signals produced by hardware can be captured and used to re-create the data, or at least metadata about the data, and the communication session.

TEMPEST is a standard that defines the study and control of electronic signals produced by various types of electronic hardware, such as computers, televisions, and phones. Its primary goal is to prevent electromagnetic interference (EMI) and radio frequency (RF) radiation from leaving a strictly defined area so as to eliminate the possibility of external radiation monitoring, eavesdropping, and signal sniffing. TEMPEST defines control zones, which generally consist of rooms or facilities that are enclosed with copper or some other kind of shielding to prevent EMI/RF from either leaving or entering the facility. Such facilities are surrounded by radiation capturing, stopping, hiding, and disrupting equipment. TEMPEST may use a form of white noise to broadcast an unintelligible worthless signal to mask the presence of a real signal. TEMPEST countermeasures are designed to protect against undetectable passive monitoring of EMI and RF.

Dumpster Diving

Dumpster diving is the act of digging through the refuse, remains, or leftovers from an organization or operation in order to discover or infer confidential information. Dumpster diving is primarily associated with digging through actual garbage. It can also include searching, investigating, and reverse-engineering an organization's website, commercial products, and publicly accessible literature (such as financial statements, brochures, product information, shareholder reports, etc.).

Scavenging is a form of dumpster diving performed electronically. Online scavenging is performed to search for useful information in the remnants of data left over after processes or tasks are completed. This could include audit trails, log files, memory dumps, variable settings, port mappings, and cached data.

Dumpster diving and scavenging can be employed as a penetration test to discover how much information about your organization is carelessly discarded into the garbage or left around after closing a facility. Countermeasures to dumpster diving and scavenging include secure disposal of all garbage. This usually means shredding all documentation. Other safeguards include maintaining physical access control.

Social Engineering

A social engineering attack is an attempt by an attacker to convince an employee to perform an unauthorized activity to subvert the security of an organization. Often the goal of social engineering is to gain access to the IT infrastructure or the physical facility.

Social engineering is a skill by which an unknown person gains the trust of someone inside of your organization. Adept individuals can convince employees that they are associated with upper management, technical support, the help desk, and so on. Once this deception is successful, the victim is often encouraged to make a change to their user account on the system, such as reset their password. Other attacks include instructing the victim to open specific e-mail attachments, launch an application, or connect to a specific URL. Whatever the actual activity is, it is usually directed toward opening a back door that the attacker can use to gain access to the network.

Social engineering attacks do not exclusively occur over the phone; they can happen in person as well. Malicious individuals impersonating repair technicians, upper management, or traveling company managers can intimidate some employees into performing activities that violate security. Countermeasures to in-person social engineering attacks include verifying the identity of the intruder/visitor via a secured photograph, contacting their source company, or finding a local manager that recognizes the individual.

Social engineering attacks can be used as penetration tests. These sorts of tests will help determine how vulnerable your frontline employees are to individuals adept at lying. For a detailed discussion of social engineering attacks, see Chapter 4, "Communications Security and Countermeasures."

Problem Management

Once auditing, monitoring, and penetration testing has occurred, the next step is problem management. *Problem management* is exactly what it sounds like: a formalized process or structure for resolving problems. For the most part, problem management is a solution developed in-house to address the various types of issues and problems encountered in your environment. Problem management is typically defined as having three goals or purposes:

- To reduce failures to a manageable level
- To prevent the occurrence or reoccurrence of a problem
- To mitigate the negative impact of problems on computing services and resources

Inappropriate Activities

Inappropriate activities are actions that may take place on a computer or over the IT infrastructure and that may not be actual crimes but are often grounds for internal punishments or termination. Some types of inappropriate activities include creating or viewing inappropriate content, sexual and racial harassment, waste, and abuse.

Inappropriate content can be defined as anything that is not related to and supportive of the work tasks of an organization. It includes, but is not limited to, pornography, sexually explicit material, entertainment, political data, and violent content. The definition of inappropriate content can be defined by example (by listing types of information deemed inappropriate) or by exclusion (by listing types of information deemed appropriate). Inappropriate content can be defined to include personal e-mail that is not work related.

Keeping inappropriate content to a minimum requires several steps. First, it must be included as an objective in the security policy. Second, staff must have awareness training in regard to inappropriate content. Third, content filtering tools can be deployed to filter data based on source or word content. It is not possible to programmatically prevent all inappropriate content, but sufficient penalties can be levied against violations, along with regular auditing/monitoring to keep its level to a minimum.

Sexual and racial harassment is a form of inappropriate content or activity on company equipment. Sexual harassment can take many forms, including distribution of images, videos, audio clips, or text information (such as jokes). Sexual and racial harassment controls include awareness training and content filtering.

Waste of resources can have a direct effect on the profitability of an organization. If the storage space, computing power, or networking bandwidth capacity is consumed by inappropriate or non-work-related data, the organization is losing money on non-profit-producing activities. Some of the more common examples of resource waste include operating a personal business over company equipment, accessing and distributing inappropriate data (pornography, entertainment, music, videos, etc.), and aimlessly surfing the Internet. Just as with inappropriate material, resource waste can be reduced but not eliminated. Some of the primary means to reduce waste include user awareness training, activity monitoring, and content filtering.

Abuse of rights and privileges is the attempt to perform activities or gain access to resources that are restricted or assigned to a higher classification and access level. When access is gained inappropriately, the confidentiality of data is violated and sensitive information can be disclosed. Countermeasures to abuse include strong implementations of access controls and activity logging.

Indistinct Threats and Countermeasures

Not all problems that an IT infrastructure will face have definitive countermeasures or are even a recognizable threat. There are numerous vulnerabilities against which there are no immediate or distinct threats and against such threats there are few countermeasures. Many of these vulnerabilities lack direct-effect countermeasures, or the deployment of available countermeasures offers little in risk reduction.

Errors and Omissions

One of the most common vulnerabilities and hardest to protect against is the occurrence of errors and omissions. Errors and omissions occur because humans interact with, program, control, and provide data for IT. There are no direct countermeasures to prevent all errors and omissions. Some safeguards against errors and omissions include input validators and user training. However, these mechanisms offer only a minimal reduction in overall errors and omissions encountered in an IT environment.

Fraud and Theft

Fraud and theft are criminal activities that can be perpetrated over computers or are made possible by computers. Most of the access controls deployed in a secured environment will reduce fraud and theft, but not every form of these crimes can be predicted and protected against. Both internal authorized users and external unauthorized intruders can exploit your IT infrastructure to perform various forms of fraud and theft. Maintaining an intensive auditing and monitoring program and prosecuting all criminal incidents will help reduce fraud and theft.

Collusion

Collusion is an agreement among multiple people to perform an unauthorized or illegal action. It is hindered by separation of duties, restricted job responsibilities, audit logging, and job rotation, which all reduce the likelihood that a coworker will be willing to collaborate on an illegal or abusive scheme due to the higher risk of detection. However, these safeguards are not primarily directed toward collusion prevention. The reduction of collusion is simply a side benefit of these security controls.

Sabotage

Employee sabotage can become an issue if an employee is knowledgeable enough about the IT infrastructure of an organization, has sufficient access to manipulate critical aspects of the environment, and has become disgruntled. Employee sabotage occurs most often when an employee suspects they will be terminated without just cause. This is one important reason terminations should be handled swiftly, including disabling all access to the infrastructure (IT and physical) and escorting the ex-employee off of the premises. Safeguards against employee sabotage are intensive auditing, monitoring for abnormal or unauthorized activity, keeping lines of communication open between employees and managers, and properly compensating and recognizing employees for excellence and extra work.

Loss of Physical and Infrastructure Support

The loss of physical and infrastructure support can be caused by power outages, natural disasters, communication interruptions, severe weather, loss of any core utility or service, disruption of transportation, strikes, and national emergencies. It may result in IT downtime and almost always significantly reduces productivity and profitability during the length of the event. It is nearly impossible to predict and protect against events that cause physical and infrastructure support loss. Disaster recovery and business continuity planning can provide restoration methods if the loss event is severe. In most cases, you must simply wait until the emergency or condition expires and things return to normal.

Unix Details

For the most part, the CISSP exam is product- and vendor-independent. However, there are a handful of issues specific to Unix that you should aware of. If you have worked with Unix or even Linux, most of these items will be simple review. If you have never touched a Unix system, then read the following items carefully.

On Unix systems, passwords are stored in a password file. The password file is stored as a shadow file so that it does not appear by default in a directory listing. The shadow setting is similar to the file setting of hidden Windows system files. Although this is an improvement, it is not a real security mechanism because everyone knows that the password file is set not to display in a directory listing by default but a simple modification of the directory command parameters reveals all hidden or shadowed files.

The most privileged account on a Unix system is known as the root. Other powerful accounts with similar levels of access are known as superusers. It is important to restrict access to these types of user accounts to only those people who absolutely need that level of access to perform their work tasks. The root or superuser accounts on Unix are similar to the administrator account(s) on Windows systems. Whenever possible, root and superuser access should be restricted to the local console so that they cannot be used over a network connection.

The two utilities, setuid and setgid, should be closely monitored and their uses logged. These two tools are used to manipulate access to resources. Thus, if they are employed by a non-administrator, or when employed by an administrator in an unapproved fashion, it can indicate security policy violations.

Another important command to monitor is the mount command, which is used to map a local drive letter to a shared network drive. This activity may seem like an efficient method to access network resources. However, it also makes malicious code and intruder attacks easier to implement. When the mount command is used when it is not authorized for use, it could indicate an intrusion or an attempt to create a security loophole.

You should also consider monitoring the use of the following commands: systat, bootp, tftp, sunrpc, snmp, snmp-trap, and nfs.

Finally, Unix systems can be configured to boot into a fixed dedicated security mode where authentication is not required. When this is done, anyone accessing the system has complete access to everything at the security level at which the system is currently operating. You can easily determine if a system has been configured to perform this operation if there is a /etc/host.equiv file present. Removing this file disables this feature.

Malicious Hackers or Crackers

Malicious hackers or crackers are individuals who actively seek to infiltrate your IT infrastructure whether for fame, access, or financial gain. These intrusions or attacks are important threats against which your security policy and your entire security infrastructure is designed to repel. Most safeguards and countermeasures protect against one specific threat or another, but it is not possible to protect against all possible threats that a cracker represents. Remaining vigilant about security, tracking activity, and implementing intrusion detection systems can provide a reasonable level of protection.

Espionage

Espionage is the malicious act of gathering proprietary, secret, private, sensitive, or confidential information about an organization for the express purpose of disclosing and often selling that data to a competitor or other interested organization (such as a foreign government). Espionage is sometimes committed by internal employees who have become dissatisfied with their jobs and have become compromised in some way. It can also be committed by a mole or plant placed into your organization to steal information for their primary secret employer. Countermeasures against espionage are to strictly control access to all non-public data, thoroughly screen new employee candidates, and efficiently track the activities of all employees.

Malicious Code

Malicious code is any script or program that performs an unwanted, unauthorized, or unknown activity on a computer system. Malicious code can take many forms, including viruses, worms, Trojan horses, documents with destructive macros, and logic bombs. Some form of malicious code exists for every type of computer or computing device. Monitoring and filtering the traffic that enters and travels within a secured environment is the only effective countermeasure to malicious code.

Traffic and Trend Analysis

The ongoing activities of a network and even a business environment may produce recognizable patterns. These patterns are known as trends or traffic patterns. A specific type of attack called *traffic* and *trend analysis* examines these patterns for what they reveal. What is interesting about these types of examinations or attacks is that they reveal only the patterns of traffic, not the actual content of the traffic. Patterns and trends can reveal operations that occur on a regular basis or that are somehow considered important. For example, suppose an attacker watches your T1 line and notices that from 3 PM to approximately 4:30 PM every Friday your organization consumes nearly 80 percent of the capacity of the T1 line. The attacker can infer that the noticeable pattern is a file or data transfer activity that is important because it always occurs at the same time every week. Thus, the attacker can schedule an attack for 2:45 PM to take out the T1 or otherwise cause a denial of service to prevent legitimate activity from occurring. Traffic and trend analysis can be used against both encrypted and nonencrypted traffic because patterns of traffic rather than contents are examined. Traffic and trend analysis can be used against physical environments and people as well. For example, a security guard can be watched to discover that it takes 12 minutes for him to walk the perimeter of a building and for 8 of those minutes, he will be unable to see a section of fence where an intruder could easily climb.

Countermeasures to traffic and trend analysis include performing traffic and trend analysis on your own environment to see what types of information you are inadvertently revealing if anyone happens to be watching. You can alter your common and mission-critical activities so as not to produce easily recognizable patterns. Other countermeasures to traffic and trend analysis are traffic padding, noise, and use of covert channels. You can pad your communication channels through traffic generation tools or broadcasting noise whenever legitimate traffic is not occurring.

Initial Program Load Vulnerabilities

There is a period of time between the moments when a device is off and when it is fully booted and operational that the system is not fully protected by its security mechanisms. This time period is known as the *initial program load (IPL)* and it has numerous vulnerabilities. Without physical security, there are no countermeasures for IPL vulnerabilities. Anyone with physical access to a device can easily exploit its weaknesses during its bootup process. Some IPL vulnerabilities are accessing alternate boot menus, booting to a mobile operating system off of a CD or floppy, and accessing CMOS to alter configuration settings, such as enabling or disabling devices.

Linux Details

Just as there are a few Unix issues to take notice of, there are a few Linux items as well:

Salts are added to Linux passwords to increase randomness and ensure uniqueness of the stored hash. Think of a salt as a random number appended to the password before hashing.

Low Water-Mark Mandatory Access Control (LOMAC) is a loadable kernel module for Linux designed to protect the integrity of processes and data. It is an OS security architecture extension or enhancement that provides flexible support for security policies.

Flask is an OS prototyped in the Fluke research OS. Flask is a security architecture for operating systems that includes flexible support for security polices. Some features of the Fluke prototype were ported into the OSKit (a programmer's toolkit for writing OSes). Many of the Flask architecture features were being incorporated into SE Linux (Security-Enhanced Linux) since it was built using the OSKit. Therefore, Flask led to the Fluke OS, which led to the OSKit, which was used to write SE Linux, which incorporates flask features.

Summary

Maintaining operations security requires directed efforts in auditing and monitoring. These efforts give rise to detecting attacks and intrusions. This in turn guides the selection of counter-measures, encourages penetration testing, and helps to limit, restrict, and prevent inappropriate activities, crimes, and other threats.

Auditing is a methodical examination or review of an environment to ensure compliance with regulations and to detect abnormalities, unauthorized occurrences, or outright crimes. Secure IT environments rely heavily on auditing. Overall, auditing serves as the primary type of detective control used by a secure environment.

Audit trails are the records created by recording information about events and occurrences into a database or log file, and they can be used to, for example, reconstruct an event, extract information about an incident, and prove or disprove culpability. Audit trails provide a passive form of detective security control and serve as a deterrent in the same manner as CCTV or security guards do. In addition, they can be essential as evidence in the prosecution of criminals.

Record retention is the organizational policy that defines what information is maintained and for how long. In most cases, the records in question are audit trails of user activity, including file and resource access, logon patterns, e-mail, and the use of privileges.

Monitoring is a form of auditing that focuses more on the active review of the audited information or the audited asset. It is most often used in conjunction with performance, but it can be used in a security context as well. The actual tools and techniques used to perform monitoring vary greatly between environments and system platforms, but there are several common forms found in most environments: warning banners, keystroke monitoring, traffic analysis and trend analysis, and other monitoring tools.

Penetration testing is a vigorous attempt to break into your protected network using any means necessary, and it is a common method for testing the strength of your security measures. Organizations often hire external consultants to perform the penetration testing so the testers are not privy to confidential elements of the security's configuration, network design, and other internal secrets. Penetration testing methods can include war dialing, sniffing, cavesdropping, radiation monitoring, dumpster diving, and social engineering.

Inappropriate activities may take place on a computer or over the IT infrastructure, and may not be actual crimes, but they are often grounds for internal punishments or termination. Inappropriate activities include creating or viewing inappropriate content, sexual and racial harassment, waste, and abuse.

An IT infrastructure can include numerous vulnerabilities against which there is no immediate or distinct threat and against such threats there are few countermeasures. These types of threats include errors, omissions, fraud, theft, collusion, sabotage, loss of physical and infrastructure support, crackers, espionage, and malicious code. There are, however, steps you can take to lessen the impact of most of these.

Exam Essentials

Understand auditing.   Auditing is a methodical examination or review of an environment to ensure compliance with regulations and to detect abnormalities, unauthorized occurrences, or outright crimes. Secure IT environments rely heavily on auditing. Overall, auditing serves as the primary type of detective control used by a secure environment.

Know the types or forms of auditing.   Auditing encompasses a wide variety of different activities, including the recording of event/occurrence data, examination of data, data reduction, the use of event/occurrence alarm triggers, log analysis, and response (some other names for these activities are logging, monitoring, examining alerts, analysis, and even intrusion detection). Be able to explain what each type of auditing activity involves.

Understand compliance checking.   Compliance checking (or compliance testing) ensures that all of the necessary and required elements of a security solution are properly deployed and functioning as expected. Compliance checks can take many forms, such as vulnerability scans and penetration testing. They can also involve auditing and be performed using log analysis tools to determine if any vulnerabilities for which countermeasures have been deployed have been realized on the system.

Understand the need for frequent security audits.   The frequency of an IT infrastructure security audit or security review is based on risk. You must determine whether sufficient risk exists to warrant the expense and interruption of a security audit on a more or less frequent basis. The frequency of audit reviews should be clearly defined and adhered to.

Understand that auditing is an aspect of due care.   Security audits and effectiveness reviews are key elements in displaying due care. Senior management must enforce compliance with regular periodic security reviews or they will be held accountable and liable for any asset losses that occur as a result.

Understand audit trails.   Audit trails are the records created by recording information about events and occurrences into a database or log file. They are used to reconstruct an event, to extract information about an incident, and to prove or disprove culpability. Using audit trails is a passive form of detective security control, and audit trails are essential evidence in the prosecution of criminals.

Understand how accountability is maintained.   Accountability is maintained for individual subjects through the use of audit trails. Activities of users and events caused by the actions of users while online can be recorded so users can be held accountable for their actions. This directly promotes good user behavior and compliance with the organization's security policy.

Know the basic elements of an audit report.   Audit reports should all address a few basic or central concepts: the purpose of the audit, the scope of the audit, and the results discovered or revealed by the audit. They often include many other details specific to the environment, such as time, date, and specific systems. Audit reports can include a wide range of content that focuses on problems/events/conditions, standards/criteria/baselines, causes/reasons, impact/effect, or solutions/recommendations/safeguards.

Understand the need to control access to audit reports. Audit reports include sensitive information and should be assigned a classification label and handled appropriately. Only people with sufficient privilege should have access to them. An audit report should also be prepared in various versions according to the hierarchy of the organization, providing only the details relevant to the position of the staff members they are prepared for.

Understand sampling. Sampling, or data extraction, is the process of extracting elements of data from a large body of data in order to construct a meaningful representation or summary of the whole. There are two forms of sampling: statistical and nonstatistical. An auditing tool using precise mathematical functions to extract meaningful information from a large volume of data performs statistical sampling. Statistical sampling is used to measure the risk associated with the sampling process.

Understand record retention. Record retention is the act of retaining and maintaining important information. There should be an organizational policy that defines what information is maintained and for how long. The records in question are usually audit trails of user activity, including file and resource access, logon patterns, e-mail, and the use of privileges. Depending upon your industry and your relationship with the government, you may need to retain records for three years, seven years, or indefinitely.

Understand monitoring and the uses of monitoring tools. Monitoring is a form of auditing that focuses more on the active review of the audited information or the audited asset. It's most often used in conjunction with performance, but it can be used in a security context as well. Monitoring can focus on events, subsystems, users, hardware, software, or any other object within the IT environment. Although the actual tools and techniques used to perform monitoring vary greatly between environments and system platforms, there are several common forms found in most environments: warning banners, keystroke monitoring, traffic analysis and trend analysis, and other monitoring tools. Be able to list the various monitoring tools and know when and how to use each tool.

Understand failure recognition and response. On systems that use manual review, failure recognition is the responsibility of the observer or auditor. In order to recognize a failure, one must understand what is normal and expected. When the monitored or audited events stray from this standard baseline, then a failure, breach, intrusion, error, or problem has occurred and a response must be initiated.

Understand what penetration testing is and be able to explain the methods used. Organizations use penetration testing to evaluate the strength of their security infrastructure. Know that it involves launching intrusion attacks on your network and be able to explain the methods used: war dialing, sniffing and eavesdropping, radiation monitoring, dumpster diving, and social engineering.

Know what TEMPEST is. TEMPEST is a standard for the study and control of electronic signals produced by various types of electronic hardware, such as computers, televisions, phones, and so on. Its primary goal is to prevent EMI and RF radiation from leaving a strictly defined area so as to eliminate the possibility of external radiation monitoring, eavesdropping, and signal sniffing.

Know what dumpster diving and scavenging are.   Dumpster diving and scavenging involve digging through the refuse, remains, or leftovers from an organization or operation in order to discover or infer confidential information. Countermeasures to dumpster diving and scavenging include secure disposal of all garbage. This usually means shredding all documentation and incinerating all shredded material and other waste. Other safeguards include maintaining physical access control and monitoring privilege activity use online.

Understand social engineering.   A social engineering attack is an attempt by an attacker to convince an employee to perform an unauthorized activity to subvert the security of an organization. Often the goal of social engineering is to gain access to the IT infrastructure or the physical facility. The only way to protect against social engineering attacks is to thoroughly train users how to respond and interact with communications as well as with unknown personnel.

Know what inappropriate activities are.   Inappropriate activities are actions that may take place on a computer or over the IT infrastructure and that may not be actual crimes but are often grounds for internal punishments or termination. Some types of inappropriate activities include creating or viewing inappropriate content, sexual and racial harassment, waste, and abuse.

Know that errors and omissions can cause security problems.   One of the most common vulnerabilities and hardest to protect against are errors and omissions. Errors and omissions occur because humans interact with, program, control, and provide data for IT. There are no direct countermeasures to prevent all errors and omissions. Some safeguards against errors and omissions include input validators and user training. However, these mechanisms offer only a minimal reduction in overall errors and omissions encountered in an IT environment.

Understand fraud and theft.   Fraud and theft are criminal activities that can be perpetrated over computers or made possible by computers. Most of the access controls deployed in a secured environment will reduce fraud and theft, but not every form of these crimes can be predicted and protected against. Both internal authorized users and external unauthorized intruders can exploit your IT infrastructure to perform various forms of fraud and theft. Maintaining an intensive auditing and monitoring program and prosecuting all criminal incidents will help reduce fraud and theft.

Know what collusion is.   Collusion is an agreement among multiple people to perform an unauthorized or illegal action. It is hindered by separation of duties, restricted job responsibilities, audits, and job rotation, which all reduce the likelihood that a coworker will be willing to collaborate on an illegal or abusive scheme due to the higher risk of detection.

Understand employee sabotage.   Employee sabotage can become an issue if an employee is knowledgeable enough about the IT infrastructure of an organization, has sufficient access to manipulate critical aspects of the environment, and has become disgruntled. Safeguards against employee sabotage are intensive auditing, monitoring for abnormal or unauthorized activity, keeping lines of communication open between employees and managers, and properly compensating and recognizing employees for excellence and extra work.

Know how loss of physical and infrastructure support can cause security problems.   The loss of physical and infrastructure support is caused by power outages, natural disasters, communication interruptions, severe weather, loss of any core utility or service, disruption of transportation, strikes, and national emergencies. It is nearly impossible to predict and protect against events of physical and infrastructure support loss. Disaster recovery and business continuity planning can provide restoration methods if the loss event is severe. In most cases, you must simply wait until the emergency or condition subsides and things return to normal.

Understand espionage.   Espionage is the malicious act by an internal employee of gathering proprietary, secret, private, sensitive, or confidential information about an organization for the express purpose of disclosing and often selling that data to a competitor or other interested organization (such as a foreign government). Countermeasures against espionage are to strictly control access to all nonpublic data, thoroughly screen new employee candidates, and efficiently track the activities of all employees.

Review Questions

1. What is a methodical examination or review of an environment to ensure compliance with regulations and to detect abnormalities, unauthorized occurrences, or outright crimes?

   A. Penetration testing

   B. Auditing

   C. Risk analysis

   D. Entrapment

2. Which of the following is not considered a type of auditing activity?

   A. Recording of event data

   B. Data reduction

   C. Log analysis

   D. Deployment of countermeasures

3. Monitoring can be used to perform all but which of the following?

   A. Detect availability of new software patches

   B. Detect malicious actions by subjects

   C. Detect attempted intrusions

   D. Detect system failures

4. What provides data for re-creating step-by-step the history of an event, intrusion, or system failure?

   A. Security policies

   B. Log files

   C. Audit reports

   D. Business continuity planning

5. What is the frequency of an IT infrastructure security audit or security review based on?

   A. Asset value

   B. Management discretion

   C. Risk

   D. Level of realized threats

6. Failure to perform which of the following can result in the perception that due care is not being maintained?

   A. Periodic security audits

   B. Deployment of all available safeguards

   C. Performance reviews

   D. Creating audit reports for shareholders

7. Audit trails are considered to be what type of security control?

    A. Administrative

    B. Passive

    C. Corrective

    D. Physical

8. Which essential element of an audit report is not considered to be a basic concept of the audit?

    A. Purpose of the audit

    B. Recommendations of the auditor

    C. Scope of the audit

    D. Results of the audit

9. Why should access to audit reports be controlled and restricted?

    A. They contain copies of confidential data stored on the network.

    B. They contain information about the vulnerabilities of the system.

    C. They are useful only to upper management.

    D. They include the details about the configuration of security controls.

10. What are used to inform would-be intruders or those who attempt to violate security policy that their intended activities are restricted and that any further activities will be audited and monitored?

    A. Security policies

    B. Interoffice memos

    C. Warning banners

    D. Honey pots

11. Which of the following focuses more on the patterns and trends of data rather than the actual content?

    A. Keystroke monitoring

    B. Traffic analysis

    C. Event logging

    D. Security auditing

12. Which of the following activities is not considered a valid form of penetration testing?

    A. Denial of service attacks

    B. Port scanning

    C. Distribution of malicious code

    D. Packet sniffing

13. The act of searching for unauthorized modems is known as _____.

    A. Scavenging

    B. Espionage

    C. System auditing

    D. War dialing

14. Which of the following is not a useful countermeasure to war dialing?

    A. Restricted and monitored Internet access

    B. Imposing strong remote access security

    C. Callback security

    D. Call logging

15. The standard for study and control of electronic signals produced by various types of electronic hardware is known as _____.

    A. Eavesdropping

    B. TEMPEST

    C. SESAME

    D. Wiretapping

16. Searching through the refuse, remains, or leftovers from an organization or operation to discover or infer confidential information is known as _____.

    A. Impersonation

    B. Dumpster diving

    C. Social engineering

    D. Inference

17. Which of the following is not an effective countermeasure against inappropriate content being hosted or distributed over a secured network?

    A. Activity logging

    B. Content filtering

    C. Intrusion detection system

    D. Penalties and termination for violations

18. One of the most common vulnerabilities of an IT infrastructure and hardest to protect against is the occurrence of _____.

    A. Errors and omissions

    B. Inference

    C. Data destruction by malicious code

    D. Data scavenging

19. The willful destruction of assets or elements within the IT infrastructure as a form of revenge or justification for perceived wrongdoing is known as _____.

    A. Espionage

    B. Entrapment

    C. Sabotage

    D. Permutation

20. What is the most common reaction to the loss of physical and infrastructure support?

    A. Deploying OS updates

    B. Vulnerability scanning

    C. Waiting for the event to expire

    D. Tightening of access controls

Answers to Review Questions

1. B. Auditing is a methodical examination or review of an environment to ensure compliance with regulations and to detect abnormalities, unauthorized occurrences, or outright crimes.

2. D. Deployment of countermeasures is not considered a type of auditing activity; rather, it's an active attempt to prevent security problems.

3. A. Monitoring is not used to detect the availability of new software patches.

4. B. Log files provide an audit trail for re-creating step-by-step the history of an event, intrusion, or system failure. An audit trail is used to reconstruct an event, to extract information about an incident, to prove or disprove culpability, and much more.

5. C. The frequency of an IT infrastructure security audit or security review is based on risk. You must establish the existence of sufficient risk to warrant the expense of and interruption caused by a security audit on a more or less frequent basis.

6. A. Failing to perform periodic security audits can result in the perception that due care is not being maintained. Such audits alert personnel that senior management is practicing due diligence in maintaining system security.

7. B. Audit trails are a passive form of detective security control. Administrative, corrective, and physical security controls are active ways to maintain security.

8. B. Recommendations of the auditor are not considered basic and essential concepts to be included in an audit report. Key elements of an audit report include the purpose, scope, and results of the audit.

9. B. Audit reports should be secured because they contain information about the vulnerabilities of the system. Disclosure of such vulnerabilities to the wrong person could lead to security breaches.

10. C. Warning banners are used to inform would-be intruders or those who attempt to violate the security policy that their intended activities are restricted and that any further activities will be audited and monitored.

11. B. Traffic analysis focuses more on the patterns and trends of data rather than the actual content. Such an analysis offers insight into primary communication routes, sources of encrypted traffic, location of primary servers, primary and backup communication pathways, amount of traffic supported by the network, typical direction of traffic flow, frequency of communications, and much more.

12. C. Distribution of malicious code will almost always result in damage or loss of assets. Thus, it is not an element of penetration testing under any circumstance, even if it's done with the approval of upper management.

13. D. War dialing is the act of searching for unauthorized modems that will accept inbound calls on an otherwise secure network in an attempt to gain access.

14. A. Users often install unauthorized modems because of restricted and monitored Internet access. Because war dialing is often used to locate unauthorized modems, restricting and monitoring Internet access wouldn't be an effective countermeasure.

15. B. TEMPEST is the standard that defines the study and control of electronic signals produced by various types of electronic hardware.

16. B. Dumpster diving is the act of searching through the refuse, remains, or leftovers from an organization or operation to discover or infer confidential information.

17. C. An IDS is not a countermeasure against inappropriate content.

18. A. One of the most common vulnerabilities and hardest to protect against is the occurrence of errors and omissions.

19. C. The willful destruction of assets or elements within the IT infrastructure as a form of revenge or justification for perceived wrongdoing is known as sabotage.

20. C. In most cases, you must simply wait until the emergency or condition expires and things return to normal.

Chapter

15

Business Continuity Planning

THE CISSP EXAM TOPICS COVERED IN THIS CHAPTER INCLUDE:

- ✓ Business Continuity Planning
- ✓ Project Scope and Planning
- ✓ Business Impact Assessment
- ✓ Containment Strategy

Despite our best wishes, disasters of one form or another eventually strike every organization. Whether it's a natural disaster like a hurricane or earthquake or a manmade disaster like a riot or explosion, every organization will encounter events that threaten their very existence. Strong organizations have plans and procedures in place to help mitigate the effects a disaster has on their continuing operations and to speed the return to normal operations. Recognizing the importance of planning for business *continuity* and disaster recovery, (ISC)² designated these two processes as the eighth domain of the Common Body of Knowledge for the CISSP program. Knowledge of these fundamental topics will help you prepare for the exam and help you prepare your organization for the unexpected.

In this chapter, we'll explore the concepts behind Business Continuity Planning. Chapter 16, "Disaster Recovery Planning," will continue our discussion.

Business Continuity Planning

Business Continuity Planning (BCP) involves the assessment of a variety of risks to organizational processes and the creation of policies, plans, and procedures to minimize the impact those risks might have on the organization if they were to occur. BCP is used to restore operations back to normal in the event of a minor disaster. A minor disaster is any event that does not fully interrupt business processes but is not handled automatically by the deployed security mechanisms. Thus, a BCP event is less disastrous than a *Disaster Recovery Planning (DRP)* event but more disastrous than a simple security violation. BCP focuses on maintaining business operations with reduced or restricted infrastructure capabilities or resources. As long as the continuity of the organization's ability to perform its mission-critical work tasks is maintained, BCP can be used to manage and restore the environment. If the continuity is broken, then business processes have stopped and the organization is in disaster mode, thus DRP takes over.

The top priority of BCP and DRP is always *people*. The primary concern is to get people out of harm's way; then you can address IT recovery and restoration issues.

The overall goal of BCP is to reduce the risk of financial loss and to enhance a company's ability to recover from a disruptive event promptly. The BCP process, as defined by (ISC)², has four main steps:

- Project Scope and Planning
- Business Impact Assessment

- Continuity Planning
- Approval and Implementation

The next three sections of this chapter cover each of these phases in detail. The last portion of this chapter will introduce some of the critical elements you should take under consideration when compiling documentation of your organization's business continuity plan.

Project Scope and Planning

As with any formalized business process, the development of a strong business continuity plan requires the use of a proven methodology. This requires a structured analysis of the business's organization from a crisis planning point of view, the creation of a BCP team with the approval of senior management, an assessment of the resources available to participate in business continuity activities, and an analysis of the legal and regulatory landscape that governs an organization's response to a catastrophic event.

Business Organization Analysis

One of the first responsibilities of the individuals responsible for business continuity planning is to perform an analysis of the business organization to identify all departments and individuals who have a stake in the Business Continuity Planning process. Some areas to consider are included in the following list:

- Operational departments that are responsible for the core services the business provides to its clients
- Critical support services, such as the information technology department, plant maintenance department, and other groups responsible for the upkeep of systems that support the operational departments
- Senior executives and other key individuals essential for the ongoing viability of the organization

This identification process is critical for two reasons. First, it provides the groundwork necessary to help identify potential members of the Business Continuity Planning team (see the next section). Second, it provides the foundation for the remainder of the BCP process.

Normally, the business organization analysis is performed by the one or two individuals spearheading the BCP effort. This is acceptable, given the fact that they normally use the output of the analysis to assist with the selection of the remaining BCP team members. However, a thorough review of this analysis should be one of the first tasks assigned to the full BCP team when it is convened. This step is critical because the individuals performing the original analysis may have overlooked critical business functions known to BCP team members that represent other parts of the organization. If the team were to continue without revising the organizational analysis, the entire BCP process may become corrupted and result in the development of a plan that does not fully address the emergency response needs of the organization as a whole.

Each location of an organization should have its own distinct plan. A single plan should not cover multiple geographic locations.

BCP Team Selection

In many organizations, the IT and/or security departments are given sole responsibility for Business Continuity Planning. Operational and other support departments are given no input in the development of the plan and may not even know of its existence until disaster strikes or is imminent. This is a critical flaw! The independent development of a business continuity plan can spell disaster in two ways. First, the plan itself may not take into account knowledge possessed only by the individuals responsible for the day-to-day operation of the business. Second, it keeps operational elements "in the dark" about plan specifics until implementation becomes necessary. This reduces the possibility that operational elements will agree with the provisions of the plan and work effectively to implement it. It also denies organizations the benefits achieved by a structured training and testing program for the plan.

To prevent these events from adversely impacting the Business Continuity Planning process, the individuals responsible for the effort should take special care when selecting the BCP team. The team should include, as a minimum, the following individuals:

- Representatives from each of the organization's departments responsible for the core services performed by the business

- Representatives from the key support departments identified by the organizational analysis

- IT representatives with technical expertise in areas covered by the BCP

- Security representatives with knowledge of the BCP process

- Legal representatives familiar with corporate legal, regulatory, and contractual responsibilities

- Representatives from senior management

Select your team carefully! You need to strike a balance between representing different points of view and creating a team with explosive personality differences. Your goal should be to create a group that is as diverse as possible and still operates in harmony.

Each one of the individuals mentioned in the preceding list brings a unique perspective to the BCP process and will have individual biases. For example, the representatives from each of the operational departments will often consider their department the most critical to the organization's continued viability. Although these biases may at first seem divisive, the leader of the BCP effort should embrace them and harness them in a productive manner. If used effectively, the biases will help achieve a healthy balance in the final plan as each representative advocates the needs of their department. On the other hand, if proper leadership isn't provided, these biases may devolve into destructive turf battles that derail the BCP effort and harm the organization as a whole.

Resource Requirements

After the team validates the business organization analysis, they should turn to an assessment of the resources required by the BCP effort. This involves the resources required by three distinct BCP phases:

BCP development   The BCP team will require some resources to perform the four elements of the BCP process (Project Scope and Planning, Business Impact Assessment, Continuity Planning, and Approval and Implementation). It's more than likely that the major resource consumed by this BCP phase will be manpower expended by members of the BCP team and the support staff they call upon to assist in the development of the plan.

BCP testing, training, and maintenance   The testing, training, and maintenance phases of BCP will require some hardware and software commitments, but once again, the major commitment in this phase will be manpower on the part of the employees involved in those activities.

BCP implementation   When a disaster strikes and the BCP team deems it necessary to conduct a full-scale implementation of the business continuity plan, significant resources will be required. This includes a large amount of manpower (BCP will likely become the focus of a large part, if not all, of the organization) and the utilization of "hard" resources. For this reason, it's important that the team uses its BCP implementation powers judiciously, yet decisively.

An effective business continuity plan requires the expenditure of a large amount of corporate resources, ranging all the way from the purchase and deployment of redundant computing facilities to the pencils and paper used by team members scratching out the first drafts of the plan.

However, as you saw earlier, one of the most significant resources consumed by the BCP process is personnel. Many security professionals overlook the importance of accounting for labor. However, you can rest assured that senior management will not. Business leaders are keenly aware of the effect that time-consuming side activities have on the operational productivity of their organizations and the real cost of personnel in terms of salary, benefits, and lost opportunities. These concerns become especially paramount when you are requesting the time of senior executives. You should expect that leaders responsible for resource utilization management will put your BCP proposal under a microscope, and you should be prepared to defend the necessity of your plan with coherent, logical arguments that address the business case for BCP.

🌐 Real World Scenario

Explaining the Benefits of BCP

One of the most common arguments against committing resources to BCP is the planned use of "seat of the pants" continuity planning, or the attitude that the business has always survived and the key leaders will figure something out in the event of a disaster. If you encounter this objection, you might want to point out to management the costs that will be incurred by the business (both direct costs and the indirect cost of lost opportunities) for each day that the business is down. Then ask them to consider how long a "seat of the pants" recovery might take when compared to an orderly, planned continuity of operations.

Legal and Regulatory Requirements

Many industries may find themselves bound by federal, state, and local laws or regulations that require them to implement various degrees of Business Continuity Planning. We've already discussed one example in this chapter—the officers and directors of publicly traded firms have a fiduciary responsibility to exercise due diligence in the execution of their business continuity duties. In other circumstances, the requirements (and consequences of failure) might be more severe. Emergency services, such as police, fire, and emergency medical operations, have a responsibility to the community to continue operations in the event of a disaster. Indeed, their services become even more critical in an emergency when the public safety is threatened. Failure on their part to implement a solid BCP could result in the loss of life and/or property and the decreased confidence of the population in their government.

In many countries, financial institutions, such as banks, brokerages, and the firms that process their data, are governed by strict government and international banking and securities regulations designed to facilitate their continued operation to ensure the viability of the national economy. When pharmaceutical manufacturers must produce products in less-than-optimal circumstances following a disaster, they are required to certify the purity of their products to government regulators. There are countless other examples of industries that are required to continue operating in the event of an emergency by various laws and regulations.

Even if you're not bound by any of these considerations, you might have contractual obligations to your clients that require you to implement sound BCP practices. If your contracts include some type of *service level agreement (SLA),* you might find yourself in breach of those contracts if a disaster interrupts your ability to service your clients. Many clients may feel sorry for you and want to continue using your products/services, but their own business requirements might force them to sever the relationship and find new suppliers.

On the flip side of the coin, developing a strong, documented business continuity plan can help your organization win new clients and additional business from existing clients. If you can show your customers the sound procedures you have in place to continue serving them in the event of a disaster, they'll place greater confidence in your firm and might be more likely to choose you as their preferred vendor. Not a bad position to be in!

All of these concerns point to one conclusion—it's essential to include your organization's legal counsel in the Business Continuity Planning process. They are intimately familiar with the legal, regulatory, and contractual obligations that apply to your organization and can help your team implement a plan that meets those requirements while ensuring the continued viability of the organization to the benefit of all—employees, shareholders, suppliers, and customers alike.

Laws regarding computing systems, business practices, and disaster management change frequently and vary from jurisdiction to jurisdiction. Be sure to keep your attorneys involved throughout the lifetime of your BCP, including the testing and maintenance phases. If you restrict their involvement to a pre-implementation review of the plan, you may not become aware of the impact that changing laws and regulations have on your corporate responsibilities.

Business Impact Assessment

Once your BCP team completes the four stages of preparing to create a business continuity plan, it's time to dive into the heart of the work—the *Business Impact Assessment (BIA)*. The BIA identifies the resources that are critical to an organization's ongoing viability and the threats posed to those resources. It also assesses the likelihood that each threat will actually occur and the impact those occurrences will have on the business. The results of the BIA provide you with quantitative measures that can help you prioritize the commitment of business continuity resources to the various risks your organization faces.

It's important to realize that there are two different types of analyses that business planners use when facing a decision:

Quantitative decision making   *Quantitative decision making* involves the use of numbers and formulas to reach a decision. This type of data often expresses options in terms of the dollar value to the business.

Qualitative decision making   *Qualitative decision making* takes nonnumerical factors, such as emotions, investor/customer confidence, workforce stability, and other concerns, into account. This type of data often results in categories of prioritization (such as high, medium, and low).

Quantitative analysis and qualitative analysis both play an important role in the Business Continuity Planning process. However, most people tend to favor one type of analysis over the other. When selecting the individual members of the BCP team, try to achieve a balance between people who prefer each strategy. This will result in the development of a well-rounded BCP and benefit the organization in the long run.

The BIA process described in this chapter approaches the problem from both quantitative and qualitative points of view. However, it's very tempting for a BCP team to "go with the numbers" and perform a quantitative assessment while neglecting the somewhat more difficult qualitative assessment. It's important that the BCP team perform a qualitative analysis of the factors affecting your BCP process. For example, if your business is highly dependent upon a few very important clients, your management team is probably willing to suffer significant short-term financial loss in order to retain those clients in the long term. The BCP team must sit down and discuss (preferably with the involvement of senior management) qualitative concerns to develop a comprehensive approach that satisfies all stakeholders.

Identify Priorities

The first BIA task facing the Business Continuity Planning team is the identification of business priorities. Depending upon your line of business, there will be certain activities that are most essential to your day-to-day operations when disaster strikes. The priority identification task, or *criticality prioritization*, involves creating a comprehensive list of business processes and ranking them in order of importance. Although this task may seem somewhat daunting, it's not as hard as it seems. A great way to divide the workload of this process among the team members is to assign each participant responsibility for drawing up a prioritized list that covers the business functions that their department is responsible for. When the entire BCP team convenes, team members can use those prioritized lists to create a master prioritized list for the entire organization.

This process helps identify business priorities from a qualitative point of view. Recall that we're describing an attempt to simultaneously develop both qualitative and quantitative BIAs. To begin the quantitative assessment, the BCP team should sit down and draw up a list of organization *assets* and then assign an *asset value (AV)* in monetary terms to each asset. These numbers will be used in the remaining BIA steps to develop a financially based BIA. The second quantitative measure that the team must develop is the *maximum tolerable downtime (MTD), or recovery time objective (RTO),* for each business function. This is the maximum length of time a business function can be inoperable without causing irreparable harm to the business. The MTD provides valuable information when performing both BCP and DRP planning.

Risk Identification

The next phase of the Business Impact Assessment is the identification of risks posed to your organization. Some elements of this organization-specific list may come to mind immediately.

The identification of other, more obscure risks might take a little creativity on the part of the BCP team.

Risks come in two forms: natural risks and man-made risks. The following list includes some events that pose natural threats:

- Violent storms/hurricanes/tornadoes/blizzards
- Earthquakes
- Mudslides/avalanches
- Volcanic eruptions

Man-made threats include the following events:

- Terrorist acts/wars/civil unrest
- Theft/vandalism
- Fires/explosions
- Prolonged power outages
- Building collapses
- Transportation failures

Remember, these are by no means all inclusive lists. They merely identify some common risks that many organizations face. You may wish to use them as a starting point, but a full listing of risks facing your organization will require input from all members of the BCP team.

The risk identification portion of the process is purely qualitative in nature. At this point in the process, the BCP team should not be concerned about the likelihood that each type of risk will actually materialize or the amount of damage such an occurrence would inflict upon the continued operation of the business. The results of this analysis will drive both the qualitative and quantitative portions of the remaining BIA tasks.

Likelihood Assessment

The preceding step consisted of the BCP team drawing up a comprehensive list of the events that can be a threat to an organization. You probably recognized that some events are much more likely to happen than others. For example, a business in Southern California is much more likely to face the risk of an earthquake than that posed by a volcanic eruption. A business based in Hawaii might have the exact opposite likelihood that each risk would occur.

To account for these differences, the next phase of the Business Impact Assessment identifies the likelihood that each risk will occur. To keep calculations consistent, this assessment is usually expressed in terms of an *annualized rate of occurrence (ARO)* that reflects the number of times a business expects to experience a given disaster each year.

The BCP team should sit down and determine an ARO for each risk identified in the previous section. These numbers should be based upon corporate history, professional experience of team members, and advice from experts, such as meteorologists, seismologists, fire prevention professionals, and other consultants, as needed.

Impact Assessment

As you may have surmised based upon its name, the impact assessment is one of the most critical portions of the Business Impact Assessment. In this phase, you analyze the data gathered during risk identification and likelihood assessment and attempt to determine what impact each one of the identified risks would have upon the business if it were to occur.

From a quantitative point of view, there are three specific metrics we will examine: the exposure factor, the single loss expectancy, and the annualized loss expectancy. Each one of these values is computed for each specific risk/asset combination evaluated during the previous phases.

The *exposure factor (EF)* is the amount of damage that the risk poses to the asset, expressed as a percentage of the asset's value. For example, if the BCP team consults with fire experts and determines that a building fire would cause 70 percent of the building to be destroyed, the exposure factor of the building to fire is 70 percent.

The *single loss expectancy (SLE)* is the monetary loss that is expected each time the risk materializes. It is computed as the product of the exposure factor (EF) and the asset value (AV). Continuing with the preceding example, if the building is worth $500,000, the single loss expectancy would be 70 percent of $500,000, or $350,000. You can interpret this figure to mean that a single fire in the building would be expected to cause $350,000 worth of damage.

The *annualized loss expectancy (ALE)* is the monetary loss that the business expects to occur as a result of the risk harming the asset over the course of a year. It is computed as the product of the annualized rate of occurrence (ARO from the previous section) and the asset value (AV). Returning once again to our building example, if fire experts predict that a fire will occur in the building once every 30 years, the ARO is 1/30, or 0.03. The ALE is then 3 percent of the $350,000 SLE, or $11,667. You can interpret this figure to mean that the business should expect to lose $11,667 each year due to a fire in the building. Obviously, a fire will not occur each year—this figure represents the average cost over the 30 years between fires. It's not especially useful for budgeting considerations but proves invaluable when attempting to prioritize the assignment of BCP resources to a given risk. These concepts were also covered in Chapter 6, "Asset Value, Policies, and Roles."

> Be certain you're familiar with the quantitative formulas contained in this chapter and the concepts of asset value (AV), exposure factor (EF), annualized rate of occurrence (ARO), single loss expectancy (SLE), and annualized loss expectancy (ALE). Know the formulas and be able to work through a scenario. The formula for figuring the single loss expectancy is SLE=AV*EF. The formula for figuring the annualized loss expectancy is ALE=SLE*ARO.

From a qualitative point of view, you must consider the nonmonetary impact that interruptions might have on your business. For example, you might want to consider the following:

- Loss of goodwill among your client base
- Loss of employees after prolonged downtime
- Social/ethical responsibilities to the community
- Negative publicity

It's difficult to put dollar values on items like these in order to include them in the quantitative portion of the impact assessment, but they are equally important. After all, if you decimate your client base, you won't have a business to return to when you're ready to resume operations!

Resource Prioritization

The final step of the BIA is to prioritize the allocation of business continuity resources to the various risks that you identified and assessed in the preceding tasks of the BIA.

From a quantitative point of view, this process is relatively straightforward. You simply create a list of all of the risks you analyzed during the BIA process and sort them in descending order by the order by the ALE computed during computed during the impact assessment phase. This provides you with a prioritized list of the risks that you should address. Simply select as many items as you're willing and able to address simultaneously from the top of the list and work your way down, adding another item to the working plate as you are satisfied that you are prepared to address an existing item. Eventually, you'll reach a point at which you've exhausted either the list of risks (unlikely!) or all of your available resources (much more likely!).

Recall from the previous section that we also stressed the importance of addressing qualitatively important concerns as well. In previous sections about the BIA, we treated quantitative and qualitative analysis as mainly separate functions with some overlap in the analysis. Now it's time to merge the two prioritized lists, which is more of an art than a science. You must sit down with the BCP team and (hopefully) representatives from the senior management team and combine the two lists into a single prioritized list. Qualitative concerns may justify elevating or lowering the priority of risks that already exist on the ALE-sorted quantitative list. For example, if you run a fire suppression company, your number one priority might be the prevention of a fire in your principal place of business, despite the fact that an earthquake might cause more physical damage. The potential loss of face within the business community resulting from the destruction of a fire suppression company by fire might be too difficult to overcome and result in the eventual collapse of the business, justifying the increased priority.

Continuity Strategy

The first two phases of the BCP process (Project Scope and Planning and the Business Impact Assessment) are focused on determining how the BCP process will work and the prioritization of the business assets that must be protected against interruption. The next phase of BCP development, Continuity Planning, focuses on the development and implementation of a continuity strategy to minimize the impact realized risks might have on protected assets.

Strategy Development

The strategy development phase of continuity planning bridges the gap between the Business Impact Assessment and the Continuity Planning phases of BCP development. The BCP team must now take the prioritized list of concerns raised by the quantitative and qualitative resource prioritization exercises and determine which risks will be addressed by the business continuity plan. Fully addressing all of the contingencies would require the implementation of provisions and processes that maintain a zero-downtime posture in the face of each and every possible risk. For obvious reasons, implementing a policy this comprehensive is simply impossible.

The BCP team should look back to the maximum tolerable downtime (MTD) estimates created during the early stages of the BIA and determine which risks are deemed acceptable and which must be mitigated by BCP continuity provisions. Some of these decisions are obvious—the risk of a blizzard striking an operations facility in Egypt is negligible and would be deemed an acceptable risk. The risk of a monsoon in New Delhi is serious enough that it must be mitigated by BCP provisions.

 Keep in mind that there are four possible responses to a risk: reduce, assign, accept, and reject. Each may be an acceptable response based upon the circumstances.

Once the BCP team determines which risks require mitigation and the level of resources that will be committed to each mitigation task, they are ready to move on to the provisions and processes phase of continuity planning.

Provisions and Processes

The provisions and processes phase of continuity planning is the meat of the entire business continuity plan. In this task, the BCP team designs the specific procedures and mechanisms that will mitigate the risks deemed unacceptable during the strategy development stage. There are three categories of assets that must be protected through BCP provisions and processes: people, buildings/facilities, and infrastructure. In the next three sections, we'll explore some of the techniques you can use to safeguard each of these categories.

People

First and foremost, you must ensure that the people within your organization are safe before, during, and after an emergency. Once you've achieved that goal, you must make provisions to allow your employees to conduct both their BCP and operational tasks in as normal a manner as possible given the circumstances.

 Don't lose sight of the fact that people are truly your most valuable asset. In almost every line of business, the safety of people must always come before the organization's business goals. Make sure that your business continuity plan makes adequate provisions for the security of your employees, customers, suppliers, and any other individuals who may be affected!

People should be provided with all of the resources they need to complete their assigned tasks. At the same time, if circumstances dictate that people be present in the workplace for extended periods of time, arrangements must be made for shelter and food. Any continuity plan that requires these provisions should include detailed instructions for the BCP team in the event of a disaster. Stockpiles of provisions sufficient to feed the operational and support teams for an extended period of time should be maintained in an accessible location and rotated periodically to prevent spoilage.

Buildings/Facilities

Many businesses require specialized facilities in order to carry out their critical operations. These might include standard office facilities, manufacturing plants, operations centers, warehouses, distribution/logistics centers, and repair/maintenance depots, among others. When you perform your BIA, you will identify those facilities that play a critical role in your organization's continued viability. Your continuity plan should address two areas for each critical facility:

Hardening provisions   Your BCP should outline mechanisms and procedures that can be put into place to protect your existing facilities against the risks defined in the strategy development phase. This might include steps as simple as patching a leaky roof or as complex as installing reinforced hurricane shutters and fireproof walls.

Alternate sites   In the event that it's not possible to harden a facility against a risk, your BCP should identify alternate sites where business activities can resume immediately (or at least in a period of time that's shorter than the maximum tolerable downtime for all affected critical business functions). The next chapter, "Disaster Recovery Planning," describes a few of the facility types that might be useful in this stage.

Infrastructure

Every business depends upon some sort of infrastructure for its critical processes. For many businesses, a critical part of this infrastructure is an IT backbone of communications and computer systems that process orders, manage the supply chain, handle customer interaction, and perform other business functions. This backbone comprises a number of servers, workstations, and critical communications links between sites. The BCP must address how these systems will be protected against risks identified during the strategy development phase. As with buildings and facilities, there are two main methods of providing this protection:

Hardening systems   You can protect systems against the risks by introducing protective measures such as computer-safe fire suppression systems and uninterruptible power supplies.

Alternative systems   You can also protect business functions by introducing redundancy (either redundant components or completely redundant systems/communications links that rely on different facilities).

These same principles apply to whatever infrastructure components serve your critical business processes—transportation systems, electrical power grids, banking and financial systems, water supplies, and so on.

Plan Approval

Once the BCP team completes the design phase of the BCP document, it's time to gain top-level management endorsement of the plan. If you were fortunate enough to have senior management involvement throughout the development phases of the plan, this should be a relatively straight-forward process. On the other hand, if this is your first time approaching management with the BCP document, you should be prepared to provide a lengthy explanation of the plan's purpose and specific provisions.

 Senior management approval and buy-in is essential to the success of the over-all BCP effort.

If possible, you should attempt to have the plan endorsed by the top executive in your business—the chief executive officer, chairman, president, or similar business leader. This move demonstrates the importance of the plan to the entire organization and showcases the business leader's commitment to business continuity. The signature of such an individual on the plan also gives it much greater weight and credibility in the eyes of other senior managers, who might otherwise brush it off as a necessary but trivial IT initiative.

Plan Implementation

Once you've received approval from senior management, it's time to dive in and start implementing your plan. The BCP team should get together and develop an implementation schedule that utilizes the resources dedicated to the program to achieve the stated process and provision goals in as prompt a manner as possible given the scope of the modifications and the organizational climate.

After all of the resources are fully deployed, the BCP team should supervise the conduct of an appropriate BCP maintenance program to ensure that the plan remains responsive to evolving business needs.

Training and Education

Training and education are essential elements of the BCP implementation. All personnel who will be involved in the plan (either directly or indirectly) should receive some sort of training on the overall plan and their individual responsibilities. Everyone in the organization should receive at least a plan overview briefing to provide them with the confidence that business leaders have considered the possible risks posed to continued operation of the business and have put a plan in place to mitigate the impact on the organization should business be disrupted. People with direct BCP responsibilities should be trained and evaluated on their specific BCP tasks to ensure that they are able to complete them efficiently when disaster strikes. Furthermore, at least one backup person should be trained for every BCP task to ensure redundancy in the event personnel are injured or cannot reach the workplace during an emergency.

Training and education are important parts of any security-related plan and the BCP process is no exception. Ensure that personnel within your organization are fully aware of their BCP responsibilities before disaster strikes!

BCP Documentation

Documentation is a critical step in the Business Continuity Planning process. Committing your BCP methodology to paper provides several important benefits:

- It ensures that BCP personnel have a written continuity document to reference in the event of an emergency, even if senior BCP team members are not present to guide the effort.

- It provides an historical record of the BCP process that will be useful to future personnel seeking to both understand the reasoning behind various procedures and implement necessary changes in the plan.

- It forces the team members to commit their thoughts to paper—a process that often facilitates the identification of flaws in the plan. Having the plan on paper also allows draft documents to be distributed to individuals not on the BCP team for a "sanity check."

In the following sections, we'll explore some of the important components of the written business continuity plan.

Continuity Planning Goals

First and foremost, the plan should describe the goals of continuity planning as set forth by the BCP team and senior management. These goals should be decided upon at or before the first BCP team meeting and will most likely remain unchanged throughout the life of the BCP.

The most common goal of the BCP is quite simple: to ensure the continuous operation of the business in the face of an emergency situation. Other goals may also be inserted in this section of the document to meet organizational needs.

Statement of Importance

The statement of importance reflects the criticality of the BCP to the organization's continued viability. This document commonly takes the form of a letter to the organization's employees stating the reason that the organization devoted significant resources to the BCP development process and requesting the cooperation of all personnel in the BCP implementation phase.

Here's where the importance of senior executive buy-in comes into play. If you can put out this letter under the signature of the CEO or an officer at a similar level, the plan itself will carry tremendous weight as you attempt to implement changes throughout the organization. If you have the signature of a lower-level manager, you may encounter resistance as you attempt to work with portions of the organization outside of that individual's direct control.

Statement of Priorities

The statement of priorities flows directly from the identify priorities phase of the Business Impact Assessment. It simply involves listing the functions considered critical to continued business operations in a prioritized order. When listing these priorities, you should also include a statement that they were developed as part of the BCP process and reflect the importance of the functions to continued business operations in the event of an emergency and nothing more. Otherwise, the list of priorities could be used for unintended purposes and result in a political turf battle between competing organizations to the detriment of the business continuity plan.

Statement of Organizational Responsibility

The statement of organizational responsibility also comes from a senior-level executive and can be incorporated into the same letter as the statement of importance. It basically echoes the sentiment that "Business Continuity Is Everyone's Responsibility!" The statement of organizational responsibility restates the organization's commitment to Business Continuity Planning and informs the organization's employees, vendors, and affiliates that they are individually expected to do everything they can to assist with the BCP process.

Statement of Urgency and Timing

The statement of urgency and timing expresses the criticality of implementing the BCP and outlines the implementation timetable decided upon by the BCP team and agreed to by upper management. The wording of this statement will depend upon the actual urgency assigned to the BCP process by the organization's leadership. If the statement itself is included in the same letter as the statement of priorities and statement of organizational responsibility, the timetable should be included as a separate document. Otherwise, the timetable and this statement can be put into the same document.

Risk Assessment

The risk assessment portion of the BCP documentation essentially recaps the decision-making process undertaken during the Business Impact Assessment. It should include a discussion of all of the risks considered during the BIA as well as the quantitative and qualitative analyses performed to assess these risks. For the quantitative analysis, the actual AV, EF, ARO, SLE, and ALE figures should be included. For the qualitative analysis, the thought process behind the risk analysis should be provided to the reader.

Risk Acceptance/Mitigation

The risk acceptance/mitigation section of the BCP documentation contains the outcome of the strategy development portion of the BCP process. It should cover each risk identified in the risk analysis portion of the document and outline one of two thought processes:

- For risks that were deemed acceptable, it should outline the reasons the risk was considered acceptable as well as potential future events that might warrant reconsideration of this determination.

- For risks that were deemed unacceptable, it should outline the risk mitigation provisions and processes put into place to reduce the risk to the organization's continued viability.

Vital Records Program

The BCP documentation should also outline a vital records program for the organization. This document states where critical business records will be stored and the procedures for making and storing backup copies of those records. This is also a critical portion of the disaster recovery plan and is discussed in Chapter 16's coverage of that topic.

Emergency Response Guidelines

The emergency response guidelines outline the organizational and individual responsibilities for immediate response to an emergency situation. This document provides the first employees to detect an emergency with the steps that should be taken to activate provisions of the BCP that do not automatically activate. These guidelines should include the following:

- Immediate response procedures (security procedures, fire suppression procedures, notification of appropriate emergency response agencies, etc.)

- Whom to notify (executives, BCP team members, etc.)

- Secondary response procedures to take while waiting for the BCP team to assemble

Maintenance

The BCP documentation and the plan itself must be living documents. Every organization encounters nearly constant change, and this dynamic nature ensures that the business's continuity requirements will also evolve. The BCP team should not be disbanded after the plan is developed but should still meet periodically to discuss the plan and review the results of plan tests to ensure that it continues to meet organizational needs. Obviously, minor changes to the plan do not require conducting the full BCP development process from scratch; they can simply be made at an informal meeting of the BCP team by unanimous consent. However, keep in mind that drastic changes in an organization's mission or resources may require going back to the BCP drawing board and beginning again. All older versions of the BCP should be physically destroyed and replaced by the most current version so that there is never any confusion as to the correct implementation of the BCP. It is also a good practice to include BCP components into job descriptions to ensure that the BCP remains fresh and correctly performed.

Testing

The BCP documentation should also outline a formalized testing program to ensure that the plan remains current and that all personnel are adequately trained to perform their duties in the event of an actual disaster. The testing process is actually quite similar to that used for the disaster recovery plan, so discussion of the specific test types will be reserved for Chapter 16.

Summary

Every organization dependent upon technological resources for its survival should have a comprehensive business continuity plan in place to ensure the sustained viability of the organization when unforeseen emergencies take place. There are a number of the important concepts that underlie solid Business Continuity Planning (BCP) practices, including Project Scope and Planning, Business Impact Assessment, Continuity Planning, and Approval and Implementation. Every organization must have plans and procedures in place to help mitigate the effects a disaster has on continuing operations and to speed the return to normal operations. To determine the risks that your business faces and that require mitigation, you must conduct a Business Impact Assessment from both quantitative and qualitative points of view. You must take the appropriate steps in developing a continuity strategy for your organization and know what to do to weather future disasters.

Finally, you must create the documentation required to ensure that your plan is effectively communicated to present and future BCP team participants. Such documentation must include continuity planning guidelines. The business continuity plan must also contain statements of importance, priorities, organizational responsibility, and urgency and timing. In addition, the documentation should include plans for risk assessment, acceptance, and mitigation, a vital records program, emergency response guidelines, and plans for maintenance and testing.

The next chapter will take this planning to the next step—developing and implementing a disaster recovery plan. The disaster recovery plan kicks in where the business continuity plan leaves off. When an emergency occurs that interrupts your business in spite of the BCP measures, the disaster recovery plan guides the recovery efforts necessary to restore your business to normal operations as quickly as possible.

Exam Essentials

Understand the four steps of the Business Continuity Planning process.   Business Continuity Planning (BCP) involves four distinct phases: Project Scope and Planning, Business Impact Assessment, Continuity Planning, and Approval and Implementation. Each task contributes to the overall goal of ensuring that business operations continue uninterrupted in the face of an emergency situation.

Describe how to perform the business organization analysis. In the business organization analysis, the individuals responsible for leading the BCP process determine which departments and individuals have a stake in the business continuity plan. This analysis is used as the foundation for BCP team selection and, after validation by the BCP team, is used to guide the next stages of BCP development.

List the necessary members of the Business Continuity Planning team. The BCP team should contain, as a minimum, representatives from each of the operational and support departments; technical experts from the IT department; security personnel with BCP skills; legal representatives familiar with corporate legal, regulatory, and contractual responsibilities; and representatives from senior management. Additional team members depend upon the structure and nature of the organization.

Know the legal and regulatory requirements that face business continuity planners. Business leaders must exercise due diligence to ensure that shareholders' interests are protected in the event disaster strikes. Some industries are also subject to federal, state, and local regulations that mandate specific BCP procedures. Many businesses also have contractual obligations to their clients that must be met, before and after a disaster.

Explain the steps of the Business Impact Assessment process. The five steps of the Business Impact Assessment process are identification of priorities, risk identification, likelihood assessment, impact assessment, and resource prioritization.

Describe the process used to develop a continuity strategy. During the strategy development phase, the BCP team determines which risks will be mitigated. In the provisions and processes phase, mechanisms and procedures that will actually mitigate the risks are designed. The plan must then be approved by senior management and implemented. Personnel must also receive training on their roles in the BCP process.

Explain the importance of fully documenting an organization's business continuity plan. Committing the plan to writing provides the organization with a written record of the procedures to follow when disaster strikes. It prevents the "it's in my head" syndrome and ensures the orderly progress of events in an emergency.

Review Questions

1. What is the first step that individuals responsible for the development of a business continuity plan should perform?

    A. BCP team selection

    B. Business organization analysis

    C. Resource requirements analysis

    D. Legal and regulatory assessment

2. Once the BCP team is selected, what should be the first item placed on the team's agenda?

    A. Business Impact Assessment

    B. Business organization analysis

    C. Resource requirements analysis

    D. Legal and regulatory assessment

3. What is the term used to describe the responsibility of a firm's officers and directors to ensure that adequate measures are in place to minimize the effect of a disaster on the organization's continued viability?

    A. Corporate responsibility

    B. Disaster requirement

    C. Due diligence

    D. Going concern responsibility

4. What will be the major resource consumed by the BCP process during the BCP phase?

    A. Hardware

    B. Software

    C. Processing time

    D. Personnel

5. What unit of measurement should be used to assign quantitative values to assets in the priority identification phase of the Business Impact Assessment?

    A. Monetary

    B. Utility

    C. Importance

    D. Time

6. Which one of the following BIA terms identifies the amount of money a business expects to lose to a given risk each year?

   A. ARO

   B. SLE

   C. ALE

   D. EF

7. What BIA metric can be used to express the longest time a business function can be unavailable without causing irreparable harm to the organization?

   A. SLE

   B. EF

   C. MTD

   D. ARO

8. You are concerned about the risk that an avalanche poses to your $3 million shipping facility. Based upon expert opinion, you determine that there is a 5 percent chance that an avalanche will occur each year. Experts advise you that an avalanche would completely destroy your building and require you to rebuild on the same land. Ninety percent of the $3 million value of the facility is attributed to the building and 10 percent is attributed to the land itself. What is the single loss expectancy of your shipping facility to avalanches?

   A. $3,000,000

   B. $2,700,000

   C. $270,000

   D. $135,000

9. Referring to the scenario in question 8, what is the annualized loss expectancy?

   A. $3,000,000

   B. $2,700,000

   C. $270,000

   D. $135,000

10. Your manager is concerned that the Business Impact Assessment recently completed by the BCP team doesn't adequately take into account the loss of goodwill among customers that might result from a particular type of disaster. Where should items like this be addressed?

    A. Continuity strategy

    B. Quantitative analysis

    C. Likelihood assessment

    D. Qualitative analysis

11. Which task of BCP bridges the gap between the Business Impact Assessment and the Continuity Planning phases?

    A. Resource prioritization

    B. Likelihood assessment

    C. Strategy development

    D. Provisions and processes

12. Which resource should you protect first when designing continuity plan provisions and processes?

    A. Physical plant

    B. Infrastructure

    C. Financial

    D. People

13. Which one of the following concerns is not suitable for quantitative measurement during the Business Impact Assessment?

    A. Loss of a plant

    B. Damage to a vehicle

    C. Negative publicity

    D. Power outage

14. Lighter Than Air Industries expects that it would lose $10 million if a tornado struck its aircraft operations facility. It expects that a tornado might strike the facility once every 100 years. What is the single loss expectancy for this scenario?

    A. 0.01

    B. $10,000,000

    C. $100,000

    D. 0.10

15. Referring to the scenario in question 13, what is the annualized loss expectancy?

    A. 0.01

    B. $10,000,000

    C. $100,000

    D. 0.10

16. In which Business Continuity Planning task would you actually design procedures and mechanisms to mitigate risks deemed unacceptable by the BCP team?

    A. Strategy development

    B. Business Impact Assessment

    C. Provisions and processes

    D. Resource prioritization

17. What type of mitigation provision is utilized when redundant communications links are installed?

    A. Hardening systems

    B. Defining systems

    C. Reducing systems

    D. Alternative systems

18. What type of plan outlines the procedures to follow when a disaster interrupts the normal operations of a business?

    A. Business continuity plan

    B. Business Impact Assessment

    C. Disaster recovery plan

    D. Vulnerability assessment

19. What is the formula used to compute the single loss expectancy for a risk scenario?

    A. SLE=AV*EF

    B. SLE= RO*EF

    C. SLE=AV*ARO

    D. SLE=EF*ARO

20. When computing an annualized loss expectancy, what is the scope of the output number?

    A. All occurrences of a risk across an organization during the life of the organization

    B. All occurrences of a risk across an organization during the next year

    C. All occurrences of a risk affecting a single organizational asset during the life of the asset

    D. All occurrences of a risk affecting a single organizational asset during the next year

Answers to Review Questions

1. B. The business organization analysis helps the initial planners select appropriate BCP team members and then guides the overall BCP process.

2. B. The first task of the BCP team should be the review and validation of the business organization analysis initially performed by those individuals responsible for spearheading the BCP effort. This ensures that the initial effort, undertaken by a small group of individuals, reflects the beliefs of the entire BCP team.

3. C. A firm's officers and directors are legally bound to exercise due diligence in conducting their activities. This concept creates a fiduciary responsibility on their part to ensure that adequate business continuity plans are in place.

4. D. During the planning phase, the most significant resource utilization will be the time dedicated by members of the BCP team to the planning process itself. This represents a significant use of business resources and is another reason that buy-in from senior management is essential.

5. A. The quantitative portion of the priority identification should assign asset values in monetary units.

6. C. The annualized loss expectancy (ALE) represents the amount of money a business expects to lose to a given risk each year. This figure is quite useful when performing a quantitative prioritization of business continuity resource allocation.

7. C. The maximum tolerable downtime (MTD) represents the longest period a business function can be unavailable before causing irreparable harm to the business. This figure is very useful when determining the level of business continuity resources to assign to a particular function.

8. B. The SLE is the product of the AV and the EF. From the scenario, you know that the AV is $3,000,000 and the EF is 90 percent, based upon the fact that the same land can be used to rebuild the facility. This yields an SLE of $2,700,000.

9. D. This problem requires you to compute the ALE, which is the product of the SLE and the ARO. From the scenario, you know that the ARO is 0.05 (or 5 percent). From question 8, you know that the SLE is $2,700,000. This yields an SLE of $135,000.

10. D. The qualitative analysis portion of the BIA allows you to introduce intangible concerns, such as loss of customer goodwill, into the BIA planning process.

11. C. The strategy development task bridges the gap between Business Impact Assessment and Continuity Planning by analyzing the prioritized list of risks developed during the BIA and determining which risks will be addressed by the BCP.

12. D. The safety of human life must always be the paramount concern in Business Continuity Planning. Be sure that your plan reflects this priority, especially in the written documentation that is disseminated to your organization's employees!

13. C. It is very difficult to put a dollar figure on the business lost due to negative publicity. Therefore, this type of concern is better evaluated through a qualitative analysis.

14. B. The single loss expectancy (SLE) is the amount of damage that would be caused by a single occurrence of the risk. In this case, the SLE is $10 million, the expected damage from one tornado. The fact that a tornado occurs only once every 100 years is not reflected in the SLE but would be reflected in the annualized loss expectancy (ALE).

15. C. The annualized loss expectancy (ALE) is computed by taking the product of the single loss expectancy (SLE), which was $10 million in this scenario, and the annualized rate of occurrence (ARO), which was 0.01 in this example. These figures yield an ALE of $100,000.

16. C. In the provisions and processes phase, the BCP team actually designs the procedures and mechanisms to mitigate risks that were deemed unacceptable during the strategy development phase.

17. D. Redundant communications links are a type of alternative system put in place to provide backup circuits in the event a primary communications link fails.

18. C. Disaster recovery plans pick up where business continuity plans leave off. After a disaster strikes and the business is interrupted, the disaster recovery plan guides response teams in their efforts to quickly restore business operations to normal levels.

19. A. The single loss expectancy (SLE) is computed as the product of the asset value (AV) and the exposure factor (EF). The other formulas displayed here do not accurately reflect this calculation.

20. D. The annualized loss expectancy, as its name implies, covers the expected loss due to a risk during a single year. ALE numbers are computed individually for each asset within an organization.

Chapter

16

Disaster Recovery Planning

THE CISSP EXAM TOPICS COVERED IN THIS CHAPTER INCLUDE:

- ✓ Recovery Strategy
- ✓ Recovery Plan Development
- ✓ Implementation
- ✓ Work Group Recovery
- ✓ Training/Testing/Maintenance
- ✓ BCP/DRP Events

In the previous chapter, you learned the essential elements of Business Continuity Planning (BCP)—the art of helping your organization avoid being interrupted by the devastating effects of an emergency. Recall that one of the main BCP principles was risk management—you must assess the likelihood that a vulnerability will be exploited and use that likelihood to determine the appropriate allocation of resources to combat the threat.

Because of this risk management principle, business continuity plans are not intended to prevent every possible disaster from affecting an organization—this would be an impossible goal. On the contrary, they are designed to limit the effects of commonly occurring disasters. Naturally, this leaves an organization vulnerable to interruption from a number of threats—those that were judged to be not worthy of mitigation or those that were unforeseen.

Disaster Recovery Planning (DRP) steps in where BCP leaves off. When a disaster strikes and the business continuity plan fails to prevent interruption of the business, the disaster recovery plan kicks into effect and guides the actions of emergency response personnel until the end goal is reached—the business is restored to full operating capacity in its primary operations facilities.

While reading this chapter, you may notice many areas of overlap between the BCP and DRP processes. Indeed, our discussion of specific disasters provides information on how to handle them from both BCP and DRP points of view. This serves to illustrate the close linkage between the two processes. In fact, although the (ISC)² CISSP curriculum draws a distinction between the two, most organizations simply have a single team/plan that addresses both business continuity and disaster recovery concerns in an effort to consolidate responsibilities.

Disaster Recovery Planning

Disaster recovery planning brings order to the chaotic events surrounding the interruption of an organization's normal activities. By its very nature, the *disaster recovery plan* is implemented only when tension is high and cooler heads might not naturally prevail. Picture the circumstances in which you might find it necessary to implement DRP measures—a hurricane just destroyed your main operations facility, a fire devastated your main processing center, terrorist activity closed off access to a major metropolitan area. Any event that stops, prevents, or interrupts your organization's ability to perform its work tasks is considered a disaster. The moment you are unable to support your mission-critical process is the moment DRP is needed to manage the restoration and recovery procedures.

The disaster recovery plan should be set up in a manner such that it can almost run on autopilot. The DRP should be designed to eliminate decision-making activities during a disaster as much as possible. Essential personnel should be well trained in their duties and responsibilities in the wake of a disaster and also know the steps they need to take to get the organization up and running as soon as possible. We'll begin by analyzing some of the possible disasters that might strike your organization and the particular threats that they pose. Many of these were mentioned in the previous chapter, but we will now explore them in further detail.

Natural Disasters

Natural disasters represent the fury of our habitat—violent occurrences that take place due to changes in the earth's surface or atmosphere that are beyond the control of mankind. In some cases, such as hurricanes, scientists have developed sophisticated prediction techniques that provide ample warning before a disaster strikes. Others, such as earthquakes, can bring unpredictable destruction at a moment's notice. Your disaster recovery plan should provide mechanisms for responding to both types of disasters, either with a gradual buildup of response forces or as an immediate reaction to a rapidly emerging crisis.

Earthquakes

Earthquakes are caused by the shifting of seismic plates and can occur almost anywhere in the world without warning. However, they are much more likely to occur along the known fault lines that exist in many areas of the world. A well-known example is the San Andreas fault, which poses a significant risk to portions of the western United States. If you live in a region along a fault line where earthquakes are likely, your DRP should address the procedures your business will implement if a seismic event interrupts your normal activities.

You might be surprised by some of the regions of the world where earthquakes are considered possible. Table 16.1 shows the parts of the United States that the Federal Emergency Management Agency (FEMA) considers moderate, high, or very high seismic hazards. Note that the states in the table comprise 80 percent of the 50 states, meaning that the majority of the country has at least a moderate risk of seismic activity.

Floods

Flooding can occur almost anywhere in the world at any time of the year. Some flooding results from the gradual accumulation of rainwater in rivers, lakes, and other bodies of water that then overflow their banks and flood the community. Other floods, known as flash floods, strike when a sudden severe storm dumps more rainwater on an area than the ground can absorb in a short period of time. Floods can also occur when dams are breached. Large waves caused by seismic activity, or tsunamis, combine the awesome power and weight of water with flooding, as we saw during the December 2004 tsunami disaster. The tsunamis obviously demonstrated the enormous destructive capabilities of water and the impact it can have on various businesses and economies.

According to government statistics, flooding is responsible for over $1 billion (that's billion with a *b!*) of damage to businesses and homes each year in the United States. It's important that your DRP make appropriate response plans for the eventuality that a flood may strike your facilities.

TABLE 16.1   Seismic Hazard Level by State

Moderate Seismic Hazard	High Seismic Hazard	Very High Seismic Hazard
Alabama	American Samoa	Alaska
Colorado	Arizona	California
Connecticut	Arkansas	Guam
Delaware	Illinois	Hawaii
Georgia	Indiana	Idaho
Maine	Kentucky	Montana
Maryland	Missouri	Nevada
Massachusetts	New Mexico	Oregon
Mississippi	South Carolina	Puerto Rico
New Hampshire	Tennessee	Virgin Islands
New Jersey	Utah	Washington
New York		Wyoming
North Carolina		
Ohio		
Oklahoma		
Pennsylvania		
Rhode Island		
Texas		
Vermont		
Virginia		
West Virginia		

When you evaluate your firm's risk of damage from flooding to develop your business continuity and disaster recovery plans, it's also a good idea to check with responsible individuals and ensure that your organization has sufficient insurance in place to protect it from the financial impact of a flood. In the United States, most general business policies do not cover flood damage, and you should investigate obtaining specialized government-backed flood insurance under FEMA's National Flood Insurance Program.

Although flooding is theoretically possible in almost any region of the world, it is much more likely to occur in certain areas. FEMA's National Flood Insurance Program is responsible for completing a flood risk assessment for the entire United States and providing this data to citizens in graphical form. You can view flood maps online at www.esri.com/hazards/. This site also provides valuable information on historic earthquakes, hurricanes, wind storms, hail storms, and other natural disasters to help you in preparing your organization's risk assessment. When viewing the flood maps, like the one shown in Figure 16.1, you'll find that the two risks often assigned to an area are the "100-year flood plain" and the "500-year flood plain." These evaluations mean that the government expects these areas to flood at least once every 100 and 500 years, respectively. For a more detailed tutorial on reading flood maps, visit www.fema.gov/mit/tsd/ot_firmr.htm.

Storms

Storms come in many forms and pose diverse risks to a business. Prolonged periods of intense rainfall bring the risk of flash flooding described in the previous section. Hurricanes and tornadoes come with the threat of severe winds exceeding 100 miles per hour that threaten the structural integrity of buildings and turn everyday objects like trees, lawn furniture, and even vehicles into deadly missiles. Hail storms bring a rapid onslaught of destructive ice chunks falling from the sky. Many storms also bring the risk of lightning, which can cause severe damage to sensitive electronic components. For this reason, your business continuity plan should detail appropriate mechanisms to protect against lightning-induced damage and your disaster recovery plan should provide adequate provisions for the power outages and equipment damage that might result from a lightning strike. Never underestimate the magnitude of damage that a single storm can bring.

If you live in an area susceptible to a certain type of severe storm, it's important that you regularly monitor weather forecasts from the responsible government agencies. For example, disaster recovery specialists in hurricane-prone areas should periodically check the website of the National Weather Service's Tropical Prediction Center (www.nhc.noaa.gov) during the hurricane season. This website allows you to monitor Atlantic and Pacific storms that may pose a risk to your region before word of them hits the local news. This allows you to begin a gradual response to the storm before time runs out.

FIGURE 16.1   Flood hazard map for Miami-Dade County, Florida

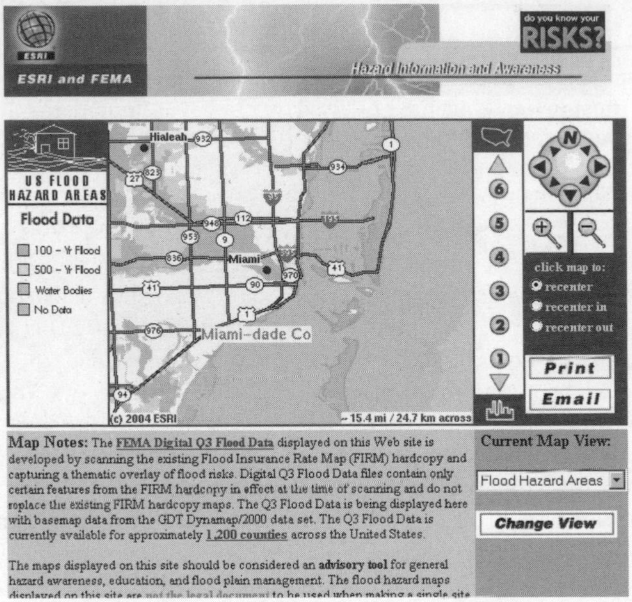

Fires

Fires can start for a variety of reasons, both natural and man-made, but both forms can be equally devastating. During the BCP/DRP process, you should evaluate the risk of fire and implement at least basic measures to mitigate that risk and prepare the business for recovery from a catastrophic fire in a critical facility.

Some regions of the world are susceptible to wildfires during the warm season. These fires, once started, spread in somewhat predictable patterns, and fire experts in conjunction with meteorologists can produce relatively accurate forecasts of a wildfire's potential path.

> As with many other types of large-scale natural disasters, you can obtain valuable information about impending threats on the Web. In the United States, the National Interagency Fire Center posts daily fire updates and forecasts on its website: www.nifc.gov/firemaps.html. Other countries have similar warning systems in place.

Other Regional Events

Some regions of the world are prone to localized types of natural disasters. During the BCP/DRP process, your assessment team should analyze all of your organization's operating locations and gauge the impact that these types of events might have on your business. For example, many regions of the world are prone to volcanic eruptions. If you conduct operations in an area in close proximity to an active or dormant volcano, your DRP should probably address this eventuality. Other localized natural occurrences include monsoons in Asia, tsunamis in the South Pacific, avalanches in mountainous regions, and mudslides in the western United States.

If your business is geographically diverse, it would be prudent to include area natives on your planning team. At the very least, make use of local resources like government emergency preparedness teams, civil defense organizations, and insurance claim offices to help guide your efforts. These organizations possess a wealth of knowledge and will usually be more than happy to help you prepare your organization for the unexpected—after all, every organization that successfully weathers a natural disaster is one less organization that requires a portion of their valuable recovery resources after disaster strikes.

Man-Made Disasters

The advanced civilization built by mankind over the centuries has become increasingly dependent upon complex interactions between technological, logistical, and natural systems. The same complex interactions that make our sophisticated society possible also present a number of potential vulnerabilities from both intentional and unintentional *man-made disasters*. In the following sections, we'll examine a few of the more common disasters to help you analyze your organization's vulnerabilities when preparing a business continuity plan and disaster recovery plan.

Fires

In the previous section, we explored how large-scale wildfires spread due to natural reasons. Many smaller-scale fires occur due to man-made causes—be it carelessness, faulty electrical wiring, improper fire protection practices, or other reasons. Studies from the Insurance Information Institute indicate that there are at least 1,000 building fires in the United States *every day*. If one of those fires struck your organization, would you have the proper preventative measures in place to quickly contain it? If the fire destroyed your facilities, how quickly would your disaster recovery plan allow you to resume operations elsewhere?

Bombings/Explosions

Explosions can result from a variety of man-made occurrences. Explosive gases from leaks might fill a room/building with explosive gases that later ignite and cause a damaging blast. In many areas, bombings are also a cause for concern. From a disaster planning point of view, the effects of bombings and explosions are similar to those caused by a large-scale fire. However, planning to avoid the impact of a bombing is much more difficult and relies upon physical security measures such as those discussed in Chapter 19, "Physical Security Requirements."

Acts of Terrorism

Since the terrorist attacks on September 11, 2001, businesses are increasingly concerned about the risks posed by a terrorist threat. The attacks on September 11 caused many small businesses to simply fold because they did not have in place business continuity/disaster recovery plans that

were adequate to ensure their continued viability. Many larger businesses experienced significant losses that caused severe long-term damage. The Insurance Information Institute issued a
study one year after the attacks that estimated the total damage from the attacks in New York
City at $40 billion (yes, that's with a *b* again!).

> Your general business insurance may not properly cover your organization against
> acts of terrorism. Prior to the September 11, 2001 terrorist attacks, most policies
> either covered acts of terrorism or didn't explicitly mention them. After suffering
> that catastrophic loss, many insurance companies responded by quickly amending
> policies to exclude losses from terrorist activity. Policy riders and endorsements are
> sometimes available, but often at an extremely high cost. If your business continu-
> ity or disaster recovery plan includes insurance as a means of financial recovery (as
> it probably should!), you'd be well advised to check your policies and contact your
> insurance professional to ensure that you're still covered.

Terrorist acts pose a unique challenge to DRP teams due to their unpredictable nature. Prior
to the September 11, 2001 terrorist attacks in New York and Washington, D.C., few DRP
teams considered the threat of an airplane crashing into their corporate headquarters significant
enough to merit mitigation. Many companies are now asking themselves a number of new
"what if" questions regarding terrorist activities. In general, these types of questions are healthy
in that they promote dialog between business elements regarding potential threats. On the other
hand, disaster recovery planners must emphasize solid risk-management principles and ensure
that resources aren't over allocated to a terrorist threat to the detriment of those DRP/BCP
activities that protect against threats more likely to materialize.

Power Outages

Even the most basic disaster recovery plan contains provisions to deal with the threat of a short
power outage. Critical business systems are often protected by uninterruptible power supply
(UPS) devices capable of running them at least long enough to shut down or long enough to get
emergency generators up and running. However, is your organization capable of operating in
the face of a sustained power outage? After Hurricane Andrew struck South Florida in 1992,
many areas were without power for weeks. Does your business continuity plan include provisions to keep your business a viable going concern during such a prolonged period without
power? Does your disaster recovery plan make ample preparations for the timely restoration of
power even if the commercial power grid remains unavailable?

> Check your UPSs regularly! These critical devices are often overlooked until
> they become necessary. Many UPSs contain self-testing mechanisms that
> report problems automatically, but it's still a good idea to subject them to reg-
> ular testing. Also, be sure to audit the number/type of devices plugged in to
> each UPS. It's amazing how many people think it's OK to add "just one more
> system" to a UPS, and you don't want to be surprised when the device can't
> handle the load during a real power outage!

Today's technology-driven organizations are increasingly dependent upon electric power, and your BCP/DRP team should consider the provisioning of alternative power sources capable of running business systems for an indefinite period of time. An adequate backup generator could mean the difference when the survival of your business is at stake.

Other Utility and Infrastructure Failures

When planners consider the impact that utility outages may have on their organizations, they naturally think first about the impact of a power outage. However, keep other utilities in mind also. Do you have critical business systems that rely on water, sewers, natural gas, or other utilities? Also consider regional infrastructure such as highways, airports, and railroads. Any of these systems can suffer failures that might not be related to weather or other conditions described in this chapter. Many businesses depend on one or more of these infrastructure services to move people or materials. A failure can paralyze your business' ability to continue functioning.

If you quickly answered no when asked if you have critical business systems that rely on water, sewers, natural gas, or other utilities, think a little more carefully. Do you consider people a critical business system? If a major storm knocked out the water supply to your facilities and you needed to keep the facilities up and running, would you be able to supply your employees with adequate drinking water to meet their biological needs?

What about your fire protection systems? If any of them are water based, is there a holding tank system in place that contains ample water to extinguish a serious building fire if the public water system were unavailable? Fires often cause serious damage in areas ravaged by storms, earthquakes, and other disasters that might also interrupt the delivery of water.

Hardware/Software Failures

Like it or not, computer systems fail. Hardware failures are the most common cause of unplanned downtime. Hardware components simply wear out and refuse to continue performing or suffer from physical damage. Software systems contain bugs or are given improper/unexpected operating instructions. For this reason, BCP/DRP teams must provide adequate redundancy in their systems. If zero downtime is a mandatory requirement, the best solution is to use fully redundant failover servers in separate locations attached to separate communications links and infrastructures. If one server is damaged or destroyed, the other will instantly take over the processing load. For more information on this concept, see the section "Remote Mirroring" later in this chapter.

Due to financial constraints, maintaining fully redundant systems is not always possible. In those circumstances, the BCP/DRP team should address how replacement parts will be quickly obtained and installed. As many parts as possible should be maintained in a local parts inventory for quick replacement; this is especially true for hard-to-find parts that must be shipped in. After all, how many organizations could do without telephones for three days while a critical PBX component is shipped from an overseas location and installed on site?

⊕ Real World Scenario

NYC Blackout

On August 14, 2003, the lights went out in New York City and large portions of the northeastern and midwestern United States when a series of cascading failures caused the collapse of a major power grid.

Fortunately, security professionals in the New York area were ready. Spurred to action by the September 11, 2001 terrorist attacks, many businesses updated their disaster recovery plans and took measures to ensure their continued operations in the wake of another disaster. The blackout served as that test, as many organizations were able to continue operating on alternate power sources or transferred control seamlessly to offsite data processing centers.

There were a few important lessons learned during the blackout that provide insight for BCP/DRP teams around the world:

Ensure that your alternate processing sites are located sufficiently far away from your main site that they won't likely be affected by the same disaster.

Remember that the threats facing your organization are both internal and external. Your next disaster may come from a terrorist attack, building fire, or malicious code running loose on your network. Take steps to ensure that your alternate sites are segregated from the main facility in a manner that protects against all of these threats.

Disasters don't usually come with advance warning. If real-time operations are critical to your organization, be sure that your backup sites are ready to assume primary status at a moment's notice.

Strikes

When designing your business continuity and disaster recovery plans, don't forget about the importance of the human factor in emergency planning. One form of man made disaster that is often overlooked is the possibility of a strike or other labor crisis. If a large segment of your employees walked out at the same time, what impact would that have on your business? How long would you be able to sustain operations without the regular full-time employees that staff a certain area? Your BCP and DRP teams should address these concerns, providing alternative plans if a labor crisis occurs.

Theft/Vandalism

In a previous section, we looked at the threat that terrorist activities pose to an organization. Theft and vandalism represent the same kind of activity on a much smaller scale. In most cases, however, there's a far greater chance that your organization will be affected by theft or vandalism than by a terrorist attack. Insurance provides some financial protection against these events (subject to deductibles and limitations of coverage), but acts of this nature can cause serious damage to your business, on both a short-term and long-term basis. Your business continuity and disaster recovery plans should include adequate preventative measures to control the frequency of these occurrences as well as contingency plans to mitigate the effects theft and vandalism have on your ongoing operations.

 Keep the impact that theft may have on your operations in mind when planning your parts inventory. It would be a good idea to keep an extra inventory of items with a high pilferage rate, such as RAM chips and laptops.

Recovery Strategy

When a disaster interrupts your business, your disaster recovery plan should be able to kick in nearly automatically and begin providing support to recovery operations. The disaster recovery plan should be designed in such a manner that the first employees on the scene can immediately begin the recovery effort in an organized fashion, even if members of the official DRP team have not yet arrived on site. In the following sections, we'll examine the critical subtasks involved in crafting an effective disaster recovery plan that will guide the rapid restoration of normal business processes and the resumption of activity at the primary business location.

In addition to improving your response capabilities, purchasing insurance can reduce risk of financial losses. When selecting insurance, be sure to purchase sufficient coverage to enable you to recover from a disaster. Simple value coverage may be insufficient to encompass actual replacement costs. If your property insurance includes an Actual Cost Evaluation (ACV) clause, then your damaged property will be compensated based on the value of the items on the date of loss plus 10 percent.

Valuable paper insurance coverage provides protection for inscribed, printed, and written documents and manuscripts and other printed business records. However, it does not cover damage to paper money and printed security certificates.

Business Unit Priorities

In order to recover your business operations with the greatest possible efficiency, you must engineer your disaster recovery plan so that the business units with the highest priority are recovered first. To achieve this goal, the DRP team must first identify those business units and agree on an order of prioritization. If this process sounds familiar, it should! This is very similar to the prioritization task the BCP team performed during the Business Impact Assessment, discussed in the previous chapter. In fact, if you have a completed BIA, you should use the resulting documentation as the basis for this prioritization task.

As a minimum requirement, the output from this task should be a simple listing of business units in prioritized order. However, a much more useful deliverable would be a more detailed list broken down into specific business processes listed in order of priority. This business process–oriented list is much more reflective of real-world conditions, but it requires considerable additional effort. It will, however, greatly assist in the recovery effort—after all, not every task performed by your highest-priority business unit will be of the highest priority. You might find that it would be best to restore the highest-priority unit to 50 percent capacity and then move on to lower-priority units to achieve some minimum operating capacity across the organization before attempting a full recovery effort.

Crisis Management

If a disaster strikes your organization, it is likely that panic will set in. The best way to combat this is with an organized disaster recovery plan. The individuals in your business who are most likely to first notice an emergency situation (i.e., security guards, technical personnel, etc.) should be fully trained in disaster recovery procedures and know the proper notification procedures and immediate response mechanisms.

Many things that normally seem like common sense (such as calling 911 in the event of a fire) may slip the minds of panicked employees seeking to flee an emergency. The best way to combat this is with continuous training on disaster recovery responsibilities. Returning to the fire example, all employees should be trained to activate the fire alarm or contact emergency officials when they spot a fire (after, of course, taking appropriate measures to protect themselves). After all, it's better that the fire department receives 10 different phone calls reporting a fire at your organization than it is for everyone to assume that someone else already took care of it.

Crisis management is a science and an art form. If your training budget permits, investing in crisis training for your key employees would be a good idea. This will ensure that at least some of your employees know the proper way to handle emergency situations and can provide the all-important "on the scene" leadership to panic-stricken coworkers.

Emergency Communications

When a disaster strikes, it is important that the organization be able to communicate internally as well as with the outside world. A disaster of any significance is easily noticed, and if the organization is unable to keep the outside world informed of its recovery status, the public is apt to fear the worst and assume that the organization is unable to recover. It is also essential that the organization be able to communicate internally during a disaster so that employees know what is expected of them—whether they are to return to work or report to another location, for instance.

In some cases, the circumstances that brought about the disaster to begin with may have also damaged some or all normal means of communications. A violent storm or an earthquake may have also knocked out telecommunications systems; at that point it's too late to try to figure out other means of communicating both internally and externally.

Work Group Recovery

When designing your disaster recovery plan, it's important to keep your goal in mind—the restoration of work groups to the point that they can resume their activities in their usual work locations. It's very easy to get sidetracked and think of disaster recovery as purely an IT effort focused on restoring systems and processes to working order.

To facilitate this effort, it's sometimes best to develop separate recovery facilities for different work groups. For example, if you have several subsidiary organizations that are in different locations and that perform tasks similar to the tasks that work groups at your office perform, you may wish to consider temporarily relocating those work groups to the other facility and having them communicate electronically and via telephone with other business units until they're ready to return to the main operations facility.

Larger organizations may have difficulty finding recovery facilities capable of handling the entire business operation. This is another example of a circumstance in which independent recovery of different work groups is appropriate.

Alternate Processing Sites

One of the most important elements of the disaster recovery plan is the selection of alternate processing sites to be used when the primary sites are unavailable. There are many options available when considering recovery facilities, limited only by the creative minds of disaster recovery planners and service providers. In the following sections, we'll take a look at the several types of sites commonly used in disaster recovery planning: cold sites, warm sites, hot sites, mobile sites, service bureaus, and multiple sites.

> When choosing any type of alternate processing site, be sure to place it far away enough from your primary location that it won't likely be affected by the same disaster that disables your primary site!

Cold Sites

Cold sites are simply standby facilities large enough to handle the processing load of an organization and with appropriate electrical and environmental support systems. They may be large warehouses, empty office buildings, or other similar structures. However, the cold site has no computing facilities (hardware or software) preinstalled and does not have activated broadband communications links. Many cold sites do have at least a few copper telephone lines, and some sites may have standby links that can be activated with minimal notification.

The major advantage of a cold site is its relatively inexpensive cost—there is no computing base to maintain and no monthly telecommunications bill when the site is not in use. However, the drawbacks of such a site are obvious—there is a tremendous lag time between the time the decision is made to activate the site and the time the site is actually ready to support business operations. Servers and workstations must be brought in and configured. Data must be restored from backup tapes. Communications links must be activated or established. The time to activate a cold site is often measured in weeks, making timely recovery close to impossible and often yielding a false sense of security.

Hot Sites

The *hot site* is the exact opposite of the cold site. In this type of configuration, a backup facility is maintained in constant working order, with a full complement of servers, workstations, and communications links ready to assume primary operations responsibilities. The servers and workstations are all preconfigured and loaded with appropriate operating system and application software.

 When choosing a facility, make sure it is far enough away from the original site so as not to be affected by the same disaster and yet close enough that it does not take all day driving to reach the backup site.

The data on the primary site servers is periodically or continuously replicated to the corresponding servers at the hot site, ensuring that the hot site has up-to-date data. Depending upon the bandwidth available between the two sites, the hot site data may be replicated instantaneously. If that is the case, operators could simply move operations to the hot site at a moment's notice. If it's not the case, disaster recovery managers have three options to activate the hot site:

- If there is sufficient time before the primary site must be shut down, they may force replication between the two sites right before the transition of operational control.

- If this is not possible, they may hand-carry backup tapes of the transaction logs from the primary site to the hot site and manually apply any transactions that took place since the last replication.

- If there aren't any available backups and it wasn't possible to force replication, the disaster recovery team may simply accept the loss of a portion of the data.

The advantages of a hot site are quite obvious—the level of disaster recovery protection provided by this type of site is unsurpassed. However, the cost is *extremely* high. Maintaining a hot site essentially doubles the organization's budget for hardware, software, and services and requires the use of additional manpower to maintain the site.

 If you use a hot site, never forget that it has copies of your production data. Be sure to provide that site with the same level of technical and physical security controls you provide at your primary site!

If an organization wishes to maintain a hot site but wants to reduce the expense of equipment and maintenance, it might opt to use a shared hot site facility managed by an outside contractor. However, the inherent danger in these facilities is that they may be overtaxed in the event of a widespread disaster and be unable to service all of their clients simultaneously. If your organization considers such an arrangement, be sure to investigate these issues thoroughly, both before signing the contract and periodically during the contract term.

Warm Sites

Warm sites are a middle ground between hot sites and cold sites for disaster recovery specialists. They always contain the equipment and data circuits necessary to rapidly establish operations.

As it is in hot sites, this equipment is usually preconfigured and ready to run appropriate applications to support the organization's operations. Unlike hot sites, however, warm sites do not typically contain copies of the client's data. The main requirement in bringing a warm site to full operational status is the transportation of appropriate backup media to the site and restoration of critical data on the standby servers.

Activation of a warm site typically takes at least 12 hours from the time a disaster is declared. However, warm sites avoid the significant telecommunications and personnel costs inherent in maintaining a near-real-time copy of the operational data environment. As with hot sites and cold sites, warm sites may also be obtained on a shared facility basis. If you choose this option, be sure that you have a "no lockout" policy written into your contract guaranteeing you the use of an appropriate facility even during a period of high demand. It's a good idea to take this concept one step further and physically inspect the facilities and the contractor's operational plan to reassure yourself that the facility will indeed be able to back up the "no lockout" guarantee when push comes to shove.

Mobile Sites

Mobile sites are non-mainstream alternatives to traditional recovery sites. They typically consist of self-contained trailers or other easily relocated units. These sites come with all of the environmental control systems necessary to maintain a safe computing environment. Larger corporations sometimes maintain these sites on a "fly-away" basis, ready to deploy them to any operating location around the world via air, rail, sea, or surface transportation. Smaller firms might contract with a mobile site vendor in the local area to provide these services on an as-needed basis.

If your disaster recovery plan depends upon a work group recovery strategy, mobile sites can be an excellent way to implement that approach. They are often large enough to accommodate entire (small!) work groups.

Mobile sites are often configured as cold sites or warm sites, depending upon the disaster recovery plan they are designed to support. It is also possible to configure a mobile site as a hot site, but this is not normally done because it is not often known in advance where a mobile site will be deployed.

Service Bureaus

A service bureau is a company that leases computer time. Service bureaus own large server farms and often fields of workstations. Any organization can purchase a contract with a service bureau to consume some portion of their processing capacity. Access can be on site or remote. A service bureau can usually provide support for all of your IT needs in the event of a disaster, even desktops for workers to use. Your contract with a service bureau will often include testing and backups as well as response time and availability. However, service bureaus regularly oversell their actual capacity by gambling that not all of the contracts will be exercised at the same time. Therefore, there is potential for resource contention in the event of a major disaster. If your company operates in an industry dense locale, this could be an important concern. You may need to select both a local and a distant service bureau in order to ensure that you can gain access to processing facilities.

Hardware Replacement Locations

One thing to consider when determining mobile sites and recovery sites in general is hardware replacement supplies. There are basically two options for hardware replacement supplies. One option is to employ "in-house" replacement whereby you warehouse extra and duplicate equipment at a different but nearby location (i.e., a warehouse on the other side of town). (In-house here means you own it already, not that it is necessarily housed under the same roof as your production environment.) If you have a hardware failure or a disaster, you can immediately pull the appropriate equipment from your stash. The other option is an SLA-type agreement with a vendor to provide quick response and delivery time in the event of a disaster. However, even a 4-, 12-, 24-, or 48-hour replacement hardware contract from a vendor does not provide a reliable guarantee that the delivery will actually occur. There are too many uncontrollable variables to rely upon this second option as your sole means of recovery.

Multiple Sites

By splitting or dividing your outfit into several divisions, branches, offices, and so on, you create multiple sites and reduce the impact of a major disaster. In fact, the more sites you employ, the less impact a major disaster on any one site will have. However, for the multiple sites to be effective, they must be separated by enough distance that a major disaster cannot affect multiple sites simultaneously. One of the drawbacks of using multiple sites is that it increases the difficulty of managing and administering the entire company when it's spread across a large geographic area in numerous locations.

Mutual Assistance Agreements

Mutual Assistance Agreements (MAAs) are popular in disaster recovery literature but are rarely implemented in real-world practice. In theory, they provide an excellent alternate processing option. Under an MAA, two organizations pledge to assist each other in the event of a disaster by sharing computing facilities or other technological resources. They appear to be extremely cost effective at first glance—it's not necessary for either organization to maintain expensive alternate processing sites (such as the hot sites, warm sites, cold sites, and mobile processing sites described in the previous sections). Indeed, many MAAs are structured to provide one of the levels of service described. In the case of a cold site, each organization may simply maintain some open space in their processing facilities for the other organization to use in the event of a disaster. In the case of a hot site, the organizations may host fully redundant servers for each other.

However, there are many drawbacks to Mutual Assistance Agreements that prevent their widespread use:

- MAAs are difficult to enforce. The parties are placing trust in each other that the support will materialize in the event of a disaster. However, when push comes to shove, the non-victim might renege on the agreement. The victim may have legal remedies available to them, but this won't help the immediate disaster recovery effort.

- Cooperating organizations should be located in relatively close proximity to each other to facilitate the transportation of employees between sites. However, this proximity means that both organizations may be vulnerable to the same threats! Your MAA won't do you much good if an earthquake levels your city, destroying the processing sites of *both* participating organizations!

- Confidentiality concerns often prevent businesses from placing their data in the hands of others. These may be legal concerns (such as in the handling of healthcare or financial data) or business concerns (such as trade secrets or other intellectual property issues).

Despite these concerns, a Mutual Assistance Agreement may be a good disaster recovery solution for your organization—especially if cost is an overriding factor. If you simply can't afford to implement any other type of alternate processing facility, an MAA might provide a degree of valuable protection in the event a localized disaster strikes your business.

Database Recovery

Many organizations rely upon databases to process and track operations, sales, logistics, and other activities vital to their continued viability. For this reason, it's essential that you include database recovery techniques in your disaster recovery plans. It's a wise idea to have a database specialist on the DRP team to provide input as to the technical feasibility of various ideas. After all, you don't want to allocate several hours to restore a database backup when it's technically impossible to complete the restoration in less than half a day!

In the following sections, we'll take a look at the three main techniques used to create offsite copies of database content: electronic vaulting, remote journaling, and remote mirroring. Each one has specific benefits and drawbacks—you'll need to analyze your organization's computing requirements and available resources to select the option best suited to your firm.

Electronic Vaulting

In an *electronic vaulting* scenario, database backups are transferred to a remote site in a bulk transfer fashion. The remote location may be a dedicated alternative recovery site (such as a hot site) or simply an offsite location managed within the company or by a contractor for the purpose of maintaining backup data. If you use electronic vaulting, keep in mind that there may be a significant time delay between the time you declare a disaster and the time your database is ready for operation with current data. If you decide to activate a recovery site, technicians will need to retrieve the appropriate backups from the electronic vault and apply them to the soon-to-be production servers at the recovery site.

WARNING   Be careful when considering vendors for an electronic vaulting contract. Definitions of electronic vaulting vary widely within the industry. Don't settle for a vague promise of "electronic vaulting capability." Insist upon a written definition of the service that will be provided, including the storage capacity, bandwidth of the communications link to the electronic vault, and the time necessary to retrieve vaulted data in the event of a disaster.

As with any type of backup scenario, be certain to periodically test your electronic vaulting setup. A great method for testing backup solutions is to give disaster recovery personnel a "surprise test," asking them to restore data from a certain day.

Remote Journaling

With *remote journaling,* data transfers are performed in a more expeditious manner. Data transfers still occur in a bulk transfer fashion, but they occur on a more frequent basis, usually once every hour or less. Unlike electronic vaulting scenarios, where database backup files are transferred, remote journaling setups transfer copies of the database transaction logs containing the transactions that occurred since the previous bulk transfer.

Remote journaling is similar to electronic vaulting in that the transaction logs transferred to the remote site are not applied to a live database server but are maintained in a backup device. When a disaster is declared, technicians retrieve the appropriate transaction logs and apply them to the production database.

Remote Mirroring

Remote mirroring is the most advanced database backup solution. Not surprisingly, it's also the most expensive! Remote mirroring goes beyond the technology used by remote journaling and electronic vaulting; with remote mirroring, a live database server is maintained at the backup site. The remote server receives copies of the database modifications at the same time they are applied to the production server at the primary site. Therefore, the mirrored server is ready to take over an operational role at a moment's notice.

Remote mirroring is a popular database backup strategy for organizations seeking to implement a hot site. However, when weighing the feasibility of a remote mirroring solution, be sure to take into account the infrastructure and personnel costs required to support the mirrored server as well as the processing overhead that will be added to each database transaction on the mirrored server.

Recovery Plan Development

Once you've established your business unit priorities and gotten a good idea of the appropriate alternative recovery sites for your organization, it's time to put pen to paper and begin drafting a true disaster recovery plan. Don't expect to sit down and write the full plan at one sitting. It's likely that the DRP team will go through many evolutions of draft documents before reaching a final written document that satisfies the operational needs of critical business units and falls within the resource, time, and expense constraints of the disaster recovery budget and available manpower.

In the following sections, we'll explore some of the important items to include in your disaster recovery plan. Depending upon the size of your organization and the number of people involved in the DRP effort, it may be a good idea to maintain several different types of plan documents, intended for different audiences. The following list includes some types of documents to consider:

- Executive summary
- Department-specific plans
- Technical guides for IT personnel responsible for implementing and maintaining critical backup systems
- Checklists for individual members of the disaster recovery team
- Full copies of the plan for critical disaster recovery team members

The use of custom-tailored documents becomes especially important when a disaster occurs or is imminent. Personnel who need to refresh themselves on the disaster recovery procedures that affect various parts of the organization will be able to refer to their department-specific plans. Critical disaster recovery team members will have checklists to help guide their actions amid the chaotic atmosphere of a disaster. IT personnel will have technical guides helping them get the alternate sites up and running. Finally, managers and public relations personnel will have a simple document that walks them through a high-level picture of the coordinated symphony of an active disaster recovery effort without requiring interpretation from team members busy with tasks directly related to the effort.

Emergency Response

The disaster recovery plan should contain simple yet comprehensive instructions for essential personnel to follow immediately upon recognition that a disaster is in progress or is imminent. These instructions will vary widely depending upon the nature of the disaster, the type of personnel responding to the incident, and the time available before facilities need to be evacuated and/or equipment shut down. For example, the instructions for a large-scale fire will be much more concise than the instructions for how to prepare for a hurricane that is still 48 hours away from a predicted landfall near an operational site. Emergency response plans are often put together in the form of checklists provided to responders. When designing these checklists, keep one essential design principle in mind: Arrange the checklist tasks in order of priority, with the most important task first!

It's essential that you keep in mind that these checklists will be executed in the midst of a crisis. It is extremely likely that responders will not be able to complete the entire checklist, especially in the event of a short-notice disaster. For this reason, you should put the most essential tasks (i.e., "Activate the building alarm") first on the checklist. The lower an item on the list, the lower the likelihood that it will be completed before an evacuation/shutdown takes place.

Personnel Notification

The disaster recovery plan should also contain a list of personnel to contact in the event of a disaster. Normally, this will include key members of the DRP team as well as those personnel who execute critical disaster recovery tasks throughout the organization. This response checklist should include alternate means of contact (i.e., pager numbers, cell phone numbers, etc.) as well as backup contacts for each role in the event the primary contact can not be reached or can not reach the recovery site for one reason or another.

The Power of Checklists

Checklists are an invaluable tool in the face of disaster. They provide a sense of order amidst the chaotic events surrounding a disaster. Take the time to ensure that your response checklists provide first responders with a clear plan that will protect life and property and ensure the continuity of operations.

A checklist for response to a building fire might include the following steps:

1. Activate the building alarm system.

2. Ensure that an orderly evacuation is in progress.

3. After leaving the building, use a cellular telephone to call 911 to ensure that emergency authorities received the alarm notification. Provide additional information on any required emergency response.

4. Ensure that any injured personnel receive appropriate medical treatment.

5. Activate the organization's disaster recovery plan to ensure continuity of operations.

Be sure to consult with the individuals in your organization responsible for privacy before assembling and disseminating a telephone notification checklist. You may need to comply with special policies regarding the use of home telephone numbers and other personal information in the checklist.

The notification checklist should be provided to all personnel who might respond to a disaster. This will enable prompt notification of key personnel. Many firms organize their notification checklists in a "telephone tree" style: each member of the tree contacts the person below them, spreading the notification burden among members of the team instead of relying upon one person to make a number of telephone calls.

If you choose to implement a telephone tree notification scheme, be sure to add a safety net. Have the last person in each chain contact the originator to confirm that their entire chain has been notified. This lets you rest assured that the disaster recovery team activation is smoothly underway.

Backups and Offsite Storage

Your disaster recovery plan (especially the technical guide) should fully address the backup strategy pursued by your organization. Indeed, this is one of the most important elements of any business continuity plan and disaster recovery plan.

Many system administrators are already familiar with the various types of backups, and you'll benefit by bringing one or more individuals with specific technical expertise in this area onto the BCP/DRP team to provide expert guidance. There are three main types of backups:

Full backups   As the name implies, *full backups* store a complete copy of the data contained on the protected device. Full backups duplicate every file on the system regardless of the setting of the archive bit. Once a full backup is complete, the archive bit on every file is reset, turned off, or set to 0.

Incremental backups   *Incremental backups* store only those files that have been modified since the time of the most recent full or incremental backup. Incremental backups duplicate only files that have the archive bit turned on, enabled, or set to 1. Once an incremental backup is complete, the archive bit on all duplicated files is reset, turned off, or set to 0.

Differential backups   *Differential backups* store all files that have been modified since the time of the most recent full backup. Differential backups duplicate only files that have the archive bit turned on, enabled, or set to 1. However, unlike full and incremental backups, the archive bit is not changed by the differential backup process.

The most important difference between incremental and differential backups is the time needed to restore data in the event of an emergency. If you use a combination of full and differential backups, you will only need to restore two backups—the most recent full backup and the most recent differential backup. On the other hand, if your strategy combines full backups with incremental backups, you will need to restore the most recent full backup as well as all incremental backups performed since that full backup. The trade-off is the time required to *create* the backups—differential backups don't take as long to restore, but they take longer to create than incremental backups.

Storage of the backup media is equally critical. It may be convenient to store backup media in or near the primary operations center to easily fulfill user requests for backup data, but you'll definitely need to keep copies of the media in at least one offsite location to provide redundancy in the event your primary operating location is suddenly destroyed.

Real World Scenario

Using Backups

In case of a system failure, many companies use one of two common methods to restore data from backups. In the first situation, they run a full backup on Monday night and then run differential backups every other night of the week. If a failure occurs Saturday morning, they restore Monday's full backup and then restore only Friday's differential backup. In the second situation, they run a full backup on Monday night and incremental backups are run every other night of the week. If a failure occurs Saturday morning, they restore Monday's full backup and then restore each incremental backup in original chronological order (i.e., Wednesday's, then Friday's, etc.).

Most organizations adopt a backup strategy that utilizes more than one of the three backup types along with a media rotation scheme. Both allow backup administrators access to a sufficiently large range of backups to complete user requests and provide fault tolerance while minimizing the amount of money that must be spent on backup media. A common strategy is to perform full backups over the weekend and incremental or differential backups on a nightly basis.

Backup Media Formats

The physical characteristics and the rotation cycle are two factors that a worthwhile backup solution should track and manage. The physical characteristics are the type of tape drive in use. This defines the physical wear placed on the media. The rotation cycle is the frequency of backups and retention length of protected data. By overseeing these characteristics, you can be assured that valuable data will be retained on serviceable backup media. Backup media has a maximum use limit; perhaps 5, 10, or 20 rewrites may be made before the media begins to lose reliability (statistically speaking). There is a wide variety of backup media formats:

- Digital Audio Tape (DAT)
- Quarter Inch Cartridge (QIC), commonly used in SOHO backups
- 8mm tape, commonly used in Helical Scan tape drives, but has been superseded by DLT
- Digital Linear Tape (DLT)
- Write Once, Read Many (WORM), a storage type often used to retain audit trails
- CDR/W media, usually requires faster file access than tape, useful for temporary storage of changeable data

Writable CDs and DVDs as well as Jaz and Zip drives are considered inappropriate for network backup solutions, primarily because of their limited capacity, but in some cases due to their speed or buffer underflow problems. Buffer underflow problems occurred before the advent of burn-proof software. Underflow is when the write buffer of the drive empties during the writing process, which causes an error on the media rendering it useless. However, these types of backup media are appropriate for end users to perform backups of limited sets of data from specific applications or for personal archiving purposes.

Backup Common Sense

No matter what the backup solution, media, or method, there are several common issues with backups that must be addressed. For instance, backup and restoration activities can be bulky and slow. Such data movement can significantly affect the performance of a network, especially during normal production hours. Thus, backups should be scheduled during the low peak periods (e.g., at night).

The amount of backup data increases over time. This causes the backup (and restoration) processes to take longer each time and to consume more space on the backup media. Thus, you need to build sufficient capacity to handle a reasonable amount of growth over a reasonable amount of time into your backup solution. What is reasonable all depends on your environment and budget.

With periodic backups (i.e., those backups that are run every 24 hours), there is always the potential for data loss up to the length of the period. In fact, Murphy's law dictates that the server crash is never immediately after a successful backup. Instead, it is always just before the next backup begins. To avoid the problem with periods, you need to deploy some form of real-time continuous backup, such as RAID, clustering, or server mirroring.

Tape Rotation

There are several commonly used tape rotation strategies for backups: the Grandfather-Father-Son strategy (GFS), the Tower of Hanoi strategy, and the Six Cartridge Weekly Backup strategy. These strategies can be fairly complex, especially with large tape sets. They can be implemented manually using a pencil and a calendar or automatically by using either commercial backup software or a fully automated Hierarchical Storage Management (HSM) system. An HSM system is an automated robotic backup jukebox consisting of 32 or 64 optical or tape backup devices. All of the drive elements within an HSM system are configured as a single drive array (a bit like RAID).

Details about the various tape rotations are beyond the scope of this book, but if you want to learn more about them, search by their names on the Internet.

Software Escrow Arrangements

A software escrow arrangement is a unique tool used to protect a company against the failure of a software developer to provide adequate support for its products or against the possibility that the developer will go out of business and no technical support will be available for the product.

Focus your efforts on negotiating software escrow agreements with those suppliers you fear may go out of business due to their size. It's not likely that you'll be able to negotiate such an agreement with a firm like Microsoft, unless you are responsible for an extremely large corporate account with serious bargaining power. On the other hand, it's equally unlikely that a firm of Microsoft's magnitude will go out of business, leaving end users high and dry.

If your organization depends upon custom-developed software or software products produced by a small firm, you may wish to consider developing this type of arrangement as part of your disaster recovery plan. Under a software escrow agreement, the developer provides copies of the application source code to an independent third-party organization. This third party then maintains updated backup copies of the source code in a secure fashion. The agreement between the end user and the developer specifies "trigger events," such as the failure of the developer to meet terms of a service level agreement (SLA) or the liquidation of the developer's firm. When a trigger event takes place, the third party releases copies of the application source code to the end user. The end user can then analyze the source code to resolve application issues or implement software updates.

External Communications

During the disaster recovery process, it will be necessary to communicate with various entities outside of your organization. You will need to contact vendors to provide supplies as they are needed to support the disaster recovery effort. Your clients will want to contact you for reassurance that you are still in operation. Public relations officials may need to contact the media or investment firms, and managers may need to speak to governmental authorities. For these reasons, it is essential that your disaster recovery plan include appropriate channels of communication to the outside world in a quantity sufficient to meet your operational needs. Usually, it is not a sound business practice or recovery practice to use the CEO as your spokesperson during a disaster. A media liaison should be hired, trained, and prepared to take on this responsibility.

Utilities

As discussed in previous sections of this chapter, your organization is reliant upon several utilities to provide critical elements of your infrastructure—electric power, water, natural gas, sewer service, and so on. Your disaster recovery plan should contain contact information and procedures to troubleshoot these services if problems arise during a disaster.

Logistics and Supplies

The logistical problems surrounding a disaster recovery operation are immense. You will suddenly face the problem of moving large numbers of people, equipment, and supplies to alternate recovery sites. It's also possible that the people will be actually living at those sites for an extended period of time, and the disaster recovery team will be responsible for providing them with food, water, shelter and appropriate facilities. Your disaster recovery plan should contain provisions for this type of operation if it falls within the scope of your expected operational needs.

Recovery vs. Restoration

It is sometimes useful to separate disaster recovery tasks from disaster restoration tasks. This is especially true when the recovery effort is expected to take a significant amount of time. A disaster recovery team may be assigned to implement and maintain operations at the recovery site while a salvage team is assigned to restore the primary site to operational capacity. These allocations should be made according to the needs of your organization and the types of disasters that you face.

The recovery team has a very short time frame in which to operate. They must put the DRP into action and restore IT capabilities as swiftly as possible. If the recovery team fails to restore business processes within the MTD/RTO, then the company fails.

Once the original site is deemed safe for people, the salvage team begins their work. Their job is to restore the company back to its full original capabilities and, if necessary, to the original location. If the original location is no longer in existence, then a new primary spot is selected. The salvage team must rebuild or repair the IT infrastructure. Since this activity is basically the same as building a new IT system, the return activity from the alternate/recovery site back to the primary/original site is itself a risky activity. Fortunately, the salvage team has more time to work than the recovery team. The salvage team must ensure the reliability of the new IT infrastructure. This is done by returning the least-mission-critical processes back to the restored original site to stress-test the rebuilt network. As the restored site shows resiliency, more important processes are transferred. A serious vulnerability exists when mission-critical processes are returned to the original site. The act of returning to the original site could cause a disaster of its own. Therefore, the state of emergency cannot be declared over until full normal operations have returned to the restored original site.

At the conclusion of any disaster recovery effort, the time will come to restore operations at the primary site and terminate any processing sites operating under the disaster recovery agreement. Your DRP should specify the criteria used to determine when it is appropriate to return to the primary site and guide the DRP recovery and salvage teams through an orderly transition.

Training and Documentation

As with the business continuity plan, it is essential that you provide training to all personnel who will be involved in the disaster recovery effort. The level of training required will vary according to an individual's role in the effort and their position within the company. When designing a training plan, you should consider including the following elements:

- Orientation training for all new employees
- Initial training for employees taking on a new disaster recovery role for the first time
- Detailed refresher training for disaster recovery team members
- Brief refresher training for all other employees (can be accomplished as part of other meetings and through a medium like e-mail newsletters sent to all employees)

> Loose-leaf binders provide an excellent option for storage of disaster recovery plans. You can distribute single-page changes to the plan without destroying a national forest!

The disaster recovery plan should also be fully documented. Earlier in this chapter, we discussed several of the documentation options available to you. Be sure that you implement the necessary documentation programs and modify the documentation as changes to the plan occur. Because of the rapidly changing nature of the disaster recovery and business continuity plans, you might consider publication on a secured portion of your organization's intranet.

Your DRP should be treated as an extremely sensitive document and provided to individuals on a compartmentalized, need-to-know basis only. Individuals who participate in the plan should fully understand their roles, but they do not need to know or have access to the entire plan. Of course, it is essential to ensure that key DRP team members and senior management have access to the entire plan and understand the high-level implementation details. You certainly don't want this knowledge to rest in the mind of one individual.

> **WARNING**
>
> Remember that a disaster may render your intranet unavailable. If you choose to distribute your disaster recovery and business continuity plans through an intranet, be sure that you maintain an adequate number of printed copies of the plan at both the primary and alternate sites and maintain *only* the most current copy!

Testing and Maintenance

Every disaster recovery plan must be tested on a periodic basis to ensure that the plan's provisions are viable and that it meets the changing needs of the organization. The types of tests that you are able to conduct will depend upon the types of recovery facilities available to you, the culture of your organization, and the availability of disaster recovery team members. The five main test types—checklist tests, structured walk-throughs, simulation tests, parallel tests, and full-interruption tests—are discussed in the remaining sections of this chapter.

Checklist Test

The *checklist test* is one of the simplest tests to conduct, but it is also one of the most critical. In this type of test, you simply distribute copies of the disaster recovery checklists to the members of the disaster recovery team for review. This allows you to simultaneously accomplish three goals. First, it ensures that key personnel are aware of their responsibilities and have that knowledge refreshed on a periodic basis. Second, it provides individuals with an opportunity to review the checklists for obsolete information and update any items that require modification due to changes within the organization. Finally, in large organizations, it aids in the identification of situations in which key personnel have left the company and nobody bothered to reassign their disaster recovery responsibilities! This is also a good reason why disaster recovery responsibilities should be included in job descriptions.

Structured Walk-Through

The *structured walk-through* takes testing one step further. In this type of test, often referred to as a "table-top exercise," members of the disaster recovery team gather in a large conference room and role-play a disaster scenario. Normally, the exact scenario is known only to the test moderator, who presents the details to the team at the meeting. The team members then refer to their copies of the disaster recovery plan and discuss the appropriate responses to that particular type of disaster.

Simulation Test

Simulation tests are similar to the structured walk-throughs. In simulation tests, disaster recovery team members are presented with a scenario and asked to develop an appropriate response. Unlike the tests previously discussed, some of these response measures are then tested. This may involve the interruption of noncritical business activities and the use of some operational personnel.

Parallel Test

Parallel tests represent the next level in testing and involve actually relocating personnel to the alternate recovery site and implementing site activation procedures. The employees relocated to the site perform their disaster recovery responsibilities in the same manner as they would for an actual disaster. The only difference is that operations at the main facility are not interrupted. That site retains full responsibility for conducting the day-to-day business of the organization.

Full-Interruption Test

Full-interruption tests operate in a manner similar to parallel tests, but they involve actually shutting down operations at the primary site and shifting them to the recovery site. For obvious reasons, full-interruption tests are extremely difficult to arrange and you often encounter resistance from management.

Maintenance

Remember that your disaster recovery plan is a living document. As your organization's needs change, you must adapt the disaster recovery plan to meet those changed needs. You will discover many necessary modifications through the use of a well-organized and coordinated testing plan. Minor changes may often be made through a series of telephone conversations or e-mails, whereas major changes may require one or more meetings of the full disaster recovery team.

Summary

Disaster recovery planning is a critical portion of a comprehensive information security program. No matter how comprehensive your business continuity plan, the day may come when your business is interrupted by a disaster and you have the task of quickly and efficiently restoring operations to the primary site. Keep in mind the old adage that an ounce of prevention is worth a pound of cure. Spending the time and effort developing a comprehensive disaster recovery plan will greatly ease the process of recovering operations in the midst of a chaotic emergency.

An organization's disaster recovery plan is one of the most important documents under the purview of security professionals. It should provide guidance to the personnel responsible for ensuring the continuity of operations in the face of disaster. The DRP provides an orderly sequence of events designed to activate alternate processing sites while simultaneously restoring the primary site to operational status. Security professionals should ensure that adequate programs are in place so that those team members charged with disaster recovery duties are well-trained for their roles under the plan.

Exam Essentials

Know the common types of natural disasters that may threaten an organization.   Natural disasters that commonly threaten organizations include earthquakes, floods, storms, fires, tsunamis, and volcanic eruptions.

Know the common types of man-made disasters that may threaten an organization.   Explosions, electrical fires, terrorist acts, power outages, other utility failures, infrastructure failures, hardware/software failures, labor difficulties, theft, and vandalism are all common man-made disasters.

Be familiar with the common types of recovery facilities.   The common types of recovery facilities are cold sites, warm sites, hot sites, mobile sites, service bureaus, and multiple sites. It is important that you understand the benefits and drawbacks of each of these facilities.

Explain the potential benefits behind Mutual Assistance Agreements as well as the reasons they are not commonly implemented in businesses today.   Mutual Assistance Agreements (MAAs) provide an inexpensive alternative to disaster recovery sites, but they are not commonly used because they are difficult to enforce. Organizations participating in an MAA may also be shut down by the same disaster, and MAAs raise confidentiality concerns.

Know the five types of disaster recovery plan tests and the impact each has on normal business operations.   The five types of disaster recovery plan tests are checklist tests, structured walk-throughs, simulation tests, parallel tests, and full-interruption tests. Checklist tests are purely paperwork exercises, whereas structured walk-throughs involve a project team meeting. Neither has an impact on business operations. Simulation tests may shut down noncritical business units. Parallel tests involve relocation of personnel but do not affect day-to-day operations. Full-interruption tests involve shutting down primary systems and shifting responsibility to the recovery facility.

Written Lab

Answer the following questions about Disaster Recovery Planning:

1. What are some of the main concerns businesses have when considering adopting a Mutual Assistance Agreement?

2. List and explain the five types of disaster recovery tests.

3. Explain the differences between the three types of backup strategies discussed in this chapter.

Review Questions

1. What is the end goal of Disaster Recovery Planning?

    A. Preventing business interruption

    B. Setting up temporary business operations

    C. Restoring normal business activity

    D. Minimizing the impact of a disaster

2. Which one of the following is an example of a man-made disaster?

    A. Tsunami

    B. Earthquake

    C. Power outage

    D. Lightning strike

3. According to the Federal Emergency Management Agency, approximately what percentage of U.S. states is considered to have at least a moderate risk of seismic activity?

    A. 20 percent

    B. 40 percent

    C. 60 percent

    D. 80 percent

4. Which one of the following disaster types is not normally covered by standard business or home-owner's insurance?

    A. Earthquake

    B. Flood

    C. Fire

    D. Theft

5. In the wake of the September 11, 2001 terrorist attacks, what industry made drastic changes that directly impact DRP/BCP activities?

    A. Tourism

    B. Banking

    C. Insurance

    D. Airline

6. Which one of the following statements about Business Continuity Planning and Disaster Recovery Planning is not correct?

   A. Business Continuity Planning is focused on keeping business functions uninterrupted when a disaster strikes.

   B. Organizations can choose whether to develop Business Continuity Planning or Disaster Recovery Planning plans.

   C. Business Continuity Planning picks up where Disaster Recovery Planning leaves off.

   D. Disaster Recovery Planning guides an organization through recovery of normal operations at the primary facility.

7. What does the term "100-year flood plain" mean to emergency preparedness officials?

   A. The last flood of any kind to hit the area was more than 100 years ago.

   B. A flood is expected to hit the area once every 100 years.

   C. The area is expected to be safe from flooding for at least 100 years.

   D. The last significant flood to hit the area was more than 100 years ago.

8. In which one of the following database recovery techniques is an exact, up-to-date copy of the database maintained at an alternative location?

   A. Transaction logging

   B. Remote journaling

   C. Electronic vaulting

   D. Remote mirroring

9. What disaster recovery principle best protects your organization against hardware failure?

   A. Consistency

   B. Efficiency

   C. Redundancy

   D. Primacy

10. What Business Continuity Planning technique can help you prepare the business unit prioritization task of Disaster Recovery Planning?

    A. Vulnerability Analysis

    B. Business Impact Assessment

    C. Risk Management

    D. Continuity Planning

11. Which one of the following alternative processing sites takes the longest time to activate?

    A. Hot site

    B. Mobile site

    C. Cold site

    D. Warm site

12. What is the typical time estimate to activate a warm site from the time a disaster is declared?

   A. 1 hour

   B. 6 hours

   C. 12 hours

   D. 24 hours

13. Which one of the following items is a characteristic of hot sites but not a characteristic of warm sites?

   A. Communications circuits

   B. Workstations

   C. Servers

   D. Current data

14. What type of database backup strategy involves bulk transfers of data to a remote site on a periodic basis but does not involve maintenance of a live backup server at the remote site?

   A. Transaction logging

   B. Remote journaling

   C. Electronic vaulting

   D. Remote mirroring

15. What type of document will help public relations specialists and other individuals who need a high-level summary of disaster recovery efforts while they are underway?

   A. Executive summary

   B. Technical guides

   C. Department-specific plans

   D. Checklists

16. What Disaster Recovery Planning tool can be used to protect an organization against the failure of a critical software firm to provide appropriate support for their products?

   A. Differential backups

   B. Business Impact Assessment

   C. Incremental backups

   D. Software escrow agreement

17. What type of backup involves always storing copies of all files modified since the most recent full backup?

   A. Differential backups

   B. Partial backup

   C. Incremental backups

   D. Database backup

18. What combination of backup strategies provides the fastest backup creation time?

A. Full backups and differential backups

B. Partial backups and incremental backups

C. Full backups and incremental backups

D. Incremental backups and differential backups

19. What combination of backup strategies provides the fastest backup restoration time?

A. Full backups and differential backups

B. Partial backups and incremental backups

C. Full backups and incremental backups

D. Incremental backups and differential backups

20. What type of disaster recovery plan test fully evaluates operations at the backup facility but does not shift primary operations responsibility from the main site?

A. Structured walk-through

B. Parallel test

C. Full-interruption test

D. Simulation test

Answers to Review Questions

1. C. Disaster Recovery Planning picks up where Business Continuity Planning leaves off. Once a disaster interrupts the business operations, the goal of DRP is to restore normal business activity as quickly as possible.

2. C. A power outage is an example of a man-made disaster. The other events listed—tsunamis, earthquakes, and lightning strikes—are all naturally occurring events.

3. D. As shown in Table 16.1, 40 of the 50 U.S. states are considered to have a moderate, high, or very high risk of seismic activity.

4. B. Most general business insurance and homeowner's insurance policies do not provide any protection against the risk of flooding or flash floods. If floods pose a risk to your organization, you should consider purchasing supplemental flood insurance under FEMA's National Flood Insurance Program.

5. C. Although all of the industries listed in the options made changes to their practices after September 11, 2004, the insurance industry's change toward noncoverage of acts of terrorism most directly impacts the BCP/DRP process.

6. C. The opposite of this statement is true—Disaster Recovery Planning picks up where Business Continuity Planning leaves off. The other three statements are all accurate reflections of the role of Business Continuity Planning and Disaster Recovery Planning.

7. B. The term "100-year flood plain" is used to describe an area where flooding is expected once every 100 years. It can also be said that there is a 1 percent probability of flooding in any given year.

8. D. When you use remote mirroring, an exact copy of the database is maintained at an alternative location. You keep the remote copy up-to-date by executing all transactions on both the primary and remote site at the same time.

9. C. Redundant systems/components provide protection against the failure of one particular piece of hardware.

10. B. During the Business Impact Assessment phase, you must identify the business priorities of your organization to assist with the allocation of BCP resources. This same information can be used to drive the DRP business unit prioritization.

11. C. The cold site contains none of the equipment necessary to restore operations. All of the equipment must be brought in and configured and data must be restored to it before operations can commence. This often takes weeks.

12. C. Warm sites typically take about 12 hours to activate from the time a disaster is declared. This is compared to the relatively instantaneous activation of a hot site and the lengthy (at least a week) time required to bring a cold site to operational status.

13. D. Warm sites and hot sites both contain workstations, servers, and the communications circuits necessary to achieve operational status. The main difference between the two alternatives is the fact that hot sites contain near real-time copies of the operational data and warm sites require the restoration of data from backup.

14. C. In an electronic vaulting scenario, bulk transfers of data occur between the primary site and the backup location on a periodic basis. These backups are stored at the remote location but are not maintained on a live database server. Once a disaster is declared, technicians retrieve the data from the vault and apply it to production servers.

15. A. The executive summary provides a high-level view of the entire organization's disaster recovery efforts. This document is useful for the managers and leaders of the firm as well as public relations personnel who need a nontechnical perspective on this complex effort.

16. D. Software escrow agreements place the application source code in the hands of an independent third party, thus providing firms with a "safety net" in the event a developer goes out of business or fails to honor the terms of a service agreement.

17. A. Differential backups involve always storing copies of all files modified since the most recent full backup regardless of any incremental or differential backups created during the intervening time period.

18. C. Any backup strategy must include full backups at some point in the process. Incremental backups are created faster than differential backups due to the number of files it is necessary to back up each time.

19. A. Any backup strategy must include full backups at some point in the process. If a combination of full and differential backups is used, a maximum of two backups must be restored. If a combination of full and incremental backups is chosen, the number of required restorations may be unlimited.

20. B. Parallel tests involve moving personnel to the recovery site and gearing up operations, but responsibility for conducting day-to-day operations of the business remains at the primary operations center.

Answers to Written Lab

Following are answers to the questions in this chapter's written lab:

1. There are three main concerns businesses have when considering the adoption of Mutual Assistance Agreements. First, the nature of an MAA often necessitates that the businesses be located in close geographical proximity. However, this requirement also increases the risk that the two businesses will fall victim to the same threat. Second, MAAs are difficult to enforce in the middle of a crisis. If one of the organizations is affected by a disaster and the other isn't, the organization not affected could back out at the last minute and the other organization is out of luck. Finally, confidentiality concerns (both legal and business related) often prevent businesses from trusting others with their sensitive operational data.

2. There are five main types of disaster recovery tests:

   - Checklist tests involve the distribution of recovery checklists to disaster recovery personnel for review.

   - Structured walk-throughs are "table-top" exercises that involve assembling the disaster recovery team to discuss a disaster scenario.

   - Simulation tests are more comprehensive and may impact one or more noncritical business units of the organization.

   - Parallel tests involve relocating personnel to the alternate site and commencing operations there.

   - Full-interruption tests involve relocating personnel to the alternate site and shutting down operations at the primary site.

3. Full backups create a copy of all data stored on a server. Incremental backups create copies of all files modified since the last full or incremental backup. Differential backups create copies of all files modified since the last full backup without regard to any previous differential or incremental backups that may have taken place.

Chapter

17

Law and Investigations

THE CISSP EXAM TOPICS COVERED IN THIS CHAPTER INCLUDE:

- ✓ Laws
- ✓ Major Categories and Types of Laws
- ✓ Investigations

In the early days of computer security, information security professionals were pretty much left on their own to defend their systems against attacks. They didn't have much help from the criminal and civil justice systems. When they did seek assistance from law enforcement, they were met with reluctance by overworked agents who didn't have a basic understanding of how something that involved a computer could actually be a crime. The legislative branch of government hadn't addressed the issue of computer crime, and the executive branch felt that they simply didn't have statutory authority or obligation to pursue those matters.

Fortunately, both our legal system and the men and women of law enforcement have come a long way over the past two decades. The legislative branches of governments around the world have at least attempted to address issues of computer crime. Many law enforcement agencies have full-time, well-trained computer crime investigators with advanced security training. Those that don't usually know where to turn when they require this sort of experience.

In this chapter, we'll take a look at the various types of laws that deal with computer security issues. We'll examine the legal issues surrounding computer crime, privacy, intellectual property, and a number of other related topics. We'll also cover basic investigative techniques, including the pros and cons of calling in assistance from law enforcement.

Categories of Laws

There are three main categories of laws that play a role in our legal system. Each is used to cover a variety of different circumstances, and the penalties for violating laws in the different categories vary widely. In the following sections, we'll take a look at how criminal law, civil law, and administrative law interact to form the complex web of our justice system.

Criminal Law

Criminal law forms the bedrock of the body of laws that preserve the peace and keep our society safe. Many high-profile court cases involve matters of criminal law; these are the laws that the police and other law enforcement agencies concern themselves with. Criminal law contains prohibitions against acts such as murder, assault, robbery, arson, and similar offenses. Penalties for violating criminal statutes fall in a range that includes mandatory hours of community service, monetary penalties in the form of fines (small and large), deprivation of civil liberties in the form of prison sentences, and in the most extreme cases, forfeiture of one's life through application of the death penalty.

There are a number of criminal laws that serve to protect society against computer crime. In later sections of this chapter, you'll learn how some laws, like the Computer Fraud and Abuse Act, the Electronic Communications Privacy Act, and the Identity Theft and Assumption Deterrence Act (among others), provide criminal penalties for serious cases of computer crime. Technically savvy prosecutors teamed with concerned law enforcement agencies have dealt serious blows to the "hacking underground" by using the court system to slap lengthy prison terms on offenders guilty of what used to be considered harmless pranks.

In the United States, legislative bodies at all levels of government establish criminal laws through elected representatives. At the federal level, both the House of Representatives and the Senate must pass criminal law bills by a majority vote (in most cases) in order for the bill to become law. Once passed, these laws then become federal law and apply in all cases where the federal government has jurisdiction (mainly cases that involve interstate commerce, cases that cross state boundaries, or cases that are offenses against the federal government itself). If federal jurisdiction does not apply, state authorities handle the case using laws passed in a similar manner by state legislators.

All federal and state laws must comply with the document that dictates how our system of government works—the U.S. Constitution. All laws are subject to judicial review by regional courts with the right of appeal all the way to the Supreme Court of the United States. If a court finds that a law is unconstitutional, it has the power to strike it down and render it invalid.

Keep in mind that criminal law is a serious matter. If you find yourself involved in a matter in which criminal authorities become involved—either as a witness, defendant, or victim of a computer crime—you'd be well advised to seek advice from an attorney familiar with the criminal justice system and specifically with matters of computer crime. It's not wise to "go it alone" in such a complex system.

Civil Law

Civil laws form the bulk of our body of laws. They are designed to provide for an orderly society and govern matters that are not crimes but require an impartial arbiter to settle between individuals and organizations. Examples of the types of matters that may be judged under civil law include contract disputes, real estate transactions, employment matters, and estate/probate procedures. Civil laws also are used to create the framework of government that the executive branch uses to carry out its responsibilities. These laws provide budgets for governmental activities and lay out the authority granted to the executive branch to create administrative laws (see the next section).

Civil laws are enacted in the same manner as criminal laws. They must pass through the legislative process before enactment and are subject to the same constitutional parameters and judicial review procedures. At the federal level, both criminal and civil laws are embodied in the United States Code (USC).

The major difference between civil laws and criminal laws is the way that they are enforced. Normally, law enforcement authorities do not become involved in matters of civil law beyond taking action necessary to restore order. In a criminal prosecution, the government, through law enforcement investigators and prosecutors, brings action against a person accused of a crime. In civil matters, it is incumbent upon the person who feels they have been wronged to obtain legal counsel and file a civil lawsuit against the person they feel is responsible for their grievance. The government (unless it is the plaintiff or defendant) does not take sides in the dispute or argue one position or the other. The only role of the government in civil matters is to provide the judges, juries, and court facilities used to hear civil cases and to play an administrative role in managing the judicial system in accordance with the law.

As with criminal law, it is best to obtain legal assistance if you feel that you need to file a civil lawsuit or you fear that a civil lawsuit may be filed against you. Although civil law does not provide for imprisonment, the losing party may face extremely severe financial penalties. One need look no further than the nightly news for examples—multimillion-dollar cases against tobacco companies, major corporations, and wealthy individuals are heard every day.

Administrative Law

The executive branch of our government charges numerous agencies with wide-ranging responsibilities to ensure that government functions effectively. It is the duty of these agencies to abide by and enforce the criminal and civil laws enacted by the legislative branch. However, as can be easily imagined, criminal and civil law can't possibly lay out rules and procedures that should be followed in any possible situation. Therefore, executive branch agencies have some leeway to enact administrative law, in the form of policies, procedures, and regulations that govern the daily operations of the agency. Administrative law covers topics as mundane as the procedures to be used within a federal agency to obtain a desk telephone to more substantial issues such as the immigration policies that will be used to enforce the laws passed by Congress. Administrative law is published in the Code of Federal Regulations, often referred to as the CFR.

Although administrative law does not require an act of the legislative branch to gain the force of law, it must comply with all existing civil and criminal law. Government agencies may not implement regulations that directly contradict existing laws passed by the legislature. Furthermore, administrative law (and the actions of government agencies) must also comply with the U.S. Constitution and are subject to judicial review.

Laws

Throughout these sections, we'll examine a number of laws that relate to information technology. By necessity, this discussion is U.S.-centric, as is the material covered by the CISSP exam. We'll look at several high-profile foreign laws, such as the European Union's data privacy act. However, if you operate in an environment that involves foreign jurisdictions, you should retain local legal counsel to guide you through the system.

WARNING   Every information security professional should have a basic understanding of the law as it relates to information technology. However, the most important lesson to be learned is knowing when it's necessary to call in a legal professional. If you feel that you're in a legal "gray area," it's best to seek professional advice.

Computer Crime

The first computer security issues addressed by legislators were those involving computer crime. Early computer crime prosecutions were attempted under traditional criminal law, and many were dismissed because judges felt that applying traditional law to this modern type of crime was too far of a stretch. Legislators responded by passing specific statutes that defined computer crime and laid out specific penalties for various crimes. In the following sections, we'll take a look at several of those statutes.

> The U.S. laws discussed in this chapter are federal laws. Almost every state in the union has enacted some form of legislation regarding computer security issues. Due to the global reach of the Internet, most computer crimes cross state lines and, therefore, fall under federal jurisdiction and are prosecuted in the federal court system. However, in some circumstances, state laws can be more restrictive than federal laws and impose harsher penalties.

Computer Fraud and Abuse Act of 1984

Congress first enacted the *Computer Fraud and Abuse Act (CFAA)* in 1984 and it remains in force today, with several amendments. This law was carefully written to exclusively cover computer crimes that crossed state boundaries to avoid infringing upon states' rights and treading on thin constitutional ice. The major provisions of the act are that it is a crime to perform the following:

- Access classified information or financial information in a federal system without authorization or in excess of authorized privileges

- Access a computer used exclusively by the federal government without authorization

- Use a federal computer to perpetrate a fraud (unless the only object of the fraud was to gain use of the computer itself)

- Cause malicious damage to a federal computer system in excess of $1,000

- Modify medical records in a computer when doing so impairs or may impair the examination, diagnosis, treatment, or medical care of an individual

- Traffic in computer passwords if the trafficking affects interstate commerce or involves a federal computer system

The CFAA was amended in 1986 to change the scope of the act. Instead of merely covering federal computers that processed sensitive information, the act was changed to cover all "federal interest" computers. This widened the coverage of the act to include the following:

- Any computer used exclusively by the U.S. government

- Any computer used exclusively by a financial institution

- Any computer used by the government or a financial institution when the offense impedes the ability of the government or institution to use that system

- Any combination of computers used to commit an offense when they are not all located in the same state

1994 CFAA Amendments

In 1994, Congress recognized that the face of computer security had drastically changed since the CFAA was last amended in 1986 and made a number of sweeping changes to the act. Collectively, these changes are referred to as the Computer Abuse Amendments Act of 1994 and included the following provisions:

- Outlawed the creation of any type of malicious code that might cause damage to a computer system

- Modified the CFAA to cover any computer used in interstate commerce rather than just "federal interest" computer systems

- Allowed for the imprisonment of offenders, regardless of whether they actually intended to cause damage

- Provided legal authority for the victims of computer crime to pursue civil action to gain injunctive relief and compensation for damages

Computer Security Act of 1987

After amending the CFAA in 1986 to cover a wider variety of computer systems, Congress turned its view inward and examined the current state of computer security in federal government systems. Members of Congress were not satisfied with what they saw and enacted the *Computer Security Act (CSA) of 1987* to mandate baseline security requirements for all federal agencies. In the introduction to the CSA, Congress specified four main purposes of the act:

- To give the National Bureau of Standards (now the National Institute of Standards and Technology, or NIST) responsibility for developing standards and guidelines for federal computer systems, including responsibility for developing standards and guidelines for federal computer systems. Drawing on the technical advice and assistance (including work products) of the National Security Agency where appropriate.

- To provide for promulgation of such standards and guidelines.

- To require establishment of security plans by all operators of federal computer systems that contain sensitive information.

- To require mandatory periodic training for all persons involved in management, use, or operation of federal computer systems that contain sensitive information.

This act clearly set out a number of requirements that formed the basis of federal computer security policy for many years. It also divided responsibility for computer security among two federal agencies. The National Security Agency (NSA), which formerly had authority over all computer security issues, now retained authority over classified systems. NIST gained responsibility for securing all other federal government systems.

Federal Sentencing Guidelines

The *Federal Sentencing Guidelines* released in 1991 provided punishment guidelines to help federal judges interpret computer crime laws. There are three major provisions of these guidelines that have had a lasting impact on the information security community:

They formalized the *prudent man rule,* which requires senior executives to take personal responsibility for ensuring the *due care* that ordinary, prudent individuals would exercise in the same situation. This rule, developed in the realm of fiscal responsibility, now applies to information security as well.

They allowed organizations and executives to minimize punishment for infractions by demonstrating that they used due diligence in the conduct of their information security duties.

They outlined three burdens of proof for *negligence.* First, there must be a legally recognized obligation of the person accused of negligence. Second, the person must have failed to comply with recognized standards. Finally, there must be a causal relationship between the act of negligence and subsequent damages.

Paperwork Reduction Act of 1995

The Paperwork Reduction Act of 1995 requires that agencies obtain Office of Management and Budget (OMB) approval before requesting most types of information from the public. Information collections include forms, interviews, record-keeping requirements, and a wide variety of other things. This act was amended by the Government Information Security Reform Act (GISRA) of 2000.

National Information Infrastructure Protection Act of 1996

In 1996, Congress passed yet another set of amendments to the Computer Fraud and Abuse Act designed to further extend the protection it provides. It included the following main new areas of coverage:

- Broadens the act to cover computer systems used in international commerce in addition to systems used in interstate commerce

- Extends similar protections to portions of the national infrastructure other than computing systems, such as railroads, gas pipelines, electric power grids, and telecommunications circuits

- Treats any intentional or reckless act that causes damage to critical portions of the national infrastructure as a felony

Government Information Security Reform Act of 2000

The *Government Information Security Reform Act of 2000* amends the United States Code to implement additional information security policies and procedures. In the text of the act, Congress laid out five basic purposes for establishing the GISRA:

- To provide a comprehensive framework for establishing and ensuring the effectiveness of controls over information resources that support federal operations and assets

- To recognize the highly networked nature of the federal computing environment, including the need for federal government interoperability, and in the implementation of improved security management measures, to assure that opportunities for interoperability are not adversely affected

- To provide effective government-wide management and oversight of the related information security risks, including coordination of information security efforts throughout the civilian, national security, and law enforcement communities

- To provide for development and maintenance of minimum controls required to protect federal information and information systems

- To provide a mechanism for improved oversight of federal agency information security programs

The provisions of the GISRA continue to charge the National Institute of Standards and Technology and the National Security Agency with security oversight responsibilities for unclassified and classified information processing systems, respectively. However, GISRA places the burden of maintaining the security and integrity of government information and information systems squarely on the shoulders of individual agency leaders.

GISRA also creates a new category of computer system. Mission-critical systems meet one of the following criteria:

- It is defined as a national security system by other provisions of law.

- It is protected by procedures established for classified information.

- The loss, misuse, disclosure, or unauthorized access to or modification of any information it processes would have a debilitating impact on the mission of an agency.

The GISRA provides specific evaluation and auditing authority for mission-critical systems to the secretary of defense and the director of central intelligence. This is an attempt to ensure that all government agencies, even those that do not routinely deal with classified national security information, implement adequate security controls on systems that are absolutely critical to the continued functioning of the agency.

Intellectual Property

America's role in the global economy is shifting away from a manufacturer of goods and toward a provider of services. This trend also shows itself in many of the world's large industrialized nations. With this shift toward providing services, intellectual property takes on an increasingly important role in many firms. Indeed, it is arguable that the most valuable assets of many large multinational companies are simply the brand names that we've all come to recognize, and company names like Dell, Proctor & Gamble, and Merck bring instant credibility to any product. Publishing companies, movie producers, and artists depend upon their creative output to earn their livelihood. Many products depend upon secret recipes or production techniques—take the legendary secret formula for Coca-Cola or the Colonel's secret blend of herbs and spices, for example.

These intangible assets are collectively referred to as *intellectual property,* and a whole host of laws exist to protect the rights of their owners. After all, it simply wouldn't be fair if a music store only bought one copy of each artist's CD and burned copies for all of their customers—that would deprive the artist of the benefits of their labor. In the following sections, we'll explore the laws surrounding the four major types of intellectual property—copyrights, trademarks, patents, and trade secrets. We'll also discuss how these concepts specifically concern information security professionals. Many countries protect (or fail to protect) these rights in different ways, but the basic concepts ring true throughout the world.

> Some countries are notorious for violating intellectual property rights. The most notable example is China. China is world-renowned for its blatant disregard of copyright and patent law. If you're planning to do business in this region of the world, you should definitely consult with an attorney who specializes in this area.

Copyrights

Copyright law guarantees the creators of "original works of authorship" protection against the unauthorized duplication of their work. There are eight broad categories of works that qualify for copyright protection:

- Literary works
- Musical works
- Dramatic works
- Pantomimes and choreographic works
- Pictorial, graphical, and sculptural works
- Motion pictures and other audiovisual works
- Sound recordings
- Architectural works

There is precedent for copyrighting computer software—it's done under the scope of literary works. However, it's important to note that copyright law only protects the expression inherent in computer software—that is, the actual source code. It does not protect the ideas or process behind the software. There has also been some question over whether copyrights can be extended to cover the "look and feel" of a software package's graphical user interface. Court decisions have gone in both directions on this matter; if you will be involved in this type of issue, you should consult a qualified intellectual property attorney to determine the current state of legislation and case law.

There is a formal procedure to obtain a copyright that involves sending copies of the protected work along with an appropriate registration fee to the Library of Congress. For more information on this process, visit the Library's website at www.loc.gov/copyright/. However, it is important to note that officially registering a copyright is not a prerequisite for copyright enforcement.

Indeed, the law states that the creator of a work has an automatic copyright from the instant the work is created. If you can prove in court that you were the creator of a work (perhaps by publishing it), you will be protected under copyright law. Official registration merely provides the government's acknowledgment that they received your work on a specific date.

Copyright ownership always defaults to the creator of a work. The exceptions to this policy are works for hire. A work is considered "for hire" when it is made for an employer during the normal course of an employee's workday. For example, when an employee in a company's public relations department writes a press release, the press release is considered a work for hire. A work may also be considered a work for hire when it is made as part of a written contract declaring it as such.

Current copyright law provides for a very lengthy period of protection. Works by one or more authors are protected until 70 years after the death of the last surviving author. Works for hire and anonymous works are provided protection for the shorter of 95 years from the date of first publication or 120 years from the date of creation.

Digital Millennium Copyright Act of 1998

In 1998, Congress recognized the rapidly changing digital landscape that was stretching the reach of existing copyright law. To help meet this challenge, it enacted the hotly debated *Digital Millennium Copyright Act*. The DMCA also serves to bring United States copyright law into compliance with terms of two World Intellectual Property Organization (WIPO) treaties.

The first major provision of the DMCA is the prohibition of attempts to circumvent copyright protection mechanisms placed on a protected work by the copyright holder. This clause was designed to protect copy-prevention mechanisms placed on digital media like CDs and DVDs. The DMCA provides for penalties of up to $1,000,000 and 10 years in prison for repeat offenders. Nonprofit institutions such as libraries and schools are exempted from this provision.

The DMCA also limits the liability of Internet service providers when their circuits are used by criminals violating the copyright law. The DMCA recognizes that ISPs have a legal status similar to the "common carrier" status of telephone companies and does not hold them liable for the "transitory activities" of their users. In order to qualify for this exemption, the service provider's activities must meet the following requirements (quoted directly from the Digital Millennium Copyright Act of 1998, U.S. Copyright Office Summary, December 1998):

- The transmission must be initiated by a person other than the provider.

- The transmission, routing, provision of connections, or copying must be carried out by an automated technical process without selection of material by the service provider.

- The service provider must not determine the recipients of the material.

- Any intermediate copies must not ordinarily be accessible to anyone other than anticipated recipients, and must not be retained for longer than reasonably necessary.

- The material must be transmitted with no modification to its content.

The DMCA also exempts activities of service providers related to system caching, search engines, and the storage of information on a network by individual users. However, in those cases, the service provider must take prompt action to remove copyrighted materials upon notification of the infringement.

Congress also included provisions in the DMCA that allow the creation of backup copies of computer software and any maintenance, testing, or routine usage activities that require software duplication. These provisions only apply if the software is licensed for use on a particular computer, the usage is in compliance with the license agreement, and any such copies are immediately deleted when no longer required for a permitted activity.

Finally, the DMCA spells out the application of copyright law principles to the emerging field of webcasting, or broadcasting audio and/or video content to recipients over the Internet. This technology is often referred to as streaming audio or streaming video. The DMCA states that these uses are to be treated as "eligible nonsubscription transmissions." The law in this area is still under development, so if you plan to engage in this type of activity, you should contact an attorney to ensure that you are in compliance with current law.

Trademarks

Copyright laws are used to protect creative works; there is also protection for *trademarks,* which are words, slogans, and logos used to identify a company and its products or services. For example, a business might obtain a copyright on its sales brochure to ensure that competitors can't duplicate its sales materials. That same business might also seek to obtain trademark protection for its company name and the names of specific products and services that it offers to its clients.

The main objective of trademark protection is to avoid confusion in the marketplace while protecting the intellectual property rights of people and organizations. As with copyright protection, trademarks do not need to be officially registered to gain protection under the law. If you use a trademark in the course of your public activities, you are automatically protected under any relevant trademark law and may use the symbol to show that you intend to protect words or slogans as trademarks. If you want official recognition of your trademark, you may register it with the United States Patent and Trademark Office (USPTO). This process generally requires an attorney to perform a "due diligence" comprehensive search for existing trademarks that might preclude your registration. The entire registration process can take over a year from start to finish. Once you've received your registration certificate from the USPTO, you may denote your mark as a registered trademark with the symbol.

One major advantage of trademark registration is that you may register a trademark that you intend to use but are not necessarily already using. This type of application is called an "intent to use" application and conveys trademark protection as of the date of filing provided that you actually use the trademark in commerce within a certain time period. If you opt not to register your trademark with the PTO, your protection begins only when you first use the trademark.

There are two main requirements for the acceptance of a trademark application in the United States:

- The trademark must not be confusingly similar to another trademark—you should determine this during your attorney's due diligence search. There will be an open opposition period during which other companies may dispute your trademark application.

- The trademark should not be descriptive of the goods and services that you will offer. For example, "Mike's Software Company" would not be a good trademark candidate because it describes the product produced by the company. The USPTO may reject an application if it considers the trademark descriptive.

In the United States, trademarks are granted for an initial period of 10 years and may be renewed for successive 10-year periods.

Patents

Patents protect the intellectual property rights of inventors. They provide a period of 20 years during which the inventor is granted exclusive rights to use the invention (whether directly or via licensing agreements). At the end of the patent exclusivity period, the invention is then in the public domain available for anyone to use.

There are three main requirements for a patent:

- The invention must be new. Inventions are only patentable if they are original ideas.

- The invention must be useful. It must actually work and accomplish some sort of task.

- The invention must be non-obvious. You could not, for example, obtain a patent for your idea to use a drinking cup to collect rainwater. This is an obvious solution. You might, however, be able to patent a specially designed cup that optimizes the amount of rainwater collected while minimizing evaporation.

In the technology field, patents have long been used to protect hardware devices and manufacturing processes. There is plenty of precedent on the side of inventors in those areas. Recent patents have also been issued covering software programs and similar mechanisms, but the jury's still out on whether these patents will hold up to the scrutiny of the courts.

One high-profile case involved Amazon.com's patent on the "One-Click Shopping" e-commerce methodology. Amazon.com claims that its patent grants the company exclusive rights to use this technique. Arguments against this claim revolve around the novelty and non-obviousness requirements of patent law.

Trade Secrets

Many companies have intellectual property that is absolutely critical to their business and would cause significant damage if it were disclosed to competitors and/or the public—in other words, *trade secrets*. We previously mentioned two examples of this type of information from popular culture—the secret formula for Coca-Cola and Kentucky Fried Chicken's "secret blend of herbs and spices." Other examples are plentiful—a manufacturing company may wish to keep secret a certain manufacturing process that only a few key employees fully understand, or a statistical analysis company might wish to safeguard an advanced model developed for in-house use.

Two of the previously discussed intellectual property tools—copyrights and patents—could be used to protect this type of information, but with two major disadvantages:

- Filing a copyright or patent application requires that you publicly disclose the details of your work or invention. This automatically removes the "secret" nature of your property and may harm your firm by removing the mystique surrounding a product or by allowing unscrupulous competitors to copy your property in violation of international intellectual property laws.

- Copyrights and patents both provide protection for a limited period of time. Once your legal protection expires, other firms are free to use your work at will (and they have all the details from the public disclosure you made during the application process!).

There actually isn't much of an official process regarding trade secrets—by their nature you don't register them with anyone. You simply must implement adequate controls within your organization to ensure that only authorized personnel who need to know the secrets have access to them in the course of their duties. You must also ensure that anyone who does have this type of access is bound by a nondisclosure agreement (NDA) or other legal document that prohibits them from sharing the information with others and provides penalties for violation of the agreement. It is important to ensure that the agreement lasts for the maximum period permitted by law.

Trade secret protection is one of the best ways to protect computer software. As discussed in the previous section, patent law does not provide adequate protection for computer software products. Copyright law only protects the actual text of the source code and doesn't prohibit others from rewriting your code in a different form and accomplishing the same objective. If you treat your source code as a trade secret, it keeps it out of the hands of your competitors in the first place. This is the technique used by large software development companies like Microsoft to protect their core base of intellectual property.

Economic Espionage Act of 1996

Trade secrets are very often the crown jewels of major corporations, and the United States government recognized the importance of protecting this type of intellectual property when Congress enacted the *Economic Espionage Act of 1996*. This law has two major provisions:

- Anyone found guilty of stealing trade secrets from a U.S. corporation with the intention of benefiting a foreign government or agent may be fined up to $500,000 and imprisoned for up to 15 years.

- Anyone found guilty of stealing trade secrets under other circumstances may be fined up to $250,000 and imprisoned for up to 10 years.

The terms of the Economic Espionage Act give true teeth to the intellectual property rights of trade secret owners. Enforcement of this law requires that companies take adequate steps to ensure that their trade secrets are well protected and not accidentally placed into the public domain.

Licensing

Security professionals should also be familiar with the legal issues surrounding software licensing agreements. There are three common types of license agreements in use today:

- *Contractual license agreements* utilize a written contract between the software vendor and the customer outlining the responsibilities of each. These agreements are commonly found for high-priced and/or highly specialized software packages.

- *Shrink-wrap license agreements* are written on the outside of the software packaging. They get their name because they commonly include a clause stating that you acknowledge agreement to the terms of the contract simply by breaking the shrink-wrap seal on the package.

- *Click-wrap license agreements* are becoming more commonplace than shrink-wrap agreements. In this type of agreement, the contract terms are either written on the software box or included in the software documentation. During the installation process, you are required to click a button indicating that you have read the terms of the agreement and agree to abide by them. This adds an active consent to the process, ensuring that the individual is aware of the agreement's existence prior to installation.

Uniform Computer Information Transactions Act

The *Uniform Computer Information Transactions Act (UCITA)* is a federal law designed for adoption by each of the 50 states to provide a common framework for the conduct of computer-related business transactions. UCITA contains provisions that address software licensing. The terms of the UCITA give legal backing to the previously questionable practices of shrink-wrap licensing and click-wrap licensing by giving them status as legally binding contracts. UCITA also requires that manufacturers provide software users with the option to reject the terms of the license agreement before completing the installation process and receive a full refund of the software's purchase price.

 Two important industry groups provide guidance and enforcement activities regarding software licensing. You can get more information from their websites. The Business Software Alliance (BSA) can be found at www.bsa.org, and SPA Anti-Piracy can be found at www.spa.org/piracy/default.asp.

Import/Export

The federal government recognizes that the very same computers and encryption technologies that drive the Internet and e-commerce also can be extremely powerful tools in the hands of a military force. For this reason, during the Cold War, the government developed a complex set of regulations governing the export of sensitive hardware and software products to other nations.

Until recently, it was very difficult to export high-powered computers outside of the United States, except to a select handful of allied nations. The controls on exporting encryption software were even more severe, rendering it virtually impossible to export any encryption technology outside of the country. Recent changes in federal policy have relaxed these restrictions and provided for more open commerce.

Computer Export Controls

Currently, U.S. firms may export high-performance computing systems to virtually any country without receiving prior approval from the government. There are exceptions to this rule for countries designated by the Department of Commerce as Tier 3 countries. This includes countries such as India, Pakistan, Afghanistan, and countries in the Middle East. The export of any computer that is capable of operating in excess of 190,000 MTOPS (million theoretical operations per second) must be preapproved by the Department of Commerce.

A complete list of countries and their corresponding computer export tiers may be found on the Department of Commerce's website at www.bxa.doc.gov/HPCs/ctpchart.htm.

The export of high-performance computers to any country currently on the Tier 4 list is prohibited. These countries include Cuba, Iran, Iraq, Libya, North Korea, Sudan, and Syria.

Encryption Export Controls

The Department of Commerce's Bureau of Industry and Security sets forth regulations on the export of encryption products outside of the United States. Under previous regulations, it was virtually impossible to export even relatively low-grade encryption technology outside of the United States. This placed U.S. software manufacturers at a great competitive disadvantage to foreign firms who faced no similar regulations. After a lengthy lobbying campaign by the software industry, the president directed the Commerce Department to revise its regulations to foster the growth of the American security software industry.

Current regulations now designate the categories of retail and mass market security software. The rules now permit firms to submit these products for review by the Commerce Department, but the review will take no longer than 30 days. After successful completion of this review, companies may freely export these products.

Privacy

The right to privacy has for years been a hotly contested issue in the United States. The main source of this contention is that the Constitution's Bill of Rights does not explicitly provide for a right to privacy. However, this right has been upheld by numerous courts and is vigorously pursued by organizations like the American Civil Liberties Union (ACLU).

Europeans have also long been concerned with their privacy. Indeed, countries like Switzerland are world-renowned for their ability to keep financial secrets. In the second half of this section, we'll examine how the new European Union data privacy laws impact companies and Internet users.

U.S. Privacy Law

Although there is no constitutional guarantee of privacy, there is a myriad of federal laws (many enacted in recent years) designed to protect the private information the government maintains about citizens as well as key portions of the private sector like financial, educational, and healthcare institutions. In this section, we'll examine a number of these federal laws.

Fourth Amendment

The basis for privacy rights is in the *Fourth Amendment* to the U.S. Constitution. It reads as follows:

"The right of the people to be secure in their persons, houses, papers, and effects, against unreasonable searches and seizures, shall not be violated, and no warrants shall issue, but upon probable cause, supported by oath or affirmation, and particularly describing the place to be searched, and the persons or things to be seized."

The direct interpretation of this amendment prohibits government agents from searching private property without a warrant and probable cause. The courts have expanded their interpretation of the Fourth Amendment to include protections against wiretapping and other invasions of privacy.

Privacy Act of 1974

The *Privacy Act of 1974* is perhaps the most significant piece of privacy legislation restricting the way the federal government may deal with private information about individual citizens. It severely limits the ability of federal government agencies to disclose private information to other persons or agencies without the prior written consent of the affected individual(s). It does provide for exceptions involving the Census, law enforcement, the National Archives, health and safety, and court orders.

The Privacy Act mandates that agencies only maintain records that are necessary for the conduct of their business and that they destroy those records when they are no longer needed for a legitimate function of government. It provides a formal procedure for individuals to gain access to records the government maintains about them and to request that incorrect records be amended.

Electronic Communications Privacy Act of 1986

The *Electronic Communications Privacy Act (ECPA)* makes it a crime to invade the electronic privacy of an individual. This act updated the Federal Wiretap Act to apply to the illegal interception of electronic (i.e., computer) communications or to the intentional, unauthorized access of electronically stored data. It prohibits the interception or disclosure of electronic communication and defines those situations in which disclosure is legal. It protects against the monitoring of e-mail and voicemail communications and prevents providers of those services from making unauthorized disclosures of their content.

One of the most notable provisions of the ECPA is the fact that it makes it illegal to monitor cellular telephone conversations. In fact, such monitoring is punishable by a fine of up to $500 and a prison term of up to five years.

Communications Assistance for Law Enforcement Act (CALEA) of 1994

The Communications Assistance for Law Enforcement Act (CALEA) of 1994 amended the Electronic Communications Privacy Act of 1986. CALEA requires all communications carriers to make wiretaps possible for law enforcement with an appropriate court order, regardless of the technology in use.

Economic and Protection of Proprietary Information Act of 1996

The Economic and Protection of Proprietary Information Act of 1996 extends the definition of property to include proprietary economic information so that the theft of this information can be considered industrial or corporate espionage. This changed the legal definition of theft so that it was no longer restricted by physical constraints.

Health Insurance Portability and Accountability Act of 1996

In 1996, Congress passed the *Health Insurance Portability and Accountability Act (HIPAA)*, which made numerous changes to the laws governing health insurance and health maintenance organizations (HMOs). Among the provisions of HIPAA are privacy regulations requiring strict security measures for hospitals, physicians, insurance companies, and other organizations that process or store private medical information about individuals.

The HIPAA privacy regulations are quite complex. You should be familiar with the broad intentions of the act, as described here. If you work in the healthcare industry, you should consider devoting time to an in-depth study of this law's provisions.

The HIPAA also clearly defines the rights of individuals who are the subject of medical records and requires organizations who maintain such records to disclose these rights in writing.

Children's Online Privacy Protection Act of 1998

In April 2000, provisions of the *Children's Online Privacy Protection Act (COPPA)* became the law of the land in the United States. COPPA makes a series of demands upon websites that cater to children or knowingly collect information from children:

- Websites must have a privacy notice that clearly states the types of information they collect and what it's used for, including whether any information is disclosed to third parties. The privacy notice must also include contact information for the operators of the site.

- Parents must be provided with the opportunity to review any information collected from their children and permanently delete it from the site's records.

- Parents must give verifiable consent to the collection of information about children under the age of 13 prior to any such collection. There are exceptions in the law that allow the site to collect minimal information solely for the purpose of obtaining such parental consent.

Gramm-Leach-Bliley Act of 1999

Until the *Gramm-Leach-Bliley Act (GLB)* became law in 1999, there were strict governmental barriers between financial institutions. Banks, insurance companies, and credit providers were severely limited in the services they could provide and the information they could share with each other. GLB somewhat relaxed the regulations concerning the services each organization could provide. When Congress passed this law, it realized that this increased latitude could have far-reaching privacy implications. Due to this concern, it included a number of limitations on the types of information that could be exchanged even among subsidiaries of the same corporation and required financial institutions to provide written privacy policies to all of their customers by July 1, 2001.

USA Patriot Act of 2001

Congress passed the *USA Patriot Act of 2001* in direct response to the 9/11 terrorist attacks. The Patriot Act greatly broadened the powers of law enforcement organizations and intelligence agencies across a number of areas, including the monitoring of electronic communications.

One of the major changes prompted by the Patriot Act revolves around the way government agencies obtain wiretapping authorizations. Previously, police could obtain warrants for only one circuit at a time, after proving that the circuit was used by someone subject to monitoring. Provisions of the Patriot Act allow authorities to obtain a blanket authorization for a person and then monitor all communications to or from that person under the single warrant.

Another major change is in the way the government deals with Internet service providers (ISPs). Under the terms of the Patriot Act, ISPs may voluntarily provide the government with a large range of information. The Patriot Act also allows the government to obtain detailed information on user activity through the use of a subpoena (as opposed to a wiretap).

Finally, the USA Patriot Act amends the Computer Fraud and Abuse Act (yes, another set of amendments!) to provide more severe penalties for criminal acts. The Patriot Act provides for jail terms of up to 20 years and once again expands the coverage of the CFAA.

Family Educational Rights and Privacy Act

The *Family Educational Rights and Privacy Act (FERPA)* is another specialized privacy bill that affects any educational institution that accepts any form of funding from the federal government (the vast majority of schools). It grants certain privacy rights to students over the age of 18 and the parents of minor students. Specific FERPA protections include the following:

- Parents/students have the right to inspect any educational records maintained by the institution on the student.

- Parents/students have the right to request correction of records they feel are erroneous and the right to include a statement in the records contesting anything that is not corrected.

- Schools may not release personal information from student records without written consent, except under certain circumstances.

Identity Theft and Assumption Deterrence Act

In 1998, the president signed the *Identity Theft and Assumption Deterrence Act* into law. In the past, the only legal victims of identity theft were the creditors who were defrauded. This act makes identity theft a crime against the person whose identity was stolen and provides severe criminal penalties (up to a 15-year prison term and/or a $250,000 fine) for anyone found guilty of violating this law.

European Union Privacy Law

On October 24, 1995, the European Union Parliament passed a sweeping directive outlining privacy measures that must be in place for protecting personal data processed by information systems. The directive went into effect three years later in October 1998. The full text of the agreement (document 95/46/EC) is available on the European Union's website (http://europa.eu.int/).

Real World Scenario

Privacy in the Workplace

As you've read in this chapter, the U.S. court system has long upheld the traditional right to privacy as an extension of basic constitutional rights. However, the courts have maintained that a key element of this right is that privacy should be guaranteed only when there is a "reasonable expectation of privacy." For example, if you mail a letter to someone in a sealed envelope, you may reasonably expect that it will be delivered without being read along the way—you have a reasonable expectation of privacy. On the other hand, if you send your message on a postcard, you do so with the awareness that one or more people might read your note before it arrives at the other end—you do not have a reasonable expectation of privacy.

Recent court rulings have found that employees do not have a reasonable expectation of privacy while using employer-owned communications equipment in the workplace. If you send a message using an employer's computer, Internet connection, telephone, or other communications device, your employer may monitor it as a routine business procedure.

That said, if you're planning to monitor the communications of your employees, you should take reasonable precautions to ensure that there is no implied expectation of privacy. Here are some common measures to consider:

- Clauses in employment contracts that state the employee has no expectation of privacy while using corporate equipment

- Similar written statements in corporate acceptable use and privacy policies

- Logon banners warning that all communications are subject to monitoring

- Warning labels on computers and telephones warning of monitoring

As with many of the issues discussed in this chapter, it's a good idea to consult with your legal counsel before undertaking any communications monitoring efforts.

The directive requires that all processing of personal data meet one of the following criteria:
- Consent
- Contract
- Legal obligation
- Vital interest of the data subject
- Balance between the interests of the data holder and the interests of data subject

The directive also outlines key rights of individuals about whom data is held and/or processed:
- Right to access the data
- Right to know the data's source

- Right to correct inaccurate data
- Right to withhold consent to process data in some situations
- Right of legal action should these rights be violated

American companies doing business in Europe may obtain protection under a treaty between the European Union and the United States that allows the Department of Commerce to certify businesses that comply with regulations and offer them "safe harbor" from prosecution.

In order to qualify for the safe harbor provision, U.S. companies conducting business in Europe must meet seven requirements for the processing of personal information:

Notice   They must inform individuals of what information they collect about them and how the information will be used.

Choice   They must allow individuals to opt out if the information will be used for any other purpose or shared with a third party. For information considered sensitive, an opt-in policy must be used.

Onward Transfer   Organizations may only share data with other organizations that comply with the safe harbor principles.

Access   Individuals must be granted access to any records kept containing their personal information.

Security   Proper mechanisms must be in place to protect data against loss, misuse, and unauthorized disclosure.

Data Integrity   Organizations must take steps to ensure the reliability of the information they maintain.

Enforcement   Organizations must make a dispute resolution process available to individuals and provide certifications to regulatory agencies that they comply with the safe harbor provisions.

For more information on the safe harbor protections available to American companies, visit the Department of Commerce's Safe Harbor website at www.export.gov/safeharbor/sh_overview.html.

Investigations

Every information security professional will, at one time or another, encounter a security incident that requires an investigation. In many cases, this investigation will be a brief, informal determination that the matter is not serious enough to warrant further action or the involvement of law enforcement authorities. However, in some cases, the threat posed or damage done will be severe enough to require a more formal inquiry. When this occurs, investigators must be careful to ensure that proper procedures are followed. Failure to abide by the correct procedures may violate the civil rights of those individual(s) being investigated and could result in a failed prosecution or even legal action against the investigator.

Evidence

In order to successfully prosecute a crime, the prosecuting attorneys must provide sufficient evidence to prove an individual's guilt beyond a reasonable doubt. In the following sections, we'll look at the requirements that evidence must meet before it is allowed in court, the various types of evidence that may be introduced, and the requirements for handling and documenting evidence.

Admissible Evidence

There are three basic requirements for evidence to be introduced into a court of law. To be considered *admissible evidence,* it must meet all three of these requirements, as determined by the judge, prior to being discussed in open court:

- The evidence must be *relevant* to determining a fact.
- The fact that the evidence seeks to determine must be *material* (i.e., related) to the case.
- The evidence must be *competent,* meaning that it must have been obtained legally. Evidence that results from an illegal search would be inadmissible because it is not competent.

Types of Evidence

There are four types of evidence that may be used in a court of law: real evidence, documentary evidence, testimonial evidence, and demonstrative evidence. Each has slightly different additional requirements for admissibility.

Real Evidence

Real evidence (also known as object evidence) consists of things that may actually be brought into a court of law. In common criminal proceedings, this may include items like a murder weapon, clothing, or other physical objects. In a computer crime case, real evidence might include seized computer equipment, such as a keyboard with fingerprints on it or a hard drive from a hacker's computer system. Depending upon the circumstances, real evidence may also be *conclusive evidence,* such as DNA, that is incontrovertible.

Documentary Evidence

Documentary evidence includes any written items brought into court to prove a fact at hand. This type of evidence must also be authenticated. For example, if an attorney wishes to introduce a computer log as evidence, they must bring a witness (e.g., the system administrator) into court to testify that the log was collected as a routine business practice and is indeed the actual log that the system collected.

There are two additional evidence rules that apply specifically to documentary evidence:

- The *best evidence rule* states that, when a document is used as evidence in a court proceeding, the original document must be introduced. Copies or descriptions of original evidence (known as *secondary evidence*) will not be accepted as evidence unless certain exceptions to the rule apply.

- The *parol evidence rule* states that, when an agreement between parties is put into written form, the written document is assumed to contain all of the terms of the agreement and no verbal agreements may modify the written agreement.

If documentary evidence meets the materiality, competency, and relevancy requirements and also complies with the best evidence and parol evidence rules, it may be admitted into court.

Chain of Evidence

Real evidence, like any type of evidence, must meet the relevancy, materiality, and competency requirements before being admitted into court. Additionally, real evidence must be authenticated. This may be done by a witness who can actually identify an object as unique (e.g., "That knife with my name on the handle is the one that the intruder took off the table in my house and stabbed me with").

In many cases, it is not possible for a witness to uniquely identify an object in court. In those cases, a *chain of evidence* (also known as a chain of custody) must be established. This involves everyone who handles evidence—including the police who originally collect it, the evidence technicians who process it, and the lawyers who use it in court. The location of the evidence must be fully documented from the moment it was collected to the moment it appears in court to ensure that it is indeed the same item. This requires thorough labeling of evidence and comprehensive logs noting who had access to the evidence at specific times and the reasons they required such access.

When evidence is labeled to preserve the chain of custody, the label should include the following types of information regarding the collection:

- General description of the evidence

- Time, date, and exact location of collection

- Name of the person collecting the evidence

- Relevant circumstances surrounding the collection

Each person who handles the evidence must sign the chain of custody log indicating the time that they took direct responsibility for the evidence and the time that they handed it off to the next person in the chain of custody. The chain must provide an unbroken sequence of events accounting for the evidence from the time it was collected until the time of the trial.

Testimonial Evidence

Testimonial evidence is, quite simply, evidence consisting of the testimony of a witness, either verbal testimony in court or written testimony in a recorded deposition. Witnesses must take an oath agreeing to tell the truth and they must have personal knowledge upon which their testimony is based. Furthermore, witnesses must remember the basis for their testimony (they may consult written notes or records to aid their memory). Witnesses can offer *direct evidence:* oral testimony that proves or disproves a claim based upon their own direct observation. The testimonial evidence of most witnesses must be strictly limited to direct evidence based upon the witness's factual observations. However, this does not apply if a witness has been accepted by the court as an expert in a certain field. In that case, the witness may offer an *expert opinion* based upon the other facts presented and their personal knowledge of the field.

Testimonial evidence must not be so-called *hearsay evidence.* That is, a witness may not testify as to what someone else told them outside of court. Computer log files that are not authenticated by a system administrator may also be considered hearsay evidence.

Investigation Process

When you initiate a computer security investigation, you should first assemble a team of competent analysts to assist with the investigation.

Calling In Law Enforcement

One of the first decisions that must be made in an investigation is whether law enforcement authorities should be called in. This is actually a relatively complicated decision that should involve senior management officials. There are many factors in favor of calling in the experts. For example, the FBI now maintains a National Computer Crime Squad that includes individuals with the following qualifications:

- Degrees in the computer sciences
- Prior work experience in industry and academic institutions
- Basic and advanced commercial training
- Knowledge of basic data and telecommunications networks
- Experience with Unix and other computer operating systems

On the other hand, there are also two major factors that may cause a company to shy away from calling in the authorities. First, the investigation will more than likely become public and may embarrass the company. Second, law enforcement authorities are bound to conduct an investigation that complies with the Fourth Amendment and other legal requirements that may not apply to a private investigation.

Search Warrants

Even the most casual viewer of American crime television is familiar with the question "Do you have a warrant?" The Fourth Amendment of the U.S. Constitution outlines the burden placed upon investigators to have a valid search warrant before conducting certain searches and the legal hurdle they must overcome to obtain a warrant:

"The right of the people to be secure in their persons, houses, papers and effects, against unreasonable searches and seizures, shall not be violated, and no warrants shall issue, but upon probable cause, supported by oath or affirmation, and particularly describing the place to be searched, and the persons or things to be seized."

This amendment contains several important provisions that guide the activities of law enforcement personnel:

- Investigators must obtain a warrant before searching a person's private belongings, assuming that there is a reasonable expectation of privacy. There are a number of documented exceptions to this requirement, such as when an individual consents to a search, the evidence of a crime is in plain view, or there is a life-threatening emergency necessitating the search.

- Warrants can be issued only based upon probable cause. There must be some type of evidence that a crime took place and that the search in question will yield evidence relating to that crime. The standard of "probable cause" required to get a warrant is much weaker than the standard of evidence required to secure a conviction. Most warrants are "sworn out" based solely upon the testimony of investigators.

- Warrants must be specific in their scope. The warrant must contain a detailed description of the legal bounds of the search and seizure.

If investigators fail to comply with even the smallest detail of these provisions, they may find their warrant invalidated and the results of the search deemed inadmissible. This leads to another one of those American colloquialisms: "He got off on a technicality."

Conducting the Investigation

If you elect not to call in law enforcement, you should still attempt to abide by the principles of a sound investigation to ensure the accuracy and fairness of your inquiry. It is important to remember a few key principles:

- Never conduct your investigation on an actual system that was compromised. Take the system offline, make a backup, and use the backup to investigate the incident.

- Never attempt to "hack back" and avenge a crime. You may inadvertently attack an innocent third party and find yourself liable for computer crime charges.

- If in doubt, call in expert assistance. If you don't wish to call in law enforcement, contact a private investigations firm with specific experience in the field of computer security investigations.

- Normally, it's best to begin the investigation process using informal interviewing techniques. These are used to gather facts and determine the substance of the case. When specific suspects are identified, they should be questioned using interrogation techniques. Again, this is an area best left untouched without specific legal advice.

Summary

Computer security necessarily entails a high degree of involvement from the legal community. In this chapter, you learned about a large number of laws that govern security issues such as computer crime, intellectual property, data privacy, and software licensing. You also learned about the procedures that must be followed when investigating an incident and collecting evidence that may later be admitted into a court of law during a civil or criminal trial.

Granted, computer security professionals can not be expected to understand the intricate details of all of the laws that cover computer security. However, the main objective of this chapter is to provide you with the foundations of that knowledge. The best legal skill that a CISSP candidate should have is ability to identify a legally questionable issue and know when to call in an attorney who specializes in computer/Internet law.

Exam Essentials

Understand the differences between criminal law, civil law, and administrative law. Criminal law protects society against acts that violate the basic principles we believe in. Violations of criminal law are prosecuted by federal and state governments. Civil law provides the framework for the transaction of business between people and organizations. Violations of civil law are brought to the court and argued by the two affected parties. Administrative law is used by government agencies to effectively carry out their day-to-day business.

Be able to explain the basic provisions of the major laws designed to protect society against computer crime. The Computer Fraud and Abuse Act (as amended) protects computers used by the government or in interstate commerce from a variety of abuses. The Computer Security Act outlines steps the government must take to protect its own systems from attack. The Government Information Security Reform Act further develops the federal government information security program.

Know the difference between copyrights, trademarks, patents, and trade secrets. Copyrights protect original works of authorship, such as books, articles, poems, and songs. Trademarks are names, slogans, and logos that identify a company, product, or service. Patents provide protection to the creators of new inventions. Trade secret law protects the operating secrets of a firm.

Be able to explain the basic provisions of the Digital Millennium Copyright Act of 1998. The Digital Millennium Copyright Act prohibits the circumvention of copy protection mechanisms placed in digital media and limits the liability of Internet service providers for the activities of their users.

Know the basic provisions of the Economic Espionage Act of 1996. The Economic Espionage Act provides penalties for individuals found guilty of the theft of trade secrets. Harsher penalties apply when the individual knows that the information will benefit a foreign government.

Understand the various types of software license agreements. Contractual license agreements are written agreements between a software vendor and user. Shrink-wrap agreements are written on software packaging and take effect when a user opens the package. Click-wrap agreements are included in a package but require the user to accept the terms during the software installation process.

Explain the impact of the Uniform Computer Information Transactions Act on software licensing. The Uniform Computer Information Transactions Act provides a framework for the enforcement of shrink-wrap and click-wrap agreements by federal and state governments.

Understand the restrictions placed upon export of high-performance hardware and encryption technology outside of the United States. No high-performance computers or encryption technology may be exported to Tier 4 countries. The export of hardware capable of operating in excess of 190,000 MTOPS to Tier 3 countries must be approved by the Department of Commerce. New rules permit the easy exporting of "mass market" encryption software.

Understand the major laws that govern privacy of personal information in both the United States and the European Union. The United States has a number of privacy laws that affect the government's use of information as well as the use of information by specific industries, like financial services companies and healthcare organizations, that handle sensitive information. The European Union has a more comprehensive directive on data privacy that regulates the use and exchange of personal information.

Know the basic requirements for evidence to be admissible in a court of law. To be admissible, evidence must be relevant to a fact at issue in the case, the fact must be material to the case, and the evidence must be competent, or legally collected.

Explain the various types of evidence that may be used in a criminal or civil trial. Real evidence consists of actual objects that may be brought into the courtroom. Documentary evidence consists of written documents that provide insight into the facts. Testimonial evidence consists of verbal or written statements made by witnesses.

Written Lab

Answer the following questions about law and investigations:

1. What are the key rights guaranteed to individuals under the European Union's directive on data privacy?

2. What are the three basic requirements that evidence must meet in order to be admissible in court?

3. What are some common steps that employers take to notify employees of system monitoring?

Review Questions

1. Which criminal law was the first to implement penalties for the creators of viruses, worms, and other types of malicious code that cause harm to computer system(s)?

   A. Computer Security Act

   B. National Infrastructure Protection Act

   C. Computer Fraud and Abuse Act

   D. Electronic Communications Privacy Act

2. Which law first required operators of federal interest computer systems to undergo periodic training in computer security issues?

   A. Computer Security Act

   B. National Infrastructure Protection Act

   C. Computer Fraud and Abuse Act

   D. Electronic Communications Privacy Act

3. What type of law does not require an act of Congress to implement at the federal level but, rather, is enacted by the executive branch in the form of regulations, policies, and procedures?

   A. Criminal law

   B. Common law

   C. Civil law

   D. Administrative law

4. Which federal government agency has responsibility for ensuring the security of government computer systems that are not used to process sensitive and/or classified information?

   A. National Security Agency

   B. Federal Bureau of Investigation

   C. National Institute of Standards and Technology

   D. Secret Service

5. What is the broadest category of computer systems protected by the Computer Fraud and Abuse Act, as amended?

   A. Government-owned systems

   B. Federal interest systems

   C. Systems used in interstate commerce

   D. Systems located in the United States

6. What law protects the right of citizens to privacy by placing restrictions on the authority granted to government agencies to search private residences and facilities?

   A. Privacy Act

   B. Fourth Amendment

   C. Second Amendment

   D. Gramm-Leach-Bliley Act

7. Matthew recently authored an innovative algorithm for solving a mathematical problem and he would like to share it with the world. However, prior to publishing the software code in a technical journal, he would like to obtain some sort of intellectual property protection. Which type of protection is best suited to his needs?

   A. Copyright

   B. Trademark

   C. Patent

   D. Trade Secret

8. Mary is the cofounder of Acme Widgets, a manufacturing firm. Together with her partner, Joe, she has developed a special oil that will dramatically improve the widget manufacturing process. To keep the formula secret, Mary and Joe plan to make large quantities of the oil by themselves in the plant after the other workers have left. They would like to protect this formula for as long as possible. What type of intellectual property protection best suits their needs?

   A. Copyright

   B. Trademark

   C. Patent

   D. Trade secret

9. Richard recently developed a great name for a new product that he plans to begin using immediately. He spoke with his attorney and filed the appropriate application to protect his product name but has not yet received a response from the government regarding his application. He would like to begin using the name immediately. What symbol should he use next to the name to indicate its protected status?

   A. ©

   B. ®

   C. ™

   D. †

10. What law prevents government agencies from disclosing personal information that an individual supplies to the government under protected circumstances?

    A. Privacy Act

    B. Electronic Communications Privacy Act

    C. Health Insurance Portability and Accountability Act

    D. Gramm-Leach-Bliley Act

11. What law formalizes many licensing arrangements used by the software industry and attempts to standardize their use from state to state?

    A. Computer Security Act

    B. Uniform Computer Information Transactions Act

    C. Digital Millennium Copyright Act

    D. Gramm-Leach-Bliley Act

12. The Children's Online Privacy Protection Act was designed to protect the privacy of children using the Internet. What is the minimum age a child must be before companies may collect personal identifying information from them without parental consent?

    A. 13

    B. 14

    C. 15

    D. 16

13. Which one of the following is not a requirement that Internet service providers must satisfy in order to gain protection under the "transitory activities" clause of the Digital Millennium Copyright Act?

    A. The service provider and the originator of the message must be located in different states.

    B. The transmission, routing, provision of connections, or copying must be carried out by an automated technical process without selection of material by the service provider.

    C. Any intermediate copies must not ordinarily be accessible to anyone other than anticipated recipients and must not be retained for longer than reasonably necessary.

    D. The transmission must be originated by a person other than the provider.

14. Which one of the following laws is not designed to protect the privacy rights of consumers and Internet users?

    A. Health Insurance Portability and Accountability Act

    B. Identity Theft Assumption and Deterrence Act

    C. USA Patriot Act

    D. Gramm-Leach-Bliley Act

15. Which one of the following types of licensing agreements is most well known because it does not require that the user take action to acknowledge that they have read the agreement prior to executing it?

    A. Standard license agreement

    B. Shrink-wrap agreement

    C. Click-wrap agreement

    D. Verbal agreement

16. What industry is most directly impacted by the provisions of the Gramm-Leach-Bliley Act?

    A. Healthcare

    B. Banking

    C. Law enforcement

    D. Defense contractors

17. What is the standard duration of patent protection in the United States?

    A. 14 years from the application date

    B. 14 years from the date the patent is granted

    C. 20 years from the application date

    D. 20 years from the date the patent is granted

18. Which one of the following is not a valid legal reason for processing information about an individual under the European Union's data privacy directive?

    A. Contract

    B. Legal obligation

    C. Marketing needs

    D. Consent

19. What type of evidence must be authenticated by a witness who can uniquely identify it or through a documented chain of custody?

    A. Documentary evidence

    B. Testimonial evidence

    C. Real evidence

    D. Hearsay evidence

20. What evidentiary principle states that a written contract is assumed to contain all of the terms of an agreement?

    A. Material evidence

    B. Best evidence

    C. Parol evidence

    D. Relevant evidence

Answers to Review Questions

1. C. The Computer Fraud and Abuse Act, as amended, provides criminal and civil penalties for those individuals convicted of using viruses, worms, Trojan horses, and other types of malicious code to cause damage to computer system(s).

2. A. The Computer Security Act requires mandatory periodic training for all persons involved in the management, use, or operation of federal computer systems that contain sensitive information.

3. D. Administrative laws do not require an act of the legislative branch to implement at the federal level. Administrative laws consist of the policies, procedures, and regulations promulgated by agencies of the executive branch of government. Although they do not require an act of Congress, these laws are subject to judicial review and must comply with criminal and civil laws enacted by the legislative branch.

4. C. The National Institute of Standards and Technology (NIST) is charged with the security management of all federal government computer systems that are not used to process sensitive national security information. The National Security Agency (part of the Department of Defense) is responsible for managing those systems that do process classified and/or sensitive information.

5. C. The original Computer Fraud and Abuse Act of 1984 covered only systems used by the government and financial institutions. The act was broadened in 1986 to include all federal interest systems. The Computer Abuse Amendments Act of 1994 further amended the CFAA to cover all systems that are used in interstate commerce, covering a large portion (but not all) of the computer systems in the United States.

6. B. The Fourth Amendment to the U.S. Constitution sets the "probable cause" standard that law enforcement officers must follow when conducting searches and/or seizures of private property. It also states that those officers must obtain a warrant before gaining involuntary access to such property.

7. A. Copyright law is the only type of intellectual property protection available to Matthew. It covers only the specific software code that Matthew used. It does not cover the process or ideas behind the software. Trademark protection is not appropriate for this type of situation. Patent protection does not apply to mathematical algorithms. Matthew can't seek trade secret protection because he plans to publish the algorithm in a public technical journal.

8. D. Mary and Joe should treat their oil formula as a trade secret. As long as they do not publicly disclose the formula, they can keep it a company secret indefinitely.

9. C. Richard's product name should be protected under trademark law. Until his registration is granted, he may use the symbol next to it to inform others that it is protected under trademark law. Once his application is approved, the name becomes a registered trademark and Richard may begin using the symbol.

10. A. The Privacy Act of 1974 limits the ways government agencies may use information that private citizens disclose to them under certain circumstances.

11. B. The Uniform Computer Information Transactions Act (UCITA) attempts to implement a standard framework of laws regarding computer transactions to be adopted by all states. One of the issues addressed by UCITA is the legality of various types of software license agreements.

12. A. The Children's Online Privacy Protection Act (COPPA) provides severe penalties for companies that collect information from young children without parental consent. COPPA states that this consent must be obtained from the parents of children under the age of 13 before any information is collected (other than basic information required to obtain that consent).

13. A. The Digital Millennium Copyright Act does not include any geographical location requirements for protection under the "transitory activities" exemption. The other options are three of the five mandatory requirements. The other two requirements are that the service provider must not determine the recipients of the material and the material must be transmitted with no modification to its content.

14. C. The USA Patriot Act was adopted in the wake of the 9/11 terrorist attacks. It broadens the powers of the government to monitor communications between private citizens and therefore actually weakens the privacy rights of consumers and Internet users. The other laws mentioned all contain provisions designed to enhance individual privacy rights.

15. B. Shrink-wrap license agreements become effective when the user opens a software package. Click-wrap agreements require the user to click a button during the installation process to accept the terms of the license agreement. Standard license agreements require that the user sign a written agreement prior to using the software. Verbal agreements are not normally used for software licensing but also require some active degree of participation by the software user.

16. B. The Gramm-Leach-Bliley Act provides, among other things, regulations regarding the way financial institutions may handle private information belonging to their customers.

17. C. United States patent law provides for an exclusivity period of 20 years beginning at the time the patent application is submitted to the Patent and Trademark Office.

18. C. Marketing needs are not a valid reason for processing personal information, as defined by the European Union privacy directive.

19. C. Real evidence must be either uniquely identified by a witness or authenticated through a documented chain of custody.

20. C. The parol evidence rule states that a written contract is assumed to contain all of the terms of an agreement and may not be modified by a verbal agreement.

Answers to Written Lab

Following are answers to the questions in this chapter's written lab:

1. Individuals have a right to access records kept about them and know the source of data included in those records. They also have the right to correct inaccurate records. Individuals have the right to withhold consent from data processors and have legal recourse if these rights are violated.

2. To be admissible, evidence must be reliable, competent, and material to the case.

3. Some common steps that employers take to notify employees of monitoring include clauses in employment contracts that state that the employee should have no expectation of privacy while using corporate equipment, similar written statements in corporate acceptable use and privacy policies, logon banners warning that all communications are subject to monitoring, and warning labels on computers and telephones warning of monitoring.

Chapter

18

Incidents and Ethics

THE CISSP EXAM TOPICS COVERED IN THIS CHAPTER INCLUDE:

✓ Major Categories of Computer Crime

✓ Incident Handling

✓ Ethics

In this chapter, we'll continue our discussion from Chapter 17 regarding the Law, Investigation, and Ethics domain of the Common Body of Knowledge (CBK) for the CISSP certification exam. This domain deals with topics and issues related to computer crime laws and regulations, investigative techniques used to determine if a computer crime has been committed and to collect evidence when appropriate, and ethics issues and code of conduct for the computer practitioner.

The first step in deciding how to respond to a computer attack is to know if and when an attack has taken place. You must know how to determine that an attack is occurring, or has occurred, before you can properly choose a course of action. Once you have determined that an incident has occurred, the next step is to conduct an investigation and collect evidence to find out what has happened and determine the extent of any damage that might have been done. You must be sure you conduct the investigation in accordance with local laws and practices.

Major Categories of Computer Crime

There are many ways to attack a computer system and many motivations to do so. Information system security practitioners generally put crimes against or involving computers into different categories. Simply put, a *computer crime* is a crime (or violation of a law or regulation) that involves a computer. The crime could be against the computer, or the computer could have been used in the actual commission of the crime. Each of the categories of computer crimes represents the purpose of an attack and its intended result.

Any individual who violates one or more of your security policies is considered to be an *attacker*. An attacker uses different techniques to achieve a specific goal. Understanding the goals helps to clarify the different types of attacks. Remember that crime is crime, and the motivations behind computer crime are no different than the motivations behind any other type of crime. The only real difference may be in the methods the attacker uses to strike.

Computer crimes are generally classified as one of the following types:

- Military and intelligence attacks
- Business attacks
- Financial attacks
- Terrorist attacks
- Grudge attacks
- "Fun" attacks

It is important to understand the differences among the categories of computer crime to best understand how to protect a system and react when an attack occurs. The type and amount of evidence left by an attacker is often dependent on their expertise. In the following sections, we'll discuss the different categories of computer crimes and what type of evidence you might find after an attack. The evidence can help you determine what the attacker did and what the intended target of the attack was. You may find that your system was only a link in the chain of network hops used to reach the real victim and possibly make the trail harder to follow back to the attacker.

Military and Intelligence Attacks

Military and intelligence attacks are launched primarily to obtain secret and restricted information from law enforcement or military and technological research sources. Disclosure of such information could compromise investigations, disrupt military planning, and threaten national security. Attacks to gather military information or other sensitive intelligence often precede other, more damaging attacks.

An attacker may be looking for the following kinds of information:

- Military descriptive information of any type, including deployment information, readiness information, and order of battle plans
- Secret intelligence gathered for military or law enforcement purposes
- Descriptions and storage locations of evidence obtained in a criminal investigation
- Any secret information that could be used in a later attack

Due to the sensitive nature of information collected and used by the military and intelligence agencies, their computer systems are often attractive targets for experienced attackers. To protect from more numerous and more sophisticated attackers, you will generally find more formal security policies in place on systems that house such information. As you learned in Chapter 5, "Security Management Concepts and Principles," data can be classified according to sensitivity and stored on systems that support the required level of security. It is common to find stringent perimeter security as well as internal controls to limit access to classified documents on military and intelligence agency systems.

You can be sure that serious attacks to acquire military or intelligence information are carried out by professionals. Professional attackers are generally very thorough in covering their tracks. There is usually very little evidence to collect after such an attack. Attackers in this category are the most successful and the most satisfied when no one is aware that an attack occurred.

Business Attacks

Business attacks focus on illegally obtaining an organization's confidential information. This could be information that is critical to the operation of the organization, such as a secret recipe, or information that could damage the organization's reputation if disclosed, such as personal information about its officers. The gathering of a competitor's confidential information, also called *industrial espionage,* is not a new phenomenon. Businesses have used illegal means to acquire competitive information for many years. The temptation to steal a competitor's secrets and the ease with which a savvy attacker can compromise some computer systems to extract files that contain valuable research or other confidential information can make this type of attack attractive.

The goal of business attacks is solely to extract confidential information. The use of the information gathered during the attack usually causes more damage than the attack itself. A business that has suffered an attack of this type can be put into a position from which it might not ever recover. It is up to you as the security professional to ensure that the systems that contain confidential data are secure. In addition, a policy must be developed that will handle such an intrusion should it occur. (For more information on security policies, see Chapter 6, "Asset Value, Policies, and Roles.")

Financial Attacks

Financial attacks are carried out to unlawfully obtain money or services. They are the type of computer crime you most commonly hear about. The goal of a financial attack could be to increase the balance in a bank account or to place "free" long-distance telephone calls. You have probably heard of individuals breaking into telephone company computers and placing free calls. This type of financial attack is called *phone phreaking*.

Shoplifting and burglary are both examples of financial attacks. You can usually tell the sophistication of the attacker by the dollar amount of the damages. Less-sophisticated attackers seek easier targets, but although the damages are usually minimal, they can add up over time.

Financial attacks launched by sophisticated attackers can result in substantial damages. Although phone phreaking causes the telephone company to lose the revenue of calls placed, serious financial attacks can result in losses amounting to millions of dollars. As with the attacks previously described, the ease with which you can detect an attack and track an attacker is largely dependent on the attacker's skill level.

Terrorist Attacks

Terrorist attacks are a reality in many different areas of our society. Our increasing reliance upon information systems makes them more and more attractive to terrorists. Such attacks differ from military and intelligence attacks. The purpose of a terrorist attack is to disrupt normal life, whereas a military or intelligence attack is designed to extract secret information. Intelligence gathering generally precedes any type of terrorist attack. The very systems that are victims of a terrorist attack were probably compromised in an earlier attack to collect intelligence. The more diligent you are in detecting attacks of any type, the better prepared you will be to intervene before more serious attacks occur.

Possible targets of a computer terrorist attack could be systems that regulate power plants or control telecommunications or power distribution. Many such control and regulatory systems are computerized and vulnerable to terrorist action. In fact, the possibility exists of a simultaneous physical and computerized terrorist attack. Our ability to respond to such an attack would be greatly diminished if the physical attack were simultaneously launched with a computer attack designed to knock out power and communications.

Most large power and communications companies have dedicated a security staff to ensure the security of their systems, but many smaller businesses that have systems connected to the Internet are more vulnerable to attacks. You must diligently monitor your systems to identify any attacks and then respond swiftly when an attack is discovered.

Grudge Attacks

Grudge attacks are attacks that are carried out to damage an organization or a person. The damage could be in the loss of information or information processing capabilities or harm to the organization or a person's reputation. The motivation behind a grudge attack is usually a feeling of resentment, and the attacker could be a current or former employee or someone who wishes ill will upon an organization. The attacker is disgruntled with the victim and takes out their frustration in the form of a grudge attack.

An employee who has recently been fired is a prime example of a person who might carry out a grudge attack to "get back" at the organization. Another example is a person who has been rejected in a personal relationship with another employee. The person who has been rejected might launch an attack to destroy data on the victim's system.

Your security policy should address the potential of attacks by disgruntled employees. For example, as soon as an employee is terminated, all system access for that employee should be terminated. This action reduces the likelihood of a grudge attack and removes unused access accounts that could be used in future attacks.

Although most grudge attackers are just disgruntled people with limited hacking and cracking abilities, some possess the skills to cause substantial damage. An unhappy cracker can be a handful for security professionals. Take extreme care when a person with known cracking ability leaves your company. At the least, you should perform a vulnerability assessment of all systems the person could access. You may be surprised to find one or more "back doors" left in the system. But even in the absence of any back doors, a former employee who is familiar with the technical architecture of the organization may know how to exploit its weaknesses.

Grudge attacks can be devastating if allowed to occur unchecked. Diligent monitoring and assessing systems for vulnerabilities is the best protection for most grudge attacks.

"Fun" Attacks

Fun attacks are the attacks that crackers with few true skills launch. Attackers who lack the ability to devise their own attacks will often download programs that do their work for them. These attackers are often called "script kiddies" because they only run other people's programs, or scripts, to launch an attack.

The main motivation behind fun attacks is the thrill of getting into a system. If you are the victim of a fun attack, the most common fate you will suffer is a service interruption. Although an attacker of this type may destroy data, the main motivation is to compromise a system and perhaps use it to launch an attack against another victim.

Evidence

Chapter 17 included a general coverage of the topic of evidence. Remember that the term *evidence* refers to any hardware, software, or data that you can use to prove the identity and actions of an attacker. Make sure you understand the importance of properly handling any and all evidence you collect after an attack. You should realize that most computer evidence is intangible, meaning it is electronic and magnetically stored information that is vulnerable to erasure, corruption, and other forms of damage.

Your ability to recover damages in a court of law may depend solely on your diligence during the evidence collection process. In fact, your ability to determine the extent of an attack depends on your evidence collecting abilities. Once an attack has been identified, you should start the evidence collection process. Always assume an attack will result in a legal battle. It is far easier to take evidence collection seriously from the beginning than to later realize an attack was more severe than first thought and then try to go back and do it right. Following standard evidence collection procedures also ensures that you conduct your investigation in an orderly, scientific manner.

Most attacks leave evidence of some kind. However, professional attackers may leave evidence that is so subtle that it is difficult or impossible to find. Another problem with evidence is that it is often time sensitive. Your logs probably roll over periodically and old information is lost. Do you know the frequency of your log purge routines? Some attacks leave traces in memory. The bulk of the evidence will be lost when you remove power from the system. Each step you take as you collect evidence should be deliberate and well documented.

You must know what your system baseline looks like and how it operates in a normal mode. Without this knowledge, you will be hard-pressed to recognize an attack or to know where to search for valuable evidence. Experienced security professionals learn how their systems operate on a daily basis and are comfortable with the regular operations of the system. The more you know your systems, the more an unusual event stands out.

Incident Handling

When an incident occurs, you must handle it in a manner that is outlined in your security policy and consistent with local laws and regulations. The first step in handling an incident properly is recognizing when one occurs. Even before recognition, you need to clearly understand what an incident is. Your security policy should define recognized incidents, but the general definition of an *incident* is a violation or the threat of a violation of your security policy.

The most common reason incidents are not reported is that they are never identified. You could have many security policy violations occurring each day, but if you don't have a way of identifying them, you will never know. Therefore, your security policy should identify and list all possible violations and ways to detect them. It's also important to update your security policy as new types of violations and attacks emerge.

What you do when you find that an incident has occurred depends on the type of incident and scope of damage. Law dictates that some incidents must be reported, such as those that impact government or federal interest computers (a federal interest computer is one that is used by financial institutions and by infrastructure systems such as water and power systems) or certain financial transactions, regardless of the amount of damage.

Next, we'll look at some of the different types of incidents and typical responses.

Common Types of Incidents

We discussed the different types of attacks in Chapter 2. An incident occurs when an attack, or other violation of your security policy, is carried out against your system. There are many ways to classify incidents; here is a general list of categories:

- Scanning
- Compromises
- Malicious code
- Denial of service

These four areas are the basic entry points for attackers to impact a system. You must focus on each of these areas to create an effective monitoring strategy that detects system incidents. Each incident area has representative signatures that can tip off an alert security administrator that an incident has occurred. Make sure you know your operating system environment and where to look for the telltale signs of each type of incident.

Scanning

Scanning attacks are incidents that usually indicate that another attack is possible. Attackers will gather as much information about your system as possible before launching a directed attack. Look for any unusual activity on any port or from any single address. A high volume of Simple Network Management Protocol (SNMP) packets can point to a systematic scan of your system.

Remember that simply scanning your system is not illegal. It is similar to "casing" a neighborhood prior to a burglary. It can indicate that illegal activity will follow, so it is a good idea to treat scans as incidents and to collect evidence of scanning activity. You may find that the evidence you collect at the time the system is scanned could be the link you need later to find the party responsible for a later attack.

Because scanning is such a common occurrence, you definitely want to automate evidence collection. Set up your firewall to log the SNMP traffic and archive your log files. The logs can become relatively large, but that is the price you pay for retained evidence.

Compromise

For a system that contains sensitive information, a compromise could be the most serious incident. A system *compromise* is any unauthorized access to the system or information the system stores. A compromise could originate inside or outside the organization. To make matters worse, a compromise could come from a valid user. An unauthorized use of a valid user ID is just as much of a compromise incident as an experienced cracker breaking in from the outside.

System compromises can be very difficult to detect. Most often, the data custodian notices something unusual about the data. It could be missing, altered, or moved; the time stamps could be different; or something else is just not right. The more you know about the normal operation of your system, the better prepared you will be to detect abnormal system behavior.

Malicious Code

When *malicious code* is mentioned, you probably think of viruses. Although a virus is a common type of malicious code, it is only one type of several. (In Chapter 4, "Communications Security and Countermeasures," we discussed different types of malicious code.) Detection of this type of a malicious code incident comes from either an end user reporting behavior caused by the malicious code or an automated alert reporting that scanned code containing a malicious component has been found.

The most effective way to protect your system from malicious code is to implement code scanners and keep the signature database up-to-date. In addition, your security policy should address the introduction of outside code. Be specific as to what code you will allow end users to install.

Denial of Service

The final type of incident is a *denial of service (DoS)*. This type of incident is often the easiest to detect. A user or automated tool reports that one or more services (or the entire machine) is unavailable. Although they're simple to detect, avoidance is a far better course of action. It is theoretically possible to dynamically alter firewall rules to reject DoS network traffic, but in recent years the sophistication and complexity of DoS attacks make them extremely difficult to defend against. Because there are so many variations of the DoS attack, implementing this strategy is a nontrivial task.

Response Teams

Many organizations now have a dedicated team responsible for investigating any computer security incidents that take place. These teams are commonly known as Computer Incident Response Teams (CIRTs) or Computer Security Incident Response Teams (CSIRTs). When an incident occurs, the response team has four primary responsibilities:

- Determine the amount and scope of damage caused by the incident
- Determine whether any confidential information was compromised during the incident
- Implement any necessary recovery procedures to restore security and recover from incident-related damages
- Supervise the implementation of any additional security measures necessary to improve security and prevent recurrence of the incident

As part of these duties, the team should facilitate a *postmortem review* of the incident within a week of the occurrence to ensure that key players in the incident share their knowledge and develop best practices to assist in future incident response efforts.

Real World Scenario

The Gibson Research Denial-of-Service Attacks: Fun or Grudge?

Steve Gibson is a well-known software developer and personality in the IT industry whose high visibility derives not only from highly regarded products associated with his company, Gibson Research, but also from his many years as a vocal and outspoken columnist for *Computer World* magazine. In recent years, he has become quite active in the field of computer security, and his site offers free vulnerability scanning services and a variety of patches and fixes for operating system vulnerabilities. He operates a website at http://grc.com that has been the subject of numerous well-documented denial of service attacks. It's interesting to speculate whether such attacks are motivated by grudges (that is, by those who seek to advance their reputations by breaking into an obvious and presumably well-defended point of attack) or by fun (that is, by those with excess time on their hands who might seek to prove themselves against a worthy adversary without necessarily expecting any gain other than notoriety from their actions).

Gibson's website has in fact been subject to two well-documented denial of service attacks that you can read about in detail on his site:

- "Distributed Reflection Denial of Service," February 22, 2002, http://grc.com/dos/drdos.htm

- "The Strange Tale of the Denial of Service Attacks Against GRC.COM," last updated March 5, 2002, http://grc.com/dos/grcdos.htm

Although his subsequent anonymous discussions with one of the perpetrators involved seem to indicate that the motive for some of these attacks was fun rather than business damage or acting on a grudge, these reports are fascinating because of the excellent model they provide for incident handling and reporting.

These documents contain a brief synopsis of the symptoms and chronology of the attacks that occurred, along with short- and long-term fixes and changes enacted to prevent recurrences. They also stress the critical importance of communication with service providers whose infrastructures may be involved in attacks as they're underway. What's extremely telling about Gibson's report on the denial of service attacks is that he experienced 17 hours of downtime because he was unable to establish contact with a knowledgeable, competent engineer at his service provider who could help define the right kinds of traffic filters to stymie the floods of traffic that characterize denial of service attacks.

Gibson's analysis also indicates his thoroughness in analyzing the sources of the distributed denial of service attacks and in documenting what he calls "an exact profile of the malicious traffic being generated during these attacks." This information permitted his ISP to define a set of filters that blocked further such traffic from transiting the final T1 links from Gibson's Internet service provider to his servers. As his experience proves so conclusively, recognizing, analyzing, and characterizing attacks is absolutely essential to defining filters or other countermeasures that can block or defeat them.

Abnormal and Suspicious Activity

The key to identifying incidents is to identify any abnormal or suspicious activity. Hopefully, any suspicious activity will also be abnormal. The only way to identify abnormal behavior is to know what normal behavior looks like. Every system is different. Although you can detect many attacks by their characteristic signatures, experienced attackers know how to "fly under the radar." You must be very aware of how your system operates normally. *Abnormal or suspicious activity* is any system activity that does not normally occur on your system.

An attacker with a high level of skills generally has little obvious impact on your system. The impact will be there, but it might take substantial skill to detect it. It is not uncommon for experienced attackers to replace common operating system monitoring utilities with copies that do not report system activity correctly. Even though you may suspect that an incident is in progress and you investigate, you may see no unusual activity. In this case, the activity exists but has been hidden from the casual administrator.

Always use multiple sources of data when investigating an incident. Be suspicious of anything that does not make sense. Ensure that you can clearly explain any activity you see is not normal for your system. If it just does not "feel" right, it could be the only clue you have to successfully intervene in an ongoing incident.

Confiscating Equipment, Software, and Data

Once you determine that an incident has occurred, the next step is to choose a course of action. Your security policy should specify steps to take for various types of incidents. Always proceed with the assumption that an incident will end up in a court of law. Treat any evidence you collect as if it must pass admissibility standards. Once you taint evidence, there is no going back. You must ensure that the chain of evidence is maintained.

It is common to confiscate equipment, software, or data to perform a proper investigation. The manner in which the evidence is confiscated is important. Confiscation of evidence must be carried out in a proper fashion. There are three basic alternatives.

First, the person who owns the evidence could *voluntarily surrender* it. This method is generally only appropriate when the attacker is not the owner. Few guilty parties willingly surrender evidence they know will incriminate them. Less-experienced attackers may believe they have successfully covered their tracks and voluntarily surrender important evidence. A good forensic investigator can extract much "covered up" information from a computer. In most cases, asking for evidence from a suspected attacker just alerts the suspect that you are close to taking legal action.

Second, you could get a court to issue a *subpoena*, or court order, that compels an individual or organization to surrender evidence and have the subpoena served by law enforcement. Again, this course of action provides sufficient notice for someone to alter the evidence and render it useless in court.

The last option is a *search warrant*. This option should be used only when you must have access to evidence without tipping off the evidence's owner or other personnel. You must have a strong suspicion with credible reasoning to convince a judge to pursue this course of action.

The three alternatives apply to confiscating equipment both inside and outside an organization, but there is another step you can take to ensure that the confiscation of equipment that belongs to your organization is carried out properly. It is becoming more common to have all new employees sign an agreement that provides consent to search and seize any necessary evidence during an investigation. In this manner, consent is provided as a term of the employment agreement. This makes confiscation much easier and reduces the chances of a loss of evidence while waiting for legal permission to seize it. Make sure your security policy addresses this important topic.

Incident Data Integrity and Retention

No matter how persuasive evidence may be, it can be thrown out of court if you change it during the evidence collection process. Make sure you can prove that you maintained the integrity of all evidence. (Chapter 17, "Law and Investigations," includes more information on evidence rules.) But what about the integrity of data before it is collected?

You may not detect all incidents as they are happening. Sometimes an investigation reveals that there were previous incidents that went undetected. It is discouraging to follow a trail of evidence and find that a key log file that could point back to an attacker has been purged. Carefully consider the fate of log files or other possible evidence locations. A simple archiving policy can help ensure that key evidence is available upon demand no matter how long ago the incident occurred.

Because many log files can contain valuable evidence, attackers often attempt to sanitize them after a successful attack. Take steps to protect the integrity of log files and to deter their modification. One technique is to implement remote logging. Although not a perfect solution, it does provide some protection from post-incident log file cleansing.

Another important forensic technique is to preserve the original evidence. Remember that the very conduct of your investigation may alter the evidence you are evaluating. Therefore, it's always best to work with a copy of the actual evidence whenever possible. For example, when conducting an investigation into the contents of a hard drive, make an image of that drive, seal the original drive in an evidence bag, and then use the disk image for your investigation.

As with every aspect of security planning, there is no single solution. Get familiar with your system and take the steps that make the most sense for your organization to protect it.

Reporting Incidents

When should you report an incident? To whom should you report it? These questions are often difficult to answer. Your security policy should contain guidelines on answering both questions. There is a fundamental problem with reporting incidents. If you report every incident, you run the very real risk of being viewed as a noisemaker. When you have a serious incident, you may be ignored. Also, reporting an unimportant incident could give the impression that your organization is more vulnerable than is the case. This can have a serious detrimental effect for organizations that must maintain strict security. For example, hearing about daily incidents from your bank would probably not instill additional confidence in their security practices.

On the other hand, escalation and legal action become more difficult if you do not report an incident soon after discovery. If you delay notifying authorities of a serious incident, you will probably have to answer questions about your motivation for delaying. Even an innocent person could look as if they were trying to hide something by not reporting an incident in a timely manner.

As with most security topics, the answer is not an easy one. In fact, you are compelled by law or regulation to report some incidents. If your organization is regulated by a government authority and the incident caused your organization to deviate from any regulation, you must report the incident. Make sure you know what incidents you must report. For example, any organization that stores personal health information must report any incident in which disclosure of such information occurred.

Before you encounter an incident, it is very wise to establish a relationship with your corporate legal personnel and the appropriate law enforcement agencies. Find out who the appropriate law enforcement contacts are for your organization and talk with them. When the time comes to report an incident, your efforts at establishing a prior working relationship will pay off. You will spend far less time in introductions and explanations if you already know the person with whom you are talking.

Once you determine to report an incident, make sure you have as much of the following information as possible:

- What is the nature of the incident, how was it initiated, and by whom?
- When did the incident occur? (Be as precise as possible with dates and times.)
- Where did the incident occur?
- If known, what tools did the attacker use?
- What was the damage resulting from the incident?

You may be asked to provide additional information. Be prepared to provide it in as timely a manner as possible. You may also be asked to quarantine your system.

As with any security action you take, keep a log of all communication and make copies of any documents you provide as you report an incident.

Ethics

Security professionals with substantial responsibilities are held to a high standard of conduct. The rules that govern personal conduct are collectively known as rules of *ethics*. Several organizations have recognized the need for standard ethics rules, or codes, and have devised guidelines for ethical behavior.

We present two codes of ethics in the following sections. These rules are not laws. They are minimum standards for professional behavior. They should provide you with a basis for sound, ethical judgment. Any security professional should be expected to abide by these guidelines regardless of their area of specialty. Make sure you understand and agree with the codes of ethics outlined in the following sections.

(ISC)² Code of Ethics

The governing body that administers the CISSP certification is the International Information Systems Security Certification Consortium (ISC)². The (ISC)² Code of Ethics was developed to provide the basis for CISSP behavior. It is a simple code with a preamble and four canons. Here is a short summary of the major concepts of the Code of Ethics.

All CISSP candidates should be familiar with the entire (ISC)² Code of Ethics because they have to sign an agreement that they will adhere to this code. We won't cover the code in depth, but you can find further details about the (ISC)²'s Code of Ethics at www.isc2.org. You need to visit this site and read the entire code.

Code of Ethics Preamble:

- Safety of the commonwealth, duty to our principals, and to each other requires that we adhere, and be seen to adhere, to the highest ethical standards of behavior.
- Therefore, strict adherence to this code is a condition of certification.

Code of Ethics Canons:

Protect society, the commonwealth, and the infrastructure.   Security professionals have great social responsibility. We are charged with the burden of ensuring that our actions benefit the common good.

Act honorably, honestly, justly, responsibly, and legally.   Integrity is essential to the conduct of our duties. We cannot carry out our duties effectively if others within our organization, the security community, or the general public have doubts about the accuracy of the guidance we provide or the motives behind our actions.

Provide diligent and competent service to principals.   Although we have responsibilities to society as a whole, we also have specific responsibilities to those who have hired us to protect their infrastructure. We must ensure that we are in a position to provide unbiased, competent service to our organization.

Advance and protect the profession.   Our chosen profession changes on a continuous basis. As security professionals, we must ensure that our knowledge remains current and that we contribute our own knowledge to the community's common body of knowledge.

Ethics and the Internet

In January 1989, the Internet Advisory Board (IAB) issued a statement of policy concerning the proper use of the Internet. The contents of this statement are valid even today. It is important that you know the basic contents of the document, titled "Ethics and the Internet," Request for Comment (RFC) 1087, because most codes of ethics can trace their roots back to this document.

The statement is a brief list of practices considered unethical. Where a code of ethics states what you should do, this document outlines what you should not do. RFC 1087 states that any activity with the following purposes is unacceptable and unethical:

- Seeks to gain unauthorized access to the resources of the Internet
- Disrupts the intended use of the Internet
- Wastes resources (people, capacity, computer) through such actions
- Destroys the integrity of computer-based information
- Compromises the privacy of users

Ten Commandments of Computer Ethics

The Computer Ethics Institute created its own code of ethics. The Ten Commandments of Computer Ethics are as follows:

1. Thou shalt not use a computer to harm other people.

2. Thou shalt not interfere with other people's computer work.

3. Thou shalt not snoop around in other people's computer files.

4. Thou shalt not use a computer to steal.

5. Thou shalt not use a computer to bear false witness.

6. Thou shalt not copy proprietary software for which you have not paid.

7. Thou shalt not use other people's computer resources without authorization or proper compensation.

8. Thou shalt not appropriate other people's intellectual output.

9. Thou shalt think about the social consequences of the program you are writing or the system you are designing.

10. Thou shalt always use a computer in ways that ensure consideration and respect for your fellow humans.

There are many ethical and moral codes of IT behavior to choose from. Another system you should consider is the Generally Accepted Systems Security Principles (GASSP). The full text of the GASSP system is found at: http://www.auerbach-publications.com/dynamic_data/2334_1221_gassp.pdf.

Summary

Computer crimes are grouped into several major categories, and the crimes in each category share common motivations and desired results. Understanding what an attacker is after can help in properly securing a system.

For example, military and intelligence attacks are launched to acquire secret information that could not be obtained legally. Business attacks are similar except that they target civilian systems. Other types of attacks include financial attacks (phone phreaking is an example of a financial attack) and terrorist attacks (which, in the context of computer crimes, are attacks designed to disrupt normal life). Finally, there are grudge attacks, the purpose of which is to cause damage by destroying data or using information to embarrass an organization or person, and fun attacks, launched by inexperienced crackers to compromise or disable a system. Although generally not sophisticated, fun attacks can be annoying and costly.

An incident is a violation or the threat of a violation of your security policy. When an incident is suspected, you should immediately begin an investigation and collect as much evidence as possible because, if you decide to report the incident, you must have enough admissible evidence to support your claims.

The set of rules that govern your personal behavior is called a code of ethics. There are several codes of ethics, from general to specific in nature, that security professionals can use to guide them. The (ISC)² makes the acceptance of its code of ethics a requirement for certification.

Exam Essentials

Know the definition of computer crime.   Computer crime is a crime (or violation of a law or regulation) that is directed against, or directly involves, a computer.

Be able to list and explain the six categories of computer crimes.   Computer crimes are grouped into six categories: military and intelligence attack, business attack, financial attack, terrorist attack, grudge attack, and fun attack. Be able to explain the motive of each type of attack.

Know the importance of collecting evidence.   As soon you discover an incident, you must begin to collect evidence and as much information about the incident as possible. The evidence can be used in a subsequent legal action or in finding the identity of the attacker. Evidence can also assist you in determining the extent of damage.

Understand that an incident is any violation, or threat of a violation, of your security policy. Incidents should be defined in your security policy. Even though specific incidents may not be outlined, the existence of the policy sets the standard for the use of your system. Any departure from the accepted use of your system is defined as an incident.

Be able to list the four common types of incidents and know the telltale signs of each.   An incident occurs when an attack or other violation of your security policy is carried out against your system. Incidents can be grouped into four categories: scanning, compromises, malicious code, and denial of service. Be able to explain what each type of incident involves and what signs to look for.

Know the importance of identifying abnormal and suspicious activity.   Attacks will generate some activity that is not normal. Recognizing abnormal and suspicious activity is the first step toward detecting incidents.

Know how to investigate intrusions and how to gather sufficient information from the equipment, software, and data.   You must have possession of equipment, software, or data to analyze it and use it as evidence. You must acquire the evidence without modifying it or allowing anyone else to modify it.

Know the three basic alternatives for confiscating evidence and when each one is appropriate. First, the person who owns the evidence could voluntarily surrender it. Second, a subpoena could be used to compel the subject to surrender the evidence. Third, a search warrant is most useful when you need to confiscate evidence without giving the subject an opportunity to alter it.

Know the importance of retaining incident data.   Because you will discover some incidents after they have occurred, you will lose valuable evidence unless you ensure that critical log files are retained for a reasonable period of time. You can retain log files and system status information either in place or in archives.

Be familiar with how to report an incident.   The first step is to establish a working relationship with the corporate and law enforcement personnel with whom you will work to resolve an incident. When you do have a need to report an incident, gather as much descriptive information as possible and make your report in a timely manner.

Understand the importance of ethics to security personnel.   Security practitioners are granted a very high level of authority and responsibility to execute their job functions. The potential for abuse exists, and without a strict code of personal behavior, security practitioners could be regarded as having unchecked power. Adherence to a code of ethics helps ensure that such power is not abused.

Know the (ISC)² Code of Ethics and RFC 1087, "Ethics and the Internet."   All CISSP candidates should be familiar with the entire (ISC)² Code of Ethics because they have to sign an agreement that they will adhere to it. In addition, be familiar with the basic statements of RFC 1087.

Review Questions

1. What is a computer crime?

    A. Any attack specifically listed in your security policy

    B. Any illegal attack that compromises a protected computer

    C. Any violation of a law or regulation that involves a computer

    D. Failure to practice due diligence in computer security

2. What is the main purpose of a military and intelligence attack?

    A. To attack the availability of military systems

    B. To obtain secret and restricted information from military or law enforcement sources

    C. To utilize military or intelligence agency systems to attack other nonmilitary sites

3. What type of attack targets trade secret information stored on a civilian organization's system?

    A. Business attack

    B. Denial of service attack

    C. Financial attack

    D. Military and intelligence attack

4. What goal is not a purpose of a financial attack?

    A. Access services you have not purchased

    B. Disclose confidential personal employee information

    C. Transfer funds from an unapproved source into your account

5. What is one possible goal of a terrorist attack?

    A. Alter sensitive trade secret documents

    B. Damage the ability to communicate and respond to a physical attack

    C. Steal unclassified information

    D. Transfer funds to other countries

6. Which of the following would not be a primary goal of a grudge attack?

    A. Disclose embarrassing personal information

    B. Launch a virus on an organization's system

    C. Send inappropriate e-mail with a spoofed origination address of the victim organization

    D. Use automated tools to scan the organization's systems for vulnerable ports

7. What are the primary reasons attackers engage in "fun" attacks? (Choose all that apply.)

   A. Bragging rights

   B. Money from the sale of stolen documents

   C. Pride of conquering a secure system

   D. Retaliation against a person or organization

8. What is the most important rule to follow when collecting evidence?

   A. Do not turn off a computer until you photograph the screen.

   B. List all people present while collecting evidence.

   C. Never modify evidence during the collection process.

   D. Transfer all equipment to a secure storage location.

9. What would be a valid argument for not immediately removing power from a machine when an incident is discovered?

   A. All of the damage has been done. Turning the machine off would not stop additional damage.

   B. There is no other system that can replace this one if it is turned off.

   C. Too many users are logged in and using the system.

   D. Valuable evidence in memory will be lost.

10. What is the reason many incidents are never reported?

   A. It involves too much paperwork.

   B. Reporting too many incidents could hurt an organization's reputation.

   C. The incident is never discovered.

   D. Too much time has passed and the evidence is gone.

11. What is an incident?

   A. Any active attack that causes damage to your system

   B. Any violation of a code of ethics

   C. Any crime (or violation of a law or regulation) that involves a computer

   D. Any violation of your security policy

12. If port scanning does no damage to a system, why is it generally considered an incident?

   A. All port scans indicate adversarial behavior.

   B. Port scans can precede attacks that cause damage and can indicate a future attack.

   C. Scanning a port damages the port.

13. What type of incident is characterized by obtaining an increased level of privilege?

   A. Compromise

   B. Denial of service

   C. Malicious code

   D. Scanning

14. What is the best way to recognize abnormal and suspicious behavior on your system?

   A. Be aware of the newest attacks.

   B. Configure your IDS to detect and report all abnormal traffic.

   C. Know what your normal system activity looks like.

   D. Study the activity signatures of the main types of attacks.

15. If you need to confiscate a PC from a suspected attacker who does not work for your organization, what legal avenue should you pursue?

   A. Consent agreement signed by employees

   B. Search warrant

   C. Subpoena

   D. Voluntary consent

16. Why should you avoid deleting log files on a daily basis?

   A. An incident may not be discovered for several days and valuable evidence could be lost.

   B. Disk space is cheap and log files are used frequently.

   C. Log files are protected and cannot be altered.

   D. Any information in a log file is useless after it is several hours old.

17. Which of the following conditions indicate that you must report an incident? (Choose all that apply.)

   A. Confidential information protected by government regulation was possibly disclosed.

   B. Damages exceeded $1,500.

   C. The incident has occurred before.

   D. The incident resulted in a violation of a law.

18. What are ethics?

   A. Mandatory actions required to fulfill job requirements

   B. Professional standards of regulations

   C. Regulations set forth by a professional organization

   D. Rules of personal behavior

19. According to the (ISC)² Code of Ethics, how are CISSPs expected to act?

   A. Honestly, diligently, responsibly, and legally

   B. Honorably, honestly, justly, responsibly, and legally

   C. Upholding the security policy and protecting the organization

   D. Trustworthy, loyally, friendly, courteously

20. Which of the following actions are considered unacceptable and unethical according to RFC 1087, "Ethics and the Internet?"

   A. Actions that compromise the privacy of classified information

   B. Actions that compromise the privacy of users

   C. Actions that disrupt organizational activities

   D. Actions in which a computer is used in a manner inconsistent with a stated security policy

Answers to Review Questions

1. C. A crime is any violation of a law or regulation. The violation stipulation defines the action as a crime. It is a computer crime if the violation involves a computer either as the target or a tool.

2. B. A military and intelligence attack is targeted at the classified data that resides on the system. To the attacker, the value of the information justifies the risk associated with such an attack. The information extracted from this type of attack is often used to plan subsequent attacks.

3. A. Confidential information that is not related to the military or intelligence agencies is the target of business attacks. The ultimate goal could be destruction, alteration, or disclosure of confidential information.

4. B. A financial attack focuses primarily on obtaining services and funds illegally.

5. B. A terrorist attack is launched to interfere with a way of life by creating an atmosphere of fear. A computer terrorist attack can reach this goal by reducing the ability to respond to a simultaneous physical attack.

6. D. Any action that can harm a person or organization, either directly or through embarrassment, would be a valid goal of a grudge attack. The purpose of such an attack is to "get back" at someone.

7. A, C. Fun attacks have no reward other than providing a boost to pride and ego. The thrill of launching a fun attack comes from the act of participating in the attack (and not getting caught).

8. C. Although the other options have some merit in individual cases, the most important rule is to never modify, or taint, evidence. If you modify evidence, it becomes inadmissible in court.

9. D. The most compelling reason for not removing power from a machine is that you will lose the contents of memory. Carefully consider the pros and cons of removing power. After all is considered, it may be the best choice.

10. C. Although an organization would not want to report a large number of incidents (unless reporting them is mandatory), the reality is that many incidents are never discovered. The lack of well-trained users results in many incidents that are never recognized.

11. D. An incident is defined by your security policy. Actions that you define as an incident may not be considered an incident in another organization. For example, your organization may prohibit Internet access while another organization encourages it. Accessing the Internet would be an incident in your organization.

12. B. Some port scans are normal. An unusually high volume of port scan activity can be a reconnaissance activity preceding a more dangerous attack. When you see unusual port scanning, you should always investigate.

13. A. Any time an attacker exceeds their authority, the incident is classified as a system compromise. This includes valid users who exceed their authority as well as invalid users who gain access through the use of a valid user ID.

14. C. Although options A, B, and D are actions that can make you aware of what attacks look like and how to detect them, you will never successfully detect most attacks until you know your system. When you know what the activity on your system looks like on a normal day, you can immediately detect any abnormal activity.

15. B. In this case, you need a search warrant to confiscate equipment without giving the suspect time to destroy evidence. If the suspect worked for your organization and you had all employees sign consent agreements, you could simply confiscate the equipment.

16. A. Log files contain a large volume of generally useless information. However, when you are trying to track down a problem or an incident, they can be invaluable. Even if an incident is discovered as it is happening, it may have been preceded by other incidents. Log files provide valuable clues and should be protected and archived.

17. A, D. You must report an incident when the incident resulted in the violation of a law or regulation. This includes any damage (or potential damage) to or disclosure of protected information.

18. D. Ethics are simply rules of personal behavior. Many professional organizations establish formal codes of ethics to govern their members, but ethics are personal rules individuals use to guide their lives.

19. B. The second canon of the (ISC)² Code of Ethics states how a CISSP should act, which is honorably, honestly, justly, responsibly, and legally.

20. B. RFC 1087 does not specifically address the statements in A, C, or D. Although each type of activity listed is unacceptable, only the activity identified in option B is identified in RFC 1087.

Chapter

19

Physical Security Requirements

THE CISSP EXAM TOPICS COVERED IN THIS CHAPTER INCLUDE:

- ✓ Physical Security Threats
- ✓ Facility Requirements
- ✓ Forms of Physical Access Controls
- ✓ Technical Controls
- ✓ Environment and Life Safety

The Physical Security domain of the Common Body of Knowledge (CBK) for the CISSP certification exam deals with topics and issues related to facility construction and location, the security features of a facility, forms of physical access control, types of physical security technical controls, and maintaining security by properly sustaining the environment and protecting human life.

The purpose of physical security is to protect against physical threats. The following types of physical threats are among the most common:

- Fire and smoke

- Water (rising/falling)

- Earth movement (earthquakes, landslides, volcanoes)

- Storms (wind, lightning, rain, snow, sleet, ice)

- Sabotage/vandalism

- Explosion/destruction

- Building collapse

- Toxic materials

- Utility loss (power, heating, cooling, air, water)

- Equipment failure

- Personnel loss (strikes, illness, access, transport)

This chapter explores each of these issues and provides discussion of safeguards and countermeasures to protect against them. In many cases, a disaster recovery plan or a business continuity plan will be needed in the event a serious physical threat (such as an explosion, sabotage, or natural disaster) becomes a reality. See Chapter 15, "Business Continuity Planning," and Chapter 16, "Disaster Recovery Planning," for additional details.

Facility Requirements

It should be blatantly obvious if you've read the previous 18 chapters that without control over the physical environment, no amount of administrative, technical, or logical access controls can provide adequate security. If a malicious person can gain physical access to your facility or equipment, they can do just about anything they want, from destruction to disclosure and alteration. Physical controls are your first line of defense, while people are your last.

There are many aspects and elements to implementing and maintaining physical security. One of the core or foundational elements is selecting or designing the facility that will house your IT infrastructure and the operations of your organization. The process of selecting or designing a secure facility must start with a plan.

Secure Facility Plan

A secure facility plan outlines the security needs of your organization and emphasizes methods or mechanisms to employ to provide security. Such a plan is developed through a process known as critical path analysis. *Critical path analysis* is a systematic effort to identify relationships between mission-critical applications, processes, and operations and all of the necessary supporting elements. For example, an e-commerce server used to sell products over the Web relies on Internet access, computer hardware, electricity, temperature control, storage facility, and so on. When critical path analysis is performed properly, a complete picture of the interdependencies and interactions necessary to sustain the organization is produced. Once the analysis is complete, the results serve as a list of items to secure. The first step in designing a secure IT infrastructure is providing security for the basic requirements of the organization and its computers. The basic requirements include electricity, environmental control (i.e., a building, air conditioning, heating, humidity control, etc.), and water/sewage.

Physical Security Controls

The security controls implemented to manage physical security can be divided into three groups: administrative, technical, and physical. Because these are the same categories used to describe access control, it is important to keep in mind the physical security nature of these groupings. *Administrative physical security controls* include facility construction and selection, site management, personnel controls, awareness training, and emergency response and procedures. *Technical physical security controls* include access controls; intrusion detection; alarms; closed-circuit television (CCTV); monitoring; heating, ventilating, and air conditioning (HVAC); power supplies; and fire detection and suppression. *Physical controls for physical security* include fencing, lighting, locks, construction materials, mantraps, dogs, and guards.

When designing the physical security for an environment, keep the functional order of controls in mind. Security controls should be deployed so that initial attempts to access physical assets are deterred (i.e, boundary restrictions). If deterrence fails, then direct access to the physical assets should be denied (for example, locked vault doors). If denial fails, then your system needs to detect intrusion (for example, using motion detectors) and the intrusion should be delayed sufficiently for response by authorities (for example, a cable lock on the asset). So, it's important to remember the order of deployment: deterrence, then denial, then detection, then delay.

Site Selection

Site selection should be based on the security needs of the organization. Cost, location, and size are important, but addressing the requirements of security should always take precedence. When choosing a site on which to build a facility or selecting a preexisting structure, be sure to carefully examine every aspect of the location.

Visibility

Visibility is important. What is the surrounding terrain? Would it be easy to approach the facility by vehicle or on foot without being seen? The makeup of the surrounding area is also important. Is it in or near a residential, business, or industrial area? What is the local crime rate? Where are the closest emergency services located (fire, medical, police)? What unique hazards are found in the area (chemical plants, homeless shelter, university, construction, etc.)?

Accessibility

The accessibility to the area is also important. Single entrances are great for providing security, but multiple entrances are better for evacuation during emergencies. What types of roads are nearby? What means of transportation are easily accessible (trains, highway, airport, shipping)? What is the level of traffic throughout the day?

Natural Disasters

Another concern is the effect of natural disasters in the area. Is the area prone to earthquakes, mud slides, sink holes, fires, floods, hurricanes, tornadoes, falling rocks, snow, rainfall, ice, humidity, heat, extreme cold, and so on? You must prepare for natural disasters and equip your IT environment to either survive an event or be easily replaceable.

Facility Design

When designing a facility for construction, you need to understand the level of security needed by your organization. The proper level of security must be planned and designed before construction begins. Some important issues to consider include the combustibility, fire rating, construction materials, load rating, placement, and control of items such as walls, doors, ceilings, flooring, HVAC, power, water, sewage, gas, and so on. Forced intrusion, emergency access, resistance to entry, direction of entries and exits, use of alarms, and conductivity are other important aspects to evaluate. Every element within a facility should be evaluated in terms of how it could be used for and against the protection of the IT infrastructure and personnel (for example, positive flows for both air and water from inside the facility to the outside of the facility).

Work Areas

The design and configuration of work areas and visitor areas should be carefully considered. There should not be equal access to all locations within a facility. Areas that contain assets of higher value or importance should have restricted access. For example, anyone who enters the facility should be able to access the restrooms and the public telephone, but only the network administrators and security staff should have access to the server room. Valuable and confidential assets should be located in the heart or center of protection provided by a facility. In effect, you should focus on deploying concentric circles of protection. This type of configuration requires increased levels of authorization to gain access into the more sensitive areas of the organization.

Walls or partitions can be used to separate similar but distinct work areas. Such divisions deter casual shoulder surfing or eavesdropping. *Shoulder surfing* is the act of gathering information from a system by observing the monitor or the use of the keyboard by the operator. Floor-to-ceiling walls should be used to separate areas with differing levels of sensitivity and confidentiality.

Each work area should be evaluated and assigned a type of classification just as IT assets are classified. Only people with clearance or classifications corresponding to the classification of the work area should be allowed access. Areas with different purposes or uses should be assigned different levels of access or restrictions. The more access to assets the equipment within an area offers, the greater the restrictions to control who enters those areas and what activities they perform should be.

Server Rooms

Server rooms, server vaults, and IT closets are enclosed, restricted and protected rooms where your mission-critical servers and network devices are housed. Centralized server rooms need not be human compatible. In fact, the more human incompatible a server room is, the more protection against both casual and determined attacks it will offer. Human incompatibility can be accomplished by including *Halon* or other oxygen-displacement fire detection and extinguishing systems, low temperatures, little or no lighting, and equipment stacked so there is little room for walking or moving. Server rooms should be designed to best support the operation of the IT infrastructure and to prevent unauthorized human access and intervention.

 The walls of your server room should also have a 1-hour minimum fire rating.

Visitors

If a facility employs restricted areas to control physical security, then a mechanism to handle visitors is required. Often an escort is assigned to visitors and their access and activities are monitored closely. Failing to track the actions of outsiders when they are granted access into a protected area can result in malicious activity against the most protected assets.

Forms of Physical Access Controls

There are many types of physical access control mechanisms that can be deployed in an environment to control, monitor, and manage access to a facility. These range from deterrents to detection mechanisms.

The various sections, divisions, or areas of a site or facility should be clearly designated as public, private, or restricted. Each of these areas requires unique and focused physical access controls, monitoring, and prevention mechanisms. The following sections discuss many of the mechanisms that can be used to separate, isolate, and control access to the various types of areas on a site.

🌐 Real World Scenario

Deploying Physical Access Controls

In the real world, you will deploy multiple layers of physical access controls to manage the traffic of authorized and unauthorized individuals within your facility. The outermost layer will be lighting. The entire outer perimeter of your site should be clearly lit. This will provide for easy identification of personnel and make it easier to notice intrusions. Just inside of the lighted area should be a fence or wall designed to prevent intrusion. Specific controlled points along that fence or wall should be entrance points. There should be gates, turnstiles, or mantraps all monitored by closed-circuit television (CCTV) and security guards. Identification and authentication should be required at these entrance points before entrance is granted.

Within the facility, areas of different sensitivity or confidentiality levels should be distinctly separated and compartmentalized. This is especially true of public areas and areas accessible to visitors. An additional identification/authentication process to validate a need to enter should be required when anyone is moving from one area to another. The most sensitive resources and systems should be isolated from all but the most privileged personnel and located at the center or core of the facility.

Fences, Gates, Turnstiles, and Mantraps

A *fence* is a perimeter-defining device. Fences are used to clearly differentiate between areas that are under a specific level of security protection and those that aren't. Fencing can include a wide range of components, materials, and construction methods. It can consist of stripes painted on the ground, chain link fences, barbed wire, concrete walls, and even invisible perimeters using laser, motion, or heat detectors. Various types of fences are effective against different types of intruders:

- Fences that are 3 to 4 feet high deter casual trespassers.
- Fences that are 6 to 7 feet high are too hard to climb easily.
- Fences that are 8 feet high with three strands of barbed wire deter determined intruders.

A *gate* is a controlled exit and entry point in a fence. The deterrent level of a gate must be equivalent to the deterrent level of the fence to sustain the effectiveness of the fence as a whole. Hinges and locking/closing mechanisms should be hardened against tampering, destruction, or removal. When a gate is closed, it should not offer any additional access vulnerabilities. Gates should be kept to a minimum. They may be manned by guards or not. When they're not protected by guards, deployment of dogs or CCTV is recommended.

A *turnstile* (see Figure 19.1) is a form of gate that prevents more than one person from gaining entry at a time and often restricts movement in one direction. It is used to gain entry but not exit or vice versa. A turnstile is basically a fencing equivalent of a secured revolving door.

A *mantrap* is a double set of doors that is often protected by a guard (see Figure 19.1). The purpose of a mantrap is to contain a subject until their identity and authentication is verified. If they are proven to be authorized for entry, the inner door opens, allowing them to enter the facility or premises. If they are not authorized, both doors remain closed and locked until an escort (typically a guard or a police officer) arrives to escort them off the property or arrest them for trespassing (this is known as a delay feature). Often a mantrap will include a scale to prevent piggybacking or tailgating.

Lighting

Lighting is one of the most commonly used forms of perimeter security control. The primary purpose of lighting is to discourage casual intruders, trespassers, prowlers, and would-be thieves who would rather perform their maliciousness in the dark. However, lighting is not a strong deterrent. It should not be used as the primary or sole protection mechanism except in areas with a low threat level.

FIGURE 19.1   A secure physical boundary with a mantrap and a turnstile

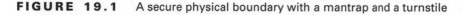

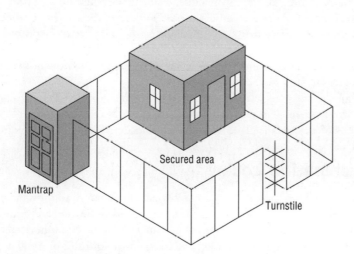

Lighting should not illuminate the positions of guards, dogs, patrol posts, or other similar security elements. It should be combined with guards, dogs, CCTV, or some form of intrusion detection or surveillance mechanism. Lighting must not cause a nuisance or problem for nearby residents, roads, railways, airports, and so on.

The National Institute of Standards and Technology (NIST) standard for perimeter protection using lighting is that critical areas should be illuminated with 2 candle feet of power at a height of 8 feet. Another common issue related to the use of lighting is the placement of the lights. Standards seem to indicate that light poles should be placed the same distance apart as the diameter of the illuminated area created by the light. So, if the lighted area is 40 feet in diameter, the poles should be 40 feet apart.

Security Guards and Dogs

All physical security controls, whether static deterrents or active detection and surveillance mechanisms, ultimately rely upon personnel to intervene and stop actual intrusions and attacks. Security guards exist to fulfill this need. Guards may be posted around a perimeter or inside to monitor access points or watch detection and surveillance monitors. The real benefit of guards is that they are able to adapt and react to any condition or situation. Guards are able to learn and recognize attack and intrusion activities and patterns, can adjust to a changing environment, and are able to make decisions and judgment calls. Security guards are often an appropriate security control when immediate, onsite, situation handling and decision making is necessary.

Unfortunately, using security guards is not a perfect solution. There are numerous disadvantages to deploying, maintaining, and relying upon security guards. Not all environments and facilities support security guards. This may be due to actual human incompatibility or to the layout, design, location, and construction of the facility. Not all security guards are themselves reliable. Prescreening, bonding, and training do not guarantee that you won't end up with an ineffective and unreliable security guard. Likewise, even if a guard is initially reliable, they are subject to physical injury and illness, take vacations, can become distracted, are vulnerable to social engineering, and can become unemployable due to substance abuse. In addition, they are sometimes focused on self-preservation instead of the preservation of the security of the guarded facility. This may mean that security guards can offer protection only up to the point at which their life is endangered. Additionally, security guards are usually unaware of the scope of the operations within a facility and are therefore not thoroughly equipped to know how to respond to every situation. Finally, security guards are expensive.

Guard dogs can be an alternative to security guards. They can often be deployed as a perimeter security control. As a detection and deterrent, dogs are extremely effective. However, dogs are costly, require a high level of maintenance, and impose serious insurance and liability requirements.

Keys and Combination Locks

Locks are used to keep closed doors closed. They are designed and deployed to prevent access to everyone without proper authorization. A lock is a crude form of an identification and authorization mechanism. If you posses the correct key or combination, you are considered authorized and permitted entry. Key-based locks are the most common and inexpensive forms of physical access control devices. These are often known as preset locks. These types of locks are often subject to picking, which is often categorized under the class of lock mechanism attacks called shimming.

Programmable or combination locks offer a broader range of control than preset locks. Some programmable locks can be configured with multiple valid access combinations or may include digital or electronic controls employing keypads, smart cards, or cipher devices. For instance, an *Electronic Access Control (EAC)* lock comprises three elements: an electromagnet to keep the door closed, a credential reader to authenticate subjects and to disable the electromagnet, and a door closed sensor to reenable the electromagnet.

Locks serve as an alternative to security guards as a perimeter entrance access control device. A gate or door can be opened and closed to allow access by a security guard who verifies your identity before granting access, or the lock itself can serve as the verification device that also grants or restricts entry.

Badges

Badges, identification cards, and *security IDs* are forms of physical identification and/or of electronic access control devices. A badge can be as simple as a name tag indicating whether you are a valid employee or a visitor. Or it can be as complex as a smart card or token device that employs multifactor authentication to verify and prove your identity and provide authentication and authorization to access a facility, specific rooms, or secured workstations. Badges often include pictures, magnetic strips with encoded data, and personal details to help a security guard verify identity.

Badges may be used in environments in which physical access is primarily controlled by security guards. In such conditions, the badge serves as a visual identification tool for the guards. They can verify your identity by comparing your picture to your person and consult a printed or electronic roster of authorized personnel to determine whether you have valid access.

Badges can also serve in environments guarded by scanning devices rather than security guards. In such conditions, the badge can be used either for identification or for authentication. When the badge is used for identification, it is swiped in a device and then the badge owner must provide one or more authentication factors, such as a password, pass phrase, or biological trait (if a biometric device is used). When the badge is used for authentication, the badge owner provides their ID, username, and so on and then swipes the badge to authenticate.

Motion Detectors

A *motion detector,* or *motion sensor,* is a device that senses the occurrence of motion in a specific area. There are many different types of motion detectors, including infrared, heat, wave pattern, capacitance, photoelectric, and passive audio. An infrared motion detector monitors for significant or meaningful changes in the infrared lighting pattern of a monitored area. A heat-based motion detector monitors for significant or meaningful changes in the heat levels and patterns in a monitored area. A wave pattern motion detector transmits a consistent low ultrasonic or high microwave frequency pattern into the monitored area and monitors for significant or meaningful changes or disturbances in the reflected pattern. A capacitance motion detector senses changes in the electrical or magnetic field surrounding a monitored object. A photoelectric motion detector senses changes in the visible light levels of the monitored area. Photoelectric motion detectors are usually deployed in internal rooms that have no windows and are kept dark. A passive audio motion detector listens for abnormal sounds in the monitored area.

Intrusion Alarms

Whenever a motion detector registers a significant or meaningful change in the environment, it triggers an alarm. An *alarm* is a separate mechanism that triggers a deterrent, a repellant, and/or a notification. Alarms that trigger deterrents may engage additional locks, shut doors, and so on. The goal of such an alarm is to make further intrusion or attack more difficult. Alarms that trigger repellants usually sound an audio siren or bell and turn on lights. These kinds of alarms are used to discourage the intruder or attacker from continuing their malicious or trespassing activities and get them to leave the premises. Alarms that trigger notification are often silent from the perspective of an intruder/attacker, but they record data about the incident and notify administrators, security guards, and law enforcement. The recording of an incident can take the form of log files and/or CCTV tapes. The purpose of a silent alarm is to bring authorized security personnel to the location of the intrusion or attack in hopes of catching the person committing the unwanted acts.

Local alarm systems must broadcast an audible alarm signal that can be easily heard up to 400 feet away. Additionally, they must be protected, usually by security guards, from tampering and disablement. For a local alarm system to be effective, there must be a security team or guards positioned nearby who can respond when the alarm is triggered. A *centralized alarm system* may not have a local alarm; a remote or centralized monitoring station is signaled when the alarm is triggered. *Auxiliary alarm systems* can be added to either local or centralized alarm systems. The purpose of an auxiliary alarm system is to notify local police or fire services when an alarm is triggered.

Secondary Verification Mechanisms

When motion detectors, sensors, and alarms are used, secondary verification mechanisms should be in place. As the sensitivity of these devices is increased, a false trigger will occur more often. Innocuous events such as the presence of animals, birds, bugs, and authorized personnel can trigger false alarms. Deploying two or more detection and sensor systems and requiring two or more triggers in quick succession to occur before an alarm is triggered may significantly reduce false alarms and increase the certainty of sensing actual intrusions or attacks.

CCTV (closed-circuit television via security cameras) is a security mechanism related to motion detectors, sensors, and alarms. However, CCTV is not an automated detection-and-response system. CCTV requires personnel to watch the captured video to detect suspicious and malicious activities and to trigger alarms. Security cameras can expand the effective visible range of a security guard, therefore increasing the scope of his oversight. In many cases, CCTV is not used as a primary detection tool due to the high cost of paying a person to sit and watch the video screens. Instead, it is used as a secondary or follow-up mechanism that is reviewed after a trigger by an automated system occurs. In fact, the same logic used on auditing and audit trails is used for CCTV and recorded events. A CCTV is a preventative measure, while reviewing recorded events is a detective measure.

Technical Controls

The technical controls most often found employed as an access control mechanism to manage physical access include smart/dumb cards and biometrics. In addition to access control, physical security mechanisms include audit trails, access logs, and intrusion detection systems (IDSs).

Smart Cards

Smart cards are credit-card-sized IDs, badges, or security passes that have a magnetic strip, bar code, or integrated circuit chip embedded in them. They can contain information about the authorized bearer that can be used for identification and/or authentication purposes. Some smart cards are even capable of processing information or can be used to store reasonable amounts of data in a memory chip. A smart card can be referred to by several phrases or terms:

- An identity token containing integrated circuits (ICs)
- A processor IC card
- An IC card with an ISO 7816 interface

Smart cards are often viewed as a complete security solution, but they should not be considered a complete solution. As with any single security mechanism, such a solution has weakness and vulnerabilities. Smart cards can be subjected to physical attacks, logical attacks, Trojan horse attacks, and social engineering attacks.

Memory cards are machine-readable ID cards with a magnetic strip. Like a credit card, debit card, or ATM card, memory cards are capable of retaining a small amount of data but are unable to process data like a smart card. Memory cards often function as a type of two-factor control in that they usually require that the user have physical possession of the card (Type 2 factor) as well as know the PIN code for the card (Type 1 factor). However, memory cards are easy to copy or duplicate and are considered insufficient for authentication purposes in a secure environment.

Dumb cards are human-readable card IDs that usually have a photo and written information about the authorized bearer. Dumb cards are for use in environments in which automated controls are infeasible or unavailable but security guards are practical.

Proximity Readers

In addition to smart and dumb cards, proximity readers can be used to control physical access. A *proximity reader* can be a passive device, a field-powered device, or a transponder. The proximity device is worn or held by the authorized bearer. When they pass a proximity reader, the reader is able to determine who the bearer is and whether they have authorized access. A passive device reflects or otherwise alters the electromagnetic field generated by the reader. This alteration is detected by the reader. The passive device has no active electronics; it is just a small magnet with specific properties (like the antitheft devices commonly found on DVDs). A field-powered device has electronics that are activated when it enters the electromagnetic field generated by the reader. Such devices actually generate electricity from the EM field to power themselves (like card readers that only require that the access card be waved within inches of the reader to unlock doors). A transponder device is self-powered and transmits a signal received by the reader. This can occur consistently or only at the press of a button (like a toll road pass or a garage door opener).

In addition to smart/dumb cards and proximity readers, physical access can be managed with biometric access control devices. See Chapter 1, "Accountability and Access Control," for a description of biometric devices.

Access Abuses

No matter what form of physical access control is used, a security guard or other monitoring system must be deployed to prevent abuse, masquerading, and piggybacking. Examples of abuses of physical access controls are propping open secured doors and bypassing locks or access controls. *Masquerading* is using someone else's security ID to gain entry into a facility. *Piggybacking* is following someone through a secured gate or doorway without being identified or authorized personally.

Audit trails and access logs are useful tools even for physical access control. They may need to be created manually by security guards. Or they can be generated automatically if sufficient automated access control mechanisms (such as smart cards and certain proximity readers) are in place. The time a subject requests entry, the result of the authentication process, and the length of time the secured gate remains open are important elements to include in audit trails and access logs. In addition to the electronic or paper trail, you should consider monitoring entry points with CCTV. CCTV enables you to compare the audit trails and access logs with a visually recorded history of the events. Such information is critical for reconstructing the events of an intrusion, breach, or attack.

Intrusion Detection Systems

Intrusion detection systems are systems—automated or manual—that are designed to detect the attempted intrusion, breach, or attack of an authorized individual; the use of an unauthorized entry point; or the committal of the event at an unauthorized or abnormal time. Intrusion detection systems used to monitor physical activity may include security guards, automated access controls, and motion detectors, as well as other specialty monitoring techniques. Physical intrusion detection systems, also called burglar alarms, detect unauthorized activities and notify the authorities (internal security or external law enforcement). Physical intrusion detection systems can monitor for vibrations, movement, temperature changes, sound, changes in electromagnetic fields, and much more. The most common type of system uses a simple circuit (a.k.a. dry contact switches) comprising foil tape in entrance points to detect when a door or window has been opened.

An intrusion detection mechanism is useful only if it is connected to an intrusion alarm. An intrusion alarm notifies authorities about a breach of physical security. There are four types of alarms:

Local alarm system   An alarm sounds locally and can be heard up to 400 feet away.

Central station system   The alarm is silent locally, but offsite monitoring agents are notified so they can respond to the security breach. Most residential security systems are of this type. Most central station systems are well-known or national security companies, such as Brinks and ADT.

Proprietary system   This is the same thing as a central station system; however, the host organization has its own onsite security staff waiting to respond to security breaches.

Auxiliary station   When the security perimeter is breached, emergency services are notified to respond to the incident and arrive at the location. This could include fire, police, and medical services.

Two or more of these types of intrusion and alarm systems can be incorporated in a single solution. However, there are two aspects of any intrusion detection and alarm system that can cause it to fail: how it gets its power and how it communicates. If the system loses power, it will not function. Thus, a reliable detection and alarm system has a battery backup with enough stored power for 24 hours of operation. If the communication lines are cut, the alarm may not function and security personnel and emergency services will not be notified. Thus, a reliable detection and alarm system has a heartbeat sensor for line supervision. A heartbeat sensor is a mechanism by which the communication pathway is either constantly or periodically checked with a test signal. If the receiving station ever detects a failed heartbeat signal, the alarm is triggered automatically. Both of these measures are designed to prevent an intruder from circumventing the detection and alarm system.

Emanation Security

Many electrical devices emanate electrical signals or radiation that can be intercepted by unauthorized individuals. These signals may contain confidential, sensitive, or private data. Obvious examples of emanation devices are wireless networking equipment and mobile phones, but there are many other devices that that are vulnerable to interception. Some possible examples could be monitors, modems, and internal and external media drives (hard drives, floppy drives, CDs, etc.). With the right equipment, unauthorized users could intercept the electromagnetic or radio frequency signals (collectively known as emanations) and extract confidential data.

TEMPEST

Clearly, if a device is sending out a signal that can be intercepted by someone outside of your organization, a security precaution is needed. The types of countermeasures and safeguards used to protect against emanation attacks are known as Transient Electromagnetic Pulse Equipment Shielding Techniques (TEMPEST) devices. TEMPEST was originally a government research study aimed at protecting electronic equipment from damage from the electromagnetic pulse (EMP) from nuclear explosions. It has since expanded to a general study of monitoring emanations and preventing emanation interception. Thus *TEMPEST* is now a formal name referencing a broad category of activities rather than an acronym for a specific purpose.

TEMPEST Countermeasures

Some TEMPEST countermeasures are Faraday cages, white noise, and control zones. A Faraday cage is a box, mobile room, or entire building that is designed with an external metal skin, often a wire mesh, that fully surrounds an area on all six sides (i.e., front, back, left, right, top, and bottom). This metal skin is slightly electrified to produce a capacitor-like effect (hence the name Faraday) that prevents all electromagnetic signals (emanations) from exiting or entering the area enclosed by the Faraday cage. Faraday cages are very effective in blocking EM signals. In fact, inside of an active Faraday cage, mobile phones do not work and neither can you pick up broadcast radio or television stations.

White noise is simply the broadcasting of false traffic at all times to mask and hide the presence of real emanations. White noise can consist of a real signal of another source that is not confidential, a constant signal of a specific frequency, a randomly variable signal (such as the white noise heard between radio stations or television stations), or even a jam signal that causes interception equipment to fail. White noise is most effective when created around the perimeter of an area so that it is broadcast outward to protect the internal area where emanations may be needed for normal operations.

The final type of TEMPEST countermeasure, a control zone, is simply the implementation of either a Faraday cage or white noise generation in an environment where a specific area is protected while the rest is not. A control zone can be a room, a floor, or an entire building. Control zones are those areas where emanation signals are supported and used by necessary equipment, such as wireless networking, mobile phones, radios, and televisions. Outside of the control zones, emanation interception is blocked or prevented through the use of various TEMPEST countermeasures.

Environment and Life Safety

An important aspect of physical access control and maintaining the security of a facility is protecting the basic elements of the environment and protecting human life. In all circumstances and under all conditions, the most important aspect of security is protecting people. Preventing harm to people is the most important goal of all security solutions.

Personnel Safety

Part of maintaining safety for personnel is maintaining the basic environment of a facility. For short periods of time, people can survive without water, food, air conditioning, and power. But in some cases, the loss of these elements can have disastrous results or they can be symptoms of more immediate and dangerous problems. Flooding, fires, release of toxic materials, and natural disasters all threaten human life as well as the stability of a facility. Physical security procedures should focus on protecting human life and then on restoring the safety of the environment and restoring the utilities necessary for the IT infrastructure to function.

People should always be your top priority. Only after personnel are safe can you consider addressing business continuity issues. Many organizations are adopting Occupant Emergency Plans (OEPs) to guide and assist with sustaining personnel safety in the event of a disaster. The OEP provides guidance on how to minimize threats to life, prevent injury, and protect property from damage in the event of a destructive physical event. The OEP does not address IT issues or business continuity, just personnel and general property. The BCP and DRP address IT and business continuity and recovery issues.

Power and Electricity

Power supplied by electric companies is not always consistent and clean. Most electronic equipment demands clean power to function properly. Equipment damage due to power fluctuations is a common occurrence. Many organizations opt to manage their own power through several means. An *uninterruptible power supply (UPS)* is a type of self-charging battery that can be used to supply consistent clean power to sensitive equipment. A UPS functions basically by taking power in from the wall outlet, storing it in a battery, pulling power out of the battery, and then feeding that power to whatever devices are connected to it. By directing current through its battery, it is able to maintain a consistent clean power supply. A UPS has a second function, one that is used most often as a selling point. A UPS provides continuous power even after the primary power source fails. A UPS can continue to supply power for minutes or hours, depending on its capacity and the amount of power the equipment needs.

Another means to ensure that equipment is not damaged by power fluctuations is the use of power strips with surge protectors. A surge protector includes a fuse that will blow before power levels change significantly enough to cause damage to equipment. However, once a surge protector's fuse or circuit is tripped, the electric flow is completely interrupted. Surge protectors should be used only when instant termination of electricity will not cause damage or loss to the equipment. Otherwise, a UPS should be employed.

If maintaining operations for considerable time in spite of a brownout or blackout is a necessity, then onsite electric generators are required. Such generators turn on automatically when a power failure is detected. Most generators operate using a fuel tank of liquid or gaseous propellant that must be maintained to ensure reliability. Electric generators are considered alternate or backup power sources.

The problems with power are numerous. Here is a list of terms associated with power issues you should be familiar with:

Fault   A momentary loss of power

Blackout   A complete loss of power

Sag   Momentary low voltage

Brownout   Prolonged low voltage

Spike   Momentary high voltage

Surge   Prolonged high voltage

Inrush   An initial surge of power usually associated with connecting to a power source, whether primary or alternate/secondary

Noise   A steady interfering disturbance

Transient   A short duration of line noise disturbance

Clean   Nonfluctuating pure power

Ground   The wire in an electrical circuit that is grounded

A brownout is an interesting power issue because its definition references the ANSI standards for power. The ANSI standards allow for an 8-percent drop in power between the power source and the facility meter and a drop of 3.5 percent between the facility meter and the wall outlet before the instance of prolonged low voltage is labeled as a brownout. The ANSI standard further distinguishes that the low voltage outside of your meter is to be repaired by the power company, while the internal brownout is your responsibility.

Noise

Noise can cause more than just problems with how equipment functions; it can also interfere with the quality of communications, transmissions, and playback. Noise generated by electric current can affect any means of data transmission that relies on electromagnetic transport mechanisms, such as telephone, cellular, television, audio, radio, and network mechanisms. There are two types of *electromagnetic interference (EMI):* common mode and traverse mode. *Common mode noise* is generated by the difference in power between the hot and ground wires of a power source or operating electrical equipment. Traverse mode noise is generated by the difference in power between the hot and neutral wires of a power source or operating electrical equipment.

A similar issue is *radio frequency interference (RFI),* which can affect many of the same systems as EMI. RFI is generated by a wide number of common electrical appliances, including fluorescent lights, electrical cables, electric space heaters, computers, elevators, motors, and electric magnets.

Protecting your power supply and your equipment from noise is an important part of maintaining a productive and functioning environment for your IT infrastructure. Steps to take for this kind of protection include providing for sufficient power conditioning, establishing proper grounding, shielding all cables, and limiting exposure to EMI and RFI sources.

Temperature, Humidity, and Static

In addition to power considerations, maintaining the environment involves control over the HVAC mechanisms. Rooms primarily containing computers should be kept at 60 to 75 degrees Fahrenheit (15 to 23 degrees Celsius). Humidity in a computer room should be maintained between 40 and 60 percent. Too much humidity can cause corrosion. Too little humidity causes static electricity. Even on nonstatic carpeting, if the environment has low humidity it is still possible to generate 20,000-volt static discharges. As you can see in Table 19.1, even minimal levels of static discharge can destroy electronic equipment.

TABLE 19.1   Static Voltage and Damage

Static Voltage	Possible Damage
40	Destruction of sensitive circuits and other electronic components
1,000	Scrambling of monitor displays
1,500	Destruction of data stored on hard drives
2,000	Abrupt system shutdown
4,000	Printer jam or component damage
17,000	Permanent circuit damage

Water

Water leakage and flooding should be addressed in your environmental safety policy and procedures. Plumbing leaks are not an everyday occurrence, but when they do happen, they often cause significant damage. Water and electricity don't mix. If your computer systems come in contact with water, especially while they are operating, damage is sure to occur. Plus water and electricity create a serious risk of electrocution to personnel. Whenever possible, locate server rooms and critical computer equipment away from any water source or transport pipes. You may also want to install water detection circuits on the floor around mission-critical systems. Water detection circuits will sound an alarm and alert you if water is encroaching upon the equipment. To minimize emergencies, be familiar with shutoff valves and drainage locations. In addition to monitoring for plumbing leaks, you should evaluate your facility's capability of handling severe rain or flooding in your area. Is the facility located on a hill or in a valley? Is there sufficient drainage? Is there a history of flooding or accumulation of standing water? Is your server room located in the basement or on the first floor?

Fire Detection and Suppression

Fire detection and suppression must not be overlooked. Protecting personnel from harm should always be the most important goal of any security or protection system. In addition to protecting people, fire detection and suppression is designed to keep damage caused by fire, smoke, heat, and suppression materials to a minimum, especially in regard to the IT infrastructure.

Basic fire education involves knowledge of the fire triangle (see Figure 19.2). The three corners of the triangle represent fire, heat, and oxygen. The center of the triangle represents the chemical reaction of the three elements. The point of the fire triangle is to illustrate that if you can remove any one of the four items from the fire triangle, the fire can be extinguished. Different suppression mediums address different aspects of the fire:

- Water suppresses the temperature.
- Soda acid and other dry powders suppress the fuel supply.
- CO_2 suppresses the oxygen supply.
- Halon (and its substitutes) interferes with the chemical reaction of combustion and/or suppresses the oxygen supply.

When selecting a suppression medium, it is important to consider what aspect of the fire triangle it addresses, what this represents in reality, how effective the suppression medium usually is, and what effect the suppression medium will have on your environment.

In addition to understanding the fire triangle, it is also helpful to understand the stages of fire. Fire has numerous stages, and Figure 19.3 addresses the four most vital stages.

Stage 1: The incipient stage   At this stage, there is only air ionization but not smoke.

Stage 2: The smoke stage   In Stage 2, smoke is visible from the point of ignition.

Stage 3: The flame stage   This is when a flame can be seen with the naked eye.

Stage 4: The heat stage   At Stage 4, the fire is considerably further down the timescale to the point where there is an intense heat buildup and everything in the area burns.

FIGURE 19.2 The fire triangle

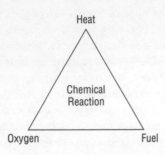

FIGURE 19.3 The four primary stages of fire

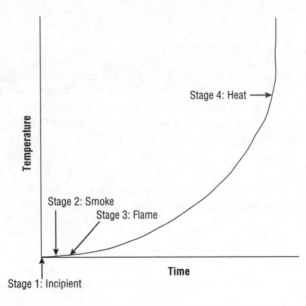

The earlier a fire is detected, the easier it is to extinguish and the less damage it and its suppression medium(s) can cause.

One of the basics of fire management is proper personnel awareness training. Everyone should be thoroughly familiar with the fire suppression mechanisms in their facility. Everyone should also be familiar with at least two evacuation routes from their primary work location and know how to locate evacuation routes elsewhere in the facility. Personnel should be trained in the location and use of fire extinguishers. Other items that can be included in fire or general emergency response training are cardiopulmonary resuscitation (CPR) training, emergency shutdown procedures, and a preestablished rendezvous location or safety verification mechanism (such as voicemail).

Most fires in a data center are caused by overloaded electrical distribution outlets.

Fire Extinguishers

There are several different types of fire extinguishers. Understanding what type to use on various forms of fire is essential to effective fire suppression. If a fire extinguisher is used improperly or the wrong form of fire extinguisher is used, the fire could spread and intensify instead of being quenched. Fire extinguishers are to be used only when a fire is still in the incipient stage. Table 19.2 lists the three common types of fire extinguishers.

TABLE 19.2   Fire Extinguisher Classes

Class	Type	Suppression Material
A	Common combustibles	Water, soda acid (a dry powder or liquid chemical)
B	Liquids	CO_2, Halon*, soda acid
C	Electrical	CO_2, Halon*
D	Metal	Dry powder

* Halon or EPA-approved Halon substitute.

Water cannot be used on Class B fires because it splashes the burning liquids and said liquids usually float. Water cannot be used on Class C fires because of the potential for electrocution. Oxygen suppression cannot be used on metal fires because burning metal produces its own oxygen.

Fire Detection Systems

To properly protect a facility from fire is to install an automated detection and suppression system. There are many types of fire detection systems. Fixed temperature detection systems trigger suppression when a specific temperature is reached. The trigger is usually a metal or plastic component that is in the sprinkler head and melts at a specific temperature. Rate of rise temperature detection systems trigger suppression when the speed at which the temperature changes reaches a specific level. Flame actuated systems trigger suppression based on the infrared energy of flames. Smoke actuated systems trigger suppression based on photoelectric or radioactive ionization sensors.

Most fire detection systems can be linked to fire response service notification mechanisms. When suppression is triggered, such linked systems will contact the local fire response team and request aid using an automated message or alarm.

To be effective, fire detectors need to be placed strategically. Don't forget to place them in dropped ceilings and raised floors, in server rooms, in private offices and public areas, in HVAC vents, in elevator shafts, in the basement, and so on.

As for the suppression mechanisms used, they can be based on water or on a fire suppression gas system. Water is the most common in human-friendly environments, whereas gaseous systems are more appropriate for computer rooms where personnel typically do not reside.

Water Suppression Systems

There are four main types of water suppression systems. A *wet pipe system* (also known as a *closed head system*) is always full of water. Water discharges immediately when suppression is triggered. A *dry pipe system* contains compressed air. Once suppression is triggered, the air escapes, opening a water valve that in turn causes the pipes to fill and discharge water into the environment. A *deluge system* is another form of dry pipe system that uses larger pipes and therefore a significantly larger volume of water. Deluge systems are inappropriate for environments that contain electronics and computers. A *preaction system* is a combination dry pipe/wet pipe system. The system exists as a dry pipe until the initial stages of a fire (smoke, heat, etc.) are detected and then the pipes are filled with water. The water is released only after the sprinkler head activation triggers are melted by sufficient heat. If the fire is quenched before the sprinklers are triggered, the pipes can be manually emptied and reset. This also allows for manual intervention to stop the release of water before sprinkler triggering occurs. Preaction systems are the most appropriate water-based system for environments that include both computers and humans in the same locations.

The most common cause of failure for a water-based system is human error, such as turning off the water source when there is a fire or triggering a water release when there is no fire.

Gas Discharge Systems

Gas discharge systems are usually more effective than water discharge systems. However, gas discharge systems should not be employed in environments in which people are located. Gas discharge systems usually remove the oxygen from the air, thus making them hazardous to personnel. They employ a pressurized gaseous suppression medium, such as CO_2, Halon, or FM-200 (a Halon replacement).

Halon is a very effective fire suppression compound, but it degrades into toxic gases at 900 degrees Fahrenheit. Additionally, it is not environmentally friendly. The EPA has banned the manufacture of Halon in the United States, but it can still be imported. However, according to the Montreal Protocol, you should contact a Halon recycling facility to make arrangements for refilling a discharged system instead of contacting a vendor or manufacturer directly. This action is encouraged so that already produced Halon will be consumed and less new Halon will be created.

Due to the issues with Halon, it is often replaced by a more ecological and less toxic medium. The following list includes EPA-approved replacements for Halon:

- FM-200 (HFC-227ea)
- CEA-410 or CEA 308
- NAF-S-III (HCFC Blend A)
- FE-13 (HCFC-23)
- Aragon (IG55) or Argonite (IG01)
- Inergen (IG541)

Halon may also be replaced by low-pressure water mists, but those systems are usually not employed in computer rooms or electrical equipment storage facilities. A low-pressure water mist is a vapor cloud used to quickly reduce the temperature of an area.

Damage

Addressing fire detection and suppression includes dealing with the possible contamination and damage caused by a fire. The destructive elements of a fire include smoke and heat, but they also include the suppression medium, such as water or soda acid. Smoke is damaging to most storage devices. Heat can damage any electronic or computer component. One hundred degrees Fahrenheit can damage storage tapes, 175 degrees can damage computer hardware (i.e., CPU and RAM), and 350 degrees can damage paper products (i.e., warping and discoloration).

Suppression mediums can cause short circuits, initiate corrosion, or otherwise render equipment useless. All of these issues must be addressed when designing a fire response system.

WARNING   Don't forget that in the event of a fire, in addition to damage caused by the fire and your selected suppression medium, members of the fire department may cause damage using their hoses to spray water and their axes while searching for hot spots.

Equipment Failure

No matter what the quality of the equipment your organization chooses to purchase and install is, eventually it will fail. Understanding this fact and preparing for it will ensure the ongoing availability of your IT infrastructure and will help you to protect the integrity and availability of your resources.

Preparing for equipment failure can take many forms. In some non-mission-critical situations, simply knowing where you can purchase replacement parts for a 48-hour replacement timeline is sufficient. In other situations, maintaining onsite replacement parts is mandatory. Keep in mind that the response time in returning a system back to a fully functioning state is directly proportional to the cost involved in maintaining such a solution. Costs include storage, transportation, prepurchasing, and maintaining onsite installation and restoration expertise. In some cases, maintaining onsite replacements is infeasible. For those cases, establishing a service level agreement (SLA) with the hardware vendor is essential. An SLA clearly defines the response time a vendor will provide in the event of an equipment failure emergency.

Aging hardware should be scheduled for replacement and/or repair. The schedule for such operations should be based on the mean time to failure (MTTF) and mean time to repair (MTTR) estimates established for each device. MTTF is the expected typical functional lifetime of the device given a specific operating environment. MTTR is the average length of time required to perform a repair on the device. A device can often undergo numerous repairs before a catastrophic failure is expected. Be sure to schedule all devices to be replaced before their MTTF expires. When a device is sent out for repairs, you need to have an alternate solution or a backup device to fill in for the duration of the repair time. Often, waiting until a minor failure occurs before a repair is performed is satisfactory, but waiting until a complete failure occurs before replacement is an unacceptable security practice.

Summary

If you don't have control over the physical environment, no amount of administrative or technical/logical access controls can provide adequate security. If a malicious person can gain physical access to your facility or equipment, they own it.

There are many aspects and elements to implementing and maintaining physical security. One of the core elements is selecting or designing the facility that will house your IT infrastructure and the operations of your organization. You must start with a plan that outlines the security needs of your organization and emphasizes methods or mechanisms to employ to provide security. Such a plan is developed through a process known as critical path analysis.

The security controls implemented to manage physical security can be divided into three groups: administrative, technical, and physical. Administrative physical security controls include facility construction and selection, site management, personnel controls, awareness training, and emergency response and procedures. Technical physical security controls include access controls, intrusion detection, alarms, CCTV, monitoring, HVAC, power supplies, and fire detection and suppression. Examples of physical controls for physical security include fencing, lighting, locks, construction materials, mantraps, dogs, and guards.

There are many types of physical access control mechanisms that can be deployed in an environment to control, monitor, and manage access to a facility. These range from deterrents to detection mechanisms. They can be fences, gates, turnstiles, mantraps, lighting, security guards, security dogs, key locks, combination locks, badges, motion detectors, sensors, and alarms.

The technical controls most often found employed as an access control mechanism to manage physical access include smart/dumb cards and biometrics. In addition to access control, physical security mechanisms can be in the form of audit trails, access logs, and intrusion detection systems.

An important aspect of physical access control and maintaining the security of a facility is protecting the basic elements of the environment and protecting human life. In all circumstance and under all conditions, the most important aspect of security is protecting people. Preventing harm is the utmost goal of all security solutions. Providing clean power sources and managing the environment are also important.

Fire detection and suppression must not be overlooked. In addition to protecting people, fire detection and suppression is designed to keep damage caused by fire, smoke, heat, and suppression materials to a minimum, especially in regard to the IT infrastructure.

Exam Essentials

Understand why there is no security without physical security.   Without control over the physical environment, no amount of administrative or technical/logical access controls can provide adequate security. If a malicious person can gain physical access to your facility or equipment, they can do just about anything they want, from destruction to disclosure and alteration.

Be able to list administrative physical security controls.   Examples of administrative physical security controls are facility construction and selection, site management, personnel controls, awareness training, and emergency response and procedures.

Be able to list the technical physical security controls.   Technical physical security controls can be access controls, intrusion detection, alarms, CCTV, monitoring, HVAC, power supplies, and fire detection and suppression.

Be able to name the physical controls for physical security.   Physical controls for physical security are fencing, lighting, locks, construction materials, mantraps, dogs, and guards.

Know the functional order of controls.   The are denial, deterrence, detection, then delay.

Know the key elements in making a site selection and designing a facility for construction. The key elements in making a site selection are visibility, composition of the surrounding area, area accessibility, and the effects of natural disasters. A key element in designing a facility for construction is understanding the level of security needed by your organization and planning for it before construction begins.

Know how to design and configure secure work areas.   There should not be equal access to all locations within a facility. Areas that contain assets of higher value or importance should have restricted access. Valuable and confidential assets should be located in the heart or center of protection provided by a facility. Also, centralized server or computer rooms need not be human compatible.

Understand how to handle visitors in a secure facility.   If a facility employs restricted areas to control physical security, then a mechanism to handle visitors is required. Often an escort is assigned to visitors and their access and activities are monitored closely. Failing to track the actions of outsiders when they are granted access into a protected area can result in malicious activity against the most protected assets.

Know the three categories of security controls implemented to manage physical security and be able to name examples of each.   The security controls implemented to manage physical security can be divided into three groups: administrative, technical, and physical. Understand when and how to use each and be able to list examples of each kind.

Know the common threats to physical access controls.   No matter what form of physical access control is used, a security guard or other monitoring system must be deployed to prevent abuse, masquerading, and piggybacking. Abuses of physical access control are propping open secured doors and bypassing locks or access controls. Masquerading is using someone else's security ID to gain entry into a facility. Piggybacking is following someone through a secured gate or doorway without being identified or authorized personally.

Understand the need for audit trails and access logs.   Audit trails and access logs are useful tools even for physical access control. They may need to be created manually by security guards. Or they can be generated automatically if sufficiently automated access control mechanisms are in place (i.e., smart cards and certain proximity readers). You should also consider monitoring entry points with CCTV. Through CCTV, you can compare the audit trails and access logs with a visually recorded history of the events. Such information is critical to reconstructing the events of an intrusion, breach, or attack.

Understand the need for clean power.   Power supplied by electric companies is not always consistent and clean. Most electronic equipment demands clean power in order to function properly. Equipment damage due to power fluctuations is a common occurrence. Many organizations opt to manage their own power through several means. A UPS (uninterruptible power supply) is a type of self-charging battery that can be used to supply consistent clean power to sensitive equipment. UPSs also provide continuous power even after the primary power source fails. A UPS can continue to supply power for minutes or hours depending on its capacity and the draw by equipment.

Know the terms commonly associated with power issues.   Know the definitions of the following: fault, blackout, sag, brownout, spike, surge, inrush, noise, transient, clean, and ground.

Understand controlling the environment.   In addition to power considerations, maintaining the environment involves control over the HVAC mechanisms. Rooms primarily containing computers should be kept at 60 to 75 degrees Fahrenheit (15 to 23 degrees Celsius). Humidity in a computer room should be maintained between 40 and 60 percent. Too much humidity can cause corrosion. Too little humidity causes static electricity.

Know about static electricity.   Even on nonstatic carpeting, if the environment has low humidity, it is still possible to generate 20,000-volt static discharges. Even minimal levels of static discharge can destroy electronic equipment.

Understand the need to manage water leakage and flooding.   Water leakage and flooding should be addressed in your environmental safety policy and procedures. Plumbing leaks are not an everyday occurrence, but when they do happen, they often cause significant damage. Water and electricity don't mix. If your computer systems come in contact with water, especially while they are operating, damage is sure to occur. Whenever possible, locate server rooms and critical computer equipment away from any water source or transport pipes.

Understand the importance of fire detection and suppression.   Fire detection and suppression must not be overlooked. Protecting personnel from harm should always be the most important goal of any security or protection system. In addition to protecting people, fire detection and suppression is designed to keep damage caused by fire, smoke, heat, and suppression materials to a minimum, especially in regard to the IT infrastructure.

Understand the possible contamination and damage caused by a fire and suppression.   The destructive elements of a fire include smoke and heat, but they also include the suppression medium, such as water or soda acid. Smoke is damaging to most storage devices. Heat can damage any electronic or computer component. Suppression mediums can cause short circuits, initiate corrosion, or otherwise render equipment useless. All of these issues must be addressed when designing a fire response system.

Review Questions

1. Which of the following is the most important aspect of security?

   A. Physical security

   B. Intrusion detection

   C. Logical security

   D. Awareness training

2. What method can be used to map out the needs of an organization for a new facility?

   A. Log file audit

   B. Critical path analysis

   C. Risk analysis

   D. Inventory

3. What type of physical security controls focus on facility construction and selection, site management, personnel controls, awareness training, and emergency response and procedures?

   A. Technical

   B. Physical

   C. Administrative

   D. Logical

4. Which of the following is not a security-focused design element of a facility or site?

   A. Separation of work and visitor areas

   B. Restricted access to areas with higher value or importance

   C. Confidential assets located in the heart or center of a facility

   D. Equal access to all locations within a facility

5. Which of the following does not need to be true in order to maintain the most efficient and secure server room?

   A. It must be human compatible.

   B. It must include the use of non-water fire suppressants.

   C. The humidity must be kept between 40 and 60 percent.

   D. The temperature must be kept between 60 and 75 degrees Fahrenheit.

6. What is a perimeter-defining device used to deter casual trespassing?

   A. Gates

   B. Fencing

   C. Security guards

   D. Motion detectors

7. Which of the following is a double set of doors that is often protected by a guard and is used to contain a subject until their identity and authentication is verified?

   A. Gate

   B. Turnstile

   C. Mantrap

   D. Proximity detector

8. What is the most common form of perimeter security devices or mechanisms?

   A. Security guards

   B. Fences

   C. CCTV

   D. Lighting

9. Which of the following is not a disadvantage of using security guards?

   A. Security guards are usually unaware of the scope of the operations within a facility.

   B. Not all environments and facilities support security guards.

   C. Not all security guards are themselves reliable.

   D. Prescreening, bonding, and training does not guarantee effective and reliable security guards.

10. What is the most common cause of failure for a water-based fire suppression system?

   A. Water shortage

   B. People

   C. Ionization detectors

   D. Placement of detectors in drop ceilings

11. What is the most common and inexpensive form of physical access control device?

   A. Lighting

   B. Security guard

   C. Key locks

   D. Fences

12. What type of motion detector senses changes in the electrical or magnetic field surrounding a monitored object?

   A. Wave

   B. Photoelectric

   C. Heat

   D. Capacitance

13. Which of the following is not a typical type of alarm that can be triggered for physical security?

  A. Preventative

  B. Deterrent

  C. Repellant

  D. Notification

14. No matter what form of physical access control is used, a security guard or other monitoring system must be deployed to prevent all but which of the following?

  A. Piggybacking

  B. Espionage

  C. Masquerading

  D. Abuse

15. What is the most important goal of all security solutions?

  A. Prevention of disclosure

  B. Maintaining integrity

  C. Human safety

  D. Sustaining availability

16. What is the ideal humidity range for a computer room?

  A. 20–40 percent

  B. 40–60 percent

  C. 60–75 percent

  D. 80–95 percent

17. At what voltage level can static electricity cause destruction of data stored on hard drives?

  A. 4,000

  B. 17,000

  C. 40

  D. 1,500

18. A Type B fire extinguisher may use all but which of the following suppression mediums?

  A. Water

  B. CO_2

  C. Halon

  D. Soda acid

19. What is the best type of water-based fire suppression system for a computer facility?

    A. Wet pipe system

    B. Dry pipe system

    C. Preaction system

    D. Deluge system

20. Which of the following is typically not a culprit in causing damage to computer equipment in the event of a fire and a triggered suppression?

    A. Heat

    B. Suppression medium

    C. Smoke

    D. Light

Answers to Review Questions

1. A. Physical security is the most important aspect of overall security. Without physical security, none of the other aspects of security is sufficient.

2. B. Critical path analysis can be used to map out the needs of an organization for a new facility. A critical path analysis is the process of identifying relationships between mission-critical applications, processes, and operations and all of the supporting elements.

3. C. Administrative physical security controls include facility construction and selection, site management, personnel controls, awareness training, and emergency response and procedures.

4. D. Equal access to all locations within a facility is not a security-focused design element. Each area containing assets or resources of different importance, value, and confidentiality should have a corresponding level of security restriction placed on it.

5. A. A computer room does not need to be human compatible to be efficient and secure. Having a human-incompatible server room provides a greater level of protection against attacks.

6. B. Fencing is a perimeter-defining device used to deter casual trespassing. Gates, security guards, and motion detectors do not define a facility's perimeter.

7. C. A mantrap is a double set of doors that is often protected by a guard and used to contain a subject until their identity and authentication is verified.

8. D. Lighting is the most common form of perimeter security devices or mechanisms. Your entire site should be clearly lit. This provides for easy identification of personnel and makes it easier to notice intrusions.

9. A. Security guards are usually unaware of the scope of the operations within a facility, which supports confidentiality and helps reduce the possibility that a security guard will be involved in disclosure of confidential information.

10. B. The most common cause of failure for a water-based system is human error. If you turn off the water source after a fire and forget to turn it back on, you'll be in trouble for the future. Also, pulling an alarm when there is no fire will trigger damaging water release throughout the office.

11. C. Key locks are the most common and inexpensive form of physical access control device. Lighting, security guards, and fences are all much more cost intensive.

12. D. A capacitance motion detector senses changes in the electrical or magnetic field surrounding a monitored object.

13. A. There is no preventative alarm. Alarms are always triggered in response to a detected intrusion or attack.

14. B. No matter what form of physical access control is used, a security guard or other monitoring system must be deployed to prevent abuse, masquerading, and piggybacking. Espionage cannot be prevented by physical access controls.

15. C. Human safety is the most important goal of all security solutions.

16. B. The humidity in a computer room should ideally be from 40 to 60 percent.

17. D. Destruction of data stored on hard drives can be caused by 1,500 volts of static electricity.

18. A. Water is never the suppression medium in Type B fire extinguishers because they are used on liquid fires.

19. C. A preaction system is the best type of water-based fire suppression system for a computer facility.

20. D. Light is usually not damaging to most computer equipment, but fire, smoke, and the suppression medium (typically water) are very destructive.

Glossary

Numbers & Symbols

* (star) Integrity Axiom (* Axiom)   An axiom of the Biba model that states that a subject at a specific classification level cannot write data to a higher classification level. This is often shortened to "no write up."

* (star) Security Property (* Property)   A property of the Bell-LaPadula model that states that a subject at a specific classification level cannot write data to a lower classification level. This is often shortened to "no write down."

1000Base-T   A form of twisted-pair cable that supports 1000Mbps or 1Gbs throughput at 100 meter distances. Often called Gigabit Ethernet.

100Base-TX   Another form of twisted-pair cable similar to 100Base-T.

10Base2   A type of coaxial cable. Often used to connect systems to backbone trunks. 10Base2 has a maximum span of 185 meters with maximum throughput of 10Mpbs. Also called thinnet.

10Base5   A type of coaxial cable. Often used as a network's backbone. 10Base5 has a maximum span of 500 meters with maximum throughput of 10Mpbs. Also called thicknet.

10Base-T   A type of network cable that is made up of four pairs of wires that are twisted around each other and then sheathed in a PVC insulator. Also called twisted-pair.

A

abnormal activity   Any system activity that does not normally occur on your system. Also referred to as suspicious activity.

abstraction   The collection of similar elements into groups, classes, or roles for the assignment of security controls, restrictions, or permissions as a collective.

acceptance testing   A form of testing that attempts to verify that a system satisfies the stated criteria for functionality and possibly also for security capabilities of a product. It is used to determine whether end users or a customer will accept the completed product.

accepting risk   The valuation by management of the cost/benefit analysis of possible safeguards and the determination that the cost of the countermeasure greatly outweighs the possible cost of loss due to a risk.

access   The transfer of information from an object to a subject.

access control   The mechanism by which subjects are granted or restricted access to objects.

access control list (ACL)   The column of an access control matrix that specifies what level of access each subject has over an object.

access control matrix   A table of subjects and objects that indicates the actions or functions that each subject can perform on each object. Each column of the matrix is an ACL. Each row of the matrix is a capability list.

access tracking   Auditing, logging, and monitoring the attempted access or activities of a subject. Also referred to as activity tracking.

account lockout   An element of the password policy's programmatic controls that disables a user account after a specified number of failed logon attempts. Account lockout is an effective countermeasure to brute force and dictionary attacks against a system's logon prompt.

accountability   The process of holding someone responsible (accountable) for something. In this context, accountability is possible if a subject's identity and actions can be tracked and verified.

accreditation   The formal declaration by the Designated Approving Authority (DAA) that an IT system is approved to operate in a particular security mode using a prescribed set of safeguards at an acceptable level of risk.

ACID model   The letters in ACID represent the four required characteristics of database transitions: *atomicity*, *consistency*, *isolation*, and *durability*.

active content   Web programs that users download to their own computer for execution rather than consuming server-side resources.

ActiveX   Microsoft's answer to Sun's Java applets. It operates in a very similar fashion, but ActiveX is implemented using any one of a variety of languages, including Visual Basic, C, C++, and Java.

Address Resolution Protocol (ARP)   A subprotocol of the TCP/IP protocol suite that operates at the Data Link layer (layer 2). ARP is used to discover the MAC address of a system by polling using its IP address.

addressing   The means by which a processor refers to various locations in memory.

administrative access controls   The policies and procedures defined by an organization's security policy to implement and enforce overall access control. Examples of administrative access controls include hiring practices, background checks, data classification, security training, vacation history reviews, work supervision, personnel controls, and testing.

administrative law   Regulations that cover a range of topics from procedures to be used within a federal agency to immigration policies that will be used to enforce the laws passed by Congress. Administrative law is published in the Code of Federal Regulations (CFR).

administrative physical security controls   Security controls that include facility construction and selection, site management, personnel controls, awareness training, and emergency response and procedures.

admissible evidence   Evidence that is relevant to determining a fact. The fact that the evidence seeks to determine must be material (i.e., related) to the case. In addition, the evidence must be competent, meaning that it must have been obtained legally. Evidence that results from an illegal search would be inadmissible because it is not competent.

Advanced Encryption Standard (AES)   The encryption standard selected in October 2000 by the National Institute for Standards and Technology (NIST) that is based on the Rijndael cipher.

advisory policy   A policy that discusses behaviors and activities that are acceptable and defines consequences of violations. An advisory policy discusses the senior management's desires for security and compliance within an organization. Most policies are advisory.

agent   Intelligent code objects that perform actions on behalf of a user. They typically take initial instructions from the user and then carry on their activity in an unattended manner for a predetermined period of time, until certain conditions are met, or for an indefinite period.

aggregate functions   SQL functions, such as COUNT(), MIN(), MAX(), SUM(), and AVG(), that can be run against a database to produce an information set.

aggregation   A number of functions that combine records from one or more tables to produce potentially useful information.

alarm   A mechanism that is separate from a motion detector and triggers a deterrent, triggers a repellant, and/or triggers a notification. Whenever a motion detector registers a significant or meaningful change in the environment, it triggers an alarm.

alarm triggers   Notifications sent to administrators when a specific event occurs.

amplifier   See *repeater*.

AND   The operation (represented by the ∧ symbol) that checks to see whether two values are both true.

analytic attack   An algebraic manipulation that attempts to reduce the complexity of a cryptographic algorithm. This attack focuses on the logic of the algorithm itself.

annualized loss expectancy (ALE)   The possible yearly cost of all instances of a specific realized threat against a specific asset. The ALE is calculated using the formula ALE = single loss expectancy (SLE) * annualized rate of occurrence (ARO).

annualized rate of occurrence (ARO)   The expected frequency that a specific threat or risk will occur (i.e., become realized) within a single year.

anomaly detection   See *behavior-based detection*.

APIPA   See *automatic private IP addressing*.

applet   Code objects sent from a server to a client to perform some action. Applets are self-contained miniature programs that execute independently of the server that sent them.

Application layer   Layer 7 of the Open Systems Interconnection (OSI) model.

application-level gateway firewall   A firewall that filters traffic based on the Internet service (i.e., application) used to transmit or receive the data. Application-level gateways are known as second-generation firewalls.

assembly language   A higher-level alternative to machine language code. Assembly languages use mnemonics to represent the basic instruction set of a CPU but still require hardware-specific knowledge.

asset   Anything within an environment that should be protected. The loss or disclosure of an asset could result in an overall security compromise, loss of productivity, reduction in profits, additional expenditures, discontinuation of the organization, and numerous intangible consequences.

asset valuation   A dollar value assigned to an asset based on actual cost and nonmonetary expenses, such as costs to develop, maintain, administer, advertise, support, repair, and replace; as well as other values, such as public confidence, industry support, productivity enhancement, knowledge equity, and ownership benefits.

asset value (AV)   A dollar value assigned to an asset based on actual cost and nonmonetary expenses.

assigning risk   See *transferring risk*.

assurance   The degree of confidence that security needs are satisfied. Assurance must be continually maintained, updated, and reverified.

asymmetric key   Algorithms that provide a cryptologic key solution for public key cryptosystems.

asynchronous dynamic password token   A token device that generates passwords based on the occurrence of an event. An event token requires that the subject press a key on the token and on the authentication server. This action advances to the next password value.

asynchronous transfer mode (ATM)   A cell-switching technology rather than a packet-switching technology like Frame Relay. ATM uses virtual circuits much like Frame Relay, but because it uses fixed-size frames or cells, it can guarantee throughput. This makes ATM an excellent WAN technology for voice and video conferencing.

atomicity   One of the four required characteristics of all database transactions. A database transaction must be an "all or nothing" affair, hence the use of *atomic*. If any part of the transaction fails, the entire transaction must be rolled back as if it never occurred.

attack   The exploitation of a vulnerability by a threat agent.

attacker   Any person who attempts to perform a malicious action against a system.

attenuation   The loss of signal strength and integrity on a cable due to the length of the cable.

attribute   A column within a table of a relational database.

audit trails The records created by recording information about events and occurrences into a database or log file. Audit trails are used to reconstruct an event, to extract information about an incident, to prove or disprove culpability, and much more.

auditing A methodical examination or review of an environment to ensure compliance with regulations and to detect abnormalities, unauthorized occurrences, or outright crimes.

auditor The person or group responsible for testing and verifying that the security policy is properly implemented and the derived security solutions are adequate.

authentication The process of verifying or testing that the identity claimed by a subject is valid.

Authentication Header (AH) An element of IPSec that provides authentication, integrity, and nonrepudiation.

authentication protocols Protocol used to provide the transport mechanism for logon credentials. May or may not provide security through traffic encryption.

Authentication Service (AS) An element of the Kerberos Key Distribution Center (KDC). The AS verifies or rejects the authenticity and timeliness of tickets.

authorization A process that ensures that the requested activity or object access is possible given the rights and privileges assigned to the authenticated identity (i.e., subject).

automatic private IP addressing (APIPA) A feature of Windows that assigns an IP address to a system should DHCP address assignment fail. APIPA assigns each failed DHCP client an IP address within the range of 169.254.0.1 to 169.254.255.254 along with a default Class B subnet mask of 255.255.0.0.

auxiliary alarm system An additional function that can be added to either local or centralized alarm systems. The purpose of an auxiliary alarm system is to notify local police or fire services when an alarm is triggered.

availability The assurance that authorized subjects are granted timely and uninterrupted access to objects.

awareness A form of security teaching that is a prerequisite to training. The goal of awareness is to bring security into the forefront and make it a recognized entity for students/users.

B

badges Forms of physical identification and/or of electronic access control devices. A badge can be as simple as a name tag indicating whether you are a valid employee or a visitor. Or it can be as complex as a smart card or token device that employs multifactor authentication to verify and prove your identity and provide authentication and authorization to access a facility, specific rooms, or secured workstations. Also referred to as identification cards and security IDs.

Base+Offset addressing   An addressing scheme that uses a value stored in one of the CPU's registers as the base location from which to begin counting. The CPU then adds the offset supplied with the instruction to that base address and retrieves the operand from the computed memory location.

baseband   A communication medium that supports only a single communication signal at a time.

baseline   The minimum level of security that every system throughout the organization must meet.

Basic Input/Output System (BIOS)   The operating-system-independent primitive instructions that a computer needs to start up and load the operating system from disk.

Basic Rate Interface (BRI)   An ISDN service type that provides two B, or data, channels and one D, or management, channel. Each B channel offers 64Kbps, and the D channel offers 16Kbps.

behavior   In the context of object-oriented programming terminology and techniques, the results or output from an object after processing a message using a method.

behavior-based detection   An intrusion discovery mechanism used by IDS. Behavior-based detection finds out about the normal activities and events on your system through watching and learning. Once it has accumulated enough data about normal activity, it can detect abnormal and possible malicious activities and events. The primary drawback of a behavior-based IDS is that it produces many false alarms. Also known as statistical intrusion detection, anomaly detection, and heuristics-based detection.

Bell-LaPadula model   A confidentiality-focused security model based on the state machine model and employing mandatory access controls and the lattice model.

best evidence rule   A rule that states that when a document is used as evidence in a court proceeding, the original document must be introduced. Copies will not be accepted as evidence unless certain exceptions to the rule apply.

Biba model   An integrity-focused security model based on the state machine model and employing mandatory access controls and the lattice model.

bind variable   A placeholder for SQL literal values, such as numbers or character strings.

biometrics   The use of human physiological or behavioral characteristics as authentication factors for logical access and identification for physical access.

birthday attack   An attack in which the malicious individual seeks to substitute in a digitally signed communication a different message that produces the same message digest, thereby maintaining the validity of the original digital signature; based on the statistical anomaly that in a room with 23 people, the probability of two of more people having the same birthday is greater than 50%.

black box testing   A form of program testing that examines the input and output of a program without focusing on its internal logical structures.

blackout   A complete loss of power.

block cipher   A cipher that applies the encryption algorithm to an entire message block at the same time. Transposition ciphers are examples of block ciphers.

Blowfish   A block cipher that operates on 64-bit blocks of text and uses variable-length keys ranging from a relatively insecure 32 bits to an extremely strong 448 bits.

boot sector   The portion of a storage device used to load the operating system and the types of viruses that attack that process.

bot   An intelligent agent that continuously crawls a variety of websites retrieving and processing data on behalf of the user.

bounds   The limits to the memory and resources a process can access.

breach   The occurrence of a security mechanism being bypassed or thwarted by a threat agent.

bridge   A network device used to connect networks with different speeds, cable types, or topologies that still use the same protocol. A bridge is a layer 2 device.

broadband   A communication medium that supports multiple communication signals simultaneously.

broadcast   A communications transmission to multiple but unidentified recipients.

broadcast address   A broadcast network address that is used during a Smurf attack.

brouter   A network device that first attempts to route and then defaults to bridging if routing fails.

brownout   A period of prolonged low voltage.

brute force attack   An attack made against a system to discover the password to a known identity (i.e., username). A brute force attack uses a systematic trial of all possible character combinations to discover an account's password.

buffer overflow   A vulnerability that can cause a system to crash or allow the user to execute shell commands and gain access to the system. Buffer overflow vulnerabilities are especially prevalent in code developed rapidly for the Web using CGI or other languages that allow unskilled programmers to quickly create interactive web pages.

business attack   An attack that focuses on illegally obtaining an organization's confidential information.

Business Continuity Planning (BCP)   The assessment of a variety of risks to organizational processes and the creation of policies, plans, and procedures to minimize the impact those risks might have on the organization if they were to occur.

Business Impact Assessment (BIA)   An analysis that identifies the resources that are critical to an organization's ongoing viability and the threats posed to those resources. It also assesses the likelihood that each threat will actually occur and the impact those occurrences will have on the business.

C

cache RAM   A process by that takes data from slower devices and temporarily stores it in higher-performance devices when its repeated use is expected.

campus area network (CAN)   A network that spans a college, university, or a multi-building office complex.

capabilities list   A list that maintains a row of security attributes for each controlled object. Although not as flexible as the token approach, capabilities lists generally offer quicker lookups when a subject requests access to an object.

capability list   Each row of an access control matrix is a capability list. A capability list is tied to the subject; it lists valid actions that can be taken on each object.

cardinality   The number of rows in a relational database.

cell suppression   The act of suppressing (or hiding) individual data items inside a database to prevent aggregation or inference attacks.

centralized access control   Method of control in which all authorization verification is performed by a single entity within a system.

centralized alarm system   An alarm system that signals a remote or centralized monitoring station when the alarm is triggered.

certificate authority   An agency that authenticates and distributes digital certificates.

certificate revocation list (CRL)   The list of certificates that have been revoked by a certificate authority before the lifetimes of the certificates have expired.

certificates   Endorsed copies of an individual's public key that verifies their identity.

certification   The comprehensive evaluation, made in support of the accreditation process, of the technical and nontechnical security features of an IT system and other safeguards to establish the extent to which a particular design and implementation meets a set of specified security requirements.

chain of evidence   The process by which an object is uniquely identified in a court of law.

Challenge Handshake Authentication Protocol (CHAP)   One of the authentication protocols used over PPP links. CHAP encrypts usernames and passwords.

challenge-response token   A token device that generates passwords or responses based on instructions from the authentication system. The authentication system displays a challenge in the form of a code or pass phrase. This challenge is entered into the token device. The token generates a response based on the challenge, and then the response is entered into the system for authentication.

change control   See *change management*.

change control management   See *change management*.

change management   The means by which changes to an environment are logged and monitored in order to ensure that any change does not lead to reduced or compromised security.

checklist test   A process in which copies of the disaster recovery checklists are distributed to the members of the disaster recovery team for their review.

Children's Online Privacy Protection Act (COPPA)   A law in the United States that places specific demands upon websites that cater to children or knowingly collect information from children.

chosen ciphertext attack   An attack in which the attacker has the ability to decrypt chosen portions of the ciphertext message.

chosen plaintext attack   An attack in which the attacker has the ability to encrypt plaintext messages of their choosing and then analyze the ciphertext output of the encryption algorithm.

CIA Triad   The three essential security principles of confidentiality, integrity, and availability. All three must be properly addressed to establish a secure environment.

cipher   A system that hides the true meaning of a message. Ciphers use a variety of techniques to alter and/or rearrange the characters or words of a message to achieve confidentiality.

Cipher Block Chaining (CBC)   A process in which each block of unencrypted text is XORed with the block of ciphertext immediately preceding it before it is encrypted using the DES algorithm.

Cipher Feedback (CFB)   A mode in which the DES algorithm is used to encrypt the preceding block of ciphertext. This block is then XORed with the next block of plaintext to produce the next block of ciphertext.

ciphertext   A message that has been encrypted for transmission.

civil laws   Laws that form the bulk of the body of laws in the United States. They are designed to provide for an orderly society and govern matters that are not crimes but require an impartial arbiter to settle disputes between individuals and organizations.

Clark-Wilson model   An model that employs limited interfaces or programs to control and maintain object integrity.

class   In the context of object-oriented programming terminology and techniques, a collection of common methods from a set of objects that defines the behavior of those objects.

classification   A label that is applied to a resource to indicate its sensitivity or value to an organization and therefore designate the level of security necessary to protect that resource.

classification level   Another term for a security label. An assigned importance or value placed on objects and subjects.

clean 1) The act of removing a virus from a system and repairing the damage caused by the virus. 2) The act of removing data from a storage media for reuse in the same security environment.

clean power Nonfluctuating pure power.

clearing A method of sufficiently deleting media that will be reused in the same secured environment. Also known as overwriting.

click-wrap license agreement A software agreement in which the contract terms are either written on the software box or included in the software documentation. During the installation process, you are required to click a button indicating that you have read the terms of the agreement and agree to abide by them.

clipping level A threshold value used in violation analysis auditing. Crossing the clipping level triggers recording of relevant event data to an audit log.

closed-circuit television (CCTV) A security system using video cameras and video recording devices.

closed head system See *wet pipe system*.

clustering (or key clustering) A weakness in cryptography where a plaintext message generates identical ciphertext messages using the same algorithm but using different keys.

coaxial cable A cable with a center core of copper wire surrounded by a layer of insulation and then by a conductive braided shielding and finally encased in an insulation sheath. Coaxial cable is fairly resistant to EMI, has a low cost, and is easy to install.

code See *cipher*.

cohesive (or cohesiveness) An object is highly cohesive if it can perform a task with little or no help from other objects. Highly cohesive objects are not as dependent upon other objects as objects with lower cohesion. Objects with higher cohesion are often better. Highly cohesive objects perform tasks alone and have low coupling.

cognitive password A variant of the password authentication factor that asks a series of questions about facts or predefined responses that only the subject should know.

cold sites Standby facilities large enough to handle the processing load of an organization and with appropriate electrical and environmental support systems.

collision attack See *birthday attack*.

collusion An agreement between multiple people to perform an unauthorized or illegal action.

commercial business/private sector classification The security labels commonly employed on secure systems used by corporations. Common corporate or commercial security labels are confidential, proprietary, private, sensitive, and public.

Committed Information Rate (CIR) A contracted minimum guaranteed bandwidth allocation for a virtual circuit.

Common Body of Knowledge (CBK)   The areas of information prescribed by (ISC)² as the source of knowledge for the CISSP exam.

common mode noise   Electromagnetic interference (EMI) noise generated by the difference in power between the hot and ground wires of a power source or operating electrical equipment.

Common Object Request Broker Architecture (CORBA)   An international standard for distributed computing. CORBA enables code operating on a computer to locate resources located elsewhere on the network.

companion virus   A variation of the file infector virus. A companion virus is a self-contained executable file that escapes detection by using a filename similar to, but slightly different from, a legitimate operating system file.

compartmented   A type of MAC environment. Compartmentalized or compartmented environments have no relationship between one security domain and another. To gain access to an object, the subject must have the exact specific clearance for that object's security domain.

compartmented mode   See *compartmented security mode.*

compartmented mode workstations   A computer system in which all users have the same clearance. The concept of need-to-know is used to control access to sensitive data and the system is able to process data from multiple sensitivity levels at the same time.

compartmented security mode   A security mode in which systems process two or more types of compartmented information. All system users must have an appropriate clearance to access all information processed by the system but do not necessarily have a need to know all of the information in the system.

compensation access control   A type of access control that provides various options to other existing controls to aid in the enforcement and support of a security policy.

competent   A distinction of evidence that means that the evidence must be obtained legally. Evidence that results from an illegal search would be inadmissible because it is not competent.

compiled languages   A computer language that is converted into machine language before distribution or execution.

compliance checking   The process by which it is ensured that all of the necessary and required elements of a security solution are properly deployed and functioning as expected.

compliance testing   Another common usage of auditing. Verification that a system complies with laws, regulations, baselines, guidelines, standards, and policies is an important part of maintaining security in any environment.

Component Object Model (COM)   Microsoft's standard for the use of components within a process or between processes running on the same system.

compromise   If system security has been broken, the system is considered compromised.

computer architecture   An engineering discipline concerned with the construction of computing systems from the logical level.

computer crime   Any crime that is perpetrated against or with the use of a computer.

Computer Fraud and Abuse Act   A United States law written to exclusively cover computer crimes that cross state boundaries to avoid infringing upon states' rights.

Computer Security Act (CSA) of 1987   A United States law that mandates baseline security requirements for all federal agencies.

concentrator   See *repeater*.

conclusive evidence   Incontrovertible evidence that overrides all other forms of evidence.

concurrency   A security mechanism that endeavors to make certain that the information stored in a database is always correct or at least has its integrity and availability protected. Concurrency uses a "lock" feature to allow an authorized user to make changes and then "unlocks" data elements only after all changes are complete.

confidential   1) A government/military classification used for data of a confidential nature. Unauthorized disclosure of confidential data will have noticeable effects and cause damage to national security. This classification is used for all data between secret and sensitive but unclassified classifications. 2) The highest level of commercial business/private sector classification. Used for data that is extremely sensitive and for internal use only. A significant negative impact could occur for the company if confidential data is disclosed.

confidentiality   The assurance that information is protected from unauthorized disclosure and the defined level of secrecy is maintained throughout all subject-object interactions.

configuration management   The process of logging, auditing, and monitoring activities related to security controls and security mechanisms over time. This data is then used to identify agents of change, whether objects, subjects, programs, communication pathways, or even the network itself.

confinement (or confinement property)   The principle that allows a process only to read from and write to certain memory locations and resources. This is an alternate name for the * (star) Security Property of the Bell-LaPadula model.

confusion   It occurs when the relationship between the plaintext and the key is complicated enough that an attacker can't just alter the plaintext and analyze the result in order to determine the key.

consistency   One of the four required characteristics of all database transactions (the other three are *atomicity*, *isolation*, and *durability*). All transactions must begin operating in an environment that is consistent with all of the database's rules.

contamination   The result of mixing of data with a different classification level and/or need-to-know requirement.

content-dependent access control   A form of access control based on the contents or payload of an object.

context-dependent access control   A form of access control based on the context or surroundings of an object.

continuity   A goal an organization can accomplish by having plans and procedures to help mitigate the effects a disaster has on its continuing operations and to speed the return to normal operations.

contractual license agreement   A written contract between the software vendor and the customer outlining the responsibilities of each.

control   The use of access rules to limit a subject's access to an object.

controls gap   The difference between total risk and residual risk.

Copper Distributed Data Interface (CDDI)   Deployment of FDDI using twisted pair (i.e., copper) wires. Reduces the maximum segment length to 100 meters and is susceptible to interference.

copyright   Law that guarantees the creators of "original works of authorship" protection against the unauthorized duplication of their work.

corrective access control   An access control deployed to restore systems to normal after an unwanted or unauthorized activity has occurred. Examples of corrective access controls include alarms, mantraps, and security policies.

corrective controls   Instructions, procedures, or guidelines used to reverse the effects of an unwanted activity, such as attacks or errors.

countermeasures   Actions taken to patch a vulnerability or secure a system against an attack. Countermeasures can include altering access controls, reconfiguring security settings, installing new security devices or mechanisms, adding or removing services, and so on.

coupling   The level of interaction between objects. Lower coupling means less interaction. Lower coupling delivers better software design because objects are more independent. Lower coupling is easier to troubleshoot and update. Objects with low cohesion require lots of assistance from other objects to perform tasks and have high coupling.

covert channel   The means by which data can be communicated outside of normal, expected, or detectable methods.

covert storage channel   A channel that conveys information by writing data to a common storage area where another process can read it.

covert timing channel   A channel that conveys information by altering the performance of a system component or modifying a resource's timing in a predictable manner. This is generally a more sophisticated method to covertly pass data and is very difficult to detect.

cracker   Malicious users intent on waging an attack against a person or system. Crackers may be motivated by greed, power, or recognition. Their actions can result in stolen property (data, ideas, etc.), disabled systems, compromised security, negative public opinion, loss of market share, reduced profitability, and lost productivity.

creeping privilege(s)   When a user account accumulates privileges over time as job roles and assigned tasks change. This can occur because new tasks are added to a user's job and the related or necessary privileges are added as well but no privileges or access are ever removed, even if related work tasks are no longer associated with or assigned to the user. Creeping privileges results in excessive privilege.

criminal law   Body of laws that the police and other law enforcement agencies enforce. Criminal law contains prohibitions against acts such as murder, assault, robbery, arson, theft, and similar offenses.

critical path analysis   A systematic effort to identify relationships between mission-critical applications, processes, and operations and all of the necessary supporting elements.

criticality prioritization   The prioritization of mission-critical assets and processes during the creation of BCP/DRP.

Crossover Error Rate (CER)   The point at which the False Acceptance Rate (FAR) equals the False Rejection Rate (FRR). This is the point from which performance is measured in order to compare the capabilities of different biometric devices.

cryptanalysis   The study of methods to defeat codes and ciphers.

cryptographic key   Data that has been protected through encryption processing. Often found on tokens to be used as identification or authentication factors. Cryptographic keys provide the "secret" for all cryptography because all good cryptographic algorithms are publicly available and known.

cryptography   Algorithms applied to data that are designed to ensure confidentiality, integrity, authentication, and nonrepudiation. Primarily assures only confidentiality, not necessarily integrity, authentication, and not nonrepudiation in the case of symmetric cryptology.

cryptology   The art and science of hiding the meaning of a message from all but the intended recipient.

cryptosystem   System in which a shared secret key or pairs of public and private keys are used by communicating parties to facilitate secure communication.

cryptovariable   Another name for the key used to perform encryption and decryption activities.

custodian   A subject that has been assigned or delegated the day-to-day responsibility of classifying and labeling objects and proper storage and protection of objects. The custodian is typically the IT staff or the system security administrator.

cyclic redundancy check (CRC)   Similar to a hash total, a value that indicates whether or not a message has been altered or damaged in transit.

D

data circuit-terminating equipment (DCE)   A networking device that performs the actual transmission of data over the Frame Relay as well as establishing and maintaining the virtual circuit for the customer.

data classification   Grouping data under labels for the purpose of applying security controls and access restrictions.

data custodian   The user who is assigned the task of implementing the prescribed protection defined by the security policy and upper management. The data custodian performs any and all activities necessary to provide adequate protection for data and to fulfill the requirements and responsibilities delegated to him from upper management.

Data Definition Language (DDL)   The database programming language that allows for the creation and modification of the database's structure (known as the schema).

data dictionary   Central repository of data elements and their relationships. Stores critical information about data usage, relationships, sources, and formats.

data diddling   The act of changing data.

Data Encryption Standard (DES)   A standard cryptosystem proposed in 1977 for all government communications. Many government entities continue to use DES for cryptographic applications today despite the fact that it was superseded by Advanced Encryption Standard (AES) in December 2001.

data extraction   The process of extracting elements of data from a large body of data to construct a meaningful representation or summary of the whole.

data hiding   The process of preventing data from being known by a subject.

Data Link layer   Layer 2 of the OSI model.

Data Manipulation Language (DML)   The database programming language that allows users to interact with the data contained within the schema.

data mart   The storage facility used to secure metadata.

data mining   A technique or tool that allows analysts to comb through data warehouses and look for potential correlated information amid the historical data.

data owner   The person who is responsible for classifying information for placement and protection within the security solution.

data terminal equipment (DTE)   A networking device that acts like a router or a switch and provides the customer's network access to the Frame Relay network.

data warehouse   Large databases used to store large amounts of information from a variety of databases for use in specialized analysis techniques.

database   An electronic filing system for organizing collections of information. Most databases are organized by files, records, and fields.

database management system (DBMS)   An application that enables the storage, modification, and extraction of information from a database.

database partitioning   The act of dividing a database up into smaller sections or individual databases; often employed to segregate content with varying sensitivity labels.

decentralized access control   System of access control in which authorization verification is performed by various entities located throughout a system.

decision support system (DSS)   An application that analyzes business data and presents it so as to make business decisions easier for users. DSS is considered an informational application more so than an operational application. Often a DSS is employed by knowledge workers (such as help desk or customer support) and by sales services (such as phone operators).

declassification   The process of moving a resource into a lower classification level once its value no longer justifies the security protections provided by a higher level of classification.

decrypt   The process of reversing a cryptographic algorithm that was used to encrypt a message.

dedicated mode   See *dedicated security mode*.

dedicated security mode   Mode in which the system is authorized to process only a specific classification level at a time. All system users must have clearance and a need to know that information.

deencapsulation   The process of stripping a layer's header and footer from a PDU as it travels up the OSI model layers.

degaussing   The act of using a magnet to return media to its original pristine unused state.

degree   The number of columns in a relational database.

delegation   In the context of object-oriented programming, the forwarding of a request by an object to another object or delegate. An object delegates if it does not have a method to handle the message.

delta rule   Also known as the learning rule. It is the feature of expert systems that allows them to learn from experience.

Delphi technique   An anonymous feedback and response process used to arrive at a group consensus.

deluge system   Another form of dry pipe (fire suppression) system that uses larger pipes and therefore a significantly larger volume of water. Deluge systems are inappropriate for environments that contain electronics and computers.

denial of service (DoS)   A type of attack that prevents a system from processing or responding to legitimate traffic or requests for resources and objects. The most common forms of denial of service attacks involve transmitting so many data packets to a server that it cannot processes them all. Other forms of denial of service attacks focus on the exploitation of a known fault or vulnerability in an operating system, service, or application.

deny risk   See *reject risk*.

detective access control   An access control deployed to discover unwanted or unauthorized activity. Examples of detective access controls include security guards, supervising users, incident investigations, and intrusion detection systems (IDSs).

detective control   See *detective access control*.

deterrent access control   An access control that discourages violations of a security policy.

dictionary attack   An attack against a system designed to discover the password to a known identity (i.e., username). In a dictionary attack, a script of common passwords and dictionary words is used to attempt to discover an account's password.

differential backup   A type of backup that stores all files that have been modified since the time of the most recent full backup.

Diffie-Hellman algorithm   A key exchange algorithm useful in situations in which two parties might need to communicate with each other but they have no physical means to exchange key material and there is no public key infrastructure in place to facilitate the exchange of secret keys.

diffusion   When a change in the plaintext results in multiple changes spread out throughout the ciphertext.

Digital Millennium Copyright Act   A law that establishes the prohibition of attempts to circumvent copyright protection mechanisms placed on a protected work by the copyright holder and limits the liability of Internet service providers when their circuits are used by criminals violating the copyright law.

digital signature   A method for ensuring a recipient that a message truly came from the claimed sender and that the message was not altered while in transit between the sender and recipient.

Digital Signature Standard (DSS)   A standard that specifies that all federally approved digital signature algorithms must use the SHA-1 hashing function.

direct addressing   A process by which the CPU is provided with the actual address of the memory location to be accessed.

direct evidence   Evidence that proves or disproves a specific act through oral testimony based on information gathered through the witness's five senses.

directive access control   An access control that directs, confines, or controls the actions of subjects to force or encourage compliance with security policy.

directive control   A security tool used to guide the security implementation of an organization. The goal or objective of directive controls is to cause or promote a desired result.

directory service   A centralized database of resources available to the network, much like a telephone directory for network services and assets. Users, clients, and processes consult the directory service to learn where a desired system or resource resides.

Direct Memory Access (DMA)   A mechanism that allows devices to exchange data directly with real memory (RAM) without requiring assistance from the CPU.

disaster   An event that brings great damage, loss, or destruction to a system or environment.

disaster recovery plan   A document that guides the recovery efforts necessary to restore your business to normal operations as quickly as possible.

Disaster Recovery Planning (DRP)   Term that describes the actions an organization takes to resume normal operations after a disaster interrupts normal activity.

discretionary access control   A mechanism used to control access to objects. The owner or creator of an object controls and defines the access other subjects have to it.

Discretionary Security Property   Property that states that the system uses an access control matrix to enforce discretionary access control.

distributed access control   A form of access control in which authorization verification is performed by various entities located throughout a system.

Distributed Component Object Model (DCOM)   An extension of COM to support distributed computing. This is Microsoft's answer to CORBA.

distributed data model   In a distributed data model, data is stored in more than one database but remains logically connected. The user perceives the database as a single entity, even though it comprises numerous parts interconnected over a network. Each field may have numerous children as well as numerous parents. Thus, the data mapping relationship is many-to-many.

distributed denial of service (DDoS)   Another form of DoS. A distributed denial of service occurs when the attacker compromises several systems to be used as launching platforms against one or more victims. The compromised systems used in the attack are often called slaves or zombies. A DDoS attack results in the victims being flooded with data from numerous sources.

distributed reflective denial of service (DRDoS)   Another form of DoS. DRDoS attacks take advantage of the normal operation mechanisms of key Internet services, such as DNS and router update protocols. DRDoS attacks function by sending numerous update, session, or control packets to various Internet service servers or routers with a spoofed source address of the intended victim. Usually these servers or routers are part of the high-speed, high-volume Internet backbone trunks. What results is a flood of update packets, session acknowledgment responses, or error messages sent to the victim. A DRDoS attack can result in so much traffic that upstream systems are adversely affected by the sheer volume of data focused on the victim.

DNS poisoning The act of altering or falsifying the information of DNS to route or misdirect legitimate traffic.

documentary evidence Any written items brought into court to prove a fact at hand. This type of evidence must also be authenticated.

domain 1) A realm of trust or a collection of subjects and objects that share a common security policy. Each domain's access control is maintained independently of other domains' access control. This results in decentralized access control when multiple domains are involved. 2) An area of study for the CISSP exam.

dry pipe system A fire suppression system that contains compressed air. Once suppression is triggered, the air escapes, which opens a water valve that in turn causes the pipes to fill and discharge water into the environment.

due care The steps taken to ensure that assets and employees of an organization have been secured and protected and that upper management has properly evaluated and assumed all unmitigated or transferred risks.

due diligence The extent to which a reasonable person will endeavor under specific circumstances to avoid harming other people or property.

dumb cards Human-readable-only card IDs that usually have a photo and written information about the authorized bearer. Dumb cards are for use in environments where automated controls are infeasible or unavailable but security guards are practical.

dumpster diving The act of digging through the refuse, remains, or leftovers from an organization or operation in order to discover or infer information about the organization.

durability One of the four required characteristics of all database transactions (the other three are *atomicity*, *consistency*, and *isolation*). The concept that database transactions must be resilient. Once a transaction is committed to the database, it must be preserved. Databases ensure durability through the use of backup mechanisms, such as transaction logs.

dwell time The length of time a key on the keyboard is pressed. This is an element of the keystroke dynamics biometric factor.

Dynamic Host Configuration Protocol (DHCP) A protocol used to assign TCP/IP configuration settings to systems upon bootup. DHCP uses port 67 for server point-to-point response and port 68 for client request broadcast. DHCP supports centralized control and management of network addressing.

dynamic packet-filtering firewalls A firewall that enables real-time modification of the filtering rules based on traffic content. Dynamic packet-filtering firewalls are known as fourth-generation firewalls.

dynamic passwords Passwords that do not remain static for an extended period of time. Dynamic passwords can change on each use or at a regular interval, such as every 30 days.

E

eavesdropping   Another term for sniffing. However, eavesdropping can include more than just capturing and recording network traffic. Eavesdropping also includes recording or listening to audio communications, faxes, radio signals, and so on.

Economic Espionage Act of 1996   A law that states that anyone found guilty of stealing trade secrets from a U.S. corporation with the intention of benefiting a foreign government or agent may be fined up to $500,000 and imprisoned for up to 15 years and that anyone found guilty of stealing trade secrets under other circumstances may be fined up to $250,000 and imprisoned for up to 10 years.

education   A detailed endeavor where students/users learn much more than they actually need to know to perform their work tasks. Education is most often associated with users pursuing certification or seeking job promotion.

El Gamal   The explanation of how the mathematical principles behind the Diffie-Hellman key exchange algorithm could be extended to support an entire public key cryptosystem used for the encryption and decryption of messages.

electronic access control (EAC)   A type of smart lock that uses a credential reader, a electro-magnet, and a door closed sensor.

electronically erasable PROM (EEPROM)   A storage system that uses electric voltages delivered to the pins of the chip to force erasure. EEPROMs can be erased without removal from the computer, giving them much greater flexibility than standard PROM and EPROM chips.

electromagnetic interference (EMI)   A type of electrical noise that can do more than just cause problems with how equipment functions; it can also interfere with the quality of communications, transmissions, and playback.

Electronic Codebook (ECB)   The simplest encryption mode to understand and the least secure. Each time the algorithm processes a 64-bit block, it simply encrypts the block using the chosen secret key. This means that if the algorithm encounters the same block multiple times, it produces the exact same encrypted block.

Electronic Communications Privacy Act (ECPA)   The law that makes it a crime to invade an individual's electronic privacy. It protects against the monitoring of e-mail and voice mail communications and prevents providers of those services from making unauthorized disclosures of their content.

electronic vaulting   A storage scenario in which database backups are transferred to a remote site in a bulk transfer fashion. The remote location may be a dedicated alternative recovery site (such as a hot site) or simply an offsite location managed within the company or by a contractor for the purpose of maintaining backup data.

elliptic curve cryptography   A new branch of public key cryptography that offers similar security to established public key cryptosystems at reduced key sizes.

elliptic curve group   Each elliptic curve has a corresponding elliptic curve group made up of the points on the elliptic curve along with the point O, located at infinity. Two points within the same elliptic curve group (P and Q) can be added together with an elliptic curve addition algorithm.

employee   Often referred to as the user when discussing IT issues. See also *user*.

employment agreement   A document that outlines an organization's rules and restrictions, security policy, and acceptable use and activities policies; details the job description; outlines violations and consequences; and defines the length of time the position is to be filled by the employee.

Encapsulating Security Payload (ESP)   An element of IPSec that provides encryption to protect the confidentiality of transmitted data but can also perform limited authentication.

encapsulation   The process of adding a header and footer to a PDU as it travels down the OSI model layers.

encrypt   The process used to convert a message into ciphertext.

encryption   The art and science of hiding the meaning or intent of a communication from recipients not meant to receive it.

end user   See *user*.

end-to-end encryption   An encryption algorithm that protects communications between two parties (i.e., a client and a server) and is performed independently of link encryption. An example of this would be the use of Privacy Enhanced Mail (PEM) to pass a message between a sender and a receiver. This protects against an intruder who might be monitoring traffic on the secure side of an encrypted link or traffic sent over an unencrypted link.

enrollment   The process of establishing a new user identity or authentication factor on a system. Secure enrollment requires physical proof of a person's identity or authentication factor. Generally, if the enrollment process takes longer than two minutes, the identification or authorization mechanism (typically a biometric device) is not approved.

entity   A subject or an object.

erasable PROM (EPROM)   A PROM chip that has a small window through which the illumination of a special ultraviolet light causes the contents of the chip to be erased. After this process is complete, the end user can burn new information into the EPROM.

erasing   A delete operation against a file, a selection of files, or the entire media. In most cases, the deletion or erasure process removes only the directory or catalog link to the data. The actual data remains on the drive.

Escrowed Encryption Standard   A failed government attempt to create a back door to all encryption solutions. The solution employed the Clipper chip, which used the Skipjack algorithm.

espionage   The malicious act of gathering proprietary, secret, private, sensitive, or confidential information about an organization for the express purpose of disclosing and often selling that data to a competitor or other interested organization (such as a foreign government).

Ethernet   A common shared media LAN technology.

ethical hacking   See *penetration testing*.

ethics   The rules that govern personal conduct. Several organizations have recognized the need for standard ethics rules, or codes, and have devised guidelines for ethical behavior. These rules are not laws but are minimum standards for professional behavior. They should provide you with a basis for sound, professional, ethical judgment.

evidence   In the context of computer crime, any hardware, software, or data that you can use to prove the identity and actions of an attacker in a court of law.

excessive privilege(s)   More access, privilege, or permission than a user's assigned work tasks dictate. If a user account is discovered to have excessive privilege, the additional and unnecessary benefits should be immediately curtailed.

exit interview   An aspect of a termination policy. The terminated employee is reminded of their legal responsibilities to prevent disclosure of confidential and sensitive information.

expert opinion   A type of evidence consisting of the opinions and facts offered by an expert. An expert is someone educated in a field and who currently works in that field.

expert system   A system that seeks to embody the accumulated knowledge of mankind on a particular subject and apply it in a consistent fashion to future decisions.

exposure   The condition of being exposed to asset loss due to a threat. Exposure involves being susceptible to the exploitation of a vulnerability by a threat agent or event.

exposure factor (EF)   The percentage of loss that an organization would experience if a specific asset were violated by a realized risk.

extranet   A cross between the Internet and an intranet. An extranet is a section of an organization's network that has been sectioned off so that it acts as an intranet for the private network but it also serves information out to the public Internet. Extranets are often used in B2B applications, between customers and suppliers.

F

face scan   An example of a biometric factor, which is a behavioral or physiological characteristic that is unique to a subject. A face scan is a process by which the shape and feature layout of a person's face is used to establish identity or provide authentication.

fail-secure   The response of a system to a failure so that it protects the security of the assets.

fail-safe   The response of a system to a failure so that it protects human safety.

fail-open   The response of a system to a failure whereby it no longer keeps assets secure.

Fair Cryptosystems   A failed government attempt to create a back door to all encryption solutions. This technology used a segmented key that was divided among several trustees.

False Acceptance Rate (FAR)   Error that occurs when a biometric device is not sensitive enough and an invalid subject is authenticated. Also referred to as a Type 2 error.

False Rejection Rate (FRR)   Error that occurs when a biometric device is too sensitive and a valid subject is not authenticated. Also referred to as a Type 1 error.

Family Educational Rights and Privacy Act (FERPA)   A specialized privacy bill that affects any educational institution that accepts any form of funding from the federal government (the vast majority of schools). It grants certain privacy rights to students over the age of 18 and the parents of minor students.

fault   A momentary loss of power.

Federal Information Processing Standard 140 (FIPS-140)   FIPS-140 defines the hardware and software requirements for cryptographic modules that the federal government uses.

Federal Sentencing Guidelines   A 1991 law that provides punishment guidelines for breaking federal laws.

fence   A perimeter-defining device. Fences are used to clearly differentiate between areas that are under a specific level of security protection and those that are not. Fencing can include a wide range of components, materials, and construction methods. It can be in the form of stripes painted on the ground, chain link fences, barbed wire, concrete walls, and even invisible perimeters using laser, motion, or heat detectors.

Fiber Distributed Data Interface (FDDI)   A high-speed token-passing technology that employs two rings with traffic flowing in opposite directions. FDDI offers transmission rates of 100Mbps and is often used as a backbone to large enterprise networks.

fiber-optic   A cabling form that transmits light instead of electrical signals. Fiber-optic cable supports throughputs up to 2Gbps and lengths of up to 2 kilometers.

file infector   Virus that infects different types of executable files and triggers when the operating system attempts to execute them. For Windows-based systems, these files end with .EXE and .COM extensions.

financial attack   A crime that is carried out to unlawfully obtain money or services.

fingerprints   The patterns of ridges on the fingers of humans. Often used as a biometric authentication factor.

firewall   A network device used to filter traffic. A firewall is typically deployed between a private network and a link to the Internet, but it can be deployed between departments within an organization. Firewalls filter traffic based on a defined set of rules.

firmware   Software that is stored in a ROM chip.

Flaw Hypothesis Methodology of Penetration Testing   "The Flaw Hypothesis Methodology is a system analysis and penetration technique where specifications and documentation for the system are analyzed and then flaws in the system are hypothesized. The list of hypothesized flaws is then prioritized on the basis of the estimated probability that a flaw actually exists and, assuming a flaw does exist, on the ease of exploiting it and on the extent of control or compromise it would provide. The prioritized list is used to direct the actual testing of the system." (Quoted from the NCSC/DOD/NIST Orange Book/TCSEC.)

flight time   The length of time between key presses. This is an element of the keystroke dynamics form of biometrics.

flooding   An attack that involves sending enough traffic to a victim to cause a DoS. Also referred to as a stream attack.

fortress mentality   In a fortress mentality security approach, a single giant master wall is built around the assets like the massive rock walls of a castle fortress. The major flaw in such an approach is that large massive structures often have minor weakness and flaws; are difficult if not impossible to reconfigure, adjust, or move; and are easily seen and avoided by would be attackers (i.e., they find easier ways into the protected area).

Fourth Amendment   An amendment to the U.S. constitution that prohibits government agents from searching private property without a warrant and probable cause. The courts have expanded their interpretation of the Fourth Amendment to include protections against wiretapping and other invasions of privacy.

fraggle   A form of denial of service attack similar to Smurf, but it uses UDP packets instead of ICMP.

fragment   When a network receives a packet larger than its maximum allowable packet size, it breaks it up into two or more fragments. These fragments are each assigned a size (corresponding to the length of the fragment) and an offset (corresponding to the starting location of the fragment).

fragmentation attacks   An attack that exploits vulnerabilities in the fragment reassembly functionality of the TCP/IP protocol stack.

Frame Relay   A shared connection medium that uses packet-switching technology to establish virtual circuits for customers.

frequency analysis   A cryptographic analysis or attack that looks for repetition of letters in an encrypted message and compares that with the statistics of letter usage for a specific language, such as the frequency of the letters *E, T, A, O, N, R, I, S,* and *H* in the English language.

full backup   A complete copy of data contained on the protected device on the backup media. Also refers to the process of making a complete copy of data, as in "performing a full backup."

full-interruption tests   A disaster recovery test that involves actually shutting down operations at the primary site and shifting them to the recovery site.

fun attacks   An attack launched by crackers with few true skills. The main motivation behind fun attacks is the thrill of getting into a system.

G

Gantt chart   A type of bar chart that shows the interrelationships over time between projects and schedules. It provides a graphical illustration of a schedule that helps to plan, coordinate, and track specific tasks in a project.

gate   A controlled exit and entry point in a fence.

gateway   A networking device that connects networks that are using different network protocols.

Government Information Security Reform Act of 2000   Act that amends the United States Code to implement additional information security policies and procedures.

government/military classification   The security labels commonly employed on secure systems used by the military. Military security labels range from highest sensitivity to lowest: top secret, secret, confidential, sensitive but unclassified, and unclassified (top secret, secret, confidential are collectively known as classified).

Gramm-Leach-Bliley (GLB) Act   A law passed in 1999 that eased the strict governmental barriers between financial institutions. Banks, insurance companies, and credit providers were severely limited in the services they could provide and the information they could share with each other. GLB somewhat relaxed the regulations concerning the services each organization could provide.

granular object control   A very specific and highly detailed level of control over the security settings of an object.

ground   The wire in an electrical circuit that is grounded (that is, connected with the earth).

group   An access control management simplification mechanism similar to a role. Similar users are made members of a group. A group is assigned access to an object. Thus, all members of the group are granted the same access to an object. The use of groups greatly simplifies the administrative overhead of managing user access to objects.

grudge attack   Attack usually motivated by a feeling of resentment and carried out to damage an organization or a person. The damage could be in the loss of information or harm to the organization or a person's reputation. Often the attacker is a current or former employee or someone who wishes ill will upon an organization.

guideline   A document that offers recommendations on how standards and baselines are implemented. Guidelines outline methodologies, include suggested actions, and are not compulsory.

H

hacker   A technology enthusiast who does not have malicious intent. Many authors and the media often use the term hacker when they are actually discussing issues relating to crackers.

Halon   A fire-suppressant material that converts to toxic gases at 900 degrees Fahrenheit and depletes the ozone layer of the atmosphere and is therefore usually replaced by an alternative material.

hand geometry   A type of biometric control that recognizes the physical dimensions of a hand. This includes width and length of the palm and fingers. It can be a mechanical or image-edge (i.e., visual silhouette) graphical solution.

handshaking   A three-way process utilized by the TCP/IP protocol stack to set up connections between two hosts.

hardware   An actual physical device, such as a hard drive, LAN card, printer, and so on.

hardware segmentation   A technique that implements process isolation at the hardware level by enforcing memory access constraints.

hash   See *hash function.*

hash function   The process of taking a potentially long message and generating a unique output value derived from the content of the message. This value is commonly referred to as the message digest.

hash total   A checksum used to verify the integrity of a transmission. See also *cyclic redundancy check (CRC).*

hash value   A number that is generated from a string of text and is substantially smaller than the text itself. A formula creates a hash value in a way that it is extremely unlikely that any other text will produce the same hash value.

Hashed Message Authentication Code (HMAC)   An algorithm that implements a partial digital signature—it guarantees the integrity of a message during transmission, but it does not provide for nonrepudiation.

Health Insurance Portability and Accountability Act (HIPAA)   A law passed in 1996 that made numerous changes to the laws governing health insurance and health maintenance organizations (HMOs). Among the provisions of HIPAA are privacy regulations requiring strict security measures for hospitals, physicians, insurance companies, and other organizations that process or store private medical information about individuals.

hearsay evidence   Evidence consisting of statements made to a witness by someone else outside of court. Computer log files that are not authenticated by a system administrator can also be considered hearsay evidence.

heart/pulse pattern   An example of a biometric factor, which is a behavioral or physiological characteristic that is unique to a subject. The heart/pulse pattern of a person is used to establish identity or provide authentication.

heuristics-based detection   See *behavior-based detection.*

hierarchical   A form of MAC environment. *Hierarchical environments* relate the various classification labels in an ordered structure from low security to medium security to high security. Each level or classification label in the structure is related. Clearance in a level grants the subject access to objects in that level as well as to all objects in all lower levels but prohibits access to all objects in higher levels.

hierarchical data model   A form of database that combines records and fields that are related in a logical tree structure. This is done so that each field can have one child or many or no children but each field can have only a single parent. Therefore, the data mapping relationship is one-to-many.

High-Speed Serial Interface (HSSI)   A layer 1 protocol used to connect routers and multiplexers to ATM or Frame Relay connection devices.

High-Level Data Link Control (HDLC)   A layer 2 protocol used to transmit data over synchronous communication lines. HDLC is an ISO standard based on IBM's SDLC. HDLC supports full-duplex communications, supports both point-to-point and multipoint connections, offers flow control, and includes error detection and correction.

high-level languages   Programming languages that are not machine languages or assembly languages. These languages are not hardware dependent and are more understandable by humans. Such languages must be converted to machine language before or during execution.

hijack attack   An attack in which a malicious user is positioned between a client and server and then interrupts the session and takes it over. Often, the malicious user impersonates the client so they can extract data from the server. The server is unaware that any change in the communication partner has occurred.

honey pot   Individual computers or entire networks created to serve as a snare for intruders. The honey pot looks and acts like a legitimate network, but it is 100 percent fake. Honey pots tempt intruders with unpatched and unprotected security vulnerabilities as well as hosting attractive, tantalizing, but faux data. Honey pots are designed to grab an intruder's attention and direct them into the restricted playground while keeping them away from the legitimate network and confidential resources.

host-based IDS   An intrusion detection system (IDS) that is installed on a single computer and can monitor the activities on that computer. A host-based IDS is able to pinpoint the files and processes compromised or employed by a malicious user to perform unauthorized activity.

hostile applet   Any piece of mobile code that attempts to perform unwanted or malicious activities.

hot site   A configuration in which a backup facility is maintained in constant working order, with a full complement of servers, workstations, and communications links ready to assume primary operations responsibilities.

hub   A network device used to connect multiple systems together in a star topology. Hubs repeat inbound traffic over all outbound ports.

hybrid   A type of MAC environment. A *hybrid environment* combines the hierarchical and compartmentalized concepts so that each hierarchical level may contain numerous subcompartments that are isolated from the rest of the security domain. A subject must have not only the correct clearance but also the need-to-know for the specific compartment in order to have access to the compartmentalized object.

hybrid attack   A form of password attack in which a dictionary attack is first attempted and then a type of brute force attack is performed. The follow-up brute force attack is used to add prefix or suffix characters to passwords from the dictionary in order to discover one-upped constructed passwords, two-upped constructed passwords, and so on.

Hypertext Transfer Protocol   The protocol used to transmit web page elements from a web server to web browsers (over the well-known service TCP/UDP port address 80).

Hypertext Transfer Protocol over Secure Sockets Layer (HTTPS)   A standard that uses port 443 to negotiate encrypted communications sessions between web servers and browser clients.

I

identification   The process by which a subject professes an identity and accountability is initiated. The identification process can consist of a user providing a username, a logon ID, a PIN, or a smart card or a process providing a process ID number.

identification card   A form of physical identification, generally contains a picture of the subject and/or a magnetic strip that contains additional information about a subject.

Identity Theft and Assumption Deterrence Act   An act that makes identity theft a crime against the person whose identity was stolen and provides severe criminal penalties (up to a 15-year prison term and/or a $250,000 fine) for anyone found guilty of violating it.

ignore risk   Denying that a risk exists and hoping that by ignoring a risk it will never be realized.

Internet Mail Authentication Protocol 4 (IMAP 4)   A protocol used to pull e-mail messages from an inbox on an e-mail server down to an e-mail client. IMAP is more secure than POP3, uses port 143, and offers the ability to pull headers down from the e-mail server as well as to store and manage messages on the e-mail server without having to download to the local client first.

immediate addressing   A way of referring to data that is supplied to the CPU as part of an instruction.

impersonation   The assumption of someone's identity or online account, usually through the mechanisms of spoofing and session replay. An impersonation attack is considered a more active attack than masquerading.

implementation attack   This type of attack exploits weaknesses in the implementation of a cryptography system. It focuses on exploiting the software code, not just errors and flaws but methodology employed to program the encryption system.

inappropriate activities   Actions that may take place on a computer or over the IT infrastructure and that may not be actual crimes but are often grounds for internal punishments or termination. Some types of inappropriate activities include viewing inappropriate content, sexual and racial harassment, waste, and abuse.

incident   The occurrence of a system intrusion.

incremental backups   A backup that stores only those files that have been modified since the time of the most recent full or incremental backup. Also the process of creating such a backup.

indirect addressing   The memory address that is supplied to the CPU as part of the instruction and doesn't contain the actual value that the CPU is to use as an operand. Instead, the memory address contains another memory address (perhaps located on a different page). The CPU then retrieves the actual operand from that address.

industrial espionage   The act of someone using illegal means to acquire competitive information.

inference   An attack that involves using a combination of several pieces of nonsensitive information to gain access to information that should be classified at a higher level.

inference engine   The second major component of an expert system that analyzes information in the knowledge base to arrive at the appropriate decision.

information flow model   A model that focuses on the flow of information to ensure that security is maintained and enforced no matter how information flows. Information flow models are based on a state machine model.

information hiding   Placing data and a subject at different security domains for the purpose of hiding the data from that subject.

informative policy   A policy that is designed to provide information or knowledge about a specific subject, such as company goals, mission statements, or how the organization interacts with partners and customers. An informative policy is nonenforceable.

inherit (or inheritance)   In object-oriented programming, inheritance refers to a class having one or more of the same methods from another class. So when a method has one or more of the same methods from another class, it is said to have "inherited" them.

initialization vector (IV)   A nonce used by numerous cryptography solutions to increase the strength of encrypted data by increasing the randomness of the input.

inrush   An initial surge of power usually associated with connecting to a power source, whether primary or alternate/secondary.

instance   In object-oriented programming, an instance can be an object, example, or representation of a class.

Integrated Services Digital Network (ISDN)   A digital end-to-end communications mechanism. ISDN was developed by telephone companies to support high-speed digital communications over the same equipment and infrastructure that is used to carry voice communications.

integrity   A state characterized by the assurance that modifications are not made by unauthorized users and authorized users do not make unauthorized modifications.

intellectual property   Intangible assets, such as secret recipes or production techniques.

International Data Encryption Algorithm (IDEA)   A block cipher that was developed in response to complaints about the insufficient key length of the DES algorithm. IDEA operates on 64-bit blocks of plain-/ciphertext, but it begins its operation with a 128-bit key.

International Organization for Standardization (ISO)   An independent oversight organization that defines and maintains computer, networking, and technology standards, along with more than 13,000 other international standards for business, government, and society.

Internet Key Exchange (IKE)   A protocol that provides for the secure exchange of cryptographic keys between IPSec participants.

Internet Message Access Protocol (IMAP)   A protocol used to transfer e-mail messages from an e-mail server to an e-mail client.

Internet Security Association and Key Management Protocol (ISAKMP)   A protocol that provides background security support services for IPSec.

interpreted languages   Programming languages that are converted to machine language one command at a time at the time of execution.

interrupt (IRQ)   A mechanism used by devices and components in a computer to get the attention of the CPU.

intranet   A private network that is designed to host the same information services found on the Internet.

intrusion   The condition in which a threat agent has gained access to an organization's infrastructure through the circumvention of security controls and is able to directly imperil assets. Also referred to as penetration.

intrusion detection   A specific form of monitoring both recorded information and real-time events to detect unwanted system access.

Intrusion detection system (IDS)   A product that automates the inspection of audit logs and real-time system events. IDSs are generally used to detect intrusion attempts, but they can also be employed to detect system failures or rate overall performance.

IP header protocol field value   An element in an IP packet header that identifies the protocol used in the IP packet payload (usually this will be 6 for TCP, 17 for UDP, or 1 for ICMP, or any of a number of other valid routing protocol numbers).

IP Payload Compression (IPcomp) protocol   A protocol that allows IPSec users to achieve enhanced performance by compression packets prior to the encryption operation.

IP probes   An attack technique that uses automated tools to ping each address in a range. Systems that respond to the ping request are logged for further analysis. Addresses that do not produce a response are assumed to be unused and are ignored.

IP Security (IPSec)   A standards-based mechanism for providing encryption for point-to-point TCP/IP traffic.

IP spoofing The process by which a malicious individual reconfigures their system so that it has the IP address of a trusted system and then attempts to gain access to other external resources.

iris scans An example of a biometric factor, which is a behavioral or physiological characteristic that is unique to a subject. The colored portion of the eye that surrounds the pupil is used to establish identity or provide authentication.

isolation A concept that ensures that any behavior will affect only the memory and resources associated with the process.

J

Java A platform-independent programming language developed by Sun Microsystems.

job description A detailed document outlining a specific position needed by an organization. A job description includes information about security classification, work tasks, and so on.

job responsibilities The specific work tasks an employee is required to perform on a regular basis.

job rotation A means by which an organization improves its overall security by rotating employees among numerous job positions. Job rotation serves two functions. First, it provides a type of knowledge redundancy. Second, moving personnel around reduces the risk of fraud, data modification, theft, sabotage, and misuse of information.

K

Kerchoff's assumption The idea that all algorithms should be public but all keys should remain private. Kerchoff's assumption is held by a large number of cryptologists, but not all of them.

Kerberos A ticket based authentication mechanism that employs a trusted third party to provide identification and authentication.

kernel The part of an operating system that always remains resident in memory (so that it can run on demand at any time).

kernel proxy firewalls A firewall that is integrated into an operating system's core to provide multiple levels of session and packet evaluation. Kernel proxy firewalls are known as fifth-generation firewalls.

key A secret value used to encrypt or decrypt messages.

Key Distribution Center (KDC) An element of the Kerberos authentication system. The KDC maintains all the secret keys of enrolled subjects and objects. A KDC is also a COMSEC facility that distributes symmetric crypto keys, especially for government entities.

key escrow system   A cryptographic recovery mechanism by which keys are stored in a database and can be recovered only by authorized key escrow agents in the event of key loss or damage.

keystroke dynamics   A biometric factor that measures how a subject uses a keyboard by analyzing flight time and dwell time.

keystroke monitoring   The act of recording the keystrokes a user performs on a physical keyboard. The act of recording can be visual (such as with a video recorder) or logical/technical (such as with a capturing hardware device or a software program).

keystroke patterns   An example of a biometric factor, which is a behavioral or physiological characteristic that is unique to a subject. The pattern and speed of a person typing a pass phrase is used to establish identity or provide authentication.

knowledge base   A component of an expert system, the knowledge base contains the rules known by an expert system and seeks to codify the knowledge of human experts in a series of "if/then" statements.

knowledge-based detection   An intrusion discovery mechanism used by IDS and based on a database of known attack signatures. The primary drawback to a knowledge-based IDS is that it is effective only against known attack methods.

known plaintext attack   An attack in which the attacker has a copy of the encrypted message along with the plaintext message used to generate the ciphertext (the copy). This greatly assists the attacker in breaking weaker codes.

KryptoKnight   A ticket-based authentication mechanism similar to Kerberos but based on peer-to-peer authentication.

L

LAN extender   A remote access, multilayer switch used to connect distant networks over WAN links. This is a strange beast of a device in that it creates WANs but marketers of this device steer clear of the term *WAN* and use only the terms *LAN* and *extended LAN*. The idea behind this device was to make the terminology easier to understand and thus make the device easier to sell than a more conventional WAN device grounded in complex concepts and terms.

land attack   A type of DoS. A land attack occurs when the attacker sends numerous SYN packets to a victim and the SYN packets have been spoofed to use the same source and destination IP address and port number as the victim's. This causes the victim to think it sent a TCP/IP session opening packet to itself, which causes a system failure, usually resulting in a freeze, crash, or reboot.

lattice-based access control   A variation of nondiscretionary access controls. Lattice-based access controls define upper and lower bounds of access for every relationship between a subject and object. These boundaries can be arbitrary, but they usually follow the military or corporate security label levels.

layer 1   The Physical layer of the OSI model.

layer 2   The Data Link layer of the OSI model.

layer 3   The Network layer of the OSI model.

layer 4   The Transport layer of the OSI model.

layer 5   The Session layer of the OSI model.

layer 6   The Presentation layer of the OSI model.

layer 7   The Application layer of the OSI model.

Layer 2 Forwarding (L2F)   A protocol developed by Cisco as a mutual authentication tunneling mechanism. L2F does not offer encryption.

Layer 2 Tunneling Protocol (L2TP)   A point-to-point tunnel protocol developed by combining elements from PPTP and L2F. L2TP lacks a built-in encryption scheme but typically relies upon IPSec as its security mechanism.

layering   The use of multiple security controls in series to provide for maximum effectiveness of security deployment.

learning rule   See *delta rule*.

licensing   A contract that states how a product is to be used.

lighting   One of the most commonly used forms of perimeter security control. The primary purpose of lighting is to discourage casual intruders, trespassers, prowlers, and would-be thieves who would rather perform their malicious activities in the dark.

link encryption   An encryption technique that protects entire communications circuits by creating a secure tunnel between two points. This is done by using either a hardware or software solution that encrypts all traffic entering one end of the tunnel and decrypts all traffic exiting the other end of the tunnel.

local alarm systems   Alarm systems that broadcast an audible signal that can be easily heard up to 400 feet away. Additionally, local alarm systems must be protected from tampering and disablement, usually by security guards. In order for a local alarm system to be effective, there must be a security team or guards positioned nearby who can respond when the alarm is triggered.

local area network (LAN)   A network that is geographically limited, such as within a single office, building, or city block.

log analysis   A detailed and systematic form of monitoring. The logged information is analyzed in detail to look for trends and patterns as well as abnormal, unauthorized, illegal, and policy-violating activities.

logging   The activity of recording information about events or occurrences to a log file or database.

logic bomb   Malicious code objects that infect a system and lie dormant until they are triggered by the occurrence of one or more conditions.

logical access control   A hardware or software mechanism used to manage access to resources and systems and provide protection for them. They are the same as technical access controls. Examples of logical or technical access controls include encryption, smart cards, passwords, biometrics, constrained interfaces, access control lists, protocols, firewalls, routers, intrusion detection systems, and clipping levels.

logon credentials   The identity and the authentication factors offered by a subject to establish access.

logon script   A script that runs at the moment of user logon. A logon script is often used to map local drive letters to network shares, to launch programs, or to open links to often accessed systems.

loopback address   The IP address used to create a software interface that connects to itself via the TCP/IP protocol. The loopback address is handled by software alone. It permits testing of the TCP/IP protocol stack even if network interfaces or their device drivers are missing or damaged.

Low Water-Mark Mandatory Access Control (LOMAC)   A loadable kernel module for Linux designed to protect the integrity of processes and data. It is an OS security architecture extension or enhancement that provides flexible support for security policies.

M

machine language   A programming language that can be directly executed by a computer.

macro viruses   A virus that utilizes crude technologies to infect documents created in the Microsoft Word environment.

mailbombing   An attack in which sufficient numbers of messages are directed to a single user's inbox or through a specific STMP server to cause a denial of service.

maintenance   The variety of tasks that are necessary to ensure continued operation in the face of changing operational, data processing, storage, and environmental requirements.

maintenance hooks   Entry points into a system that only the developer of the system knows; also called back doors.

malicious code   Code objects that include a broad range of programmed computer security threats that exploit various network, operating system, software, and physical security vulnerabilities to spread malicious payloads to computer systems.

mandatory access control   An access control mechanism that uses security labels to regulate subject access to objects.

mandatory vacations   A security policy that requires all employees to take vacations annually so their work tasks and privileges can be audited and verified. This often results in easy detection of abuse, fraud, or negligence.

man-in-the-middle attack   A type of attack that occurs when malicious users are able to position themselves between the two endpoints of a communication's link. The client and server are unaware that there is a third party intercepting and facilitating their communication session.

man-made disasters   Disasters cause by humans, including explosions, electrical fires, terrorist acts, power outages, utility failures, hardware/software failures, labor difficulties, theft, and vandalism.

mantrap   A double set of doors that is often protected by a guard. The purpose of a mantrap is to contain a subject until their identity and authentication is verified.

masquerading   Using someone else's security ID to gain entry into a facility or system.

massively parallel processing (MPP)   Technology used to create systems that house hundreds or even thousands of processors, each of which has its own operating system and memory/bus resources.

Master Boot Record (MBR)   The portion of a hard drive or floppy disk that the computer uses to load the operating system during the boot process.

Master Boot Record (MBR) virus   Virus that attacks the MBR. When the system reads the infected MBR, the virus instructs it to read and execute the code stored in an alternate location, thereby loading the entire virus into memory and potentially triggering the delivery of the virus's payload.

maximum tolerable downtime (MTD)   The maximum length of time a business function can be inoperable without causing irreparable harm to the business.

MD2 (Message Digest 2)   A hash algorithm developed by Ronald Rivest in 1989 to provide a secure hash function for 8-bit processors.

MD4   An enhanced version of the MD2 algorithm, released in 1990. MD4 pads the message to ensure that the message length is 64 bits smaller than a multiple of 512 bits.

MD5   The next version the MD algorithm, released in 1991, which processes 512-bit blocks of the message, but it uses four distinct rounds of computation to produce a digest of the same length as the MD2 and MD4 algorithms (128 bits).

mean time to failure (MTTF)   The length of time or number of uses a hardware or media component can endure before its reliability is questionable and it should be replaced.

Media Access Control (MAC) address   A 6-byte address written in hexadecimal. The first three bytes of the address indicate the vendor or manufacturer of the physical network interface. The last three bytes make up a unique number assigned to that interface by the manufacturer. No two devices on the same network can have the same MAC address.

meet-in-the-middle attack   An attack in which the attacker uses a known plaintext message. The plaintext is then encrypted using every possible key (k1), while the equivalent ciphertext is decrypted using all possible keys (k2). When a match is found, the corresponding pair (k1, k2) represents both portions of the double encryption. This type of attack generally takes only double the time necessary to break a single round of encryption (or $2^{(n+1)}$ rather than the anticipated $2^n * 2^n$), offering minimal added protection.

memory   The main memory resources directly available to a system's CPU. Primary memory normally consists of volatile random access memory (RAM) and is usually the most high-performance storage resource available to a system.

memory card   A device that can store data but cannot process it; often built around some form of flash memory.

memory page   A single chunk of memory that can be moved to and from RAM and the paging file on a hard drive as part of a virtual memory system.

memory-mapped I/O   A technique used to manage input/output between system components and the CPU.

Message   The communications to or input for an object (in the context of object-oriented programming terminology and concepts).

message digest (MD)   A summary of a message's content (not unlike a file checksum) produced by a hashing algorithm.

metadata   The results of a data mining operation on a data warehouse.

meta-model   A model of models. Because the spiral model encapsulates a number of iterations of another model (the waterfall model), it is known as a *meta-model*.

methods   The actions or functions performed on input (messages) to produce output (behaviors) by objects in an object-oriented programming environment.

microcode   A term used to describe software that is stored in a ROM chip. Also called firmware.

middle management   See *security professional*.

military and intelligence attacks   Attacks that are launched primarily to obtain secret and restricted information from law enforcement or military and technological research sources.

MIME Object Security Services (MOSS)   Standard that provides authenticity, confidentiality, integrity, and nonrepudiation for e-mail messages.

mitigated   The process by which a risk is removed.

mitigate risk   See *reducing risk*.

mobile sites   Non-mainstream alternatives to traditional recovery sites that typically consist of self-contained trailers or other easily relocated units.

module testing   In module testing, each independent or self-contained segment of code for which there exists a distinct and separate specification is tested independently of all other modules. This can also be called component testing. This can be seen as a parent or super-class of unit testing.

modulo   The remainder value left over after a division operation is performed.

MONDEX   A type of electronic payment system and protocol designed to manage cash on smart cards.

monitoring   The activity of manually or programmatically reviewing logged information looking for specific information.

motion detector   A device that senses the occurrence of motion in a specific area.

motion sensor   See *motion detector*.

multicast   A communications transmission to multiple identified recipients.

multilevel mode   See *multilevel security mode*.

multilevel security mode   A system that is authorized to process information at more than one level of security even when all system users do not have appropriate clearances or a need to know for all information processed by the system.

multipartite virus   A virus that uses more than one propagation technique in an attempt to penetrate systems that defend against only one method or the other.

multiprocessing   A technology that makes it possible for a computing system to harness the power of more than one processor to complete the execution of a single application.

multiprogramming   The pseudo-simultaneous execution of two tasks on a single processor coordinated by the operating system for the purpose of increasing operational efficiency. Multiprogramming is considered a relatively obsolete technology and is rarely found in use today except in legacy systems.

multistate   Term used to describe a system that is certified to handle multiple security levels simultaneously by using specialized security mechanisms that are designed to prevent information from crossing between security levels.

multitasking   A system handling two or more tasks simultaneously.

multithreading   A process that allows multiple users to make use of the same process without interfering with each other.

Mutual Assistance Agreement (MAA)   An agreement in which two organizations pledge to assist each other in the event of a disaster by sharing computing facilities or other technological resources.

N

natural disaster   A disaster that is not caused by man, such as earthquakes, mud slides, sink holes, fires, floods, hurricanes, tornadoes, falling rocks, snow, rainfall, ice, humidity, heat, extreme cold, and so on.

need-to-know   The requirement to have access to, knowledge about, or possession of data or a resource in order to perform specific work tasks. A user must have a need to know in order to gain access to data or resources. Even if that user has an equal or greater security classification than the requested information, if they do not have a need to know, they are denied access.

negligence   Failure to exercise the degree of care considered reasonable under the circumstances, resulting in an unintended injury to another party.

NetSP   A single sign-on product based on KryptoKnight.

Network Address Translation (NAT)   A mechanism for converting the internal nonroutable IP addresses found in packet headers into public IP addresses for transmission over the Internet.

Network layer   Layer 3 of the OSI model.

network-based IDS   An IDS installed onto a host to monitor a network. Network-based IDSs detect attacks or event anomalies through the capture and evaluation of network packets.

neural network   A system in which a long chain of computational decisions that feed into each other and eventually add up to produce the desired output is set up.

noise   A steady interfering disturbance.

nonce   A random number generator variable used in cryptography software and creates a new and unique value every time it is used often based on a timestamp based seed value.

nondisclosure agreement (NDA)   A document used to protect the confidential information within an organization from being disclosed by a former employee. When a person signs an NDA, they agree not to disclose any information that is defined as confidential to anyone outside of the organization. Often, violations of an NDA are met with strict penalties.

nondiscretionary access control   An access control mechanism that regulates subject access to objects by using roles or tasks.

noninterference model   A model loosely based on the information flow model. The noninterference model is concerned with the actions of one subject affecting the system state or actions of another subject.

nonrepudiation   A feature of a security control or an application that prevents the sender of a message or the subject of an activity or event from denying that the event occurred.

nonvolatile   See *nonvolatile storage*.

nonvolatile storage   A storage system that does not depend upon the presence of power to maintain its contents, such as magnetic/optical media and nonvolatile RAM (NVRAM).

normalization   The database process that removes redundant data and ensures that all attributes are dependent on the primary key.

NOT   An operation (represented by the ~ or ! symbol) that reverses the value of an input variable. This function operates on only one variable at a time.

O

object   A passive entity that provides information or data to subjects. An object can be a file, a database, a computer, a program, a process, a file, a printer, a storage media, and so on.

object linking and embedding (OLE)   A Microsoft technology used to link data objects into or from multiple files or sources on a computer.

object-oriented programming (OOP)   A method of programming that uses encapsulated code sets called *objects*. OOP is best suited for eliminating error propagation and mimicking or modeling the real world.

object-relational database   A relational database combined with an object-oriented programming environment.

one-time pad   An extremely powerful type of substitution cipher that uses a different key for each message. The key length is the same length as the message.

one-time password   A variant of dynamic passwords that is changed every time it is used.

one-upped constructed password   A password with a single-character difference from its present form in a dictionary list.

one-way encryption   A mathematical function performed on passwords, messages, CRCs, and so on that creates a cryptographic code that cannot be reversed.

one-way function   A mathematical operation that easily produces output values for each possible combination of inputs but makes it impossible to retrieve the input values. Public key cryptosystems are all based upon some sort of one-way function.

Open Systems Interconnection (OSI) model   A standard model developed to establish a common communication structure or standard for all computer systems.

operational plans   Short-term and highly detailed plans based on the strategic and tactical plans. Operational plans are valid or useful only for a short time. They must be updated often (such as monthly or quarterly) to retain compliance with tactical plans. Operational plans are detailed plans on how to accomplish the various goals of the organization.

operations security triple   The relationship between asset, vulnerability, and threat.

OR   An operation (represented by the ∨ symbol) that checks to see whether at least one of the input values is true.

organizational owner   See *senior management*.

OSI model   See *Open Systems Interconnection (OSI) model*.

Output Feedback (OFB)   A mode in which DES XORs plaintext with a seed value. For the first encrypted block, an initialization vector is used to create the seed value. Future seed values are derived by running the DES algorithm on the preceding seed value. The major advantage of OFB mode is that transmission errors do not propagate to affect the decryption of future blocks.

overt channel   An obvious, visible, detectable, known method of communicating that is addressed by a security policy and subsequently controlled by logical or technical access controls.

overwriting   See *clearing*.

owner   The person who has final corporate responsibility for the protection and storage of data. The owner may be liable for negligence if they fail to perform due diligence in establishing and enforcing security policy to protect and sustain sensitive data. The owner is typically the CEO, president, or department head.

P

package   In the context of the Common Criteria for information technology security evaluation, a package is a set of security features that can be added or removed from a target system.

packet   A portion of a message that contains data and the destination address; also called a datagram.

padded cell   Similar to a honey pot. When an intruder is detected by an IDS, the intruder is transferred to a padded cell. The padded cell has the look and layout of the actual network, but within the padded cell the intruder can neither perform malicious activities nor access any confidential data. A padded cell is a simulated environment that may offer fake data to retain an intruder's interest.

palm geography   An example of a biometric factor, which is a behavioral or physiological characteristic that is unique to a subject. The shape of a person's hand is used to establish identity or provide authentication.

palm scan   See *palm topography*.

palm topography   An example of a biometric factor, which is a behavioral or physiological characteristic that is unique to a subject. The layout of ridges, creases, and grooves on a person's palm is used to establish identity or provide authentication. Same as a palm scan and similar to a fingerprint.

parallel run   A type of new system deployment testing in which the new system and the old system are run in parallel.

parallel tests   Testing that involves actually relocating personnel to an alternate recovery site and implementing site activation procedures.

parole evidence rule   An rule that states that when an agreement between parties is put into written form, the written document is assumed to contain all of the terms of the agreement and no verbal agreements may modify the written agreement.

pass phrase   A string of characters usually much longer than a password. Once the pass phrase is entered, the system converts it into a virtual password for use by the authentication process. Pass phrases are often natural language sentences to allow for simplified memorization.

password   A string of characters entered by a subject as an authentication factor.

Password Authentication Protocol (PAP)   A standardized authentication protocol for PPP. PAP transmits usernames and passwords in the clear. PAP offers no form of encryption; it simply provides a means to transport the logon credentials from the client to the authentication server.

password policy   The section of an organization's security policy that dictates the rules, restrictions, and requirements of passwords. Can also indicate the programmatic controls deployed on a system to improve the strength of passwords.

password restrictions   The rules that define the minimal requirements of passwords, such as length, character composition, and age.

patent   A governmental grant that bestows upon an invention's creator the sole right to make, use, and sell that invention for a set period of time.

pattern-matching detection   See *knowledge-based detection*.

penetration   See *intrusion*.

penetration testing   An activity used to test the strength and effectiveness of deployed security measures with an authorized attempted intrusion attack. Penetration testing should be performed only with the consent and knowledge of the management staff.

permanent virtual circuit (PVC)   A predefined virtual circuit that is always available for a Frame Relay customer.

personal identification number (PIN)   A number or code assigned to a person to be used as an identification factor. PINs should be kept secret.

personnel management   An important factor in maintaining operations security. Personnel management is a form of administrative control or administrative management.

phone phreaking   The process of breaking into telephone company computers to place free calls.

physical access control   A physical barrier deployed to prevent direct contact with systems. Examples of physical access controls include guards, fences, motion detectors, locked doors, sealed windows, lights, cable protection, laptop locks, swipe cards, dogs, CCTV, mantraps, and alarms.

physical controls for physical security   See *physical access control*.

Physical layer   Layer 1 of the OSI model.

piggybacking   The act of following someone through a secured gate or doorway without being identified or authorized personally.

ping   A utility used to troubleshoot a connection to test whether a particular IP address is accessible.

ping of death attack   A type of DoS. A ping of death attack employs an oversized ping packet. Using special tools, an attacker can send numerous oversized ping packets to a victim. In many cases, when the victimized system attempts to process the packets, an error occurs causing the system to freeze, crash, or reboot.

plain old telephone service (POTS)   Normal telephone service.

plaintext   A message that has not been encrypted.

playback attack   See *replay attack*.

Point-to-Point Protocol (PPP)   A full-duplex protocol used for the transmission of TCP/IP packets over various non-LAN connections, such as modems, ISDN, VPNs, Frame Relay, and so on. PPP is widely supported and is the transport protocol of choice for dial-up Internet connections.

Point to Point Tunneling Protocol (PPTP)   An enhancement of PPP that creates encrypted tunnels between communication endpoints. PPTP is used on VPNs but is often replaced by L2TP.

policy   See *security policy*.

polyalphabetic substitution   A cryptographic transformation that encrypts a message using letter-by-letter conversion and multiple alphabets from different languages or countries.

polyinstantiation   The event that occurs when two or more rows in the same table appear to have identical primary key elements but contain different data for use at differing classification levels. Polyinstantiation is often used as a defense against some types of inference attacks.

polymorphic virus   A virus that modifies its own code as it travels from system to system. The virus's propagation and destruction techniques remain exactly the same, but the signature of the virus is somewhat different each time it infects a new system.

polymorphism   In the context of object-oriented programming terminology and concepts, the characteristic of an object to provide different behaviors based upon the same message and methods owing to variances in external conditions.

port   A connection address within a protocol.

Port Address Translation (PAT)   A mechanism for converting the internal nonroutable IP addresses found in packet headers into public IP addresses and port numbers for transmission over the Internet. PAT supports a many-to-one mapping of internal to external IP addresses by using ports.

port scan   Software used by an intruder to probe all of the active systems on a network and determine what public services are running on each machine.

postmortem review   An analysis and review of an activity after its completion to determine its success and whether processes and procedures need to be improved.

Post Office Protocol, version 3 (POP3)   A protocol used to transfer e-mail messages from an e-mail server to an e-mail client.

preaction system   A combination dry pipe/wet pipe system. The system exists as a dry pipe until the initial stages of a fire (smoke, heat, etc.) are detected and then the pipes are filled with water. The water is released only after the sprinkler head activation triggers are melted by sufficient heat. If the fire is quenched before the sprinklers are triggered, the pipes can be manually emptied and reset. This also allows for manual intervention to stop the release of water before sprinkler triggering occurs. Preaction systems are the most appropriate water-based system for environments that include both computers and humans in the same locations.

Presentation layer   Layer 6 of the OSI model.

Pretty Good Privacy (PGP)   A public/private key system that uses the IDEA algorithm to encrypt files and e-mail messages. PGP is not a standard but rather an independently developed product that has wide Internet grassroots support.

preventative access control   An access control deployed to stop an unwanted or unauthorized activity from occurring. Examples of preventative access controls include fences, security policies, security awareness training, and anti-virus software.

preventive access control   See *preventative access control*.

preventive control   See *preventative access control*.

primary memory   Storage that normally consists of volatile random access memory (RAM) and is usually the most high-performance storage resource available to a system.

Primary Rate Interface (PRI)   An ISDN service type that provides up to 23 B channels and one D channel. Thus, a full PRI ISDN connection offers 1.544Mbps throughput, the same as a T1 line.

primary storage   The RAM that a computer uses to keep necessary information readily available.

principle of least privilege   An access control philosophy that states that subjects are granted the minimal access possible for the completion of their work tasks.

privacy   An element of confidentiality aimed at preventing personal or sensitive information about an individual or organization from being disclosed.

Privacy Act of 1974   A law that mandates that agencies maintain only records that are necessary for the conduct of their business and destroy those records when they are no longer needed for a legitimate function of government. It provides a formal procedure for individuals to gain access to records the government maintains about them and to request that incorrect records be amended. The Privacy Act also restricts the way the federal government can deal with private information about individual citizens.

Privacy Enhanced Mail (PEM)   An e-mail encryption mechanism that provides authentication, integrity, confidentiality, and nonrepudiation. PEM is a layer 7 protocol. PEM uses RSA, DES, and X.509.

private   A commercial business/private sector classification used for data of a private or personal nature that is intended for internal use only. A significant negative impact could occur for the company or individuals if private data is disclosed.

private branch exchange (PBX)   A sophisticated telephone system often used by organizations to provide inbound call support, extension-to-extension calling, conference calling, and voice mail. Implemented as a stand-alone phone system network or can be integrated with the IT infrastructure.

private key   A secret value that is used to encrypt or decrypt messages and is kept secret and known only to the user; used in conjunction with a public key in asymmetrical cryptography.

privileged entity controls   See *privileged operations functions.*

privileged mode   The mode designed to give the operating system access to the full range of instructions supported by the CPU.

privileged operations functions   Activities that require special access or privilege to perform within a secured IT environment. In most cases, these functions are restricted to administrators and system operators.

problem state   The state in which a process is actively executing.

procedure   In the context of security, a detailed step-by-step how-to document describing the exact actions necessary to implement a specific security mechanism, control, or solution.

process isolation   One of the fundamental security procedures put into place during system design. Basically, using process isolation mechanisms (whether part of the operating system or part of the hardware itself) ensures that each process has its own isolated memory space for storage of data and the actual executing application code itself.

processor   The central processing unit in a PC; it handles all functions on the system.

Program Evaluation Review Technique (PERT)   A project scheduling tool. It is a method used to judge the size of a software product in development and calculate the Standard Deviation (SD) for risk assessment. PERT relates the estimated lowest possible size, the most likely size, and the highest possible size of each component. PERT is used to direct improvements to project management and software coding in order to produce more efficient software. As the capabilities of programming and management improve, the actual produced size of software should be smaller.

programmable read-only memory (PROM)   A PROM chip that does not have its contents "burncd in" at the factory as is done with standard ROM chips. Instead, special functionality is installed that allows the end user to burn in the contents of the chip.

proprietary   A form of commercial business/private sector confidential information. If proprietary data is disclosed, it can have drastic effects on the competitive edge of an organization.

protection profile   From the Common Criteria for information technology security evaluation, the evaluation element in which a subject states its security needs.

protocol   A set of rules and restrictions that define how data is transmitted over a network medium (e.g., twisted-pair cable, wireless transmission, etc.). Protocols make computer-to-computer communications possible.

proximity reader   A passive device, field-powered device, or transponder that detects the presence of authorized personnel and grants them physical entry into a facility. The proximity device is worn or held by the authorized bearer. When they pass a proximity reader, the reader is able to determine who the bearer is and whether they have authorized access.

proxy   A mechanism that copies packets from one network into another. The copy process also changes the source and destination address to protect the identity of the internal or private network.

prudent man rule   Invoked by the Federal Sentencing Guidelines, the rule that requires senior officials to perform their duties with the care that ordinary, prudent people would exercise under similar circumstances.

pseudo-flaws   A technique often used on honey pot systems and on critical resources to emulate well-known operating system vulnerabilities.

public   The lowest level of commercial business/private sector classification. Used for all data that does not fit in one of the higher classifications. This information is not readily disclosed, but if it is it should not have a serious negative impact on the organization.

public IP addresses   The addresses defined in RFC 1918, which are not routed over the Internet.

public key   A value that is used to encrypt or decrypt messages and is made public to any user and used with a private key in asymmetric cryptography.

public key infrastructure (PKI)   A hierarchy of trust relationships that makes it possible to facilitate communication between parties previously unknown to each other.

purging   The process of erasing of media so it can be reused in a less secure environment.

Q

qualitative decision making   A decision making process that takes nonnumerical factors, such as emotions, investor/customer confidence, workforce stability, and other concerns, into account. This type of data often results in categories of prioritization (such as high, medium, and low).

qualitative risk analysis   Scenario-oriented analysis using ranking and grading for exposure ratings and decisions.

quality assurance check   A form of personnel management and project management that oversees the development of a product. QA checks ensure that the product in development is consistent with stated standards, methods of practice, efficiency, and so on.

quantitative decision making   The use of numbers and formulas to reach a decision. Options are often expressed in terms of the dollar value to the business.

quantitative risk analysis   A method that assigns real dollar figures to the loss of an asset.

R

radiation monitoring   A specific form of sniffing or eavesdropping that involves the detection, capture, and recording of radio frequency signals and other radiated communication methods, including sound and light.

radio frequency interference (RFI)   A type of noise that is generated by a wide number of common electrical appliances, including florescent lights, electrical cables, electric space heaters, computers, elevators, motors, electric magnets, and so on. RFI can affect many of the same systems EMI affects.

RADIUS   See *Remote Authentication Dial-In User Service (RADIUS)*.

random access memory (RAM)   Readable and writeable memory that contains information the computer uses during processing. RAM retains its contents only when power is continuously supplied to it.

random access storage   Devices, such as RAM and hard drives, that allow the operating system to request contents from any point within the media.

read-only memory (ROM)   Memory that can be read but cannot be written to.

ready state   The state in which a process is ready to execute but is waiting for its turn on the CPU.

real evidence   Items that can actually be brought into a court of law; also known as object evidence.

real memory   Typically the largest RAM storage resource available to a computer. It is normally composed of a number of dynamic RAM chips and therefore must be refreshed by the CPU on a periodic basis; also known as main memory or primary memory.

realized risk   The incident, occurrence, or event when a risk becomes a reality and a breach, attack, penetration, or intrusion has occurred that may or may not result in loss, damage, or disclosure of assets.

record   Contents of a table in a relational database.

record retention   The organizational policy that defines what information is maintained and for how long. In most cases, the records in question are audit trails of user activity. This may include file and resource access, logon patterns, e-mail, and the use of privileges.

record sequence checking   Similar to hash total checking, but instead of verifying content integrity, it involves verifying packet or message sequence integrity.

recovery access control   A type of access control that is used to repair or restore resources, functions, and capabilities after a security policy violation.

recovery time objective (RTO)   See *maximum tolerable downtime*.

reducing risk   The implementation of safeguards and countermeasures. Also referred to as mitigating risk.

reference monitor   A portion of the security kernel that validates user requests against the system's access control mechanisms.

reference profile   The digitally stored sample of a biometric factor.

reference template   See *reference profile*.

referential integrity   Used to enforce relationships between two tables. One table in the relationship contains a foreign key that corresponds to the primary key of the other table in the relationship.

register   A limited amount of onboard memory in a CPU.

register address   The address of a register, which is a small memory locations directly on the CPU. When the CPU needs information from one of those registers to complete an operation, it can simply use the register address (e.g., "register one") to access the information.

registration authority (RA)   A read-only version of a certificate authority that is able to distribute the CRL and perform certificate verification processes but is not able to create new certificates. An RA is used to share the workload of a CA.

regulatory policy   A policy that is required whenever industry or legal standards are applicable to your organization. This policy discusses the regulations that must be followed and outlines the procedures that should be used to elicit compliance.

reject risk   To deny that a risk exists or hope that by ignoring a risk, it will never be realized. It is an unacceptable response to risk. Also referred to as deny risk.

relational database   A database that consists of tables that contain a set of related records.

relationship   The association of information in tables of a relational database.

relevant Characteristic of evidence that is applicable in determining a fact in a court of law.

Remote Authentication Dial-In User Service (RADIUS) A service used to centralize the authentication of remote dial-up connections.

remote journaling Transferring copies of the database transaction logs containing the transactions that occurred since the previous bulk transfer.

remote mirroring Maintaining a live database server at the backup site. It is the most advanced database backup solution.

repeater A network device used to amplify signals on network cabling to allow for longer distances between nodes. Can also be called a concentrator or amplifier.

replay attack An attack in which a malicious user records the traffic between a client and server. The packets sent from the client to the server are then played back or retransmitted to the server with slight variations of the time stamp and source IP address (i.e., spoofing). In some cases, this allows the malicious user to restart an old communication link with a server. Also referred to as a playback attack.

residual risk Risk that comprises specific threats to specific assets against which upper management chooses not to implement a safeguard. In other words, residual risk is the risk that management has chosen to accept rather than mitigate.

restricted interface model A model that uses classification-based restrictions to offer only subject-specific authorized information and functions. One subject at one classification level will see one set of data and have access to one set of functions while another subject at a different classification level will see a different set of data and have access to a different set of functions.

retina scan An example of a biometric factor, which is a behavioral or physiological characteristic that is unique to a subject. The blood vessel pattern at the back of the eyeball is used to establish identity or provide authentication.

Reverse Address Resolution Protocol (RARP) A subprotocol of the TCP/IP protocol suite that operates at the Data Link layer (layer 2). RARP is used to discover the IP address of a system by polling using its MAC address.

reverse engineering This is considered an unethical form of engineering. Programmers decompile code to understand all the intricate details of its functionality, especially when employed for the purpose of creating a similar, competing, or compatible product.

reverse hash matching The process of discovering the original message that has been hashed by generating potential messages, hashing them, and comparing their hash value to the original. When H(M)=H(M'), then M=M'.

revocation A mechanism that allows a PKI certificate to be canceled, effectively removing a user from the system.

RFC 1918 The public standard that defines public and private IP addresses.

Rijndael block cipher   A block cipher that was selected to replace DES. The Rijndael cipher allows the use of three key strengths: 128 bits, 192 bits, and 256 bits.

risk   The likelihood that any specific threat will exploit a specific vulnerability to cause harm to an asset. Risk is an assessment of probability, possibility, or chance. Risk = threat + vulnerability.

risk analysis   An element of risk management that includes analyzing an environment for risks, evaluating each risk as to its likelihood of occurring and cost of damage, assessing the cost of various countermeasures for each risk, and creating a cost/benefit report for safeguards to present to upper management.

risk management   A detailed process of identifying factors that could damage or disclose data, evaluating those factors in light of data value and countermeasure cost, and implementing cost-effective solutions for mitigating or reducing risk.

risk tolerance   The ability of an organization to absorb the losses associated with realized risks.

Rivest, Shamir, and Adleman (RSA)   A public key encryption algorithm named after Rivest, Shamir, and Adleman, its inventors.

role-based access control   A form of nondiscretionary access controls that employs job function roles to regulate subject access to objects.

root   The administrator level of a system.

rootkit   A specialized software package that allows hackers to gain expanded access to a system.

router   A network device used to control traffic flow on networks. Routers are often used to connect similar networks together and control traffic flow between them. They can function using statically defined routing tables or employ a dynamic routing system.

RSA   See *Rivest, Shamir, and Adleman (RSA)*.

rule-based access control   A variation of mandatory access controls. A rule-based system uses a set of rules, restrictions, or filters to determine what can and cannot occur on the system, such as granting subject access, performing an action on an object, or accessing a resource. Firewalls, proxies, and routers are common examples of rule-based access control systems.

running key cipher   A form of cryptography in which the key is a designation of a changing source, such as the third page of the *New York Times*.

running state   The state in which a process is actively executing. This is another name for problem state.

S

S/MIME   See *Secure Multipurpose Internet Mail Extensions (S/MIME)*.

safeguard   Anything that removes a vulnerability or protects against one or more specific threats. Also referred to as a countermeasure.

sag   Momentary low voltage.

salami attack   An attack performed by gathering small amounts of data to construct something of greater value or higher sensitivity.

salt   A random number appended to a password before hashing to increase randomness and ensure uniqueness in the resulting stored hash value.

sampling   A form of data reduction that allows an auditor to quickly determine the important issues or events from an audit trail.

sandbox   A security boundary within which a Java applet executes.

sanitization   Any number of processes that prepares media for destruction. Sanitization is the process that ensures that data cannot be recovered by any means from destroyed or discarded media. Sanitization can also be the actual means by which media is destroyed. Media can be sanitized by purging or degaussing without physically destroying the media.

scanning   Similar to "casing" a neighborhood prior to a burglary, the process by which a potential intruder looks for possible entryways into a system. Scanning can indicate that illegal activity will follow, so it is a good idea to treat scans as incidents and to collect evidence of scanning activity.

scavenging   A form of dumpster diving performed electronically. Online scavenging searches for useful information in the remnants of data left over after processes or tasks are completed. This could include audit trails, log files, memory dumps, variable settings, port mappings, cached data, and so on.

schema   The structure that holds the data that defines or describes a database. The schema is written using a Data Definition Language (DDL).

scripted access   A method to automate the logon process with a script that provides the logon credentials to a system. It is considered a form of single sign-on.

search warrant   A document obtained through the judicial system that allows law enforcement personnel to acquire evidence from a location without first alerting the individual believed to have perpetrated a crime.

secondary evidence   A copy of evidence or an oral description of the contents of best evidence.

secondary memory   Magnetic/optical media and other storage devices that contain data not immediately available to the CPU.

secondary storage   Data repositories that include magnetic and optical media, such as tapes, disks, hard drives, and CD/DVD storage.

second-tier attack   An assault that relies upon information or data gained from eavesdropping or other similar data-gathering techniques. In other words, it is an attack that is launched only after some other attack is completed.

secret   A government/military classification, used for data of a secret nature. Unauthorized disclosure of secret data could cause serious damage to national security.

secure communication protocol   A protocol that uses encryption to provide security for the data transmitted by it.

Secure Electronic Transaction (SET)   A security protocol for the transmission of transactions over the Internet. SET is based on RSA encryption and DES. SET has the support of major credit card companies, such as Visa and MasterCard.

Secure Hash Algorithm (SHA)   A government standard hash function developed by the National Institute of Standards and Technology (NIST) and specified in an official government publication.

Secure HTTP (S-HTTP)   The second major protocol used to provide security on the World Wide Web.

Secure Multipurpose Internet Mail Extensions (S/MIME)   A protocol used to secure the transmission of e-mail and attachments.

Secure Remote Procedure Call (S-RPC)   An authentication service. S-RPC is simply a means to prevent unauthorized execution of code on remote systems.

Secure Shell (SSH)   An end-to-end encryption technique. This suite of programs provide encrypted alternatives to common Internet applications like FTP, Telnet, and rlogin. There are actually two versions of SSH. SSH1 supports the DES, 3DES, IDEA, and Blowfish algorithms. SSH2 drops support for DES and IDEA but adds support for several other algorithms.

Secure Sockets Layer (SSL)   An encryption protocol developed by Netscape to protect the communications between a web server and a web browser.

security association (SA)   In an IPSec session, the representation of the communication session and process of recording any configuration and status information about the connection.

security ID   A form of physical identification, generally contains a picture of the subject and/or a magnetic strip that contains additional information about a subject.

security kernel   The core set of operating system services that handles all user/application requests for access to system resources.

security label   An assigned classification or sensitivity level used in security models to determine the level of security required to protect an object and prevent unauthorized access.

security management planning   The act of thoroughly and systematically designing procedural and policy documentation to reduce risk and then to maintain risk at an acceptable level for a given environment.

security perimeter   The imaginary boundary that separates the trusted computing base from the rest of the system.

security policy   A document that defines the scope of security needs of an organization, prescribes solutions to manage security issues, and discusses the assets that need protection, and the extent to which security solutions should go to provide the necessary protection.

security professional   Trained and experienced network, systems, and security engineer who is responsible for following the directives mandated by senior management.

security role   The part an individual plays in the overall scheme of security implementation and administration within an organization.

security target   The evaluation element from the Common Criteria for information technology security evaluation in which a vendor states the security features of its product.

senior management   A person or group who is ultimately responsible for the security maintained by an organization and who should be most concerned about the protection of its assets. They must sign off on all policy issues, and they will be held liable for overall success or failure of a security solution. It is the responsibility of senior management to show prudent due care. Also referred to as organizational owner and upper management.

sensitive   A commercial business/private sector classification used for data that is more sensitive than public data. A negative impact could occur for the company if sensitive data is disclosed.

sensitive but unclassified   A government/military classification used for data of a sensitive or private nature but significant damage would not occur if disclosed.

sensitivity   In regard to biometric devices, the level at which the device is configured for scanning.

separation of duties and responsibilities   A common practice to prevent any single subject from being able to circumvent or disable security mechanisms. By dividing core administration or high-authority responsibilities among several subjects, no one subject has sufficient access to perform significant malicious activities or bypass imposed security controls.

separation of privilege   The principle that builds upon the principle of least privilege. It requires the use of granular access permissions; that is, different permissions for each type of privileged operation. This allows designers to assign some processes rights to perform certain supervisory functions without granting them unrestricted access to the system.

Sequenced Packet Exchange (SPX)   The Transport layer protocol of the IPX/SPX protocol suite from Novell.

sequential storage   Devices that require that you read (or speed past) all of the data physically stored prior to the desired location. A common example of a sequential storage device is a magnetic tape drive.

Serial Line Internet Protocol (SLIP)   An older technology developed to support TCP/IP communications over asynchronous serial connections, such as serial cables or modem dial-up.

Service Level Agreement (SLA)   A contractual obligation to your clients that requires you to implement sound BCP practices. Also used to assure acceptable levels of service from suppliers for sound BCP practices.

SESAME   A ticket-based authentication mechanism similar to Kerberos.

session hijacking   An attack that occurs when a malicious individual intercepts part of a communication between an authorized user and a resource and then uses a hijacking technique to take over the session and assume the identity of the authorized user.

Session layer   Layer 5 of the OSI model.

shielded twisted-pair (STP)   A twisted-pair wire that includes a metal foil wrapper inside of the outer sheath to provide additional protection from EMI.

shoulder surfing   The act of gathering information from a system by observing the monitor or the use of the keyboard by the operator.

shrink-wrap license agreement   A license written on the outside of software packaging. Such licenses get their name because they commonly include a clause stating that you acknowledge agreement to the terms of the contract simply by breaking the shrink-wrap seal on the package.

signature-based detection   The process used by antivirus software to identify potential virus infections on a system.

signature dynamics   When used as a biometric, the use of the pattern and speed of a person writing their signature to establish identity or provide authentication.

Simple Integrity Axiom (SI Axiom)   An axiom of the Biba model that states that a subject at a specific classification level cannot read data with a lower classification level. This is often shortened to "no read down."

Simple Key Management for IP (SKIP)   An encryption tool used to protect sessionless datagram protocols.

Simple Mail Transfer Protocol (SMTP)   The primary protocol used to move e-mail messages from clients to servers and from server to server.

Simple Security Property (SS property)   A property of the Bell-LaPadula model that states that a subject at a specific classification level cannot read data with a higher classification level. This is often shortened to "no read up."

simulation tests   A test in which disaster recovery team members are presented with a scenario and asked to develop an appropriate response. Some of these response measures are then tested. This may involve the interruption of noncritical business activities and the use of some operational personnel.

single loss expectancy (SLE)   The cost associated with a single realized risk against a specific asset. The SLE indicates the exact amount of loss an organization would experience if an asset were harmed by a specific threat. SLE = asset value ($) * exposure factor (EF).

Single Sign On (SSO)   A mechanism that allows subjects to authenticate themselves only once to a system. With SSO, once subjects are authenticated, they can freely roam the network and access resources and service without being rechallenged for authentication.

single state   Systems that require the use of policy mechanisms to manage information at different levels. In this type of arrangement, security administrators approve a processor and system to handle only one security level at a time.

single-use passwords   A variant of dynamic passwords that are changed every time they are used.

Skipjack   Associated with the Escrowed Encryption Standard, an algorithm that operates on 64-bit blocks of text. It uses an 80-bit key and supports the same four modes of operation supported by DES. Skipjack was proposed but never implemented by the U.S. government. It provides the cryptographic routines supporting the Clipper and Capstone high-speed encryption chips designed for mainstream commercial use.

smart card   Credit-card-sized ID, badge, or security pass that has a magnetic strip, bar code, or integrated circuit chip embedded in it. Smart cards can contain information about the authorized bearer that can be used for identification and/or authentication purposes.

Smurf attack   A type of DoS. A Smurf attack occurs when an amplifying server or network is used to flood a victim with useless data.

sniffer attack   Any activity that results in a malicious user obtaining information about a network or the traffic over that network. A sniffer is often a packet-capturing program that duplicates the contents of packets traveling over the network medium into a file. Also referred to as a snooping attack.

sniffing   A form of network traffic monitoring. Sniffing often involves the capture or duplication of network traffic for examination, re-creation, and extraction.

snooping attack   See *sniffer attack*.

social engineering   A skill by which an unknown person gains the trust of someone inside of your organization and encourages them to make a change to IT system in order to grant them access.

socket   Another name for a port.

software IP encryption (SWIPE)   A layer 3 security protocol for IP. It provides authentication, integrity, and confidentiality using an encapsulation protocol.

spam   The term describing unwanted e-mail, newsgroup, or discussion forum messages. Spam can be as innocuous as an advertisement from a well-meaning vendor or as malignant as floods of unrequested messages with viruses or Trojan horses attached.

spamming attacks   Sending significant amounts of spam to a system in order to cause a DoS or general irritation, consume storage space, or consume bandwidth and processing capabilities.

spike   Momentary high voltage.

split knowledge   The specific application of the ideas of separation of duties and two-man control into a single solution. The basic idea is that the information or privilege required to perform an operation is divided among multiple users. This ensures that no single person has sufficient privileges to compromise the security of the environment.

spoofing   The act of replacing the valid source and/or destination IP address and node numbers with false ones.

spoofing attack   Any attack that involves spoofed or modified packets.

standards   Documents that define compulsory requirements for the homogenous use of hardware, software, technology, and security controls. They provide a course of action by which technology and procedures are uniformly implemented throughout an organization. Standards are tactical documents that define steps or methods to accomplish the goals and overall direction defined by security policies.

state   A snapshot of a system at a specific instance in time.

state machine model   A system that is designed so that no matter what function is performed, it is always a secure system.

stateful inspection firewall   A firewall that evaluates the state or the context of network traffic. By examining source and destination address, application usage, source of origin, and the relationship between current packets with the previous packets of the same session, stateful inspection firewalls are able to grant a broader range of access for authorized users and activities and actively watch for and block unauthorized users and activities. Stateful inspection firewalls are known as third-generation firewalls.

static packet-filtering firewall   A firewall that filters traffic by examining data from a message header. Usually the rules are concerned with source, destination, and port addresses. Static packet-filtering firewalls as known as first-generation firewalls.

static password   Password that does not change over time or that remains the same for a significant period of time.

static token   A physical means to provide identity, usually not employed as an authentication factor. Examples include a swipe card, a smart card, a floppy disk, a USB RAM dongle, or even something as simple as a key to operate a physical lock.

statistical attack   This type of attack exploits statistical weaknesses in a cryptosystem, such as such as floating point errors or an inability to produce random numbers. It attempts to find vulnerabilities in the hardware or operating system hosting the cryptography application.

statistical intrusion detection   See *behavior-based detection.*

stealth virus   A virus that hides itself by actually tampering with the operating system to fool antivirus packages into thinking that everything is functioning normally.

steganography   The act of embedding messages within another message, commonly used within an image or a WAV file.

stop error   The security response of an operating system, such as Windows, when an application performs an illegal operation, such as accessing hardware or modifying/accessing the memory space of another process.

stopped state   The state in which a process is finished or must be terminated. At this point, the operating system can recover all memory and other resources allocated to the process and reuse them for other processes as needed.

strategic plan   A long-term plan that is fairly stable. It defines the organization's goals, mission, and objectives. A strategic plan is useful for about five years if it is maintained and updated annually. The strategic plan also serves as the planning horizon.

stream attack   A type of DoS. A stream attack occurs when a large number of packets are sent to numerous ports on the victim system using random source and sequence numbers. The processing performed by the victim system attempting to make sense of the data will result in a DoS. Also referred to as flooding.

stream ciphers   Ciphers that operate on each character or bit of a message (or data stream) one character/bit at a time.

strong password   Password that is resistant to dictionary and brute force attacks.

Structured Query Language (SQL)   The standard language used by relational databases to enter and extract the information stored in them.

structured walk-through   A type of disaster recovery test, often referred to as a "table-top exercise," in which members of the disaster recovery team gather in a large conference room and role-play a disaster scenario.

subject   An active entity that seeks information about or data from passive objects through the exercise of access. A subject can be a user, a program, a process, a file, a computer, a database, and so on.

subpoena   A court order that compels an individual or organization to surrender evidence or to appear in court.

substitution cipher   Cipher that uses an encryption algorithm to replace each character or bit of the plaintext message with a different character, such as a Caesar cipher.

supervisor state (or supervisory state)   The state in which a process is operating in a privileged, all-access mode.

supervisory mode   Mode in which processes at layer 0 run, which is the ring where the operating system itself resides.

surge   Prolonged high voltage.

SWIPE   See *software IP encryption (SWIPE)*.

switch   A network device that is an intelligent hub because it knows the addresses of the systems connected on each outbound port. Instead of repeating traffic on every outbound port, a switch repeats only traffic out of the port on which the destination is known to exist. Switches offer greater efficiency for traffic delivery, create separate broadcast and collision domains, and improve the overall throughput of data.

Switched Multimegabit Data Services (SMDS)   A connectionless network communication service. SMDS provides bandwidth on demand. SMDS is a preferred connection mechanism for linking remote LANs that communicate infrequently.

switched virtual circuit (SVC)   A virtual circuit that must be rebuilt each time it is used; similar to a dial-up connection.

semantic integrity mechanisms   A common security feature of a DBMS. This feature ensures that no structural or semantic rules are violated. It also checks that all stored data types are within valid domain ranges, that only logical values exist, and that any and all uniqueness constraints are met.

symmetric key   An algorithm that relies upon a "shared secret" encryption key that is distributed to all members who participate in communications. This key is used by all parties to both encrypt and decrypt messages.

symmetric multiprocessing (SMP)   A type of system in which the processors share not only a common operating system, but also a common data bus and memory resources. In this type of arrangement, it is not normally possible to use more than 16 processors.

SYN flood attack   A type of DoS. A SYN flood attack is waged by not sending the final ACK packet, which breaks the standard three-way handshake used by TCP/IP to initiate communication sessions.

Synchronous Data Link Control (SDLC)   A layer 2 protocol employed by networks with dedicated or leased lines. SDLC was developed by IBM for remote communications with SNA systems. SDLC is a bit-oriented synchronous protocol.

synchronous dynamic password token   Tokens used in a token device that generates passwords at fixed time intervals. Time interval tokens require that the clock of the authentication server and the token device be synchronized. The generated password is entered by the subject along with a PIN, pass phrase, or password.

system call   A process by which an object in a less-trusted protection ring requests access to resources or functionality by objects in more-trusted protection rings.

system high mode   See *system-high security mode*.

system-high security mode   Mode in which systems are authorized to process only information that all system users are cleared to read and have a valid need to know. Systems running in this mode are not trusted to maintain separation between security levels, and all information processed by these systems must be handled as if it were classified at the same level as the most highly classified information processed by the system.

T

table   The main building block of a relational database; also known as a relation.

TACACS   See *Terminal Access Controller Access Control System (TACACS).*

tactical plan   A midterm plan developed to provide more details on accomplishing the goals set forth in the strategic plan. A tactical plan is typically useful for about a year. It often prescribes and schedules the tasks necessary to accomplish organizational goals.

Take-Grant model   A model that employs a directed graph to dictate how rights can be passed from one subject to another or from a subject to an object. Simply put, a subject with the grant right can grant another subject or another object any other right they possess. Likewise, a subject with the take right can take a right from another subject.

task-based   An access control methodology in which access is granted based on work tasks or operations.

TCP wrapper   An application that can serve as a basic firewall by restricting access based on user IDs or systems IDs.

teardrop attack   A type of DoS. A teardrop attack occurs when an attacker exploits a bug in operating systems. The bug exists in the routines used to reassemble fragmented packets. An attacker sends numerous specially formatted fragmented packets to the victim, which causes the system to freeze or crash.

technical access control   The hardware or software mechanisms used to manage access to resources and systems and provide protection for those resources and systems. Examples of logical or technical access controls include encryption, smart cards, passwords, biometrics, constrained interfaces, access control lists, protocols, firewalls, routers, IDEs, and clipping levels. The same as logical access control.

technical physical security controls   Security controls that use technology to implement some form of physical security, including intrusion detection systems, alarms, CCTV, monitoring, HVAC, power supplies, and fire detection and suppression.

TEMPEST   The study and control of electronic signals produced by various types of electronic hardware, such as computers, televisions, phones, and so on. Its primary goal is to prevent EM and RF radiation from leaving a strictly defined area so as to eliminate the possibility of external radiation monitoring, eavesdropping, and signal sniffing.

Terminal Access Controller Access Control System (TACACS)   An alternative to RADIUS. TACACS is available in three versions: original TACACS, XTACACS (eXtended TACACS), and TACACS+. TACACS integrates the authentication and authorization processes. XTACACS keeps the authentication, authorization, and accounting processes separate. TACACS+ improves XTACACS by adding two-factor authentication.

terrorist attacks   Attacks that differ from military and intelligence attacks in that the purpose is to disrupt normal life, whereas a military or intelligence attack is designed to extract secret information.

test data method   A form of program testing that examines the extent of the system testing to locate untested program logic.

testimonial evidence   Evidence that consists of the testimony of a witness, either verbal testimony in court or written testimony in a recorded deposition.

thicknet   See *10Base5*.

thin client   A term used to describe a workstation that has little or no local processing or storage capacity. A thin client is used to connect to and operate a remote system.

thinnet   See *10Base2*.

threat   A potential occurrence that may cause an undesirable or unwanted outcome on an organization or to a specific asset.

threat agents   People, programs, hardware, or systems that intentionally exploit vulnerabilities.

threat events   Accidental exploitations of vulnerabilities.

throughput rate   The rate at which a biometric device can scan and authenticate subjects. A rate of about six seconds or faster is required for general acceptance of a specific biometric control.

ticket   A electronic authentication factor used by the Kerberos authentication system.

Ticket Granting Service (TGS)   An element of the Kerberos authentication system. The TGS manages the assignment and expiration of tickets. Tickets are used by subjects to gain access to objects.

time-of-check (TOC)   The time at which a subject checks on the status of an object.

time-of-check-to-time-of-use (TOCTTOU)   A timing vulnerability that occurs when a program checks access permissions too far in advance of a resource request.

time-of-use (TOU)   The time at which the decision is made by a subject to access an object.

time slice   A single chunk or division of processing time.

token   See *token device*.

token device   A password-generating device that subjects must carry with them. Token devices are a form of a "something you have" (Type 2) authentication factor.

token ring   A token-passing LAN technology.

top secret   The highest level of government/military classification. Unauthorized disclosure of top secret data will cause exceptionally grave damage to national security.

topology   The physical layout of network devices and connective cabling. The common network topologies are ring, bus, star, and mesh.

total risk   The amount of risk an organization would face if no safeguards were implemented. Threats * vulnerabilities * asset value = total risk.

trade secret   Intellectual property that is absolutely critical to a business and would cause significant damage if it were disclosed to competitors and/or the public.

trademark   A registered word, slogan, or logos used to identify a company and its products or services.

traffic analysis   A form of monitoring that in which the flow of packets rather than the actual content of packets is examined. Also referred to as trend analysis.

training   The task of teaching employees to perform their work tasks and to comply with the security policy. All new employees require some level of training so they will be able to properly comply with all standards, guidelines, and procedures mandated by the security policy.

transferring risk   Placing the cost of loss from a realized risk onto another entity or organization, such as purchasing insurance. Also referred to as assigning risk.

transient   A short duration of line noise disturbance.

Transmission Control Protocol (TCP)   A connection-oriented protocol located at layer 4 of the OSI model.

transmission error correction   A capability built into connection- or session-oriented protocols and services. If it is determined that a message, in whole or in part, was corrupted, altered, or lost, a request can be made for the source to resend all or part of the message.

transmission logging   A form of auditing focused on communications. Transmission logging records the details about source, destination, time stamps, identification codes, transmission status, number of packets, size of message, and so on.

transparency   A characteristic of a service, security control, or access mechanism that is unseen by users. Transparency is often a desirable feature for security controls.

Transport layer   Layer 4 of the OSI model.

transport mode   A mode of IPSec when used in a VPN. In transport mode, the IP packet data is encrypted but the header of the packet is not.

transposition cipher   Cipher that uses an encryption algorithm to rearrange the letters of a plaintext message to form the ciphertext message.

trap door   Undocumented command sequence that allows software developers to bypass normal access restrictions.

traverse mode noise   EMI noise generated by the difference in power between the hot and neutral wires of a power source or operating electrical equipment.

trend analysis See *traffic analysis*.

Triple DES (3DES) A standard that uses three iterations of DES with two or three different keys to increase the effective key strength to 112 bits.

Trojan horse A malicious code object that appears to be a benevolent program—such as a game or simple utility that performs the "cover" functions as advertised but also carries an unknown payload, such as a virus.

trust A security bridge established to share resources from one domain to another. A trust is established between two domains to allow users from one domain to access resources in another. Trusts can be one-way only or they can be two-way.

trusted computing base (TCB) The combination of hardware, software, and controls that form a trusted base that enforces your security policy.

trusted path Secure channel used by the TCB to communicate with the rest of the system.

trusted recovery process On a secured system, a process that ensures the system always returns to a secure state after an error, failure, or reboot.

trusted system A secured computer system.

tunnel mode A mode of IPSec when used in a VPN. In tunnel mode, the entire IP packet is encrypted and a new header is added to the packet to govern transmission through the tunnel.

tunneling A network communications process that protects the contents of protocol packets by encapsulating them in packets of another protocol.

turnstile A form of gate that prevents more than one person at a time from gaining entry and often restricts movement in one direction.

twisted-pair See *10Base-T*.

two-factor authentication Authentication that requires two factors.

Type 1 authentication factor Something you know, such as a password, personal identification number (PIN), combination lock, pass phrase, mother's maiden name, and favorite color.

Type 2 authentication factor Something you have, such as a smart card, ATM card, token device, and memory card.

Type 3 authentication factor Something you are, such as fingerprints, voice print, retina pattern, iris pattern, face shape, palm topology, and hand geometry.

Type 1 error See *False Rejection Rate (FRR)*.

Type 2 error See *False Acceptance Rate (FAR)*.

U

unclassified   The lowest level of government/military classification. Used for data that is neither sensitive nor classified. Disclosure of unclassified data does not compromise confidentiality, nor does it cause any noticeable damage.

unicast   A communications transmission to a single identified recipient.

Uniform Computer Information Transactions Act (UCITA)   A federal law designed for adoption by each of the 50 states to provide a common framework for the conduct of computer-related business transactions.

uninterruptible power supply (UPS)   A type of self-charging battery that can be used to supply consistent clean power to sensitive equipment. A UPS functions basically by taking power in from the wall outlet, storing it in a battery, pulling power out of the battery, and then feeding that power to whatever devices are connected to it. By directing current through its battery, it is able to maintain a consistent clean power supply.

unit testing   A method of testing software. Each unit of code is tested independently to discover any errors or omissions and to ensure that it functions properly. Unit testing should be performed by the development staff.

unshielded twisted-pair (UTP)   A twisted-pair wire that does not include additional EMI protection. Most twisted-pair wiring is UTP.

upper management   See *senior management*.

USA Patriot Act of 2001   An act implemented after the September 11, 2001 terrorist attacks. It greatly broadened the powers of law enforcement organizations and intelligence agencies across a number of areas, including the monitoring of electronic communications.

user   Any person who has access to the secured system. A user's access is tied to their work tasks and is limited so they have only enough access to perform the tasks necessary for their job position (i.e., principle of least privilege). Also referred to as end user and employee.

User Datagram Protocol (UDP)   A connectionless protocol located at layer 4 of the OSI model.

user mode   The basic mode used by the CPU when executing user applications.

V

Vernam cipher   A device that implements a 26-character modulo 26 substitution cipher. It functions as a one-time pad.

view   A client interface used to interact with a database. The view limits what clients can see and what functions they can perform.

Vigenere cipher   A polyalphabetic substitution cipher.

violation analysis   A form of auditing that uses clipping levels.

virtual machine   A software simulation of a computer within which a process executes. Each virtual machine has its own memory address space and communication between virtual machines is securely controlled.

virtual memory   A special type of secondary memory that is managed by the operating system in such a manner that it appears to be real memory.

virtual private network (VPN)   A network connection established between two systems over an existing private or public network. A VPN provides confidentiality and integrity for network traffic through the use of encryption.

virtual private network (VPN) protocol   The protocols, such as PPTP, L2TP, and IPSec, that are used to create VPNs.

virus   The oldest form of malicious code objects that plague cyberspace. Once they are in a system, they attach themselves to legitimate operating system and user files and applications and normally perform some sort of undesirable action, ranging from the somewhat innocuous display of an annoying message on the screen to the more malicious destruction of the entire local file system.

Voice over IP (VoIP)   A network service that provides voice communication services by transporting the voice traffic as network packets over an IP network.

voice pattern   An example of a biometric factor, which is a behavioral or physiological characteristic that is unique to a subject. The speech, tone, modulation, and pitch patterns of a person's voice is used to establish identity or provide authentication.

volatile   See *volatile storage*.

volatile storage   A storage medium, such as RAM, that loses its contents when power is removed from the resource.

voluntarily surrender   The act of willingly handing over evidence.

vulnerability   The absence or weakness of a safeguard or countermeasure. In other words, a vulnerability is the existence of a flaw, loophole, oversight, error, limitation, frailty, or susceptibility in the IT infrastructure or any other aspect of an organization.

vulnerability scan   A test performed on a system to find weaknesses in the security infrastructure.

vulnerability scanner   A tool used to test a system for known security vulnerabilities and weaknesses. Vulnerability scanners are used to generate reports that indicate the areas or aspects of the system that need to be managed to improve security.

W

wait state   The state in which a process is ready to execute but is waiting for an operation such as keyboard input, printing, or file writing to complete.

war dialing   The act of using a modem to search for a system that will accept inbound connection attempts.

warm site   A middle ground between hot sites and cold sites for disaster recovery specialists. A warm site always contains the equipment and data circuits necessary to rapidly establish operations but does not typically contain copies of the client's data.

warning banners   Messages used to inform would-be intruders or attempted security policy violators that their intended activities are restricted and that any further activities will be audited and monitored. A warning banner is basically an electronic equivalent of a no trespassing sign.

well-known ports   The first 1,024 ports of TCP and UDP. They are usually assigned to commonly used services and applications.

wet pipe system   A fire suppression system that is always full of water. Water discharges immediately when triggered by a fire or smoke. Also known as a closed head system.

white box testing   A form of program testing that examines the internal logical structures of a program.

wide area network (WAN)   A network or a network of LANs that is geographically diverse. Often dedicated leased lines are used to establish connections between distant components.

WinNuke attack   A type of DoS. A WinNuke attack is a specialized assault against Windows 95 systems. Out-of-band TCP data is sent to a victim's system, which causes the OS to freeze.

Wireless Application Protocol (WAP)   A protocol used by portable devices like cell phones and PDAs to support Internet connectivity via your telco or carrier provider.

Wired Equivalency Protocol (WEP)   A protocol that provides both 40- and 128-bit encryption options to protect communications within the wireless LAN.

work function or work factor   A way of measuring the strength of a cryptography system by measuring the effort in terms of cost and/or time. Usually the time and effort required to perform a complete brute force attack against an encryption system is what the work function rating represents. The security and protection offered by a cryptosystem is directly proportional to the value of the work function/factor.

worm   A form of malicious code that is self-replicating but is not designed to impose direct harm on host systems. The primary purpose of a worm is to replicate itself to other systems and gather information. Worms are usually very prolific and often cause a denial of service due to their consumption of system resources and network bandwidth in their attempt to self-replicate.

X

X.25   An older WAN protocol that uses carrier switching to provide end-to-end connections over a shared network medium.

XOR   A function that returns a true value when only one of the input values is true. If both values are false or both values are true, the output of the XOR function is false.

Z

zero knowledge proof   A concept of communication whereby a specific type of information is exchanged but no real data is exchanged. Great examples of this idea are digital signatures and digital certificates.

Index

Note to the Reader: Throughout this index **boldfaced** page numbers indicate primary discussions of a topic. *Italicized* page numbers indicate illustrations.

J

T